D0005420

DATE DUE

Shakespeare's
Contemporaries

with an introductory essay by
Alfred Harbage, Harvard University

PRENTICE-HALL INC., Englewood Cliffs, New Jersey

Shakespeare's Contemporaries:
Modern Studies in English Renaissance Drama

SECOND EDITION

edited by

MAX BLUESTONE
*University of Massachusetts
at Boston*

NORMAN RABKIN
*University of California
at Berkeley*

to the memory of our fathers

SAMUEL BLUESTONE
WILLIAM RABKIN

© 1970 Prentice-Hall, Inc., Englewood Cliffs, New Jersey

C-13-807677-4
P-13-807651-0

Library of Congress Catalog Card Number: 69-12627

Printed in the United States of America

Current Printing (last number):

10 9 8 7 6 5 4 3 2 1

PRENTICE-HALL ENGLISH LITERATURE SERIES

Maynard Mack

Editor

PRENTICE-HALL INTERNATIONAL, INC., London
PRENTICE-HALL OF AUSTRALIA, PTY. LTD., Sydney
PRENTICE-HALL OF CANADA, LTD., Toronto
PRENTICE-HALL OF INDIA PRIVATE, LIMITED, New Delhi
PRENTICE-HALL OF JAPAN, INC., Tokyo

Preface
to the First Edition

This collection of writings testifies to the continuing vitality of the English Renaissance drama, which, apart from its intimate association with Shakespeare, has elicited in our time a significant body of serious criticism and fruitful scholarship. Together the essays present a comprehensive introduction not only to a number of plays but also to various methods of study indulged by modern students of this drama. Taking their departure from a variety of critical scholarly persuasions, the studies examine a selection of the best plays produced by Shakespeare's contemporaries, and range widely among such subjects as Renaissance intellectual history, dramatic rhetoric and structure, textual bibliography, and theory of tragedy. Diverse though they be, these writers nevertheless contribute to a communal enterprise that preserves and promulgates an important and precious part of modern man's cultural heritage. If their efforts make more accessible the plays here considered, this anthology will have fulfilled its purpose.

Placing emphasis largely where it has been placed by modern scholars and critics themselves, the collection devotes a considerable share of attention to Marlowe and Jonson. The Marlowe materials tend to weight the collection toward the Elizabethans rather than the Jacobeans, thus "environing Shakespeare," in Felix Schelling's phrase, more fully by his predecessors than by his followers. Wherever possible we have chosen essays which—whatever particular methodology they employ—address themselves to the illumination of individual plays. Given various strictures and our own eclectic aims, we cannot sanction everything we have printed, but we paraphrase Rosalind by charging the partisan reader "to like as much of this [book] as please you." We hope, however, that the bibliographies will redress whatever imbalance our choices have created. Highly selective as they are, the bibliographies largely list writings, like the essays in the collection itself, which deal with individual plays and which suggest lines of further inquiry and study.

We are indebted to the kind encouragement of our teacher, Alfred Harbage, whose *Shakespeare and the Rival Traditions* and other studies have deepened so effectively the modern understanding of this body of drama. Although they are not responsible for the faults in our work, the following have helped us in various ways: Joanne Bluestone and Martha Rabkin, Jonas A. Barish, Rita and Robert M. Durling, P. H. Fine, Mrs. Frederick W. Harrison, Bernard S. Levy, Maynard Mack, Anne Saxon, Priscilla Shaw, the staffs of the Harvard College Library, the Harvard Medical School Library, the Library of the University of California at Berkeley, the Photographic Department of the Massachusetts Institute of Technology, the Wellesley College Library, and a relay team of amateur radio operators, who attempted in a trying moment to speed our communication with each other.

N. R.
M. B.

Preface
to the Second Edition

As we prepared this second edition of *Shakespeare's Contemporaries,*
we found it increasingly difficult to believe that only eight years have
passed since the first. In that time over three hundred books and
articles on its subject have appeared. But their number alone scarcely
suggests how they have transformed the landscape of modern studies
of English Renaissance drama. This is not to say that the changes
which impress one have occurred since our first edition, but rather
that the increased vigor of the criticism has reinforced, established, and
promulgated what a few years ago could hardly have been forecast as
trends. Plays whose names were unfamiliar to all but a handful of
scholars in 1961 have been published in large and widely distributed
editions. The Marlowe quadricentennial, like the Shakespeare celebration of the same year, stimulated the publication of a great deal of new
work on the University wits and their successors. Two annual publications, Samuel Schoenbaum's enterprising *Renaissance Drama* and the
annual number of *Studies in English Literature, 1500–1900* devoted
exclusively to the subject, provide scholars a greater opportunity than
before to make their voices heard effectively. Critical methods available
only to an academic avant-garde and applied only tentatively to Renaissance drama have become a language in which communication among
large numbers of sensitive readers is now possible. Reading the work
produced by a new generation, one senses the emergence of something
closer than it was a decade ago to a true scholarly community, which
has come to realize more fully than before that it shares its borders
with other intellectual principalities. More than ever the study of
English Renaissance drama is profitably bound up with the disciplines
of history and theology, rhetorical analysis and psychoanalysis, and
with the problems of the world we inhabit.

The quality and quantity of the new work have made the preparation of the second edition easier in some ways than that of the first.
For the first edition we faced the need to establish a canon of the best

or most significant plays by Shakespeare's contemporaries and to insure that the critical traditions we presented were adequately eclectic. The favorable reception of the first edition and the direction of studies since its appearance encouraged us to think that our choice of plays concurred with the general judgment as to what is most significant. The criticism and scholarship published since 1961 have enabled us to see more clearly which material from the first half of the century has proved most seminal; in some instances, as in that of Arthur Mizener's study of *A King and No King* reprinted in this second edition, a study several decades old seems even more important now than it did when it first appeared. The lengthening of our bibliographies to include citations of the most useful criticism and scholarship since the first edition has been, though arduous, a fairly straightforward matter. (The reader will note that the abbreviations used for the journals referred to in these bibliographies are the standard PMLA ones.) In our first edition we needed to represent work on Marlowe and Jonson in proportion to its actual frequency and with the danger of unbalancing the collection; in the second we have been able to reduce the sections on these playwrights in deference to the judiciously edited and readily available Twentieth Century Views collections by Clifford Leech and Jonas A. Barish, and we have therefore been able to increase the offerings on Peele, Kyd, Tourneur, Beaumont and Fletcher, Middleton, and Ford. (We regret that exigencies of space required the late deletion of one excellent essay on Marlowe, Witold Ostrowski's "The Interplay of the Subjective and the Objective in Marlowe's *Doctor Faustus*," and we are grateful to Wilbur Sanders for revising part of his just-published *The Dramatist and the Received Idea* so that we might print it.)

In other ways our editorial task has been harder. The proliferation of series of editions such as the Regents Renaissance Drama Series, the Revels Plays, the New Mermaids, and the Yale Ben Jonson testifies to the vitality we earlier asserted of the plays. But since these editions are easy to come by, we decided that reprinting introductions from them, illuminating as some of them are, is not a valuable service. We have therefore replaced with other kinds of material some introductions included in our first edition. Some noteworthy contributions to our subject have been published too recently for us to take advantage of them: Arthur Freeman's study of Kyd, Charlotte Spivack's work on Chapman, and David Bevington's work on Tudor drama. (We are especially pleased, however, to be able to reprint an excellent essay from Philip J. Finkelpearl's *John Marston of the Middle Temple* concurrently with its appearance at the Harvard University Press.) Our greatest difficulty, however, has been our greatest pleasure as well. As we said above, each new essay transforms the entire landscape of which it is a part, and choosing from so large a number of first-rate essays has required radical reconsideration of the entire book.

The vicissitudes of editing the collection are less interesting than the novelty, the incisiveness, and the critical luminousness of the new essays (we must leave to others, however, the evaluation of our own two essays included in this edition). The new work suggests, as do the increasingly frequent stage productions of the plays, that English Renaissance drama is more firmly rooted than ever in our literary and theatrical heritage.

We are grateful, as before, to our wives, our families, our colleagues, and our institutions for support of various kinds. Maynard Mack has cast a knowledgeable and generous eye on our enterprise, but no more than others can he be held responsible for our choices, which, we hope, will betray in deepest consequences neither the playwrights and their plays, nor the community of critics and scholars, nor, least significant of all, the attendant lords, the editors.

M. B.

N. R.

Boston and Berkeley, January, 1969

Introduction

Among the plays treated in this volume, *Gammer Gurton's Needle* and *Cambises* may be viewed as a kind of prologue, a promise of things to come. Within a few decades, the plays of Lyly and Marlowe began to appear on the London stage. An alert young man of twenty-one who, in 1584, saw the first performance of Lyly's first play, could have seen all the plays of Lyly, Marlowe, Peele, Kyd, and Greene while still in his twenties, and the best of the plays of Jonson, Heywood, Dekker, Marston, Webster, Chapman, Middleton, Tourneur, and Beaumont and Fletcher before he had passed his forties. Meanwhile he could have seen all the plays of Shakespeare, and hundreds more by a score of other playwrights. The prime of Elizabethan drama fitted a span no longer than the prime of a single human life.

My task is to say something about the criticism of this drama, but first a word about its nature and early standing. After centuries of slow preparation, the sudden flowering of the 1580's and the teeming fruitfulness of the next few decades are a marvel of cultural history. This drama has sometimes proved too pungent for classical tastes, but no one has been able to deny at least its plenitude, vitality, and infinite variety. It is deadly to appraise art in terms of the *average,* since whatever endures is whatever excels the average, but an Elizabethan play chosen almost at random shows certain admirable traits. It will be "dramatic" in the root sense, full of "doings," full enough indeed to furnish out a dozen modern plays. It will be richly peopled, projecting many characters in sharp contrast with each other. It will be truly dialectal, in the sense that the speech will seem to issue from the speakers, not from an author-ventriloquist. And this speech will be colorful, energetic, resourceful—reflecting the time's delight in words. In addition there will be moments of poetry and flashes of insight into the nature of man and his eternal dilemma. When the poetry and insight prevail, the play is above average. There are a number of such plays, and not all of them are by Shakespeare.

In view of its distinction, it is odd that this drama won little critical attention in its own day. The spectators no doubt talked about it, but they did not write about it. Perhaps the interested writers were too busy creating drama to create dramatic criticism. Elizabethan criticism of popular Elizabethan drama may be treated in four words: it does not exist. What we have is not criticism but a few laudatory or damnatory remarks, panegyric defenses or satiric attacks, along with a few rationalizations by the playwrights themselves, usually Ben Jonson. However, it may be viewed as an act of critical approbation when the age began to print individual plays and then the collected works of individual authors. Ben Jonson issued the first installment of his works in 1616, and his admirers completed the project in 1640. Shakespeare's fellow actors issued his collected works in 1623, and the volume was reissued in 1632. Six plays by Lyly were issued collectively by a publisher in 1632, and six by Marston in 1633. That is all for the period proper, but after the closing of the theatres in 1642, the plays of Beaumont and Fletcher were collected in 1647 and 1679. Publishers were prepared to issue other playwrights in collected form, but the plans were dropped as the climate of critical opinion became hostile. Sadly enough, the typical late seventeenth-century record of Elizabethan drama is a stationer's catalogue of single plays, in print or languishing in manuscript.

The Restoration period had decided that Ben Jonson, Beaumont and Fletcher, and Shakespeare were all it wanted from the former age; and even these received mixed notices in the critical writings of the time. The others were sometimes plagiarized by the new dramatists, but they were dismissed with contempt by the critics. Heywood especially served as a convenient whipping-boy. In the eighteenth century, plays by the same survivors but in a new order: Shakespeare, Jonson, and Beaumont and Fletcher, continued to be performed, usually in adapted versions, and continued to be published in collected form. Those of Philip Massinger were added to the list, but the other playwrights receded further and further from sight. Individual plays might be pilfered in grotesque stage presentations, but the original authors were not mentioned or not regarded seriously. It was enough to enumerate them and their plays in works of reference. If the typical late seventeenth-century record is a stationer's catalogue, the typical eighteenth-century record is a dictionary of the drama.

So far as criticism is concerned, the eighteenth century devoted its whole energies to Shakespeare, who was fast dimming the stars of even Jonson and Beaumont and Fletcher. Concern for the other Elizabethan dramatists was mainly antiquarian, and their plays—if published at all —were published in the same spirit as the ancient ballads. Robert Dodsley's twelve-volume compendium of 1744 was called *A Select Collection of Old English Plays*. The word "old" persisted in the many later revisions and off-shoots of this collection, suggesting not that the plays were *good* but simply that they were *old*. If Charles Lamb had performed no other service when he published in 1808 his famous sampling, *Specimens of English Dramatic Poets who Lived about the Time of Shakespeare,* he would still deserve a palm for banishing the word "old" and introducing the word "poets." Non-Shakespearean Elizabethan drama was rescued by the Romantic Movement. In this rescue, the crusading Shakespeareans, Schlegel and Coleridge, played little if any part. Both turned from Shakespeare only long enough for a few perfunctory remarks about the other "accredited" playwrights, Jonson, Beaumont and Fletcher, and Massinger. On behalf of Coleridge it may at least be said that he was not guilty of curt words of dismissal, like those of Schlegel. It is strange to hear so good a critic as Schlegel saying in his lectures of 1809 that Lyly is only a "learned witling," the verses of Marlowe are "flowing but without energy," and the whole of *The Spanish Tragedy* is "like the drawings of children." Coleridge is often accused of having listened more attentively than he was willing to admit to Schlegel's appraisal of Shakespeare. It would have been well if Schlegel could have listened attentively to the appraisal of Shakespeare's contemporaries by Lamb and William Hazlitt.

Charles Lamb picked up quartos of Elizabethan plays on the book-stalls of London with an ease which makes modern collectors sigh. He opened them in a spirit of adventure. What he found filled him with delighted surprise. In the excerpts he published in 1808, he is neither systematic nor always discriminating, but the total effect of the excerpts and his too-brief notes of appreciation was to emancipate Elizabethan drama. He constantly mentioned Shakespeare, but not at the expense of the others; rather it was to give them a share of Shakespeare's qualities, or to show they possessed some of their own. His notes are still a pleasure to read, warm, imaginative, generous, and nearly always apt. An even greater landmark is William Hazlitt's *Lectures on the Dramatic Literature of the Age of Elizabeth,* 1820. Hazlitt begins his second lecture by saying that here is a "forgotten mine of wealth" which "only wants exploring to fill the inquiring mind with wonder." It is astonishing for a modern student to read in a relatively modern work that the dramatists "whose names are now little known and their writings nearly obsolete, are Lyly, Marlowe, Marston, Chapman, Middleton and Rowley, Heywood, Webster, Dekker, and Ford." Working with no critical tradition behind him, Hazlitt proceeded to create one. When we read of Marlowe that "There is a lust of power in his writings, a hunger and thirst after unrighteousness, a glow of imagination, un-hallowed by anything but its own energies," we see the contrast with Schlegel's "flowing but without energy," and discover also the seed-pod of nearly all subsequent criticism of Marlowe. The remarks on the "gentle-hearted Dekker" owe more to Charles Lamb, but they also have sent echoes down the years. Hazlitt's criticism is not only original, but also good, perhaps too good, or at least too persuasive for the good of later critics. Considerable nineteenth-century criticism simply worked variations upon Hazlitt's themes.

Now came, belatedly, the collected editions, prepared by Alexander Dyce and others: Marlowe in 1826, Webster in 1830, Greene in 1831, Shirley in 1833, Peele in 1828–39, Middleton in 1840, Heywood in 1842–51, Chapman in 1873, Dekker also in 1873, Tourneur in 1878, and at last Kyd in 1901. Ford preceded this procession by achieving collection in 1811. Considerable criticism of Elizabethan drama accompanies the publication of the works, in the above and subsequent editings, but, as we shall see in a moment, it was usually of a summary character. An impetus was given to public interest by the *Mermaid Series,* in which selected plays of individual dramatists were inexpensively issued with critical introductions between 1887 and 1909. The wretched editing and annotation was compensated by the excellent choice of plays from among the works of the various authors. In the closing decades of the nineteenth century and the opening ones of the twentieth there was considerable evidence of interest in Elizabethan drama: fine "histories" like A. W. Ward's of 1875 and Felix E. Schelling's of 1908; provocative aesthetic judgments like those of J. A. Symonds, Algernon Swinburne, Arthur Symons, T. S. Eliot, and others; and even performances, usually by experimental societies, of plays banished from the stage for centuries. In this same period something of a reaction set in, articulated chiefly by adherents of the school of Ibsen and Shaw. After a performance of Webster's *Duchess of Malfi* by the Phoenix Society in 1920 William Archer coolly affirmed:

> Its performance will bring home to playgoers the hollowness of the old uncritical praise of the great Elizabethan dramatists. Charles Lamb's gentle enthusiasm and Swinburne's boisterous panegyrics have made a legend of Elizabethan drama not founded on fact, as most critical students have known for a long time.

The characterization of a whole century of appraisal in England, Europe, and America as "Charles Lamb's gentle enthusiasm and Swinburne's boisterous panegyrics" is more startling than just, but it brings home the fact that there had been few critical documents which would convince a skeptic. They are excellent in their kind, but they are rarely solidly analytical; we hear the voices of converts speaking to other converts rather than the voice of the teacher and exegete. Impressionistic criticism is defenseless against impressionistic countercriticism. Elizabethan drama was in 1920 in need of a supplementary *kind* of criticism, and the contents of the present volume represent something which might well be considered an answer to William Archer and his "not founded on fact."

All the essays here presented have been written since 1920. Although I have been associated with the editors in their student days and since, I have not suggested their project, its plan, or the inclusion or exclusion of any item; hence I feel free to express my admiration for what they have done. Their selections all meet the fundamental test of honesty: the critics believe in what they are doing, respect the works they are discussing, and grant those works rather than themselves the center of the stage. This does not mean that they affect an arid impersonality. . . . The analytical bias, the sense of fact, has not banished appreciation. The first essay is mainly appreciation, but appreciation fortified by a strong historical consciousness. The second essay is mainly historical criticism, but appreciation is there—appreciation which some have found hard to achieve in the case of such a play as *Cambises*. And so it goes: the essays are good criticism and good reading, and fortified as they are by invaluable bibliographies of additional criticism, they perform a notable service.

It was not enough to saȳ that the Elizabethan plays with more than one plot may still have "a kind of unity," and that this unity will be "organic" rather than "mechanic." It was necessary to get down to cases, and to identify the structural and thematic devices by which this unity is achieved. Several essays in this volume do precisely that. Others attack similar problems and tie up loose ends long left dangling in the air. The items included range from treatment of the general characteristics of a dramatist's entire output . . . to analysis of a single characteristic of a single play. . . . Most of them, quite properly, aim to give an inclusive view of a single play. Nothing is rejected in this collection in the way of critical approach; it follows no "line" and adheres to no "school." Philosophical and social backgrounds, sources of material and inspiration, coeval critical tenets, and the nature of other plays are all levied upon by some of the critics, while others stick closely to structural, verbal, and thematic analysis. When several essays upon the same play appear, they do not cancel but supplement each other; the first essay does not shrink in stature as a result of juxtaposition with a second employing a different critical approach. The editors are not sponsoring a dispute, but conducting a symposium.

The collection should function in several ways. For the casual reader of Elizabethan drama it should sharpen the reading sense, and add to understanding and enjoyment. For the critic, it should suggest a program. The method of approach used with one play might with equal success be used with others. Elizabethan drama in general still sorely needs the kind of critical attention it receives in these essays. Since Shakespeare is in no danger of neglect, one may reasonably suggest that some of the effort lavished upon his plays might well be re-directed toward the plays of his contemporaries.

A number of the present essays do not even mention Shakespeare, and this is always refreshing, but the prestige of Shakespeare's fellows does not depend upon the blanking out of his august figure. They can endure comparison; they suffer only when placed in competition. They have often been put in such a posture by students of the period including the present writer; one can only say *culpa mea* and plead his good intentions at the time. It has sometimes been asserted that the lesser dramatists have profited by their status as Shakespeare's contemporaries, that they have ridden to repute upon his coat-tails. The charge would be hard to maintain. Certainly Marlowe's status as Shakespeare's contemporary did not save him from two centuries of utter neglect; and certainly Jonson has suffered enormously from the mere fact that he was, conspicuously, not Shakespeare. The lovers of Elizabethan drama made a tactical blunder in speaking of Shakespeare as only the brightest star in a bright constellation. He was not that. Like Homer and Dante and other universal figures he dwarfed his immediate literary context. He was more nearly the moon than the brightest star. But what of that? To say that the moon is a thing of wonder is not to say that the sky has no wonder on a moonless night. What Hazlitt said was true, that Elizabethan drama will "fill the inquiring mind with wonder," and the editors of this collection have assembled fine products of the inquiring mind.

Alfred Harbage
1961

Contents

Gammer Gurton's Needle

THE HYBRID IMAGE IN FARCE *

Bernard Spivack

THE only known early edition of *Gammer Gurton's Needle*, "Played on Stage, not longe ago in Christes Colledge in Cambridge" and "Made by Mr. S. Mr. of Art," belongs to 1575, but the play itself is undoubtedly a good deal earlier. It is probably the same as the "Dyccon of Bedlam, &c." licensed in 1563, and it may go back to the last years of Edward VI if its author, as seems reasonably certain now, is William Stevenson, a fellow of Christ's in 1551–54 and again in 1559–61. The college records for 1559–60 contain an item of five shillings "Spent at Mr. Stevenson's plaie," but this performance may be no more than a revival from the earlier period of Stevenson's fellowship, when he was also credited with a play.[1] At any rate, *Gammer Gurton's Needle* is one of the few surviving examples of vernacular comedy at the universities in the sixteenth century. No doubt this distinction explains in part another: unlike the popular drama of the same period, it is completely free from the homiletic tradition, which it does not even acknowledge by way of apology or valediction. The scholarship of its author appears in its obedience to the formal

* From *Shakespeare and the Allegory of Evil*, Bernard Spivack. New York, 1958, pp. 322–327. Reprinted by permission of the Columbia University Press.

1 See Henry Bradley, introd. to *Gammer Gurton's Needle*, in *Representative English Comedies*, ed. Charles M. Gayley (New York, 1903–1914), I, 197–202.

structure of classic comedy: five-act division, change of scene for each entrance and departure, a single locale abutted by several houses, an action contained within one day. Unlike *Roister Doister*, however, its plot and characters have not even a derived affinity with Latin comedy but originate in the life and manners of rural England. For all its classic technique the play is native to its core. Hodge, Tib, Dame Chat, and Gammer Gurton herself are the primitive human scenery of the English countryside. They speak its dialect with lusty vulgarity and spend their lives upon its major issues—cats, poultry, livestock, middens, clouted breeches, and jolly good ale and old. Dr. Rat, the curate in this genre piece, is a cut above them in language but in little else. Master Bailiff, who restores them all to peace after their war of the needle, is a cut above them in sophistication, but no less native to their rustic society on the manorial estate.

Diccon the Bedlam, whose name supplies the title by which the play was licensed and whose devices supply its plot, belongs to a different fellowship. He is in the country but not quite of it, a visitor upon the scene after having, as he explains to the audience, covered "Many a myle ...diuers and sundry waies" and tasted hospitality at "many a good mans house." His unprovoked aggressions against practically everyone in the play are subject to a kind of explanation in the fact that by his name he belongs to the race of crackbrained vagrants out of St. Mary of Bethlehem, with a reputation for thievery and mischief. But the play itself never urges such an explanation, and he shows, in fact, none of the fantasticality associated with this type of madman-beggar elsewhere in the literature of the times, of which Edgar's speech in *Lear* is a summary:

> My face I'll grime with filth,
> Blanket my loins, elf all my hair in knots,
> And with presented nakedness outface
> The winds and persecutions of the sky.
> The country gives me proof and precedent
> Of Bedlam beggars, who, with roaring voices,
> Strike in their numb'd and mortified bare arms
> Pins, wooden pricks, nails, sprigs of rosemary;
> And with this horrible object, from low farms,
> Poor pelting villages, sheepcotes, and mills,
> Sometime with lunatic bans, sometime with prayers,
> Enforce their charity.

(II. iii. 9–19)

Such a description has nothing to do with Diccon. His clothing is sober, his language trim and sophisticated, his behavior sane and efficient. Nor is he treated by the others like a tolerable lunatic, but as a welcome visitor and counselor at first. In the end, when he stands uncovered, they are content to know no more than that they have been victimized by a "villain knaue" and "false varlet." To a deeper curiosity he is none of all these

THE HYBRID IMAGE IN FARCE 3

things essentially, but the Vice once more adjusted to farce and once more assimilated to a formal image of humanity. He moves against his dupes by an impetus that has lost sight of its origin, but retains the unmistakable features of his heredity.

Although the loss of the needle is none of his doing, all its consequences are. On the strength of it he weaves a net of bedevilment around everyone within reach, inciting them by his lies to reciprocal mayhem; and his whole program unrolls in a speech whose style and content are familiar:

> Here is a matter worthy glosynge,
> Of Gammer Gurtons nedle losynge,
>   And a foule peece of warke!
> A man, I thyncke, myght make a playe,
> And nede no worde to this they saye,
>   Being but half a clarke.
>
> Softe, let me alone! I will take the charge
> This matter further to enlarge
>   Within a tyme shorte.
> If ye will marke my toyes, and note,
> I will geue ye leaue to cut my throte
>   If I make not good sporte.

(II. ii. 7–18)[2]

The "sporte" he provides is rough, but his devices are subtle. Extracting a promise of secrecy in respect to himself, he arouses Dame Chat with the finespun lie ("Because I knew you are my friend, hide it I cold not") that Gammer Gurton accuses her of the theft of a favorite rooster. Leaving that redoubtable female to nurse her wrath, he stokes up a contrary fury in Gammer Gurton and her man Hodge, desperate for the recovery of the needle because of his torn breeches. His instigation is wonderfully astute. To Hodge, who ran away previously in great fright from Diccon's conjuration of the Devil, he now imparts (at Hodge's request) what that demon is supposed to have told him:

> The horson talked to mee I know not well of what:
> One whyle his tonge it ran and paltered of a cat;
> Another whyle he stamered styll vppon a rat;
> Last of all, there was nothing but euery word chat! chat!
> But this I well perceyued, before I wolde him rid,
> Betweene chat and the rat and the cat, the nedle is hyd.
> Now, wether Gyb, our cat, haue eate it in her mawe,
> Or Doctor Rat, our curat, haue found it in the straw,
> Or this Dame Chat, your neighbour, haue stollen it, God he knoweth!

(II. iii. 19–27)

<hr>

2 *Gammer Gurton's Needle,* in *Specimens of the Pre-Shakespearean Drama,* ed. J. M. Manly (Boston, 1897).

To Gammer Gurton he recites a circumstantial tale of how he saw Dame Chat stoop down before the Gurton gate and pick up "a nedle or a pyn." He remonstrated with her, he continues, but the "crafty drab" outfaced him: "Ech other worde I was a knaue, and you a hore of hores." Having fired passions all around to the boiling point, he delivers his typical communique to the audience on the sport about to begin. Thereafter he gets out of the way of the impending carnage, leaving Gammer Gurton and Hodge to advance upon Dame Chat and clash with that amazon in a long scene of primitive violence, both verbal and physical.

With three of his puppets thus manipulated into mutual discomfiture, Diccon turns his skill upon a new victim. To Dr. Rat, who has been summoned by Gammer Gurton to help recover her property, he gives the advice that he has only to creep into Dame Chat's house in the night to catch her red-handed with the needle. To Dame Chat he imparts that Hodge, in revenge for his beating, will break in upon her to steal her poultry. The curate, in consequence, is received in the darkness by a cudgel that sends him out again with a broken head and fury in his heart. He summons the bailiff to redress his injuries, and the latter patiently unweaves the enormous confusion, while everyone talks at cross-purposes, until he penetrates to the agent of all their troubles:

> I weene the ende will proue this brawle did first arise
> Upon no other ground but only Diccons lyes.
>
> . . . .
>
> My Gammer here he made a foole, and drest hir as she was;
> And goodwife Chat he set to scole, till both parties cried alas:
> And D[octor] Rat was not behind, whiles Chat his crown did pare;
> I wold the knaue had ben starke blind, if Hodg had not his share!

(V. ii. 166–203)

Diccon, summoned, readily admits his guilt but is sorry for nothing. In reply to the bailiff's question: "Hast thou not made a lie or two, to set these two by the eares?" he asserts—and it is the Vice speaking—his prescriptive right to his habitual activity:

> What if I haue? fiue hundred such haue I seene within these seuen yeares.
> I am sory for nothing else but that I see not the sport
> Which was betwene them when they met, as they them-selues report.

(V. ii. 223–25)

He is roundly cursed by all his victims, and the curate strikes him. Under pressure from the bailiff, however, who can appreciate a jest of which he is not the butt, they ultimately let him off with a mock penance, during which, by taking his oath with a vigorous hand on Hodge's breeches, he makes the latter feelingly aware of the precious needle sticking in them.

The end is a celebration in the tavern with ale provided by Gammer Gurton's halfpenny.

The nature of his victims converts to farce the deceit and injury he inflicts on them, and in farce he is under no great pressure to acquire moral plausibility. As Diccon the Bedlam he conforms sufficiently to the world he enters to deflect a deeper scrutiny. But the temper of his performance, no less than the familiar character of his actions, reveals to our acquired perspective what he really is and where he comes from. The demonstration, no longer homiletic, is still a demonstration:

> Ye see, masters, that one end tapt of this my short deuise!
> Now must we broche tother, to, before the smoke arise.
>
> (II. iii. 1–2)

The Vice survives in him even more minutely—in the "gear" he promotes, in his conspiratorial intimacy with the audience, and in his urging that they make room for the action on the stage:

> Now this gere must forward goe, for here my gammer commeth.
> Be still a-while and say nothing, make here a litle romth!
>
> (II. iv. 1–2)

> Now, sirs, do you no more, but kepe my counsaile iuste,
> And Doctor Rat shall thus catch some good, I trust.
>
> (IV. iii. 1–2)

And if farce is where we find him specialized at present, out of the medley of dramatic moods in which he originated, one scholar at least, in dealing with the play before us, was able to divine what Diccon could become:

> In the central figure of the piece, Diccon the Bedlam, a merry-spirited village Iago, laying plot upon plot with no other purpose than the gratification of his own super-subtle imagination, English drama received the very finest comic creation which it had yet to show.[3]

[3] Tucker Brooke, *The Tudor Drama* (Boston, 1911), p. 163.

GAMMER GURTON'S NEEDLE

Boas, Frederick S. *University Drama in the Tudor Age*. Oxford, 1914, pp. 70–80.

Ingram, Reginald W. "*Gammer Gurton's Needle:* Comedy Not Quite of the Lowest Order?" *SEL,* VII (1967), 257–268.

Roberts, Charles W. "The Authorship of *Gammer Gurton's Nedle,*" *PQ,* XIX (1940), 97–113.

Watt, Homer A. "The Staging of *Gammer Gurton's Nedle,*" in *Elizabethan Studies and Other Essays in Honor of George F. Reynolds*. Boulder, Colorado, 1945, pp. 85–92.

Whiting, Barrett Jere. "Diccon's French Cousin," *SP,* XLII (1945), 31–40.

Thomas Preston

CAMBISES *

Willard Farnham

THE third of the "classical" morality-tragedies, Preston's *Cambises*, suffers like Pickering's *Horestes* from the author's disinclination to depart very far from the book in which he finds his story. What book this is can be demonstrated beyond question. In 1539, Richard Taverner published *The Garden of Wysdom*, a compilation of anecdotes concerning various great men of classical antiquity. It proved popular and went through new editions into the 1550's. Taverner had an M.A. in Greek from Cambridge, and his literary work in general was humanistic translation and adaptation. He had a bent for moralizing the material which he compiled. The larger part of the contents of *The Garden of Wysdom* is translation from the *Apophthegmata* of Erasmus, but about a third of Book II, which was published separately from Book I in the same year, is otherwise obtained. In this *Secōd booke of the Garden of wysedome, wherin are conteyned wytty, pleasaunt, and nette sayenges of renowmed personages,* one section which cannot be traced to Erasmus is "Of Cambyses." The account of the Persian king here given is closely followed by Preston in the serious scenes of his play.

* From *The Medieval Heritage of Elizabethan Tragedy*, Willard Farnham. Berkeley, 1936, pp. 263–270, 467–468. Reprinted by permission of the University of California Press.

6

If one considers what Taverner does with Cambyses, one can well understand how Preston, seeking matter for a moral play, could have been caught by it. In a short section dealing with "The Egyptians," Taverner praises the extreme care taken by certain Egyptian kings to obtain incorruptible judges and then furnishes an end link with his next section by alluding to "a certayn iuge of whome I shall nowe make relation." Thus he begins his section "Of Cambyses" with the story of the unjust judge Sisamnes. He sagely remarks: "Cambyses Kynge of Persia was otherwyse a verye wycked and cruell tyraunte. Yet there is no prynce of so disperat an hope of so naughtye a lyfe, but that at the lest waye other whyles doth some honest acte."[1] In all the histories, he says, Cambyses is commended for one good deed: when the king learned that Sisamnes, a deputy of his in Asia, had allowed bribery to corrupt justice, he put him to death and commanded that he should be flayed. The skin of Sisamnes was placed over the judgment seat, and the son of Sisamnes, who succeeded to his father's office, was thereby constantly admonished to be upright in his dealings. "Thys exemple," says Taverner, "teacheth them y^t beare offyce & rule to remēber, y^t god suffereth not iniustice nor iniury vnreuenged." But, he proceeds, since he has begun to talk of Cambyses, who otherwise lived a very tyrannous and wicked life, he may as well report certain of his notorious crimes and his end, so that rulers may take further example. For though Cambyses at the beginning "subdued & conquered Egypte, yet anone he forgatte all goodnes and degendred quyte & cleane frō the renowmed & excellent vertues of hys father." The crimes of Cambyses which Taverner sketches are three. First, when Prexaspes, one of his chosen counselors, urged the king to abandon his besetting vice of drunkenness, Cambyses appealed to other lords of the realm, and when they flattered him instead of seconding Prexaspes, he visited terrible punishment upon his counselor. He commanded that the young son of Prexaspes be brought before him. The king, after he had "throughly washed hys braynes wyth wyne," shot the boy through the heart with an arrow, and had the transfixed heart cut out to prove that he was no drunkard. Second, Cambyses murdered his own brother Smerdis lest he might at any time be king. Third, he sinned against nature by marrying his "owne suster germayne," and then he put her to death. At a feast with this queen he arranged a combat between a young lion and a dog for pleasure and sport. Another dog of the same litter as the first broke his bonds to help his brother vanquish the lion. When the queen shed tears and reminded the king that he had treated his own brother otherwise, he slew her. "Wherfore," concludes Taverner, "not long after, wyth a greuouse vengeaunce, God plaged him. For as he was comming out of Egypte in to Persia, when he shulde mownt on horsbacke, his swerd felle out of the skaberd and sore wounded hym in suche

---

1 Fol. 17 of the first edition, 1539.

wyse that he dyed of it. This exēple testifyeth, that god woll not longe suffre tyrantes to reygne."

All this is to be found in Herodotus, though it is not there related in the same order and though some of the minor details are different. In Herodotus the story of Sisamnes is told in a separate book following that in which the three crimes appear, and the three crimes are not described in Taverner's sequence.[2] Wherever Taverner got the matter for his section on Cambyses, it was doubtless not directly from Herodotus, and the same thing may be said of his moral attitude.[3] His "plague of God" moralizing is somewhat reminiscent of the pointed way in which Herodotus says that the sword of Cambyses gave the king a fatal wound in the thigh, in that part where he had once stabbed the Egyptian god Apis, but Taverner's moral manner is essentially one which the skeptical Herodotus does not in the least attempt.

Here, then, Preston could find a moral play and a tragedy of sorts very neatly made to order, with even the moralizing fully supplied according to the fashion of the day for discovering examples of God's vengeance. That he made thorough use of the opportunity is proved by the fact that he offers the good deed and the three crimes nearly as they are in Taverner, and exactly in Taverner's order, for the serious action of *Cambises,* emphasizing the one good deed done by the king just as Taverner emphasizes it and upon occasion employing distinctive words and phrases to be found in Taverner. Preston more than once makes the garrulous Vice direct attention to the one good deed of the king, as in the following lines:

> As he for the good deed, on the Judge was commended,
> For all his deeds els he is reprehended.[4]

The places in which Preston's words and phrases are the same as Taverner's are few but noticeable. In dramatizing the story of Prexaspes (Praxaspes in the play), Preston seems definitely to have kept his finger on the text of *The Garden of Wysdom* and let it provide some of his wording. Taverner has Prexaspes say to the king "that the Persians praysed

---

[2] Herodotus, III, 30 ff., and V, 25.

[3] It has recently been remarked that Johann Carion, in his *Chronicorum Libri Tres* (edition of 1550), deals with Cambyses in a way quite similar to Preston's. See D. C. Allen, "A Source for *Cambises*," *Modern Language Notes,* XLIX (1934), 384 ff. Obviously there is a close relationship between Carion's and Taverner's accounts, though in Carion the incident of Sisamnes is dealt with last and in Taverner (as in Preston) it is dealt with first. This relationship and what lies behind it I have not had opportunity to investigate. Cambyses was well known in the Middle Ages as a horrible example of vicious life. See Arthur Lincke, "Kambyses in der Sage, Litteratur und Kunst des Mittelalters," *Aegyptiaca, Festschrift für Georg Ebers,* Leipsic, 1897, pp. 41 ff.

[4] *Cambyses King of Persia,* ed. J. S. Farmer (Tudor Facsimile Texts), 1910, sig. D *verso.* See also sig. F 3 *verso.*

hym very much, but thys one thyng dyspleased them, that he was so subiecte to the vyce of dronkēnes." Preston gives this speech to Praxaspes as:

> The Persians much doo praise your grace, but one thing discommend:
> In that to wine subiect you be, wherin you doo offend.

Taverner's king asks his lord "whether in any thyng he were worthy to be reprehēded." Preston's king asks:

> Am I worthy of any crime once to be reprehended?

Finally, Taverner's king says to the father that the murdered child's heart is well hit, "wherfore he mought esteme full well herby, y^t he was no drōkard." Preston's king comes about as close to saying these very words as he could come in a line of morality verse:

> Esteem thou maist right well therby, no drunkard is ye King.[5]

The play might have been far better if Preston had not found it so easy to let Taverner's arrangement of anecdotes take on dramatic meaning and be sufficient in themselves for the main business of the action. Preston might otherwise have been stimulated to the discovery of further material in history or legend and to purposeful organization. Yet, disconnected anecdotal structure was relatively no great blemish upon a play in the 1560's, and if the level of achievement demanded by his age be considered, Preston must be praised. He recognized tragic possibilities in an outrageously cruel protagonist stalking through a succession of bloody crimes to a bloody doom, and hit for the first time an Elizabethan dramatic taste to which Marlowe and the immature Shakespeare were to cater. Also, he utilized Taverner with a kind of shrewd economy.

Preston's modicum of dramatic shrewdness makes itself plain at once in the dramatization of his first incident, that of Sisamnes. Taverner begins with the punishment by Cambyses of the unjust judge simply because his comment on Egyptian kings and Egyptian judges has led him to do so. He does not place this one good deed among the first exercises of power by the Persian king; he tells of it as an interlude in the king's later viciousness. As he observes, Cambyses began his reign by approaching the greatness of his father Cyrus in another matter, that of conquering Egypt. Preston magnifies the incident of Sisamnes and combines it with the conquest of Egypt to make them both together represent the level of statesmanship and goodness at which the king began his reign and from which he declined and fell. He lets the king appoint Sisamnes as his deputy at home when he departs for Egypt. Also, Preston uses Sisamnes quite effectively in introducing the inevitable Vice, in this play named

---

[5] Phrasing as quoted for the Praxaspes incident may be found in the 1539 edition of *The Garden of Wysdom,* fols. 18 *verso* and 19 *verso,* and in the Tudor Facsimile Text of the play, sigs. C 3 *verso* and D *recto.*

Ambidexter because he "plays with both hands," doing both good and evil though always intending mischief. Ambidexter helps to corrupt Sisamnes, and later, of course, speeds the king upon his mad career of crime. In intervals between the more serious scenes, Ambidexter turns to orthodox low comedy with such company as the ruffians Huf, Ruf, and Snuf, and the country bumpkins Hob and Lob. In his character as a politic player with both hands, getting much evil done but some good, Ambidexter is a legitimate extension of Taverner's ruling idea that good may somehow come to be done in the midst of vice.

The final moralizing of the action Preston leaves practically as it is in Taverner, except to make sure that it shall not suffer for any lack of emphasis. His king dies with these last words:

A iust reward for my misdeeds, my death doth plaine declare.

Ambidexter, deserting a scene in which he can do nothing more, reminds us that events have worked neatly toward their logical conclusion and that he has rejoiced to point out their working all along:

I did prognosticate of his end by the Masse.

And one of the lords of the court immediately makes the moral triply sure:

A iust reward for his misdeeds, the God aboue hath wrought:
For certainly the life he led was to be counted nought.[6]

In *Cambises,* the English morality comes to the climax of its concern with mundane retribution and truly becomes simple tragedy, without any of the older morality spirit which stood in the way of tragic finality. Preston's play has no touch at all of mercy. It centers in a single concrete sinner and leaves him with the utmost lack of hesitancy to the wages of sin which his acts might be expected to gather in this world.

By its unification in the melodramatic fall of a single tragic figure, *Cambises* has a certain effective superiority over either *Apius and Virginia* or *Horestes,* even though its structure is loosely episodic. All three plays are plainly from the same popular mold. Each lacks division into acts and scenes. Each has its lone Vice who gives some impulse to the major action and who draws with him into the play a troop of comic figures from vulgar life. Each has generally a marked distinction in versification between the "heroic" scenes and the scenes of low comedy, giving to the former a measure which may be scanned as seven-foot iambic and to the latter a measure which may only be scanned as tumbling verse. Each is in the fullest sense native to the English stage; the author of each is so far from being directly stirred by classic learning that he is content to depend almost wholly upon a single secondary source in English for his classic subject-matter.

Scorn for the failure of these three plays to show, either by form or by

---

[6] *Ed. cit.,* sig. F 4 *recto.*

choice of subject-matter, a broader classic background than they do can easily obscure their very real achievement. They demonstrate that English popular drama at the beginning of Elizabeth's reign was ready to profit by the example of classic tragedy because English popular drama had been able to develop a crudely tragic force of its own. But before their promise was to be converted into established reality, the popular taste for tragedy was to be further confirmed in nondramatic literature.

CAMBISES

Armstrong, William A. "The Authorship and Political Meaning of *Cambises*," *English Studies*, XXXVI (1955), 289–299.

Bevington, David M. *From* Mankind *to* Marlowe: Growth *of* Structure *in the* Popular Drama *of* Tudor England. Cambridge, Mass., 1962, pp. 183–189, *et passim.*

Clemen, Wolfgang. *English Tragedy Before Shakespeare.* London, 1961.

Rossiter, Arthur P. *English Drama from Early Times to the Elizabethans.* London, 1950, pp. 142–144.

John Lyly

LYLY *

G. Wilson Knight

ELIZABETHAN thought was more linguistically alive than ours. Perhaps the reputation of puns and word-play varies according to an age's literary strength—we find them in Hebrew literature and Greek drama. Word-play sees similarity in opposites. Metaphor is a sort of pun; and Elizabethan conversation may have held, weakly, the metaphoric and allusive quality of Bacon's prose. That Elizabethan tragedy depended on a verbal joy now lost is generally allowed; that *Ralph Roister Doister* is a word-farce only slightly dependent on situation and action has not been, I think, noticed; hence its surges of doggerel absurdity rising at high moments to nonsensical word-makings of a rough syllabic music. Lyly's verbal and allusive extravagances, and their contemporary popularity, must not be too sharply dismissed: his dramatic work relates significantly to his Euphuism. Before turning to the plays I would make two points concerning *Euphues* itself.

The style is neatly balanced and heavily antithetical in word, phrase, sentence, paragraph. Complex cross-antitheses are usual. Consider this one:

* From *Review of English Studies*, Vol. 15, 1939, pp. 146–163. Reprinted in abridged form by permission of the author and the Clarendon Press, Oxford.

What is he, Euphues, that, knowing thy wit and seeing thy folly, but will rather punish thy lewdness than pity thy heaviness?

(*Euphues,* Bond, Vol. I, p. 208)[1]

Observe that the technical essence can be characterized—and if it can be it must be—as substance. This sentence expresses a lively awareness of opposites. Now Lyly's style plays constantly round psychological contradictions. In *Euphues* soliloquy, letters, dramatic argument regularly express mental conflict. Lyly's "Ay, but..." connections in fictional self-communing serve continually to introduce battalions of opposing reasons to what precedes. Implicit in his method—which is also his matter—there is therefore dramatic conflict. The antithetic style of *Euphues* reflects that balancing of contradictions that is also the core of Elizabethan drama. However luxuriant and leisurely the book, as a whole, may seem, it has thus a dramatic immediacy and tension faintly analogous to the very different, yet also epistolary, manner of Richardson. A certain wisdom of accepted uncertainty is always at the back of the opposing parties or principles rooted in the nature of drama: this wisdom is Lyly's, pre-eminently.

Second, we have a mass of pseudo-scientific, natural, and classical comparisons. Though there is gross exaggeration, the thing exaggerated is of vital poetic importance. Lyly continually refers human and psychological issues to the natural universe. True morality must be in some sense truth to nature: it is Hooker's problem in Book I of his *Ecclesiastical Polity.* It is everybody's problem, rooted in the very structure of poetic expression. Consider this typical passage:

> The similitude you rehearse of the wax, argueth your waxing and melting brain, and your example of the hot and hard iron showeth in you but cold and weak disposition. Do you not know that which all men do affirm and know, that black will take no other colour? That the stone abeston being once made hot will never be made cold? That fire cannot be forced downward? That nature will have force after kind? That everything will dispose itself according to nature? Can the Aethiope change or alter his skin? or the leopard his hue? Is it possible to gather grapes of thorns or figs of thistles? or to cause anything to strive against nature?

(V. I, p. 191)

The explicit human-natural reference here is implicit throughout the multitudinous crazy similitudes of *Euphues:* a desire at once to read the human mind in terms of the living physical universe and see that universe and its properties—including inorganic matter—as a vital extension of

---

[1] The references follow R. Warwick Bond's edition of Lyly's works, Oxford, 1902.

the human mind. In Wordsworth you have the philosophy of it; in all poets the practice of it. Certainly, Lyly's references smell overstrong of mediaeval bestiaries and alchemy; but the Renaissance mind in wording a new consciousness of nature is often driven to expression in mediaeval terms—as we shall find, too, in Marlowe. The generalized and intentional force of Lyly's comparisons blends easily into his use of a well-known proverb near the end of my quotation, followed by the transcription, similar in both substance and direction, of a famous New Testament passage. The fundamentally serious quality and the profound intention are thus clear.

Lyly's numerous mythological, especially Greek, references tone with the upsurge of Renaissance Hellenism generally: and this, too, relates to my last argument, since Greek mythology is continually for Renaissance and Romantic poets the natural grammar for a consciousness that has broken the man-nature opacity. In *Euphues* the stress falls mostly on pseudo-scientific learning; in the plays, on Greek mythology.

The neat antitheses of *Euphues* recur in the balanced parties and general symmetry of design in the plays. These show vital conflicts though no powerful train of action: they are static and spatialized rather than narrative, yet their vivid immediacy never lacks excitement. The conclusions to the first two scenes of *Endimion* will illustrate this technical mastery. Scene beginnings also consistently rivet the eye. Though the action is slow to advance, its very static unrest is so emphasized at a re-entry that suspense is strong:

> No rest, Endimion? Still uncertain how to settle thy steps by day, or thy thoughts by night?

> *(Endimion, II. iii. 1)*

A trick Shakespeare assimilated thoroughly: soliloquy often exquisitely expands the dualized personality of a central figure, whetting your attention to the outcome. As you read, you see:

> Yonder I espy Endimion. I will seem to suspect nothing, but soothe him, that seeing I cannot obtain the depth of his love, I may learn the height of his dissembling.

> *(Endimion, II. i.47)*

You are jerked into a stage-awareness and your anxiety sharpened. All that tires in *Euphues* under strict compression ignites. Instead of listening, you see; instead of knowing, experience. Dramatic suspense adds a dimension to your receptivity: and Lyly's progress from *Euphues* to the plays miniatures neatly the movement from *The Faery Queen* to Shakespeare. Effects are narrowed and intensified under a tight dramatic technique. There is far less pseudo-science but new vital personifications of Hellenic myth.

As in Spenser different sorts of allegory or symbolism jostle each other. Lyly, like Spenser, is a court-poet: the title-page to *Euphues* says: "Very pleasant for all gentlemen to read, and most necessary to remember." He is even closer to court life than Spenser. He transmits the electric torch of contemporary social eroticism; rather like Pope. In all poetry we expect a particular event or person to be at one with a generalized significance: but in Spenser and Lyly there is the additional complication of masked contemporary meanings. If these are too organic something may be lost for future ages: the work is too closely bedded in its own birth. With Spenser I feel this, but less with Lyly. Most of his drama can, like Shakespeare's, be read without searching too exactly for such origins; and when, as in *Endimion,* such independence in reading is not possible, there is somehow a pleasing necessity about our very mystification. Lyly's plays more precisely than any others reflect the court of Elizabeth; our interest is closely involved in this; his pregnant love-analyses come hot, as it were, from knowledge of court-flirtations; and we rather like to feel there are points in the dialogue and sometimes the whole structure to which we cannot respond as directly as his first audience. The very flavor, as it were, of the plays would be different were he always transmuting, instead of reflecting, his day. Lyly is not, and is not wanted to be, Shakespeare. The conventional choice of *Endimion* as Lyly's most representative play is probably fortunate enough. It distils and intensifies his general qualities. Its various allegories are of shifting importance. There is Cynthia = Elizabeth, Tellus = Mary Queen of Scots, and the otherwise-to-be-interpreted other persons; parallel with this, and of changing importance, is Cynthia = the Moon and Tellus = the Earth, without further correspondences; and last, the more generalized sense of a hero set between a high and divine love and earthy and unscrupulous passions. Cynthia rules the action from the start and statuesquely takes charge at the close. That Cynthia-Elizabeth should so dominate Lyly's most dense and weighty single play is apt, since the Queen is necessarily the focal point of all that courtly eroticism at the back of his work. The imaginative and factual coalesce. The Queen is close-involved in the mysterious dream allegories at the play's heart; so that Lyly's most deeply imaginative, even mystic, apprehension is appropriately locked, as by a navelstring, to the age of its birth. Cynthia's particularity as Elizabeth becomes itself a universal.

Often, however, his persons and plots, and continually isolated exquisite movements of dialogue, have symbolic or poetic force of the most normal kind. There is a new strength in advance of the moralities. Those started with a rigid abstraction: poverty, good-deeds, or such like, and set it walking in human form. The resulting personality either outgrows the conception and general plan, or stays severely limited. The Elizabethan recognizes the complexity and contradictions and dramatic oppositions *within* the single personality and the baffling indecisiveness of all moral categories. So he starts with a concrete, often mythical or pseudo-historical, figure and lets his abstract thinking play round and into its growth. The ideas within his human delineation will be many and paradoxical. Where there is a seeming figure of the mediaeval sort, it will shadow some vast and universal idea such as Cupid = Love: itself, in Lyly, one tissue of contradictions. The weakness of the moralities is suggested by their name. Moral categories are on a plane below that of poetic creation (which is not therefore independent of them), and, if allowed to direct autonomously the plan, tend to impose a seeming simplicity on a real complexity. "Death" or "love" are realities so ultimate that they hold power beyond the shifting concepts of the moral order, and can safely be personified in any age. The communistic or pacifist propagandist art of to-day might study, with profit, this problem. Of course, a Christian propaganda does not exactly incur this limitation, Christianity being itself a complex poetry first, and an ethic, if at all, afterwards. It is significant that when Lyly uses a mediaeval touch in *The Woman in the Moon* his personified qualities are vast and non-ethical: Nature, Concord, Discord—the two last, under their own names or in symbols of Music and Tempest being the rooted dualism throughout Shakespeare. But generally Lyly lets his plays grow from and form about some concretely conceived story.

I pass to consider Lyly's more direct content, what the plays say to us. Love, as in *Euphues,* is his whole theme. He is as aware as Spenser of its complexities: he is more aware than Spenser of its inward contradictions. His understanding is at once purer and more realistic. He can refer to crude, and in a sense healthy, lust but seems to have little or no sense, as have Spenser, Marlowe, and Milton, of the sexual nature in subtle mental disease: in this he is with Shakespeare.

Campaspe dramatizes a typical Renaissance conflict, of soldiership and love. The whole play is redolently Elizabethan. The choice of an Alexander story is apt; since Alexander and Caesar have here an almost Messianic authority. The Elizabethan ideal must be a soldier, yet a Christian gentleman. Shakespeare's Theseus and Lyly's Alexander are correspondent, precisely: strong and masterful, yet gentle:

> Alexander as he tendereth virtue, so he will you; he drinketh not blood, but thirsteth after honour, he is greedy of victory, but never satisfied with mercy. In fight terrible, as becometh a captain; in conquest mild, as beseemeth a king. In all things, than which nothing can be greater, he is Alexander.

(I. i. 48)

As in *A Midsummer Night's Dream* the poet shows his hero returning from conquests, not actually seen at any bloody-work: so exploiting the positive while not the negative aspect of valor. Alexander is anxious to

have as great care to govern in peace, as conquer in war: that whilst
arms cease, arts may flourish, and, joining letters with lances, we
endeavour to be as good philosophers as soldiers, knowing it no less
praise to be wise than commendable to be valiant.

(I. i. 80)

Which is answered by Hephaestion's:

Needs must that commonwealth be fortunate, whose Captain is a
Philosopher and whose Philosopher is a Captain.

(I. i. 85)

The typically Elizabethan conception shows how close we are in this
(earlier) play to the equation of Cynthia with Elizabeth in *Endimion*.
The play's central problem is the age's problem, intrinsic to such a book
as Castiglione's *Courtier*. What is the perfect courtly, humanistic, existence? Notice Alexander's courteous and delightful conversation with
Apelles: and how exquisitely the warrior-king is balanced against the
artist. The Elizabethan aims at the paradox of a Christlike warrior:
Alexander, and Theseus. And when his foes are vanquished, how must
he act? What is left to do? The solution is, dramatically at least, obvious:
he must fall in love. Which Alexander does, shocking his soldier retainer,
Hephaestion:

What! is the son of Philip, king of Macedon, become the subject of
Campaspe, the captive of Thebes? Is that mind, whose greatness the
world could not contain, drawn within the compass of an idle alluring
eye?

(II. ii. 31)

He reminds Alexander of Campaspe's mortality. This is Lyly's recurrent
problem—if love is divine, why so brittle? and so sternly to be controlled?
Yet, if it be not, then what is? Alexander is given a typically neat defence:

My case were light, Hephaestion, and not worthy to be called love, if
reason were a remedy, or sentences could salve, that (which) sense
cannot conceive.

(II. ii. 77)

Being a king, he says, his passions are greater than others'. Hephaestion
must cease

With arguments to seek to repel that which with their deity the gods
cannot resist.

(II. ii. 89)

Again, a typical thought of Lyly's—love's superb strength. Moreover, says Alexander, is it not likely and reasonable that the captive Campaspe should return an Alexander's love? But note the exquisite reply:

> You say that in love there is no reason, and therefore there can be no likelihood.

(II. ii. 110)

The light dialogue plays over psychological profundities. Alexander's arguments are turned against himself. Lyly's persons are often so tangled in the mysterious contradictions and irrationalities of their own love. Hephaestion turns out to be right, Campaspe loves Apelles, the painter:

> I perceive Alexander cannot subdue the affections of men, though he conquer their countries. Love falleth like dew as well upon the low grass, as upon the high cedar.

(V. iv. 127)

Which holds a lucid and lovely truth comparable to its New Testament original. Alexander ends the fine, generous-hearted hero, as little subdued by a selfish passion as Theseus is taken in by the seething imaginations of lunatic, lover, or poet. He leaves love to "seamsters and scholars" and "fancies out of books," like Theseus; while Apelles takes Campaspe. This is not strange. The king, the soldier, man of action, is often greater than poet or philosopher to the Elizabethan; as Christ is greater, apart from all theology, than a Dante or a Shakespeare—the man who lives, not writes, his record. So

> HEPHAESTION: The conquering of Thebes was not so honourable as the subduing of these thoughts.
>
> ALEXANDER: It were a shame Alexander should desire to command the world, if he could not command himself.

(V. iv. 148)

This touches, for an instant, something beyond both love and warriorship. But—and it is a big one—the play ends on a delightfully pregnant remark:

> And, good Hephaestion, when all the world is won, and every country is thine and mine, either find me out another to subdue, or, of my word, I will fall in love.

(V. iv. 153)

If we thought Love dethroned, we are wrong: so often a seeming conclusion in Lyly turns into its opposite. Every separate statement is, by itself, a shadow only of the profound movement of his dialogue, something bigger, heavier than his delicate phrases at first suggest. So here the problem of an ultimate good remains.

· · · ·

Lyly's love-apprehension is new and striking. His faith in the naked impulse of sexual attraction is exceptionally pure and independent of all moralizings. He is more interested in studying and projecting the impulse than in judging its results. The eros-perception is dramatically best consummated in marriage: but his analyses concern the thing itself, in which positive and negative impressions are inseparable. His conflicts are subtle and intricate with no easy black-and-white solutions. Spenser's *Bower of Bliss,* which is parasitic on a sin-consciousness, is to him an unknown field. The stream of romantic love welling from Provence and fertilizing mediaeval allegory is locked now in the tight reservoirs of Lyly's dramatic work, forming new depths. Love has become for the first time dramatic, challenging the religious consciousness which through the centuries preceding held a monopoly over drama.[2]

· · · ·

Shakespeare's debt to Lyly has been often emphasized; though it is as much a natural kinship as a debt. Thought-parallels bristle on page after page. I would stress a wider parallel of design, a measured and purposive working out of complications unfurling to a satisfying, often somewhat ritualistic, close. This, so beautifully executed in Lyly, is part of the Shakespearian art always. And I do not mean only Shakespeare's lighter work: Lyly's thought points the mind as much to the metaphysic of love in *Troilus and Cressida* and *Antony and Cleopatra* as to *Love's Labour's Lost* and the sonnets. So, too, the central dream in *Endimion* and its recapitulation at the end forecast Posthumus' dream and description in *Cymbeline:* note the part played by the eagle in both plays. And the conclusions, and indeed the whole designs, are so ceremoniously satisfying through use especially of two sorts of *centrality,* both throwing forward to Shakespeare.

First, there are central dominating figures: Cynthia, Venus, Cupid, Alexander. All the plays reflect Elizabethan royalism in that each possesses some dominant and central figure of worldly or divine authority or, as in *Endimion,* of both; persons of power on whom everything depends, and who yet do not steal the whole action like Marlowe's protagonists. This reflects, of course, the Queen-centred court-life of the plays' origin. Lyly and Shakespeare constructed admirable art-forms partly because the Queen-centred life around Elizabeth was itself of art-form quality: they had a hub on which to revolve. Moreover, a hub that could inspire a belief—however transient—like this:

2 The more esoteric aspects of Lyly's love-apprehension will be discussed in my forthcoming study of British drama, *The Golden Labyrinth.*

GYPTES: They are thrice fortunate that live in your palace, where Truth is not in colours, but life, virtues not in imagination, but execution.

CYNTHIA: I have always studied to have rather living virtues than painted Gods; the body of Truth, than the tomb.

(*Endimion,* IV. iii. 48)

An earthly paradise was, or seemed, at hand to the Elizabethan imagination. The actual was eros-impregnated on a grand scale, and Elizabethan literature is one of the results. The synthesis of loyalty and eroticism in Endimion's adoration for Cynthia points ahead to the twin positive forces of Shakespeare's work: the romantic and kingly ideals, not so distinct then as now. Kindred dual feelings are blent into Shakespeare's sonnets, neither flattery nor sexual emotion, but something to us slightly alien, made of both.

There are, secondly, central symbols, the impregnating of some object with a central significance, such as the Well, or the sleeping figure of the hero himself, in *Endimion,* or the Tree both in *Gallathea* and *Love's Metamorphoses.* Such a symbol, taking as it were the stage-centre of the play's massed area (and often it will therefore be an object central on the actual stage), lends concreteness and focal length to the action round it; serves as a heart to the organism, as the central person is its spine and head and the ceremonial conclusion its crown. Time and again art forms of Shakespearian texture, whether in poem, play, or novel, show such central symbolisms: something both created by and reacting on, the dominant conflicts concerned; the body's heart.

Lyly's formalized and ceremonious designs enclose acts of sacrifice or other ritual and devotion to one or other of his gods. A fervent piety breathes in all these, especially in the sublimation and victory of Cupid over the chastity of Ceres' nymphs in *Love's Metamorphoses,* and the friendly exchange of sacrifices between the two divinities, Cupid and Ceres; reflecting a synthesis of naked desire and marriage fertility, perhaps of all Lyly's most significant symbolic stroke of art. Sacrifice and piety are intrinsic to Lyly's conception of love; a humble, rich, sweetly human thing. Campaspe and Apelles talk of Venus, who can, of course, almost be equated with Cupid:

CAMPASPE: How is she hired? by prayer, by sacrifice, or bribes?

APELLES: By prayer, sacrifice, and bribes.

CAMPASPE: What prayer?

APELLES: Vows irrevocable.

CAMPASPE: What sacrifice?

APELLES: Hearts ever sighing, never dissembling.

CAMPASPE: What bribes?

APELLES: Roses and kisses: but were you never in love?

CAMPASPE: No, nor love in me.

(*Campaspe,* III. iii. 34)

Notice the religious tonings. Lyly's religious feeling in the plays may recall his more specifically Christian and Biblical moralizings in *Euphues.* He was saturated in all that first before becoming an artistic devotee of his eros-cult. This is correspondingly sweetened and ennobled. It is his essential humility and purity before direct human experience that brings Lyly closest to Shakespeare and makes his humor sympathetic and kindly, the antithesis of Jonson's: compare his satire on alchemists in *Gallathea* with Jonson's. Lyly's comedy there with the Astronomer, who falls into a ditch whilst studying the stars, is, characteristically, a humor playing around the philosophic. Such humor of Shakespearian sort is, like his dialogue, dependent often on a sudden awareness of a big simplicity breaking through a slight complexity. Remember his delightful fun with Latin tags in *Endimion;* with Sir Tophas as "three quarters of a noun-substantive"; and remember he is a schoolmaster, producing with his boys as players. A deeper wisdom puts learning in its place: yet surely no Elizabethan used learning to better purpose; nor any literary genius of the first order in English literature was more fit to be, as well, a teacher of children.

For this is, in short, his humanistic message

> There is no man so savage in whom resteth not this divine particle, that there is an omnipotent, eternal, and divine mover, which may be called God.

(*Campaspe,* I. iii. 35)

And, yet paradoxically—and to be true to him we must preserve a paradox:

> I cannot see, Montanus, why it is feigned by the poets that love sat upon the chaos and created the world; since in the world there is so little love.

(*Love's Metamorphoses,* I. i. 1)

That may be. But it is not the fault of Lyly's plays.

CAMPASPE AND ENDIMION

Baker, George, ed. *Campaspe,* in *Representative English Comedies,* ed. Charles Mills Gayley. 3 vols. New York, 1912–1914, I, 268–275.

Baker, George, ed. *Endymion: The Man in the Moon.* New York, 1894, pp. xi–xciii.

Bennett, Josephine Waters. "Oxford and *Endimion,*" *PMLA,* LVII (1942), 354–369.

Bevington, David M. "John Lyly and Queen Elizabeth: Royal Flattery in *Campaspe* and *Sapho* and Phao," *RenP* (1966), 37–67.

Boas, Frederick S. *An Introduction to Tudor Drama.* Oxford, 1933, pp. 87–91.

Bond, R. W., ed. *The Complete Works of John Lyly.* 3 vols. Oxford, 1902, II, 251–261, 274–276, 302–312; III, 6–15, 81–103.

Bryant, J. A., Jr. "The Nature of the Allegory in Lyly's *Endymion,*" in *Renaissance Papers 1956,* ed. Hennig Cohen and J. Woodrow Hassell, Jr. Durham, N.C. and Columbia, S.C., 1956, pp. 4–11.

Feuillerat, Albert. *John Lyly: Contribution à l'Histoire de la Renaissance en Angleterre.* Cambridge, Eng., 1910, pp. 98–106, 141–190, 314ff.

Hunter, G. K. *John Lyly: The Humanist as Courtier.* London, and Cambridge, Mass., 1962, pp. 159–257.

Huppé, Bernard. "Allegory of Love in Lyly's Court Comedies," *ELH,* XIV (1947), 93–133.

Jeffery, Violet M. *John Lyly and the Italian Renaissance.* Paris, 1928, pp. 95–102.

Powell, Jocelyn. "John Lyly and the Language of Play," in *Elizabethan Theatre,* ed. John Russell Brown and Bernard Harris. Stratford-upon-Avon Studies 9, London, 1966, pp. 147–167.

Turner, Robert Y. "Some Dialogues of Love in Lyly's Comedies," *ELH,* XXIX (1962), 276–288.

Wilson, John Dover. *John Lyly.* Cambridge, Eng. 1905, pp. 99–102, 107–110.

George Peele

PEELE'S *OLD WIVES' TALE:*
A PLAY OF ENCHANTMENT *

M. C. Bradbrook

As its form emerged from pageant shews and rhetorical set speeches, Elizabethan courtly comedy was defined as a dream or shadow of the courtly life and distanced by a remote mythological setting.[1] Although he early mastered the transition from dream to waking, myth to court—at the end of *The Arraignement of Paris* Diana delivers the apple of gold into Elizabeth's own hands—George Peele (1556–96) achieved his masterpiece in a more traditional kind. *The Old Wives' Tale,* surviving only in an uncertain text dating from 1595, but possibly originating in the late eighties, rests half-way between shew and drama. Weaving in folk themes and recollections of other plays, Peele achieved "a rare condition of complete simplicity" that invited the audience to "piece the play out with their thoughts."

The play belonged to the Queen's Men, who in the mid-eighties led the London stage, but in the late eighties and early nineties were scarcely

* Reprinted from *English Studies,* Vol. 63, 1962, pp. 323–330, by permission of the publishers.

[1] The emergence of drama from the rhetorical set speeches has been studied by Wolfgang Clemen, *Die Tragödie vor Shakespeare* (1955). For Lyly's definition of comedy, see especially the prologues to *Endimion* and *The Woman in the Moon.*

seen there; driven out by new actors, especially Alleyn's and Henslowe's company, they divided into two groups, who sank to country strollers. *The Old Wives' Tale,* with twenty-four named parts, for a company of seven men and two boys needed much doubling; so that characters succeed each other rapidly in small groups and may never reappear to tell the end of their adventures. Some of the many prophecies are not fulfilled, others are fulfilled but not noted; it is clear that the play has been shortened, but one or two silent parts have been kept, because variety was a prime need.[2] The play was set elaborately in old-fashioned "simultaneous" style, presenting on the stage at least two separate "pavilions" with curtains (the old wife's cottage and Sacrapant's study); a wood with a cross-roads and a "well of life" from which an enchanted head arose; a piece of "enchanted ground," with a hillock, where some characters dug and others were blasted with flames of fire.[3] These sets, which in medieval times at least were miniature in scale,[4] must have been carried round in property carts. A country audience, as Shakespeare's Holofernes knew, would be delighted with "a shew, or ostentation or firework," accompanied here by an "invisible" character, a magic banquet and much other spectacle. But it seems unlikely that they would enjoy literary satire or burlesque, or be prepared to recognise Gabriel Harvey in the figure of Huanebango. They would not know Harvey from Adam. It is unlikely too that a company which was still apparently acting plays like *Clyomon and Clamydes*—another of the Queen's Men's works which they did not release till 1595, though it was then about twenty years old —would at the same time burlesque the tradition of the romance.[5]

The Queen's Men did not share the light mockery of the boys' troupes

2 For a discussion of textual problems see Harold Jenkins, *Modern Language Review,* vol. 34, 1939, pp. 177–185. The prophecy made to Eumenides is fulfilled but not noted; the prophecy to the brothers is fulfilled by Eumenides; the end of Huanebango's and the Clown's adventures is missing. Venelia's important part in the plot is unsupported by speech but her miming would be eloquent, as would the Furies' also.

3 The well was evidently an important property, which the Revels Office once borrowed from the wardrobe kept at the Bell Inn in Gracechurch Street (Feuillerat, *Documents relating to the Revels,* 1908, p. 277). By 1601 it is treated as a jest in the Oxford play of *Narcissus.* The magic head which rose from the well is probably the same as that used in Greene's *Alphonsus of Aragon, Friar Bacon and Friar Bungay,* etc. The pavilions were used in *The Cobbler's Prophecy,* another Queen's Men's play. For a recent discussion of stage properties see Morton Pearson in *Studies in the Elizabethan Theatre,* ed. Charles T. Prouty, 1961.

4 See Allardyce Nicoll, *Masks, Mimes and Miracles,* 1931, p. 196.

5 The view that *The Old Wives' Tale* was satiric or burlesque is now fairly generally discarded. For modern views, see A. K. McIlwraith, *Five Elizabethan Comedies* (Oxford, 1934) p. xiii; Harold Jenkins, *op. cit.*; Herbert Goldstone, *Boston University Studies in English,* IV, 1960, pp. 202–213. Mockery of scholastic pretension was a regular part of country sports; compare the clowns' use of the form of disputation, ll. 593–605; the dispraise of scholars in Nashe's *Summer's Last Will*

under Lyly, or their more robust mockery under Nashe. The repertoire consisted of close-packed plays like the old *King Leire, The Famous Victories of Henry V,* or *Five Plays in One;* when it was first formed, the leaders of this troupe dealt in lusty, extemporal clowning—they included Tarlton (who dressed as a countryman), Laneham, and Robert Wilson. Peele, perhaps an actor and certainly a great deviser of city pageants, had gone up to Oxford in 1571, and so grew up in the decade before the rise of Alleyn, Greene, Marlowe, and Nashe. He is placed where he really belongs by the traditional, apocryphal *Merry Jests of George Peele,* that is, as a companion of Tarlton, Knell, and Bentley—which last two he challenged young Alleyn to equal.[6]

In *The Old Wives' Tale* there is no need for information, orderly sequence of plot, or dramatic connexion, since the enchanted princess "as white as snow and as red as blood," her two brothers, who seek her; the wicked enchanter; the wandering knight; the beggar with his two daughters, one fair and curst, the other foul and patient; the Spanish Knight with his two-handed sword have all been met with by the audience many times before the play began. They had no need to play an action: merely to display themselves for what they were. "When I was a little one, you might have drawne me a mile after you with such a discourse."

So, whether as the result of the actors' cutting or not, when the Two Brothers meet Erestus, the enchanted knight—who is also addressed as "the white bear of England's wood" (a title from medieval romance) and once as "Father Time"—he does not need to be told their story, but can ask at once "Is she fair?" In performance, this seems perfectly natural; the perplexity felt by a reader melts away. When, through simultaneous setting, the audience is released from the confines of place, they cannot be tied to narrative progression.

The fluid life of such plays, like that of ballads, belonged within folk tradition, where the marvellous must always be familiar, though it cannot be rational. Recognition of the familiar and delight by the unexpected must be evenly balanced for the audience to be "rapt." Consistency of mood, the power to absorb the fancy and lull the feelings, binds simplified characters together in a fantastic action, dependent on riddles and magic shews. Each figure was so familiar that as he came forward to give his sequence, it would have been natural for the audience, if pleased, to demand a little more—to cry for the braggart to come back; in Bottom's phrase, "Let him roar again." In fact the first sequence of the boastful Spaniard, Juan y Bango (Huanebango) may have been inserted as an addition in this way; it is somewhat out of key with the rest of the play, the Clown is given a different name in it, and it contains specific literary

---

and Testament, put into the mouth of Winter; the clowns' play in *John a Kent and John a Cumber.* See also note 13 below.

6 See David Horne, *Life and Minor Works of George Peele,* 1952, pp. 85–86.

allusions which place it in or about 1591.[7] The core of the play consists of adventures familiar from tales of wandering knights, many of which had been turned into plays;[8] but the groupings of these characters are drawn from medley plays, which the Queen's Men had given at other times. In these plays there is no narrative sequence: instead, variety of spectacle effects unity of mood or temper.

Medleys usually included two or more pairs of lovers, a hermit or magician, a speaker of riddles and prophecies, and a clown. *The Cobbler's Prophecy* (published 1594) was written by Wilson of the Queen's Men; in it, the Cobbler is given the gift of riddling prophecy that in Peele belongs to Erestus: The Cobbler's mad wife Zelota destroys the villain as Erestus' mad betrothed wife, Venelia, destroys the enchantments of Sacrapant. Both plays require simultaneous settings with two pavilions; in *The Cobbler's Prophecy* smoke arises as "the Cabin of Contempt is set on fire" for the finale. In one of the plays of Derby's Men, *The Rare Triumphs of Love and Fortune* (1582/3), a brother pursues his fleeing sister, and is struck dumb by an enchanter; whereas in Peele, two brothers in seeking a sister are reduced to servitude, and the clown and braggart knight struck blind and deaf. The hermit of the one play is all-powerful: in the other, he is a victim of enchantment. In each, the princess is threatened with death in the final scene, but by meek submission dissolves the last spells.

It seems therefore that much of the material of *The Old Wives' Tale* was common to the stages of the eighties; and when a few lines from Greene's *Orlando Furioso* (1591) (another Queen's play) together with the name Sacrapant are found to have crept in, this may illustrate a general habit of building up scenes fairly freely upon the basis of a scenario or "plot." *The Old Wives' Tale* as it stands, adapted to the needs of a small troupe of country strollers, consists of brief sequences, with as much scenic variety and multiplication of characters as could be achieved. As a later apologist was to say

> Of actors we did lack a many,
> Therefore we clipt our play into a shew.

[7] Harold Jenkins thinks this passage—lines 312–410—was intended for deletion, and that ll. 651–656 were intended to replace it. It seems to me more likely to be an accretion; the later writer has forgotten the Clown's grand name of Corebus, which he perhaps was meant originally to assume on becoming a 'knight' errant. Change of name was important for change of role; so Delia is renamed Berecynthia. (Compare the wholesale renaming of characters in the sub-plot of Shakespeare's *Taming of the Shrew*.) Perhaps there was still some memory of the old habit of the player's name being written on a scroll pinned to his breast.

[8] William of Palerne, hero of a fourteenth-century romance, is turned into a White Bear, like Erestus. Lost plays on Sir Eglamour and Degrebell and on 'a knight called Florence' were given as early as 1443. A number of lost plays from the eighties must belong to the same kind as *Clyomon and Clamydes*—e.g. *Hepatulus the Blue Knight*. Shakespeare's Flute hopes Thisbe is a wandering knight.

The illusion of variety pleased. Familiar parts would have been recognisable even in mime; the outline could be filled out to whatever extent the audience desired and the occasion warranted. To extend a part would be as plausible as to repeat a song; the Queen's Men had long been famous for extemporising. It has recently been suggested that "plots" or scenarios were supplied by playwrights to the actors, and that Antony Mundy's fame as "our best plotter" depended on his ability to do this.[9]

The poetry of Peele's play lives in the songs, transforming another folk tradition—that of rural seasonal games. A company of harvesters suddenly enter the scene, singing of love:

All ye that lovely lovers be, pray you for me,
Lo, here we come a sowing, a sowing,
And sow sweet fruits of love:
In your sweet hearts well may it prove.

Perhaps, like Ceres in *The Cobbler's Prophecy,* at this point they "sowed" sweetmeats among the audience. Later they appear with harvest women, to sing their second verse: "Lo, here we come a-reaping. . . ."

As long before as 1244, plays "of the bringing in of autumn" were forbidden in the diocese of Lincoln; they were the counterpart of May Games. "The thesher with his flail" is referred to as an expected figure, in the prologue to Robert Wilson's *Three Ladies of London* (1583), while in Nashe's *Summer's Last Will and Testament* (1592/3), also based on seasonal sports, harvesters enter to a drinking song:

Merry, merry, merry, cheary, cheary, cheary,
Trole the blacke bowl to me
Hey derry derry, with a poupe and a lerrie,
Ile trole it again to thee.
Hookie, hookie, we have shorn and we have bound,
And we have brought harvest home to town.[10]

Though Nashe's work is as long-drawn-out as Peele's is brief, it too substitutes thematic imaginative coherence for narrative order. In contrast with their dream-like flatness of dialogue, both shews (Nashe's is introduced as "no play neither, but a shew") are filled out by rich poetic sensuousness of pastoral description, ripe fullness of the songs; these

[9] See I. A. Shapiro, in *Shakespeare Survey,* vol. 14. 1960, pp. 30–31. What has been retained here is the skeleton of action—the riddles—and the regular pattern of leading characters. Incidents in classic pantomime can still be fitted in to skeleton plots (as anyone who has been to the Tivoli pantomime at Copenhagen will realize.) For the habits of the Queen's Men, see W. W. Greg, *Two Elizabethan Stage Abridgements* (1923), on *Orlando Furioso.*

[10] In Cambridgeshire villages today, the harvest feast is known as 'horkey' supper. 'Horkey' is the last load home. Compare the harvesters who enter as part of Prospero's masque in *The Tempest.* For a general discussion of harvest plays, especially in relation no Nashe's play and to Shakespeare, see C. L. Barber, *Shakespheare's Festive Comedy,* 1959, pp. 58–79.

embody a lyric gorgeousness which no scenic display could give to
the eye.

> When as the Rie reach to the chin,
> And chopcherrie, chopcherrie, ripe within,
> Strawberries swimming in the cream,
> And schoolboys playing in the stream,
> Then O, then O, then O, my true love said,
> Till that time come again,
> She could not live a maid.

The clustered images, spreading summer pleasure, and carrying only by
suggestion the beautiful wantonness of a woman's body, are sung by one
of the more sophisticated characters in Peele's Induction. In contrast,
later in his play, the Enchanted Head which rises from the Well of Life
bearing ears of corn and showers of gold recites a country spell, where
the harvest of love and fertility is celebrated more wantonly.

> Gently dip; but not too deepe;
> For fear thou make the golden beard to weep.
> Fair maiden, white and red,
> Combe me smooth and stroke my head,
> And thou shalt have some cockell bread.

The country manners that went to the making of cockell bread were
coarse enough;[11] yet Peele's fancy remains "clean...without spavin or
windgall."

Jack, the dead man that comes back to help the friendly stranger who
out of charity had interred him, prances in to a mummer's jingle:

> Are you not the man, sir,
> Deny it if you can, sir...

and Juan y Bango reflects the glancing mockery of the mummers; for
though in his linguistic and amorous exploits he is the prototype of
Shakespeare's Don Adriano de Armado, in another light he represents
Bold Slasher.

Both Nashe and Peele reserve their heaviest mockery for learning;
both are quite exceptional in the extent of their reliance on folk material,
and the way in which they set it at a distance through complex Inductions.
Perhaps to contemporaries this would have recalled *The Canterbury Tales*
—Chaucer being an unskilled old gaffer in Elizabethan eyes. To Peele's
fellow-authors a movement "Back to Chaucer" was familiar enough.

The jesting ghost of old Will Summers draws the audience into Nashe's
shew, but constantly breaks the illusion of the scene by the kind of ritual
abuse common in country merriment; nor unknown at court festivities,
where the audience frequently tried to "dash" the players. Played by

---

[11] Cockell bread was a marriage charm. See *The New English Dictionary* s.v.
cocklebreads and cf. Eric Partridge, *A Dictionary of Slang*, s.v. cockles.

an adult actor named Toy, Summers would dominate physically the boy players of Nashe. He is the only human figure to appear in the allegory; his irony both controls and anticipates the audience's response.

Peele's Induction is less striking to a modern audience than his fairy tale, because the fairy world is now less familiar. Drama however lives most fully in the Induction, as poetry resides in the songs. It is the Induction that prevents the play from being merely another medley; it supplies natural intercourse, action that follows natural laws.

Three servants of a noble lord, whose names proclaim them actors, lost in a wood, find the creature comforts of food, fire, and sleep in the cottage of Clunch and Madge. Antic goes to bed and to dream offstage, while Frolic and Fantastic sit up with old Madge that they may be "ready...extempore" for the morning. The tale she tells, "of the Gyant and the Kings Daughter and I know not what," comes to life, and before the end old Madge is asleep. Dream perspective justifies the medley, as Madge's half-told, half-dreamt tale. The original and complex tradition of the medieval dream-vision was not fully accessible to Elizabethans, but Peele made some use of it in his own dream-vision, *The Honour of the Garter.*

Written for noble players, who, fallen on evil days, gave it to country audiences, an Induction which shewed country folk entertaining strayed courtly players supplied a looking glass or mirror for actual performance. Actors and audience would find their representatives here, yet in such a manner that the simpler part of the spectators might respond directly, while the lord of the manor would laugh at and recognise old Madge. Contrary to the general practice of using allegorical figures for the Induction, it is here more naturalistic than the main play. Sometimes, of course, a play was presented by a grave figure representing the author; and more than a century earlier Lydgate had described a story teller reciting his tale in a theatre, while mute actors came out of a tent and mimed the story as he told it.[12]

The presence of Madge, Frolic, and Fantastic throws a special colour or tone over the fairy tale, deepening the bare simplicity of the writing— its spareness or "parsimony' as one critic has termed it. Their speech relieves the pastoral lusciousness of the poetry with studied plainness.

> When this was done, I took a piece of bread and cheese and came my way, and so shall you have too, before you go, to your breakefast.

Romance, though still potent when Peele wrote, was diminished—like the miniature wood of his stage or like "far-off mountains turned into

---

[12] For a discussion of this passage from Lydgate's *Tale of Troy,* see Glynne Wickham, *Early English Stages,* Oxford 1959, pp. 193–4. A late use of Induction with the author as presenter is that of *Pericles,* where Gower appears, The Induction represents an attempt to transfer from a predominantly narrative to a predominantly dramatic way of writing. The 'shew' with its 'truchman' survived as a subordinate form well into Elizabeth's reign and developed into the masque.

clouds"—as Shakespeare later described a woodland dream. Ben Jonson mocked the wandering knight in *Every Man out of His Humour* (1599) ; when in the Induction to *The Knight of the Burning Pestle* (1607), Ralph and his mistress disrupt the play, their dreams of romance are farcical. Ralph the grocer's boy is at one time set to woo the King of Cracovia's daughter, at another to make a May Day speech in his own person. Yet, a year or so later, Shakespeare in his last plays wonderfully transformed and revived the old Romances of his youth.

In the 1580's, George Peele and his friends of the Queen's Men were still enjoying that happy moment when "the obvious was supremely satisfying." They could rely on their audience:

> the common people, who rejoice much to be at plays and enterludes and...have at such times their ears...attentive to the matter and their eyes upon the shews of the stage.[13]

This audience would supply for each brief scene an amplification from its own store of legend: so that the dream play achieves with the utmost economy both theatrical depth and poetic lucidity. It belongs to a theatre of presentation and statement, where the unfolding of the action does not consist in dramatic interplay between characters, but rather in different levels of the imaginative life itself. It is a theatre in which poetry is active as recitative and song, not yet active as fully developed dramatic exchange.[14] *The Old Wives' Tale* might most fittingly have begun to be told in the late eighties, halfway between the desert wastes of rant in *Sir Clyomon and Sir Clamydes,* and the full splendor of Shakespeare's *Love's Labour's Lost* or *Midsummer Night's Dream.*

[13] George Puttenham, *The Arte of English Poesie,* (c. 1583), edited A. Walker and G. Willcock, Cambridge 1936, p. 82. Puttenham says that the common people enjoy 'words of exceeding great length' and that while they are attentive to 'matter' and 'shew', yet 'they take little heed to the conning of the rime'. As he has just been advocating classical metres, this passage would suggest that Huanebango's use of hexameters would not be noticed by a common country audience, and that they would enjoy his long words with no thought of literary parody. The notion that in a theatre *any* audience is capable of this kind of literary source-hunting seems to me very largely a figment of scholarly fancy.

[14] I have tried to trace the significance of spectacles and shows in the seventies and the literary development of the eighties in ...*The Rise of the Common Player: A Study of Actor and Society in Shakespeare's England* (London, 1962). The rhetorical questions have been considered by Clemen, and to some extent by Madeline Doran in *Endeavors of Art* (Madison, 1954). Also, more recently by G. K. Hunter in his study, *John Lyly, the Humanist as Courtier* (London, 1962).

See Peele bibliography, below, p. 41.

INTERPLAY IN PEELE'S
THE OLD WIVES' TALE *

Herbert Goldstone

OF Peele's five dramatic works, *The Old Wives' Tale* stands out as the most successful. In all the others he so playfully imitates themes and forms of his contemporaries that he ends up with no more than a pastiche. *The Arraignment of Paris*, for all of its graceful pageantry, never does harmonize the pastoral theme of unrequited love and the mythological one of the fate of Paris. And, though *David and Bethsabe* has some exotically sensual love poetry and some striking insights into sin and expiation, it never does quite reconcile its morality-play account of David and Bethsabe's sin and its *Tamburlaine*-like handling of the battle scenes. But in *The Old Wives' Tale* Peele seems able to use his playfulness to greater advantage, and, as a result, he has fashioned one of the freshest and most quixotically charming of Elizabethan comedies. A very important secret of his success is his resourceful use of different literary worlds —a method he may have learned from Lyly. However, Peele goes beyond Lyly, and, in fact, most of his other contemporaries, for he does not stop at simple contrast but has these different worlds interact upon one another and blend together.

A very important starting point for understanding what Peele has done in *The Old Wives' Tale* is Gummere's introduction to the play, which combines keen appreciation of its humor and just analysis of its technique. According to Gummere, Peele has created an interplay between realistic speech (of ordinary people) and romantic subject matter (such as that of folklore), and between the induction and the play as a whole.[1] The interplay of speech and subject matter makes fantastic situations and actions seem quite down-to-earth because of the everyday language. A good example would be the scene in which Eumenides, the folklore hero, and Jack, the ghost of the young man

---

* From *Boston University Studies in English*, Vol. 4, 1960, pp. 202–213. Reprinted by permission of the publishers and the author.

[1] F. B. Gummere, "Critical Essay on *The Old Wives' Tale*," in *Representative English Comedies*, ed. Charles Mills Gayley (New York: The Macmillan Company, 1903), I, 341, 344.

for whose burial he has arranged, become partners. Here the two work out important details of the folklore source story of "The Grateful Dead" in folksy conversation that makes the whole action seem merely a good business deal.[2] "Well, my lad," remarks Eumenides to his helper, "since thou art so importunate, I am content to entertain thee not as a servant but a copartner in my journey. But whither shall we goe for I have not any money more than one bare three halfe-pence" (898–902).[3] This folksy business tone also makes the scene humorous, because it shows that Eumenides really has no idea of what can happen in his relationship with Jack. As for the interplay between the induction and the play proper, Gummere suggests that the two so interact that it is difficult to differentiate one from the other.[4] Such confusion between the two, he feels, creates the proper mood for accepting the seemingly fantastic events that keep occurring, though in the play proper confusion seems to indicate defective plot arrangement. The sudden appearance of the pages, for example, and their pretending to be characters in their songs, the abrupt entrance of Clunch the smith and his pretending to be an enchanter whose domain they are entering, the way the pages change their tack and start teasing the smith and his wife, the disorganized way Madge tells the old wives' tale that the pages urge her to tell, and the amazing speed with which the very characters in her story suddenly appear in the flesh to take over the story—all create a bewildering succession of events and moods. Yet, oddly enough, all the shifting and confusion create a context that makes it possible for the ordinary and fantastic events to complement one another.

However, there are simply too many other features in the play that Gummere's analysis does not account for. One of the most humorous incidents of all is that in which Sacrapant, the enchanter, realizes that he is losing his magical power. He bursts out, not in realistic, earthy prose, as Gummere would have us believe, but in bombastic blank verse:

> What hand inuades the head of *Sacrapant?*
> What hatefull fury doth enuy my happy state?
> Then *Sacrapant* these are thy latest dayes,
> Alas my vaines are numd, my sinews shrinke,
> My bloud is pearst, my breath fleeting away,
> And now my timelesse date is come to end:
> He in whose life his actions hath beene so foule,
> Now in his death to hell desends his soule.

(1014–1021)

2 For a discussion of Peele's use of "The Grateful Dead," see Gordon K. Gerould, *The Grateful Dead* (London: D. Nutt, for The Folk-lore Society, 1908), pp. 71–73.

3 All line references are to *The Old Wives' Tale,* ed. W. W. Greg (London: Oxford University Press [Malone Society reprints], 1908).

4 Gummere, p. 344.

This speech, in its references to hell and the dissolution of the body, may be a deliberate echo of Faustus' dying speech:

> O, it strikes, it strikes! Now, body, turn to air,
> Or Lucifer will bear thee quick to hell!
> O soul, be changed into little water-drops,
> And fall into the ocean, ne'er be found!
> *Thunder and enter the Devils.*
> My God, my God, look not so fierce on me!
> Adders and serpents, let me breathe awhile!
> Ugly hell, gape not! Come not, Lucifer!
> I'll burn my books!—Ah, Mephistophilis![5]

Sacrapant need not be exactly paraphrasing Faustus, but he could be echoing a stock speech of a dramatic character facing death and given to Marlovian hyperbole, especially when we know how widely imitated Marlowe was by his contemporaries. Here Sacrapant is very amusing because he is really a puny, frightened enchanter and yet, by echoing Faustus or a similar character, he dares imagine himself a heroic figure.

Other examples which do not depend upon realistic speech expressing romantic subject matter include Eumenides' extravagant joy in his reunion with his beloved Delia, when he speaks in blank verse echoing a passage from Robert Greene's play *Orlando Furioso*,[6] or the foolish Huanebango's

---

[5] *The Tragical History of Doctor Faustus,* ed. Frederick S. Boas, in *The Work and Life of Christopher Marlowe,* Vol. V (London: Methuen & Co., Ltd., 1932), V.ii.187–195.

[6] Eumenides pours out his feelings in these lines:

> Thou fairest flower of these westerne parts:
> Whose beautie so reflecteth in my sight,
> As doth a Christall mirror in the sonne:
> For thy sweet sake I haue crost the frosen *Rhine,*
> Leauing faire *Po,* I saild vp *Danuby,*
> As farre as Saba whose inhansing streames,
> Cuts twixt the *Tartars* and the *Russians,*
> These haue I crost for thee faire *Delia:*
> Then grant me that which I haue sude for long.   (1069–1077)

Similarly, one of the knights in Greene's play, *Orlando Furioso,* decribes his love for Angelica [*The Plays and Poems of Robert Greene,* ed. J. Churton Collins (Oxford: Clarendon Press, 1905), I, 225]:

> From thence, mounted vpon a Spanish Barke,
> Such as transported Iason to the fleece,
> Come from the South, I furrowed Neptunes Seas,
> Northeast as far as is the frosen Rhene;
> Leauing faire Voya, crost vp Danuby,
> As hie as Saba, whose inhaunsing streames,
> Cuts twixt the Tartares and the Russians:
> There did I act as many braue attempts,
> As did Pirothous for his Proserpine.   (I.i.63–69)

pompously learned denunciation of others and his fantastic boasts of his renown.

A second criticism of Gummere's essay is that in emphasizing confusion in the play proper he gives the impression that the plot structure is very weak, whereas actually it is clear and logical. Even Madge's apparently chaotic introduction of her story really explains things pretty clearly. She does introduce all of the major folklore characters, except the hero Eumenides, and she even makes his appearance plausible by stating that everyone went looking for the kidnapped princess, his beloved Delia. In addition, by mentioning the enchanter and the prophetic young man, Erestus, she calls attention to the two characters around whom just about all of the plot action, even including that of the nonfolklore characters, revolves. All of the characters either come to Erestus and then meet Sacrapant, who significantly determines their final fate, or they have their future determined by the actions of Sacrapant and Erestus.

What is necessary, then, is to explain the sources of humor in the play more thoroughly and to point out the clear plot structure. And these can be done by extending Gummere's remarks about speech and subject matter and qualifying those concerning the relationship of the Induction to the rest of the play. To begin with, the humor of speech and subject matter is really one manifestation of a much broader interplay that results from the interaction of folklore and many other literary worlds. This more inclusive interplay expresses itself in the relationship between characters and in the presentation of individual characters.

In the first type, characters from widely different literary worlds find common ground, and, despite their apparent differences, accept one another readily. A good example is the poignantly amusing scene between Erestus and Lampriscus, who certainly come from very different literary traditions. Erestus, of course, is a folklore character from Madge's story. Lampriscus, as a man plagued by women all his life, suggests the stock character of the patient, mistreated man exemplified by the husband in Heywood's realistic farce *Iohan Iohan*. The two are able to communicate not only because Lampriscus values Erestus' prophetic advice but because each provides such an appreciative audience for the other's trouble. Therefore, the more each complains the happier the scene becomes. Encouraged by Erestus, Lampriscus berates women so exuberantly that his attack becomes comic art. "As curst as a waspe," Lampriscus sums up his mean daughter Zantyppa, "and as frowarde as a childe new taken from the mothers teate, shee is to my age, as smoake to the eyes, or as vinegar to the teeth" (277–280). Like a discerning critic, Erestus commends his performance, "Holily praised, neighbour, as much for the next" (281–282).

Another example of this type of interplay is the scene in which Eumenides pays for the burial of Jack the pauper after he has listened to a violent argument between village church officials and Jack's friends.

Eumenides, like Erestus, is a folklore character, while the villagers, like Lampriscus, come from realistic comedy. The scene differs from that involving Lampriscus and Erestus in that the characters accept one another unconsciously; neither Eumenides nor the villagers are aware of how different they are from each other. One might think that this scene merely illustrates Gummere's thesis because the racy realistic dialogue between Eumenides and the villagers does ironically work out an important part of the folklore story of "The Grateful Dead." However, the real humor of the scene depends upon the fact that it is simultaneously a realistic comedy dispute about burial and a folklore story about the grateful dead and that none of the characters present recognizes this fact. Eumenides, in particular, stands out because in a completely foreign situation he instinctively acts generously and unknowingly fulfills Erestus' folklore prophecy of the preceding scene.[7] The characters' mutual acceptance of one another becomes apparent as the mood of the scene changes from violent discord to final harmony. At first the villagers quarrel outlandishly, heaping insults upon one another. Yet, apparently having enjoyed their raillery, they go off together at the end to have a drink.

The second type of interplay depends more upon complex and shifting interaction of literary worlds and seems to individualize the characters. Peele takes stock types, like the folklore heroine, the enchanter, or the *miles gloriosus,* and has them constantly echo themes, lines, or actions of stock characters from other Elizabethan literary words. The result of this constant echoing is that each character becomes a composite of types and evokes in the audience varied feelings associated with the literary worlds from which he is drawn. Yet each character is more than the sum of his parts, for the various echoings make the characters more distinctively individual than they might otherwise be.

If Sacrapant, for example, were just a routine enchanter, he would merely act consistently as an all-powerful figure, for this, as W. W. Herrington points out, is what such magicians were prone to do.[8] But, though Sacrapant does show himself to be powerful until he is overcome, he also has endearing human failings. When he first appears, he laments his fate much as the unhappy lover of pastoral whom he apparently resembles:

> The day is cleare, the Welkin bright and gray,
> The Larke is merrie, and records hir notes;

---

[7] Not until after Eumenides has paid for the burial does he realize that he has followed Erestus' instructions: "Heere hould it then" he remarks, "and I haue left me but one poore three halfe pence; now do I remember the wordes the old man spake as the crosse; bestowe all thou hast, and this all, tille dead mens bones come at thy call" (621–624).

[8] W. W. Herrington, "Witchcraft and Magic in The Elizabethan Drama," in *Journal of American Folklore,* XXXII (1919), 458.

Each thing reioyeth vnderneath the Skie,
But onely I whom heauen hath in hate:
Wretched and miserable *Sacrapant,*
In *Thessalie* was I borne and brought vp,
My mother *Meroe* hight a famous witch. . .

(413–419)

Then, as Sacrapant looks at Delia and blames her for his misery, he sounds like the languishing lover of the sonnet sequences flourishing in the 1590's. "See where she comes from whence my sorrowes grow," Sacrapant complains, "How now faire *Delya* where haue you bin?" (432–433). He continues in this conventionally despairing vein, admitting his mistress' beauty and lamenting her cruelty: "Ah *Delya,* fairer art thou than the running water, yet harder farre than steele or Adamant" (438–439). Sacrapant understandably compares Delia to plain running water because Delia has just told him that she has been near the water. Yet his doing this may represent Peele's satire of the exalted comparisons of the Petrarchist lovers in the sonnet sequences: though Sacrapant is as absurd as the Petrarchist lover, he is at least more down-to-earth in his comparisons.

In succeeding speeches, Sacrapant shows himself even more ardent by wanting to please Delia so much. In getting her the best wine, the best meat, and "the veriest knaue in all Spain" (461–466), he may be echoing Faustus' obtaining grapes for the Duchess of Vanholt. He seems no more foolish than Faustus, who is only showing off before the Duchess, whereas Sacrapant at least acts out of love for Delia. In his final speech he again reminds us of Dr. Faustus, as has been noted above. These different echoings make Sacrapant amusing because, despite his power as an enchanter, he is so insecure and unhappy; but they also make him humanly appealing because he can fall in love and be so easily hurt.

Certainly Delia shows herself to be a standard captured folklore princess, for she does have to be rescued and she does graciously thank Eumenides, her lover, for saving her:

Thou gentle knight, whose fortune is so good:
To finde me out, and set my brothers free
My faith, my heart, my hand I giue to thee.

(1079–1081)

But the rest of the time she acts like a princess *manqué.* In the first place, judging from Sacrapant's feelings toward her, she seems like the cruel Petrarchist mistress. In fact, her name itself may have been suggested by Daniel's sonnet sequence, parts of which appeared in 1591 and 1592.[9]

---

[9] Thorleif Larsen, "The Date of Peele's *Old Wives' Tale,*" MP, XXX (1932), 23–28. The exact date of composition of *The Old Wives' Tale* is uncertain; Larsen

Yet she also seems submissive and deferential to Sacrapant as she waits on him and asks, "Will it please you to sit downe sir?" (440). When she asks Sacrapant for the best meat, etc., she seems vain, foolish, and completely unaware of Sacrapant's feelings for her. Whether in these instances Peele is reminding us of the actions of other stock characters, is not clear; he may merely be making a second implied contrast by showing us that Delia is not really the conventional Petrarchist mistress to whom she is being compared. Such a double comparison may make Delia seem, because of her unawareness of Sacrapant's love, more amusing than the conventional Petrarchist mistress and yet also a bit more human because of her docility and naïveté.

In a later scene, Delia seems even more unlike a fairy-tale princess as Sacrapant by means of a magic potion transforms her into Berecynthia so that she will not recognize her brothers. When Delia does act as Berecynthia, she speaks like the stock character of the virago so popular in English drama from the cycle plays on:

> What tell you mee of *Delya* prating swaines?
> I know no *Delya* nor know I what you meane,
> Ply your work or else you are like to smart. . .   (718–720)

> Yet more of *Delya,* then take this and smart:
> What faine you shifts for to defer your labor?
> Worke villaines worke, it is for gold you digg.

(726–728)

Like Noah's wife in the Wakefield play, for example, she beats her brothers and ridicules them. The changing of Delia into a shrew is a master stroke of comedy, for she almost seems unconsciously to be ridiculing herself as a folklore princess when she berates her brothers for their insisting that she *is* the princess Delia.

The change involved in her gracious acceptance of Eumenides at the end of the play is, of course, justified in the plot action, since her rescue by Eumenides releases her from Sacrapant's spell. But the transformation is also justified in terms of Delia's character, for throughout all the changes she remains ingenuous and unable to see that she really *is* a princess and not a deferential child, a virago, or a cruel mistress. Moreover, the changes endow her with the supreme feminine trait of unpredictability.

Huanebango, like Sacrapant and Delia, also keeps suggesting resem-

suggests that a number of references to the play seem to come from the 1592 phase of the Nashe-Harvey quarrel, and argues that 1592 is a distinct possibility. On the other hand, P. H. Cheffaud, *George Peele* (Paris: Alcan, 1913), p. 127, argues that it is the 1590 phase that Peele had in mind. These two estimates are not necessarily contradictory, for if one regards 1592 as the date he could accept the evidence of both Larsen and Cheffaud.

blances to other stock characters. But, unlike them, the more Huanebango sounds like other characters, the more truly he shows himself the foolish boaster. In his very first appearance with his companion Booby, Huanebango explicitly links himself to the original *miles gloriosus,* Plautus' Pergopolinices, by his reference to similar names and family backgrounds: "If shee bee mine, as I assure my selfe the heauens will doo somewhat to reward my worthines; shee shall bee allied to none of the meanest gods; but bee inuested in the most famous *Polimackroeplacidus,* my Grandfather: my father *Pergopolyneo*: my mother, *Dyonora de Sardynya*: famouslie descended" (350–357). Later in the scene he makes his boasting more apparent when he acts like a pedant, a commonly recognized subtype of the *miles glorious*: "...if this Ladie [Delia] be so faire as she is said to bee," Huanebango pontificates, "She is mine: she is mine. Meus, mea, meum in contemptium omnium Grammaticorum" (343–346). In themselves, these speeches may not seem humorous, but in context they do, for, while Huanebango is raving on, Booby is openly ridiculing him. When Huanebango reappears later, he continues boasting by echoing the folklore themes of magic passwords and gallant rescues:

> Fee, fa, fum here is the Englishman,
> Conquer him that can, came for his lady bright,
> To prooue himself a knight,
> And win her loue in fight.

(659–662)

Immediately after this speech, we see even more clearly how foolish is his boasting when Sacrapant causes him to become deaf and throws him into the well. Still not cured of his boasting, Huanebango rises from the well, and, when he sees Zantyppa, the shrewish daughter of Lampriscus, he begins to woo her by spouting this apparent gibberish:

> Phylyda phylerdos, Pamphylyda floryda flortos,
> Dub dub a dub, bounce quoth the gums, with a sulphorous huffe snuffe:
> Wakte with a wench, pretty peat, pretty loue, and my sweet prettie pigsnie;
> Iust by thy side shall sit surnamed great *Huanebango*
> Safe in my arms will I keepe thee, threat *Mars* or thunder *Olympus*.

(799–808)

Here he is echoing Stanyhurst's horrendous translation of *The Aeneid* and some verses of Gabriel Harvey, who was then a butt of satire because of his quarrel with Nashe.[10] In context this speech is even more outlandishly amusing because Zantyppa herself ridicules Huanebango in scorching, vitriolic prose which is the complete antithesis to his own

10 *The Works of Peele,* ed. Arthur H. Bullen (London: Nimmo, 1888), I, 333n.

language: "Foe, what greasie groome haue wee here? Hee lookes as though hee crept out of the backeside of the well; and speakes like a Drum perisht at the West end" (809–811). Unable, of course, to hear Zantyppa, Huanebango boasts on and asks her to marry him, believing that she is deeply in love with him.

Foolish as Huanebango appears, he nevertheless displays some intelligence, which his very boasting brings out. Sometimes in talking to Booby, for example, he deftly echoes themes from folklore and Petrarchism: "Beautie I tell thee is peerelesse, and she precious whom thou affectest: do off these desires good countriman, good friend runne away from thy selfe, and so soone as thou canst, forget her; whom none must inherit but he that can monsters tame, laboures atchiue, riddles absolue, loose inchantments, murther magicke, and kill coniuring: and that is the great and mighty *Huanebango*" (326–334). Here Huanebango has almost a poetic talent that comes out as he makes fun of his companion. Even when he foolishly lets Zantyppa trap him, he still expresses a very charming feeling for beauty in praising his beloved:

> Hir Corall lippes, hir crimson chinne
> Hir siluer teeth so white within:
> Hir golden locks hir rowling eye
> Hir pretty parts let them goe by:
> Hey ho hath wounded me,
> That I must die this day to see.

> (838–843)

Furthermore, in cataloguing and praising his mistress' features, he may very well be echoing a typical Elizabethan song about beauty, for such cataloguing was very typical. All in all, Huanebango's varied boasts expressed through these diverse echoes make him outrageously foolish; but they also show that he is somewhat imaginative, and that even a *miles gloriosus* can have some endearing traits.

When we look more closely at the plot, we discover that it is pretty carefully worked out, especially since the interplay of characters from different literary worlds strengthens the connection between various groups of incidents. First of all, the fact that a folklore character such as Erestus and a realistic comedy figure such as Lampriscus do accept one another makes the folklore action seem more within the realm of ordinary human experience to the audience watching the play. Such an audience (Elizabethan or modern) can identify with a character such as Lampriscus because he is close to ordinary human experience, and, if he can accept folklore events and conventions of action, so can they. The action involving Huanebango and Booby, the only characters who scoff at folklore and yet the two most adversely affected by it, establishes a negative proof for the plausibility of the folklore characters. At the very least, these characters are no more absurd than the two fools, if only because they have enough sense not to scorn enchantment and mystery. Second, all of the plot action involving nonfolklore characters, except that of a group of harvesters who appear briefly, ironically contrasts with the main plot. The main plot has a search for a missing daughter (started by her father), while the plot involving Lampriscus reverses this, for here a father is trying to get rid of his daughters. (It is true that the parallel is not exact because of the additional daughter brought in, but there are enough other similarities since both plots depend upon meetings with Erestus and Sacrapant.) Huanebango and Booby also ironically contrast with Eumenides the hero, for the two fools are competing with him—if indirectly—in rescuing Delia. As for the harvesters, though they have no direct connection with the plot action, they, too, make what happens more likely by foreshadowing the happy ending. When they first appear, they create a mood of amorous expectation as they sing:

> All yee that louely louers be, pray you for me,
> Loe here we come a sowing, a sowing,
> And sowe sweete fruits of loue:
> In your sweete heartes well may it proue.

(308–311)

Later they reappear and sing about reaping. The effect of the songs is to suggest more strongly that the folklore story will end happily by creating a parallel between reaping and sowing in the cycle of the seasons and in love, both of which are parts of nature. Third, the incidents in both the main and subplots effectively create suspense. The very fact that the characters in the subplots are also searching for Delia means that they are competing with Eumenides and therefore may beat him to the rescue, especially since he is naïve and slow-witted. However, the subplots also serve as effective delaying actions and create new complications just when everything seems safe for Eumenides, the hero. For example, when Eumenides and Jack are finally ready to confront Sacrapant, the scene shifts to Booby the clown and Celanta, the ugly daughter of Lampriscus. Again, even after Eumenides has freed Delia, he has to contend with his helper, Jack, who in accordance with a previous agreement between the two of them, demands half of what Eumenides has gained, namely Delia.

Though other writers, such as Lyly, Shakespeare, and Beaumont, have played with different literary worlds, none of them has gone as far as Peele. Lyly in *Endimion* contrasts such different worlds as the aristocratic, courtly circle of Endimion and Eumenides and the low-life realistic comedy milieu of Bagoa and Dipsas to show the different ways in which love affects human beings. However, he always keeps these worlds separate and neither has much effect upon the other. Shakespeare in

As You Like It playfully contrasts such different ideal literary worlds as Petrarchism in Orlando's versifying and pastoralism in Duke Senior's exaggerated praise of the simple life. Yet each still retains its own conventions and feelings. Beaumont in *The Knight of the Burning Pestle* would surely seem to be doing what Peele is, for he also echoes other literary worlds and seems constantly to be shifting from the quixotic adventures of Ralph the grocer to the apparently different mercantile world of the Venturewells. But, actually, all the time he is merely satirizing middle-class ideals which are common to both of the worlds that he presents. Peele, however, not only echoes many more worlds but also subtly modifies them to create his own—a miniature one as fresh as a country landscape and as strange as that of a dream. In so doing, he is not only demonstrating how folklore is an organic part of all the other literary worlds familiar to the Elizabethans, but how the ordinary and the fantastic, the strange and the everyday, can somehow be part of a unified whole. In short, Peele in *The Old Wives' Tale* is really dramatizing by means of interplay the working of the imagination and showing how it enlarges, unifies, and yet refreshingly complicates human life.

PEELE

Boas, Frederick S. *An Introduction to Tudor Drama.* Oxford, 1933, pp. 151–160.

Cheffaud, P. H. *George Peele (1558–1596?).* Paris, 1913.

Clemen, Wolfgang. *English Tragedy Before Shakespeare.* London, 1961.

Gummere, Francis B., ed. *The Old Wive's Tale,* in *Representative English Comedies,* ed. Charles Mills Gayley. 3 vols. New York, 1912–1914, I, 336–347.

Jenkins, Harold, "Peele's *Old Wives' Tale,*" *MLR,* XXXIV (1939), 177–185.

Musgrove, S. "Peele's *Old Wives' Tale:* An Afterpiece?" *Journal of the Australasian Universities Language and Literature Association,* No. 23 (1965), pp. 86–95.

Robert Greene

THE FUNCTION OF THE DOUBLE PLOT *

William Empson

THE mode of action of a double plot is the sort of thing critics are liable to neglect; it does not depend on being noticed for its operation, so is neither an easy nor an obviously useful thing to notice. Deciding which sub-plot to put with which main plot must be like deciding what order to put the turns in at a music hall, a form of creative work on which I know of no critical dissertation, but at which one may succeed or fail. As in the music hall, the parts may be by different hands, different in tone and subject matter, hardly connected by plot, and yet the result may be excellent; *The Changeling* is the best example of this I can find. It is an easy-going device, often used simply to fill out a play, and has an obvious effect in the Elizabethans of making you feel the play deals with life as a whole, with any one who comes onto the street the scene so often represents; this may be why criticism has not taken it seriously when it deserved to be. Just because of this carelessness much can be put into it; to those who miss the connections the thing still seems sensible, and queer connections can be insinuated powerfully and unobtrusively; especially if they fit in with ideas the audience already has at the back of its mind. The old quarrel about tragi-comedy, which deals with part of the question, shows that the drama in England has always at its best had a certain looseness of structure; one might almost say that the English drama did not outlive the double plot. The matter is not only of theoretical interest; it seems likely that the double plot needs to be revived and must first be understood.

Probably the earliest form of double plot is the comic interlude, often in prose between serious verse scenes. Even here the relation between the two is neither obvious nor constant; the comic part relieves boredom and the strain of belief in the serious part, but this need not imply criticism of it. Falstaff may carry a half-secret doubt about the value of the kings and their quarrels, but the form derived from the Miracle Plays, and Mac's wife in the Nativity is doing something more peculiar. To hide a stolen sheep in the cradle and call it her newborn child is a very detailed parallel to the Paschal Lamb, hidden in the appearance of a newborn child, open to scandal because without a legal father, and kept among animals in the manger. The Logos enters humanity from above as this sheep does from below, or takes on the animal nature of man which is like a man becoming a sheep, or sustains all nature and its laws so that in one sense it is as truly present in the sheep as the man. The searchers think this a very peculiar child, a "natural" sent from the supernatural, and Mac's wife tries to quiet them by a powerful joke on the eating of Christ in the Sacrament:

> If ever I you beguiled
> May I eat this child,
> That lies in this cradle.

This parody must have had its effect on the many critics who have praised the scene, but I don't remember to have read one of them who mentioned it; I suppose those who were conscious of what was affecting them thought it obvious. The effect is hard to tape down; it seems a sort of test of the belief in the Incarnation strong enough to prove it to be massive and to make the humorous thieves into fundamental symbols of humanity.

Wyndham Lewis's excellent book, for one, points out that the Miracle Play tradition gave a hint of magic to Elizabethan drama; with nationalism and the disorder of religion, the Renaissance Magnificent Man took the place of the patron saint, anyway on the stage; hence the tragic hero was a king on sacrificial as well as Aristotelian grounds; his death was somehow Christlike, somehow on his tribe's account, something like an atonement for his tribe that put it in harmony with God or nature. This seems a less wild notion if one remembers that a sixteenth-century critic would be interested in magical theories about kings; he would not be blankly surprised as at the psychoanalyst on Hamlet. In the obscure suggestions of the two plots one would expect to find this as a typical submerged concept, and in fact their fundamental use was to show the labor of the king or saint in the serious part and in the comic part the people, as "popular" as possible, for whom he labored. This gave a sort of reality to the sentiments about the king or saint (*Marriage à la Mode* is an odd example—they needed giving reality there); even here the relation between the two parts is that of symbol and things symbolized.

This in itself can hardly be kept from irony, and the comic part, once licensed, has an obvious subject for its jokes. Usually it provides a sort of parody or parallel in low life to the serious part; Faustus' servant gets dangerously mixed up with the devils like his master. This gives as impression of dealing with life completely, so that critics sometimes say that *Henry IV* deals with the whole of English life at some date, either Shakespeare's or Henry's; this is palpable nonsense, but what the device wants to make you feel. Also the play can thus anticipate the parody a hearer might have in mind without losing its dignity, which again has a sort of completeness. It is hard to feel that Mac's wife was meant to do this, but she is only the less conscious end of a scale, and perhaps no example occupies only one point of it. A remark by Middleton on clowns seems a comment on this process:

> There's nothing in a play to a clown, if he
> Have but the grace to hit on't; that's the thing indeed:
> The king shows well, but he sets off the king.

The ideas of *foil* to a jewel and *soil* from which a flower grows give the different views of such a character, and with a long "s" the words are almost indistinguishable; it may be significant that the first edition of Tamburlane's Beauty speech reads *soil* for the accepted "foil," a variant I have never seen listed, but the line is at some distance from interpreting either word. A clear case of "foil" is given by the play of heroic swashbucklers which has a comic cowardly swashbuckler (Parolles), not at all to parody the heroes but to stop you from doing so: "If you want to laugh at this sort of thing laugh now and get it over." I believe the Soviet Government in its early days paid two clowns, Bim and Bom, to say as jokes the things everybody else would have been shot for saying. . . .

Some critics have called Greene's plays "a heap of isolated episodes, with clumsy devices to explain the course of the action"; others have said that his invention of the double plot, as apart from the comic sub-plot, required the wide overriding grasp of detail of a brain trained in the law. But I don't know who has tried to say what the point of the method is; why it is an advantage, in the early *Friar Bacon and Friar Bungay,* that the story of King Edward's love for Margaret, the keeper's daughter, and his magnanimity in letting himself be cut out by the Earl of Lincoln, should be told side by side with the story of Bacon and the Brazen Head; why, if these stories have nothing to do with each other, they should form a unity by being juxtaposed.

One connection is that Margaret and Bacon, like Faustus and Tamburlane, are low-born people who by their own qualities have obtained respect and power; both stories are democratic and individualist. But such powers are dangerous; at one point there is a very firm parallel between Margaret and Bacon to make this clear. It has been called a specially shameless piece of episodic writing that Edward should forgive the Earl of Lincoln so early as the third act, thus leaving time, while the earl is "testing" her by pretending to break it off, for two country gentlemen to become rivals for her hand and kill each other in a duel. In any case this is the repetition of a situation with new characters to show all its possibilities; also how wise the king has been, and how humble Margaret is still, and how it is a fatal hubris for mere gentry to love this demi-goddess, and how they are sure to do so in any pause of the story. But its main use is to compare her to Bacon. While the duel is going on two scholars at Oxford have asked to see their fathers in Bacon's perspective glass; they see them kill each other, so they kill each other too. Bacon cracks his glass and forswears necromancy, and we next see Margaret preparing to turn nun; they are well-meaning, but their powers are fatal. (One may add that she marries the earl, and that Bacon uses his powers at least once more to have his servant carried off by the devil.) This incident had to come late, not till we have learned to respect them both will we find it natural to compare them; it had to be applied to minor lovers of Margaret, or it would spoil the happy ending. So if you start with the two legends and the intention of making this comparison Greene's "episodic" plot is the only possible one.

On seeing the calamity the friars say:

> BUNGAY: O strange stratagem!
> [as if it was intentional].
>
> BACON: See, friar, where the fathers both lie dead.
> Bacon, thy magic doth effect this massacre.

The sense must be "Not a trick of mine intended to kill the sons; the fathers are really dead. Still I have killed the sons with my magic." This stress is then on *this* ("not [on] the fathers"). But the rough impression is that Bungay is accustomed to villainy and that Bacon admits he has killed all four. His magic is somehow the same as Margaret's magic, which has also killed all four.

The process is simply that of dramatising a literary metaphor—"the power of beauty is like the power of magic"; both are individualist, dangerous, and outside the social order. But it is so strong that it brings out other ideas which were at the back of the metaphor. It lets Margaret's continual insistence that she is humble and only the keeper's daughter make her into a sort of earth-goddess, and Bacon's magic, though not from Black Magic like Faust's, is from an earth-magic he must repent of; his pupil Bungay actually defends the claims of the earth-spirits, in an argument with the foreign magician Vandermast, against Vandermast's more ethereal spirits of the fire. Here at least M. Saurat's theory of the influence of the cabbalists is not fanciful, for they are quoted, and Bungay is making just that claim for the value of matter—

I tell thee, German, magic haunts the ground

which M. Saurat takes as the essential novelty of the Renaissance. (Matter is not evil and made from nothing but part of God from which God willingly removed his will; one can therefore put more trust in the flesh, the sciences, the natural man, and so on.)

The effect on the friars is to make them "jolly," connected with low life or the people as a whole. That is why Bacon depends on his servant Miles at the crucial moment of preparing the head; it shows the importance of the common people for this sort of magic, and yet we are to feel that Miles was right (so that he too is the fool who becomes the critic) in letting the head spoil. Also it was not very wicked of Bacon to let the devil carry him off; it is only an earth-devil and it suits him; he rides on its back. And it does not seem an irrelevant piece of flattery when Bacon produces a final prophecy in praise of Elizabeth; it was this Renaissance half-worship of Elizabeth and the success of England under her rule that gave conviction to the whole set of ideas. One need not suppose that Greene invented these implications any more than the stories themselves; what I want to point out is that the double plot was an excellent vehicle for them, if only because it could suggest so powerfully without stating anything open to objection.

FRIAR BACON AND FRIAR BUNGAY

Boas, Frederick S. *An Introduction to Tudor Drama.* Oxford, 1933, pp. 160–167.

Bradbrook, Muriel C. *The Growth and Structure of Elizabethan Comedy.* London, 1955, pp. 69–71.

Cellini, Benvenuto, ed. *Friar Bacon and Friar Bungay.* . . . Florence, 1952, pp. xi–xviii.

Clemen, Wolfgang. *English Tragedy Before Shakespeare.* London, 1961.

Ellis-Fermor, Una. "Marlowe and Greene: A Note on their Relations as Dramatic Artists," in *Studies in Honor of T. W. Baldwin,* ed. Don Cameron Allen. Urbana, Ill., 1958, pp. 136–149.

Harrison, G. B. *Elizabethan Plays and Players.* London, 1940, pp. 91–93.

Muir, Kenneth. "Robert Greene as Dramatist," in *Essays on Shakespeare and the Elizabethan Drama in Honor of Hardin Craig,* ed. Richard Hosley. Columbia, Missouri, 1962, pp. 45–54.

Parrott, Thomas Marc, and Robert H. Ball. *A Short View of Elizabethan Drama.* New York, 1943, pp. 71–74.

Seltzer, Daniel, ed. *Friar Bacon and Friar Bungay.* Regents Renaissance Drama Series. Lincoln, Nebraska, 1963, pp. ix–xxi.

Thomas Kyd

THE USES OF RHETORIC *

Wolfgang Clemen

THAT Kyd was much more successful in his attempt to reconcile the classical and the native styles of drama is obvious in *The Spanish Tragedy*.[1] In this play we see how a gifted playwright with a strongly marked sense of theatre managed to fuse the heterogeneous and discordant elements of earlier types of play, and from them produced a striking and original composition of his own. With its skilful exploitation and combination of different stylistic levels and different kinds of dramatic artifice and stage-effect, *The Spanish Tragedy* was bound to be a success; moreover, Kyd sensibly took into account the various tendencies of contemporary taste. However, his mastery is grounded in matters of technique rather than in any dramatic urge that took its rise from his own personal experience, and as a result *The Spanish Tragedy* fails to move us today; furthermore, we are offended by the lapses in taste which

---

* From *English Tragedy Before Shakespeare*, trans. T. S. Dorsch. London, 1961. Reprinted by permission of Methuen & Co., Ltd.

[1] This is well studied by P. W. Biesterfeldt, *Die dramatische Technik Thomas Kyds*, Halle, 1936. Cf. also Fischer, *Zur Kunstentwicklung der englischen Tragödie*, p. 94; Tucker Brooke, *The Tudor Drama*, pp. 209 ff.; J. Schick, Introduction to his edition of *The Spanish Tragedy* in the Temple Dramatists, 1898.

Schlegel deplored.[2] However, the prodigious success of the play on the Elizabethan stage is evidence that Kyd's contemporaries must have felt otherwise. Its exaggerated theatricality and its combination of a highly emotional rhetoric with an intricate and exciting plot are the very qualities which are likely to have roused their admiration, the qualities which gave the play its exceptional appeal.

What effect has this new skill in the techniques of dramatic composition on the handling of the set speech? Kyd knew how to pull out all the stops, how to exploit every linguistic and theatrical trick at his disposal in the theatre of the day; naturally he also recognized the potentialities of the declamatory set speech, and he showed some skill in adapting it to his purposes as a whole. In contrast to *Locrine, The Spanish Tragedy* offers us a coherent and artistically constructed plot[3] in which the threads of the action are skilfully interwoven and complicated. Although a number of subsidiary episodes are introduced, the course of the main plot remains perfectly clear; with all his tricks of mystification and delayed action and contrast, Kyd shows a conscious virtuosity in his handling of plot, and steadily advances the action through its various stages. Within this framework, the set speeches which periodically occur are strategically placed. Even when, as often happens, their subject-matter goes beyond the requirements of the immediate context, the mere fact that they are part of a coherent plot prevents them from losing touch with the action of the play.

Furthermore, even the *visible* structure of the work, the distribution of the longer speeches through its pages, shows the skill and the conscious artistry with which they have been introduced. There are no longer any scenes in which a number of long set speeches just follow one another without variation. Equally striking is the fact that situations which in the earlier tradition would have been represented entirely by means of long set speeches are now dealt with in other ways. For example, the second part of the second scene (I. ii) corresponds in its outlines to the familiar "tribunal scene"; it is a scene in which a dispute between two nobles is arbitrated and settled by the King. This settlement is brought about, not by means of long-drawn statements, but in rapid, dramatically exciting dialogue.[4] Where the longer set speeches or monologues do occur, they are generally placed next to passages of stichomythia—concise, quickly-changing single-line dialogue that moves at a great pace. Thus the tempo of the play is speeded up, and by a situation's being consciously worked up to a climax, the relevant phase of the action is advanced. In

---

[2] *August Wilhelm v. Schlegels Vorlesungen über dramatische Kunst und Literatur,* ed. G. V. Amoretti. Bonn, 1923. Vol. II, p. 233.

[3] On this and later points cf. Biesterfeldt's excellent analyses, *op. cit.*

[4] Cf. also I. iii. 43 ff., where the news of Balthazar's still being alive is imparted in some dramatically effective dialogue.

the set speeches and monologues, however, this forward movement is checked, and by means of the deliberation upon a course of conduct or the declamatory set piece we are transported to a higher, more universal level, and thus lose contact with the specific situation that is being presented. This rise and fall in the dramatic tempo, and the diversity in the method of presentation—with its claims alike upon the eye and the ear—give rise to a structural pattern which far surpasses anything with a similar tendency up to that time found in English drama.

Even in the structure of the individual scene we may observe, in the distribution of the longer speeches, the deliberate application of a structural principle. In Act II, Scene i, for instance, the two long speeches of Balthazar are placed at the beginning and the end; these are the speeches in which, in his highly rhetorical and antithetic style, he discusses the objects respectively of his love and his hate, Bellimperia and Horatio. The first speech is devoted entirely to Bellimperia; the second, after Pedringano's disclosure of the love-affair between Horatio and Bellimperia, concerns itself with Horatio alone. Thus the two goals of Balthazar's future endeavours are brought into sharp relief, not only in dialogue enlivened by action, but also through the rhetorical emphasis of the set speeches; and the significant new turn given to events in the central part of the scene, in the disclosures made in the exciting, fast-moving dialogue of Lorenzo and Pedringano, is shown for what it is by means of the two corner-posts of the scene, that is, the two set speeches of Balthazar. Comparable corner-posts in Act III, Scene ii, are the long soliloquy of Hieronimo at the beginning of the scene, and the closing soliloquy in which Lorenzo reveals his purposes; by their means we find out all about the two contending forces which, in the course of the ensuing scenes, are to be engaged in intrigue and conflict against each other.

A structural device of another kind may be seen in Act I, Scene iv. In the first part of this scene the meeting between Horatio and Bellimperia takes place. On this occasion Horatio has once more to tell the story of Don Andrea's death. There follows, together with Bellimperia's symbolic action in bestowing Don Andrea's scarf on Horatio, an ambiguous conversation, which is rounded off, on Horatio's departure, with a soliloquy by Bellimperia. In this first section of the scene the longer speeches impose a slower tempo, and this is in keeping with the situation, in which the recapitulated account of Don Andrea's death gradually draws Horatio and Bellimperia together. Now comes some dialogue employing a very different technique. The encounter between Bellimperia and her future adversaries Lorenzo and Balthazar—shortly to be broken in upon by Horatio—is conducted in a rapid exchange of polished, witty, single-line questions and answers. By means of this rapid cross-fire of questions asked and countered, these tactics of evasion and pointed rejoinder, tension is raised, and the main lines of the conflict are sketched in, its significance being emphasized by the by-play with the glove which Bellimperia drops and Horatio picks up. Both times, therefore, the outward form and the tempo of the dialogue are adapted to the situation, and an impressive sense of contrast is produced by the clash of the two different techniques. As far as concerns the distribution of long and short speeches, of duologue and colloquy divided between several speakers, the same observations might be applied to a number of other scenes.

Even when the speeches disconcert us by their length, as in Act I, Scene ii, suggesting a reversion to the technique of detailed narrative report characteristic of the earlier classical plays,[5] we find on closer study that the long-drawn recapitulation serves a definite dramatic purpose in the complication of the plot. *The Spanish Tragedy* is a tragedy of revenge;[6] it is introduced by an Induction in which Don Andrea appears in the company of Revenge.[7] What Andrea here discloses about his death was not sufficient, however, to establish an urgent revenge-motif; this motif had to be impressed on us again and made quite obvious in a detailed report of the battle, when at the same time the true circumstances of Balthazar's capture could be recounted. This dispassionate report of the Spanish General's is in its turn contrasted with the distortions and misrepresentations of Villuppo in the next scene (I. iii), and these are followed yet again by Horatio's corrective account of the facts (I. iv). According to the convention hitherto followed, any report given in a play had to be accepted as being objective, and hence it would have been superfluous to give several versions of the same event. Here, as a contrast, we have reports given from several different points of view, to be apprehended according to their relative value; among them there is even one utterly false report. These varied reports in turn have their consequences in the dramatic events of later scenes; they become mainsprings in the action of the play.[8] Moreover, the retrospective narration is thus in a certain sense woven into the texture of the plot. Of course Kyd could not have drawn out to such a length the Spanish General's

---

5 Cf. Biesterfeldt, *op. cit.*, p. 65. F. S. Boas indeed still sees here an excessive weight of epic elements (Kyd, *Works*, Oxford, 1901, p. xxxii).

6 Cf. F. T. Bowers, *Elizabethan Revenge Tragedy, 1587–1642*, Princeton, 1940.

7 Don Andrea's Ghost and Revenge form the Chorus, which comes in after each act and speaks its commentary. But even the Chorus-speeches, which in the classical plays commented on events and gave a didactic exposition of them, have been given some dramatic quality by Kyd. Don Andrea's Ghost and Revenge together constitute the Spirit of Revenge directing events from the background; they are no longer mere anonymous onlookers.

8 Apart from this, the report of the battle in a sense establishes the atmosphere of the tragedy in that it strikes the note, fundamental to the play, of bitter strife and slaughter. The strife here portrayed continues an underground course in the hidden intrigues of the succeeding acts, and comes out into the open again in the final scene. Moreover, in the last part of this battle report, from l. 63 onwards, a neutral account of the character and role of Horatio as well as of Balthazar is given, and this is important for what happens later.

account of the battle, which indeed in its earlier part (up to 1. 54) has no real relevance to the plot, had not his audience expected showy and elaborately rhetorical[9] report-speeches of this kind, and valued then as "good theatre" and as the peculiar glory of a play.

That the set speeches are more closely integrated with the structure of the plot than had up till then been the case does not mean that their speakers are brought into a close relationship with each other. Where the longer speeches are concerned, even in *The Spanish Tragedy* the characters are much more prone to talk at cross purposes than to make contact with one another's minds. Only in the genuine dialogue-passages does any interplay develop in which the speakers are delicately attuned to one another and establish a real contact. When the device of "speaking past one another" is employed in such a context, it is usually done as a deliberate dramatic artifice; understanding and misunderstanding are by this means deftly and ironically played off against each other, and in such a way as to bring out more subtle contrasts between the speakers.[10] However, scarcely a single one of the longer speeches is fully attuned to the person addressed, except in those few instances where it is a matter of giving instructions or of announcing a decision (e.g., I. ii. 179 ff.); and in any case these are not rhetorical set speeches as we have been using the term. In fact there are no long speeches that could be classified as conventional "conversion-speeches," "dissuasion-speeches," or "instigation-speeches";[11] where an attempt is made to influence a person, it is done in dialogue. The inference may be drawn that Kyd found the long set speech inappropriate for the development of close personal relationships; he assigned this function to his dialogue.

From the early classical tragedies we are familiar with the two ends normally and chiefly served by the long set speech: those of moralizing self-revelation and dissection of the emotions. The novelty of Kyd's method may be illustrated by a couple of examples. The two speeches of the Viceroy at the beginning of Act I, Scene iii, and Act III, Scene i, are not essentially different in theme from that of Gorboduc at the beginning of Act II in *Gorboduc*. The main difference lies in the stronger dramatic quality imparted to the Viceroy's speeches, especially the first one (I. iii), where his throwing himself on the ground and the gesture with which he offers to give away his crown are intended to add to the theatricality. There is a further difference in the effective way in which the climax is worked up in the Viceroy's speech, with all its rhetorical figures and its pointedly antithetic phraseology; for in the place of Gorboduc's dispassionate reflections he gives us an impassioned display of

---

[9] E.g., ll. 116–20.

[10] Cf. Biesterfeldt, *op. cit.,* pp. 73–74.

[11] There is, however, the long speech (IV. i. 1–28) in which Bellimperia reproaches Hieronimo for his passivity and thus drives him to act.

a man reasoning with himself. We get the impression of a mind-probing self-communion, a quasi-psychological soliloquy, as the Viceroy enters into judgments with himself and with the goddess Fortune.[12]

We find the same tendency to break up the thought into antitheses, and to analyze a situation by means of argument and counter-argument, in Balthazar's first speech in Act II, Scene i (ll. 9–28). This speech is actually intended as an answer to Lorenzo's attempt to allay his despair at his repulse by Bellimperia. However, finding a self-sufficing pleasure in the rhetorical development of his theme, he draws out through twenty lines of ingenious antithesis his contrast between his wooing of Bellimperia and her rejection of his advances, as well as his examination of his prospects as a lover.[13] The rhetorical "type" underlying this effusion is the Senecan "deliberation-speech." In Seneca, however, in spite of all the rhetorical coloring, a continuous train of thought emerges, whereas here the thought is split up into a series of symmetrically ordered antitheses for the sake of the rhetorical pattern. By this procedure, which Kyd also follows in other passages, thought and feeling are trimmed and shaped in such a way as to adapt them to the rationalistic see-saw of argument and counter-argument.

Balthazar's speech at the end of the scene (II. i. 113–35), in which all his thoughts are concentrated on Horatio, shows us another form of this verbal ingenuity by means of which the facts of a case are "dressed up" for the sake of a rhetorical pattern. In this case Horatio's fight with him and his fate as a lover are, by the rhetorical devices of epiploke and climax, given the appearance of a logical chain of cause and effect in which the one circumstance is a necessary consequence of the other. But this logic is of the most superficial kind, and moreover it is only one component of the ingenious verbal byplay which is at this point being carried on. Certainly it cannot have been by accident that Kyd here allows Balthazar in particular to indulge in a pointed, rhetorical turn of speech of just this nature (cf. his speeches at I. ii. 138–44, 161–65; I. iv. 93–97). For the lack of substance in this repetitive style of his, tediously amplified by antithesis and other rhetorical figures, is exactly in keeping with the irresolute, dependent, puppet-like role that Balthazar is to sustain in the play. The replies and retorts that his words receive

---

12 The Viceroy's opening speech in III. i lacks this peculiar tone. It might equally well belong to *Gorboduc,* and, with some allied scenes, might serve to exemplify Schücking's view that even the original text of *The Spanish Tragedy* is not uniform (Levin L. Schücking, *Die Zusätze zur Spanish Tragedy,* Sächs. Akad. d. Wissenschaft z. Leipzig, 1938, Vol. 2. p. 37).

13 Lorenzo's remark, "My Lord, for my sake leaue this ecstasie," is a criticism of the artificiality of this speech-technique, which employs several of the antithetical figures belonging to "topics of invention." Cf. Sister Miriam Joseph, *Shakespeare's Use of the Arts of Language,* p. 322.

from Lorenzo and Bellimperia seem to provide some hint as to the way in which his manner of speech is to be understood (I. iv. 90, "Tush, tush, my lord! let goe these ambages"; I. iv. 98, "Alas, my Lord, these are but words of course"; II. i. 29, "My Lord, for my sake leaue this extasie"). Although this technique of characterizing a person by his habits of speech is not consistently followed (see, e.g., III. xiv. 95 ff.), the passages that have been referred to may be taken as an attempt to indicate character by the use of overworked or misused rhetorical tricks. This dramatic contrivance was later considerably developed by Shakespeare.

Much more significant of course are Hieronimo's soliloquies and set speeches, which to a large degree determine the peculiar character of *The Spanish Tragedy,* and which helped to give to the famous role of Hieronimo its outstanding success. Not only are they the pith and marrow of this play itself; they also form a kind of core for the whole body of drama that immediately preceded Shakespeare, for they were imitated by many playwrights; and by a few playwrights somewhat later they were also burlesqued.[14] By means of these soliloquies, and of other speeches that are virtually soliloquies, Kyd added to a play already abounding in action and intrigue something which was designed to provide a complement, as it were, to the theatrically effective world of outward event and action, of underhand conspiracies, murders, and tangled enmities; he added the inward drama which is played out in the soul of the protagonist, Hieronimo, and which causes him to lead a solitary existence in the midst of the affairs of this world and drives him to the verge of madness. Hieronimo's emotional and declamatory set speeches, therefore, though they remain strongly indebted to the style of Seneca,[15] acquire a new significance. In the classical tragedies all the leading characters as a rule delivered set speeches and soliloquies in which their deepest thoughts and feelings were brought to the surface and laid bare. In *The Spanish Tragedy* it is especially Hieronimo who does this; only the soliloquy of Isabella which ends in her suicide (IV. ii), and which is to be regarded as a kind of prelude to what is yet to come, might also be named in this connexion. Lorenzo's soliloquies are of a different order; they are not soliloquies in which his deepest feelings are involved, but the self-revelatory soliloquies of a villain in which his scheming is disclosed, together with the explanation of his motives.

In Hieronimo, on the other hand, Kyd has created a figure[16] who, by his singular and eccentric nature, his brooding over his sorrow, his

14 Cf. Schücking, *op. cit.,* p. 25; Schick, *op. cit.,* p. xxix.

15 Hieronimo's important speeches in the "additions" are excluded from our discussion.

16 He is not of course a fully consistent "character," but the representation of certain obvious traits in particular situations.

mistrust and vacillation and procrastination, is set apart in a very marked
fashion from the other characters. Hieronimo becomes a solitary. He is
forced into a lonely isolation by the terrible suffering that falls upon him.
He has to keep his own plans secret, and in his reflections on the murder,
his tactics of delay, and his investigation of the outrage, he has to act
quite alone. Hieronimo's part in the play is therefore planned in terms of
soliloquy, and Kyd has thus given his numerous soliloquies a new basis
in their function of revealing a type of character and establishing its role
in the plot. Already in Seneca, of course, there were the beginnings of
such a process, and these might have served as a model; yet Kyd appears
to have been the first playwright in the history of English drama who
from these beginnings succeeded in creating a convincing character by
means of soliloquy.

In spite of the rhetorical commonplaces of classical origin in Hieronimo's utterances of grief and despair, and in spite of Kyd's obvious
endeavour wherever possible to out-Seneca Seneca within the framework
of classical conventions of rhetoric,[17] a whole range of new qualities
emerged in his work. Let us glance at Hieronimo's first soliloquy (II. v.
1–33). As Schücking has shown with some probability, the second part of
this speech, with its conventional apostrophes of lament, may well have
been replaced in the later version of the play by the expanded form of it
which occurs in lines 46–98.[18] The first part, however, is not in the
manner of the soliloquies with which we have so far been familiar.

> What out-cries pluck me from my naked bed,
> And chill my throbbing hart with trembling feare,
> Which neuer danger yet could daunt before?
> Who cals *Hieronimo?* speak, heere I am.
> I did not slumber; therefore twas no dreame.
> No, no, it was some woman cride for helpe;
> And heere within this garden did she crie;
> And in this garden must I rescue her.
> But stay, what murdrous spectacle is this?
> A man hanged vp and all the murderers gone:
> And in my bower, to lay the guilt on me.
> This place was made for pleasure, not for death.

(II. v. 1–12)

---

[17] Nashe's disparaging remark in his famous Preface to *Menaphon* (1589) is an
attempt to hit off Kyd's borrowings from Seneca; he was of course unwilling to
concede that in other ways *The Spanish Tragedy* was striking out in fresh directions. ("Yet English Seneca, read by candle-light, yields many good sentences. . . .
The sea exhaled by drops will in continuance be dry, and Seneca let blood line by
line, and page by page, at length must needs die for our stage. . . .") Cf. Schick,
op. cit., pp. ix–xiii.

[18] Cf. Schücking, *op. cit.,* p. 31.

This is a soliloquy which is not only spoken, but also acted. Hieronimo comes running into the garden in his night-shirt, Bellimperia's screams still ringing in his ears, so that they cannot have been a dream or a figment of his imagination. In the darkness of the garden he searches for this woman who has cried out for help, and comes upon the body of a dead man hanging from a tree. Up to this point the soliloquy is not a mere passage of emotional rhetoric unaccompanied by action; it is a speech which accurately reflects what Hieronimo is experiencing, at the same time indicating his actions by means of internal stage-directions. We still find this technique used by Shakespeare, though by him it is as a rule more subtly and more covertly managed.

Hieronimo's soliloquies are on several occasions, though not invariably, attended by stage-business; they demand properties or appropriate gesture. At such times we see the hand of the true man of the theatre; declamatory as it may be, the soliloquy is made an integral part of the plot, and at the same time turned into a piece of good theatre. That great cry of grief, "Oh eies, no eies..." (III. ii. 1 ff.), one of the most famous pieces of rhetoric in Elizabethan drama, is given actuality on the stage by the direction, *A Letter falleth*. From this point onwards the soliloquy is carried on in much less rhetorical language, for Hieronimo picks up the letter, reads it, and from its contents draws deductions as to his future course of conduct. In the same way, his soliloquy at the end of Act III, Scene vii, is largely taken up by the reading of the letter handed to him by the Hangman, the information it gives him about the circumstances of Horatio's murder, and the deliberations to which it gives rise. Even the outbursts of grief, "Woe to the cause of these constrained warres..." etc., are associated with direct references to action; only the soliloquy with which the scene opens consists of unmixed lamentation. Similarly, at the beginning of Act III, Scene xii, when Hieronimo enters with a dagger in one hand and a rope in the other to await the arrival of the King, is an "acted" soliloquy. It is true that it contains that lurid image of the fiery tower of judgment beside the lake of hell; but immediately after this it is again linked with the action, and Hieronimo engages in some stage-business with the properties:

> Downe by the dale that flowes with purple gore,
> Standeth a firie Tower; there sits a iudge
> Vpon a seat of steele and molten brasse,
> And twixt his teeth he holdes a fire-brand,
> That leades vnto the lake where hell doth stand.
> Away, *Hieronimo,* to him be gone:
> Heele doe thee iustice for *Horatios* death.
> Turne downe this path: thou shalt be with him straite;
> Or this, and then thou needst not take thy breth:
> This we, or that way:—soft and faire, not so:
> For if I hang or kill my selfe, lets know

Who will reuenge *Horatios* murther then?
No, no; fie, no: pardon me, ile none of that.
He flings away the dagger and halter.

(III. xii. 7–19)

There is nothing of the kind in Seneca. The histrionic quality of the popular drama has here forced its way into the static, declamatory monologue
of the classical tradition. Only with regard to the lament at the beginning
of Act III, Scene vii, can it be said that the conventional form of the
rhetorical lament has been preserved in its entirety. On all other occasions
the action of the play is advanced in one way or another in the course
of the soliloquies, and the speaking is accompanied by gesture or by
stage-business. Even in Isabella's final soliloquy (IV. ii) this histrionic
and theatrically effective quality is manifested;[19] for in the form of a
soliloquy we are given what is essentially a short "action-scene," in the
course of which Isabella tears down the leaves and branches of the tree
on which Horatio was hanged, lays her curse on the garden in which
the tree is growing, and finally stabs herself.

What is to be said of the speeches of Hieronimo that are not soliloquies, those which occur in dialogue-scenes? In these scenes his speeches
for the most part tend to deviate into monologue, and the use of this
type of speech is particularly effective in reinforcing the sense of isolation
in Hieronimo's mind. In *Gorboduc* and the tragedies that succeeded it
the speech that veers away into monologue had been employed because
the playwright needs it as a vehicle for moral reflections or passionate
lament. Kyd, however, makes Hieronimo address his words to himself
in a fashion that is wholly appropriate to his spiritual condition; he
consciously and deliberately isolates him from the other characters present
in these dialogues. The grief-stricken old man, who is obsessed by thoughts
which remain hidden from the other characters, and who appears distracted (and indeed wants to appear so), must with his very strange
manner and speech have produced an uncanny effect on the stage. The
set speech deviating into monologue, a mere convention with Kyd's
predecessors, is now well on the way to becoming an organic and
dramatically significant form of expression, even if it is not yet so on all
occasions.[20] Other good examples occur in the twelfth and thirteenth
scenes of Act III; both times Hieronimo breaks up a dialogue sequence.
He is so strongly reminded of his grief by a catch-word—"Horatio" at
III. xii. 58, and the Old Man's petition "for his murdred Sonne" at

[19] The beginning of this monologue is unusual: "Tell me no more!"
[20] Thus the reflection with which Hieronimo begins his dialogue with the Deputy
in III, vi employs the old technique of elucidation. On the other hand, his speeches
in the "additions" show Kyd's approaches to true soliloquy developing further and
taking on a new psychological realism which, in the later style of the "additions,"
opens up new forms of expression for soliloquy. Cf. Schücking, *op. cit.*

III. xiii. 78—that he lets the despair he has with difficulty been holding in check break out into wild whirling words.[21]

The calculated failure to understand, the talking at cross-purposes, the breaking away from a dialogue-sequence: all these devices, up till now the peculiar property of comic drama, have in this exhibition of Hieronimo's pretended madness been given a new function, which is dramatically effective, and at the same time sound psychology. Herein, too, Kyd reveals himself as a master craftsman, one who knew how to make dramatic capital out of the greatest variety of dramatic artifices.

[21] Cf. Biesterfeldt, *op. cit.*, pp. 73–75.
See bibliography for *The Spanish Tragedy*, p. 74.

THE DRAMATIC FUNCTION
OF THE ALEXANDRO-VILLUPPO EPISODE
IN *THE SPANISH TRAGEDY* *

William K. Wiatt

THE two brief scenes in *The Spanish Tragedy* that constitute the Alexandro-Villuppo episode have had very little attention, even in the most detailed studies of the play. J. Schick found them "most unnecessary,"[1] and Frederick S. Boas, in the standard edition of Kyd's works, says nothing at all about the second scene and considers the first part of a "superfluity of narrative [that] clogs the wheels of the action in the opening Scenes."[2] Peter Wilheld Biesterfeldt, who has made the most detailed study of the structure of the play, considers the matter of Alexandro and Villuppo an independent episode which has scarcely any connection with the main dramatic action. Biesterfeldt does, however, suggest that these two scenes afford striking contrasts in tone with the

* From *Notes and Queries*, Vol. 5, 1958, pp. 327–329. Reprinted by permission of Oxford University Press.

1 J. Schick, ed., *The Spanish Tragedy* (The Temple Dramatists, London [1898]), p. 136.

2 Frederick S. Boas, ed., *The Works of Thomas Kyd* (Oxford, 1901), p. xxxiii.

events that precede them in the main action of the play.[3] In the most recent study of *The Spanish Tragedy*, Félix Carrère finds the Alexandro-Villuppo episode useless to the play.[4]

If, as these critics have suggested, the episode is unnecessary, or even if it does no more than afford contrasts in tone with the main action of the play, we may well ask why Kyd put it into the play. But to answer that question, we must examine the episode in its context. The first part of the story—scene 3, Act I—shows the Viceroy of Portugal grieving over his country's recent defeat by the Spanish. Most of all he laments the loss of his son, Balthazar, whom he believes dead.

> My best beloued, my sweete and onely Sonne.
> O wherefore went I not to warre my selfe?
> The cause was mine; I might haue died for both:
> My yeeres were mellow, his but young and greene,
> My death were naturall, but his was forced.

(I, iii, 37–42)[5]

Alexandro tries to comfort the Viceroy by suggesting that Balthazar may yet live, that he may be a prisoner in Spain; but another courtier, Villuppo, swears that he saw Alexandro shoot Balthazar in the back and thus turn the tide of battle against the Portuguese. Alexandro immediately denies this charge, but the grief-stricken Viceroy is ready to believe the worst. He orders Alexandro to be seized, saying,

> Away with him; his sight is second hell.
> Keepe him till we determine of his death:
> If *Balthazar* be dead, he shall not liue.

(I, iii, 89–91)

The second part of the episode—Scene 1, Act III—follows the murder of Horatio and immediately precedes Hieronimo's discovery of the letter charging Lorenzo and Balthazar with the murder. This scene, also set in the Portuguese court, finds the Viceroy still lamenting the loss of his only son. At last, stung to action by Villuppo's repeated allusions to the treachery of Alexandro, the Viceroy cries out

> No more, *Villuppo,* thou hast said enough,
> And with thy words thou staiest our wounded thoughts;
> Nor shall I longer dally with the world,
> Procrastinating *Alexandros* death:

[3] Peter Wilhelm Biesterfeldt, *Die dramatische Technik Thomas Kyds* (Halle, 1936), p. 61.

[4] Félix Carrère, *Le Théâtre de Thomas Kyd* (Toulouse, 1951), p. 78.

[5] The quotations and the numbering of scenes and lines are from Boas's edition of Kyd's works (Oxford, 1901).

> Goe, some of you, and fetch the traitor forth,
> That, as he is condemned, he may dye.
>
> (III, i, 25–30)

At the last minute, when Alexandro is about to be burned to death, the Viceroy's ambassador arrives from Spain and reports that Balthazar lives. As the scene ends, Alexandro is welcomed again into the Viceroy's good graces, and Villuppo, instead, is condemned to die.

From this point the similarities between the Alexandro-Villuppo episode and the main action of the play are striking. The Viceroy and Hieronimo are fathers who believe their only sons to have been treacherously murdered. Furthermore, both men are distracted: the Viceroy worries over the lost battle and the alleged murder of Balthazar, and Hieronimo is, of course, distracted to the point of madness by the murder of Horatio. Once the similarity has been clearly established the differences become significant. The Viceroy, unlike Hieronimo, has an eyewitness to the murder of his son and a word-of-mouth account of the deed from an apparently trustworthy courtier. Furthermore, he is under no obligation to seek justice through legal processes; he not only outranks both Villuppo and Alexandro; he is the supreme authority in Portugal.

Now, having witnessed the sensational last-minute acquittal of Alexandro, the playgoer must shudder as he considers the consequences of hasty action upon insufficient evidence. Indeed, with these thoughts in mind, the playgoer next sees Hieronimo find Bel-imperia's letter and thus get his first clue to the identity of the murderers of his son. Surely the spectator is now somewhat more willing than he might have been, without having seen the Alexandro-Villuppo episode, to allow Hieronimo these doubts concerning the genuineness of the letter:

> what might mooue thee, *Bel-imperia,*
> To accuse thy brother, had he beene the meane?
> *Hieronimo,* beware, thou art betraide,
> And to intrap thy life this traine is laide.
> Aduise thee therefore, be not credulous.
>
> (III, ii, 35–39)

If the playgoer remembers here the credulity of the Viceroy, he should be willing to wait with Hieronimo for better evidence. He will realize that Hieronimo cannot, like the Viceroy, act when and as he chooses, and that, unlike the Viceroy, he must first seek justice through the law. The playgoer should also remember that Hieronimo, unlike the Viceroy, is below his enemies in rank; and if that fact should have slipped his mind, these lines will remind him of it. They are spoken by Hieronimo, shortly after his unsuccessful attempt to plead his case before the king.

> Nor aught auailes it me to menace them
> Who, as a wintrie storme vpon a plaine,

Will beare me downe with their nobilitie.
No, no, *Hieronimo,* thou must enioyne
Thine eies to obseruation, and thy tung
To milder speeches then thy spirit affords;
Thy hart to patience, and thy hands to rest,
Thy Cappe to curtesie, and thy knee to bow,
Till to reuenge thou know when, where, and how.

(III, xiii, 36–44)

Above all, the spectator will realize that Hieronimo, unlike the Viceroy, cannot for all his distraction afford to err. He must catch Lorenzo and Balthazar together and strike both men quickly and surely, or all is lost. This vital point is emphasized again near the end of the third act and not long before Hieronimo sets his plan of vengeance into motion. These lines, spoken by Lorenzo in the presence of Hieronimo, take on new meaning when we realize that they not only explain Hieronimo's strange behaviour, but also suggest again the close parallel between the Alexandro-Villuppo episode and the main action of the play:

But whats a silly man, distract in minde
To thinke vpon the murder of his sonne?
Alas, how easie is it for him to erre.

(III, xiv, 87–89)

Thus the Alexandro-Villuppo episode helps to justify to the audience Hieronimo's delay in exacting vengeance on the murderers of his son.

Critics have long recognized that a major problem in *The Spanish Tragedy* is the justification of Hieronimo's procrastination. Fredson Bowers has found that after Hieronimo's unsuccessful attempt to see the king (III, xii), "the reasons for his delay, previously logical, break down."[6] But Hieronimo still has a very good, and logical, reason for his delay. Professor Boas declares that the "cardinal weakness in the play, which prevents its ranking among dramatic masterpieces, is Kyd's failure in an adequate psychological analysis of [Hieronimo's] motives for this delay."[7] The Alexandro-Villuppo episode does not provide the psychological analysis that Professor Boas wants; it does, however, help to justify to the audience Hieronimo's otherwise inexplicable delay. Kyd has undertaken to do this not by manipulating his character, but by manipulating his audience.

[6] Fredson Bowers, *Elizabethan Revenge Tragedy* (Princeton, 1940), p. 70.

[7] Boas, p. xxxv. See also Biesterfeldt (pp. 97–98) and Carrère (pp. 114–122), who quote and agree with Boas.

IRONIES OF JUSTICE
IN *THE SPANISH TRAGEDY* *

G. K. Hunter

THE assumption that *The Spanish Tragedy* is usefully categorized as a "revenge play" and that this categorization gives us a means of differentiating what is essential in the text from what is peripheral—this has governed most that has been said about Kyd's play. And this a pity, because the play when looked at in these terms shows up as rather a botched piece of work.

It is no doubt an inevitable part of the tendency of literary historians that they should look everywhere for indications of historical progress. Certainly this has caused them to search among the "amorphous" (i.e., nonmodern) dramatic forms of the Elizabethans for signs and portents of the coming of Scribe and the "well-made" play. The revenge motif, in particular, has been seen as important because (to quote Moody Prior) it

> had the advantage of imposing a fairly strict pattern on the play. It thus assisted in discouraging multiple narratives and irrelevant episodes, and, in general, acted as a check on the tendency toward diffuseness and digression which was a common defect of popular Eilzabethan drama.[1]

Percy Simpson, in the same general terms, sees the revenge motif as imposing on Elizabethan dramaturgy the Aristotelian virtues of beginning, middle, and end: "The beginning is effectively supplied by the murder; the end should be effectively supplied by the vengeance. The problem for the working dramatist was skilfully to bridge the gap between the two."[2]

Unfortunately this pattern of progress shows the actual products it seeks to explain as rather unsatisfactory parts of the very progression which is adduced to explain them. Prior finds *The Spanish Tragedy* to be ensnared in the very "multiple narratives and irrelevant episodes" that the revenge motif was supposed to discourage. He speaks of "the dis-

---

* From *Renaissance Drama*, Vol. VIII, 1965, pp. 89–104. Reprinted by permission of Northwestern University Press.

[1] Moody E. Prior, *The Language of Tragedy* (New York, 1947), p. 47.

[2] Percy Simpson, "The Theme of Revenge in Elizabethan Tragedy," British Academy Shakespeare Lecture for 1935, p. 9.

proportionate amount of preliminary preparation necessary before Hieronimo is introduced as the avenging agent,"[3] and also of "the introduction of the story of the treacherous noble in the Portuguese Court, which has no bearing on the main action."[4] Fredson Bowers tells us that "the ghost has no real concern with the play" and that "the fundamental motive for the tragic action...is not conceived until midway in the play."[5] Simpson has much the same attitude. After the passage quoted above, he goes on to apply it to Kyd:

> Now Kyd, who had a keen eye for dramatic situation and, in his happy moments, a powerful style, does at critical points fumble the action. His main theme, as the early title-page announces, is "the lamentable end of Don Horatio," avenged at the cost of his own life by his aged father Hieronimo. But the induction brings in the ghost of Horatio's friend, Don Andrea, and the personified figure of Revenge.[6]

Later Simpson speaks more unequivocally of

> the disconnectedness, the waste of opportunity, and the dramatic unevenness of much of the writing.[7]

This attitude toward the revenge play in general and *The Spanish Tragedy* in particular has persisted in criticism. Philip Edwards' recent and excellent edition of the play (1959) speaks of the "prolix early scenes" and tells us that "it is very hard to justify the sub-plot...the relevance of theme is very slight" (p. liii). But at the same time as these attitudes persist, their historical foundations are disappearing. The assumption that the Elizabethan play inherited from the Tudor interlude a diffuse form which reflects mere incompetence—this becomes increasingly difficult to sustain in the light of recent studies of the interlude by Craik,[8] Spivack,[9] Bevington,[10] and Habicht.[11] These, in their different ways, present the interlude as a serious form, in which flat characterization, repetitiveness, and dependence on a multiplicity of short episodes are not defects, but rather means perfectly adapted to express that age's moral and religious (rather than psychological or social) view of human destiny. Persons are

---

3 Prior, pp. 46 f.

4 *Ibid.*, p. 46.

5 F. T. Bowers, *Elizabethan Revenge Tragedy* (Princeton, 1940, 1959), p. 71.

6 Simpson, pp. 9 ff.

7 *Ibid.*, p. 14.

8 T. W. Craik, *The Tudor Interlude* (Leicester, 1958).

9 Bernard Spivack, *Shakespeare and the Allegory of Evil* (New York, 1958).

10 D. M. Bevington, *From* Mankind *to* Marlowe (Cambridge, Mass., 1962).

11 Werner Habicht, "Sénèque et le théâtre pré-Shakespearien," in *Sénèque et le théâtre de la Renaissance*, ed. Jacquot (Paris, 1964). Dr. Habicht's book *Studien zur Dramenform vor Shakespeare* is due to appear (Winter Verlag, Heidelberg) in 1966.

seen to be less important than theme; they exist to illustrate rather than represent; and narrative line gives way to the illustration of doctrine. I may quote Bevington's remarks on the late morality, Lupton's *All for Money* (*c.* 1577):

> The unity of *All for Money,* as in so many popular "episodic" plays, is the singleness of theme (man's greed) manifested in a variety of episodes. This theme becomes more important than the fate of individuals. Characters are drawn to illustrate a single motif of human behavior, and are given no more depth than is necessary to make a point. The full course of their lives has no relevance here. It is the course of the moral formula that is all-important: the genealogy of sin, the analysis of its origins, motivations, and processes, the depiction of its worldly success and ultimate downfall—all seen in the perspective of moral uprightness, the beginning and end of virtuous living. The parts succeed each other as *exempla* to a homily, written for an audience that perceived a rich totality in matters of faith. The success of the play lies in varied illustration, in "multiple unity" and gathering of impact, not in the crisis of the individual moment.[12]

If *The Spanish Tragedy* is seen not so much as the harbinger of *Hamlet* (not to mention Scribe), but more as the inheritor of a complex and rich tradition of moralizing dramaturgy, the actual structure of the play begins to make more sense, and the traditional strictures that Prior and Simpson re-echo lose much of their relevance. The text of the play does not appear to give its complete attention to the enactment of revenge. True. But this may be because the play is not centrally concerned with the enactment of revenge. Much more obsessive is the question of justice. Indeed we may hazard an initial statement that if revenge provides the plot line of the play (i.e., play structure as seen from Scribe's point of view), justice provides the thematic center of the play (i.e., play structure as seen from the point of view of the Tudor interlude).

The centrality of the concept of justice serves to explain much of the so-called "preliminary preparation" of the first two acts. The play opens with Don Andrea, who has been slain in the late war between Spain and Portugal. Don Andrea's journey after death is through an infernal landscape devoted to working out justice. He is set before Minos, Rhadamanthus, and Aeacus, the judges of the classical afterlife; they are unable to resolve his legal status and refer him to a higher authority—to the monarchs of the underworld, Pluto and Proserpine. On his way to their court he passes through the enactments of Hell's precisely organized justice—horribly poetic justice indeed:

> Where bloudie furies shakes their whips of steele,
> And poore *Ixion* turnes an endles wheele;
> Where vsurers are choakt with melting golde,

12 Bevington, p. 166.

And wantons are imbraste with ouglie Snakes,
And murderers grone with neuer killing wounds,
And periurde wightes scalded in boyling lead,
And all foule sinnes with torments ouerwhelmd.

(I.i.65–71)[13]

But Don Andrea is not allowed to complete his search for justice amid the palpable abstractions of Hell. What the higher court orders is that he should be sent back to earth to observe how the gods operate *there,* and for this purpose he is given Revenge as his companion and guide:

Forthwith, *Revenge,* she rounded thee in th' eare,
And bad thee lead me through the gates of Horn,
Where dreames haue passage in the silent night.
No sooner had she spoke, but we were heere,
I wot not how, in twinkling of an eye.

REVENGE

Then know, *Andrea,* that thou art ariu'd
Where thou shalt see the author of thy death,

. . . .

Depriu'd of life by *Bel-imperia.*

(I.i.81–87, 89)

Revenge here seems to bear the same relation to justice as Talus (in Book V of *The Faerie Queene*) does to Artegall—that is, he is the emotionless and terrifyingly nonhuman executive arm of the legality that is being demonstrated. But Revenge, unlike Talus, does not act in his own person; his presence guarantees that the human action will work out justly, but he is not seen to make it do so. The departure of Andrea and Revenge through the gates of horn, Virgil's *porta*—

Cornea, qua veris facilis datur exitus umbris—

and their arrival at the Spanish court, can indeed be seen as dramatic equivalents to the introductory sequences of medieval dream allegory. The play may be viewed in this sense as what Andrea dreams, as an allegory of perfect justice: "The gods are indeed just; and now you shall see how their justice works out." We are promised a mathematical perfection of total recompense, where justice and revenge are identical. From this point of view the human beings who appear in Andrea's dream—the characters of the play, scheming, complaining, and hoping—are not to be taken by the audience as the independent and self-willed individuals they suppose themselves to be, but in fact only as the puppets of a predetermined and omnicompetent justice that they (the characters) cannot

[13]The text of quotations from *The Spanish Tragedy* is that of F. S. Boas (Oxford, 1901, 1955).

see and never really understand. But *we* (watching the whole stage) must never lose sight of this piece of knowledge.

The concern with justice in the opening scenes establishes an ironic set of responses for the audience and an ironic mode of construction for the play. The structure, indeed, may remind us of a ptolemaic model of the universe, one level of awareness outside another level of awareness and, outside the whole, the unsleeping eye of God.

The disjunction between what the audience knows and what is known in the Spanish court is established straightaway when the "play proper" starts. The Spaniards congratulate themselves on the late victory and stress the unimportance of the losses:

> All wel, my soueraigne Liege, except some few
> That are deceast by fortune of the warre.

> (I.ii.2–3)

And again: "Victorie, my Liege, and that with little losse." *We,* seeing Andrea sitting on the stage, know that the "little losse" can be too easily discounted and that the "some few" may yet blemish the complacency of the court and the overconfident assumption that justice is already achieved:

> Then blest be heauen, and guider of the heauens,
> From whose faire influence such iustice flowes.

> (I.ii.10–11)

We now see assembled before us the characters who are to be involved in the final demonstration of justice, centrally Don Balthazar, who is to die (we have been told) by the hand of Bel-imperia. But what we see in the opening scenes is no movement that can be understood as leading toward the death of Balthazar. What happens involves Balthazar with a variety of different kinds of justice, but the play is obviously more interested in exploring thematic comprehensiveness than in moving toward any narrative consequence.

The problem of deciding justly between competing claims to truth, which has appeared already in the dispute between Aeacus and Rhadamanthus, recurs in the contest between Lorenzo and Horatio, who dispute which of them, in law, has Balthazar as prisoner; and the king shows a Solomon-like wisdom in making a just decision:

> Then by my iudgement thus your strife shall end:
> You both deserue, and both shall haue reward.
> Nephew, thou tookst his weapon and his horse:
> His weapons and his horse are thy reward.
> *Horatio,* thou didst force him first to yeeld:
> His ransome therefore is thy valours fee; [etc.].

> (I.ii.178–183)

Expectation is tuned into a competency of human justice that *we* know cannot finally be sustained against the meddling of divine justice in this human scene.

The next scene introduces the Portuguese episode so famous for its irrelevance to the main action. The first scene of the "play proper" showed the Spaniards rejoicing over their victory and absorbing Balthazar into their court life. What the second (Portuguese) scene does is to show us the other side of the coin—the Portingales bewailing their defeat. And actually the Portuguese scenes serve as a continuous counterpoint against the earlier stages of *The Spanish Tragedy*, not only setting Portuguese sorrow against the Spanish mirth of the first scene, but later inverting the counterpoint and setting the viceroy's joy at his son's recovery against Hieronimo's cry of sorrow and demand for vengeance. Moreover, the long aria of grief put into the viceroy's mouth in I.iii gives the first statement of what is to become the central theme of *The Spanish Tragedy*, certainly the central and most famous impulse in its rhetoric —that frantic poetry of loss and sense of universal injustice which was to give Hieronimo his fame. We can see that, in spatial terms, the viceroy prepares the way for Hieronimo by living through the same class of experience—the loss of a son. Hieronimo makes this point quite explicitly when he says at the end of the play:

> Speake, Portaguise, whose losse resembles mine:
> If thou canst weepe vpon thy *Balthazar,*
> Tis like I wailde for my *Horatio.*

(IV.iv.114–116)

The viceroy does not weep at this point, when Balthazar is really dead, but the opening scenes and the speeches in which he bewails his supposed death sustain our sense of what Hieronimo is referring to. Moreover, the connection between national sin and individual sorrow which seems to be implied in the main story of Hieronimo and Horatio is quite explicit in the Portuguese episode:

> My late ambition hath distaind my faith;
> My breach of faith occasioned bloudie warres;
> Those bloudie warres haue spent my treasure;
> And with my treasure my peoples blood;
> And with their blood, my ioy and best beloued,
> My best beloued, my sweete and onely Sonne.

(I.iii.33–38)

But this scene of sorrow does more than prepare for the second and central lost son, Don Horatio; it establishes an ironic countercurrent inside the framework of the general information that has been given us by Andrea and Revenge. Not only is it deeply ironic to see the viceroy bewailing the death of a son, who is at that moment involved in the

murder of another son, Horatio, and the bereavement of another father
(and we should note that this second bereavement is one which cannot,
this time, be avoided as if by a miracle [see III.xiv.34]). But more, the
general framework of the play tells us that it is ironic even when the
viceroy changes from lamentation to rejoicing; for *we* know that the relationship with Bel-imperia which looks so auspicious from inside the play
will be the actual cause of his death.

The short fable of human fallibility and divine concern which supplies
the narrative (as against the thematic) substance of the Portuguese
episode—this feeds into the main plot an expectation that "...murder
cannot be hid: / Time is the author both of truth and right, / And time
will bring this trecherie to light" (II.v.58–60) ; it strengthens the expectation which Revenge and Andrea arouse by their very presence—that
wrong must soon, and inevitably, be followed by retribution. It is no
accident that places the second Portuguese scene (III.i)—which shows
Alexandro rescued from death, as if by miracle, at the very last moment
—immediately after the death of Horatio and the first sounds of
Hieronimo's passion: "What out-cries pluck me from my naked bed,
[etc.]" (II.v.1) The discovery of Horatio is the center of the main plot,
being the reenactment in real life of the death which began the action
of the play; for Don Horatio is, as it were, the living surrogate for the
ghost Andrea. As he was friend and revenger to Andrea on the battlefield,
so he has taken on the role of lover to Bel-imperia, and so too he falls
victim to Balthazar (and his confederates). And this is the point in the
play where the sense of just gods directing a revenge on Balthazar is at
its lowest ebb. As Andrea understandably exclaims to Revenge:

> Broughtst thou me hether to encrease my paine?
> I lookt that *Balthazar* should haue beene slaine:
> But tis my freend *Horatio* that is slaine,
> And they abuse fair *Bel-imperia,*
> On whom I doted more then all the world,
> Because she lou'd me more then all the world.

(II.vi.1–6)

The reinforcement of the justice theme at this point is, therefore,
particularly useful. Even if the Portuguese episode had no other function,
this one would seem to justify it.

Andrea was returned to earth by the just gods, to witness a parable
of perfect recompense, a parable which would reenact the story of his life,
but cleared of the ambiguities and uncertainties that had surrounded him.
The death of Horatio re-presents the death of Andrea, but presents it
as a definite crime (as the death of Andrea was not) and makes
Balthazar into a definite criminal (as in the battle he was not). More
important, the death of Horatio raises up an agent of recompense who
has the best claim to justification in his action—the father of the victim
and a man renowned for state service, the chief judicial functionary of

the court. Kyd goes out of his way to show Hieronimo in this function
and to make the first citizen tell us that

> ...for learning and for law,
> There is not any Aduocate in Spaine
> That can preuaile, or will take halfe the paine
> That he will in pursuit of equite.

(III.xiii.51–54)

Hieronimo is justly at the center of *The Spanish Tragedy* because he is
constructed to embody perfectly the central question about justice that
the play poses: the question, "How can a human being pursue the path
of justice?" Hieronimo is constructed to suggest both complete justification of motive (his outraged fatherhood) and the strongest advantages
in social position. And as such he is groomed to be the perfect victim of
a justice machine that uses up and destroys even this paragon. Herein
lies the truly cathartic quality of *The Spanish Tragedy:* If this man, Kyd
seems to be saying, fails to find any secure way of justice on earth, how
will it fare with you and me? For Hieronimo, for all his devotion to the
cause of justice, is as much a puppet of the play's divine system of
recompense as are other characters in the action. He is stuck on the ironic
pin of his ignorance; we watch his struggles to keep the action at a legal
and human level with involvement, with sympathy, but with assurance of
their predestinate failure:

> Thus must we toyle in other mens extreames,
> That know not how to remedie our owne;
> And doe them iustice, when uniustly we,
> For all our wrongs, can compasse no redresse.
> But shall I neuer liue to see the day,
> That I may come (by iustice of the heauens)
> To know the cause that may my cares allay?
> This toyles my body, this consumeth age,
> That onely I to all men iust must be,
> And neither Gods nor men be iust to me.
>
> DEPUTY
>
> Worthy *Hieronimo,* your office askes
> A care to punish such as doe transgresse.
>
> HIERONIMO
>
> So ist my duety to regarde his death,
> Who, when he liued, deserued my dearest blood.

(III.vi.1–14)

He calls on heavenly justice; what he cannot know is that his agony
and frustration are part of the process of heavenly justice. As his madness
takes him nearer and nearer the nightmare world of Revenge and Andrea,
this mode of irony is reinforced. Hieronimo tells us:

> Though on this earth iustice will not be found,
> Ile downe to hell, and in this passion
> Knock at the dismall gates of *Plutos* Court,
>
> . . . .
>
> Till we do gaine that *Proserpine* may grant
> Reuenge on them that murd [e] red my Sonne.

(III.xiii.108–110,120–121)

What he cannot know is that this is precisely what Don Andrea has already done—indeed the explanation of the whole action of the play up to this point. Again and again he calls on the justices of Hell:

> Goe backe, my sonne, complaine to *Eacus,*
> For heeres no iustice; gentle boy, be gone,
> For iustice is exiled from the earth:
> *Hieronimo* will beare thee company.
> Thy mother cries on righteous *Radamant*
> For iust reuenge against the murderers.

(III.xiii.137–142)

> . . .thou then a furie art,
> Sent from the emptie Kingdome of blacke night,
> To sommon me to make appearance
> Before grim *Mynos* and iust *Radamant,*
> To plague *Hieronimo* that is remisse,
> And seekes not vengeance for *Horatioes* death.

(III.xiii.152–157)

But these infernal judges have already acted. All that Hieronimo can see is that he, the justice, the magistrate, the proponent of civil order, is living in a world where justice is impossible, where

> . . .neither pietie nor pittie mooues
> The King to iustice or compasion,

(IV.ii.2–3)

and where heavenly justice does not seem to be filling in the lacuna left by the failure of civil justice:

> O sacred heauens, if this vnhallowed deed,
> If this inhumane and barberous attempt,
> If this incomparable murder thus
> Of mine, but now no more my sonne,
> Shall vnreueald and vnreuenged passe,
> How should we tearme your dealings to be iust,
> If you vniustly deale with those, that in your iustice trust?

(III.ii.5–11)

The heavens are not asleep, in fact, but their wakefulness has a different aspect from that which mortals expect. Hieronimo knows the orthodox Christian doctrine of Romans XII.19, which tells us ("Vindicta mihi, ego retribuam, dicit Dominus") to leave revenge to God:

> *Vindicta mihi.*
> I, heauen will be reuenged of euery ill;
> Nor will they suffer murder vnrepaide.
> Then stay, *Hieronimo,* attend their will:
> For mortall men may not appoint their time.
>
> (III.xiii.1–5)

But no more than Andrea can he apply this knowledge or relate it to what is happening to himself and to those around him. Andrea feels that everything is going the wrong way:

> I look that *Balthazar* should haue beene slaine:
> But tis my freend *Horatio* that is slaine.
>
> (II.vi.2–3)

And when (in the next act) he finds that Revenge has actually been sleeping while the wicked continued their triumph, Heaven's conspiracy with injustice seems to be complete. But Revenge is coldly contemptuous of these passionate human outcries:

> Thus worldlings ground, what they haue dreamd, vpon.
> Content thy selfe, *Andrea;* though I sleepe,
> Yet is my mood soliciting their soules.
>
> . . . .
>
> Nor dies *Reuenge,* although he sleepe awhile;
> For in vnquiet quietnes is faind,
> And slumbring is a common worldly wile.
> Beholde, *Andrea,* for an instance, how
> *Reuenge* hath slept, and then imagine thou
> What tis to be subiect to destinie.
> [*Enter a dumme shew.*]
>
> (III.xv.17–19,22–27)

The menace and even horror of Revenge's outlook, for those who are "subject to destiny," needs to stressed. The presence of a justice machine in this play is no more cozily reassuring than in Kafka's *Strafkolonie.* For the irony of its operation works against Andrea and Hieronimo no less than against Lorenzo and Balthazar.

All in *The Spanish Tragedy* are caught in the toils of their ignorance and incomprehension, each with his own sense of knowledge and power preserved intact, and blindly confident of his own (baseless) understanding, even down to the level of the boy with the box (III.v). This episode—the only clearly comic piece of business in *The Spanish Tragedy* —catches the basic irony of the play in its simplest form. The boy's preliminary explanation of the trap set up, and his key sentence, "Ist not a scuruie iest that a man should iest himself to death?" establishes the usual Kydian disjunction in the levels of comprehension. Throughout the following trial scene (III.vi) the boy stands pointing to the empty box, like a cynical emblem of man's hope for justice; and yet the irony has also (as is usual in the play) further levels of complexity. For Lorenzo, the organizer of the ironic show which seals Pedringano's lips even while it betrays his body to the hangman, is himself a victim, not only in the larger irony of Revenge's scrutiny but also in the minor irony that it is his very cleverness that betrays him: It is Pedringano's letter that confirms Hieronimo's knowledge of the murderers of Horatio. Lorenzo, indeed, as Hieronimo remarks, "marcht in a net and thought himselfe unseen" even at the time he was entrapping others.

Hieronimo prides himself on his devotion to justice and his thoroughness as a judge, but he serves divine justice by ceasing to be just at all in any human sense. The feeling of incomprehension, of not knowing where he is, in terms of the standards by which he has ordered his life—this drives him mad; but even here he reinforces the play's constant concern with justice by his mad fantasies of journeys into the hellish landscape of infernal justice.

> *Hieronimo,* tis time for thee to trudge:
> Downe by the dale that flowes with purple gore,
> Standeth a firie Tower; there sits a iudge
> Vpon a seat of steele and molten brasse, [etc.]
>
> (III.xii.6–9)

His incomprehension is inescapable because it is a function of his humanity. His madness is a direct result of the collision of his human sense of justice with the quite different processes of divine justice; for it is a fearful thing to fall into the hands of a just God. The absorption of the human into the divine justice machine is the destruction of the human, and Hieronimo becomes the instrument of Revenge by becoming inhuman. He becomes part of the hellish landscape of his imagination. In the play of Soliman and Perseda that he organizes we have yet another reenactment of the situation that began with Don Andrea. Bel-imperia (certainly resolute even if not certainly chaste) plays the part of "Perseda chaste and resolute." Balthazar, the princely lover who hoped to win Bel-imperia from her common lovers (Andrea, Horatio), plays the Emperor Soliman, who hopes to win Perseda from her common love. The crimes and killings in the play are organized by the Bashaw or Pasha, and this is the part to be played by Hieronimo himself. When asked, "But which of us is to performe that parte?" he replies:

> O, that will I, my Lords, make no doubt of it:
> Ile play the murderer, I warrant you,
> For I already haue conceited that.
>
> (IV.i.130–133)

The Spanish Tragedy as a whole has continuously set the marionette-like action of the man whose destiny is predetermined against the sense of choice or willpower in the passionate and self-confident individual. Continuously we have had actors watching actors but being watched themselves by still other actors (watched by the audience). *We* watch Revenge and Andrea watching Lorenzo watching Horatio and Belimperia; we watch Revenge and Andrea watching Hieronimo watching Pedringano watching the boy with the box; and at each point in this chain what seems free will to the individual seems only a predetermined *act* to the onlookers.

In the play within the play, in Hieronimo's playlet of Soliman and Perseda, this interest reaches its climax. The illusion of free will is suspended. The four central characters are absorbed into an action which acts out their just relationships *for them*. The net has closed, character has become role, speech has changed to ritual; the end is now totally predetermined. The play itself is a flat puppet-like action with a total absence of personal involvement; but as the characters intone their flat, liturgical responses to one another there is an enormous *frisson* of irony or disparity between what they say and what *we* know to be meant.

Hieronimo himself has become *instrument* rather than agent. *He* knows that his life has been absorbed into the ritual and that he cannot escape back into humanity, and he accepts this Hegelian kind of freedom (freedom as the knowledge of necessity) with a resolution at once noble and inhuman. At the end of his play he comes forward to speak his own epilogue:

> Heere breake we off our sundrie languages,
>
> . . . .
>
> And, Princes, now beholde *Hieronimo*,
> Author and actor in this Tragedie,
> Bearing his latest fortune in his fist;
> And will as resolute conclude his parte
> As any of the Actors gone before.
> And, Gentles, thus I end my play.

(IV.iv.74,146–151)

Commentators on the denouement of *The Spanish Tragedy* usually concentrate on the human *mess* which follows Hieronimo's failure to complete his life in ritual, noticing the break in the pattern rather than the pattern itself. But I think that the nature of the final actions is only kept in focus if we see them as measuring the gap between the dream of justice and the haphazard and inefficient human actions that so often must embody it. This is a recurrent interest of a writer like Seneca. When he describes the suicide of Cato Uticensis, his greatest hero, he is not content to relate his fortitude in doing the deed; he stresses the horror of Cato's failure to finish himself in one clean blow. What he is concerned to show is the persistence of Cato's will to die, in spite of his own inefficiency. And I think a similar concern to contrast the will to martyrdom with the *mess* of actual martyrdom can be seen at the end of *The Spanish Tragedy*.

A martyr is rather exceptional if his suffering is not prolonged and humanly degrading; a martyr whose soul had been antiseptically abstracted from his body would be rather unlike those whose histories thronged the Elizabethan imagination, whether from *The Golden Legend* or from its local equivalent, Foxe's *Acts and Monuments*. We should remember that it was not simply Zeno who anticipated Hieronimo by biting out his own tongue, but St. Christina as well. Much ink has been spilled in sympathy for Castile, who is struck down at the end of the play, simply because he stands too close to the protagonist. But Castile is, of course, identified with the tormenters who seek to interrupt the ritual and prevent it from completing itself. It is Castile who suggests that torture is still of use, to compel Hieronimo to *write* the names of his confederates. And the death of Castile confers another dramatic advantage: It transfers mourning to the highest personage on the stage. The king of Spain has hitherto been concerned with the miseries of existence only at second hand. Now, at the end of the play, he himself becomes a principal mourner, as is indicated well enough in the final stage direction:

> *The Trumpets sound a dead march, the* King of Spaine *mourning after his brothers body, and the* King of Portingale *bearing the body of his sonne.*

In the final episode we return to the justice of Hell, where the characters of the play now supply the classical examples of sin and wickedness with which the play began ("Place *Don Lorenzo* on *Ixions* Wheele," [IV.v.33]). A last judgment places everyone where he morally belongs (as in the *Last Judgment* play at the end of the mystery cycles), but we would do less than justice to the complexity of this play if we did not notice that humanity has been sacrificed so that justice can be fulfilled. Revenge has been completed; we have seen what Fulke Greville describes as the mode of modern tragedy: "God's revenging aspect upon every particular sin to the despair and confusion of mortality."

THE SPANISH TRAGEDY

Baker, Howard. *Induction to Tragedy*. University, Louisiana, 1939, pp. 98–118, 214–218.

Barish, Jonas. "*The Spanish Tragedy*, or the Pleasures and Perils of Rhetoric," in *Elizabethan Theatre*, ed. John Russell Brown and Bernard Harris. Stratford-upon-Avon Studies 9. London, 1966, pp. 59–85.

Boas, Frederick S. *An Introduction to Tudor Drama*. Oxford, 1933, pp. 96–100.

_____, ed. *The Works of Thomas Kyd*. Oxford, 1901, pp. xxxi–xxxix.

Bowers, Fredson T. *Elizabethan Revenge Tragedy, 1587–1642*. Princeton, 1940, pp. 65–73.

Carrère, Felix. *Le Théâtre de Thomas Kyd: Contribution à l'Etude du Drame Elizabéthain.* Toulouse, 1951, pp. 67–80.

Chickera, Ernest de. "Divine Justice and Private Revenge in *The Spanish Tragedy*," *MLR*, LVII (1962), 228–232.

Cole, Douglas, *Suffering and Evil in the Plays of Christopher Marlowe.* Princeton, N.J., 1962, pp. 62–70.

Cunningham, John E. *Elizabethan and Early Stuart Drama.* London, 1965, pp. 52–55.

Edwards, Philip, ed. *The Spanish Tragedy.* The Revels Plays. Cambridge, Mass., 1959, pp. l–lxi.

Empson, William. "*The Spanish Tragedy*," *Nimbus,* III (Summer 1956), 16–29. Reprinted in *Elizabethan Drama: Modern Essays in Criticism,* ed. R. J. Kaufmann. New York, 1961, pp. 60–80.

Farnham, Willard. *The Medieval Heritage of Elizabethan Tragedy.* Berkeley and Los Angeles, 1936, pp. 391–395.

Freeman, Arthur. *Thomas Kyd: Facts and Problems.* Oxford, 1967, pp. 80–115.

Fuzier, Jean. "Thomas Kyd et l'éthique du spectacle populaire," *LanM,* LIX (1965), 451–458.

Harbage, Alfred. "Intrigue in Elizabethan Tragedy," in *Essays on Shakespeare and the Elizabethan Drama in Honor of Hardin Craig,* ed. Richard Hosley. Columbia, Missouri, 1962, pp. 37–44.

Jensen, Ejner J. "Kyd's *Spanish Tragedy:* The Play Explains Itself," *JEGP,* LXIV (1965), 7–16.

Johnson, S. F. "*The Spanish Tragedy,* or Babylon Revisited," in *Essays on Shakespeare and the Elizabethan Drama in Honor of Hardin Craig,* ed. Richard Hosley. Columbia, Missouri, 1962, pp. 23–36.

Joseph, B. L. "*The Spanish Tragedy* and *Hamlet:* Two Exercises in English Seneca," in *Classical Drama and its Influence,* ed. M. J. Anderson. London, 1965, pp. 121–134.

Kernan, Alvin. *The Cankered Muse: Satire of the English Renaissance.* New Haven, 1959, pp. 221–232.

Levin, Michael Henry. " 'Vindicta mihi!': Meaning, Morality, and Motivation in *The Spanish Tragedy*," *SEL,* IV (1964), 307–324.

Palmer, D. J. "Elizabethan Tragic Heroes," in *Elizabethan Theatre,* ed. John Russell Brown and Bernard Harris. Stratford-upon-Avon Studies 9. London, 1966, pp. 18–25.

Prior, Moody E. *The Language of Tragedy.* New York, 1947, pp. 46–59.

Ratliff, John D. "Hieronimo Explains Himself," *SP,* LIV (1957), 112–118.

Talbert, Ernest William. *Elizabethan Drama and Shakespeare's Early Plays: An Essay in Historical Criticism.* Chapel Hill, N.C., 1963, pp. 62–64, 72–79, 133–140.

Tomlinson, T. B. *A Study of Elizabethan and Jacobean Tragedy.* Cambridge, Eng., and Melbourne, 1964, pp. 73–85.

Christopher Marlowe

MARLOWE AND THE JADES OF ASIA *

Eugene M. Waith

MARLOWE'S power as a writer has never been doubted, and that power has commonly been associated with the portrayal of the passions. Shortly after his death, he was described by Peele as "Fitte to write passions for the soules below, / If any wretched soules in passion speake."[1] Drayton spoke of him as a prototypical poet, inspired by a prototypical *furor poeticus*:

> Neat Marlowe, bathed in the *Thespian* springs,
> Had in him those brave translunary things
> That the first Poets had, his raptures were
> All ayre, and fire, which made his verses cleere,
> For that fine madness still he did retaine,
> Which rightly should possesse a Poet's braine.[2]

Toward the end of the last century A. W. Ward wrote in much the same vein of Marlowe's power to move pity and terror:

* From *Studies in English Literature, 1500–1900,* Vol. 5, 1965, pp. 229–245. Reprinted by permission of the editor of *SEL* (Rice University).

[1] *The Minor Works of George Peele,* ed. David H. Horne (New Haven: Yale University Press, 1952), p. 246.

[2] "To Henry Reynolds Esq.," *The Works of Michael Drayton,* ed. J. W. Hebel (Oxford: Blackwell, 1932), III, 228–229.

But during his brief poetic career he had not learnt the art of mingling, except very incidentally, the operation of other human motives of action with those upon which his ardent spirit more especially dwelt; and of the divine gift of humour, which lies so close to that of pathos, he at the most exhibits occasional signs. The element in which as a poet he lived was passion. . . .[3]

As Shakespeare warbled his native woodnotes wild, Marlowe, according to these critics, rent the air with an unending sequence of *cris de coeur*.

Ward seems to suggest what others have also thought, that Marlowe fails to deal adequately with complementary aspects of whatever experience he is portraying. This amounts to a complaint that Marlowe is restricted in vision and lacking in balance. I hope to adduce some evidence that this criticism is unfair and that, on the contrary, one remarkable feature of Marlowe's work is the multiplicity of his vision and his insistence on balancing one view against another. This is not to deny Marlowe's effectiveness in the portrayal of passion but to claim that in a variety of ways he constantly controls his portrayal.

Before going any further we must ask ourselves whose passions are to be the subject of discussion. Peele, speaking of Marlowe's fitness "to write passions for the soules below," clearly refers to dramatic characters, while Drayton, also thinking of the plays, refers to the poet's own feelings —his "raptures." Ward implies, I think, that the raptures produced the passions, and he is also concerned with the emotions aroused in the audience. The emotions of author, character, and audience must all enter into the discussion. Though we cannot assume that the author feels exactly as one of his characters does, it is reasonable to suppose that he will seek to elicit a response corresponding to his own feelings *about* the characters and situations he is presenting—to make the audience share the emotions of the characters only to the extent that he does. When I speak of control, I have in mind the means by which the author may not only indicate the nature and intensity of the feelings of his characters but also determine the way in which the audience is to react. By so doing be reveals his own attitude toward the story he is dramatizing—an attitude which may be assumed temporarily and experimentally or may be rooted in his normal outlook on life. Because this attitude is an important part of his meaning, the control I refer to is an aspect of his technique not to be overlooked.

A scene in Part II of *Tamburlaine,* to which Shakespeare paid the tribute of a parody, will serve both for an example and a symbol. A stage direction announces: "Tamburlaine, drawn in his chariot by Trebizon and Soria, with bits in their mouths, reins in his left hand, and in his right hand a whip with which he scourgeth them. . . ." From the chariot Tamburlaine shouts his famous lines:

[3] *A History of English Dramatic Literature* (London: Macmillan & Company, Ltd., 1875), p. 203.

Holla, ye pampered jades of Asia!
What, can ye draw but twenty miles a day,
And have so proud a chariot at your heels,
And such a coachman as great Tamburlaine. . . ?
The horse that guide the golden eye of heaven
And blow the morning from their nosterils,
Making their fiery gait above the clouds,
Are not so honored in their governor
As you, ye slaves, in mighty Tamburlaine.
The headstrong jades of Thrace Alcides tamed,
That King Aegeus fed with human flesh
And made so wanton that they knew their strengths,
Were not subdued with valor more divine
Than you by this unconquered arm of mine.[4]

It is a theatrical image of unforgettable brilliance, presenting eye and ear with this conqueror of conquerors who calls himself "the scourge of God." Let me sketch in the remainder of this brief scene. Tamburlaine is accompanied by his sons, his three faithful followers, and two more captive kings, who will draw the chariot tomorrow. These protest their treatment and are cruelly mocked and punished. The concubines of the captive kings are brought out and distributed among Tamburlaine's soldiers for their recreation. Stage direction: "They run away with the ladies." The scene ends with a long speech in which Tamburlaine outlines further conquests and imagines his triumphal return to Samarcand, describing the plumes he will wear in lines which Spenser found appropriate to use for the plumes of Prince Arthur in *The Faerie Queene*. Rising to an ecstatic pitch, Tamburlaine compares himself in his chariot first to Apollo and then to Jove:

So will I ride through Samarcanda streets,
Until my soul, dissevered from this flesh,
Shall mount the milk-white way, and meet Him there.
To Babylon, my lords, to Babylon!

(ll.130–133)

No scene in all ten acts of this play depicts more clearly Tamburlaine's lust for power. Is this a passion which Marlowe shares or commends? Does he expect the audience to thrill with Tamburlaine at the prospect of more bloody victories, more cruel jokes? The questions are unexpectedly difficult to answer with assurance. The connotations of the triumphal chariot itself are various—glory, cruelty, pride. Many years before, the young gentlemen of Gray's Inn had been entertained with a classical tragedy of *Jocasta,* in which there occurred a dumb show of a king sitting in a chariot, "drawne in by foure Kinges. . . Representing

---

[4] *II Tamburlaine,* IV.iv.1–4, 7–16; *The Complete Plays of Christopher Marlowe,* ed. Irving Ribner (New York: Odyssey Press, 1963). All references to Marlowe are to this edition.

unto us Ambition. . . ."[5] Running counter to any such moral interpretation of Tamburlaine's chariot, the rhetoric points to the chariot of the
sun, bringing light or even enlightment, and to the taming of wild
mares by Hercules as one of his labors. There is cruelty in that story
too, for King Aegeus is thrown to the wild mares to be devoured, but
Marlowe reminds us that this wicked king had made them "wanton"
by feeding them on human flesh. The violence of Hercules is both
appropriate punishment and homeopathic cure, for immediately after
feasting on King Aegeus, the mares become tame; a natural order has
been restored. The allusion to these mares of the Thracian king has
a special interest, since it probably points to the source of Tamburlaine's
first words in this scene. It has been pointed out that Golding, in his
translation of Ovid's story of the taming of the wild mares, called them
"pampered jades of Thrace."[6] This labor of Hercules must be very close
to the center of the meaning of Tamburlaine and his royal team.

There is nothing heroic, however, about the brutality of Tamburlaine's
henchmen to the other captive kings, nor about handing out their concubines to the soldiers like so many pieces of candy. These episodes color
the whole enterprise with a savage humor which rapidly degenerates
toward farce as the soldiers presumably chase the concubines around the
stage and then run off with them—a burlesque rape of the Sabine
women. One recalls the statement of the printer of *Tamburlaine* that
he has omitted some "fond and frivolous gestures" which in his opinion
detracted from the play but made a great hit in the theater. Were there
some of these high jinks here? And if so, did Marlowe devise them,
or did the eager actors of bit parts? All we can say for sure is that the
text we have certainly invites comic treatment, and thus, momentarily
at least, undercuts Herculean nobility. Then, as you will recall, the theme
of Tamburlaine's immortal longings is sounded fortissimo, as his imagination soars from a roster of yet unconquered kingdoms to his entry into
the heavens.

In this scene both Tambulaine and his enemies give vent to strong
passions, but I hope you will agree that in presenting them Marlowe
has contrived to make the response to them complex. Excitement and
awe mingle with revulsion and possibly even contempt. Thus the dramatist, like his hero, seems to whip forward with one hand while he
reins in with the other, always determining the speed and guiding the
direction of his chariot.

Certain of his devices for exerting artistic control have already become
apparent. His use of allusion, his strange juxtapositions, and his unex-

---

5 *The Complete Works of George Gascoigne,* ed. J. W. Cunliffe (Cambridge:
Cambridge University Press, 1907), I, 246.

6 M. M. Wills, "Marlowe's Role in Borrowed Lines," *PMLA,* LII (1937), 902–
903.

pected strokes of humor will bear further examination, but there are also other devices to be examined; one is the use of a dramatic introduction. Marlowe's earliest play, *Dido, Queen of Carthage*, may have been written while he was still at Cambridge University, and its title page proclaims the collaboration of his fellow Cantabrigian, Thomas Nashe, though there are no clear evidences of Nashe's work in the play as it stands. I shall refer to it as Marlowe's play. The theme, of course, is the familiar love-tragedy of Dido and Aeneas in Virgil's epic. There can be no secret for any literate member of the audience about the nature of the story he is about to see; it must be heroic in so far as it concerns the high destiny of Aeneas and pathetic in its portrayal of his desertion of Dido, who is to be the principal character. Knowing this much, one is startled by the un-Virgilian opening scene in which Jupiter is discovered "dandling Ganymede upon his knee," pulling feathers out of Mercury's wing to give his young favorite, offering these and other presents in return for love, and defying Juno to spoil his fun. The tone of the scene is flippant, worldly, and satirical. This is the way Jupiter disports himself when he is supposed to be ruling heaven and earth. When Venus enters, she loses no time in rebuking her father for his lascivious neglect of duty while her son Aeneas is being tossed about by a storm arranged by Juno. Goaded into responsibility, Jupiter goes about his business, though taking Ganymede along.

Virgil's story is now launched, but after this opening we no longer know what to expect. It might seem likely that all the rest would be in the vein of burlesque, though in fact nothing could be farther from the truth. When we have reached the funeral pyre, the bitter prophecy of the Punic Wars, and the triple suicide with which the play ends, we may look back to ask why the play starts as it does.

Marlowe accomplishes several things with his introduction. Its novelty has in itself some virtue—the suggestion of a fresh look at an old story. Its comic realism may also suggest that the author knows how the most respected gods and men behave, and can be trusted not to falsify his play with idealized characters. However, the chief effect of the introduction is to put the main story in perspective, not merely by showing, as Virgil does, how dependent human affairs are upon the whims of the gods, but also by adopting temporarily the viewpoint of gods, concerned but aloof. After Jupiter's departure, we move with Venus from Mount Olympus to near Carthage, where she disguises herself and hides to observe Aeneas and Achates. With her asides she maintains direct contact with the audience while the hero converses with his friend and looks for some trace of human habitation. We seem to see them through her eyes, and only when she leaves do we get what might be called a close-up of Aeneas. The effect of perspective is strengthened by a series of parallels which extend from the introduction into the main story in a disconcerting way. As Jupiter promises treats and gifts to his "little love," so

Venus lures Ascanius, when she is abducting him, with similar offers, and so Dido takes Cupid in her lap, thinking he is Ascanius, and promises him to love Aeneas for his sake. Later on, it is Aeneas himself to whom she offers every luxury in return for his love. It is daring to present the great hero as the last in this sequence of love-objects, preceded by three spoiled boys. The emphasis is thereby thrown on the power of infatuation rather than on the greatness of the hero, and since this is Dido's story, the adjustment is appropriate. Her consuming passion is what counts. To the extent that Aeneas is analogous to Ganymede, Dido, of course, is analogous to Jupiter, and if her infatuation makes her oblivious of everything else, she is hardly more irresponsible than he is. What is merely pastime for Jupiter, however, is fatal to her, and thus the comparison of comic and tragic infatuation may lead to a somber reflection on human, as opposed to divine, existence. What Pope might have called the "machinery" of the play reveals and requires a complex attitude to Dido's passion.

Closely related to the device of an introduction is the presenter, who appears in three plays. In *Tamburlaine* he is called the Prologue, in *The Jew of Malta* he is Machiavel, and in *Doctor Faustus* Chorus. In each case he works in a different way. The Prologue of *Tamburlaine, Part I* is the envoy of the author and the players who commends the play to our attention with the equivalent of a brief "commercial": this is to be a serious play in elevated language, a better buy than the standard fare. But he commits himself to no judgment upon the hero:

> View but his picture in this tragic glass,
> And then applaud his fortunes as you please.

> (Prologue, ll. 7–8)

In *Part II* there is a little more publicity when he tells us that the great success of *Part I* encouraged the author to write a sequel, in which "death cuts off the progress of his pomp / And murderous Fates throws all his triumphs down" (Prologue ll. 4–5). Again the attitude toward the hero seems neutral except for the suggestion that his fall may be an awe-inspiring spectacle.

In contrast to this Prologue, the Machiavel of *The Jew of Malta* expounds his cynical views with engaging frankness, and having thus taken us into his confidence, makes his sympathy for the hero apparent. To be sure, we are told to "grace him as he deserves," but also urged: "And let him not be entertained the worse / Because he favors me" (Prologue, ll. 33–35). The Chorus of Doctor Faustus again represents the players ("we must now perform / The form of Faustus' fortunes"), but also makes an unequivocal judgment upon the hero, "swoll'n with cunning of a self-conceit," and "falling to a devilish exercise' (Prologue, ll. 7–8, 20, 23). At his appearance during the course of the play, the Chorus confines himself to narrative, but at the end he draws the moral:

Regard his hellish fall,
Whose fiendful fortune may exhort the wise
Only to wonder at unlawful things,
Whose deepness doth entice such forward wits
To practise more than heavenly power permits.

(Epilogue, ll. 4–8)

The attitudes of these three presenters are closely allied to Marlowe's manipulation of contexts. The failure of the Prologue to pass judgment on Tamburlaine coincides with the absence of clear moral criteria within the play. The hero gives allegiance to neither Christ nor Mahomet, and normally prays to Jove. However, the Christian and pagan rulers appear to have no more enlightened moral standards than the cruel and ambitious Tamburlaine. Since no ethic is clearly established as a basis for judging the hero's conduct, the audience is singularly free to "applaud his fortunes as they please," following the admonition of the Prologue. Such a freedom is essential if the response to Tamburlaine in his chariot, for example, is to be the complex one I have described. In the context of a firmly established Christian ethic disapproval would heavily over-balance admiration.

In *Doctor Faustus* the situation is almost reversed. Here is a man whose desires are much more sympathetic to the average man than those of Tamburlaine. He longs for knowledge, and though he also seeks power, he would not harness his enemies to his chariot, massacre virgins, or kill his own child. Yet disapproval of Faustus's ambitions is an essential part of the meaning of the story. The Christian context must be preserved; the audience must not be free to applaud his fortunes as they please, but must be constantly reminded of the nature of his error. To this end the Chorus makes his plain statements at the beginning and the conclusion, and a Good and Bad Angel keep black and white clearly distinct in the morality-play tradition. Against a background of con-ventional moral judgment Marlowe develops all that is appealing in his hero in the poetry which made the play famous. The effectiveness of the tragedy is due in part to this tension.

In *The Jew of Malta* Marlowe again makes use of stock attitudes but in an ironic fashion. The Machiavel, by proclaiming a highly unpopular point of view, damns in advance the hero to whom he is sympathetic. The avaricious Jew should in any case be anathema to a right-minded audience of the time, but especially so if he is also Machiavellian. It would seem that we know from the start how we must respond to Barabas. However, in the first scenes of the play, the representatives of Christian orthodoxy are so presented that the Machiavel's cynical view of the world seems almost justified. Is Barabas, like Tamburlaine, preferable to his enemies? The ironies of the presenter combine with ironies in the play to form a tissue of contradictory attitudes. At times they seem even to cancel each other out, rather than to support the complex balance seen in *Tamburlaine*. The obliqueness of presentation, brilliant as it is, comes near to defeating its own ends.

Although Marlowe's devices for qualifying or shifting opinion, for distancing characters or encouraging us to take them to our bosoms, are not uniformly successful, their virtuosity can always be admired, and they can be seen to great advantage even in a play in which they do not work perfectly. *The Famous Tragedy of The Rich Jew of Malta* is a case in point. It is a little disappointing in its totality, and yet it achieves some extraordinary effects. The complexities of Marlowe's presentation of Barabas are not limited to the use of the Machiavel as prologue and the exposure of Christian hypocrisy. They include the treatment of the company Barabas keeps—his friends and his daughter. He is seen near the opening of the play with three other Jews, who readily capitulate to Christian demands for half their money. Barabas refuses until too late and is punished. When he rages against the Christians, his friends behave like Job's comforters, tamely counselling patience. In contrast to them Barabas, miser that he is, can be seen as a man of spirit. As he says, they

> Think me to be a senseless lump of clay
> That will with every water wash to dirt.
> No, Barabas is born to better chance
> And framed of finer mold than common men
> That measure nought but by the present time.

> (I.ii.217–221)

But then we may also contrast him with his daughter. Abigail is treated as badly as the innocent heroine of any melodrama, and her father is the chief offender. Much as he claims to love her, she is no more than a means to his ends, as we see in often quoted lines which inspired an even better known passage in *The Merchant of Venice*. When Abigail rescues Barabas's money bags for him, he cries, "O my girl, / My gold, my fortune, my felicity..." and then: "O girl! O gold! O beauty! O my bliss!" as he "hugs his bags" (II.i. 47–48, 54). It is a marvellously humorous moment in which his confusion of values stigmatizes him beyond doubt. When Abigail, in love, is compelled to be the means of luring her Christian lover to his death, the pathos of her plight is more marked and the cruelty of her father's behavior more repellent. If a certain grandeur in his character stands out in the company of his friends, it is meanness that we notice in his dealings with Abigail.

Her part in the story comes to an abrupt end when she decides to become a Christian and Barabas poisons her along with a conventful of nuns. Marlowe's attitude to this event is an uneasy blend of opposites. The girl is given an affecting little soliloquy just before her entry into the convent. Then at the moment of death she confesses to a friar, and pleads that her father's crimes be kept secret. In both instances pathos dominates, but the tone of the death scene suddenly shifts to something resembling *Ruthless Rhymes for Heartless Homes:*

> ABIGAIL: And witness that I die a Christian.
> FRIAR BERNARDINE: Ay, and a virgin, too—that grieves me most.

> (III.vi.39–40)

The comment of Barabas is more poetic: "How sweet the bells ring now the nuns are dead" (IV.i.2). If incongruity is the soul of comedy, this must be one of the most intensely comic of situations, yet it is an uncomfortable kind of laughter that the scene produces. After such a buffeting by contrary winds one may wonder, "What next?" In this play Marlowe anticipates such devotees of the sudden change of mood as Bertolt Brecht.

The most interesting of all Marlowe's manipulations in *The Jew of Malta* is his regulation of the amount of individuality his hero is allowed to have at a given moment. Constant readjustments cause Barabas to appear now as a stock figure—melodramatic villain or comic butt—now as an aspiring and suffering man. Bernard Spivack and Douglas Cole have written well about Barabas as a morality-play Vice, as a stage Jew, and as a Machiavel.[7] At the very outset the prologue leads us to expect a stereotype, and the initial stage-image of the Jew, possibly in the traditional red Judas-wig, counting over his heaps of gold, can only confirm the expectation. Then the long first speech with its glittering references to "fiery opals, sapphires, amethysts," and "beauteous rubies" stamps the portrait of an individual upon the stereotype. To express the goal as the inclosure of "Infinite riches in a little room" is to reveal an intensity of spirit which goes beyond routine avarice and what was thought to be Machiavellianism. The contrast between Barabas and his Jewish friends further stresses individuality. Next there is a scene with Abigail and a friar, in which Barabas feigns to be angry with her, while in asides he tells her how to fool the Christians and get some of his money back. Here he is obviously playing a part, but in doing so he is also becoming more of a Machiavel. As the man disappears beneath the disguise, the individual begins to disappear into the stereotype.

In the following scene he enters alone and once again reveals something of his inner feeling, in this case the anguish of his present situation:

> Thus, like the sad presaging raven...
> Vexed and tormented runs poor Barabas.

> (II.i.1.5)

Then comes the scene with Abigail and the money bags, in which the

---

7 Bernard Spivack, *Shakespeare and the Allegory of Evil* (New York: Columbia University Press, 1958), pp. 346–353; Douglas Cole, *Suffering and Evil in the Plays of Christopher Marlowe* (Princeton: Princeton University Press, 1962), pp. 123–144.

stereotype takes over. Soon he is schooling himself to play the role of the villainous deceiver:

> We Jews can fawn like spaniels when we please,
> And when we grin, we bite; yet are our looks
> As innocent and harmless as a lamb's.
> I learned in Florence how to kiss my hand. . . .

(II.iii.20–23)

His speech to the slave Ithamore, when he tells how he kills sick people groaning under walls and goes about poisoning wells, seems almost a caricature of Machiavellianism, as if the stereotype were deliberately put on by Barabas to test the reactions of Ithamore. And shortly after this, he tells Abigail to behave "like a cunning Jew" in order to deceive the Christians. These suggestions that Barabas is aware of acting in accordance with the common stereotype of a Jew and a Machiavel add further complexity to the portrayal.

Ithamore, a basically simple character, is never anything but a Machiavellian villain, whose heartlessness is even more outrageous than that of Barabas, but so automatic that it is less shocking. Barabas refers to him as his "second self" (III.iv.15) and, though not sincerely fond of him, makes the surprising, nearly fatal mistake of trusting him. Here and in the later trusting of Ferneze there appear to be chinks in the Machiavellian armor, but it is hard to say whether they have any meaning beyond their obvious contribution to the plot.

In the latter part of the play Barabas is almost as completely the stereotype as Ithamore. There is no longer any pathos in his complaints about being tormented as he plans his poisonings; for he and his enemies are clearly "weasels fighting in a hole." The ending, where Barabas drops into the cauldron prepared for the Turk, is farce of a savage kind, as Eliot recognized years ago. Only Barabas's indomitable vitality remains to draw us to him, and that is not enough to balk applause and a heartless laugh. Marlowe's shifting attitudes towards his protagonist are fascinating, but they seem at last to warp rather than add depth to the characterization.

The mixture of humor with pathos or horror, one of the conspicuous features of *The Jew of Malta,* poses, if possible, an even more difficult problem of interpretation in *Doctor Faustus,* where comic scenes of various sorts seem to come near destroying the effects created by the poetry. I shall not try to deal with the much discussed problem of the authorship of the comic scenes, but in my opinion Marlowe might have written most of them. The author of a special version of the play in which almost all comedy has been cut out poses the problem even more clearly than he may have supposed in saying:

As a result of the removal of non-Marlovian dross from *Dr. Faustus*

I realize I may have laid myself open to the charge of having left the play too short for performance in the theatre. Yet, as a practical producer, I cannot see that there is any real difficulty. Any producer, by the use of imagination, music, ballet and magical effects, could make the play into a full evening's entertainment.[8]

Indeed this version is far too short, and it is doubtful that "entertainment" of the sort envisaged would be any improvement over the comic scenes which have been excised. Whether or not Marlowe himself wrote these scenes, he must have intended to have something of the sort in the play. Most of the material, like that of the serious scenes, comes directly from the so-called *English Faust Book*.

There are two sorts of comedy to be considered. The first consists in burlesque of the main action, as in those scenes where clownish minor characters undertake some conjuring on their own. This kind of comedy belongs to a tradition going back at least to the *Second Shepherds' Play*. It is thoroughly congruent with other devices Marlowe uses for forcing a shift of point of view.

Another sort of comic effect appears in the scenes where Faustus is found using his powers for no more exalted purposes than playing tricks on the Pope, putting horns on the head of a doubting knight, or scaring a horse-courser. These are the scenes which are most likely to contain non-Marlovian additions; yet the disparity to which they point is an essential part of the story, for there is a basic frivolity in the learned doctor. Confusion of values is the source of his tragedy. The trouble with these scenes, artistically speaking, is that they prolong the mood of trivial fooling until the fate of Faustus's soul is almost forgotten.

The point which this second sort of comic scene should make is presented elsewhere more subtly and more satisfactorily by other means. In the early scenes, which everyone attributes to Marlowe, we can see how he balances the opposed characteristics of his hero. The poetry does full justice to the dynamics of aspiration, encouraging us to share Faustus's feelings as he says:

> O, what a world of profit and delight,
> Of power, of honor, of omnipotence,
> Is promised to the studious artisan!

(I.i.54–56)

But when he adds "How am I glutted with conceit of this!" his words equate aspiration with appetite as surely as the conventional comments of the chorus, who says, "glutted now with learning's golden gifts, / He surfeits upon cursèd necromancy." When he plans to have spirits bring him gold and fruits, read him strange philosophy, wall Germany with

---

[8] *Doctor Faustus in a special version by Basil Ashmore* (London: Blandford Press, 1948), p. 99.

brass, and clothe students in silk, his want of discrimination shows that he is not only young in heart but also in brain—boyish if not infantile. In the scene where Faustus questions Mephistophilis about hell and accuses him of taking it much too seriously, it is the devil who has the orthodox and sensible scale of values and, in shocked tones, accuses Faustus of frivolity. Mephistophilis here plays the *eiron* to Faustus's *alazon*. The man who will not know what to do with his power when he gets it is plainly set forth, and the sympathy we have for him is qualified by awareness that he is making a fool of himself.

The final presentation of this fatal confusion of values is the scene at the end of the play where Faustus requests torture for the Old Man who has given him godly counsel and then addresses his magnificent lines to Helen of Troy. In context this speech functions precisely to show the choice of the lesser good dressed in all the beauty which sensitivity and imagination can contrive. Helen and the Old Man are emblematic as the representatives of Pleasure and Virtue who came to Hercules, but Faustus makes an un-Herculean choice, for "all is dross that is not Helena" (V.i.105). The lesson is crystal clear to the audience, and yet, thanks to Marlowe's poetry, so is the attraction of Helen. In all the best scenes of *Doctor Faustus* a delicately balanced view of the hero is maintained.

In *The Massacre at Paris* and *Edward II* Marlowe divides the interest among several characters instead of focussing so exclusively on one, as in *Tamburlaine, The Jew of Malta,* and *Doctor Faustus.* It is character-istic of him that he exploits this division of interest to achieve a multi-plicity of points of view. The Duke of Guise, the Duke of Anjou (later Henry III), Catherine, the Queen-Mother, and Henry of Navarre are all major characters in *The Massacre at Paris.* I shall deal with only the first two. In the present state of the text not much can be concluded, but it is at least apparent that an aspiring individual, one who lusts after political power like Tamburlaine, is here set in a context which guaran-tees disapprobation of his goal. The Duke of Guise is shown as the chief instigator of the massacre of Protestant leaders which took place on the feast of St. Bartholomew about twenty years before the writing of the play. He is introduced dispatching poisoned gloves to an enemy in the best Machiavellian tradition. However, immediately afterward, he reveals his ambitions in a speech worthy of Tamburlaine:

> Oft have I levelled, and at last have learned
> That peril is the chiefest way to happiness,
> And resolution honor's fairest aim.
> What glory is there in a common good
> That hangs for every peasant to achieve?
> That like I best that flies beyond my reach.
> Set me to scale the high pyramidès
> And thereon set the diadem of France;
> I'll either rend it with my nails to naught

Or mount the top with my aspiring wings,
Although my downfall be the deepest hell.

(ii.37–47)

Even the most Protestant and the most English man in the audience
could hardly resist some slight quickening of the pulse. It is rhetoric of
the sort that Edward Alleyn knew how to make thrilling. There is, alas,
very little more of it in the play as we have it, but this sample shows
what Marlowe was up to. It is as if he had chosen to elicit some measure
of admiration in the most difficult circumstances possible.

We get another glimpse of his plan in the treatment of the Duke of
Anjòu. At first he is shown participating with Guise in the appalling
massacre, though not sharing in the rhetorical splendor of mighty
aspirations. He is eager enough for power but always takes the easiest
path, and appears as something of a voluptuary, infatuated with his
minions. At the end of the play, however, Marlowe exploits the very
national and religious feelings which tell against the perpetrators of the
massacre to swing opinion around to the dying Henry III. Murdered at
the instigation of the Guise family, Henry turns against Rome and with
his last breath sends greetings to the Queen of England: ". . . tell her
Henry dies her faithful friend." How Marlowe loved such turns! Because
the play as it stands is crudely articulated, they are all the more apparent.

In *Edward II* the manipulation of feelings toward the main characters
is accomplished with far greater subtlety. This dexterity, added to the
structural sophistication and the highly effective portrayal of frustrated
passion, makes the play one of Marlowe's most impressive. Its whole
design is to give dramatic substance to the suffering of the King—to
make the audience experience them with an immediacy which transcends
moral judgment. In Holinshed's history, which Marlowe used, Edward's
"troublesome reign" had a practical political moral:

> . . . he wanted judgment and prudent discretion to make choice of sage
> and discreet councellors, receiving those into his favour, that abused
> the same to their private gaine and advantage, not respecting the
> advancement of the common-wealth. . . .[9]

I agree with such recent critics of the play as Harry Levin, Clifford Leech,
and Douglas Cole, that the main emphasis of Marlowe's play does not
fall here.[10] However, if Edward's personal tragedy is to be made persuasive, judgments of him as a ruler and as a man must be dealt with, and
Marlowe does so by forcing revaluations of every important character—

[9] *Chronicles* (London, 1587), 342.

[10] Harry Levin, *The Overreacher* (Cambridge: Harvard University Press, 1952),
p. 88; Clifford Leech, "Marlowe's *Edward II*: Power and Suffering," *Critical
Quarterly*, I (1959), 181–196; Cole, pp. 161–187.

of those by whom and because of whom the King is judged, and of the King himself.

In the opening scenes the faults of the King are ruthlessly exposed. He is tactless, irresponsible, and self-centered, willing to disregard the feelings of the Queen and the good of the state to indulge himself with his minion Gaveston. He appears to have no redeeming virtues. As the play progresses, however, it becomes possible to feel differently about King Edward as a result of Marlowe's treatment of other characters. Gaveston, for example, is revealed in the first speech as an opportunist, planning to exploit the King's homosexual infatuation for him. Edward's feelings, however ill-advised, seem at least to be sincere. The more outrageously Gaveston behaves, the more Edward seems to be a victim. Then, when the barons, fiercely opposed to Gaveston, succeed in capturing him, his behavior changes surprisingly, and he gives some evidence of a genuine emotional commitment. His last moments are pitiful, and through him some of the pity is directed toward the King. The career of his successor, the younger Spencer, is almost identical in shape though not so fully portrayed. He too starts as an exploiter and ends as an admirer. When, toward the end of the play, he is captured with the King and Edward is led off to prison, Spencer is given the most eloquent praise of the King to be found anywhere.

The character of the Queen becomes another instrument for altering the opinion of the King. Pathetic at first, when Edward has turned from her to Gaveston, her loyalty to him only makes his behavior the more despicable. She even intercedes with the barons to have Gaveston recalled, hoping thus to win her husband's approval. But as he continues to neglect her she drifts into an affair with Mortimer and then into plots against the King. Similarly Mortimer, at first a sincere patriot whose concern for England makes Edward seem irresponsible, becomes increasingly interested in power for himself, and after seducing the Queen, aspires to the throne. By the time that these two have Edward in their power, and Mortimer is planning the King's murder, the sympathy we had for them at first has been transferred to their victim. Kent, the King's brother, is an excellent indication of the shifts in feeling which an audience might be expected to experience. At first he is loyal though disapproving; then he deserts to the barons; but after the defection of the Queen and Mortimer, he returns to the King's side and is beheaded for trying to rescue him from prison.

Thus the treatment of each of these characters contributes to the chief revaluation, that of the King, by damaging in various ways the case against him. In the last act Marlowe is free to concentrate on the horror of the King's confinement and murder. These episodes, which in themselves compel pity, are made the more moving by a marked rise in the pitch of Marlowe's rhetoric. Though the style is less flashy than that of *Tamburlaine,* there are many moving speeches in the last part of

Edward II. One of the finest occurs in the scene where Edward is compelled to surrender his crown and is thereby brought to full recognition of the weakness which has ruined him:

> But what are kings when regiment is gone,
> But perfect shadows in a sunshine day?
> My nobles rule, I bear the name of king;
> I wear the crown, but am controlled by them,
> By Mortimer and my unconstant queen,
> Who spots my nuptial bed with infamy,
> Whilst I am lodged within this cave of care,
> Where sorrow at my elbow still attends,
> To company my heart with sad laments,
> That bleeds within me for this strange exchange.

(V.i.26–34)

This is not a better king than the one who wanted only to frolic with his Gaveston at the opening, but Marlowe has made us painfully aware of his sufferings—of that inward bleeding caused by Edward's years of frustration. Our initial feelings have been eradicated.

Tamburlaine provided an approach to this topic by way of a symbol for Marlowe's guidance of his chariot. Another passage from the same play suggests a way of summarizing the evidence for Marlowe's control of his material. In a set-piece in the last act of Part I, Tamburlaine reflects on beauty:

> What is beauty, saith my sufferings, then?
> If all the pens that ever poets held
> Had fed the feeling of their masters' thoughts,
> And every sweetness that inspired their hearts,
> Their minds, and muses on admirèd themes;
> If all the heavenly quintessence they still
> From their immortal flowers of poesy,
> Wherein, as in a mirror, we perceive
> The highest reaches of a human wit;
> If these had made one poem's period,
> And all combined in beauty's worthiness,
> Yet should there hover in their restless heads
> One thought, one grace, one wonder, at the least,
> Which into words no virtue can digest.

(V.ii.97–110)

Here is the aspiring poet who longs like his hero to conquer more and more territory, though he knows that there will always remain some unconquered region. No doubt the true meaning of the passage is very general: that no poetic endeavor can achieve absolute perfection; but it may be permissible to find a special application to Marlowe, suggested particularly by the word "restless." In the seven plays he wrote in his very brief career he appears as a vastly ambitious and gifted experimenter. No two of them use quite the same techniques. If something of his vision failed to be digested into words, if the conquered kings, those "jades of Asia," tired after going only twenty miles, Marlowe yet showed himself to be a remarkable coachman.

TAMBURLAINE

Armstrong, William A. *Marlowe's* Tamburlaine: *The Image and the Stage,* Hull, England, 1966.

Barber, C. L. "The Death of Zenocrate: 'Conceiving and Subduing Both' in Marlowe's *Tamburlaine,*" *L&P,* XVI (1966), 15–26.

Battenhouse, Roy W. "Tamburlaine, the Scourge of God," *PMLA,* LVI (1941), 337–348.

_____. *Marlowe's Tamburlaine: A Study in Renaissance Moral Philosophy.* Nashville, 1941, pp. 243–258.

Duthie, G. I. "The Dramatic Structure of Marlowe's *Tamburlaine the Great,* Parts I and II," in *English Studies: Essays and Studies Collected for the English Association,* I (1948), 101–126.

Ellis-Fermor, Una, ed. *Tamburlaine the Great: In Two Parts.* 2nd rev. ed. in *The Works and Life of Christopher Marlowe,* ed. R. H. Case. London, 1951, pp. 52–61.

Gardner, Helen. "The Second Part of *Tamburlaine the Great,*" *MLR,* XXXVII (1942), 18–24.

Jacquot, Jean. "La Pensée de Marlowe dans *Tamburlaine the Great,*" *Études Anglaises,* VI (1953), 322–345.

Jump, John D., ed. *Tamburlaine the Great: Parts 1 and 2,* Regents Renaissance Drama Series, Lincoln, Nebraska, 1967.

Kimbrough, Robert. "*1 Tamburlaine:* A Speaking Picture in a Tragic Glass," *RenD,* VII (1964), 20–34.

Leech, Clifford. "The Structure of *Tamburlaine,*" *TDR,* VIII, No. 4 (1964), 32–46.

LePage, Peter V. "The Search for Godhead in Marlowe's *Tamburlaine,*" *CE,* XXVI (1965), 604–609.

Lever, Katherine. "The Image of Man in *Tamburlaine, Part I,*" *PQ,* XXXV (1956), 421–427.

Parr, Johnstone. *Tamburlaine's Malady and Other Essays.* Tuscaloosa, Alabama, 1953, pp. 3–31.

Pearce, T. M. "Tamburlaine's 'Discipline to his Three Sonnes,' an Interpretation of *Tamburlaine, Part II,*" *MLQ,* XV (1945), 18–27.

Peet, Donald. "The Rhetoric of *Tamburlaine,*" *ELH,* XXVI (1959), 137–155.

Prior, Moody E. *The Language of Tragedy.* New York, 1947, pp. 33–46.

Quinn, Michael. "The Freedom of Tamburlaine," *MLQ,* XXI (1960), 315–320.

Ribner, Irving. "The Idea of History in Marlowe's *Tamburlaine*," *ELH*, XX (1954), 251–266.

Richards, Susan. "Marlowe's *Tamburlaine II*: A Drama of Death," *MLQ*, *XXVI* (1965), 375–387.

Schuster, Erika, and Horst Oppel. "Die Bankett-Szene in Marlowes *Tamburlaine*," *Anglia*, LXXVII (1959), 310–345.

Smith, Hallett D. "Tamburlaine and the Renaissance," in *Elizabethan Studies and Other Essays in Honor of George F. Reynolds*. Boulder, Colo., 1945, pp. 126–131.

Thorp, Willard. "The Ethical Problem in Marlowe's *Tamburlaine*," *JEGP*, XXIX (1930), 385–389.

Waith, Eugene M. *The Herculean Hero in Marlowe, Chapman, Shakespeare, and Dryden*. New York, 1962, pp. 59–87, *et passim*.

Wild, Friedrich. "Studien zu Marlowes *Tamburlaine*," in *Studies in English Language and Literature Presented to Professor Dr. Karl Brunner...*, ed. Siegfried Korninger. *WBEP*, Band LXV, Vienna, 1958, pp. 232–251.

See other studies in Marlowe bibliography (below, p. 170).

"THE FORM OF FAUSTUS' FORTUNES GOOD OR BAD" *

C. L. Barber

DOCTOR FAUSTUS tends to come apart in paraphrase. It can be turned into a fable about a Modern Man who seeks to break out of Medieval limitations. On the other hand, when one retells the story in religious terms, it tends to come out as though it were Marlowe's source, *The History of the Damnable Life and Deserved Death of Doctor John Faustus*. The truth is that the play is irreducibly dramatic. Marlowe dramatizes blasphemy, but not with the single perspective of a religious point of view: he dramatizes blasphemy as heroic endeavor. The play is an expression of the Reformation; it is profoundly shaped by sixteenth-century religious thought and ritual. But in presenting a search for

* Reprinted in abridged form from the *Tulane Drama Review*, Vol. 8, No. 4, 1964 (T24), pp. 92–119, by permission of the author and the publishers. Copyright 1964 *Tulane Drama Review;* copyright 1967 *The Drama Review.*

magical dominion, Marlowe makes blasphemy a Promethean enterprise, heroic and tragic, an expression of the Renaissance.[1]

The emergence of a new art form puts man in a new relation to his experience. Marlowe could present blasphemy as heroic endeavor, and the tragic ironies of such endeavor, because he had the new poetic drama, which put poetry in dynamic relation to action—indeed he himself had been the most important single pioneer in creating this form, in *Tamburlaine*. This creation, in turn, depended on the new professional repertory theatre to which, when he came down from Cambridge in 1587, he brought his talents, and his need to project possibilities of human omnipotence. The London theatre was a "place apart" of a new kind, where drama was not presented as part of a seasonal or other social occasion but in its own right. Its stage gave a special vantage on experience:

> Only this (Gentlemen) we must perform
> The form of Faustus' fortunes good or bad.
> To patient judgements we appeal our plaud...

> (7–9)[2]

Marlowe, with characteristic modernity, calls his play just what we call it—a form. He has an audience which includes gentlemen, to whose patient judgments he appeals. In this new situation, blasphemy can be "good or bad."

. . .

Professor Lily B. Campbell has related *Doctor Faustus* to fundamental tensions in Reformation religious experience in an essay which considers Marlowe's hero, against the background of Protestant casuistry, as "a case of Conscience."[3] She focuses on Faustus' sin of despair, his inability to believe in his own salvation, a sin to which Protestants, and particularly Calvinistic Protestants, were especially subject. They had to cope with the immense distance of Calvin's God from the worshipper, and with

---

[1] This essay is adapted from a study centering on *Tamburlaine* and *Doctor Faustus*, to be entitled *Marlowe and the Creation of Elizabethan Tragedy*.

[2] Line references for Marlowe's plays are to *The Works of Christopher Marlowe*, edited by C. F. Tucker Brooke, 1946 (first edition, 1910). I have modernized the spelling. The punctuation has been modernized with one exception, the use of the colon to indicate a pause; this feature of Marlowe's punctuation is so effectively and consistently used that to substitute full stop or comma often involves losing part of the sense. Almost everything I find occasion to use is in the 1604 Quarto; and I find its readings almost always superior to those of 1616. This experience inclines me to regard most of the 1604 text (with some obvious interpolations) as Marlowe's, or close to Marlowe's, whereas most of the additional matter in the 1616 version seems to me to lack imaginative and stylistic relation to the core of the play. Thus my experience as a reader runs counter to the conclusions in favor of the 1616 Quarto which W. W. Greg arrives at from textual study and hypothesis.

[3] *"Doctor Faustus:* a Case of Conscience," PMLA, LXVII, No. 2 (March, 1952), 219–39.

God's terrifying, inclusive justice, just alike to the predestined elect and the predestined reprobate. And they had to do without much of the intercession provided by the Roman church, its Holy Mother, its Saints, its Masses and other works of salvation. Faustus' entrance into magic is grounded in despair. . . . It can help in understanding his turning to magic —and, indirectly, Marlowe's turning to poetic drama—if we consider the tensions which were involved, for the Elizabethan church, in the use and understanding of Holy Communion.

. . .

The piety of the late Middle Ages had dwelt on miracles where a host dripped actual blood, and had depicted scenes where blood streamed down directly from Christ's wounds into the chalice on the altar. The Counter-Reformation, in its own way, pursued such physical imagery and literal conceptions, which remained viable for the Roman Catholic world as embodiments of Grace. A hunger for this kind of physical resource appears in the way that Faustus envisages Christ's blood, visibly streaming in the firmament, in drops to be drunk. But for the Elizabethan church, such thinking about Communion was "but to dream of a gross carnal feeding," in the words of the homily "Of the worthy taking of the Sacraments.[4] We have good reason to think that Marlowe had encountered Catholic ceremony during his absences from Cambridge, when the reasonable assumption is that he was working at intervals as a secret agent among Catholic English exiles and students on the Continent. The letter from the Privy Council which secured him his degree is best explained on that hypothesis, since it denies a rumor that he is "determined to have gone beyond the seas to Reims and there to remain" (as secret Catholics were doing after graduation) and speaks of his having been employed "in matters touching the benefit of his country."[5] To have acted the part of a possible student convert would have involved understanding the Catholic point of view. And we have Marlowe the Scorner's talk, filtered through Baines, "That if there be any god or any good religion, then it is in the Papists' because the service of god is performed with more ceremonies, as elevation of the mass, organs, singing men, shaven crowns, etc. . . . That all protestants are hypocritical asses. . . ."[6]

What concerns us here is the way *Doctor Faustus* reflects the tension

[4] The homily was issued in the *Seconde Tome of Homilies,* sanctioned by the Convocation of Canterbury in 1563 and "appointed to be read in all churches." It is quoted by C. W. Dugmore in *The Mass and the English Reformers* (London: 1958), p. 233. I am greately indebted to Professor Dugmore's book, and to Dom Gregory Dix's *The Shape of the Liturgy,* throughout this discussion. Professor Dugmore, in exploring in detail Tudor views of the real presence in the elements of the Lord's Supper, and their background, brings into focus exactly the tensions that are relevant to *Doctor Faustus.*

[5] John Bakeless, *The Tragical History of Christopher Marlowe,* I, 77.

[6] Bakeless, *op. cit.,* I, 111.

involved in the Protestant world's denying itself miracle in a central area of experience. Things that had seemed supernatural events and were still felt as such in Reims, were superstition or magic from the standpoint of the new Protestant focus on individual experience. Thus the abusive Bishop Bale calls the Roman priests' consecration of the elements "such a charm of enchantment as may not be done but by an oiled officer of the pope's generation."[7] Yet the Anglican church kept the basic physical gestures of the Mass, with a service and words of administration which leave open the question of how Christ's body and blood are consumed. And Anglican divines, while occasionally going all the way to the Zwinglian view of the service as simply a memorial, characteristically maintained a real presence, insisting, in Bishop Jewell's words, that "We feed not the people of God with bare signs and figures."[8] Semantic tensions were involved in this position; the whole great controversy centered on fundamental issues about the nature of signs and acts, through which the age pursued its new sense of reality.

In the church of the Elizabethan settlement, there was still, along with the Reformation's insistence that "Christ's Gospel is not a ceremonial law...but it is a religion to serve God, not in bondage to the figure and shadow,"[9] an ingrained assumption that the crucial physical acts of worship had, or should have, independent meaning. This was supported by the doctrine of a real though not physical presence of Christ. But for many worshippers the physical elements themselves tended to keep a sacred or taboo quality in line with the old need for physical embodiment. We can, I think, connect the restriction of the impulse for physical embodiment in the new Protestant worship with a compensatory fascination in the drama with magical possibilities and the incarnation of meaning in physical gesture and ceremony: the drama carries on, for the most part in secular terms, the preoccupation with a kind of realization of meaning which had been curtailed but not eliminated in religion. In secular life, the cult of royalty, as for example Elizabeth's magical virginity, carried it on also—bulking of course far larger than the drama for the age itself if not for posterity.

In *Doctor Faustus* we have the special case where religious ritual, and blasphemous substitutes for ritual, are central in a drama. The Prayer Book's admonition about the abuse of Holy Communion strikingly illuminates Marlowe's dramatization of blasphemy:

Dearly beloved in the Lord: ye that mind to come to the holy Com-

---

[7] Dugmore, *op. cit.,* p. 234, from *Selected Works,* P. S., 197. An Order of Council under Warwick in 1549 characteristically refers to "their Latin service, their conjured bread and water, with such like vain and superstitious ceremonies." *Ibid.,* 142.

[8] Dugmore, *op. cit.,* p. 229.

[9] *The First and Second Prayer Books of Edward VI* (London: 1949 [Everyman's Library, No. 448]). p. 3.

munion of the body and blood of our Saviour Christ, must consider what S. Paul writeth to the Corinthians, how he exhorteth all persons diligently to try and examine themselves, before they presume to eat of that bread, and drink of that cup: for as the benefit is great, if with a truly penitent heart and lively faith we receive that holy sacrament (for then we spiritually eat the flesh of Christ, and drink his blood, then we dwell in Christ and Christ in us, we be one with Christ, and Christ with us:) so is the danger great, if we receive the same unworthily. For then we be guilty of the body and blood of Chirst our Saviour. We eat and drink our own damnation, not considering the Lord's body.[10]

To eat and drink damnation describes not only Faustus' attitude but the physical embodiment of it, as we shall see in considering the ramifications of gluttony in the play.

Blasphemy implies belief of some sort, as T. S. Eliot observed in pointing, in his seminal 1918 essay, to blasphemy as crucial in Marlowe's work; blasphemy involves also, consciously or unconsciously, the magical assumption that signs can be identified with what they signify. Ministers were warned by several rubrics in the Tudor Prayer Books against allowing parishioners to convey the bread of the sacrament secretly away, lest they "abuse it to superstition and wickedness."[11] Such abuse depends on believing, or feeling, that, regardless of its context, the bread is God, so that by appropriating it one can magically take advantage of God. Spelled out in this way, the magical thinking which identifies sign and significance seems so implausible as to be trivial. But for the sort of experience expressed in *Doctor Faustus,* the identifications and displacements that matter take place at the levels where everyone is ignorant, the regions where desire seeks blindly to discover or recover its objects. Faustus repeatedly moves through a circular pattern, from thinking of the joys of heaven, through despairing of ever possessing them, to embracing magical dominion as a blasphemous substitute. The blasphemous pleasures lead back, by an involuntary logic, to a renewed sense of the lost heavenly joys for which blasphemy comes to seem a hollow substitute —like a stolen Host found to be only bread after all. And so the unsatisfied need starts his Ixion's wheel on another cycle.

The irony which attends Faustus' use of religious language to describe

---

10 *Liturgical Services...in the Reign of Queen Elizabeth,* Parker Society, Vol. XXX, ed. William K. Clay (Cambridge: 1847), p. 189.

11 From a rubric of the first Prayer Book of Edward VI, where the danger of such theft is made an argument against allowing the communicants to take the bread in their own hands. (*The Two Liturgies, A.D. 1549, and A.D. 1552:* etc., Parker Society, Vol. XXIX, ed. Joseph Ketley [Cambridge: 1844], p. 97.) The Second Prayer Book of Edward and the Prayer Book of Elizabeth provided that "to take away the superstition which any person hath, or might have in the bread and wine, it shall suffice that the bread be such, as is usual to be eaten at the table..." and that "if any of the bread or wine remain, the Curate shall have it to his own use." (*Ibid.,* pp. 282–3, and Clay, *op. cit.,* p. 198.)

magic enforces an awareness of this circular dramatic movement. "Divinity, adieu! / These...necromantic books are heavenly" (76–77). What seems to be a departure is betrayed by "heavenly" to be also an effort to return. "Come," Faustus says to Valdes and Cornelius, "make me blest by your sage conference" (126–127). And Valdes answers that their combined skill in magic will "make all nations to canonize us" (149). In repeatedly using such expressions, which often "come naturally" in the colloquial language of a Christian society, the rebels seem to stumble uncannily upon words which condemn them by the logic of a situation larger than they are. So Mephistophilis, when he wants to praise the beauty of the courtesans whom he can give to Faustus, falls into saying:

> As wise as Saba, or as beautiful
> As was bright Lucifer before his fall.

> (589–590)

The auditor experiences a qualm of awe in recognizing how Mephisto-philis has undercut himself by this allusion to Lucifer when he was still the star of the morning, bright with an altitude and innocence now lost.

The last and largest of these revolutions is the one that begins with showing Helen to the students, moves through the Old Man's effort to guide Faustus' steps "unto the way of life," (1274) and ends with Helen. In urging the reality of Grace, the Old Man performs the role of Spenser's Una in the Cave of Despair, but Faustus can only think "Hell calls for right" (1287). Mephistophilis, like Spenser's Despair, is ready with a dagger for suicide; Marlowe at this point is almost dramatizing Spenser. Faustus asks for "heavenly Helen," "To glut the longing of my heart's desire" and "extinguish clean / Those thoughts that do dissuade me from my vow" (1320–1324). The speech to Helen is a wonderful poetic fusion of many elements, combining chivalric worship of a mistress with human-ist intoxication over the project of recovering antiquity. In characteristic Renaissance fashion, Faustus proposes to relive classical myth in a Medieval way: "I will be Paris...wear thy colors" (1335, 1338). But these secular elements do not account for the peculiar power of the speech; the full awe and beauty of it depend on hoping to find the holy in the profane. The prose source can provide a useful contrast here; Helen is described there so as to emphasize a forthright sexual appeal:

> her hair hanged down as fair as the beaten gold, and of such length that it reached down to her hams, with amorous coal-black eyes, a sweet and pleasant face, her lips red as a cherry, her cheeks of rose all colour, her mouth small, her neck white as the swan, tall and slender of personage...she looked round about her with a rolling hawk's eye, a smiling and wanton countenance...

On the stage, of course, a full description was not necessary; but Marlowe in any case was after a different kind of meaning. He gives us nothing

of the sort of enjoyment that the Faust book describes in saying that
Helen was "so beautiful and delightful a piece" that Faustus "made her
his common concubine and bedfellow" and "could not be one hour
from her...and to his seeming, in time she was with child."[12] There is
nothing sublime about this account, but it has its own kind of strength—
an easy, open-eyed relishing which implies that sensual fulfillment is
possible and satisfying in its place within a larger whole. The writer of
the Faust book looked at Helen with his own eyes and his own assumption that the profane and the holy are separate. But for Marlowe—it was
his great, transforming contribution to the Faust myth—the magical
dominion and pleasures of Dr. Faustus ambiguously mingle the divine and
the human, giving to the temporal world a wonder and excitement which
is appropriated, daringly and precariously, from the supernatural.

The famous lines are so familiar, out of context, as an apotheosis of
love, that one needs to blink to see them as they fit into the play's
motion, with the play's ironies. (Eartha Kitt, telling *Life* magazine about
playing Helen opposite Orson Welles, ignored all irony, saying simply
"I made him immortal with a kiss.") By contrast with the Helen of the
source, who has legs, Marlowe's Helen is described only in terms of her
face and lips; and her beauty is *power:*

> Was this the face that launch'd a thousand ships,
> And burnt the topless towers of Ilium?

> (1328–1329)

The kiss which follows is a way of reaching this source of power; it goes
with a prayer, "Make me immortal with a kiss," and the action is like
taking communion, promising, like communion, a way to immortality.
It leads immediately to an ecstacy in which the soul seems to leave the
body: "Her lips suck forth my soul: see where it flies!" The speech ends
with a series of worshipping gestures expressing wonder, awe, and a yearning towards encountering a fatal power. It is striking that Helen comes
to be compared to Jupiter, god of power, rather than to a goddess:

> O thou art fairer than the evening air
> Clad in the beauty of a thousand stars:
> Brighter art thou than flaming Jupiter
> When he appeared to hapless Semele:
> More lovely than the monarch of the sky
> In wanton Arethusa's azured arms;
> And none but thou shall be my paramour.

> (1341–1347)

Upward gestures are suggested by "the evening air" and "the monarch

12 *The History of the Damnable Life and Deserved Death of Dr. John Faustus*
(1592), ed. by William Rose, London, n.d., p. 179 and pp. 193–4.

of the sky"; Faustus' attitude towards Helen is linked to that of hapless Semele when Jupiter descended as a flame, and to that of the fountain nymph Arethusa when she embraced Jupiter in her spraylike, watery, and sky-reflecting arms. Consummation with the power first described in Helen's face is envisaged as dissolution in fire or water. . . .

. . .Marlowe's art gives the encounter meaning both as a particular kind of sexual experience *and* as blasphemy.

The stage directions of the 1604 text bring the Old Man back just at the moment when Faustus in so many words is making Helen into heaven:

> Here will I dwell, for heaven be in these lips
> And all is dross that is not Helena:
>
> *Enter old man.*
>
> (1333–1334)

This figure of piety is a presence during the rest of the speech; his perspective is summarized after its close: "Accursed Faustus, miserable man, / That from thy soul exclud'st the grace of Heaven."

Another perspective comes from the earlier scenes in the play where the nature of heaven and the relation to it of man and devil is established in conversations between Mephistophilis and Faustus. For example, the large and final line in the later scene, "And all is dross that is not Helena," has almost exactly the same movement as an earlier line of Mephistophilis' which ends in "heaven."

> And, to be short, when all the world dissolves,
> And every creature shall be purified,
> All place shall be hell that is not heaven.
>
> (556–558)

One does not need to assume a conscious recognition by the audience of this parallel, wonderfully ironic as it is when we come to hear it as an echo.[13] What matters is the recurrence of similar gestures in language about heaven and its substitutes, so that a meaning of heaven, and postures towards it, are established.

The most striking element in this poetic complex is a series of passages involving a face:

> Why, this is hell, nor am I out of it:
> Think'st thou that I, that saw the face of God,
> And tasted the eternal joys of heaven,
> Am not tormented with ten thousand hells,
> In being depriv'd of everlasting bliss?
>
> (312–316)

---

[13] The echo was first pointed out to me by Professor James Alfred Martin, Jr. of Union Theological Seminary.

Just as Faustus' rapt look at Helen's face is followed by his kiss, so in the lines of Mephistophilis, "saw the face of God" is followed by "tasted the eternal joys of heaven."

Both face and taste are of course traditional religious imagery, as is motion upward and downward. Marlowe's shaping power composes traditional elements into a single complex gesture and imaginative situation which appears repeatedly. The face is always high, something above to look up to, reach or leap up to, or to be thrown down from:

> FAUSTUS: Was not that Lucifer an angel once?
>
> MEPHISTOPHILIS: Yes, Faustus, and most dearly lov'd of God.
>
> FAUSTUS: How comes it then that he is prince of devils?
>
> MEPHISTOPHILIS: Oh, by aspiring pride and insolence;
> For which God threw him from the face of heaven.
>
> (300–304)

A leaping-up complementary to this throwing-down, with a related sense of guilt, is expressed in Faustus' lines as he enters at midnight, about to conjure and eagerly hoping to have "these joys in full possession":

> Now that the gloomy shadow of the night,
> Longing to view Orion's drizzling look,
> Leaps from th' antarctic world unto the sky,
> And dims the welkin with her pitchy breath,
> Faustus, begin thine incantations...
>
> (235–239)

Here the reaching upward in *leaps* is dramatized by the word's position as a heavy stress at the opening of the line. There is a guilty suggestion in *gloomy*—both discontented and dark—linked with *longing to view*. An open-mouthed panting is suggested by *pitchy breath,* again with dark associations of guilt which carry through to Faustus' own breath as he says his *incantations* (itself an open-throated word). The whole passage has a grotesque, contorted quality appropriate to the expression of an almost unutterable desire, at the same time that it magnificently affirms this desire by throwing its shadow up across the heavens.

A more benign vision appears in the preceding scene, where the magician Valdes promises Faustus that "serviceable spirits" will attend:

> Sometimes like women, or unwedded maids,
> Shadowing more beauty in their airy brows
> Than has the white breasts of the queen of love.
>
> (156–158)

Here we get an association of the breast with the face corresponding to the linkage elsewhere of tasting power and joy with seeing a face. The lines suggest by "airy brows" that the faces are high (as well as that the women are unsubstantial spirits).

The complex we have been following gets its fullest and most intense expression in a passage of Faustus' final speech, where the imagery of communion with which we began is one element. To present it in this fuller context, I quote again:

> The stars move still, time runs, the clock will strike,
> The devil will come, and Faustus must be damn'd.
> O I'll leap up to my God: who pulls me down?
> See, see, where Christ's blood streams in the firmament.
> One drop would save my soul, half a drop, ah, my Christ.
> Ah, rend not my heart for naming of my Christ,
> Yet will I call on him: O, spare me, Lucifer!
> Where is it now? 'tis gone: and see, where God
> Stretcheth out his arm, and bends his ireful brows:

> (1429–1437)

Here the leap is discovered to be unrealizable. Faustus' blasphemous vision of his own soul with Helen—"See, where it flies"—is matched now by "See, see, where Christ's blood streams." It is "in the firmament," as was Orion's drizzling look. A paroxysm of choking tension at once overtakes Faustus when he actually envisages drinking Christ's blood. And yet—"one drop would save my soul." Such communion is denied by the companion vision of the face, now dreadful, "ireful brows" instead of "airy brows," above and bending down in overwhelming anger....

When we turn to consider the presentation of the underside of Faustus' motive, complementary to his exalted longings, the Prayer Book, again, can help us understand Marlowe. The Seventeenth of the Thirty-Nine Articles contains a warning remarkably applicable to Faustus:

> As the godly consideration of Predestination, and our election in Christ, is full of sweet, pleasant, and unspeakable comfort to godly persons.... So, for curious and carnal persons, lacking the spirit of Christ, to have continually before their eyes the sentence of God's Predestination, is a most dangerous downfall, whereby the Devil doth thrust them either into desperation, or into wretchlessness of most unclean living, no less perilous than desperation.[14]

Faustus is certainly a "curious and carnal person," and he has "the sentence of God's Predestination" continually before his eyes, without "the spirit of Christ." The Article relates this characteristically Calvinist predicament to the effort to use the body to escape despair: "wretchlessness" (for which the New English Dictionary cites only this instance) seems to combine wretchedness and recklessness. The phrase "most

---

[14] Clay, *op. cit.,* p. 189.

unclean living" suggests that the appetites become both inordinate and perverse.

The psychoanalytic understanding of the genesis of perversions can help us to understand how, as the Article says, such unclean living is spiritually motivated—like blasphemy, with which it is closely associated. We have noticed how blasphemy involves a magical identification of action with meaning, of sign with significance. A similar identification appears in perversion as Freud has described it. Freud sees in perversions a continuation of the secondary sexual satisfactions dominant in childhood. The pervert, in this view, is attempting, by repeating a way of using the body in relation to a certain limited sexual object, to recover or continue in adult life the meaning of a relationship fixed on this action and object in childhood; the sucking perversions may seek to establish a relationship of dependence by eating someone more powerful.

. . .

The perverse too can have an element of worship in it. When we consider the imagery in *Doctor Faustus* in psychoanalytic terms, an oral emphasis is very marked, both in the expression of longings that reach towards the sublime and in the gluttony which pervades the play and tends towards the comic, the grotesque, and the terrible. It is perhaps not fanciful to link the recurrent need to leap up which we have seen with an infant's reaching upward to mother or breast, as this becomes fused in later life with desire for women as sources of intoxicating strength: the face as a source of power, to be obliviously kissed, "airy brows" linked to "the white breasts of the queen of love." The two parents seem to be confused or identified so that the need appears in fantasies of somehow eating the father, panting for Orion's drizzling look. This imagery neighbors directly religious images, Christ's streaming blood, the taste of heavenly joys.

It is because Faustus has the same fundamentally acquisitive attitude towards both secular and religious objects that the religious joys are unreachable. The ground of the attitude that sustenance must be gained by special knowledge or an illicit bargain with an ultimately hostile power is the deep conviction that sustenance will not be given freely, that life and power must come from a being who condemns and rejects Faustus. We can see his blasphemous need, in psychoanalytic terms, as fixation or regression to infantile objects and attitudes, verging towards perverse developments of the infantile pursued and avoided in obscure images of sexual degradation. But to keep the experience in the perspective with which Marlowe's culture saw it, we must recognize that Faustus' despair and obsessive hunger go with his inability to take part in Holy Communion. In Holy Communion, he would, in the words of the Prayer Book, "spiritually eat the flesh of Christ, and drink his blood...dwell in Christ...be one with Christ." In the Lord's Supper the very action towards which the infantile, potentially disruptive motive tends are transformed, for the successful communicant, into a way of reconciliation with society and the ultimate source and sanction of society. But communion can only be reached by "a truly contrite heart" which recognizes human finitude, and with "a lively faith" in the possibility of God's love. Psychoanalytic interpretation can easily lead to the misconception that when we encounter infantile or potentially perverse imagery in a traditional culture it indicates, *a priori,* neurosis or degradation. Frequently, on the contrary, such imagery is enacted in ritual and used in art as a way of controlling what is potentially disruptive.[15] We are led by these considerations to difficult issues about the status and limits of psychoanalytic interpretation beyond the scope of this essay, and to ultimate issues about whether worship is necessary which each of us must settle as we can.

But for our purposes here, the necessary point is the perspective which the possibility of Holy Communion gives within Marlowe's play. Tragedy involves a social perspective on individual experience; frequently this perspective is expressed by reference to ritual or ceremonial acts, acts whose social and moral meaning is felt immediately and spontaneously. The hero one way or another abuses the ritual because he is swept away by the currents of deep aberrant motives associated with it, motives which it ordinarily serves to control. In *Doctor Faustus* this public, social ritual is Holy Communion. How deeply it is built into sensibility appears, for example, when Faustus stabs his arm:

> My blood congeals, and I can write no more.
>
> .   .   .   .
>
> *Faustus gives thee his soul.* Ah, there it stayed.
> Why shouldst thou not? Is not thy soul thy own?

$$(494, 499-500)$$

This is the crucial moment of the black mass, for Faustus is imitating Christ in sacrificing himself—but to Satan instead of to God. A moment later he will repeat Christ's last words, "Consummatus est." His flesh cringes to close the self-inflicted wound, so deeply is its meaning understood by his body.

The deep assumption that all strength must come from consuming another accounts not only for the desperate need to leap up again to the source of life, but also for the moments of reckless elation in fantasy. Faustus uses the word "fantasy" in exactly its modern psychological sense:

---

15 In an essay on "Magical Hair" (*Journal of the Royal Anthropological Institute,* V. 88, Pt. II, pp. 147–169) the anthropologist Edmund Leach has made this point in a most telling way in evaluating the psychoanalytic assumptions of the late Dr. Charles Berg in his book *The Unconscious Significance of Hair.*

...your words have won me at the last,
To practice magic and concealed arts:
Yet not your words only, but mine own fantasy,
Which will receive no object, for my head
But ruminates on necromantic skill.

(129–133)

Here "ruminates" carries on the imagery of gluttony. Moving restlessly round the circle of his desires, Faustus wants more from nature than nature can give, and gluttony is the form his "unclean living" characteristically takes. The verb "glut" recurs: "How am I glutted with conceit of this!" "That heavenly Helen... to glut the longing. ..." The Prologue summarizes his career in the same terms,[16] introducing like an overture the theme of rising up by linking gluttony with a flight of Icarus:

Till swoll'n with cunning, of a self conceit,
His waxen wings did mount above his reach,
And melting heavens conspir'd his overthrow.
For falling to a devilish exercise,
And glutted now with learnings golden gifts,
He surfeits upon cursed Negromancy.

(20–25)

On the final night, when his fellow scholars try to cheer Faustus, one of them says, "'Tis but a surfeit, never fear, man." He answers, "A surfeit of deadly sin, that hath damn'd both body and soul" (1364–1367). How accurately this exchange defines the spiritual, blasphemous motivation of his hunger!

Grotesque and perverse versions of hunger appear in the comedy. Like much of Shakespeare's low comedy, the best clowning in *Doctor Faustus* spells out literally what is metaphorical in the poetry. No doubt some of the prose comedy, even in the 1604 Quarto, is not by Marlowe; but when the comic action is a burlesque that uses imaginative associations present in the poetry, its authenticity is hard to doubt. Commentators are often very patronizing about the scene with the Pope, for example; but it carries out the motive of gluttony in a delightful and appropriate way by presenting a Pope "whose *summum bonum* is in belly cheer" (855), and by having Faustus snatch his meat and wine away

---

16 I first became aware of this pattern of gluttonous imagery in teaching a cooperative course at Amherst College in 1947—before I was conscious of the blasphemous complex of taste, face, etc. Professor R. A. Brower pointed to the prologue's talk of glut and surfeit as a key to the way Faustus' career is presented by imagery of eating. His remark proved an Open Sesame to the exploration of an "imaginative design" comparable to those he exhibits so delicately and effectively in his book, *The Fields of Light* (Oxford: 1951). This pattern later fell into place for me in relation to the play's expression of the blasphemous motives which I am analyzing.

and render his exorcism ludicrous, baffling magic with magic. Later
Wagner tells of Faustus himself carousing and swilling amongst the
students with "such belly-cheer / As Wagner in his life ne're saw the like"
(1343–1344). The presentation of the Seven Deadly Sins, though of
course traditional, comes back to hunger again and again, in gross and
obscene forms; after the show is over, Faustus exclaims "O, this feeds
my soul!" One could go on and on.

Complementary to the active imagery of eating is imagery of being
devoured. Such imagery was of course traditional, as for example in
cathedral carvings of the Last Judgment and in the Hell's mouth of the
stage. With being devoured goes the idea of giving blood, also traditional
but handled, like all the imagery, in a way to bring together deep
implications. To give blood is for Faustus a propitiatory substitute for
being devoured or torn in pieces. The relation is made explicit when,
near the end, Mephistophilis threatens that if he repents, "I'll in piece-
meal tear thy flesh." Faustus collapses at once into propitiation, signalled
poignantly by the epithet "sweet" which is always on his hungry lips:

> Sweet Mephistophilis, intreat thy Lord
> To pardon my unjust presumption,
> And with my blood again I will confirm
> My former vow I made to Lucifer.

> (1307–1310)

By his pact Faustus agrees to be devoured later provided that he can do
the devouring in the meantime. Before the signing, he speaks of paying
by using other people's blood:

> The god thou servest is thine own appetite,
> Wherein is fix'd the love of Belsabub.
> To him I'll build an altar and a church,
> And offer luke warm blood of new born babes.

> (443–446)

But it has to be his own blood. The identification of his blood with his
soul (a very common traditional idea) is underscored by the fact that
his blood congeals just as he writes "gives thee his soul," and by Mephistophilis' vampire-like exclamation, as the blood clears again under the
influence of his ominous fire: "O what will I not do to obtain his soul."

Faustus' relation to the Devil here is expressed in a way that was
characteristic of witchcraft—or perhaps one should say, of the fantasies
of witchhunters about witchcraft. Witch lore often embodies the assumption that power can be conveyed by giving and taking the contents of
the body, with which the soul is identified, especially the blood. To give
blood to the devil—and to various animal familiars—was the ritual
expression of submission, for which in return one got special powers.

Witches could be detected by the "devil's mark" from which the blood was drawn. In stabbing his arm, Faustus is making a "devil's mark" or "witch's mark" on himself.[17]

The clown contributes to this theme in his role as a common-sense prose foil to the heroic, poetic action of the protagonist. Between the scene where Faustus proposes a pact to buy Mephistophilis' service and the scene of the signing, Wagner buys a ragged but shrewd old "clown" into his service. He counts on hunger:

> ...the villain is bare, and out of service, and so hungry that I know he would give his soul to the Devil for a shoulder of mutton, though it were blood raw.

(358–361)

We have just heard Faustus exclaim:

> Had I as many souls as there be stars,
> I'd give them all for Mephistophilis.

(338–339)

But the clown is not so gullibly willing to pay all:

> How, my soul to the Devil for a shoulder of mutton, though 'twere blood raw? Not so, good friend, by 'rlady I had need to have it well roasted, and good sauce to it, if I pay so dear.

(362–365)

After making game of the sturdy old beggar's ignorance of Latin tags, Wagner assumes the role of the all-powerful magician:

> Bind yourself presently unto me for seven years, or I'll turn all the lice about thee into familiars, and they shall tear thee in pieces.

(377–380)

But again the clown's feet are on the ground:

> Do you hear sir? you may save that labour, they are too familiar with me already. Swounds, they are as bold with my flesh, as if they paid for me meat and drink.

This scene has been referred to as irrelevant padding put in by other hands to please the groundlings! Clearly the clown's independence, and the *detente* of his common man's wit which brings things down to the

---

[17] These notions, which are summarized in most accounts of witchcraft, are spelled out at length in M. A. Murray, *The Witch-Cult in Western Europe* (Oxford: 1921), pp. 86–96 and *passim*. One may have reservations as to how far what Miss Murray describes was acted out and how far it was fantasy; but the pattern is clear.

physical, is designed to set off the folly of Faustus' elation in his bargain. Mephistophilis, who is to become the hero's "familiar spirit" (as the Emperor calls him later at line 1011), "pays for" his meat and drink, and in due course will "make bold" with his flesh. The old fellow understands such consequences, after his fashion, as the high-flown hero does not.

One final, extraordinarily complex image of surfeit appears in the last soliloquy, when Faustus, frantic to escape from his own greedy identity, conceives of his whole body being swallowed up by a cloud and then vomited away:

> Then will I headlong run into the earth:
> Earth gape. O no, it will not harbour me:
> You stars that reign'd at my nativity,
> Whose influence hath allotted death and hell,
> Now draw up Faustus like a foggy mist
> Into the entrails of yon labouring cloud,
> That when you vomit forth into the air,
> My limbs may issue from your smoky mouths,
> So that my soul may but ascend to heaven:
>
> (1441–1449)

Taken by themselves, these lines might seem to present a very far-fetched imagery. In relation to the imaginative design we have been tracing they express self-disgust in terms exactly appropriate to Faustus' earlier efforts at self-aggrandizement. The hero asks to be swallowed and disgorged, anticipating the fate his sin expects and attempting to elude damnation by separating body and soul. Yet the dreadful fact is that these lines envisage death in a way which makes it a consummation of desires expressed earlier. Thus in calling up to the "stars which reigned at my nativity," Faustus is still adopting a posture of helpless entreaty towards powers above. He assumes their influence to be hostile but nevertheless inescapable; he is still unable to believe in love. And he asks to be "drawn up," "like a foggy mist," as earlier the "gloomy shadow," with its "pitchy breath," sought to leap up. The whole plea is couched as an eat-or-be-eaten bargain: you may eat my body if you will save my soul.

In the second half of the soliloquy Faustus keeps returning to this effort to distinguish body and soul. As the clock finally strikes, he asks for escape in physical dissolution:

> Now, body, turn to air,
> Or Lucifer will bear thee quick to hell:
>
> *Thunder and lightning.*
>
> Oh soul, be chang'd into little water-drops,
> And fall into the ocean, ne'er be found:
>
> (1470–1473)

It is striking that death here is envisaged in a way closely similar to the visions of sexual consummation in the Helen speech. The "body, turn to air," with the thunder and lightning, can be related to the consummation of hapless Semele with flaming Jupiter; the soul becoming little water-drops recalls the showery consummation of Arethusa. Of course the auditor need not notice these relations, which in part spring naturally from a pervasive human tendency to equate sexual release with death. The auditor does feel, however, in these sublime and terrible entreaties, that Faustus is still Faustus. Analysis brings out what we all feel—that Faustus cannot repent. Despite the fact that his attitude towards his motive has changed from exaltation to horror, he is still dominated by the same motive—body and soul are one, as he himself said in the previous scene: "hath damned both body and soul." The final pleas themselves confirm his despair, shaped as they are by the body's desires and the assumptions those desires carry.

. . .

I said at the outset that because Marlowe dramatizes blasphemy as heroic endeavor, his play is irreducibly dramatic. But in the analytical process of following out the themes of blasphemy and gluttony, I have been largely ignoring the heroic side of the protagonist, the "Renaissance" side of the play. It is high time to emphasize that Marlowe was able to present blasphemy as he did, and gluttony as he did, only because he was able to envisage them as something more or something else: "his dominion that exceeds in this / Stretcheth as far as doth the mind of man." We have been considering how the play presents a shape of longing and fear which might have lost itself in the fulfillment of the Lord's Supper or become obscene and hateful in the perversions of a witches' sabbath. But in fact Faustus is neither a saint nor a witch—he is Faustus, a particular man whose particular fortunes are defined not by ritual but by drama.

When the Good Angel tells Faustus to "lay that damned book aside ...that is blasphemy," the Evil Angel can answer in terms that are not moral but heroic:

> Go forward, Faustus, in that famous art
> Wherein all nature's treasury is contain'd:
> Be thou on earth as Jove is in the sky,
> Lord and commander of these elements.

(102–105)

It is because the alternatives are not simply good or evil that Marlowe has not written a morality play but a tragedy: there is the further, heroic alternative. In dealing with the blasphemy, I have emphasized how the vision of magic joys invests earthly things with divine attributes; but the heroic quality of the magic depends on fusing these divine suggestions with tangible values and resources of the secular world.

This ennobling fusion depends, of course, on the poetry, which brings into play an extraordinary range of contemporary life:

> From Venice shall they drag huge argosies
> And from America the golden fleece
> That yearly stuffs old Philip's treasury.

(159–161)

Here three lines draw in sixteenth-century classical studies, exploration and commercial adventure, national rivalries, and the stimulating disruptive influence of the new supply of gold bullion. Marlowe's poetry is sublime because it extends desire so as to envisage as objects of passion the larger life of society and nature: "Was this the face that..."—that did what? "...launched a thousand ships." "Clad in the beauty of..." —of what? "...a thousand stars." *Doctor Faustus* is a sublime play because Marlowe was able to occupy so much actual thought and life by following the form of Faustus' desire. At the same time, it is a remorselessly objective, ironic play, because it dramatizes the ground of the desire which needs to ransack the world for objects; and so it expresses the precariousness of the whole enterprise along with its magnificence.

Thus Faustus' gluttonous preoccupation with satisfactions of the mouth and throat is also a delight in the power and beauty of language: "I see there's virtue in my heavenly words." Physical hunger is also hunger for knowledge; his need to depend on others, and to show power by compelling others to depend on him, is also a passion for learning and teaching. Academic vices and weaknesses shadow luminous academic virtues: there is a fine, lonely, generous mastery about Faustus when he is with his colleagues and the students; and Mephistophilis too has a moving dignity in expounding unflinchingly the dreadful logic of damnation to Faustus as to a disciple. The inordinate fascination with secrets, with what cannot be named, as Mephistophilis cannot name God, includes the exploring, inquiring attitude of "Tell me, are there many heavens above the moon?" The need to leap up becomes such aspirations as the plan to "make a bridge through the moving air / To pass the ocean with a band of men." Here we have in germ that sense of man's destiny as a vector moving through open space which Spengler described as the Faustian soul form. Faustus' alienation, which we have discussed chiefly as it produces a need for blasphemy, also motivates the rejection of limitations, the readiness to alter and appropriate the created universe— make the moon drop or ocean rise—appropriating them for *man* instead of for the greater glory of God, because the heavens are "the book of Jove's high firmament," and one can hope for nothing from Jove. Perhaps most fundamental of all is the assumption that power is something outside oneself, something one does not become (as a child becomes a man); something beyond and stronger than oneself (as God remains stronger than man); *and yet* something one can capture and ride—by manipulating symbols.

Marlowe of course does not anticipate the kind of manipulation of symbols which actually has, in natural science, produced this sort of power; Mephistophilis answers Faustus with Ptolemy, not Copernicus— let alone the calculus. But Marlowe was able to exemplify the creative function of controlling symbols by the way the form of poetic drama which he developed uses poetry. He made poetic speech an integral part of drama by exhibiting it as a mode of action: Faustus can assert about himself, "This word damnation terrifies not him, / For he confounds hell in Elysium." The extraordinary pun in "confounds hell in Elysium" suggests that Faustus is able to change the world by the way he names it, to *destroy* or *baffle* hell by *equating* or *mixing* it with Elysium.[18]

Professor Scott Buchanan, in his discussion of tragedy in *Poetry and Mathematics,* suggested that we can see tragedy as an experiment where the protagonist tests reality by trying to live a hypothesis. Elizabethan tragedy, seen in this way, can be set beside the tentatively emerging science of the period. The ritualistic assumptions of alchemy were beginning to be replaced by ideas of observation; a clean-cut conception of the experimental testing of hypothesis had not developed, but Bacon was soon to speak of putting nature on the rack to make her yield up her secrets. Marlowe knew Thomas Harriot: Baines reports his saying "That Moses was but a juggler, and that one Heriots being Sir W. Raleigh's man can do more than he." Faustus' scientific questions and Mephistophilis' answers are disappointing; but the hero's whole enterprise is an experiment, or "experience" as the Elizabethans would have termed it. We watch as the author puts him on the rack.

> FAUSTUS: Come, I think hell's a fable.
>
> MEPHISTOPHILIS: Ay, think so still, 'till experience change thy mind.

(559–560)

In *Tamburlaine,* Marlowe had invented a hero who creates himself out of nothing by naming himself a demigod. By contrast with the universe assumed in a play like *Everyman,* where everything has its right name, *Tamburlaine* assumes an open situation where new right names are created by the hero's combination of powers: he conceives a God-like identity for himself, persuades others to accept his name by the "strong enchantments" of an Orphic speech, and imposes his name on stubborn enemies by the physical action of "his conquering sword." This self-creating process is dramatized by tensions between what is expressed

---

[18] In a commentary on the Virgilian and Averroist precedents for this line, in *English Studies,* XLI, No. 6 (Dec. 1960), 365–368, Bernard Fabian argues for a sense of it consistent with my reading here.

in words and what is conveyed by physical action on the stage: the hero declares what is to happen, and we watch to see whether words will become deeds—whether, in the case of Tamburlaine, man will become demigod.

The high poetry, the bombast, of Marlowe and kindred Elizabethans is not shaped to express what is, whether a passion or a fact, but to make something happen or become—it is incantation, a willful, self-made sort of liturgy. The verbs are typically future and imperative, not present indicative. And the hero constantly talks about himself as though from the outside, using his own name so as to develop a self-consciousness which aggrandizes his identity, or cherishes it, or grieves for it: "Settle thy studies, Faustus, and begin..." (29); "What shall become of Faustus, being in hell forever?" (1382–1383). In the opening speech, Faustus uses his own name seven times in trying on the selves provided by the various arts. In each unit of the speech, the words are in tension with physical gestures. As Faustus "levels at the end of every art," he reaches for successive volumes; he is looking in books for a miracle. But the tension breaks as he puts each book aside because "Yet art thou still but Faustus and a man." When finally he takes up the necromantic works, there is a temporary consummation, a present-indicative simultaneity of words and gestures: "Ay, these are those that Faustus most desires." At this point, the actor can use gesture to express the new being which has been seized, standing up and spreading his arms as he speaks the tremendous future-tense affirmation: "All things that move between the quiet poles. / Shall be at my command...." At the very end of the play Faustus' language is still demanding miracles, while the *absence* of corroborating physical actions make clear that the universe cannot be equated with his self: "Stand still, you ever-moving spheres of heaven...." King Lear in the storm, at the summit of Elizabethan tragedy, is similarly trying (and failing) to realize a magical omnipotence of mind: "...all-shaking thunder, / Smite flat the thick rotundity of the world...."

The double medium of poetic drama was peculiarly effective to express this sort of struggle for omnipotence and transcendent incarnation along with its tragic and comic failure. The dramatist of genius can do two things at once: Marlowe can "vaunt his heavenly verse," animating the reach of Faustus' motive—and putting into his hero much that, on the evidence of his other plays and of his life (beyond our scope here), was in himself. At the same time he is judge and executioner, bringing his hero remorselessly to his terrible conclusion. At the end of the text of *Doctor Faustus*, Marlowe wrote *"Terminat hora diem, Terminat Author opus."* As my friend Professor John Moore has remarked, it is as though he finished the play at midnight! The final hour ends Faustus' day; but Marlowe is still alive. As the author, he has been in control: *he* has terminated the work and its hero. This is another kind of power from that of magical dominion, a power that depends on the resources of art, realized in alliance with the "patient judgements" in an audience. It has not been a drumhead trial and execution, moreover, based on arbitrary, public-safety law. Though the final Chorus pulls back, in relief, to such a position, we have seen in detail, notably in the final soliloquy, how the fate of the hero is integral with his motive. In *Tamburlaine,* it was the hero who said "I thus conceiving and subduing both. . . . Shall give the world to note for all my birth, / That Vertue solely is the sum of glorie." Fundamental artistic limitations resulted from the identification of Marlowe with his protagonist in that play. But now, at the end of *Doctor Faustus,* Marlowe has earned an identity apart from his hero's—he is the author. He has done so by at once conceiving and subduing the protagonist.

The analogy between tragedy and a scapegoat ritual is very clear here: Faustus the hero has carried off into death the evil of the motive he embodied, freeing from its sin, for the moment, the author-executioner and the participating audience. The crop of stories which grew up about one devil too many, a real one, among the actors shows how popular tendencies to project evil in demons were put to work (and controlled, so far as "patient judgements" were concerned) by Marlowe. Popular experience of public executions provided, as Mr. John Holloway has recently pointed out (and Wyndham Lewis before him),[19] another paradigm for tragedy. We can add that, in Marlowe's case at least, some of the taboo quality which tends to stick to an executioner attached to the tragedian, a sense of his contamination by the sin of the victim. He proudly claims, in classical terms, the prerogative of the author who terminates the work, has done with it. But in his own life what was working in the work caught up with him by the summons to appear before the Privy Council, and the subsequent death at Deptford— whether it was a consequence of his own tendency to give way to "sudden cruelty," or a successfully camouflaged murder to get rid of a scandalous client of Thomas Walsingham. Art, even such austere art as *Doctor Faustus,* did not save the man in the author. But the author did save, within the limits of art, and with art's permanence, much that was in the man, to become part of the evolving culture in which his own place was so precarious.

[19] *The Story of the Night* (London: 1961); *The Lion and the Fox* (London: 1927).

See *Doctor Faustus* bibliography (below, pp. 127–129) and other studies in Marlowe bibliography (below, p. 170).

MARLOWE'S *DOCTOR FAUSTUS* *

Wilbur Sanders

It must be a fairly common experience to come away from a performance (or a reading) of *Doctor Faustus* with very mixed feelings. The scene of Faustus' death is sufficient to convince us that, in Marlowe, we are dealing with a mind of some distinction; but like so many of the play's high points, the soliloquy is followed by a scene of baffling banality, if not naivety:

> Oh, help us, heaven! see, here are Faustus' limbs,
> All torn asunder by the hand of death.

> > (Revels Plays edn., xx, 6–7)

The descent from authentic imaginative vision to the perfunctory and the commonplace can occur within the space of a line. The justly famous definition of hell ("Hell hath no limits, nor is circumscrib'd...") is immediately succeeded by

> And, to be short, when all the world dissolves
> And every creature shall be purify'd,
> All places shall be hell that is not heaven.

> > (v, 122 ff.)

Although this expands discursively the vision of a hell co-extensive with the consciousness of the damned, the poetic flame has died to an ember— "to be short" is the key to the tone: Marlowe's fitful muse has deserted him again. The same contradiction runs throughout the play, the most obvious and frequently deplored sign of it being the comparative barrenness of the comic scenes (probably written in collaboration with others) that occupy the central section.

Then there are those subtle felicities which are no sooner perceived than you start wondering whether they are not perhaps accidental; there is that curious loose-jointed fragmentariness of Marlowe's writing—a quality consistent with the assumption that the verse was assembled piece by piece from a stock-pile of previously written lines and paragraphs;

* Adapted by the author from his "Marlowe's *Doctor Faustus*," *Melbourne Critical Review*, No. 7, 1964, pp. 78–91 and his *The Dramatist and the Received Idea: Studies in the Plays of Marlowe and Shakespeare,* Cambridge: Cambridge University Press, 1968, pp. 237–242. Reprinted by permission of the author and Cambridge University Press.

112

and there are all the minor inconsistencies of a work insufficiently digested, ideas which have not undergone that inner chemistry of creation which could assimilate them to one complex imaginative organism, but which survive on the surface of the work as excrescences belonging to one historical epoch, not to all time. As I shall try to show, the unity of *Doctor Faustus* is, in many respects, something that we have to create for ourselves, answering questions that were for Marlowe insoluble, pursuing implications further than he was able or prepared to pursue them, making choices between incompatibles that appear side by side in the play as we have it. All of which makes it extremely difficult to find a *point d'appui* from which to tackle the play.

After such a comprehensive vote of no-confidence in an author, it may seem odd to undertake an investigation at all; but what is good in *Faustus* is good in such a uniquely interesting way, that none of these obvious deficiencies has been sufficient to keep the play off our stages or our bookshelves. We continue to be fascinated, though we are at the same time dissatisfied.

The diabolism in which the play deals is, I believe, one of Marlowe's unsolved problems. When he undertook to dramatize that handbook of demonological conservatism, the *English Faust Book,* Marlowe was immediately committed to accepting as a premiss something which was in process of becoming an anachronism—the phenomenon of witchcraft itself (for, though this is not the place to demonstrate it, there was in sixteenth-century England a strong, sceptical, anti-witchmongery party). The complications arising from this commitment were likely to prove troublesome in a play which, on one level at least, concerned itself with the "unsatiable speculation" of a newly emancipated humanism. Yet Marlowe's introduction of devils who are medieval in temper is, I am sure, deliberate—just as the revival of the earlier psychomachia form (the "battle for a soul" of which *Everyman* is the best-known example) is deliberate. Marlowe is studying the collision between the old wisdom of sin, grace and redemption, and the new wisdom of humanist perfectibility; and the archaic flavour of both fable and treatment is a way of giving body to the historical dimension of his theme. It is in order to preserve the integrity of the older view, too, that he refuses to rationalize witchcraft as "natural magic," the exploitation of the occult but natural virtues of things with the assistance of good spirits—though he could have found good precedents for seeing it in this light. But it is axiomatic in the play that witchcraft is damnable: Faustus' incantation includes the direct invocation of Lucifer and a deliberate blasphemy against the Trinity (iii, 16–20).

Nevertheless, in accepting the older diabolism, with its strong sense of the objectivity of the demonic world and its fairly literal view of the methods by which a man could become entangled with that world, Marlowe involved himself in a contradiction which runs deep into the play. For he also has a strong predisposition to see the matter of diabolic liaison in a markedly metaphorical light. Faustus' incantation, Mephostophilis declares, was the cause of his appearance, yet only *per accidens*.

> For when we hear one rack the name of God,
> Abjure the Scriptures and his saviour Christ,
> We fly, in hope to get his glorious soul.

(iii, 49–51)

In place of Faustus' philosophy of manipulation ("Did not my conjuring speeches raise thee? Speak."), rises the vision of a separate and autonomous order of spiritual forces which respond to human action according to laws of their own nature and with which Faustus has unwittingly become embroiled. This more complex relationship between tempter and tempted opens ironic vistas which lie beyond the compass of a mechanical view of the incantation as effective cause. By hinting that Mephostophilis is a metaphysical resultant of events in Faustus' consciousness, the sense of evil that the fiend represents is given increased depth and power. Yet the disturbing thing is that these lines are spoken by an actor who, only a few minutes before, has appeared in all the trappings of the old ranter who used so amiably to distribute fireworks, advice and cracked pates among his auditors in the old days. Furthermore, he's attended by a troop of slapstick clowns of the same kidney and is provided not only with the traditional hell-mouth, but with a specially constructed dragon as well (iii, 21).

The contradiction is woven into the entire dramatic fabric. In part it results from the resurgence of an older, but still powerful, dramatic tradition which, by rendering the demons so irrevocably "other," prevents Marlowe from doing justice to their subjective dimension. But I think it is also a heroic attempt to wed the imaginative efficiency of the old to the psychological profundity of the new. In the case of the demons, we usually get no more than an oscillation, or two alternative accounts of the one event. Thus, the perilous capacity of a man for being his own tempter, so clearly enacted in the first scene, is reduced near the end of the play to a simple matter of demonic violation:

> 'Twas I that, when thou wert i' the way to heaven,
> Damm'd up thy passage; when thou took'st the book
> To view the scriptures, then I turn'd the leaves
> And led thine eye.

(xix, 93–6)

Or Mephostophilis, requested to describe hell, gives first of all the traditional, localized underworld—

> Within the bowels of these elements,
> Where we are tortur'd and remain for ever,

(v, 120–1)

but then replaces it with the uncircumscribed state of mental torment to which I have already referred (v, 122–7). The juxtaposition may perhaps be made workable by treating Mephostophilis' first answer as an attempt to fob Faustus off with the "scholarism" he already knows. But the "vast perpetual torture-house" image persists throughout the play, and is physically "discovered" in the penultimate scene:

> There are the furies, tossing damned souls
> On burning forks; their bodies boil in lead:
> There are live quarters broiling on the coals,
> That ne'er can die...

(xix, 118–21)

I suppose there is a sense in which these lines reflect Faustus' bondage to the medieval horrors of his own consciousness. But the bondage is also Marlowe's, as is the hint of schoolboy sadism in the facilities of the rhythm. In any case, this gross physical hell combines with the "Shagge-hayr'd Deuills" and the dismembered corpse of the last scene to super-impose a relatively superficial image of hell upon a dramatic metaphor of great force and range. Hell can never be an anachronism as long as it is used to give shape to the forces which are felt to be ultimately destructive of human significance; but a hell which destroys a man by tearing him limb from limb is an anachronism in the world of *Doctor Faustus*. Its relative superficiality is reflected in the verse which presents it, relying as it does so heavily on the external and the sensational.

Marlowe is, however, more successful in moulding the Angels he inherited from the older drama, into a new artistic instrument. It is true they are abstractions, belonging to no specific time and place, speaking an unmoved, formalized verse from some point clearly outside the area where the play's decisions are taken. Yet the very abstraction keeps them sufficiently un-individualized to be functions of Faustus' conscience, and sufficiently removed from the sphere of dramatic action to symbolize an order outside it.

> Bad Angel: Go forward, Faustus, in that famous art.
> Good Angel: Sweet Faustus, leave that execrable art.
> Faustus: Contrition, prayer, repentance, what of these?
> Good Angel: O, they are means to bring thee unto heaven.
> Bad Angel: Rather illusions, fruits of lunacy,
> That make men foolish that do use them most.
> Good Angel: Sweet Faustus, think of heaven and heavenly things.
> Bad Angel: No, Faustus, think of honour and of wealth.
> [*Exeunt* Angels]
> Faustus: Wealth!

(v, 15–23)

Far from being clumsily primitive, this is an immensely dramatic procedure. The first effect of the interruption is to arrest all action on stage, and to focus attention on the protagonist suspended in the act of choice. Not until he speaks do we know to which voice he has been attending. It's the act of choice in slow motion, a dramatization of his strained attention to the faint voices of unconscious judgment. At the same time, his unawareness of their presence has the effect of revealing his blindness to the real issues at stake: what he takes to be a decision between contrition and wealth is really a primal decision between good and evil. And his unconscious echoing of their words is a parable of his inability to evade moral categories. The course of self-gratification on which he's embarked is no more his own than are the angels; yet it is, by the same token, as much his own as they are. He is an involuntary participant in the moral order, yet he shapes that order by his action.

By the device of the Angels, Marlowe breaks down the subjective-objective dualism which dogs other parts of the play, and appeals beyond it to a psychological realism rooted in the individual consciousness of Faustus himself. His dramatic point is not that evil is only the basin-eyed monster of legend and good the angelic visitant—i.e. merely objective; nor that they are only manifestations of states of consciousness—i.e. merely subjective; but rather that they have the kind of reality which is appropriately represented by an actor in a play. They are real enough to have voices of their own. It is as if the play moved on a plane at right-angles to the one whose axes are "subjective" and "objective"; its co-ordinates are heaven and hell considered as primal symbols, and ranging in their suggested provenance from the purely subjective hallucination to the stonily objective fact.

At times the same break-through is achieved with the demonic order. In Scene iii, Faustus' conjuring is presided over by "Lucifer and four devils above," again embodying the radical moral polarization implicit in all human activity. But, nevertheless, his incantations do have a specific result: Mephostophilis does appear, less "pliant" than Faustus imagines, but a palpable change in the moral landscape which must in some measure be attributed to Faustus' activity. The evil he invokes is both his own and not his own.

The insight shown at times in the handling of the supernatural, yet the disturbing dissonance between metaphorical and literal views, suggest a Marlowe dangerously entangled with the material of his art, still wrestling with unresolved paradoxes which frustrate his grand aim of harmonizing the old and the new wisdoms.

There are similar divided aims in the characterization of the sin for which Faustus is ultimately damned. Several critics (notably Una Ellis-Fermor, *Christopher Marlowe,* 1927, pp. 62–3) have tried to prove that it is the sin of humanist aspiration and that, consequently, Marlowe the humanist is obliged to condemn it only because he has been guilty of "intellectual apostasy" in the face of a menacing orthodoxy. It's true that many of Faustus' power fantasies in the early scenes are connected with the expanding world of the Renaissance in the sixteenth century. It's true that he proposes to "search all corners of the new-found world," but for what? "For pleasant fruits and princely delicates" (i, 83–4). Helen may be the paradigm of classical beauty, the resuscitated body of antique learning, but she is raised in order to become Faustus' paramour, and to "extinguish clear / Those thoughts that do dissuade me from my vow" (xviii, 94–5). Indeed, most of Faustus' "humanist" impulses closely scrutinized resolve themselves into a familiar form of hedonism and epicurean self-indulgence. There is no doubt that Marlowe sets out to place very firmly the damnable nature of Faustus' ambition; and if we are to allow any force at all to Ellis-Fermor's mitigating contentions, we must do so by positing a Marlowe divided against himself, here as elsewhere. In fact, I believe, he was. But it is necessary, first of all, to see how hard he worked to show us the dangers of the Faustian path.

When one considers Faustus' motives for taking up the magical arts, it becomes clear that Marlowe wants us to detect a serious moral weakness at the root of the decision. There is, for instance, his contempt for the laborious particularity of the academic disciplines—"too servile and illiberal for me": the revealing stress on the personal pronoun ("Thou art too ugly to attend on *me*") is the dramatic embodiment of the psychological state which Marlowe sees to be attendant on such an intellectual attitude. Faustus prefers the grandiose cult of universals: he will "level at the end of every art." But there must be no hard work: the servile drudgery is to be deputed to his "servile spirits" (i, 96). The irksome burden of unanswered questions can be shrugged off, for the spirits will "Resolve me of all ambiguities" (i, 79); and it's a desire for the fruits of knowledge without its pains which makes him long to "see hell and return again safe" (vi, 172). He shares that perennial human conviction that there's a short cut to knowledge, some formula that makes it unnecessary to go about and about the hill of Truth—a conviction that is aptly symbolized in the delusions of magic. The art into which the two infamous magicians initiate him is one of those reassuring skills which demand exactly the knowledge one possesses—astrology, "tongues," mineralogy (i, 137–9)—yet promises immediate and infallible results. Cornelius and Valdes are the direct ancestors of our Pelmanists and Scientologists, and Faustus has plainly been reading their illustrated brochure when he remarks

> Their conference will be a greater help to me
> Than all my labours, plod I ne'er so fast.

> (i, 67–8)

There is, besides, a certain passion for ostentation which tempts him to aspire to the status of an Agrippa "whose shadows made all Europe honour him" (i, 116–7). "Be a physician, Faustus", he advises himself, "and be eterniz'd for some wondrous cure" (i, 14–5). (The vaguely indefinite "some" is an index of the extent to which aspiration is divorced from reality, while "eterniz'd" reminds us how constantly Faustus makes his felicity reside in the mouths of men.) For such an academic mega-lomaniac, the triumphant university disputation is the most delectable of memories:

> I...have with concise syllogisms
> Gravell'd the pastors of the German church,
> And made the flowering pride of Wittenberg
> Swarm to my problems as the infernal spirits
> On sweet Musaeus when he came to hell. . . .

> (i, 111–15)

If there is one key motif to the scenes before the signing of the pact, it is the "humour of monarchising," an obsessive pre-occupation with power. Power over the grand forces of nature, winds, storms (i, 58), the Rhine (i, 88), the ocean (iii, 41), the air (iii, 107); power over national and international destinies (i, 86, 91–5; iii, 111–3); power over the storehouses of nature (i, 74, 81–4, 143–6) and the plate fleets of Spain (i, 130); even the disposition of the continental land masses (iii, 109–10) and the movements of celestial bodies (iii, 40) are to be at his command. They are all variations on one theme—"I'll be great emperor of the world" (iii, 106)—and his mind, like Epicure Mammon's, thrown into near delirium at this prospect, casts up this strange farrago of preposterous fantasies in the future tense ("I'll...I'll...I'll...").

In terms of the chosen peripetia this is clearly to be regarded as arrant folly and presumption. But Marlowe, we recall, is the author of *Tamburlaine* (*Tamburlaine* the indulgence *ad absurdum* of the "humour of monarchising," not the moral fable critics have made out of it). And the more I look at the verse in which Faustus' grandiose visions are expounded the less certain I am that Marlowe has wholly dissociated himself from his hero—any more than the anonymous author of the *Faust Book* had done. In both the play and its source book, there are long stretches where a naive wonder at the subtleties of the witch completely submerges the moral condemnation of witchcraft—an ambiguity which results from the shallowness of the initial condemnation. At such points in the play (and I would include nearly all the central section, Scenes viii-xvii, under this heading) the verse is strangely neutral morally— Mammon's foamings at the mouth provide an instructive contrast—has no clearly placed tone, only a shallow fluency and prolixity that suggest it came a trifle too easily to its author. It is neither the clear moral evaluation of a diseased mind, nor the enactment of a kindling imagination, but the indulgence of an abiding mood or mode in Marlowe's rhetorical poetic. This becomes clear if we consider one passage where we do get a genuine enactment of the quickened pulse and soaring imagination of a man awestruck before a new universe of meaning and potentiality:

> O, what a world of profit and delight
> Of power, of honour, of omnipotence,
> Is promis'd to the studious artisan!
> All things that move between the quiet poles
> Shall be at my command: emperors and kings
> Are but obey'd in their several provinces,
> Nor can they raise the wind or rend the clouds;
> But his dominion that exceeds in this
> Stretcheth as far as doth the mind of man.

(i, 52–60)

By charting so subtly the accumulating emotion behind the words, this masterfully articulated crescendo gives to the word "dominion" a richer and more human meaning than it has elsewhere. If this vein had been more diligently uncovered in the rest of the play, we might have had a tragedy. But even this fine passage is immediately followed by a piece of rant in the Tamburlaine vein, which tips the delicate balance between an imaginative sympathy which is itself a judgment, and a top-heavy moral censure:

> A sound magician is a demi-god;
> Here tire, my brains, to get a deity!

(i, 61–2)

The overstrain in the verse is that of homiletic demonstration.

This element of demonstration is strong in *Faustus*, especially in the rejection of learning which opens the play. Faustus here indulges in a traditional mode, the "Dispraise of Learning"; but far from indicating, in the traditional manner, the shortcomings of human wit, by showing how far each "science" falls short of its own avowed aims and of divine omniscience, Faustus refers all learning to his private satisfaction. He will read no further in the Logic whose aim is "to dispute well," because he has already "attain'd that end" (i, 8–10). Physic, which merely achieves "our body's health," holds no attraction because that end, too, he has attained, with all its concomitant glories (i, 17–23). Nor will he be a "mercenary drudge" to sweat over "a petty case of paltry legacies" as a lawyer (i, 30–6). Now it may be that we have here Faustus' mental history in a conventionalized form, but it's the mental history of a shallow mind— a sophist's mind: and the telescoping of time (if that is what it is) has the dramatic effect of heightening the sense of shallowness. It's of the utmost importance to realise that the investigation is no more than a facade (note the glib transitions, as if the books were all ready with markers at the relevant pages) and that the real decision has been taken in the first four lines, where Faustus exhorts himself to "be a divine in show / Yet level at the end of every art." Divinity, of course, was the science which claimed to do just this, and Faustus has already made "the end of every art" antithetical to the study of God. There is consequently a peremptory wilfulness in the formal dismissal of divinity (i, 39–47) — a piece of logical sleight of hand accomplished by a violent wresting of context which any member of Marlowe's audience must have spotted (*vide* Romans vi, 23 and 1 John i, 8–9). The seriousness of Faustus' commitment to a thorough-going rationalism is subsequently indicated by the interesting, though not surprising fact that he does not apply the same syllogistic canons to the "arte magick": it is enough that "these are those that Faustus most desires" (i, 51). Faustus' condemnation is thus writ large (too large, as I see it) in the opening scene. In order to regard him as a premature promethean hero of the Enlightenment, one must either regard all enlightened Prometheans as damnable, or admit that, judged by enlightened criteria, he is a decidedly damp squib. In anybody's book the attitudes he adopts are unworthy.

And yet there is this same absence of moral orientation of the *energies* of the verse, however loudly the attitudes expressed may call out for censure. As with the presentation of Faustus' power fantasies, there is an emotional indirection making it almost impossible to be sure that Marlowe has not gone a-whoring after the strange gods that he appears to abominate. To a dangerous degree Faustus *is* Marlowe, and the play is a vehement attempt to impose order on a realm of consciousness which is still in insurrection.

Perhaps this is why Marlowe overdoes the condemnation. This frivolous academic opportunist, who has clearly learned very little from his encyclopaedic education, cannot engage our sympathies very deeply. The narrow moral categories of the Prologue seem entirely adequate to encompass the significance of such a presumptuous Icarus:

> ...swollen with cunning of a self-conceit,
> His waxen wings did mount above his reach,
> And melting heavens conspir'd his overthrow.

> (Prologue, 20–2)

This is the tone and manner of homiletic demonstration, not of tragic paradox, and it is in harmony with the Faustus of the early scenes.

Yet although Faustus' initial rejection of divinity displays only his frivolity, the subsequent developments which his unbelief undergoes show Marlowe pressing nearer to the heart of things. Faustus' debates with Mephostophilis, for instance, have a persistent and revealing tendency to circle round pressing personal questions. In Scene vi, by a series of astronomical queries, he stalks nearer his quarry, hoping to find some crack that the diabolic intelligence alone can locate in the providentially-ordered universe. But Mephostophilis is stonily orthodox—indeed reactionary—in his answers. So that Faustus is obliged to come into the open: "Now tell me who made the world." Mephostophilis' menacing anger and abrupt departure, and his subsequent return with Lucifer and Beelzebub at precisely the moment when Faustus calls upon Christ, is an apt representation of the emotional upheaval which the very asking of the question provokes in Faustus' consciousness. For his particular form of scepticism is accompanied by, perhaps derived from, a profound emotional involvement with the ideas he rejects, and if his atheism is superficial, it is superficial because his theism is ineradicable. This tension between attraction and repulsion is discernible in the exaggerated gestures with which he dismisses the "vain trifles of men's souls" (iii, 64), and the "old wives' tales" of an after-life (v, 136), but especially in the ambiguous attitudes that he adopts towards hell itself. At times, hell is only a "fable" (v, 128); but if it is "sleeping, eating, walking and disputing", as Mephostophilis suggests, then he'll "willingly be damn'd" (v, 139–40). On the one hand he "confounds hell in Elysium"—meaning, I take it, that the two are a single state, the classical Hades where his ghost will be "with the old philosophers" (iii, 62–3); on the other hand, Mephostophilis is exhorted to "scorn those *joys* thou never shalt possess" (iii, 88) and Faustus acknowledges that he has "incurr'd eternal death" (iii, 90). It is only after he has asked for and received a description of hell from a being to whom he is talking only because he believes him to have come from hell, that Faustus declares hell to be a fable. Yet, a few scenes later, Lucifer's genial assurance that "in hell is all manner of delight" (vi, 171) sends him grovelling for a sight of the fabulous place.

But there's a deep consistency here. Hell is a fable only as long at it's a place "where we are tortur'd and remain forever." If it affords "all manner of delight," he believes in it. He'll scorn the joys he'll never possess only because he does not believe them to be joys. He'll willingly be damned provided he can have damnation on his own terms—"sleeping, eating, walking and disputing." The consistency resides in his determination to submit all moral categories to his personal convenience; and the ultimate failure of such an enterprise is figured in the continual presence of the melancholy fiend who knows better than to attempt it. On Mephostophilis' terms—being in hell and knowing it—one can be damned and preserve one's dignity; on Faustus'—being in hell and pretending it's heaven—one can only prevaricate and rationalize, writhing on the pin which holds one fast to an inexorably moral universe.

It's when this monumental wishful thinking collides with the demands of a nature still fundamentally religious, that the play again moves into a region of tragic potential.

> GOOD ANGEL: Faustus, repent; yet God will pity thee.
> BAD ANGEL: Thou art a spirit; God cannot pity thee.
> FAUSTUS: Who buzzeth in mine ears I am a spirit?

> Be I a devil, yet God may pity me;
> Yea, God will pity me if I repent.
> BAD ANGEL: Ay, but Faustus never shall repent.
> FAUSTUS: My heart is harden'd, I cannot repent.

(vi, 12–18)

Beneath the patterned simplicity of this—"repent," "pity," "pity," "will," "cannot," "may," "never shall"—lies the tragic paradox of a consciousness ruinously divided against itself—a consciousness powerfully drawn by "salvation, faith and heaven," yet deafened by the "fearful echoes" that thunder in Faustus' ears when he names them, by those magnified reverberations of his own despairing self-knowledge. If one had to select a single scene as the imaginative heart of the action, it might well be this one (Scene vi) with its appalling and giddy oscillation between the profundities of despair and the escapist frivolities of the Pageant of the Sins. If Faustus is torn more violently than this by his divided nature, he cannot survive.

But increasingly from this point onwards, the hardness of heart, and the corresponding stiffness of mind, provide him with an assured resting place—"Now, Faustus, must / Thou needs be damn'd...Despair in God, and trust in Beelzebub" (v, 1–5). He resolves the agonies of choice by falling back on an assumed external fate; and though he wavers and has to exhort himself to "be resolute," his resolution never comes into any fruitful contact with his repentance. He seems to prefer damnation; for, as a reprobate, he is in a position to exercise that limited variety of "manly fortitude" which consists in scorning the joys he never shall possess. His is the kind of mind which prefers consistency to integrity. He is stiff to maintain any purpose. And in that stiffness he goes to hell.

I have called this movement in the play (the movement concerned with Faustus' desperate attempt to defy a reality of his own nature) tragic, because it leads us beyond the homiletic framework of the opening scenes, and asks us to conceive of a conflict between immovable conviction and irresistible doubt on the battleground of the individual consciousness. At such moments, the evaluation of Faustus' moral condition is no longer possible in terms like the Chorus's "swollen with cunning of a self-conceit." Marlowe's attempt to impose order on his rebellion moves out of the sphere of moralistic abstraction into a world where the felt reality of the heavenly values constitutes their sole claim to serious attention. Yet it is a basic element in Faustus' damnation that salvation and the means to it should never seem more than "illusions, fruits of lunacy." Although that salvation is a continual possibility, there's a blockage in Faustus' consciousness which makes "contrition, prayer, repentance" appear always to be unreal alternatives. And it emerges that the blockage is Marlowe's too. Why else can it be that the heavenly can only be represented in the faint efflorescence of the Good Angel's utterances, or in the Old Man's appeal to a "faith" which he claims will triumph over "vile hell," but which is in fact imprisoned within its own theological concepts (Scene xviii)? The final declaration of Marlowe's failure to give body to the heavenly order is the creaking machinery of the descending "throne" in Scene xix. The only face of God that we see is one from which Faustus recoils in horror:

> Mountains and hills, come, come, and fall on me,
> And hide me from the heavy wrath of God;
>
> (xix, 152–3)

and the conception of divine justice which prevails is the Luciferian— "Christ cannot save thy soul, for he is just" (vi, 87).

It is in the sense that the world of the play is hostile to the only values that can redeem it that Faustus' damnation may be said to be imposed from above. Yet there is an urgency and a personal heat behind this terrible paradox which, though it defeats the synthesizing activity of Marlowe's art, commands attention and, indeed, a regretful respect. Though the play's grasp of reality is sporadic, its reach is tremendous. It is Marlowe, I suspect, locked in a death-embrace with the agonizing God he can neither reject nor love.

Yet, though this may be the tragedy of Christopher Marlowe, it isn't *The Tragicall History of Doctor Faustus.* Marlowe comes within hailing distance of that internalization of moral sanctions by which drama can *lead* into wisdom instead of *pointing* at it, only to abandon it in the Epilogue:

> Faustus is gone: regard his hellish fall,
> Whose fiendful fortune may exhort the wise
> Only to wonder at unlawful things,
> Whose deepness doth entice such forward wits
> To practise more than heavenly power permits.
>
> (Epilogue, 4–8)

This, cheek by jowl with the final soliloquy, is the critical paradox of *Faustus* at its most acute. It might be argued that the Epilogue merely condenses into conventional and manageable form a dramatic experience too vast and chaotic to be left unformulated. But the longer I ponder the scene of Faustus' diabolic apotheosis the less satisfied I am with the formulation—In what sense are these things "unlawful"? Whose word do we have for what heavenly power does or doesn't permit? If this is damnation, why is it so much more real than anything else in the play?

Something has happened to the Faustus of these last scenes—or perhaps it would be more accurate to say that something has happened to the way in which Marlowe imagines him; because it isn't a "character development." It is too sudden, too unmodulated, and goes with a new poetic conviction which has been totally lacking since Faustus boarded his dragon for Rome. There is an entirely new maturity of tone, appropriate perhaps to an Oedipus manfully enduring the torments of the just gods, but hardly to the vain and frivolous academic adventurer who rejects all human learning, dreams of universal empery and beats friars about the head with their beads. After the inept flounderings of the central section, something has again gripped Marlowe's imagination. It is not the possibility of repentance, for the moments where Faustus toys with this idea are the flattest and feeblest in the final section. It is the possibility of irretrievable catastrophe, damnation deserved and beyond appeal. Given that possibility, Faustus can recover his dignity, and Marlowe his seriousness—which happens most impressively in the prose scene with the Scholars.

This is a piece of chamber music finer, I think, than the symphonic grandeurs of the subsequent soliloquy—finer, because more assured, more poised, and less frenetic. The cheerful, well-meaning superficiality of the "sweet chamber-fellows" ("'Tis but a surfeit, sir; fear nothing") is a foil for Faustus' unflinching contemplation of his own state ("A surfeit of deadly sin..."). He is gentle, but inexorable:

> Ay, pray for me, pray for me; and, what noise soever ye hear, come not unto me, for nothing can rescue me.
>
> (xix, 80)

There is a human warmth, there's humility, and there is a new maturity in this Faustus. He has passed beyond egotism, yet not far beyond, for there is a momentary resurgence of the old braggart self, which has to be soberly checked. Above all, the prose charts meticulously the ebb and flow, the very pulse beat of consciousness as Faustus works his way painfully to the enormously difficult confession—"Ah, gentlemen, I gave them my soul for my cunning." Note how skilfully the improvisatory syntax is used to render Faustus' faltering progress:

> Ah, gentlemen, hear me with patience, and tremble not at my speeches. Though my heart pants and quivers to remember that I have been a student here these thirty years, O, would I had never seen Wittenberg, never read book! and what wonders I have done all Germany can witness, yea, all the world, for which Faustus hath lost both Germany and the world, yea, heaven itself—heaven, the seat of God, the throne of the blessed, the kingdom of joy—and must remain in hell for ever. Hell, ah, hell for ever! Sweet friends, what shall become of Faustus, being in hell for ever?
>
> (xix, 42)

There is nothing histrionic about this utterance: it is not "O, I'll leap up to my God! Who pulls me down?" which implies some unseemly stage acrobatics, but "I would lift up my hands, but see, they hold them, they hold them"—the perfect verbal enactment of Faustus' nightmare impotence.

The discomforted Scholars depart in awkward haste. Mephostophilis and the Angels make their last appearance, and the total destitution and isolation of the damned soul, towards which the play has been moving, is complete. Faustus faces his destiny. It is clearly the culmination of all that has gone before. In order to deal with it, Marlowe invents—and I think the word is justified—a new kind of blank verse and a mode of utterance which has excited admiration now for four centuries. It is not by way of belittling that achievement that I want to suggest the soliloquy has some flaws. It is simply that the same mingled yarn of profoundly imaginative insight and crude artistic opportunism is discernible here as elsewhere.

In a damaging sense, the speech is "an actor's vehicle"—which is to say, it looks like a fine thumping drama, but tends to turn embarrassingly stagey in the speaking lines—

> Earth gape! O, no, it will not harbour me.
>
> Yet will I call on him. O, spare me, Lucifer!—
> Where is it now? 'This gone: and see...
>
> No, no.
>
> (xix, 149–56)

—all of them, with incipiently comic gestural implications, and dependent for their functioning upon an actor who can emotionally intimidate an audience.

This implied mode of delivery goes with a very heavy reliance on the vocative case and the imperative mood—something to which English style is never very friendly—on apostrophe and on rhetorical question (in sixty-two lines Faustus apostrophises twenty times). The result, to my ears, is an oratorical overloading and a hectoring note, as Marlowe falls back on that rhetorical afflatus, that impetuous, swelling force of unharnessed energy which is so characteristic of him:

> You stars that reign'd at my nativity,
> Whose influence hath allotted death and hell,
> Now draw up Faustus like a foggy mist...
>
> (xix, 157–9)

These objections are not "technical" but human: for all the elements of self-consciousness and artificiality tend to dissolve Faustus as the focus of human awareness that he has very nearly become. And what we get is not the flow, the stream of thought, but a series of rapid oscillations. The speech jumps from one mental position to the next; with an irrelevant kind of agility:

> Curs'd be the parents that engender'd me!
> No, Faustus, curse thyself, curse Lucifer.   (xix, 180–1)
>
> Let Faustus live in hell a thousand years,
> A hundred thousand, and at last be sav'd.
> O, no end is limited to damn'd souls.   (xix, 169–71)

It's possible, I suppose, to regard these rather obvious *volte-faces* as a triumphant presentation of a personality in torment and panic disorder, rebounding from one red-hot surface to the next. But one has only to think of Leontes' comparable torment and near-delirium—so deeply and *involuntarily* frightening—to realize that, whether as actors or readers, we are here being invited to simulate emotion by means of the will.

The oscillation between extremes—faith and despair, heaven and hell, God and Lucifer ("Yet will I call on him. O, spare me, Lucifer!")— reveals itself finally as part of the homiletic simplification that so sadly dogs the play, sign of a sensibility too geometrical, too prone to simple oppositions, operating at one remove from the complex flux of sensation and thought.

Yet there remain unmistakable signs of that imaginative grip and utter seriousness for which one returns to *Faustus*: things like the halluci-nated vision of a firmament streaming with blood, as the very medium of Faustus' redemption turns to a nightmare of horror and retribution; or the potent imaging of that wrathful deity under whose looming tyranny the individual stands dwarfed and obliterated; or Faustus' agony of prayer with its abject and poignant *non sequitur* ("O God, / If thou wilt not have mercy on my soul,...Let Faustus...at last be sav'd"). These moments are the more impressive in that they show Marlowe establishing imaginative control over his most appalling fear—the fear of final destitution and rejection.

And at the end he rises superbly to the occasion with an electrically vital rendering of the very moment of dissolution:

> O, it strikes, it strikes! Now, body, turn to air,
> Or Lucifer will bear thee quick to hell!
> O soul, be chang'd into little water drops,
> And fall into the ocean, ne'er be found.   (*Enter* Devils)
> My God, my God! Look not so fierce on me!
> Adders and serpents, let me breathe awhile!
> Ugly hell, gape not! Come not, Lucifer;
> I'll burn my books!—Ah, Mephostophilis!
>
>   (xix, 183–90)

Here there's a physical particularity, an astonishing evocation of sensa-tion (the body turning to air and water, magically weightless and fluid, yet stung into frenzy by adders and serpents of physical agony that will not let it breathe), and a strange compound of terror at, and longing for, extinction. The flat either / or of heaven and hell becomes a fusion in which "My God" may be addressed either to the Deity or to the Devils. That irreducible love-hate that Faustus bears towards both God and Lucifer becomes a cry of erotic self-surrender *and* horrified revulsion as he yields to the embrace of his demon lover—"Ah, Mephostophilis!" Marlowe here masters the central paradox of his theism and makes of it a unique dramatic reality which is genuinely tragic.

There it would be pleasant to leave the final emphasis—if Marlowe would let us. But he adds the Epilogue. And the stringency and shallowness of the "morality" deployed there goes a long way towards explaining the final incoherence of *Doctor Faustus*: any extensive humanization, any development in depth will escape the coarse meshes of this net and assume equivocal control of the play's imaginative energies. Yet Marlowe, by scoring his final bars for such a consort of archaic viols, shows himself sublimely unaware of how revolutionary the drama is that he has just written.

DOCTOR FAUSTUS

Bradbrook, Muriel C. "Marlowe's *Doctor Faustus* and the Eldritch Tradition," in *Essays on Shakespeare and the Elizabethan Drama in Honor of Hardin Craig*, ed. Richard Hosley. Columbia, Missouri, 1962, pp. 55–68.

Brockbank, J. P. *Marlowe: Dr. Faustus*. Studies in English Literature No. 6, London, 1962.

Brooke, Nicholas. "The Moral Tragedy of Doctor Faustus," *Cambridge Journal,* V (1952), 662–687.

Campbell, Lily B. "*Doctor Faustus:* A Case of Conscience," *PMLA,* LXVII (1952), 219–239.

Crabtree, John H., Jr. "The Comedy in Marlowe's *Dr. Faustus,*" *FurmS,* IX, No. 1 (1961), 1–9.

Davidson, Clifford. "Doctor Faustus of Wittenberg," *SP,* LIX (1962), 514–523.

Duthie, G. I. "Some Observations on Marlowe's *Doctor Faustus,*" *Archiv,* CCIII (1966), 81–96.

Frey, Leonard H. "Antithetical Balance in the Opening and Close of *Doctor Faustus,*" *MLQ,* XXIV (1963), 350–353.

Frye, Roland M. "Marlowe's *Doctor Faustus:* The Repudiation of Humanity," *South Atlantic Quarterly,* LV (1956), 322–328.

Gardner, Helen. "Milton's Satan and the Theme of Damnation in Elizabethan Tragedy," *E & S,* N.S., I (1948), 48–53.

Gill, Roma, ed. *Doctor Faustus.* The New Mermaids, London, 1965, pp. xix–xxvii.

Green, Clarence. "*Doctor Faustus:* Tragedy of Individualism," *Science & Society,* X (1946), 275–283.

Greg, W. W. "The Damnation of Faustus," *MLR,* XLI (1946), 97–107.

Hawkins, Sherman. "The Education of Faustus," *SEL,* VI (1966), 193–209.

Heilman, Robert B. "The Tragedy of Knowledge: Marlowe's Treatment of Faustus," *QRL,* II (1945–1946), 316–332.

Homan, Sidney R., Jr. *"Doctor Faustus,* Dekker's *Old Fortunatus,* and the Morality Plays," *Modern Language Quarterly,* XXVI (1965), 497–505.

Hunter, G. K. "Five-Act Structure in *Doctor Faustus,*" *TDR,* VIII, No. 4 (1964), 77–91.

Jump, John D., ed. *Doctor Faustus.* The Revels Plays. London, 1962, pp. xlvii–lx.

Kaula, David, "Time and the Timeless in *Everyman* and *Dr. Faustus,*" *CE,* XXII (1960), 9–14.

Kirschbaum, Leo. "Marlowe's *Faustus:* A Reconsideration," *RES,* XIX (1943), 225–241.

Maxwell, J. C. "The Sin of Faustus," *The Wind and the Rain,* IV, No. 1 (Summer 1947), 49–52.

McCloskey, John C. "The Theme of Despair in Marlowe's *Faustus,*" *CE,* IV (1942), 110–113.

McCullen, Joseph T. "Dr. Faustus and Renaissance Learning," *MLR,* LI (1956), 6–16.

Mizener, Arthur. "The Tragedy of Marlowe's *Doctor Faustus,*" *CE,* V (1943), 70–75.

Morgan, Gerald. "Harlequin Faustus: Marlowe's Comedy of Hell," *HAB,* XVIII (1967), 22–34.

Ornstein, Robert. "The Comic Synthesis in *Doctor Faustus,*" *ELH,* XXII (1955), 165–172.

Ostrowski, Witold. "The Interplay of the Subjective and the Objective in Marlowe's *Dr. Faustus,*" in *Studies in Language in Honour of Margaret Schlauch,* ed. Mieczyslaw Brahmer, Stanislaw Helsztynski, and Julian Krzyzanowski. Warsaw, 1966, pp. 293–305.

Palmer, D. J. "Magic and Poetry in *Doctor Faustus,*" *CritQ,* VI (1964), 56–67.

Sachs, Arieh. "The Religious Despair of Doctor Faustus," *JEGP,* LXIII (1964), 625–647.

Sewall, Richard B. *The Vision of Tragedy.* New Haven, 1959, pp. 57–67.

Simpson, Percy. "Marlowe's 'Tragical History of Doctor Faustus,'" in *Studies in Elizabethan Drama.* Oxford, 1955, pp. 95–111.

Smith, James. "Marlowe's 'Dr. Faustus,'" *Scrutiny,* VIII (1939), 36–55.

Smith, Warren D. "The Nature of Evil in *Doctor Faustus,*" *MLR,* LX (1965), 171–175.

Snyder, Susan. "Marlowe's *Doctor Faustus* as an Inverted Saint's Life," *SP,* LXIII (1966), 565–577.

Traci, Phillip J. "Marlowe's Faustus as Artist: A Suggestion About a Theme in the Play," *RenP* (1966), 3–9.

Versfeld, Martin. "Some Remarks on Marlowe's *Faustus,*" *ESA,* I (1958), 134–143.

Westlund, Joseph. "The Orthodox Christian Framework of Marlowe's *Faustus*," *SEL*, III (1963), 191–205.

Wright, Louis B., and Virginia A. LaMar, eds. *The Tragedy of Doctor Faustus*. Folger General Reader's Edition. New York, 1959, pp. xvi–xxiv.

See other studies in Marlowe bibliography (below, p. 170).

STRUCTURE AS MEANING
IN *THE JEW OF MALTA* *

Eric Rothstein

"Tragedy" and "Marlowe" produced until recently a sort of Pavlovian salivation for pity and fear, Renaissance libido, and the pleasures of catharsis. Judged by these expectations, *The Jew of Malta* was severely botched tragedy, "beginning," as Symonds colorfully put it, "with the face and torso of a Centaur, ending in the impotent and flabby coils of a poisonous reptile."[1] As later scholars have pointed out, however, there are serious flaws in assuming that any Renaissance dramatist would have been likely to make a Machiavellian Jewish usurer heroic: Symonds' is an un-Marlovian as well as an un-Linnaean beast.[2] These scholars have

---

* From *The Journal of English and Germanic Philology*, Vol. 65, 1966, pp. 260–273. Reprinted by permission of the University of Illinois Press.

[1] A. E. Symonds, *Shakspere's Predecessors in the English Drama* (London, 1924), p. 494.

[2] See, for instance, the chapters on *The Jew of Malta* in Douglas Cole's *Suffering and Evil in the Plays of Christopher Marlowe* (Princeton, 1962) and David M. Bevington's *From "Mankind" to Marlowe: Growth of Structure in the Popular Drama of Tudor England* (Cambridge, Mass., 1962), with both of which I am in general agreement and to both of which I am in places indebted. Cole and Beving-

gone on to place Barabas within the tradition of the morality Vice, and have accepted, with some qualification, Eliot's brilliant generic description of the play as "savage farce." I should like to develop, rather than challenge, this description, to suggest that *The Jew* is a controlled work of art, moderately complex in statement and technique.

I

The so-called "Elizabethan world picture," refreshed hebdomadally from the pulpit, provided not only a set of norms by which action could be judged, but also the possibility of a parodic technique in which form and content, structure and theme, might merge. *The Jew* employs such a parodic technique almost continuously, gaining force and meaning through the unwritten but always heard counterpoint that Elizabethan culture ideally provided. Most of the parody relates directly to Barabas, establishing his position; he in turn is used by Marlowe to set off and expose the rest of the characters.

Barabas bears the stigmata of his Jewishness, his usury, his Machiavellianism, his physical grotesqueness, and also his name. If one assumes that Marlowe is merely trying to alienate sympathy from Barabas, these derogations, all announced within the first eighty-five lines, are surely excessive: Marlowe has stacked the cards, marked the deck, and played the hand with crammed sleeves. A more plausible assumption, one which gives Marlowe credit for greater economy and precision, is that each of these derogations sets up one of the mutually implicatory themes of the play. Of these themes, the most personal, the least directly social, is that implied by "Barabas." Levin suggests that "if Christ died for all men, he died most immediately for Barrabas," and the *Glossa Ordinaria* says

---

ton, along with Bernard Spivack's *Shakespeare and the Allegory of Evil* (New York, 1958), are excellent in providing the historical background that makes it plausible for Marlowe to have written a play such as they and I envision. The violence of Elizabethan feelings toward dramatic Jews is documented by Myer Landa's *The Jew in Drama* (London, 1926), and by E. E. Stoll's *Shakespeare Studies* (New York, 1927), in his chapter "Shylock," especially pp. 269–95; for Elizabethan abhorrence of usurers, see Celeste T. Wright, "The Usurer's Sin in Elizabethan Literature," *SP*, XXXV (1938), 178–94. The excellent article by G. K. Hunter, "The Theology of Marlowe's *The Jew of Malta*" (*Jour. War. Court. Inst.*, XXVII [1964], 211–40), appeared too late for me to have made use of it. Save for differences with Mr. Hunter about the "degree of sympathy and admiration that Barabas is capable of exciting," I am in general agreement with the arguments advanced in this article, many of which parallel or coincide with those that I advance here, and with those advanced by Cole or Bevington. Hunter's documentation of his points is extensive and significant, and supplements that presented here.

tersely, "Ipse est Antichristus."[3] As the Antichrist, the inversion of Christ, Barabas has the function of bringing *cupiditas* through works of malice. Politically, in terms of social action, Barabas' malice is expressed in Machiavellian *Realpolitik,* of which the historical Barabas, a rebel and a murderer (Mark 15:7, Luke 23:19), seems to have been one of the earlier practitioners. Ethically, in terms of social justification, his malice is expressed in Jewishness, the assertion of the reductive materialism of the Old Law and the denial of the *caritas* of the New.

Against this pattern of demonic action, Marlowe's brief analogy of Barabas with Job, made explicit at the moment of its rejection, is particularly amusing, for as St. Gregory the Great wrote in his *Libri Moralium,* "cuncti [sancti] Christum praenuntiarunt, maxime Job."[4] Like Job, Barabas is, at the beginning of the play, "the greatest of all the men of the East" (Job 1:3), commercial heir to the Uz trade. Like Job, he is, during the course of the play, injured in his goods, his family, and his body. Marlowe has even given him comforters whose names suggest Job's.[5] These similarities are, of course, undercut by Barabas' materialism, which measures disaster in portagues and pearls, in the letter rather than the spirit, the Old Law rather than the New; and thus desires revenge, not patient submission. His solution to the terrors of mutability is not grace but prudence: while "common men" "measure nought but by the present time,"

A reaching thought will search his deepest wits,

---

[3] Harry Levin, *The Overreacher* (Cambridge, Mass., 1952), p. 64; *Walafridi Strabi...Opera Omnia,* ed. J. P. Migne, Vol. II, *Patrologiae Latinae Tomus CXIV* (Paris, 1879), pp. 173, 345.

[4] St. Gregory the Great, in *Opera Omnia,* ed. J. P. Migne, Vol. I, *Patrologiae Latinae Tomus LXXV* (Paris, 1849), p. 524.

[5] The text, l. 215, gives "Zaareth" and "Temainte" as the Jews' names. I would hypothesize that these are misprints for "Naareth" and "Temanite," since the names as they stand seem meaningless, while of Job's comforters, Eliphaz is a Temanite and Zophar comes from Naareth ("Naamath" in the *KJV,* Job 2:11, but "Naareth" in earlier editions of the Geneva Bible, which were current when Marlowe wrote; Biblical quotations in this article are from the Geneva Bible). Cole, pp. 124–25, also discusses the analogy between Barabas and Job, concluding, "It does not really matter that this point-for-point contrast may not be dramatically evident to the audience; it reveals, most importantly, the dramatist's *conception* behind the presentation of the character, which is grounded on the complete and consistent inversion of accepted values and virtues." This statement seems to me a wise qualification. Barabas mentions Uz in l. 39. Succeeding line references to *The Jew of Malta* will be given parenthetically in my text. I use the edition of C. F. Tucker Brooke, *The Works of Christopher Marlowe* (Oxford, 1910), but have availed myself of the annotations in *The Jew of Malta and The Massacre at Paris,* ed. H. S. Bennett (London, 1931).

> And cast with cunning for the time to come:
> For euils are apt to happen euery day.

                                              (ll. 453–57)

"The time to come" is in this world; the "Blessings promis'd to the Iewes" (l. 143), the "Infinite riches," are all hard cash.

Together with this materialism comes an inversion of Job's charity, for Barabas' avarice is not primarily a humor, a controlling limitation; it functions, rather, as logical part of a ferocious ethic. One expects that if Job "caused the widowes heart to reioyce" (Job 29:13), Barabas might make that of Mathias' widowed mother grieve. If Barabas, like Job, has fed the hungry, his *specialité de la maison* is the alms of poison. And it follows that when the game is done, when Barabas has emulated Job, and therefore Christ, in returning from spiritual death (made crudely physical) to regain his realm, the tenure of Malta, he should fulfill the punishment of the wicked described in Job 18:

> 7 The steps of his strength shall be straitened, and his own counsel shall cast him down.
> 8 For he is cast into a net by his own feet, and he walketh upon a snare. . . .
> 10 The snare is laid for him in the ground, and a trap for him in the way.

As Job's wife, the voice of carnal reason, invites her husband to "Blaspheme God, and die" (Job 2:9), so Barabas, trapped, cries out, "tongue curse thy fill and dye" (l. 2373).

Job's children have a spiritual significance like that of his goods, and indeed, ironically, so do Barabas'. Child is converted into property: this is literally true of the slave Ithamore, his owned and adopted son; and Abigail, disaffiliated when she renounces Jewishness, is earlier equated with gold in double apostrophe: "Oh girle, oh gold, oh beauty, oh my blisse!" (l. 695). Gold, in turn, stands in a filial relationship to Barabas:

> Now *Phoebus* ope the eye-lids of the day,
> And for the Rauen wake the morning Larke,
> That I may houer with her in the Ayre,
> Singing ore these, as she does ore her young.

                                              (ll. 701–704)

Abigail herself, whose name means "father's joy," is Barabas' joy here, casting gold to him, as she inverts the function of her Biblical namesake, who stole from a "wicked man" to give to David, the soldier of the Lord (I Sam. 25:14–31). The star of annunciation ("starre shin[ing] yonder in the *East*" [l. 680]) heralding the birth of successful burglary, she is the agent of financial grace in Christianity: her conversion for the sake of the purse is paralleled by her going to uncover the hidden gold to the foot of the cross, the cross with which her father has marked the upper chamber plank (l. 598). It is fitting that her epiphany on the nunnery roof be led up to with Barabas' absurdly ironic prayer:

> Oh thou that with a fiery piller led'st
> The sonnes of *Israel* through the dismall shades,
> Light *Abrahams* off-spring; and direct the hand
> Of *Abigall* this night. . . .

(ll. 651–54)

God is evoked as celestial guide for the sake of the gold, and the gold assumes through the allusion the typological significance of the journey to the promised land, that is, salvation.

But Abigail pays limited profits. Like the Biblical Abigail, she eventually moves from a liaison with a son of Belial to the proper service of the Lord; in doing so, she becomes forfeit property, a replaceable (by Ithamore) sacrifice. Her default would seem to be the proleptic reason for "*Abrahams* off-spring" in the passage quoted above—Abraham has nothing to do with the Mosaic exodus, but his "off-spring" Isaac is, like Abigail, a sacrifice; her default is almost certainly the proleptic reason for Barabas' first mentioning his "one sole Daughter" in the context of the love of Agamemnon for "his *Iphigen*" (l. 176). The Chaldaean and Mycenaean potentates both submitted their children to the block for divine grace; the potentate of Malta prefers prudence, human contrivance for safety. Thus Barabas condemns Abigail to "perish vnderneath my bitter curse / Like *Cain* by *Adam,* for his brother's death" (ll. 1334–35): the obvious and immediate irony of the Scriptural distortion and inversion, that Barabas' curse is that of the old Adam, deepens the force of Barabas' hoisting himself into the place of the Lord by whom Cain was cursed. Indeed, Barabas goes God one better, for whereas Cain's life was spared and protected, Abigail's is aborted by her Adamic father.

Ithamore's career parallels Abigail's. After his adoption, the two plots in which he engages, poisoning the nuns and ensnaring the friars, are versions of those in which Abigail is involved, plundering the nunnery and deceiving the suitors. And like Abigail, Ithamore falls through romantic attachment to a Christian. In each of these cases, of course, Ithamore is a viler counterpart. The poisoning is not only an extension of the plunder, but is also, like the suitors' plot which directly precedes it, murderous; the friars' plot not only extends the suitors' (the murder now, like the poisoning, committed by Ithamore's own hands), but also involves an exploitation of the law which foreshadows the increasingly public character of the last act. Finally, surpassing Abigail, Ithamore appropriately loves a whore, love rendered material. He is thus plausibly Barabas' son, though (or because) a slave and a Turk: while the Biblical

Ithamar is the son and executive agent of the high priest Aaron, Marlowe's is son and agent of the high priest of Maltese Jewry.

Parodic action in the Barabas-Ithamore relationship includes specific mockery of two romantic conventions, the code of friendship and the pastoral. Barabas' professions of friendship to Ithamore are on the face of them bizarre, since the characters are grotesque and the protestations hypocritical as well as excessive:

> ...Oh Ithimore come neere;
> Come neere, my loue, come neere thy masters life,
> My trusty seruant, nay, my second self;
> For I haue no hope but euen in thee;
> And on that hope my happinesse is built.

> (ll. 1315–19)

And "trusty Ithimore; no seruant, but my friend" (l. 1344) replies in kind, offering to plunge into the sea for Barabas: "Why I'le doe any thing for your sweet sake" (l. 1343). As L. J. Mills has shown, these appellations and protestations take on added meaning as part of a friendship tradition, in which amicus is alter ipse, and "the sharing of property is a constant element." "Another situation common in friendship narratives is based on the desire of a person to save his friend even by sacrifice of himself." And finally, there is a "traditional preference of friendship over love."[6] Marlowe makes each of these points of friendship ironic. If Ithamore is Barabas' "second self," theirs is a communion of villainy that absolutely bars any of the other points, sharing, sacrifice, and idealistic hierarchy of relationships. But although Barabas' offers are insincere, Ithamore, in giving up his master for his mistress, redeems friendship's pledges by forced sharing of gold and, in the process of blackmail, by the sacrifice of his dear friend.

As the viciousness of the relationship between Barabas and Ithamore is pointed up by the language of friendship, innocent love's language points up the folly of Ithamore's infatuation. Overcome with furor poeticus, Ithamore breaks into rapturous couplets that parody Marlowe's own "Passionate Shepherd" (ll. 1806–16). Here the pastoral world is made material and common: the "Woods and Forrests" are conceived as dressed pedestrians who "goe in goodly greene," the meadows require carpeting, and the natural vegetation of "Sugar Canes' suggests not beauty but a sweet tooth. Appropriately enough, Ithamore begins with money ("I'le be thy Iason, thou my golden Fleece") and ends by promoting the good of the underworld to preside over his amours: "Thou in those Groues, by Dis aboue, / Shalt liue with me and be my loue." Barabas, always adaptable, presently appears as a minstrel with nature

---

6 L. J. Mills, "The Meaning of Edward II," MP, XXXII (1934), 11–31; quotations from pp. 17, 19, 21, 23.

and harmony, flower and lute, poisoning the company with the one and accompanying drunken lies with the other. Et in Arcadia Barabas; at least in this Arcadia, this proper pastoral of lust and greed, of whore, thief, and Ithamore.

The last mode of formal parody that I shall discuss, an ubiquitous mode, is dictional. There is at least one direct parody of *The Spanish Tragedy*: Abigail professes herself "The hopelesse daughter of a haplesse Iew" (l. 557) so as to gain admission to the nunnery, a line that echoes Hieronymo's "The hopeless father of a hapless son" (*Spanish Tragedy*, IV.iii.116). Marlowe has inverted the parent-child relationship, and has awarded a financial plot the dignity of Kyd's climactic revelation. Similarly, Barabas' "Oh girle, oh, gold, oh beauty, oh my blisse!" (l. 695) may recall such lines as Kyd's "O, my son, my son; O, my son Horatio!" (*Spanish Tragedy*, III.xii.237); but most of the "many passages of patterned verse in the manner of *The Spanish Tragedy*"[7] do not seem to have specific referents. They serve, like the "poetic" passages, to pump up action so that it can be loudly or sibilantly punctured. One example is Barabas' "fiery piller" invocation quoted above; another, Barabas' curse on the rice:

> As fatall be it to her as the draught
> Of which great *Alexander* drunke, and dyed:
> And with her let it worke like *Borgias* wine,
> Whereof his sire, the Pope, was poyson'd.
> In few, the blood of *Hydra,* Lerna's bane;
> The iouyce of *Hebon,* and *Cocitus* breath,
> And all the poysons of the Stygian poole
> Breake from the fiery kingdome; and in this
> Vomit your venome, and inuenome her
> That like a fiend hath left her father thus.

(ll. 1399–1408)

Ithamore promptly undercuts the curse: "What a blessing has he giu'nt? was ever pot of Rice porredge so sauc't? what shall I doe with it?" In the same way Barabas' lamentations to the other Jews for "forlorne *Barabas,*" his "extreme sorrowes," his "months of vanity and losse of time, / And painefulle nights" and "trouble of my spirit," turn out a fraud, as does his stoic loftiness to Abigail:

> No, *Abigail,* things past recouery
> Are hardly cur'd with exclamations.
> Be silent, Daughter, sufferance breeds ease,
> And time may yeeld vs an occasion
> Which on the sudden cannot serue the turne.

(ll. 425–74, *passim*)

---

7 Philip Henderson, *And Morning in His Eyes* (London, 1937), p. 258.

It is a convenient sufferance that can beguile its pain with ten thousand hidden portagues (not to mention jewels).

The Barabas plots, then, amplify his motto, "Ego mihimet sum semper proximus" (l. 228), words given by Terence to the "pessimum hominum genus," who "malis gaudeant atque ex incommodis alterius sua ut comparent commoda" (*Andria*, IV.627–29). I have been indicating the ways in which Marlowe carries out this amplification through parody and undercutting relative to Barabas and his active extensions, Abigail and Ithamore. But if Barabas is the supreme *poseur*, producing parody and reversal through the doubleness of his pose, he is also the supreme agent for exposing others. Sometimes these exposures are deliberate, a satisfying response to his faith in the badness of human nature; sometimes they are merely stimulated by his gold; at all times, he supplies a negative norm of judgment. Since *The Jew of Malta* is primarily concerned—like all other Elizabethan tragedies, I would venture—with character as expression of moral action rather than of personality, and since Barabas is tropologically totally simple, it seems likely that his dramatic function is more significant than his "personality."

II

When Ferneze, the governor of Malta, confiscates Barabas' fortune, his argument is that with which Caiaphas justified the killing of Christ: Ferneze's "better one want for a common good, / Than many perish for a priuate man" (ll. 331–32) clearly echoes Caiaphas' "Nor yet doe you consider that it is expedient for us, that one man die for the people, and that the whole nation perish not" (John 11:50). When the governor acts thus, and proceeds, with his men, to more sophistry (ll. 340–42, 356–57), one may suspect his ingenious deceits of less wit than wickedness. In fact, Christianity—Catholicism, that is—in Malta verges on the rancid, and to the extent that the play is topical, it is anti-Catholic, not (pointlessly) anti-Semitic.[8] Catholic Malta is politically leagued with the Turks until the end of the play; Catholic Malta is ethically controlled by Barabas.

The linkage of Barabas and the Catholics is made first through Machiavelli. "The opinion that Machiavelli was under the control of the devil had been seriously advanced...by Cardinal Pole, and in the course of time became popular."[9] He is thus a true analogue for Barabas, an analogue chosen, I suggest, with specific anti-Catholic intentions. "Macheuill" identifies himself in the third line of the play with the Duke

---

8 I have not been able to see an article in which a similar point seems to be made: Charles E. Peavy, "*The Jew of Malta*—Anti-Semitic or Anti-Catholic," *McNeese Review*, XI (1959–60), 57–60—abstracted in *AES*, VI (1963), item 1326.

9 Clarence V. Boyer, *The Villain as Hero in Elizabethan Drama* (London, 1914), p. 51.

of Guise, who had epitomized Catholic violence and deceit not only in the St. Bartholomew's Day Massacre and the Armada, but more particularly in sponsoring the Babington Conspiracy on the Queen's life, a crime of which Marlowe has him accused in *The Massacre at Paris* (ll. 1042–46). Machiavelli's works were also associated with the Duke's *de facto* ruler, the Catholic Queen Catherine de Medicis, who was supposed to have imported them into England.

Once having set up this possibility for topical attack, Marlowe continues to link Barabas with the Catholic powers: he is protected by the Spanish (ll. 133–35), furnished with Italian poisons (ll. 1371–75) and hypocrisy (l. 784), and provided by both nations with oaths and maxims (ll. 323, 678, 705, 1528); nearer the end of the play, Marlowe generously includes the French, by having Barabas murder his pastoral comrades as a French lutanist (ll. 1950 ff.) and threaten with a French phrase (l. 1857). The principle that one may legitimately deceive heathens, continually practiced by Barabas and explicitly recommended both by him and by Ithamore (ll. 993–95, 2001), has long been charged to Catholics —by Dennis attacking Pope and by Kingsley, Newman—and is so charged by Marlowe himself in *II Tamburlaine,* lines 2821–57. It was specifically charged to the Jesuits, who were "held in abhorrence as teaching that the end justified the means,"[10] the same Jesuits trained by Guise and deep in the Babington Plot. It is to these Babington plotters that an Elizabethan moralist applies lines from Psalm 7 like those from Job:

> Behold hee trauaileth with mischiefe (or iniquitie) hee hath conceiued sorrowe, and brought foorth a lie (or vaine thing.) Hee hath grauen and digged vp a pit, and is fallen himselfe into the pit (or destruction) that he hath made: for his trauaile shall come vpon his owne head, and his wickednes shall fall vpon his own pate....[11]

But the Catholics in this play demonstrate more than connotative guilt: they react in reasonable consistency with the same greed, lust, and violence that mark Barabas and Ithamore. The friendship of Lodowick and Mathias, and that of Jacomo and Barnadine, are structurally halvings of that of Barabas and Ithamore, of the friendship of Jews and a Turk destroyed for lust (like the lovers') and avarice (like the friars'). And indeed, why should this not be true when Malta is financed with Barabas' wealth and its Church sheltered in Barabas' house? If Lodowick, the governor's son, chooses to league himself (here in marriage) with a Jew, *defendit numerus;* and characterically his prolonged conceit in conferring about Abigail is financial (ll. 809–29). Lodowick's conduct as friend and lover makes Barabas' task simple. As

[10] *The Oxford Dictionary of the Christian Church,* ed. F. L. Cross (London, 1957), article "Jesuits," p. 722.

[11] Michael Renniger, *A Treatise Conteining Two Parts* (London, 1587), part II, "Against Treasons, Rebellions, and such like disloyalties." sig. H2.

soon as Mathias confides his passion, Lodowick tries to possess Abigail himself, conduct that Mathias, who knows his man, fears (1. 904); Mathias' "Oh treacherous *Lodowicke!*" (1. 1031) is only just, and the friends' invective hardly needs Barabas' encouragements. The mourning at their deaths is thus ridiculous, with its claims of love and its pledge to bury this foolish and unscrupled pair "Within one sacred monument of stone" (1. 1212). Marlowe's scenic juxtaposition of Barabas' prospects of a Christian son-in-law with Barabas' acquisition of a Turkish son—Ithamore—does not appear to be coincidental.

Other than Ferneze, whom I shall discuss, Lodowick and Mathias are the only significant Maltese laymen. (Discussion of the whore and the thief, Lust and Greed, seems unnecessary.) Maltese ecclesiastics are no better. Marlowe says little about the nuns, who are tangential, but he offers innuendo. "Abbess" and "nunnery" had possible sexual meanings that Marlowe exploits. Ithamore directly asks Abigail "a very feeling" question: "haue not the Nuns fine sport with the Fryars now and then?" (ll. 1254–55). The suggestion is amplified in the preparation of the poison:

> ITHAMORE: Here's a drench to poyson a whole stable of Flanders mares: I'le carry't to the Nuns with a powder.
> BARABAS: And the horse pestilence to boot; away.

> (ll. 1414–16)

("Flanders mares" were particularly riotous beats; "mare" itself, like "nag," appears in Shakespeare for "a girl, or a woman, regarded as the bearer of amorous man." "Powder," as in "powdering tub," refers to the cure of venereal disease, the "whore's pestilence."[12]) Further, one friar, as his friend is presumably deserting priestly duties to attend "faire *Maria*," exclaims about the dying nuns, "Oh what a sad confession will there be" (1. 1460); and his later lament over Abigail's having died a virgin (1. 1497) implies that she might not have died one had she lived longer in the nunnery. Finally, Barabas remarks that the nuns "swell" "euery yeare," and that the monks, "now the Nuns are dead," "dye with griefe" (ll. 1514, 1523–24). Again, the structural parallel to Abigail's death, that in which poison is given to the second apostate, Ithamore, with a whore and a pimp, is not fortuitous.

About the friars little has to be said, except that they die true to their order of St. Jacques (St. James): Barnardine follows St. James the Less in being struck with a staff so that "his brains drop out on's nose" (ll.

---

12 "Flanders mares" was used (*OED*) by William Browne in *Britannia's Pastorals*, I, v, 505 ff; Browne uses the term in a simile describing riot. For "mare" and "nag" see Eric Partridge, *Shakespeare's Bawdy* (New York, 1955); for "powdering tub" (also in *Shakespeare's Bawdy*) and "horse pestilence" (entry under "horse pox"), see Partridge, *A Dictionary of Slang and Unconventional English*, 5th ed. (New York, 1961).

1687–88), while Jacomo stands patron, like St. James the Great, to hanged men. (Both saints, one might note, were killed by the Jews.[13]) Barnardine and Jacomo are a little lower than the saints, avid for Barabas' gold as Lodowick and Mathias are for his daughter; and punished, like Lodowick and Mathias, in accordance with justice. Barnardine is strangled with his own noose, and the law of Malta, duplicating Barabas' private law, strangles Jacomo for the murder that his will has committed. Their attempted blackmail, thematically following the confiscation by Ferneze, anticipates that by Ithamore and Pilia-Borza, with whom they must be ethically, if not tonally, equated. Behind Barabas' and Ithamore's ironic taunts at Jacomo, there is truth:

> ITHAMORE: Fie vpon 'em, Mr.: will you turne Christian, when holy Friars turne deuils and murder one another.
> BARABAS: No, for this example I'le remaine a Iew:
> Heauen blesse me; what, a Fryar a murderer?
> When shall you see a Iew commit the like?
> ITHAMORE: Why, a Turke could ha done no more.

(ll. 1703–08)

As governor of the island, the force of Maltese law, Ferneze is oddly impotent, since not honor and law but Jewishness and Machiavellian contrivance characterize his subjects. His two moments of success are his moments of betrayal, thieving from Barabas in the first act and undermining him in the last. Between extralegal but effective maneuvers, he is ludicrous. Lodowick tries to marry a Jew, and gets himself pierced, leaving Ferneze remediless; when heaven (Bellamira and Pilia-Borza) eventually does reveal "the causers of our smarts" (l. 1216)), Ferneze is still unable to act, because Barabas' narcotic dupes him. He thereupon calms Del Bosco's legitimate suspicions with a smug assertion of Providence ("Wonder not at it, Sir, the heauens are just"—l. 2057), and proceeds to dispose of the "body" in precisely the wrong way, causing his citadel's capture. His record in foreign affairs is not much of an improvement. When the play begins, his island of Malta is leagued humiliatingly with the pagan Turks, who "liue vpon our spoyle" (l. 1432) just as the domestic heathens do. However, pressed by the Spaniard Del Bosco, he vows annihilation if necessary: to Del Bosco's account of the

---

[13] Louis Réau (*Iconographie de l'art Chrétien,* 3 vols. in 6 parts [Paris, 1955–59], III, Pt. ii, p. 702) says that St. James the Less was killed by a staff, which, "en lui fracassant le crâne d'un coup de bâton, fit jaillir sa cervelle." He lists St. James the Great as a protector against "pendaison (III, Pt. iii, p. 1477) and a patron of "pendus" (p. 1466). Marlowe might have learned something of the iconography by looking at the windows of Canterbury Cathedral, which he had innumerable opportunities to do in his boyhood. See Bernard Rackham, *The Ancient Glass of Canterbury* (London, 1949). Such allusions to hagiography were not limited to Marlowe. Shakespeare, for instance, ironically chose the patron saint of the battle against the pagan Moors, Sant' Iago, to name the villain in *Othello* after.

battle of Rhodes, in which "not a man suruiu'd / To bring the haplesse newes to Christendome," Ferneze rashly replies, "So will we fight it out" (ll. 755–57). He pledges a scorched earth policy (ll. 1431–38), and proclaims through his knight that "we will neuer yeeld" (l. 2007). It follows logically that at his next appearance, after Barabas' trip through the sluice, Ferneze is tame and glum: "What should I say? we are captiues and must yeeld" (l. 2106). His wars and rallying are completely ineffectual, although he makes an efficient Machiavellian, given the chance.

One might construct a metaphor for the ironies of Ferneze's action by observing that Calymath's men are blown up in a monastery. The monastery, destructive to Malta through its ethical betrayals during the play, preserves Malta by continuing in character, just as Ferneze, helpless when he has moral and political power, becomes a savior by reneging both. His final comment, that due praise must "be giuen / Neither to Fate nor Fortune, but to Heauen" (ll. 2409–10), is not convincing, unless one is to take Heaven as Barabas' Heaven, where Dis presides, not Christ.

III

The narrative of *The Jew of Malta* moves along straightforwardly, bare of the artful richness achieved by Shakespeare through development of imagery and juxtaposition of scene. Even when Marlowe does deviate from straight narrative, as he does four times, his effects are rather simple. The first (ll. 608–39) introduces Lodowick and Mathias between the scenes of Abigail's first novitiate and its golden ending. Her false conversion to Christianity is set against their true conversion to Jewishness; the pair of scenes is part of the theme of conversion occurring at the beginning of the play (ll. 305–24) and in the friars' plot as well as here: Jews feign agreement with Christianity, while Christians act Jewishly. Second, two scenes of breaking allegiance, Abigail's plunder and Ferneze's decision to abandon his "Tributory league" (ll. 640–761), both of which involve the consolidation of wealth and the taking back of extorted tribute, are placed against the scene in the slave market (ll. 762–967), in which Abigail's plunder is seen to have included Lodowick and Mathias, while Ferneze's abrogation permits Barabas to create a league with the Turk Ithamore. I have indicated above the connection between the two searches for a son, and Marlowe amplifies this connection in the third digression, by introducing Bellamira and Ithamore's infatuation at the same time that he presents the bloody ending of Lodowick's and Mathias' (ll. 1150–90). As in romances, these children revolt against their parents —Abigail deserts Barabas in the very next scene—for love, if one is to call it that. The last digression (ll. 1420–56) shows Ferneze menacing the heathen with destruction and violence; meanwhile the poisoning of the nuns (ll. 1350–1419, 1457–1508) shows the domestic heathen victorious. Thus both of Ferneze's scenes of vaunting are undercut by significant juxtapositions.

But significant juxtapositions are not really Marlowe's method of work. The play in general proceeds, as I have been trying to show, by exploiting thematic parodies of an initially stated set of ideas. These ideas themselves are not explored, but used to give body and connection to otherwise disparate episodes, which qualify each other only insofar as they indicate, through structural analogy, the proper rubrics of judgment. All values are inverted by a central diabolism in grotesque form, expressing itself through materialism ("Jewishness") and a Machiavellian ethic. To this Marlowe remains consistent. If Ferneze succeeds, as Barabas does, by vice, Barabas himself is brought down by his trust, the smallest unit of civil relationship. He is betrayed by all three people he trusts, Abigail, Ithamore, and Ferneze, just as every trusting character in every major situation throughout the entire play is betrayed. Since virtue is folly and the pitfall of vice, Marlowe can carry the paradox of inversion still farther. Until Ferneze's final triumph, there is not one action taken by any character that does not recoil, directly or indirectly, upon that character, save only the bearing off of the bodies of Lodowick and Mathias.

The manipulation of themes does not absolutely dictate emotional response, which probably depended, in the Elizabethan theater, on the audience's degree of *pity* for the characters. But just as Marlowe has set up the themes at the beginning, he has carefully indicated the level of reaction by making Barabas physically grotesque, giving him a huge nose that swelled up to tiny eyes and hooked down to a great red beard.[14] Lest the nose grow familiar, Marlowe reminds the audience of it on occasion:

> ITHAMORE: Oh braue, master, I worship your nose for this.

> (l. 938)

> ITHAMORE: Oh Mistris! I haue the brauest, grauest, secret, subtile, bottle-nos'd knaue to my Master, that euer Gentleman had.

> (ll. 1228–30)

> ITHAMORE: Look, look, Mr. here come two religious Caterpillers.
> BARABAS: I smelt 'em e're they came.
> ITHAMORE: God-a-mercy nose; come let's begone.

> (ll. 1529–31)

He also supplies some unmistakable humor in the main plot, such as the friars' scene of tentative blackmail (ll. 1529–1607) or the masquerade

---

14 Bennett, p. 88, quotes Rowley as evidence for this traditional make-up.

as French musician (ll. 1950–2001). Barabas is also made the master of *double-entendre* and the undercutting aside (ll. 212, 601–607, 810–48 *passim*, 993, etc.), so that his character as *poseur*, and his dupe's as gull, may be kept in view. Such use of deliberate humor in the main plot permits the assumption that the pervasive irony of the play is also to be taken pitilessly, and that devices like concealment and imposture, inversion, repetition, exposure, and exaggeration, which might theoretically form part of a serious plot, have been used by Marlowe to secure "alienation." Further support for such a conclusion comes from his having chosen to destroy the only potentially tragic moment by confirming suspicions about monastic lechery:

> ABIGAIL: Death seizeth on my heart: ah gentle Fryar,
> Conuert my father that he may be sau'd,
> And witnesse that I dye a Christian.   (*Dies.*)
> 2 FRYAR: I, and a Virgin too, that grieues me most. . . .

(ll. 1494–97)

The generic question, how such a play can be called "tragedy," is, I believe, factitious. *The Jew of Malta,* with its deaths and downfalls, is technically a tragedy, even if it does not satisfy the unhistoric expectations and the eagerness for "tragic mystery" and pathos characteristic of a more sentimental age than Marlowe's. The play as I would read it is skillfully constructed, and effective, if not in stimulating our emotions, then in placing before us the image of a morally crippled world, a complex emblem of un-Christian action. That world is not England, for Marlowe is neither cynic nor nihilist, but its unarable land is part of England and Englishmen. Marlowe asks us to laugh at it and leave it to scorn.

THE JEW OF MALTA

Babb, Howard S. "Policy in Marlowe's *The Jew of Malta,*" *ELH,* XXIV (1957), 85–94.

Craik, Thomas W., ed. *The Jew of Malta.* The New Mermaids, London, 1966, and New York, 1967, pp. viii–xviii.

D'Andrea, Antonio. "Studies in Machiavelli and His Reputation in the Sixteenth Century, I: Marlowe's Prologue to *The Jew of Malta,*" *Medieval and Renaissance Studies,* V (1961), 214–248.

Friedman, Alan Warren. "The Shackling of Accidents in Marlowe's *Jew of Malta,*" *TSLL,* VIII (1966), 155–167.

Harbage, Alfred. "Innocent Barabas," *TDR,* VIII, No. 4 (1964), 47–58.

Hunter, G. K. "The Theology of Marlowe's *The Jew of Malta,*" *JWCI,* XXVII (1964), 211–240.

Marlowe's The Jew of Malta: *Grammar of Policy.* Midwest Monographs, Series

1, No. 2, Urbana, Illinois, 1967. (Essays by Leonard F. Dean, Michael Bristol, and Neil Kleinman.)

Peavy, Charles E. *"The Jew of Malta*—Anti-Semitic or Anti-Catholic?" *McNR,* XI (1959–60), 57–60.

Purcell, H. D. "Whetstone's *Englysh Myrror* and Marlowe's *Jew of Malta,"* *N&Q,* XIII (1966), 288–290.

Van Fossen, Richard W., ed. *The Jew of Malta,* Regents Renaissance Drama Series. Lincoln, Nebraska, 1964, pp. xii–xxv.

See other studies in Marlowe bibliography (below, p. 170).

———••——

STATE OVERTURNED *

Harry Levin

THE tragic view is never a simple one. It is not a spontaneous reaction to a given situation, but a gradual recognition of the sternest facts that govern the whole of life. It came as the hard-won guerdon of maturity to Sophocles and Shakespeare; and even Marlowe, for all his precocity, had to ripen into it. *The Jew of Malta* provokes less pity than terror; most of its terrors, indeed, are merely horrors; and in so far as it subordinates everything else to contrivance, it deserves to be classed as a farce —or, at any rate, a melodrama. That little room, that self-contained island are quite incommensurable with the geopolitical expanses of *Tamburlaine;* but their angularity and narrowness frame a more realistic picture of society, as scaled down by the law of diminishing returns. The tragedy that overtakes Tamburlaine is almost an afterthought, although his centrifugal route is strewn with lesser tragedies. Similarly, *The Tragedy of Dido* is incidental to the epic adventures of Æneas. In those plays which we have thus far considered, Marlowe seems to stand like his Leander, poised upon the very brink of tragedy. He has provided a *sine qua non* by creating extraordinarily powerful protagonists; had he stopped there, his genre would have been monodrama; and though effective drama has been built around single figures—Eugene O'Neill's

* Reprinted by permission of the publishers, Harvard University Press and Faber & Faber Ltd., from Harry Levin, *The Overreacher: A Study of Christopher Marlowe,* pp. 82–104. Cambridge, Mass.: Harvard University Press, copyright 1952 by The President and Fellows of Harvard College.

Emperor Jones, Büchner's *Dantons Tod,* to some extent *Macbeth*—the overbalance is too precarious to be long sustained. Marlowe has taken another step, and introduced a framework of ethical reference, by stigmatizing his hero as a villain. If he does nothing else in *The Massacre at Paris,* he exorcises this devil that he has raised. And in *Edward II* he sets forth his discovery that tragic life needs no villains; that plots are spun by passions; that men betray themselves. . . .

Marlowe had already investigated the problem of kingship from the side of the legitimate monarch who forfeits his crown, the unheroic hero at whose expense the interloper achieves his self-made greatness, the weak and unambitious inheritor of high place caught in the conflict of strong and ambitious men. Marlowe's cult of strength, from the beginning, carried along its explicit corollary, the scorn of weakness. *Tamburlaine* begins with a sketch of the weakling Mycetes, lacking in wit but interested in poetry, esthetically preoccupied with the sight of blood on the battle-field, wistfully clinging to the smooth-spoken courtier whom he terms his "Damon" (58). Though Tamburlaine is all that Mycetes is not, the strain of effeteness turns up again in Calyphas, the Phaëthon-like son who proves incapable of taking over his father's reins. Tamburlaine's virtue is capable of both conceiving and subduing, as he asserts in one of his rare moments of introspection; but his behavior is so externalized that we scarcely see him when he is not subduing. The conceiving is actually done by Marlowe, who accompanies his conqueror—as poets do—"in conceit" (260). As his dramaturgy matured, he would concentrate more upon passion and less upon action, less upon externals and more upon feeling. *The Jew of Malta* glanced behind obvious surfaces and purchased with grief its glimpse of experience. But with Barabas, as with Tamburlaine and the Guise, the impact is registered on us—as on their victims—from the outside; whereas with Edward, because he is the victim, we feel the effect of people and circumstances on him. Because he is passive rather than active, he cuts much less of a figure; but he is more deeply grounded within the psychological range of his creator; and his sensations are relayed to us more fully and faithfully.

Above all, he is a man who lives by his senses, an exponent of *libido sentiendi.* Being a king, he has no need to seek power; it is thrust upon him; and, being a hedonist, he wants to enjoy it. He is kept from doing so by the agitations of those careerists who surround and harass him. In his vacillations with them, his yearning for affection, and his continual yielding, he utterly reverses the pattern of *Tamburlaine.* Tucker Brooke stresses the fact that *Edward II,* unlike Marlowe's more characteristic plays, was not performed by Henslowe's companies, and draws the interesting inference that Marlowe, unable for once to count upon Edward Alleyn for a dominating role, was attempting to distribute the equilibrium more evenly among the dramatis personæ. This is the kind of functional side-light that is seldom irrelevant to our understanding of Elizabethan drama; it illuminates both the technique of the one-man play and the emergence of an ampler and more varied characterization. But it should not deflect our attention from Marlowe's increasing flexibility, his maturing sympathies, and his unexpected insight into human frailties. Nor should it, within the precincts of the theater, persuade us that Edward's part is somehow negligible. Rather, what is envisaged may be a new style of acting, more rounded and subtle than Alleyn's elocution, ultimately to be associated with Richard Burbage and the major Shakespearean roles. We are reminded, as we enter the 1590's, that Shakespeare will soon be catching up with Marlowe. He will be imitating his contemporary, out-Marlowing the Marlovian idiom, in *Richard III*. But Shakespeare may have meanwhile established, with *Henry VI,* a dramatic balance and a lyrical modulation which Marlowe may well be emulating in *Edward II.*

During the patriotic decade between the rout of the Spanish Armada and the downfall of the Earl of Essex, between *Tamburlaine* and Shakespeare's *Henry V,* the dramatic repertory was dominated by the vogue of the chronicle history. In trying his hand at it, Marlowe addressed his iconoclastic talent to a highly traditional form, which was fast becoming a quasi-official vehicle for keeping tradition alive. Tragedy, which was also founded on some historical matter, differed from the history play by being set in some other country than England. Hence, while the tragic playwright could take many liberties in the interest of his artistic conception, the historical playwright was obliged to respect the common preconception of his material as crystallized by legend, if not by history more rigorously construed. Much of this material, in fact, was taken from the Elizabethan historians, notably from the second edition of Raphael Holinshed's *Chronicles,* published in 1587. These chronicles are essentially annals, recording events as they happened, year by year and reign by reign. The result, transferred to the stage, was bound to be clumsily episodic in structure, and to derive such unity as it possessed from the personality of the reigning monarch. Much could be done if he was a popular hero, like Henry V. When he was a villainous usurper, like Richard III, Shakespeare could blend in him the qualities of Tamburlaine and Barabas, and motivate the plot by the interplay of ambition and revenge. But those were the great exceptions, and they remain among the few English kings who have continued to live in the theater. The long-drawn-out and unhappy reign of Henry VI was more difficult to resolve dramatically. Marlowe might have been attracted by that ill-fated ruler, who would so much rather have been a shepherd; but Shakespeare relegates him to the background, where he does all too little to unify the three plays treating York and Lancaster, Joan of Arc and Jack Cade, and a miscellany of problems, foreign and domestic.

The grand design of Shakespeare's histories is delineated through a series of lessons in ethics and politics. In general, the king can do no wrong; sometimes, alas, he is led astray by evil counselors and false favorites; yet nothing ever justifies the dethronement of God's anointed. On the other hand, the commons are usually right, except when they are misled by demagogues. The sovereign and the people working happily together, in a popular monarchy where the feudal barons are kept well under control, fulfill the Tudor ideal of commonwealth. The primary function of the dramatic chronicler is to reinforce such precepts as these by examples—as crudely and naïvely, more often than not, as Peele in his jingoistic *Edward I*. No one would or could have questioned this ethos, but Marlowe shows no special concern to apply it; he is not concerned with the state, but, as always, with the individual, and, in this case, it is a poignant irony that the individual happens to be the head of a state. Where Shakespeare's rulers prefigure Queen Elizabeth in various ways, the court of Edward almost seems to anticipate the absolutism and favoritism of the Stuarts. Thomas Heywood claims, in his *Apology for Actors,* that the whole of English history has been dramatized, from the landing of the legendary Brut up to the day of writing in 1612. Out of that continuous procession, Marlowe's single choice is significant. Other University Wits, if they preceded him in taking up the chronicle history, brought to it techniques he had used in his tragedies: the blank verse, the pageantry, the handling of conquests and conspiracies. His unique contribution was to bring the chronicle within the perspective of tragedy, to adapt the most public of forms to the most private of emotions.

The prologue to *Doctor Faustus,* apologizing for the private nature of the story, casts a backward glance at certain other plays. One is about Carthaginians, though it can hardly be *Dido;* another might well be *Tamburlaine,* aptly summed up in "the pompe of prowd audacious deedes" (5). Still another may be *Edward II,* whose issue is sharply presented when the Chorus speaks of

> sporting in the dalliance of loue,
> In courts of Kings where state is ouerturned.

(3–4)

Love is an unseasonable motive, in the face of political responsibility, as Æneas demonstrated when he abandoned Dido. *"Quam male conueniunt"*—the fragment cited from Ovid in *Edward II* (308) is completed and translated when the effeminate Henry III in *The Massacre at Paris* speaks of "loue and Maiestie" (609). *Amor et maiestas*—how badly they suit each other! The complaint has been softened from Machiavelli's hard-boiled remarks on whether princes ought to be loved or feared. The pride of the Guise is conveyed, in an image of overeating, as a "surfet of ambitious thoughts" (960). The tragic flaw of *Edward II,* as Gaveston conveys it in his opening soliloquy, is to "surfet with delight" (3). Where the Guise exultantly contemplated the prospect of a Roman triumph over Henry III, Gaveston evokes it metaphorically as the measure of his relationship with Edward:

It shall suffice me to enjoy your loue,
Which whiles I haue, I thinke my selfe as great,
As *Cæsar* riding in the Romaine streete,
With captiue kings at his triumphant Carre.

(171–4)

This was an actuality for Tamburlaine, and these last two lines appear to be echoes from both *Edward I* and *Henry VI*. There the procession is taken quite literally, whereas in *Edward II* amorous fulfillment is preferred to military victory. When the future Richard III panegyrizes the sweetness of a crown, in the third part of *Henry VI*, he outdoes Tamburlaine by exclaiming:

How sweet a thing it is to weare a Crowne,
Within whose Circuits is *Elizium*,
And all that Poets faine of Blisse and Ioy.

(I, ii, 29–31)

Tamburlaine made the identical value-judgment, in equating the diadem with bliss and felicity, that Barabas did in evaluating his gold. Somewhat differently, the returning Gaveston salutes London as his Elysium and finds no greater bliss than to bask in the sunshine of royalty, to "liue and be the fauorit of a king"(5). Nemesis manages, when he is executed, to repeat the key-word in his final speech:

O must this day be period of my life!
Center of all my blisse!

(1290–1)

His affinity with the King is reaffirmed, across an eventful interval, when Edward meets his fate:

O day! the last of all my blisse on earth,
Center of all misfortune.

(1928–9)

Edward's admission of defeat it a reversal for all that Marlowe's heroes have represented:

To wretched men death is felicitie.

(2114)

While other playwrights were following Marlowe's lead and dramatizing kingly success, he chose to occupy himself with conspicuous failure. There are no unhappier pages in English history than those which record "the pitiful tragedie of this kings time"—for even Holinshed so described the regime of Edward II. Holinshed sympathized with the baronial party in its internal struggle against the King, and deplored the loss of national prestige that England suffered in its wars with Ireland, Scotland, and France. Marlowe touches upon these very lightly, treats the King much more sympathetically, and centers his dramatization on Edward's relations with his antagonist, Mortimer, and his favorite, Gaveston. Since the latter has to be executed midway through the drama, Marlowe fills in the gap and preserves the dramatic continuity by introducing the two Spencers, as Gaveston's protégés, ten years before their historical models emerged as Edward's favorites. The chronological sequence, which extends from Edward's accession in 1307 to Mortimer's execution in 1330, is concentrated into a time scheme which seems fairly short and consecutive, albeit Edward progresses from youth to old age. Early editions, which yield a more satisfactory text than we have for any of Marlowe's other plays, indicate his emphasis on the title page: *The troublesome raigne and lamentable death of Edward the second, King of England: with the tragicall fall of proud Mortimer.* Edward's reign was a time of troubles, yet his death is to be lamented. His brother, Edmund of Kent, blames "the ruine of the realme" first on Gaveston and later on Edward (1011, 1832). But when Edward is deposed, "the murmuring commons," as Mortimer recognizes, "begins to pitie him" (962, 2334). Mortimer is emphasized, as a more distinctively Marlovian figure, in the octavo of 1594; but the quartos of 1598 and thereafter add another flourish to the subtitle: *And also the life and death of Peirs Gaueston, the great Earle of Cornewall and mighty fauorite of King Edward the second.*

With Gaveston, Marlowe goes beyond Tamburlaine and Barabas in charting a new and dangerous way to rise in the world, to out-Herod monarchs. To charm their affections is to be exposed to the hatred of all their other courtiers, as was the actual Piers Gaveston, the leader of the French party at the court of the Plantagenets. Mortimer voices the attitude of the barons when he scorns "that slie inueigling Frenchman" (264), and what is said about Gaveston's aspirations and extravagances seems to be historically warranted. But Marlowe goes out of his way to make Gaveston a baseborn social climber, a "night growne mushrump" (581), just as he makes parvenus out of the respectable Spencers, in order to humble the pride of their courtly rivals. Gaveston inaugurates the drama by reading aloud the "amorous lines," the welcoming letter of Edward,

> The king, vpon whose bosome let me die,
> And with the world be still at enmitie.

(14–5)

Gaveston's insouciant hostility toward the peers is matched by his cynical contempt for the multitude, which he exhibits next in his encounter with the three poor men. This is not the right chorus for his mounting fortunes, he soliloquizes, as soon as he has dismissed them:

> I must haue wanton Poets, pleasant wits,
> Musitians, that with touching of a string
> May draw the pliant king which way I please:
> Musicke and poetrie is his delight,
> Therefore ile haue Italian maskes by night,
> Sweete speeches, comedies, and pleasing showes,
> And in the day when he shall walke abroad,
> Like *Syluan* Nimphes my pages shall be clad.

(51–8)

Marlowe is here refining on Holinshed's description of Edward "passing his time in voluptuous pleasure, and riotous excesse," corrupted by Gaveston, who "furnished his court with companies of iesters, ruffians, flattering parasites, musicians, and other vile and naughtie ribalds, that the king might spend both daies and nights in iesting, plaieng, blanketing [*sic*], and in such other filthie and dishonorable exercises." Between that medieval brawl and Marlowe's Renaissance pageant, the contrast is brilliantly illuminating. Marlowe's anachronistic Gaveston, in anticipation of such entertainments as the Earl of Leicester gave for Queen Elizabeth at Kenilworth, becomes a lord of misrule, a master of the revels, as well as a stage manager of palace intrigue. The Machiavellian becomes an Epicurean, maintaining his sway through the elusive and disturbing power of the arts. The Marlovian flattery, the speech of esthetic persuasion, is embellished with scenery and choreography; sound and spectacle are bracketed together by the casual couplet that rhymes "night" with "delight." And Gaveston proceeds to imagine a masque which can be taken as a portent, since its hero, Actæon, was hunted down for having gazed on a sight forbidden to men.

Its heroine is sexually ambiguous, a "louelie boye in *Dians* shape" (61), like the epicene pages or—for that matter—the boys who took feminine parts in the Elizabethan theater. The heroine of the play, the Queen neglected by Edward, wishes that her own shape had been changed by Circe (469), while Gaveston himself is compared to *"Proteus* god of shapes" (708). Examples of metamorphosis are frequently adduced, along with such standard mythological prototypes as Phaëthon; and the elder Mortimer evokes a long series of classical precedents to show that heroes and wise men "haue had their minions" (688)—Achilles and Patroclus, Socrates and Alcibiades, and other names still cited by apologists. Comparisons of Gaveston to Ganymede, and to Leander as well, link *Edward II* with *Dido* on the one hand and with *Hero and Leander* on the other. But the most suggestive comparison looks back to Tamburlaine's lament for Zenocrate and ahead to Faustus' vision of Helen of Troy, when Lancaster addresses Gaveston as

> Monster of men,
> That like the Greekish strumpet traind to armes
> And bloudie warres, so many valiant knights.

(1182–4)

The epithet most commonly applied to Gaveston, "minion," is ety-
mologically the French term of endearment, *mignon,* which now begins
to acquire pejorative overtones. Though it is sounded only nine times, it
charges the atmosphere, just as "policy" does in *The Jew of Malta.* The
King, says Mortimer, "is loue-sick for his minion" (382). As the Queen
says, "his minde runs on his minion" (806). And again, and always:

> Harke how he harpes vpon his minion.

(608)

His obsession is carefully underlined by the repetition of the proper name,
"Gaveston." The very word is like a charm, like "Tamburlaine" and
"Barabas" in their different ways; and all three are alike in being
amphimacers, which fit so effectively into Marlovian verse: "Bajazeth,"
"Abigall," "Mortimer." Beginning with the first line, and largely confined
to the first half of the play, "Gaveston" is sounded 110 times, fifty-six
times at the end of a line. Thus Edward, posing the absolute alternative,
will "eyther die, or liue with *Gaueston*" (138). He is perfectly willing to
divide his kingdom among his nobles,

> So I may haue some nooke or corner left,
> To frolike with my deerest Gaueston.

(367–8)

It is the old story, so often renewed by life and repeated by drama, of
neglecting one's duty to realize one's individuality: *All for Love, or the
World Well Lost.* By dwelling upon the emotional conflict between
majesty and love, Marlowe resolves the technical conflict between the
claims of history and of tragedy. Edward's infatuation, though it impels
him in the opposite direction, is just as extreme as Tamburlaine's domina-
tion or Barabas' cunning. His irresponsibility is rendered peculiarly
flagrant by the unsanctioned nature of his indulgences. It cannot pass
without comment that this, the most wholehearted treatment of love in
any of Marlowe's plays, involves the erotic attachment of man to man.
Friendship, as classically illustrated by Richard Edwardes' tragicomedy
of *Damon and Pythias,* was a major Elizabethan theme; but to glance
no farther than Shakespeare's sonnets, the ardor with which both sexes
are celebrated is such as to elude academic distinctions between the
sensual and the Platonic. Gaveston is more and less than a friend to
Edward, who devotes to him an overt warmth which Marlowe never
displays toward the female sex. The invitation to love, "Come live with

me," the mode of enticement so richly elaborated in Gaveston's monologue on music and poetry, soon found its echo in Richard Barnfield's amorous appeal of a swain to a youth, *The Affectionate Shepherd,* thereby joining a literary tradition of homoeroticism which can be traced through Vergil's second Eclogue to the Greek bucolic poets. To ignore the presence or to minimize the impact of such motivation in *Edward II,* as most of its critics discreetly tend to do, is to distort the meaning of the play. According to the testimony of Kyd, Marlowe dared to suspect "an extraordinary loue" between Saint John and Jesus—even comparing them, according to Baines, with "the sinners of Sodoma." It seems unlikely, when the chronicles hinted at such a scandal as he had read into the Gospels, that Marlowe should have looked the other way.

In Michael Drayton's *Legend of Piers Gaveston,* the monologuist adapts a familiar Marlovian symbol to characterize his relationship with the King:

> I waxt his winges, and taught him art to flye,
> Who on his back might beare me through the skye.

(281–2)

When the "mounting thoughts" (879) of Marlowe's Gaveston are blocked by the opposition, there is a residue of genuine pathos in his response to Edward's commiseration:

> Tis something to be pitied of a king.

(426)

Their dalliance, which could be profitable to Gaveston, can only be harmful to Edward, who is the lone disinterested character; or rather, as a lover, he projects his innate egoism into a second self which transcends the rest of the world. Pliant to the caprices of his flattering favorite, "the brainsick king" (125) is petulant with his "head-strong Barons" (1065), vainly commanding and pleading by turns, a spoiled child now cajoling and now capitulating. "Ile haue my will" (78), he declares on his first entrance, and a moment later: "I will haue *Gaueston*" (96). But Mortimer and the other nobles, taking their stand upon an absolute alternative, decide to be resolute,

> And either haue our wils, or lose our liues.

(341)

In the ensuing battle of wills, Edward is predestined to be "ouerrulde" by his "ouerdaring peeres" (333, 342):

> The Barons ouerbeare me with their pride.

(1315)

Every other speech of the King's is an order, which is generally flouted and countermanded, while the Mortimers issue orders of their own. When Edward decrees of the younger,

> Lay thy hands on that traitor *Mortimer,*

(315)

the elder Mortimer treasonably retorts,

> Lay hands on that traitor *Gaueston.*

(316)

Edward has the regal habit of likening himself, or being likened, to the king of beasts; he is a lion, not to be intimidated by the crowing of "these cockerels" (1005). Yet, after he has fallen, he is a wren, striving against "the Lions strength" of Mortimer (2299)—or, more appropriately, "a lambe, encompassed by Woolues" (2027). It is perversely characteristic of him that he reads his destiny in the emblems of eagles and flying fish, the heraldic devices of temporary reconciliation that Mortimer and Lancaster bear to his "generall tilt and turnament" (673).

Edward is good at such charades, his enemies concede, at "idle triumphes, maskes, lasciuious showes" (959). Mortimer understands him as well as Gaveston does, and Mortimer's reproach is as pertinent as Gaveston's artistic plan of campaign:

> When wert thou in the field with banner spread?
> But once, and then thy souldiers marcht like players,
> With garish robes, not armor.

(984–6)

For Edward is not a soldier or a commander, he is an esthete and a voluptuary. Glorified by masques or defamed by ballads, he is a king with the soul of an actor, where Tamburlaine was more like an actor in the role of a king. Rhetoric and pageantry existed on the surface in *Tamburlaine,* objective and unreal; but in *Edward II* they are of the essence, subjective and real. Here the theatricality is not conventional but psychological, conceived as a trait of Edward's character. No longer is it taken for granted that words and deeds must coincide; on the contrary, his chronic fault is his inability to substantiate his vaunts. He is steeled by the news of Gaveston's death to make the one vow that he is able to execute. Then, when the parasite is avenged at Boroughbridge, Edward must stage a triumphal ceremony in his memory and in honor of newer favorites:

> Thus after many threats of wrathfull warre,
> Triumpheth Englands *Edward* with his friends,
> And triumph *Edward* with his friends vncontrould.

(1695–7)

But his triumph, like the Guise's, is short-lived, and shortly he has reason to complain that he is "contrould" by the Queen and Mortimer (2015). When his infelicitous crown is demanded, he prays that it be transmuted into "a blaze of quenchelesse fier" (2030). Then, in accordance with the stage direction, *"The king rageth."* In his eagerness before the battle, he invoked the sun, with an invocation that Juliet would use at a happier juncture: "Gallop a pace" (1738). His vain command, on the point of abdication, is for the elements to stand still. Now he feels, as Gaveston did when banished, "a hell of greefe" (412, 2538). But, just as Gaveston nonchalantly surrendered with the maxim that "death is all" (1199), so Edward asserts in yielding that "death ends all" (2140). That is a pagan sentiment which sorts, at all events, with his prayer to "immortal *Ioue*." In the dark and muddy dungeon where he encounters his end, he prays the most ironic penalties for the frolicking prodigality of his kingship. Tortured physically and mentally, humiliated by the loss of his beard, shaved and washed in puddle water, he rises to a sense of his tragic role with his remembrance of a forgotten victory:

> Tell *Isabell* the Queene, I lookt not thus,
> When for her sake I ran at tilt in Fraunce,
> And there vnhorste the duke of *Cleremont*.

(2516–8)

It is a far cry of triumph, more theatrical than chivalric; but Shakespeare must have borne it in mind when Othello, on the verge of suicide, remembered his victory over the Turk at Aleppo. The striking feature of Edward's catastrophe is the total absence of anything spectacular. After all the talk about pageants, the tourneys and processions, they seem to have completely melted away. We are left with a bare stage which pretends to be nothing more, and with a hero stripped of any claim to distinction except his suffering.

> Hence fained weeds, vnfained are my woes.

(1964)

Edward, on his imaginative flights, is the heir of Marlowe's earlier and more exotic heroes.

> Ere my sweete *Gaueston* shall part from me,
> This Ile shall fleete vpon the Ocean,
> And wander to the vnfrequented Inde.

(343–5)

Such is his vaunt, at least, but harsh reality tests and deflates the gorgeous hyperbole. The state rests secure, the island remains terra firma, while Gaveston is whirled away by the currents of lawless dalliance. And

Edward's recognition of his own powerlessness, hyperbolic though it sounds, is quite literal:

> Ah *Spencer,* not the riches of my realme
> Can ransome him, ah he is markt to die.

(1309–10)

The style of the play, toned down to accord with its subject matter, has its pedestrian stretches as well as its minor harmonies. Numerous commas indicate varying pauses, as well as improvement upon the other texts in punctuation, and lines run over more limpidly than before. The dialogue makes flexible use of short speeches, sharp interchanges, and subdivided lines; yet, in the later scenes particularly, it crystallizes again into monologues, soliloquies, and set pieces. Marlovian allusion sounds out of place when—to cite an anticlimactic example—the Queen, setting out for Hainault in near-by Belgium, avows her willingness to travel as far as the Don,

> euen to the vtmost verge
> Of *Europe,* or the shore of *Tanaise.*

(1640–1)

The blare of Marlowe's nomenclature is subdued when his characters' names are domesticated, and the verse halts when the Earl of Lancaster boasts of his four other earldoms,

> Darbie, Salsburie, Lincolne, Leicester.

(103)

Gaveston mocks at those titles in a subsequent scene which comprises a single speech, five lines of ironic exposition while he is crossing the stage with the Earl of Kent. Such is Marlowe's technical self-consciousness that, when the Queen breaks down in the midst of a formal utterance, she is interrupted by Mortimer:

> Nay madam, if you be a warriar
> Ye must not grow so passionate in speeches.

(1762–3)

The Queen's rhetorical abilities are put to an even severer test when Edward forces her to plead for the repeal of her rival's banishment. The usual plea is reversed, and persuasion gives way to dissuasion, when she dissuades Mortimer and he dissuades the barons from standing by their resolve. He complies out of love for her, while she has complied out of love for her husband; and Gaveston, the object of her husband's love, completes the unnatural quadrangle of compliance by virtually driving her into Mortimer's arms. Meanwhile Edward, reconciled with her, ironically accepts the situation as "a second mariage" (632).

Isabell, his queen, is a split personality. Though she does not live up to the accusation of being "subtill" (1581), it would be unfair to assume that characterization of women had as yet been developed to any degree of subtlety. She is more alive, at any rate, than the corpse of Zenocrate or the wraith of Helen. The theater was still a man's world; its heroines, as played by boys, were not unnaturally somewhat androgynous; they could behave without effort like shrews or viragoes or the proverbial Hyrcanian tigresses. Somewhat more feminine, though awkwardly depicted, was the saintly, long-suffering type of the patient Griselda, like the women so consistently neglected by the men in the plays of Robert Greene. Isabell enacts both types with manic-depressive inconsistency. She is pathetically devoted to Edward when, prompted by Gaveston, he repels her as a "French strumpet" (441). Subsequently, it is he who talks of "outragious passions" and denounces her as "vnnatural" (2003). But the interim, and the downfall of her rival, have changed the forlorn wife into the scheming adulteress; and the transition is abruptly made in two brief soliloquies, which stand no more than a page or a scene apart. Despite the modifications that have been effected in order to give the drama a semblance of unity, the elaborate construction that differentiates it from all the others, there is still a break in the middle of *Edward II,* a watershed which divides our sympathies. Up to that point, Edward's follies alienate us, and afterward his trials win us back; while Isabell, who starts by being ungallantly abused, ends by justifying his antipathy. Amid these bewildering shifts of the moral winds, Kent is a sort of weathervane whose turnings veer with the rectitude of the situation, not unlike his namesake in *King Lear*—or possibly a Shakespearean *raisonneur* like John of Gaunt or Humphrey, the good Duke of Gloucester.

Our impression of Mortimer, too, is jeopardized by the same discontinuity that splits the characters of Edward and Isabell. Originally, when the King is so unreasonable, Mortimer seems not merely reasonable but exceptionally downright and hearty, the very antithesis of the intriguing courtier. One of the play's most observant commentators, W. D. Briggs, has even observed in him a model for Hotspur. In that respect he is the natural spokesman for Gaveston's enemies, ultimately becoming a foil for Edward himself, and maintaining a hold upon Isabell that parallels Gaveston's ascendancy over the King. But, as the play moves from open hostilities to more devious conspirations, Mortimer becomes increasingly Machiavellian and thus more characteristically Marlovian. Whereas Edward and Gaveston cling to each other, he stands—and falls—by himself. When Edward, "Englands scourge" (1567), defeats the barons, and Mortimer is taken prisoner, the latter asks himself:

> What *Mortimer?* can ragged stonie walles
> Immure thy vertue that aspires to heauen?

(1565–6)

Soon enough he "surmounts his fortune" and makes his escape from the Tower of London; before long he has dethroned the King and become the Lord Protector. In his quickly accumulating *hubris,* quoting a verse from Ovid, he declares that greatness has placed him beyond the reach of fortune; in Senecan terms, he is the Olympian oak, to whom all others are but humble shrubs: yet the shrub is safer than the lofty tree from the whirlwind. He exults, as Tamburlaine did, that he can make "Fortunes wheele turne as he please" (2197). But his own death, compressing three years of history into a crowded final scene, is the immediate consequence of Edward's. Young Edward, having succeeded his late father as King, at once denounces Mortimer as "Villaine" (2593). Mortimer's acceptance of the fatal decree is a belated recognition that his strivings do not exempt him from the common lot:

> Base fortune, now I see, that in thy wheele
> There is a point, to which when men aspire,
> They tumble hedlong downe: that point I touchte,
> And seeing there was no place to mount vp higher,
> Why should I greeue at my declining fall?

(2627–31)

Mortimer has viewed himself, in his heyday, rather as Fortune's successful foe than as her erstwhile favorite. With her triumph and his decline, he still may depend on his virtue; but virtue, at this point, devolves from Machiavelli's conception back to Seneca's. The individual, in a narrowing world, has less room to act and more occasion to suffer. The ethical criterion is the stoical resignation with which he meets inevitable and overwhelming odds. Where Barabas died cursing, Mortimer's last lines are profoundly meditative. In the seriocomic realm of *The Jew of Malta,* sin could be temporarily dismissed as something that happened in another country. Tragedy, however, must face consequences. Mortimer faces them with curiosity as well as fortitude, readily dismissing the limited sphere of his worldly activities and welcoming death as a further adventure, an Elizabethan voyage of exploration:

> Farewell faire Queene, weepe not for *Mortimer,*
> That scornes the world, and as a traueller,
> Goes to discouer countries yet vnknowne.

(2632–4)

Not Hotspur but Hamlet is adumbrated by Mortimer, when he sets out toward that undiscovered country from whose bourne no traveler returns. His augmented stature, outshadowing the other characters, largely determines the after-effect of the play. Ben Jonson apparently thought of expanding Marlowe's denouement into a neoclassical tragedy, *The Fall of Mortimer;* and though he left no more than a page or two, it constitutes another link between his work and Marlowe's, and projects a course for the hero-villains of Jonson's two completed tragedies. Michael Drayton was so impressed by Mortimer, "that some-what more then Man" (147), that he cast him as hero in his epic of Edward's reign, *The Barons' Wars,* which in its early version was entitled *Mortimeriados.* In addition to chanting—as Lucan had done—"a farre worse, then Civill Warre" (8), Drayton poetized the romance between Isabell and Mortimer with a pair of his Ovidian *Epistles.* It is noteworthy that Bertolt Brecht, in adapting *Edward II* to the modern German stage, vulgarizes Gaveston, whose music and poetry are reduced to drinking ale and playing whist, while refining and rationalizing Mortimer into a classical scholar turned politician. Marlowe may offer a cue for that interpretation in the soliloquy where Mortimer cites Ovid, and looks upon the Prince with the furrowed brow of a pedantic schoolmaster. Somewhere, conceivably during his short imprisonment in the Tower, Mortimer has picked up his sudden flair for disguises, equivocating letters, and the other ruses of Machiavellianism: his sentence of death for Edward has its counterpart in Ferdinand's condemnation of Antonio in *The Duchess of Malfi.* Edward, hesitating to commit Mortimer, acknowledged that "the people loue him well" (1036). Mortimer, in his Machiavellian phase, acknowledges: "Feard am I more than lou'd" (2383). The sinister aspect of his character is shadowed in the accomplice he chooses for Edward's assassination. The assassin, Lightborne, naïvely and proudly boasting of his Italianate poisons and more ingenious professional tricks, is to Mortimer what the slave Ithamore was to Barabas. And Lightborne's name reveals the cloven hoof; for it had also belonged to one of the devils in the Chester cycle, and is neither more nor less than an Anglicization of "Lucifer."

In his grimly diabolical banter with Mortimer, Lightborne undertakes to murder the King by "a brauer way" than any of the tortures he has enumerated (2369). The horrendous details are decently obscured, both in the dialogue and in the business; but legend was painfully explicit in specifying how a red-hot spit had been plunged into Edward's intestines. The sight of the instrument would have been enough to raise an excruciating shudder in the audience; and subtler minds may have perceived, as does William Empson, an ironic parody of Edward's vice. It is when he beholds the frown of Lightborne that Edward knows the worst:

> I see my tragedie written in thy browes.

> (2522)

So, in the next scene, Isabell tells Mortimer: "Now . . . begins our tragedie"

(2591). Edward's tragical history, like Tamburlaine's, is compounded of many tragedies. That of the Mortimers stood out among the stock narratives of unlucky statesmanship in the *Mirror for Magistrates*. Marlowe's Edward self-consciously catches the exemplary tone of that compilation:

> Stately and proud, in riches and in traine,
> Whilom I was powerfull and full of pompe,
> But what is he, whome rule and emperie
> Haue not in life or death made miserable?

(1879–82)

The Earl of Leicester, in arresting him, garbs the humiliation in borrowed garments of Roman sententiousness:

> *Quem dies vidit veniens superbum,*
> *Hunc dies vidit fugiens iacentem*

(1920–1)

This was Seneca's formula for Thyestes, yet it applies to all tragic vicissitudes. Thus Jonson translates it, at the conclusion of *Sejanus:*

> For, whom the morning saw so great, and high,
> Thus low, and little, 'fore the 'euen doth lie.

(V, 902–3)

Classical or medieval, the peripety is the same, the overturn from grandeur to misery. Edward, the slave of passion, diverges from the man of action, Tamburlaine, by suddenly moving away from the grandeurs of morning and lingering over the miseries of night. Should we conclude that Marlowe was moving back toward a more traditional concept of tragedy? "All liue to die," as Edward tells Spencer, "and rise to fall" (1979). All are corrupted by life, except for his son—who survives to exhibit, in Heywood's *Edward III*, the manly qualities his father has lacked. Marlowe's boyish Edward III, with the innocent wisdom of the stage-child, proclaims in three last words his "greefe and innocencie" (2670). Yet the process of corruption, as Marlowe implied in *The Jew of Malta*, has been a kind of experience purchased with grief and repaid by an awareness of the difference of things. The relative maturity of *Edward II* seems to mark some progression from innocence into experience. Lightborne's spit is an unspeakable counterpart for the scourge of the Scythian conqueror; and the moral advantage of masochism over sadism is, to say the least, a delicate question. But it marks a psychological advance, from terror to pity, when the protagonist experiences genuine agony; while, in philosophical terms, it replaces the values of Epicureanism with those of Stoicism.

Resignation is not the attitude that we intrinsically associate with Marlowe. The frailty of the body, the fallibility of the mind, and the transience of human glory come as highly reluctant admissions in his other tragedies. *Edward II* would prove, if it proved no more, Marlowe's ability to challenge his own assumptions. To see him reverse himself, to see his idiosyncrasies stamped upon a conventional formula, to see for once the would-be tyrant tyrannized over, is more than we might have expected.

> But what are kings, when regiment is gone,
> But perfect shadowes in a sun-shine day?

> (2012–3)

Shakespeare could hardly push that line of inquiry much farther. "The reluctant pangs of abdicating Royalty," Charles Lamb would argue, are often as poignantly rendered in *Edward II* as in *Richard II;* and Edward's death scene was as moving, to Lamb, as anything in ancient or modern drama. Shakespeare could balance his tragedy by handling the counter-claims of the opponents more sympathetically, envisioning the whole as a problem in statecraft, where Marlowe saw little save individual rivalries. Richard's mistakes are due to lack of judgment, where Edward's are attributable to will; and in his willfulness he knows his mind, as Richard in his vacillation does not. The inconsistencies of the latter, his frivolity and his dignity, are more consistently portrayed; yet it is the former whose maladjustment seems more fundamental and whose suffering seems more intense. Richard's death, unlike his life, is an imitation of Christ, a passion play in which an earthly crown is superseded by a crown of thorns. Yet Shakespeare seems to be universalizing the plight that Marlowe had discerned and isolated; and Shakespeare's king is illuminated, like a gilded page from a medieval manuscript, by such lyrical trappings and masquerading embellishments as Marlowe had devised. Richard, descending symbolically into the base court, visualizes himself as Phaëthon. He plays his climactic scene, the deposition, even more histrionically than his predecessor. When he dashes the looking-glass to the floor, his gesture is a farewell to the *Mirror for Magistrates.* The reflection that has been conveyed to him is a reverberation, not from *Edward II,* but from *Doctor Faustus:*

> Was this Face, the Face,
> That euery day, vnder his House-hold Roofe,
> Did keepe ten thousand men?

> (IV, i, 281–3)

When Marlowe's Edward finds brief sanctuary in the Abbey of Neath, for a fleeting moment of serenity he feels that he may have missed his real vocation, that he might better have lived in philosophical retreat, and that "this life contemplatiue is heauen" (1887). He exhorts his companions, and especially Baldock, to console themselves with Plato and

Aristotle, counselors whom they have all too cynically laid aside for careers of action. The minor character Baldock, "that smoothe toongd scholler" (1845) who has urged the King not to behave like a schoolboy, is the representative of *libido sciendi* in this play, in so far as Edward and Mortimer represent *libido sentiendi* and *libido dominandi*. Baldock's gentry, as he puts it, derives "from Oxford, not from Heraldrie" (1046). Thence he has brought "a speciall gift to forme a verbe" (775)—the talent for putting words together, in Quintilian's phrase—and now he would like "to court it like a Gentleman" (752). Having graduated into the world as the tutor of Gaveston's future countess, he is prepared, when we meet him, to join the Spencers in their campaign for Edward's patronage. The elder Spencer, advising him to "cast the scholler off" along with his curate-like attire, reads him a Machiavellian lecture on worldly wisdom:

> You must be proud, bold, pleasant, resolute,
> And now and then, stab as occasion serues.

> (762–3)

Interesting advice which a young Cambridge scholar, smooth-tongued and gifted at forming verbs, would take at his everlasting peril. Though prophecy doubtless went beyond Marlowe's intention, he may have deliberately added one or two strokes of self-caricature to this University Wit who comes to grief among the intrigues and politics of court. Since the historical Sir Robert Baldock had been Edward's Lord Chancellor, a man of affairs whose origin was by no means obscure and whose background was not specially academic, Marlowe must have gone out of his way to manifest the wry preoccupation he shared with Nashe and Greene and the other masters of arts who had rashly decided to practice the dubious trade of literature in the wicked city of London. It is as if a painter, half in earnest and half in jest, had painted himself in the corner of some panoramic canvas.

See *Edward II* bibliography (p. 169) and other studies in Marlowe bibliography (p. 170).

MARLOWE'S *EDWARD II*
AND THE TUDOR HISTORY PLAY *

Irving Ribner

IN a recent essay I have proposed as a definition of the Tudor history play that its primary distinction as a dramatic genre lay in the purpose of its author: that the history play attempted to accomplish in drama the purposes of the Tudor historian. It embodied a conscious philosophy of history. It used the past as documentation for political theory and for the light which it might throw upon contemporary political problems and thus serve as a guide for present political behavior. In doing this it freely altered its sources, for the didactic utility of history was considered by Renaissance historians to be far more important than any intrinsic claim it might have to truth. I have further suggested that current critical distinctions between history and tragedy as dramatic genres are meaningless and unnecessary, for the Elizabethans themselves made no distinction between them, and there is no necessary conflict between the two. We may regard tragedy as merely one dramatic type in which a dramatist may further historical purposes.[1]

I should like now to measure against this definition Christopher Marlowe's *Edward II,* written almost certainly in late 1591 or 1592.[2] I choose this play for several reasons. To begin with, it is the drama with which the Elizabethan history play attains maturity and some degree of aesthetic greatness. Critics have generally recognized its superiority as a work of art to any of the history plays which preceded it, but they have tended to consider it apart from the main stream of historical drama. Writers like Harry Levin, for instance, have held that although Marlowe took his matter from history, "he is not concerned with the state but, as always, with the individual; and, in this case, it is a poignant irony that the individual happens to be the head of a state."[3] Marlowe's play has

* From *ELH: A Journal of English Literary History*, Vol. 22, 1955, pp. 243–253. Reprinted by permission of the Johns Hopkins Press.

1 "The Tudor History Play: An Essay in Definition," *PMLA,* LXIX (1954), 591–609.

2 H. B. Charlton and R. D. Waller, eds., *Edward II* (London, 1933), p. 20.

3 *The Overreacher* (Cambridge, Mass., 1952), p. 88. [Cf. this volume, p. 143—ED.]

an immediate bearing upon the problem of the relation of history to tragedy in the English Renaissance both because it is our first important tragedy based upon the chronicles and because it heralded in a new type of historical tragedy from which Shakespeare learned vital lessons to be applied in *Richard II*. In it we have a conscious and deliberate molding of chronicle matter into the shape of tragedy, but I believe that at the same time the identity of the work as a history play is in no way destroyed. I should like to demonstrate that *Edward II*, while achieving the dimensions of tragedy, accomplishes also the purposes of the Elizabethan historian.

In Marlowe's *Edward II* we have, perhaps for the first time in Elizabethan drama, a mature tragedy of character in which a potentially good man comes to destruction because of inherent weaknesses which make him incapable of coping with a crisis which he himself has helped to create. And in his downfall he is able to win the sympathy of an audience already hostile to him because of his behavior before the beginning of his fall. Like the traditional tragic hero, he is a king, and his downfall is thus intimately involved with the life of the state; but in this instance Marlowe gives us a king drawn from the English chronicles, and in effecting his tragedy he accomplishes also the purposes of the Elizabethan historian. He interprets an earlier political situation which was of particular interest to Elizabethans, as we can tell from the many treatments of it in prose and verse, for it mirrored the type of civil war they most dreaded, and which many feared might return should Elizabeth fail to heed the lessons implicit in the reigns of earlier monarchs. In *Edward II* the sins of the hero are sins of government; the crisis he faces is a political one, and his disaster is also ruin to his kingdom in the form of civil war.

Marlowe's play covers a long and involved period of history, from the accession of Edward II in 1307 to the execution of Roger Mortimer in 1330. For almost all of his material he went to Holinshed, but he also consulted Stow, from whom he took the episode of the shaving of Edward in puddle water, and he must have read Fabyan, from whom he took the jig on England's disgrace at Bannockburn which is quoted by the Earl of Lancaster.[4] He thus had read in at least several places accounts of a highly varied period in English history. The quantity of incident and conflict in his sources was enormous. Marlowe approached this vast storehouse of material with a sure awareness of his purposes and perhaps a keener dramatic skill than had ever before been exercised in the history play, for he selected out of this great mass of data only what he needed for a well integrated tragedy. He omitted most of Edward's long and involved relations with the barons, his wars in France and Scotland, with the disastrous defeat at Bannockburn. He condensed the events of

---

[4] ll. 992–997. I use *The Works of Christopher Marlowe*, ed. C. F. Tucker Brooke (Oxford, 1910).

almost thirty years into what appears to be about one year, although the play gives us little real indication of the passage of time. The resulting inconsistencies and chronological errors are too numerous to list, but all of Marlowe's manipulation of his sources serves the functions of his play, and there is very little invented matter, his only significant addition to the chronicles being in Edward's refusal to ransom old Mortimer, an invention which apparently afforded some suggestion to Shakespeare in I *Henry IV*. By this compression and rearrangement of his sources, Marlowe achieved an economy and effectiveness which had not before been seen in the history play.[5]

Marlowe had long been concerned with the meaning of history, and as one of the most thoughtful dramatists of his age, it is almost inconceivable that he should not have been. In his *Tamburlaine,* written some years before, he had already expressed a deliberate philosophy of history. In another paper I have argued that this philosophy was largely classical in origin. It incorporated the substantialist metaphysics of classical history which rendered impossible any evolution or change in human character, and it saw the events of history, in the manner of classical humanism, as the products of human agents operating independently of any supernatural control or guidance.[6] Marlowe's ideas about history, however, appear to have undergone some development between the two plays. The classical substantialism of *Tamburlaine,* with its theme of the expansion of an initially complete and fully established force, and with its resulting fixity of character, is now gone, and we find instead characters who change and develop under the pressure of events. This is as true of Mortimer and Isabell as it is of Edward: the ruthless schemer and the adulterous wife of the final acts are hardly recognizable from the loyal Englishman and the long suffering queen of the play's beginning. If the change seems overly sudden and inadequately prepared for, we must remember that the English drama had not yet developed great subtlety in the art of characterization. The tragedy of Edward would have been impossible within the substantialist framework of *Tamburlaine,* and only by abandoning it was Marlowe able to attain the stature of tragedy. As Mortimer and Isabell steadily degenerate, Edward matures and develops under the pressure of disaster, and his brother, Edmund, serves as a kind of chorus to guide the shifting sympathies of the audience as the king's character develops.

In its larger aspects the humanism of *Tamburlaine,* however, persists in *Edward II.* Marlowe sees the events of history not as the working out

5 See Tucker Brooke, *The Tudor Drama* (Boston, 1911), p. 323; W. D. Briggs, ed., *Marlowe's Edward II* (London, 1914), pp. cviii–cix.

6 "The Idea of History in Marlowe's *Tamburlaine*," *ELH,* **XX** (1953), 251–266. For discussion of humanism and substantialism as two cardinal elements of classical history, see R. G. Collingwood, *The Idea of History* (Oxford, 1946), pp. 40–45.

in human affairs of a divine providence, but rather as the products of human strength and will which shape worldly events independently of any supernatural power. This humanistic attitude—characteristic both of the classical and the Italian Renaissance historians—is not so strongly emphasized in this play at it is in *Tamburlaine,* and it is tempered by a kind of pessimistic fatalism which is wholly absent from the earlier play. This is most evident in Mortimer's final speech:

> Base fortune, now I see, that in thy wheele
> There is a point, to which when men aspire,
> They tumble hedlong downe: that point I touchte,
> And seeing there was no place to mount vp higher,
> Why should I greeue at my declining fall?

(2627–2631)

There is nothing here of the Christian attitude which would emphasize man's fall as divine retribution for his sins, merely a calm acceptance of the inevitable destruction at the hands of fate of all who aspire beyond a certain point. What we have here is a stoical acceptance of fortune in the manner of classical historians such as Polybius.[7]

It is in this pessimism that the view of history to which Marlowe came in *Edward II* differs further from that in *Tamburlaine,* where there are no limits to what the ever-triumphant superman may attain, and ruthless self-sufficiency alone may create empires. The flamboyant optimism of his early play is now replaced by a more tragic view of life, perhaps most evident in the decline of Mortimer. For as he achieves success his character steadily degenerates. His initial concern for England soon becomes a concern only for his own aggrandizement, and there is no baseness to which he will not resort for his own advancement. When he is cut off by fortune, he has lost all sympathy which the audience may have had for him at first. Marlowe incorporates into *Edward II* the ancient *de casibus* theme of rise and fall, which Shakespeare had used before him in the *Henry VI* plays. The play becomes a series of successive waves, with Mortimer rising as Edward II falls, and the young Edward III rising again as Mortimer declines.[8] Marlowe's abandonment of substantialist fixity of character and his tempering of his humanism with this fatalistic perspective account for much of the difference in tone between *Tamburlaine* and *Edward II,* and they make possible a tragedy which was not possible before.

The tragedy of Mortimer, moreover, indicates some departure from the Machiavellian philosophy which Marlowe had embodied in *Tambur-*

---

[7] See M. L. W. Laistner, *The Greater Roman Historians* (Berkeley, 1947), p. 19.

[8] See R. Fricker, "The Dramatic Structure of *Edward II*," *English Studies,* **XXXIV** (1953), 204–217.

laine.[9] Mortimer is an embodiment of Machiavellian self-sufficiency, strength, and aspiring will, but he nevertheless degenerates and is destroyed, and it is because of his lack of private virtue that he does so. Marlowe fashioned Edward and Mortimer as parallel characters, each serving as foil to the other. All of Edward's lack of public virtue is mirrored in Mortimer's supreme possession of it, and similarly what private virtue Edward possesses is mirrored in Mortimer's utter lack of it. Just as a deficiency of public virtue destroys Edward, a deficiency of the private destroys Mortimer. It is in this portrayal of the impossibility of the divorce of public from private virtue that Marlowe departs chiefly from the Machiavellianism he had espoused in *Tamburlaine*. In short, although Machiavelli's humanistic, nonprovidential view of history is still in *Edward II*, Marlowe's enthusiasm for the Machiavellian superman is considerably diminished. He has come to see the moving spirits of history not as prototypes of an impossible ideal, but as men who are molded themselves by the pressure of events, who develop and change. He has come to recognize that to rule well in the secular absolutist state, the Machiavellian brand of *virtù* alone will not suffice. Combined with it must be a private humanity.

E. M. W. Tillyard has commented that there is in *Edward II* "no sense of any sweep or pattern of history," such as we find in Shakespeare's history plays,[10] and F. P. Wilson has made essentially the same observation.[11] This is so simply because Marlowe, unlike Shakespeare, does not see in history the working out of any divine providence, and therefore he cannot see in it any large scheme encompassing God's plans for men and extending over many decades, with the sins of usurping kings and treacherous nobles being visited upon their descendants to the third generation. Marlowe sees history entirely as the actions of men who bring about their triumph or destruction entirely by their own ability to cope with events, and without reference to the vices or virtues of their ancestors. This is the humanistic attitude of classical and of Italian humanist history, and if it is not proclaimed in *Edward II* so loudly and flamboyantly as it is in *Tamburlaine*, it is nevertheless present.

Tillyard has called the political doctrine in *Edward II* impeccably orthodox.[12] But if this were so, it would be indeed strange to note, as Alfred Hart has done,[13] that there is in the play not a single reference to the divine right of kings. Nor is there any mention of a king's responsibility

---

9 See Irving Ribner, "Marlowe and Machiavelli," *Comparative Literature*, VI (1954), 349–356.

10 *Shakespeare's History Plays* (New York, 1947), pp. 108–109.

11 *Marlowe and the Early Shakespeare* (Oxford, 1953), p. 125.

12 *Shakespeare's History Plays*, pp. 107–108.

13 *Shakespeare and the Homilies* (Melbourne, 1943), p. 25.

to God, a cornerstone of orthodox Elizabethan doctrine. The truth is that the theory of sovereignty underlying *Edward II* is the same as that of *Tamburlaine,* in which the unquestioned absolutism of the king is based not upon divine appointment but upon human power, and in which the king is not controlled by any responsibility to a God who will destroy him if he neglects his duties to his people, but only the limits of the king's own ability to maintain his power in spite of any opposition.[14] This calls for the Machiavellian superman like Tamburlaine, and perhaps something more as the tragedy of Mortimer may indicate. The tragedy of Edward is that he is born into a position where he must be such a superman in order to survive; he attempts to be one, but since he can not, he is doomed to destruction. Michel Poirier has summed up the play's content very neatly: "It is the story of a feudal monarch who attempts to govern as an absolute monarch and fails."[15] But we must note that it is not in the divinely sanctioned absolutism of Elizabeth and her ecclesiastical political theorists that he attempts to rule, but rather in the powerful secular autocracy of Italian Renaissance political theory, in which the king is self-sufficient and acknowledges no supernatural master. In his failure to maintain his position in such a state Edward loses all of the appurtenances of kingship, as he himself affirms:

> But what are kings, when regiment is gone,
> But perfect shadowes in a sun-shine day?

(2012–2013)

The play thus embodies both a philosophy of history and a distinctive theory of political sovereignty, in each case considerably removed form the norm of Elizabethan orthodoxy. Marlowe further accomplishes the political purposes of the Elizabethan historian in the very tragedy of Edward II, for in his downfall Marlowe delineates the qualities which will bring a king to ruin in the absolutist state. Some of Edward's shortcomings had already been indicated by Holinshed:

> ...he wanted iudgement and prudent discretion to make choise of sage and discreet councellors, receiuing those into his fauour, that abused the same to their priuate advauntage, not respecting the aduancement of the commonwealth.[16]

It was the "couetous rapine, spoile and immoderate ambition" of these favorites which alienated the nobles and caused them to rise up against their king. Marlowe thus warns that a king must be prudent in his choice

---

[14] See Paul H. Kocher, *Christopher Marlowe: A Study of his Thought, Learning and Character* (Chapel Hill, 1946), p. 189; Irving Ribner, "*Tamburlaine* and *The Wars of Cyrus,*" *JEGP*, LIII (1954), 569–573.

[15] *Christopher Marlowe* (London, 1951), p. 173.

[16] *Chronicles* (London, 1587), III, 327.

of counsellors. He must further be strong, able to control his nobles, cut off those who oppose him, which Edward manifestly can not do. But a successful king does not alienate his nobles in the first place, for they are an important bulwark of his power. At Edward's brief reconciliation with the barons, Queen Isabell directs an important bit of didacticism to the audience:

> Nowe is the king of England riche and strong,
> Hauing the loue of his renowned peers.

> (663–664)

This theme of a king's relation to his nobles is one of the principal political themes in *Edward II*.

Edward would be an absolute ruler. He regards his kingdom as personal property which he is free to give to his parasitic Gaveston if he chooses:

> If for these dignities thou be enuied,
> Ile giue thee more, for but to honour thee,
> Is Edward pleazd with kinglie regiment.
> Fearst thou thy person? though shalt haue a guard;
> Wants thou gold? go to my treasurie,
> Wouldst thou be loude and fearde? receiue my seale,
> Saue or condemne, and in our name commaund,
> What so thy minde affects or fancie likes.

> (163–170)

He places his personal pleasures above the interests of his government, and perhaps worst of all, he has no real desire to rule. He will see England quartered and reduced to chaos rather than forgo his homosexual attachment to his minion:

> Make seuerall kingdomes of this monarchie,
> And share it equally amongst you all,
> So I may haue some nooke or corner left,
> To frolike with my deerest *Gaueston*.

> (365–368)

The horror of a divided kingdom was very great in Elizabethan England, and the centering of a tragic hero's weakness in such a division of England was a common device in Elizabethan drama, where we can see it in *Gorboduc,* I *Henry IV,* and *King Lear*. In coupling a division of his kingdom with an abandonment of his rule, Marlowe in these lines makes Edward guilty of two of the greatest sins in the Renaissance catalogue of political crimes. If a Renaissance absolute monarch required anything to maintain himself in power it was a paramount desire to rule a united kingdom and a concern above all else with the maintenance of his power in spite of all opposition.

Paul H. Kocher has found in *Edward II* two political considerations which are not in any of Marlowe's earlier plays: "one is the fundamental principle of Renaissance political science that the sovereign must observe justice. The second is the elementary awareness that the nobles and the commoners are political forces of prime importance."[17] Edward's violation of these principles are violations of political ethics which the Renaissance had come generally to accept. The absolute ruler must rule justly, and this Edward does not. His failure to ransom the elder Mortimer who has been captured fighting the king's battles—an incident which is in none of the chronicles—was invented by Marlowe to emphasize this point. The necessity for justice in no way mitigates the absolutism of the king. The people, moreover, both noble and common, are a potent political force which may make its pressure felt in a kingdom, no matter how absolute a ruler may be. The absolute monarch must be aware of this force, as Machiavelli's prince always is, and if he does not learn to handle it properly, he may be overwhelmed by it. In short, through the fall of Edward II Marlowe tells his audience that an absolute ruler may continue to be one only so long as he knows how to rule: with strength, justice, and an awareness of both the power and the needs of his subjects.[18]

There are further at least two minor political issues in *Edward II*. In one important passage Marlowe disposes of the ever present problem in Elizabethan England of the relation of king to Pope, and his statement is one to gladden the hearts of patriotic Elizabethan Protestants:

> Proud Rome, that hatchest such imperiall groomes,
> For these thy superstitious taperlights,
> Wherewith thy antichristian churches blaze,
> Ile fire thy crased buildings, and enforce
> The papall towers to kisse the lowlie ground,
> With slaughtered priests make *Tibers* channel swell,
> And bankes raised higher with their sepulchers:
> As for the peeres that backe the cleargie thus,
> If I be king, not one of them shall liue.

(392–401)

This strong speech, coming from the weak King Edward, is entirely out of character, and it indicates that Marlowe is merely seizing an occasion to express a political sentiment of some concern to him.

---

[17] *Christopher Marlowe,* p. 207.

[18] John Berdan, "Marlowe's *Edward II,*" PQ, III (1924), 197–207, sees in the play a defense of monarchy and a warning to all those who might seek to oppose the crown, with the reign of Edward II being chosen for its strong analogy to the contemporary relation of James of Scotland (later James I of England) to his favorites on the one hand and to the Scottish barons on the other. Such an interpretation of the political implications in the play, however, calls for a more favorable estimate of Edward's virtues as a king than I believe a reading of the play will warrant.

A second such minor issue is in the relation of kingship and nobility to birth. In *Tamburlaine* Marlowe had proclaimed defiantly that there was no relation between kingship and birth, that it was in the nature of every man to aspire to kingship, that only the man of merit could achieve and maintain a throne. In *Edward II* this notion has been greatly modified and tempered, but a slight note of it nevertheless persists. Although there can be no doubt that Marlowe shares the abhorrence of the barons for Piers Gaveston,[19] he does not scorn Gaveston for his lowly birth, as Mortimer does (ll. 355, 700 etc.). We detect a note of sympathy in Edward's defense of the lowly born against the overbearing barons who scorn him for his origins:

> Were he a peasant, being my minion,
> Ile make the prowdest of you stoope to him.
>
> (325–326)

One wonders why Marlowe insisted that Gaveston be of lowly birth, when the chronicles report no such thing, if it were not for the opportunity which this afforded him to repeat, although in a greatly subdued manner, the doctrine he had so loudly and defiantly proclaimed in *Tamburlaine*, that kingship and nobility have small relation to birth.

We thus find in *Edward II* a carefully constructed tragedy capable of producing the tragic emotions, but embodying also a distinct philosophy of history and casting its crises and conflicts in political terms. Both in its central tragic theme and in several minor themes it uses the past to illustrate political doctrine which Marlowe apparently considered important to the present. While in no way mitigating its effect as tragedy, it thus accomplished also the purposes of the Tudor historian. In *Edward II* tragedy and history are completely fused.

[19] This is so in spite of Marlowe's apologies for Gaveston's homosexuality in terms of classical and Renaissance friendship theory. See L. J. Mills, "The Meaning of *Edward II*," *MP*, XXXII (1934), 11–32.

EDWARD II

Berdan, John M. "Marlowe's *Edward II*," *PQ*, III (1924), 197–207.

Briggs, William Dinsmore, ed. *Marlowe's Edward II*. London, 1914.

Charlton, H. B. and Waller, R. D., eds. *Edward II*, in *The Works and Life of Christopher Marlowe*. Revised by F. N. Lees. 2nd ed. London, 1955, pp. 53–64.

Fricker, Robert. "The Dramatic Structure of *Edward II*," *English Studies*, XXXIV (1953), 204–217.

Gill, Roma, ed. *Edward II*. London, 1967.

Leech, Clifford. "Marlowe's *Edward II*: Power and Suffering," *CritQ*, I (1959), 181–196.

Merchant, W. Moelwyn, ed. *Edward the Second*. The New Mermaids, London, 1967, pp. xiv–xxv.

Mills, L. J. "The Meaning of *Edward II*," *MP*, XXII (1934), 11–32.

Perret, Marion, *"Edward II:* Marlowe's Dramatic Technique," *REL*, VII, No. 4 (1966), 87–91.

Ribner, Irving. *The English History Play in the Age of Shakespeare.* Princeton, 1957, pp. 127–136.

Schelling, Felix. *The English Chronicle Play: A Study in the Popular Historical Literature Environing Shakespeare.* New York, 1902, pp. 64–74.

Waith, Eugene M., *"Edward II:* The Shadow of Action," *TDR*, VIII, No. 4 (1964), 59–76.

See other studies in Marlowe bibliography below.

MARLOWE

Tamburlaine, Part One = 1T	*Doctor Faustus* = F
Tamburlaine, Part Two = 2T	*Edward II* = E
Jew of Malta = JM	

Anon. "Marlowe and the Absolute," *TLS*, February 24, 1956, p. 116.

Baker, George P. "Dramatic Technique in Marlowe," *Essays and Studies*, IV (1913), 172–182.

Battenhouse, Roy W. "Marlowe Reconsidered: Some Reflections on Levin's *Overreacher*," *JEGP*, LII (1953), 531–542.

Bevington, David M. *From* Mankind to *Marlowe: Growth of Structure in the Popular Drama of Tudor England.* Cambridge, Mass., 1962, pp. 199–217(1T, 2T), 218–233(JM), 234–249(E), 251–262(F).

Boas, Frederick S. *Christopher Marlowe: A Biographical and Critical Study.* Oxford, 1940, pp. 69–87(1T), 88–100(2T), 132–147(JM), 172–191(E), 203–217(F).

Bradbrook, Muriel C. "The Inheritance of Christopher Marlowe," *Theology: A Monthly Review*, LXVII (July 1964 and August 1964), 298–305, 347–353.

_____. *Themes and Conventions of Elizabethan Tragedy.* Cambridge, Eng., 1935, rptd. 1957, pp. 137–147(T), 156–160(JM), 161–164(E), 148–155(F).

Brereton, J. LeGay. *Writings on Elizabethan Drama.* Melbourne, 1948, pp. 41–64; 65–80(1T); 76–80(2T).

Brooke, Nicholas. "Marlowe the Dramatist," in *Elizabethan Theatre*, ed. John Russell Brown and Bernard Harris. Stratford-upon-Avon Studies 9. London, 1966, pp. 91–98(T, JM), 98–101(F), 101–104(E).

Brown, John Russell. "Marlowe and the Actors," *TDR*, VIII, No. 4 (1964), 155–173.

Clemen, Wolfgang. *Die Tragödie vor Shakespeare; ihre Entwicklung im Spiegel der dramatischen Rede*. Heidelberg, 1955, pp. 102–113 and 248–253(T), 133–138(JM), 138–144(E), 126–132(F).

Cole, Douglas. *Suffering and Evil in the Plays of Christopher Marlowe*. Princeton, 1962, pp. 86–103(1T), 103–120(2T), 123–144(JM), 161–187(E), 191–243(F).

Cunningham, John E. *Elizabethan and Early Stuart Drama*. London, 1965, pp. 35–40(T), 40–43(JM), 43–44(E), 45–50(F).

D'Agostino, Nicola. *Christopher Marlowe*. Rome, 1950. Preface by Mario Praz.

Eliot, T. S. *Selected Essays*. New Edition. New York, 1950, pp. 100–106.

Ellis-Fermor, U. M. *Christopher Marlowe*. London, 1926, pp. 24–60(T); 61–87(F); 88–104(JM); 110–122(E).

Empson, William. "Christopher Marlowe", *Nation*, CLXIII (1946), 444–445.

Farnham, Willard. *The Medieval Heritage of Elizabethan Tragedy*. Berkeley, 1936, pp. 368–374(T), 401–404(F), 407–410(E).

Henderson, Philip. *Christopher Marlowe*. London, 1952, pp. 83–100(T), 100–109(JM), 116–126(E), 126–135(F).

Hiller Ricard I. "The Imagery of Color, Light, and Darkness in the Poetry of Christopher Marlowe," in *Elizabethan Studies and Other Essays in Honor of George F. Reynolds*. Boulder, Colo., 1945, pp. 101–125.

Kirschbaum, Leo, ed. *The Plays of Christopher Marlowe*. Cleveland and New York, 1962, pp. 28–66(1T, 2T), 66–100(E), 101–130(F), 130–154(JM).

Knights, L. C. "The Strange Case of Christopher Marlowe," in *Further Explorations*. London and Palo Alto, Calif., 1965, pp. 85–89(1T), 90–93(JM), 94–98(F).

Kocher, Paul H. *Christopher Marlowe: A Study of His Thought, Learning, and Character*. Chapel Hill, N. C., 1946, pp. 69–103, 180–192, 267–277(T); 120–130, 193–302, and 279–289(JM); 130–143(E); 139–172, 192–195, and 277–279(F).

Leech, Clifford, ed. *Marlowe: A Collection of Critical Essays,* Englewood Cliffs, N.J., 1964.

_____. "Marlowe's Humor," in *Essays on Shakespeare and the Elizabethan Drama in Honor of Hardin Craig,* ed. Richard Hosley. Columbia, Missouri, pp. 69–81.

Levin, Harry. "Marlowe Today," *TDR,* VIII, No. 4 (1964), 22–31.

_____. *The Overreacher: A Study of Christopher Marlowe*. Cambridge, Mass., 1952, pp. 30–53(T), 56–80(JM), 108–135(F).

Mahood, M. M. *Poetry and Humanism*. London, 1950, pp. 55–64(T), 64–74(F), 74–81(JM), 81–86(E).

Maxwell, J. C. "The Plays of Christopher Marlowe," in *The Age of Shakespeare,* ed. Boris Ford. Baltimore, 1955, pp. 162–178.

McAlindon, T. "Classical Mythology and Christian Tradition in Marlowe's *Doctor Faustus,*" *PMLA,* LXXI (1966), 214–223.

Morris, Harry. "Marlowe's [Dramatic] Poetry," *TDR,* VIII, No. 4 (1964), 134–154.

Palmer, D. J. "Elizabethan Tragic Heroes," in *Elizabethan Theatre,* ed. John Russsell Brown and Bernard Harris. Stratford-upon-Avon Studies 9. London, 1966, pp. 25–30(T,F), 30–33(JM,E).

Poirier, Michel. *Christopher Marlowe.* London, 1951, pp. 90–120(T), 121–145(F), 146–163(JM), 173–192(E).

Powell, Jocelyn. "Marlowe's Spectacle," *TDR,* VIII, No. 4 (1964), 195–210.

Praz, Mario. "Christopher Marlowe," *English Studies,* XIII (1931), 209–223.

Ribner, Irving. "Marlowe and the Critics," *TDR,* VIII No. 4 (1964), 211–224.

_____. "Marlowe's 'Tragique Glasse,' " in *Essays on Shakespeare and the Elizabethan Drama in Honor of Hardin Craig,* ed. Richard Hosley. Columbia, Missouri, 1962, pp. 91–114.

Röhrman, H. *Marlowe and Shakespeare: A Thematic Exposition of Their Plays.* Arnhem, 1953.

Rossiter, A. P. *English Drama from Early Times to the Elizabethans.* London, 1950, pp. 154–159.

Rowse, A. L. *Christopher Marlowe: A Biography.* London, 1964, pp. 50–80(1T, 2T), 81–99(JM), 128–141(E), 165–189(F).

Sanders, Wilbur. *The Dramatist and the Received Idea: Studies in the Plays of Marlowe and Shakespeare.* London, 1968.

Santayana, George. *Three Philosophical Poets.* Cambridge, Mass., 1910 and later editions, pp. 146–150.

Seaton, Ethel. "Marlowe's Light Reading," in *Elizabethan and Jacobean Studies Presented to Frank Percy Wilson in Honour of His Seventieth Birthday,* ed. Herbert Davis and Helen Gardner. Oxford, 1959, pp. 17–35.

Smith, Marion Bodwell. *Marlowe's Imagery and the Marlowe Canon.* Philadelphia, 1940.

Speaight, Robert. "Marlowe: The Forerunner," *REL,* VII, No. 4 (1966), 25–41.

Steane, J. B. *Marlowe: A Critical Study.* Cambridge, Eng., 1964, pp. 62–116(1T), 117–165(F), 365–369(F), 166–203(JM), 204–235(E).

Talbert, Ernest William. *Elizabethan Drama and Shakespeare's Early Plays: An Essay in Historical Criticism.* Chapel Hill, N.C., 1963, pp. 79–87(JM), 95–110(E), 110–121(1T).

Thorp, Willard. *The Triumph of Realism in Elizabethan Drama: 1558–1612.* Princeton, 1928, pp. 40–49; 133–135(JM).

Tomlinson, T. B. *A Study of Elizabethan and Jacobean Tragedy.* Cambridge, Eng., and Melbourne, 1964, pp. 48–58(1T), 58–71(F), 87–94(JM).

Wickham, Glynne. "*Exeunt to the Cave:* Notes on the Staging of Marlowe's Plays," TDR, VIII, No. 4 (1964), 184–194.

Wilson, Frank P. *Marlowe and the Early Shakespeare.* Oxford, 1954, pp. 18–56(T), 57–68(JM), 68–85(F), 86–87, and 90–103(E).

Arden of Feversham

THE IMAGERY OF TRAGIC MELODRAMA
IN *ARDEN OF FEVERSHAM* *

Max Bluestone

ALTHOUGH Holinshed considers the story of Arden of Feversham "impertinent to [his] Hystorie," he includes it in his *Chronicles* "for the horribleness thereof."[1] The story has three sensational ingredients: the cuckolded husband, Arden, sanctions his wife's infidelity; Arden's death fulfills a curse by a victim of his apparent hardhandedness in land dealings; and his wife Alice, her lover Mosbie, and their hired assassins repeatedly bungle the killing of Arden. Otherwise undistinguished, it is the sort of story Rymer might fairly have called, as he calls *Othello,* but unfairly, a bloody farce.

A record of *Arden of Feversham,* the anonymous dramatic adaptation of the *Chronicles* story, appears in the Stationer's Register for April, 1592. The running title of the play summarizes "the lamentable tragedie of M. Arden of Feversham in Kent. Who was most wickedlye murdered by the meanes of his disloyall and wanton wyfe, who for the loue she bare to one Mosbie, hyred two desperat ruffins Blackwill and Shakbag, to kill him. Wherein is shewed the great mallice and discimulation of wicked woman, the vnsatiable desire of filthie lust and the shamefull end of all murderers."[2] This summary omits, however, the complicity

---

* From *Drama Survey,* Vol. 5, 1966, pp. 171–181. Reprinted by permission of the publishers.

1 The pertinent passages from Holinshed's *Chronicles* appear conveniently in Karl Warnke and Ludwig Proescholdt, eds., *Arden of Feversham,* Halle, 1888, pp. x–xix.

2 Warnke and Proescholdt, p. viii.

of Greene, the vengeful neighbor who agrees to arrange Arden's murder in order to retrieve the lands Arden has wrested from him, of Clarke, a painter who supplies the poison for the first of six attempts on Arden's life and who thus hopes to win the hand of Mosbie's sister Susan, and of Michael, Arden's servant, who also participates in the plot on the promise of Susan's hand. Both Susan and one Bradshaw, though both innocent of the crime itself, suffer execution along with all the conspirators except the painter, who escapes.

The running title phrase, "lamentable tragedie," seems inadequate to the generic status of the play, which only approximates to high tragedy. Emphasizing the suspenseful events of the conspiracy, the play seems to suppress their tragic import. Compared with the source, however, the play can be seen much more thoroughly than the story in Holinshed to explore the divided sensibilities of the characters caught in the bloody web of the events. The world of the play encompasses more than melodramatic scandal, more than the thrill of mere suspense. If melodrama juxtaposes virtue and vice in simple conflict simply resolved in justice triumphant, if melodrama simplifies the problematical nature of things, *Arden of Feversham* transcends mere melodrama and approaches something we may call tragic melodrama.

To overestimate the merit of the play is easy. Swinburne thought it the work of "a poet of the first order, writing at a time when there were but two such poets writing for the stage—Marlowe and Shakespeare."[3] Saintsbury celebrated the "grasp of character" as evincing "a touch of [Shakespeare's] hand."[4] Arguing from verbal parallels, the first editor of the play assigned it to Shakespeare in 1770, and in the nineteenth century, at least thirteen English, German, French, and Dutch scholars, editors, and translators agreed that in whole or in part the play is Shakespeare's. Four others denied that Shakespeare had had anything to do with it. Fleay suggested in 1891 that it belonged to Kyd, and others in our time have agreed. Tucker Brooke called it the *Agamemnon* of English middle-class life, and others have compared it with works not only by Aeschylus but by Dostoevski, Proust, and Tolstoi. There being no external evidence for doing otherwise, one editor quietly asserts that "the only reason for ascribing the play to Shakespeare is its merit."[5]

[3] Algernon Charles Swinburne, *A Study of Shakespeare,* London, 1879, p. 135.

[4] George Saintsbury, *History of Elizabethan Literature,* London, 1887, quoted in Warnke and Proescholdt, p. xxvii.

[5] Ronald Bayne, ed., *Arden of Feversham,* London, 1897, p. ix. On the authorship question, see Bayne's succinct summary, pp. ix–x; Warnke and Proescholdt, pp. viii–ix; Charles Crawford, "The Authorship of *Arden of Feversham,*" *Shakespeare Jahrbuch,* XXXIX (1903), 74–86; Tucker Brooke in Albert C. Baugh, *et al., A Literary History of England,* New York, 1948, p. 469; H. D. Sykes, *Sidelights on Shakespeare,* Stratford-upon-Avon, 1919, pp. 48–76; Louis Gillet, "Arden of Feversham," in *Le Théâtre Elizabéthain,* ed. Georgette Camille and Pierre d'Exideuil, Paris, 1940, pp. 197–207 (reprinted in *Shakespeare's Contemporaries,* ed. Max Bluestone and Norman Rabkin, 1st ed. Englewood Cliffs, N.J., 1961, pp. 149–

An incontrovertible ascription to Shakespeare could still leave us with an inconsiderable play, but the language, which owes nothing to the source, stimulates respect, despite the epilogue's apology for "this naked tragedy, / Wherein no filed points are foisted in / To make it gracious to the ear" (5.6.14–16). In a recent study of the imagery, Sarah Young-blood traces the image patterns of religion, nature, and light-and-dark to redress earlier critical assumptions that "the tragic action...[is] limited in depth and scope."[6] Miss Youngblood nevertheless asserts that the play falls short of tragedy, because there "is no 'good' character or action in the play, only apparent good or relative good. For this reason, as a tragedy *Arden of Feversham* has more of terror than pity, more of woe than wonder in its effect" (p. 218). But there are "good" characters in the play. Susan, for one, becomes enmeshed in the conspiracy only after the murder of Arden and out of love for her mistress and for Michael. Bradshaw is completely innocent. Both are nevertheless executed. Arden's friend, Franklin, a character invented by the playwright, is also "good." If he is only relatively good, it may be because he too avidly assists the authorities in tracking down and punishing the murderers. We might equally well assert that Malcolm is only relatively good for the same reason and perhaps for abandoning his country to Macbeth.

The struggle between good and evil within the murderous characters is more impressive, however, than the struggle between good and evil characters. This recurrent inner struggle lifts the play above the merely melodramatic, but Miss Youngblood rightly notes a deficiency in "moral regeneration" and thus reveals one cause of the play's melodramatic taint. When, however, she asserts that by the end of the play "a moral order... has been, however artificially, restored and reaffirmed" (p. 208), she seems to ignore the execution of Susan and Bradshaw, whose justice seems no justice at all. But nothing formulaic will decide the issue. The merit of the play resides as much in the divided sensibilities of the murderers as in the divided sensibility of their victim, Arden, a good man touched somewhat by avarice. Even this vice in him becomes ambiguous, however, when the playwright departs from the source and invents Arden's denial of charges that he has been guilty, as in the source, of brutal land appropriation. This ambiguity renders questionable Miss Youngblood's judgment that Arden "is a victim whose avarice is the justification of his death" (p. 208). And at least one of the instruments of Arden's death, Greene, is equally on the gasp after the contested land: "For I had rather die than lose my land" (1.519).

Although the play generates no fully tragic *anagnorisis* for any one of the characters and becomes by at least so much the naked tragedy of the epilogue, the dramaturgy and the inner life of the characters achieve powerful correlations with the intensity of the language. Compare, for example, the source passage for the moment when Arden's servant, Michael, changes his mind about admitting the assassins to Arden's house: "Fearing least *black Will* woulde kill him as well as his maister, ...he rose agayne and shut the doores, bolting them fast."[7] In the same moment in the play, Michael's fears ravage his moral sensibilities and thus enhance his status as a tragic figure:

> Conflicting thoughts, encampèd in my breast,
> Awake me with the echo of their strokes,
> And I, a judge to censure either side,
> Can give to neither wishèd victory.
> My master's kindness pleads to me for life
> With just demand, and I must grant it him:...
> That grim-faced fellow, pitiless Black Will,
> And Shakebag, stern in bloody stratagem,...
> Methinks I see them with their bolstered hair
> Staring and grinning in thy gentle face,
> And in their ruthless hands their daggers drawn,
> Insulting o'er thee with a peck of oaths,...
> The wrinkles in [Black Will's] death-threatening face
> Gapes open wide, like graves to swallow man.

> (3.1.59–83)

The play consistently reinterprets the source with Shakespearean forms of complication; it dramatizes, even if insufficiently for final greatness, the problematical relations between cause and effect, will and necessity, good and evil, choice and justice.

Its world is a world of bloody deeds and purposes mistook, of coincidence seemingly uncontrived, of division and discrepancy, of personality called into doubt, an untidy world whose way of life becomes conspiracy, pursuit, torment, and capture, a world whose imagined corners go askew and atremble.

In such a world, the human figure undergoes transformation in animal imagery, conventional but not derived from the source. We hear of perjured beasts, prick-eared curs, tongues that must be bridled, hunted deer, foraging lions, a hunger-bitten wolf, a lamb led to the slaughter. Arden's assassins quarrel, by the playwright's invention, like Aesopian dogs who struggle for a bone only to lose it to another cur.[8] Should he fail of his murderous mission, Shakebag sees himself a reviled animal in a den

---

[7] Warnke and Proescholdt, p. xii.

[8] The basic image patterns will appear here and there in this essay without quotation marks and without text references; occasionally these patterns are summarized and paraphrased. For a study of the relation between the animal imagery and a paganism motif in the light of the murderers' solipsistic world view as justification for their designs on Arden, see Youngblood, "Theme and Imagery," *passim*.

spat at by passersby (3.2.52ff.). To Mosbie Alice Arden becomes a serpent who can "insinuate, / And clear a trespass with [her] sweet-set tongue" (3.5.146–147).

The imagery transforms the human figure further by subjecting it to commercial transaction and to other forms of violation. The person in its full theological sense undergoes sale and purchase, laceration and conflagration. Thus to fail in love is to be clean out of the lover's books; for Arden to die is for him to be paid home. Black Will complains: "I have had ten pound to steal a dog, and we have no more here to kill a man; but that a bargain is a bargain and so forth, you should do it yourself" (2.2.75–77). The lacerated-body imagery appears in such allusions as the forging of distressful looks to wound a breast, the whetting of a knife to search the closet of Arden's heart, sweet words erasing the flint walls of a woman's breasts, curses like arrows lighting on the shooter's head, a frowning look cutting off another's legs, a face furrowed, a nose cut and trampled, a torso crawling on bloody stumps of legs, of love being murdered. Alice's sighs, we hear, are deep "pathaires, like to a cannon's burst / Discharged against a ruinated wall" and breaking Mosbie's "heart in a thousand pieces" (3.5.53ff.). Alice's "love is as the lightning flame, / Which even in bursting forth consumes itself" (ll.208–209); her fitful conscience—invented by the playwright—is a fire to be dammed up in her breast until it consumes itself or until it can be shared with Mosbie, for "fire divided burns with lesser force" (3.5.47). Almost entirely barren of metaphor, the source includes only one image of the violence associated with passion or conflict: that of an Alice enflamed by lust for her paramour.[9] Although the imagery in the play never quite achieves Shakespearean prevalence and consistency, it is not less than kin to that language which exposes poor forked animals to tragic torment. The catastrophe enacts the imagery of the violated body when the murderers throttle, bludgeon, and stab Arden and when the Mayor sentences Alice to execution by burning.

From Holinshed's fable of a marriage ending not in fruition but in death, the playwright appropriately omits a daughter of the source Ardens. He plucks from the source what Northrop Frye calls perhaps too exclusively *the* mythos of tragedy, the autumn not of successful generation but only of the sere and yellow leaf.[10] The play opens with a speech alluding to Arden's appropriation of certain sequestered lands on which account Franklin, Arden's friend, urges him to "cheer up [his] spirits, and droop no more!" (1.1) despite rumors of Alice's infidelity, which are said to have "grown." The play closes with an epilogue announcing that the plot of land where the murderers cast Arden's body so withered that "in the grass his body's print was seen / Two years and more after the deed was done" (5.6.12–14); Arden's assassins hope that

---

9 Warnke and Proescholdt, p. x.

10 *Anatomy of Criticism,* Princeton, N.J., 1957, pp. 206–223.

the earth will swallow up his blood, as it does, but not sufficiently to prevent their detection. The image of blighted generation recurs especially in Alice Arden's relations with her husband and lover. To Arden she complains of her deserts and his desires *decaying*. The play opens at sunrise, Alice dissimulating chagrin over Arden's early rising, he in turn reminding her of their past, when like the lovers in the *Amores* (1.13), they had "Ovid-like" often "chid the morning when it 'gan to peep. / And often wished that dark night's purblind steeds" (1.60–62) would forestall the day. But on this morning Arden leaves the marriage bed before day, because in the night he had heard Alice call out her lover's name. The sun brings not fruition but plans for Arden's death and progress towards a darkness; the play closes with Arden's murder at the supper hour after his various escapes in night, mist, and fog. Day and night undergo a double inversion, the Ovidian night first the occasion for love, last the occasion for death. In mid-course, Alice experiences momentary remorse and begs her lover Mosbie to give up the conspiracy against Arden: "let our springtime wither; / Our harvest will yield but loathsome weeds" (3.5.67–68). She defers to Mosbie's obduracy, however, prostrates herself before him, and chokes down her contempt for his lower social station: "Flowers do sometimes spring in fallow lands, / Weeds in gardens, roses, grow on thorns" (3.5.143–144). In a new commitment to Arden's death, she cries out, "Why should he thrust his sickle in our corn" (4.1.85). Arden himself thinks that nothing will prevent dishonor from *budding,* nothing make Alice repent and "sorrow for her dissolution; / But she is rooted in her wickedness, ... Good counsel is to her as rain to weeds, / And reprehension makes her vice to grow / As Hydra's head that plenished by decay" (3.1.8–13). The curse of inverted generation takes on mythic proportions; evil becomes as inevitable as biology, Arden a bourgeois corn-king whose sacrificial slaughter yields not release but utter sterility. The murderers abandon his corpse on the snow-covered land that was to have cheered up his drooping spirits. The misalliance of the adulterers begins in an inn named after the fleur-de-lis, a blossom but funereal. Although the source Arden dies on St. Valentine's Day, the play fails to adopt the ironies of that festive occasion. Instead it substitutes an ironic allusion to another festive folk ritual. In one of the few comic episodes, a Charon-like ferryman tries to help one of the assassins who has fallen into a ditch:

> FERRYMAN: Did you ever see such a mist as this?
> BLACK WILL: No, nor such a fool as will rather be hought [i.e., hamstrung] then get [on] his way.
> FERRYMAN: Why, sir, this is no Hough-Monday; you are deceived.

> (4.3.36–41)

On Hough-Monday (Hock-Monday), following the second Sunday after Easter, pious parishioners customarily lay in wait along the highway to hock, or hamstring, travellers—that is, to snare them with a rope, and to elicit from them a ransom later converted to charitable uses. Tragic sterility grotesquely parodies this ritual, the playwright perhaps taking his cue from Alice's cry in the source, when she is exposed: "Oh the bloud of God help, for this bloud have I shed."[11] No piety or charity in the play. No Hough-Monday, indeed.

The Hock-Monday snare introduces another conventional image for Renaissance tragedy, that of the net. Again, the imagery is wholly the playwright's invention: Arden's nightmare of his being trapped like a deer in a toil, the hired assassins liming their twigs to catch this wary bird, Arden, Alice's complaint of having been "tangled with [Mosbie's] 'ticing speech," and her vision of being entwined in her husband's arms, which seem to her the snakes of Tisiphone. If he fails to kill Arden, Shakebag expects never to "draw a sword again, / Nor prosper in the twilight, cockshut light" (3.2.46–47), that is, the time of day suitable for catching woodcocks in a large net, or cockshut, that is, after sunset. Unlike Holinshed's characters, the playwright's exercise will, they quarrel, they retreat and advance, they struggle with their consciences; they undergo various kinds of *agon*. In a key soliloquy, Mosbie examines his precarious condition as a conspirator. The speech re-states all the basic images, including that of the net, now linked with the idea of things that grow but do not release: "The way I seek to find, where pleasure dwells, / Is *hedged* behind me that I cannot back" (3.5.20–21):

> Disturbèd thoughts drives me from company
> And dries my marrow with their watchfulness;...
> And nips me as the bitter north-east wind
> Doth check the tender blossoms in the spring....
> And he but pines amongst his delicates,
> Whose troubled mind is stuffed with discontent.
> My golden time was when I had no gold;
> Though then I wanted, yet I slept secure;
> My daily toil begat my night's repose,
> My night's repose made daylight fresh to me.
> But since I climbed the top-bough of the tree
> And sought to build my nest amongst the clouds,
> Each gentle stirry gale doth shake my bed,
> And makes me dread my downfall to the earth.
> But whither doth contemplation carry me?
> The way I seek to find, where pleasure dwells,
> Is hedged behind me that I cannot back,
> But needs must on, although to danger's gate.
> Then Arden, perish thou by that decree;
> For Greene doth ear the land and weed thee up
> To make my harvest nothing but pure corn.

11 Warnke and Proescholdt, p. xx.

And for his pains I'll hive him up a while,
And after smother him to have his wax:
Such bees as Greene must never live to sting. . . .
Then there is Michael, and the painter too,
Chief actors to Arden's overthrow;. . .
I'll none of [them], for I can cast a bone
To make these curs pluck out each other's throat,
And then am I sole ruler of mine own.
Yet Mistress Arden lives; but she's myself,
And holy Church rites makes us two but one.
But what for that? I may not trust you, Alice:
You have supplanted Arden for my sake,
And will extirpen me to plant another.
'Tis fearful sleeping in a serpent's bed.
And I will cleanly rid my hands of her.

(3.5.1ff.)

And as in many other passages, the soliloquy combines language, theme, and occasion into an impressively coherent whole, ironic, pathetic, awesomely brutal in its struggle with fear and time, and in its catalogue of death. Mosbie's hopes achieve fulfillment, but not by his hand. When the tragic net closes around the conspirators as well as around Arden, it closes also around Mosbie himself. The image of the net rises to dramaturgically literal action when Black Will initiates the murder of Arden under the stage direction: *Then Will pulls [Arden] down with a towel* (5.1.238), throttling him, entrammeling him. And Alice plays her part, too: "What! groans thou? nay, then give me the weapon! / Take this for hindering Mosbie's love and mine" (5.1.243–244). She blots out the least vestige of life; in the name of love, she extirpates seed, as Mosbie had foreseen.

Both Mosbie and Alice, like Macbeth and Lady Macbeth, attempt the impossible: to trammel up the consequences by feeling the future in the instant. Their hyperbolic hope makes time a theme in the play. Alice confidently asserts early that Arden's time is but short, and to Mosbie's wish that Arden's date were completed and expired, she adds, "Ah, would it were! Then comes my happy hour" (3.5.161–162). Mosbie hopes that their "loves be rocks of adamant, / Which time nor place nor tempest can asunder" (4.1.100–101). But the tempest comes. Under the cover of a snowstorm they carry Arden's body into the fields. And the tempest goes, too. It fails to conceal their telltale footprints in the snow and thus makes possible their arrest and execution.

As a verbal correlative for the melodramatic pursuit of Arden, for his seeming good luck in escaping the assassins so often, for the mysterious force seemingly balking the murder and yet allowing it finally to occur, and for the divided passions of the characters, hyperbole permeates the language of the play. Hyperbole, to cite Peacham's definition, puts "a

greater word for a lesse, as to call a proude man *Lucifer*,"[12] and throughout the play it consistently implies the cosmic import with which the
playwright suffuses his "lamentable tragedie" as he lifts his mattter above
mere melodramatic journalism. Suspecting Alice's infidelity, for example,
Arden thinks life so odious in his very first speech as to wish hyperbolically
that "for this veil of heaven / The earth hung over [his] head and covered
[him]" (11.13–14). Thus also Love is a God, and woman never loved
husband better than Alice pretends to love Arden, yet she hopes to see
him gallop across the ocean on a horse that will throw him into the
waves; for her there is no nectar but on Mosbie's lips; yet at another
time Mosbie seems to usurp his room and make a royal triumph of his
absence, and he seems to her as mad as raving Hercules; Arden's grief
rends his powers worse than the conflict at the hour of death; for love
to be jealous is for the traveller to look on the basilisk; Black Will is so
vile a rogue that not another like him lives upon the earth unless it be
he, and he has cracked as many blades as others have nuts; the assassins
are as confident of killing Arden as if his death had been decreed by
Parliament, and in the fog they think themselves almost in Hell's mouth;
and the world will dissolve, we hear, before Mosbie will overthrow Alice.
About Arden's escapes, we hear that he has wondrous holy luck, that
the Lord of Heaven has preserved him, and that doubtless he is preserved by a miracle. None of this language is in the source, and none
of it is ornamental. Its function is tragic irony of the highest kind. Thus
Alice dissimulates: "Sweet Arden, come again / Within a day or two,
or else I die" (11.85–86), and she does. Thus Mosbie, completely unaware
of the truth of his hyperbole: "Mayst thou enjoy her long: / Hell-fire
and wrathful vengeance light on me, / If I dishonour her or injure thee"
(11.336–338). In the end, hyperbole becomes thoroughly and ironically
literal. The facile assurances yield to catastrophe, not only for the guilty
but for the innocent. Thus Arden: "God grant this vision bedeem me
any good" (3.3.31), and "God frame it for the best" (3.3.56), but
Arden's hopes, like those of his enemies, fail, too. As if further to
enhance the ironic reverberations of the action he imitates, the playwright makes Arden far less culpable and Alice and Mosbie far more
tormented than their counterparts in the source.

The inversion of hyperbole, *meiosis*, also plays a part in the poise
of language, theme, and action, but its part is a lesser one. *Meiosis* is
a diminishing similitude. In reply to the opinion that divine intervention
has at first preserved Arden from death, Black Will snorts, "Preserved
a fig!" (3.6.143) and puts the cause down to the passers-by who interrupt
the ambush. The dramaturgy enacts the figure of *meiosis* even as the

---

[12] *The Garden of Eloquence,* quoted in Sister Miriam Joseph, *Shakespeare's Use
of the Arts of Language,* New York, 1947, p. 330. In defining *auxesis,* Sister Joseph
discusses both *hyperbole* and *meiosis,* the former an enlarging, the latter a diminishing, metaphorical similitude.

murderers finally succeed in killing Arden while he sits at backgammon in what he assumes is the domestic peace of his home:

> ARDEN: Mosbie! Michael! Alice! what will you do?
> WILL: Nothing but take you up, sir, nothing else.

(5.1.237–240)

A catchword for backgammon ("take you up") becomes *meiosis* for murder. Recreation becomes destruction, both in act and in word. The uncommonly skillful hand that fashioned these ironies deserves the celebration implied in the unproved ascriptions to Shakespeare. A thorough account of the playwright's handling of his source would easily demonstrate his assured responsiveness to the stage—to its spatial resources, to its capacity for rendering the flux of time, to its emblematic use of the gesturing and suffering figure of the actor, and to its demand for effective mimesis of meaningful mutability. Although Holinshed's narrative moves through time and event, it cannot render, like the play, so powerful a sense of motion or so remarkable a gallery of portraits in passion. The playwright invents the dissociated sensibilities in Alice's brilliant dissimulations and uncertainties, in Mosbie's fearful speculations, even in Black Will and Shakebag's comic frustrations, and he thus memorably sharpens the edges of betrayal, or cross-purposes, of loss, of isolation, terror, and despair.

Of tragedies superior to *Arden of Feversham* we are reminded that if the guilty get what they deserve in life, "the tragedians reply, 'Perhaps so, but will the innocent?' The preachers excuse God from any responsibility for the anguish of human experience. The tragedians see that all suffering is not merited or explicable. The preachers predict that all tears will be dried in heaven. For the tragedians the rest is silence."[13] *Arden of Feversham* many times approaches such silence. The richness of its language, the expertness of its dramaturgy, and the intensity of its characters seem purposefully to set off the plain style of its last lines. Invented by the playwright, they compellingly record a series of highly individualized responses to justice and injustice. When autumn descends, the net closes, and innocence goes under with guilt. To their sentences of death, the characters respond variously in a litany of repentance, hatred, despair, hope, a near-jest, and a curse.

> ALICE: Let my death make amends for all my sins.
> MOSBIE: Fie: upon women! this shall be my song;
> But bear me hence, for I have lived too long.
> SUSAN: Seeing no hope on earth, in heaven is my hope.
> MICHAEL: Faith, I care not, seeing I die with Susan.

[13] Robert Ornstein, *The Moral Vision of Jacobean Tragedy,* Madison, Wisconsin, 1960, p. 18.

BRADSHAW: My blood be on his head that gave the sentence.
MAYOR: To speedy execution with them all! *Exeunt*

(5.5.33–39)

Because Susan and Bradshaw are innocent, woe and wonder rush in, and we cannot assent easily to the justice of this ending. Like its running title, which heralds a tragedy and thus indulges an error of overestimation, its epilogue also assumes a tragedy of sorts: "This naked tragedy," we hear, reveals "simple truth," which is "gracious enough, / And needs no other points of glosing stuff." The play needs neither the glosing stuff of criticism nor the apology implied in the allusion to its nakedness. The playwright, whoever he was, wrought better than he knew or was willing to acknowledge. As tragic melodrama, the play, as Louis Gillet has argued on other grounds, is far more than a mere "precursor...of... bourgeois drama."[14]

---

[14] "Arden of Feversham," *Shakespeare's Contemporaries*, 1st ed., p. 150.

ARDEN OF FEVERSHAM

Adams, Henry Hitch. *English Domestic or, Homiletic Tragedy: 1575 to 1642.* New York, 1943, pp. 100–108.

Boas, Frederick S. *An Introduction to Tudor Drama.* Oxford, 1933, pp. 107–108.

Brooke, C. F. T., ed. *The Shakespeare Apocrypha.* Oxford, 1918, pp. xiii–xv.

Chapman, Raymond. *"Arden of Feversham:* Its Interest Today," *English,* XI (1956), 15–17.

Cust, Lionel. *Arden of Feversham.* London, 1920, pp. 1–22.

Gillet, Louis. *"Arden of Feversham,"* in *Le Théâtre Élizabéthain,* ed. Georgette Camille and Pierre d'Exideuil. Paris, 1940, pp. 197–207.

Greg, W. W. "Shakespeare and *Arden of Feversham,"* *RES,* XXI (1945), 134–136.

Thorp, Willard. *The Triumph of Realism in Elizabethan Drama: 1558–1612.* Princeton, 1928, pp. 108–110.

Youngblood, Sara. "Theme and Imagery in *Arden of Feversham,"* *SEL,* III (1963), 207–218.

Thomas Dekker

THE SHOEMAKER'S HOLIDAY : THEME AND IMAGE *

Harold E. Toliver

THOMAS Dekker will not likely share the lot of rediscovered minor figures. *The Shoemaker's Holiday,* to be sure, frequently appears in selections of Elizabethan comedy; but Dekker had the misfortune of being overmatched by Jonson in satire and overshadowed by Shakespeare in romantic comedy. An uncertain canon sprinkled with collaborations has made him more attractive to textual studies than to criticism. Like the rest of Dekker's comedies, *The Shoemaker's Holiday* is occasionally commended for its delightful realism, or in Mary Leland Hunt's words, for being "the most attractive picture of citizen life presented on the Elizabethan stage, and perhaps...the truest," and for manifesting Dekker's "sane, sweet, and democratic mind."[1] But the implication is that the "picture" is spontaneous, untidy, and without enduring significance for an age which does not turn excitedly to a drama of sweetness and sanity.

I think, however, that the play's vagabond madness has a method and that its lighthearted "democracy" has a shape and coherence which might tend to raise our estimation of Dekker's craftsmanship if observed. The thematic goal of the play is not to exalt one segment of Elizabethan society above others, to be a trade manual for shoemaker apprentices, or to offer a guidebook to late fifteenth-century London; rather, it is to show that the deficiencies of various social levels are symptomatic

---

* From *Boston University Studies in English,* Vol. 5, 1961, pp. 208–213. Reprinted by permission of the publishers and the author.

[1] See *Thomas Dekker: A Study* (New York: Columbia University Press, 1911), p. 58; cf. Alexis F. Lange, "Critical Essay" in *Representative English Comedies,* ed. Charles M. Gayley (New York: Macmillan, 1914), III; while the play "afforded an excellent opportunity for representing dramatically a cross-section of community life from shoemaker's shop to Lord Mayor's mansion and nobleman's palace," Dekker in general falls short in "artistic workmanship" (pp. 7, 13).

of enduring human faults, faults which may be remedied by the right kind of discipline and the right kind of holiday freedom. The special areas of deficiency and their remedies may be divided into a few imagistic and thematic categories. The shoemakers, especially Firk, are addicted to sensual "feasting" while those of higher standing entertain at a falsely civil and arid table; these two are transcended in the ceremonial-sensuous banquet which Simon Eyre, the shoemaker-mayor, serves the King. A false love for position and wealth threatens the two central love affairs from above while poverty threatens them from below; these dangers are dissolved in love matches-with-blessings. Likewise, a false sense of honor seems momentarily to promise rewards while true honor results only in a crippling lameness and a life of hardship. This condition, the world being what it is, cannot be entirely cured, but is set straight as far as possible. And last, in the shoemakers' lives a holiday atmosphere of irresponsible festivity and the crude necessities of life stand opposed; this condition, too, is ameliorated by the power of the King in conjunction with the shoemaker-mayor. If any of these is central, it would seem to be the last, though the opposition might be more broadly phrased as a struggle between the exigencies imposed upon one's free will by a life of commodity and compromise, and the desire to escape these necessities, to be an entirely free and romantic agent perpetually on a "holiday."

Freedom is not entirely dependent upon money: even those with money must learn to compromise and the unpropertied can find a way to direct their own affairs and to have their own means of creating holidays. "Prince am I none," Simon says, "yet am I princely born," receiving his proper inheritance as the "sole" son of a shoemaker. Honor can in fact be gained in a life of commodity: "I am a handicraftsman," he adds, "yet my heart is without craft" (V.v.10).[2] But the conflict between life as it is and life as the romantic spirit would have it be is nevertheless intimately involved in the differences between social and economic levels, as the two contrasting songs which serve as prelude suggest in their own oblique way. The first of the two combines natural harmony and serenity with comic lowness:

> "Now the Nightingale, the pretty Nightingale,
> The sweetest singer in all the forest's choir,
> Entreats thee, sweet Peggy, to hear thy true love's tale;
> Lo, yonder she sitteth, her breast against a brier.

> "But O, I spy the Cuckoo, the Cuckoo, the Cuckoo;
> See where she sitteth: come away, my joy;
> Come away, I prithee, I do not like the Cuckoo

---

2 Line, Scene, and act numbers are according to Fredson Bowers' standard edition, *The Dramatic Works of Thomas Dekker* (Cambridge: Cambridge University Press, 1953), I; but I have quoted from A. K. McIlwraith's edition in *Five Elizabethan Comedies* (London: Oxford University Press, 1934) because of the modernized spelling.

> Should sing where my Peggy and I kiss and toy."
>
> O the month of May, the merry month of May,
> So frolic, so gay, and so green, so green, so green!
> And then did I unto my true love say:
> "Sweet Peg, thou shalt be my summer's queen!"

The poetry of the love holiday is thus "impure." Merely setting a romantic "true-love's tale" in the context of the "brier" would not in itself make it so—the holiday atmosphere of romantic comedy is customarily intensified by a token resistance which, it is apparent from the beginning, will be overcome. But romance is confronted also by the formidable challenge of the cuckoo, which, unlike the aristocratic "sweetest singer" of the forest, is common, bourgeois, and a little absurd: love can withstand rich uncles, but can it survive domestication? The singer, at any rate, apparently fears not; he must take his joy "away" from the cuckoo's song. An uncomfortable awareness of creaturely realities impinges itself upon lovers even as they "kiss and toy," which predicts what the play itself will demonstrate, namely, that romantic loves like that of "Rose" and "Lacy" must be considered in the context of the more prosaic life of the shoemakers, especially the marital life of Simon and Margery and the sensual life of Firk.

These two views of love are part of a complex of interrelated class levels and "planes of reality" (in E. M. W. Tillyard's phrase) which the play presents. But other kinds of love besides these two are also possible. The second song resolves the conflict between romantic merriment and disenchanted reality by proposing a spirited resignation and an open-eyed love (reminiscent of Jane's and Ralph's, as we shall see later):

> Trowl the bowl, the jolly nut-brown bowl,
>   And here, kind mate, to thee:
> Let's sing a dirge for Saint Hugh's soul,
>   And down it merrily.
>
> . . . .
>
> Cold's the wind, and wet's the rain,
>   Saint Hugh be our good speed:
> Ill is the weather that bringeth no gain,
>   Nor helps good hearts in need.

If romance is tested by comic realism in the first song, in the second indoor security and warmth contain a measure of sorrow and necessity. Desire for an ideal "summer's queen" and fear of a wife who might make the cuckoos sing are both exchanged for a stable bond with a "kind mate"—an endearing but well-tried love. Likewise, nature's spontaneous tutelary powers are exchanged for society's martyr (Saint Hugh being the patron saint of shoemakers) and the light hearted songs of the May for trowling of the bowl and a "dirge." It is not the best of all possible worlds but festivity is possible—"sing a dirge," but "down it merrily."

The season itself, which is thus a mixture of winter cold and summer merriment, is to be judged partly by what can be "gained" from it. Perhaps the free and light of heart can afford to have the nightingale for a patron, but the shoemakers need Saint Hugh, or as the prologue suggests to the Queen, a goddess who will care for her "meanest vassals," as the King cares for Simon (the implication being that the Elizabethan theater, like Simon's banquet hall, is also a kind of festive meeting place where, "on bended knees," the shoemakers may properly ask for tribute).

The theme of gain is immediately taken up in the first scene by Lincoln and Lord Mayor Oteley, whose feasting together has become a mere outward form, as indeed love and honor have also. Though they are decidedly not "good hearts" in need, money is a commanding power capable of arousing distrust between them. "Poor citizens must not with courtiers wed" (I.i.12) who will spend more in a year on "silks and gay apparel" than the mayor is worth. To make the point sure, Lincoln describes at length the dissolute spending of his nephew, who has become the lowest of the humble, a shoemaker in Wittenberg, "A goodly science for a gentleman/Of such descent!" (I.i.30). Rose, the object of Lacy's love, Lincoln describes as a "gay, wanton, painted citizen" though, as we discover, she presents the only opportunity for Lacy to exchange the bright scarves, the "bunch of feathers," and "the monstrous garters" which characterize his affectation, for the true garland of festivity (I.ii.1). She in turn is enabled by him to be bound "prentice to the Gentle Trade" (III.iii.87). His disguise as a shoemaker is in a sense his own creation of identity; paradoxically, only by becoming a shoemaker can he and Rose share in the "frolic, so gay, and so green, so green. . . ." To this extent, his love takes on the qualities which modify the romantic spirit of the second song—his disguise is a symbolic acquisition of the sturdiness of the lower classes.

The issue is more clearly drawn in Lincoln's instructions to Lacy (I.i.71 f.). The Lord Mayor, "this churl. . .in the height of scorn," according to this Polonius in the height of worldly wisdom, has attempted to "buy" Lacy off. Honor, family position, and the image one puts before the world hinge upon defining love in the "proper" way, not, as the King will tell Lincoln, as that which "respects no blood,/Cares not for difference of birth or state" (V.v.104), but as the essence and achievement of birth and state:

> Remember, coz,
> What honourable fortunes wait on thee:
> Increase the king's love, which so brightly shines,
> And gilds thy hopes. I have no heir but thee,—
> And yet not thee, if with a wayward spirit
> Thou start from the true bias of my love.

(I.i.80)

The implications are that a "mixture" of bloods will destroy the social hierarchy rather than bestowing benefits on each level; the King's love functions to "gild" one's personal hopes with an external grace; and "my love" has the "true bias," which cannot be left for the wayward infatuation of romantic love without incurring the risk of disinheritance. As a comparatively free aristocrat, Lincoln misses all the advantages of his station and acquires the disadvantages of those who by necessity must be concerned for "gain." When Lacy falls into the game, Lincoln rewards him with "thirty Portigues" for his fair words of acquiescence. And while Lacy secretly rejects Lincoln's command to seek "fair Honour in her loftiest eminence" in the wars in France, policy is as yet his only remedy for policy. He implicitly endorses a superficial sense of values, while self-flagellation for not living up to them stifles festivity as surely as parental authority and false honor could have. Love is powerful only in changing "High birth to baseness, and a nobler mind/To the mean semblance of a shoemaker!" (I.iii.10). But he also sees another side of things which will develop in the course of the play until the threat of disinheritance ceases to matter:

> Then cheer my hoping spirits, be not dismay'd,
> Thou canst not want, do Fortune what she can,
> The Gentle Craft is living for a man.

Simon Eyre's version of the last line shows "living" to mean not only possessing the minimum necessities but having real life. According to the standards of Lincoln, missing the war in France to become a shoemaker-lover is not to gain a way of living but to kill the real man, the "name": "Lacy, thy name/Liv'd once in honour, now 'tis dead in shame" (II.iv.52). It is to destroy the self and the bankbook, as though identical, in the same fire, "The fire of that love's lunacy" in which Lacy has "burnt up himself, consum'd his credit" (II.iv.41). But Lincoln's economics of love are gradually turned against him. Lacy becomes "surfeit with excess of joy" and is made happy by Rose's "rich perfection," which pays "sweet interest" to his hopes and "redoubles love on love":

> let me once more
> Like to a bold-fac'd debtor crave of thee,
> This night to steal abroad...

> (IV.iii.12)

Only by the sweet theft of love can important debts be paid. In spite of her father's anger and his uncle's hate ("This traffic of hot love shall yield cold gains," IV.iv.139), trading false honor for love can be consummated in "happy nuptials" blessed by the King himself. As Firk aptly says of this "humble" marriage of the new shoemaker, "They shall be knit like a pair of stockings in matrimony."

The love of Ralph and Jane, on the other hand, is beset more by necessity than by false honor; shoemakers go to France because pressed into service, not to gain a name but to lose the full use of their limbs. The intercession of Simon is not sufficient to keep the newly married couple together, but even shoemakers can be worthy soldiers if forced to be: "take him, brave men; Hector of Troy was an hackney to him, Hercules and Termagant scoundrels." Simon's advice is somewhat more sound if less delicate than Lincoln's to Lacy; it is not, of course, without its own concern for social class and honor:

> fight for the honour of the Gentle Craft, for the gentlemen shoemakers, the courageous cordwainers, the flower of St. Martin's, the mad knaves of Bedlam, Fleet Street, Tower Street and Whitechapel; crack me the crowns of the French knaves, a pox on them, crack them; fight, by the Lord Ludgate, fight, my fine boy!

(I.i.211)

(And as Firk shows, shoemakers can also turn necessity to gain: "God send thee to cram thy slops [pockets] with French crowns, and thy enemies' bellies with bullets," I.i.221.)

Ralph himself understands clearly the contrast between the poor and the rich as they go to war. Rich men "give their wives rich gifts,/Jewels and rings, to grace their lily hands," while those of his trade make "rings for women's heels." His gift of a pair of shoes, besides being practical, becomes a symbol of fidelity and humbleness. It offers a metaphorical language for the poor to talk about love without ostentation ("These true-love knots I prick'd; I hold my life,/By this old shoe I shall find out my wife"), though to Firk love sentiments are but an "ague-fit of foolishness" (IV.ii.46). And by the shoes Ralph is enabled to find Jane as she is about to accept a countergift of Hammon's "rings," which will give her a chance to have "lily hands" of grace rather than the working hands of craft pompously described by Eyre: "Let me see thy hand, Jane. This fine hand, this white hand, these pretty fingers must spin, must card, must work; work, you bombast-cotton-queen; work for your living..." (I.i.208).

It is Jane, in fact, who is most clearly faced with the choice between an honorable poverty and a fair name. Her dilemma is this: to choose wealth is to sacrifice romance, but to choose romance is perhaps to destroy it, for it cannot survive without holidays. Hammon would make festivity possible by buying her "hand"; but she finds festivity and necessity incompatible: "I cannot *live* by keeping holiday" (III.iv.31). She would rather, she asserts, be wife of a poor man "than a king's whore" (III.iv.79), and, if her breath will make him "rich," Ralph's death makes her "poor" (III.iv.124). When set between the crippled Ralph and Hammon, like Everyman between vice and virtue, and forced to distinguish between false and true honor, she has little difficulty in choosing, but the choice, considered in context, is not a facile one. "Whom should I choose? Whom should my thoughts affect/But him whom Heaven hath made to be my love?" she asks, turning to Ralph; "Thou art my husband, and these humble weeds/Make thee more beautiful than all his wealth" (V.ii.53). The dilemma is dissolved by submission to a higher order ("for wedding and hanging goes by destiny,"

Firk remarks) and by a discovery of values in keeping with that order. While it is not possible to achieve an unrestricted self-fulfillment, one can acquiesce in providence and grasp whatever beauty exists in "humble weeds." The original choice lay with heaven, perhaps, but it can be endorsed by an act of free will which, within the limits of contingency, is an act of self-determination. Neither Jane nor Ralph is quite complete until this choice is made, but afterward they alone require no gifts from the King. Hammon is left as he began, requiring the "sunny eyes" of a kind mate to warm a "cold heart" but achieving nothing. His position in the cold street outside Jane's warm (and thoroughly honest) shop in which she sits, "a light burning by her," has revealed symbolically a "winter" nature which finds love a "lunacy" when it makes a single look "as rich...as a king's crown" (III.iv.12 f.).

Hammon's attempt to deter Ralph with "fair gold" offers a way to bring the virtues of the gentle trade into the love-honor-money complex: "dost thou think a shoemaker is so base to be a bawd to his own wife for commodity? Take thy gold, choke with it! Were I not lame, I would make thee eat thy words" (V.ii.82). A choking "feast" of gold and words might be more appropriate for Lincoln, but the point is well made, and properly conditioned by necessity—"were I not lame...." Fidelity and honor, having survived the test, get their reward and the tables are turned upon their false counterparts. Oteley and Lincoln, mistaking appearance for reality, rush in to "unmask" what is, of course, no disguise but the genuine "article." Rather than easing "her blindness," theirs is lifted:

> LINCOLN: O base wretch!
> Nay, hide thy face, the horror of thy guilt
> Can hardly be wash'd off. Where are thy powers?
> What battles have you made? O yes, I see,
> Thou fought'st with Shame, and Shame hath conquer'd thee.
> This lameness will not serve.
>
> (V.ii.121)

Ironically, he speaks more truly than he knows. Real guilt cannot indeed be "washed off" like gilt, and lameness will not "serve" one, though, in another sense, this lameness has served the state, and without a visible entourage of "powers."

In the symmetrical cross-referencing of the two love plots, Jane rejects Hammon for someone lower in the social scale while Rose rejects him for someone higher pretending to be lower; both reject him not because he is personally undesirable—by and large he is sympathetically portrayed to remove that possibility—but because "summer love" cannot be arranged or politic. The democracy of shoemakers, with its levelling of social barriers, would seem to win in both cases. Actually, a countersatire operates throughout which shows that commodity and authority inevitably have their place and that shoemakers as well as courtiers can exalt these things beyond their due. Simon's conveniently quick return on an invest-ment enables him to spread the affectations of the rich thinly over a crude, good-hearted sensuousness. It is significantly a shipload of sweet wares, enough "prunes, almonds, and sugar-candy" to send Firk into raptures and Margery into a French hood, which makes him Lord Mayor. If Margery feels "honour creep upon" her and "a certain rising" in her flesh, meaning a rise in nobility, Firk can correctly interpret it as simply growing fat: "Rising in your flesh do you feel, say you? Ay, you may be with child . . . . But you are such a shrew, you'll soon pull him down" (II.iii.136). While putting on as much finery as the "pishery-pashery" of "those silken fellows, . . . painted beings, outsides, outsides," whose "inner linings are torn," she is quick to reprove Ralph's mourning with a glib morality: "Ralph, why doest thou weep? Thou knowest that naked we came out of our mother's womb, and naked we must return; and, therefore, thank God for all things" (III.ii.91).

Firk himself is not entirely immune to the money-disease, but, like Simon, he is more apt to err on the side of crudity than on that of "finery." True festivity, as we learn from the last scene, should not be entirely without discipline, as he tends to make it: the banquet over which the new mayor and the King preside, like the love of Ralph and Jane, has an appointed order and time. That Simon is both shoemaker and mayor, the King both supreme ruler and "feaster," is significant. And "when all our sports and banquetings are done, / Wars must right wrongs which Frenchmen have begun" (V.v.190) : holidays, by the nature of things, cannot last forever. To be sure, both Simon's democracy and his discipline cease when he deals with his wife, and his feast of language is anything but a gourmet's dish: "Away, you Islington whitepot! hence, you hopperarse! you barley-pudding full of maggots! you broil'd carbo-nado!"; but he is not merely an irresponsible king of misrule designed to carry off subversive and aberrant impulses. Though he is a "wild ruffian," even noblemen praise him as a man "as serious, provident, and wise, / As full of gravity amongst the grave, / As any mayor hath been these many years" (V.iii.7).

Perhaps the nature of the final compromise, which brings out the best in the social hierarchy as well as in love, honor, and the working-festive life of the "gentle craft," can best be seen in the feasting imagery, some examples of which I have already quoted. There have been several false starts towards the final concept of the communal banquet. The only agreement Lincoln and Mayor Oteley can achieve over their "sundry" feasts, as we have seen, is that it is a "shame / To join a Lacy with an Oteley's name." Hammon, the hunter of his "dear," having lost his venison, expects to "find a wife," only to become ironically the prey at Oteley's "hunter's feast." Switching the hunt to Jane, his "poor famish'd eyes do feed on that / Which made them famish" (III.iv.5), but he is finally excluded altogether from the shoemakers' banquet, as he is excluded from the harmony and festivity of love itself (V.ii.91), because he has not been willing to sacrifice station to love. His is a false quest, not without appeal, but clearly misdirected. Before the final banquet a preliminary feast is held during which Eyre dominates and becomes the envy of those who have more money but less gaiety. Margery's suggestion to "put on gravity" (III.iii.11) is found unacceptable and Rose is advised to marry "a grocer," since "grocer is a sweet trade: plums, plums." And so Hodge and Firk, as I have indicated, conceive of the feast of life in sensual terms only:

> HODGE: . . .Let's feed and be fat with my lord's bounty.
> FIRK: O musical bell, still! O Hodge, O my brethren! There's cheer for the heavens: venison pasties walk up and down piping hot, like sergeants; beef and brewis comes marching in dry-fats, fritters and pancakes comes trowling in in wheel-barrows; hens and oranges hopping in porters' baskets, collops and eggs in scuttles, and tarts and custards comes quavering in in malt-shovels.

> (V.ii.187)

This kind of dream, so full of childlike personification, is, of course, quite different from the aristocratic dream of ideal love, but it, too, rests on the borderline between innocence and irresponsibility. The final shoemakers' banquet, while satisfying these appetites and giving gaiety its due, places controls upon the impulse to take a prolonged vacation. When the pancake bell rings, the shoemakers can be "as free as my lord mayor," shut up their shops, and make holiday, and it may seem that the holiday will "continue for ever"; but in fact it will cease and come again under the cyclical restrictions and discipline of nature and under the sanctions of a social decorum. Except for Ralph, Jane, and Hammon, everyone comes to the banquet to receive his proper reward or retribution. "Care and cold lodgings bring white hairs" (V.v.31), but "mirth lengtheneth long life," as Dekker says in the dedicatory epistle to "all good fellows. . . of the Gentle Craft"; and it causes the King to rule by the promptings of the heart rather than by the promptings of the senior citizens. He perhaps speaks better than he knows when telling Simon that it does him good to see the mayor in a merry mood, as though among his shoemakers (V.v.15). He sends Rose and Lacy to bed and by simple commandment redeems lost honor to one willing to "stoop / To bare necessity," and, forgetting courtly pleasures, to gain love by becoming a shoemaker. As the temporal head of social order, he asserts his power against false divisions. No hand on earth "should dare untie / The sacred knot, knit by God's majesty" which unites unequals "in holy nuptial bands" (V.v.63). God's majesty at the spiritual head of all hierarchies joins with the shoemakers to sustain that democratic union. Not all India's wealth would cause Lacy to forgo his love; for Rose to leave him would be like a separation of body and soul. Festive celebration thus depends upon a harmonious community which fulfills the demands of body and soul through the legal bonds of the "sacred knot," rather than through factitious differences of birth or state, or a sensual indulgence in the feast as such. Finally, even Lincoln and the former mayor are made more or less content in the general harmony.

"Ill is the weather that bringeth no gain," however, and so Simon uses the festive occasion to win a concession from the King allowing the shoemakers to buy and sell leather in the mayor's new hall twice a week. With that gift, the banquet may be concluded. In an exchange of courtesies, Simon asks the King to taste of his "poor banquet" which "stands sweetly waiting" his "sweet presence," served by none but shoemakers:

> Yet add more honour to the Gentle Trade,
> Taste of Eyre's banquet, Simon's happy made.

> (V.v.182)

In the semi-ritualistic mixture of prose and poetry and in the gesture of the King eating from the shoemakers' holiday table, feast and work, nobility and the gentle trade, honor and love, find their festive blessing and their "gain."

THE SHOEMAKER'S HOLIDAY

Berlin, Normand. "Thomas Dekker: A Partial Reappraisal," *SEL*, VI (1966), 263–277.

Boas, Frederick S. *An Introduction to Stuart Drama.* Oxford, 1946, pp. 147–165.

Bradbrook, Muriel C. *The Growth and Structure of Elizabethan Comedy.* London, 1955, pp. 119–132.

Brown, Arthur. "Citizen Comedy and Domestic Drama," in *Jacobean Theatre,* ed. John Russell Brown. Stratford-upon-Avon Studies 1. New York, 1960, pp. 64–69.

Fluchère, Henri. "Thomas Dekker et le Drame Bourgeois," in *Le Théâtre Elizabéthain,* ed. Georgette Camille *et al.* Paris, 1940, pp. 248–254.

Hunt, Mary Leland. *Thomas Dekker: A Study.* New York, 1911, pp. 56–59.

Jones-Davies, Marie Thérèse. *Un Peintre de la Vie Londienne: Thomas Dekker (circa 1572–1632).* Collection des Etudes Anglaises. 2 vols. Paris, 1958, I, 126–129.

Knights, L. C. *Drama and Society in the Age of Jonson.* London, 1937, pp. 236–240.

Koszul, A., ed. *The Shoemaker's Holiday: Fête Chez le Cordonnier.* Collection du Théâtre de la Renaissance Paris, 1955.

Lange, Alexis F., ed. *The Shoemaker's Holiday,* in *Representative English Comedies,* ed. Charles Mills Gayley. 3 Vols. New York, 1912–1914, III, 3–17.

Novarr, David. "Dekker's Gentle Craft and the Lord Mayor of London," *MP,* LVII (1960), 233–239.

Spender, Constance. "The Plays of Thomas Dekker," *The Contemporary Review,* CXXX (1926), 332–339.

Steane, J. B., ed. *The Shoemaker's Holiday.* Cambridge, Eng., 1965, pp. 1–23.

Thomas Heywood

MARRIAGE AND THE DOMESTIC DRAMA
IN *A WOMAN KILLED WITH KINDNESS* *

Peter Ure

I

THE new murder play, so formlessly topical, and the old prodigal son play, with its didactic symmetries, both help to compose the Elizabethan domestic drama. If the citizen rank·of the characters and "the sensibility of ordinary people in ordinary life"[1] are looked upon as characteristic of this kind of drama, it is difficult to deny the claims of *The Glasse of Governement* and *Arden of Feversham* to be included in the discussion every time a consideration of the domestic theme is attempted. And if

* From Peter Ure, "Marriage and the Domestic Drama in Heywood and Ford," *English Studies,* Vol. 32, 1951, pp. 200–216. Reprinted by permission of the publishers.

1 Mr. Eliot's phrase, *Selected Essays* (London, 1934), p. 175.

the "common man as hero" is the criterion, as it is for Mr. Adams,[2] we will be constrained, like him, to include not only *'Tis Pity She's a Whore* but also perhaps *The Roman Actor* and even *Romeo and Juliet,* and countless others, in the genre. What is of interest here is not so much to define more precisely a kind whose shifting edges leave the historian uneasy as to find some central characteristic which, even if it severely limits the number of plays to be considered, will permit the revaluation of some fine plays that have, from time to time, been accepted into the category. If we add to the three criteria already mentioned a fourth— that the play concern itself with the relationship between husband and wife—we arrive at a convenient limitation. This is not to propose the use of another label—the "marriage play" or some such term—with the threat of another formula lurking beneath it. The term, used as a label, would obviously take us far outside the domestic genre—to *Othello* and beyond—and its edges would be as indefinite as any. But it suggests that the strength of the three plays, written at different times between 1603 and the 1630's and to be considered here in each others' light, lies in the way that they dramatize husband and wife. This eliminates most of the murder plays, too, where the interest is in the murder and not in the marriage; it gives us some chance of escaping from the pressure of various kinds of homiletic tradition—best exemplified in the prodigal son plays—and allows us to read the plays as something less unscrupulously formalized than mere versions of homily. For, while it is a code of marriage that lies at their basis, the tragedies (for such they mainly are) would not have occurred without that order being disturbed by the aberration of one or other partner. A play as impressive as *A Woman Killed with Kindness* is not simply, as Mr. Adams would have it, *a pièce à thèse.*

It is true that a playwright would be sustained in his use of the theme by common agreements about marriage amongst his audience. Chilton Powell and L. B. Wright have shown the variety and wide distribution of popular books on marriage: the citizen doctrine of marriage is already settle before the earliest of the plays appears, nor does it alter much in the years that follow.[3] There is little trace in these decent and godly treatises of those preoccupations of the courtly literature for which the Elizabethan period is justly renowned: the conventions of passionate love preserved in the sonnet, the impossible shees, the "Platonic" masquerades, the Phillidas and Coridons—all these are inconceivably remote from the interests of the authors of *The Glasse of Godly Loue, A Discourse of Marriage and Wiving,* and *A Happy Husband: or Direc-*

2 H. H. Adams, *English Domestic* or *Homiletic Tragedy, 1575–1642* (New York, 1943), p. 1.

3 L. B. Wright, *Middle Class Culture in Elizabethan England* (Chapel Hill, 1935), p. 226. Wright is speaking of a period of citizen treatise writing extending from 1558 to 1640.

tions for a Maid to Chuse her Mate. Not quite so remote, perhaps, are the ecclesiological discriminations of sectary and catholic about the doctrine of matrimony.[4] There are many points where a particular play may read like a version of the conduct books, as when Mistress Arthur in *How a Man may Choose a Good Wife from a Bad* refuses to divorce her termagant husband and he, repentant, draws the moral at the conclusion:

> he that will choose
> A good wife from a bad, come learn of me,
> That have tried both in wealth and misery...[5]

The ethical basis of the play is the doctrine, reiterated everywhere in the treatises, that the wife should win her mate with mildness:

> for each crosse
> Answer'd with *anger,* is to both a losse[6]

—a theme of the two *Patient Grissell* plays, just as the husband's duty of ungrudging tolerance is emphasized throughout Henry Porter's entertainment *The Two Angry Women of Abingdon.* A distich in Field's *Amends for Ladies:*

> Who falls, because her husband so hath done,
> Cures not his wound, but in herself makes one,[7]

is, applied to either partner, the unshakeable doctrine of marriage play and domestic conduct book alike.[8] But even such plays as these are not

[4] The current argument between Puritans and sectarians on the one hand and Catholics on the other as to whether marriage is a necessary evil (the Catholic view) or an "honourable and natural association between men and women of which children were the proper result but not the prime cause" (the Puritan view) is discussed by Chilton Powell, *English Domestic Relations, 1487–1653* (New York, 1917), p. 120. And cf. William Haller, *The Rise of Puritanism* (New York, 1938), pp. 120 f., and Wright, *op. cit.,* pp. 203–226. But neither domestic play nor middle-class domestic conduct book are much concerned with the ontology of marriage; they are practical affairs which very often confine themselves to formulating sensible *post factum* rules for domestic living in a bourgeois milieu. Nor do the plays argue the current controversy about the relative importance of the civil contract and the ecclesiastical solemnization (on which consult Powell, *op. cit.,* p. 37), or delve into the question that agitated Calvin (*Institutes,* tr. Norton, London n.d. [?1599] IV. 19. 34) whether marriage was or was not a sacrament.

[5] Text in Hazlitt's Dodsley (London, 1874), IX. 96.

[6] "A Wiues behaviour," *The Poetical Works of Patrick Hannay,* Hunterian Club Edition (London, 1875), p. 172.

[7] *Nero and other Plays,* Mermaid Edition (London, 1888), p. 441.

[8] Cf. for example Niccholes's *Discourse,* Harleian Miscellany (London, 1809), III, 280 f. It was not of course necessary for play to borrow from treatise or treatise from play; the ideas in both are "the reflection of current though rather than an influence from one field to another" (Powell, *op. cit.,* p. 205).

simply homiletic, since the playwright's purpose is not the same as the treatise-maker's. Niccholes and Hannay and the others who write on marriage wish to advise their readers on choice and instruct them in conduct; they have, as Haller writes of the Puritan John Dod, "the practical utilitarian [purpose] of directing behaviour to moral ends...in plain straightforward prose [or pedestrian verse], neither eloquent nor inspiring but apt and well salted." The playwright, although he accepts the morality from which the treatises proceed, is concerned with more complex problems. No matter how closely we juxtapose the plays with their analogous treatises, we are obliged to remember, even in considering the meagre excellences of Porter or Field, that the dramatists had to handle character and incident before an audience, and have, therefore, the right to be judged as dramatists and not as homilists. This absolves us from indicating all the points where play matches treatise. We need remember only that the plays belong to the same world as the middle-class treatise—a world that is not very interested in nice discriminations about the theology of marriage, that tends to reject "Platonic" and passionate love as impartially as an ascetic or suspicious attitude to marriage; a world, indeed, that is no satellite of the aristocratic culture that produced Donne's love poems, the antilogies of the curious Burton, or the insinuating realism of Bacon's essay on marriage. As Burton remarked, "What cares *vulgus hominum* what they say?"⁹

II

That the play should be looked at without the intrusion of too many preconceptions about ruling formulae is particularly important in the case of what has always been justly considered the finest example of the genre, Thomas Heywood's *A Woman Killed with Kindness*. It is apposite that in this play the theme of marriage is handled in a way that contributes immensely to the dramatic force of the work, yet without any departure from an accepted code. It is the agreement about this code, which Heywood could assume in his audience—an agreement reinforced by the powerful appeal of the theme quite apart from any conscious formulation of it—that contributed to its effect and can still contribute today.¹⁰ Those who have written on this play have not done

9 *The Anatomy of Melancholy* (London, 1881), p. 624 (Part 3, Sec. 2, Mem. 5, Subs. 5).

10 Powell (*op. cit.*, p. 124) says that marriage as an institution was not so highly valued then as nowadays. Certainly, neither the Anglican-Catholic view of marriage as a necessary evil nor Calvin's equation, proceeding from a quite opposite

it justice. It is worth while to reconsider the whole work with special attention to the objections that it has had to meet.

The relation between the main plot, the story of the Frankfords and Wendoll, and the subsidiary action has always caused difficulty.[11] We may agree that an underplot should not merely distract our attention with a set of irrelevant events thrown in for good measure, which even constrict the dramatist's freedom in his handling of the main action. Dr. Clark makes a double objection that this underplot is distracting in just that way and that the appearance of a Lucrece in the fields of Yorkshire is an incongruity sharply pointed by the domestic realism of her setting. Miss Townsend has discerned, in answer to this objection, the thematic unity which binds the two plots together in the form of a contrast between Mistress Frankford's easy yielding of her honour and Susan's Roman staunchness.[12] Even more striking than this play upon Honour is the way the underplot takes up the paradox of the drama's title. Sir Charles must discharge the burden of moral debt which his enemy's kindness has laid upon him;[13] similarly, Mistress Frankford

---

principle, that "it is a good and holy ordinance of God, so tillage, carpentrie, shooemakers craft, barbers craft, are lawfull ordinances of God," would be very sympathetically recived nowadays. But whatever the theory may have been, it is surely safe to assert that the depiction of suffering husband or wife betrayed would have an appeal to an audience of husbands and wives and their children quite unaffected by the relatively low value which churchmen continued to set on the institution of matrimony right up to the time when post-Calvinistic Puritanism began to glorify it.

[11] See the various observations of Courthope (*History of English Poetry,* Oxford, 1910, IV. 215), A. M. Clark (*Thomas Heywood,* Oxford, 1931, p. 230), McIlwraith (*Five Elizabethan Tragedies,* London, 1938, pp. xvii–xviii) and others cited by Miss Townsend in "The Artistry of Thomas Heywood's Double Plots," *P.Q.* XXV (1946), pp. 97f. Since Clark says of the sub-plot that "We endure it, but it escapes the memory," I give a summary. It is the story of Sir Charles Mountford who quarrels with Sir Francis Acton, another member of the Yorkshire squirearchy, during a hawking match. Mountford and his men fight with Acton and his men, and Mountford kills two of Acton's retainers. He is put on trial and acquitted, but the legal expenses ruin him. All he has left is a small house and garden to which he retires with his sister Susan. He falls into a moneylender's power and is finally deprived of his remaining estate and thrown into the counter. Acton, who up to now has been implacable, falls in love with Susan, and for her sake secretly pays her brother's debts and releases him. Mountford is shamed by this kindness, and, unable to repay Acton in any other way, offers to prostitute his sister Susan to him. As in *The Rape of Lucrece* and Webster's *Appius and Virginia* (which may be partly Heywood's work) we have a scene in which Susan prefers death to dishonour. But Acton greatly refuses his opportunity and takes the hand of the penniless girl in marriage, himself providing the dowry. Mountford gives up the unequal battle with his enemy's kindness and the two men are reconciled.

[12] *Loc. cit.,* p. 101. Miss Townsend adds the balance of Wendoll's dishonour with Acton's honour.

[13] V. i. 63. The text used is that of McIlwraith in *Five Elizabethan Tragedies.*

must find a way to repay with interest the kindness of Frankford after his discovery of her adultery. Cheated of her rightful punishment, in which she expects to suffer the part of a Tamyra or a Penthea (IV. v. 90–91), she must herself inflict upon herself the appropriate penalty in order to discharge the mounting debt to husband and conscience. Frankford's improper kindness has surcharged her and in the end kills her— it is the paradox at the heart of the play, suitably pointed by the concluding lines of the fifth act. Both plots thus explore this strange paradox and run a concurrent course: Sir Charles suffers under the monstrous burden of being forgiven by a bitter enemy and is driven to an immorality (the prostitution of his sister) in order to free himself of it; Mistress Frankford, pardoned by a deeply injured husband, has to rid herself of the debt by an act of contrition that proceeds far beyond Christian penitence. She starves herself to death. In the conclusion, Acton's magnanimity to Susan is balanced by Frankford's passionate compassion as his wife dies. Both men have been consistently kind and these final mercies are a consummation of their virtuous Magnificence. Heywood was not writing a problem play, and it is true that the stark unusualness of Mistress Frankford's action and fate is softened by the conventional lines of the sin-repentance-forgiveness scheme which is all that Adams sees in the play. But Heywood *was* concerned, as his title suggests, to exploit a paradox which perhaps ran deeper than he knew. It is at least difficult, in the age of Ibsen, to refrain from asking why the increasing disproportion between the kindness of Acton and the indebtedness of Sir Charles should cease to worry the latter at the point it does, or to forget that the depiction of a justifiable self-slaughter in *Samson Agonistes* led even Milton into some obliquity and wresting of doctrine.[14] Heywood, of all writers, had least wish to divellicate such problems. The fact, however, that his play evades the question goes closer to an explanation of why it is not a *very* great work than any attempts by later critics, applying criteria never very clearly articulated, to charge its author with dramaturgical incompetence.

If the thematic unities of Honour and Kindness hold good, the point satisfies, at least, the requirement that an underplot should help to give structure, solidity, and verisimilitude to the architecture of the play world and underpin our understanding of the principal action. We can, in that case, derive some added pleasure from the shapeliness of the correspondences; we can recognize that Mistress Frankford's attempt to discharge her debt is not so incredible when we view the motive operating with strange results in a man of honour like Sir Charles. But an underplot may also be asked to give us a different kind of pace and rhythm from that of the main plot. In *A Woman Killed with Kindness* we cannot, by any abrupt removals from banqueting hall to porter's lodge, enjoy the

14 H. J. C. Grierson, *Milton and Wordsworth* (London, 1937), pp. 146–7.

relief that clownish gambols supposedly afford to the tensions engendered by princely circumstance. Though the source be ultimately in the *novelle*, the story of Susan has, in every sense, been domesticated. Heywood does seem, however, to have tried to make the Susan story go faster than the Frankford story: the great trajectory of Sir Charles's descent from prosperous country gentleman, whose fall stands not in the prospect of belief, to hind and prisoner, and his recovery from these declined conditions, contrasts, in the rapidity with which we absorb it all, to the slow working of the other tale—the arrival of Wendoll the seducer, his honourable resistances, Nick's suspicion of him, Nick's discovery, followed by the slow-dropping agonies of the central scenes. This may be an impression difficult to substantiate, but it bears closely upon another, and final, question about the relationship between the two plots; why it is in the nature of the subplot, admitting its thematic correspondence with the main plot, that it should end happily, and in the nature of the main plot that it should end solemnly. The difference can be explained thus: what happens to Sir Charles is something external to his deeper self, the kind of misfortune that can be spoken of plainly in terms of debts, land, and gentle status. Although he twice hovers on the verge of dissolution, when conscience-stricken after the falconry affray and when he meditates the surrender of his sister's honour, his agony never marches with Frankford's—Heywood does not trench him to the heart. He can mount aloft and resume gentility by a mere twist of Fortune's wheel. But Frankford has been flung from the wheel. His is a burrowing grief, inward and slower, like Geraldine's in *The English Traveller;* he is betrayed in a point of deepest consequences, his marriage, and when he recovers he is a changed man, existent in a world he had not formerly known, the world of repentance, exalted pardon, and imminent death. Thus, though thematically the two plots encourage understanding of one another, the contrast between the way Mountford's character is sketched and Frankford's graved, is one feature which helps to keep the subsidiary plot, as it should be, decorously subordinate to the main plot, which has digged deeper in love's mine. The cohesion between the two plots is one of moral themes which increases our understanding of the play's rationale; the difference between the two characters is the point where the dramatist's (as distinct from the moralist's) task begins. And in the Frankford story we are inducted into a world where the profound theme of marriage, unknown to the underplot, is stated not in terms of moral formulae but by the more potent agencies of dramatic character and poetic speech. We look in it not for understanding but for katharsis.

When we enter upon the main plot we have to dispose of one more objection. Heywood was not the first writer of domestic dramas to handle the theme of a virtuous woman fallen. The author of *A Warning for Fair Women* (1599) had simply fobbed his audience off with a dumb show,[15] and Heywood himself made no attempt to represent the seduction of Wincott's wife by Delavil in *The English Traveller*. In *A Woman Killed with Kindness* he was ill-advised, or courageous, enough to put the incident on the stage. The sudden breakdown of Mistress Frankford's resistance to Wendoll in II. iii (152–4) is condemned as, by modern standards, psychologically implausible—the result, according to Clark, of the constriction of the main plot by the underplot—or hardily justified as a fragment of obsolete psychology having to do with old beliefs about man's dominance by a single passion and the debility of virtuous women placed in Eve's situation.[16] It may be that we must gulp down these dry morsels; but it is fair to Heywood to remember the necessary time-scheme and architectonic of the whole play. The three great incidents of the Frankford story, the seduction, the discovery, and the death, to all of which the wedding-scene is an important prologue, are three blocks of time dramaturgically handled. To the first naturally belong the struggle of conscience, the seduction, the yielding. Seduction and surrender are the *données* of the succeeding incidents on which Heywood's special interest and the originality of the play are centred. Heywood could not delay with this early effect without disrupting the structure, which is in itself quite satisfying, and, because the audience are not baulked, much more satisfying than the reticence of *The English Traveller*. Further, since the play so utterly disregards the unity of time in the interest of extracting full pathos from the marriage theme, it was all the more desirable that Heywood should achieve a shape for it by a forthright representation of the main incidents of the marriage's chequered course, each being allotted only that share of stage time proportionate to its importance in the total scheme.

That scheme, and its moving effect, depend very largely upon the marriage theme, for the tragic powers of *A Woman Killed with Kindness* derive from the broken marriage. It is a domestic play in this narrower sense, as well as in its setting and literary affinities. The first scene opens with the wedding festivities, with Mistress Frankford already cast for the part of the dutiful wife favoured by the makers of conduct books:

> A perfect wife already, meek and patient;
> How strangely the world "husband" fits your mouth,
> Not married three hours since! Sister, 'tis good;
> You, that begin betimes thus, must needs prove
> Pliant and duteous in your husband's love.

(I. i. 37–41)

[15] *A Warning for Faire Women*, II, ed. Simpson, *The School of Shakespeare* (London, 1879), ii. 269.

[16] See Hardin Craig's remarks on the play in *The Enchanted Glass* (New York, 1936), pp. 128–136, and cf. Wright on "The Controversy over Women," *op. cit.*, Chap. XIII.

Sir Charles's next speech celebrates in what is perhaps the finest of all passages of homespun domestic verse the happiness of the marriage and the rightness of Frankford's choice (I. i. 55–72). It is of these scenes, of the country measures—

> Hark, they are all on the hoigh;
> They toil like mill-horses, and turn as round, —
> Marry, not on the toe. Ay, and they caper,
> Not without cutting; you shall see, tomorrow,
> The hall-floor peck'd and dinted like a mill-stone,
> Made with their high shoes...

(I. i 85–91)

and of the footing in parlour and yard that we are reminded during the discovery scenes of the fourth act. For a key to these scenes is recollection, the desire to undo what has been done and to return to the former happy state (IV. v. 51 f.). The strongest emphasis is placed upon the way this early happiness has been destroyed by the breaking of the marriage bond:

> This is the key that opes my outward gate;
> This is the hall-door; this my withdrawing chamber;
> But this, that door that's bawd unto my shame,
> Fountain and spring of all my bleeding thoughts,
> Where the most hallowed order and true knot
> Of nuptial sanctity hath been profan'd;
> It leads to my polluted bed-chamber,
> Once my terrestrial heaven, now my earth's hell,
> The place where sins in all their ripeness dwell

(IV. v. 8–16)

And, later, it is his desire not to suffer the unbearable tension between what is and what was that urges Frankford to rid the house of everything that may remind him of his wife (V. ii. 1–11) and that leads to the famous scenes with the abandoned lute (V. ii and iii), scenes of an artistry not less great, though more extended, than that moment in *Othello* where the Moor remembers that he can no longer speak of "my wife." In all these scenes Heywood's mastery is complete, displaying a perfect control of stage effect and timing and a complete reconciliation between character and theme—that is, we are enabled to feel with Frankford's sufferings and yet contemplate the firm development of the moral tale of the broken marriage. It is a point where the social seriousness with which the marriage contract is viewed expertly supports the *agon* in the individual before us. To realize the extent of Heywood's achievement here we need only compare it with the management of the discovery scene in *The English Traveller* (IV. iii): in Young Geraldine's long speech we find the same trajectory from happiness to misfortune described—the lover's fond recollection of his contract, the discovery, the suppressed movement of revenge, and the sudden stripping of the man of all his comforts. Yet the scene is less commendable because the audience are as unprepared for the surprise as Geraldine himslef. It is an effective stage situation, a thrilling jolt, but we are not able, as we are in the earlier play, to bring our previous knowledge of the broken contract, and the moral and social gravity which that theme has engendered in us, to bear at just that point where it is stated in terms of a particular individual's endurance of it in his own life—where, in fact, the moral theme becomes incarnate in the suffering husband. (The surrender of Mistress Frankford herself in II. iii, which is the ground of these scenes, is, rightly, not felt as they are: there we are merely presented with the act itself, the datum only of the theorem of tragic consequences which are the substance of drama-as distinct from morality. Consequently, our reaction there is one of regret, tinged with moral reproof, and an acceptance that this is a part of the unfolding of the story.) . . .

See other studies in Heywood bibliography (below, p. 218).

DRAMATIC DECEPTION IN HEYWOOD'S
THE ENGLISH TRAVELLER *

Norman Rabkin

THE most difficult but essential thing for us to realize as audience of a theater now dead is the extent and vitality of the compact between playwright and playgoer which we call convention. Like ourselves as movie goers, the Elizabethan audience knew pretty much what to expect at a play, and—again as in the movies—the dramatist's greatest capital lay in the audience's conventional expectations. Because of them the audience was immediately at home as a play began; and because of its comfortable assurance, the audience was peculiarly susceptible to surprise when the

* From *Studies in English Literature, 1500–1900*, Vol. 1, No. 2, 1961, pp. 1–16. Reprinted by permission of the editor of *SEL* (Rice University).

playwright rang unexpected changes on a particular convention. Thus, for example, Jonson jolted his auditors by variations on the established principles of the distribution of comic justice in *The Alchemist*. In *The English Traveller* Thomas Heywood reaches the height of his achievement in comedy.[1] His skill is manifest in the use of a double plot to convey a complex theme, the full implications of which are not seen until the independent plots have been brought to their conclusions and the two actions considered together. The unique mastery of the play, however, is the remarkable control over his material which enables Heywood, by brilliantly manipulating a number of dramatic conventions, to delude and mystify the audience through most of the action. And this device, which produces a great deal of dramatic excitement, is itself a means of presenting the theme of the play.

For the sake of convenience the two plots will be rehearsed briefly here. The main action is as follows. Young Geraldine, a gentleman of London, is intimate at the home of old Wincott, who is married to a woman of Geraldine's age; the two young people have been acquainted from childhood, and had even contemplated marriage until old Wincott's suit intervened. Geraldine spends a good deal of time in the house in the company of his friend Dalavill, who is courting Prudentilla, the sister of Wincott's wife. There is no illicit affair between Geraldine and Wincott's wife; in fact, the two of them in a closet scene make their innocence explicit and plight their troth for some time after the expected death of the old husband. Dalavill, however, suggests to Geraldine's father that there is such a relationship, or at least the appearance of one, and old Geraldine, in order to end either the affair or its bad appearance, requests that his son no longer frequent the home of Wincott, a request which young Geraldine agrees to obey. Wincott, disturbed by the young man's unexplained absence, asks him to violate his father's orders to the extent of coming to his house and accounting for his apparent coolness. Young Geraldine does so, covertly, and after telling his story to the old man, decides to pay a call on Wincott's wife in her bedroom. To his complete surprise, he finds her in bed with Dalavill, who boasts to her of having skillfully removed young Geraldine from the house in order to protect his own friendship, and Mistress Wincott's relationship, with Geraldine. Young Geraldine resolves to leave England and say nothing, but his father insists that before his inexplicable voyage he should accept

[1] A. M. Clark, *Thomas Heywood: Playwright and Miscellanist* (Oxford, 1931), p. 119, asserts that *The English Traveller* was "fairly certainly written...in the early twenties of the seventeenth century"; he favors 1624, but G. E. Bentley, *The Jacobean and Caroline Stage*, IV (Oxford, 1956), 565–566, prefers *c.* 1627. All citations are from the text in *The Dramatic Works of Thomas Heywood*, reprinted by John Pearson (London, 1874), Vol. IV. Since Pearson did not number the lines of the plays he printed, I shall refer to page numbers for the reader's convenience.

old Wincott's invitation to a farewell banquet at his home. At this final scene, the wife's hypocrisy forces young Geraldine to tell her the reason for his indifference to her; she is overcome by shame and grief, confesses all to her husband, and dies. Dalavill flees, and young Geraldine decides to remain in England.

The subplot is as follows. Young Lionel's father, a London merchant travelling abroad on business, has left his son the management of his house and business. Under the influence of his servant, Reignald, young Lionel has thrown open the house to rioters, low women, and profligates. Unexpectedly old Lionel returns from abroad; Reignald hides all the rioters in the house, locks it, and by a tale of murder and ghosts holds off the old man. For a short time, through quick thinking and clever handling of Lionel's neighbor Ricott, Reignald makes the old man believe that his son has enriched his estate and been a model young man, but the truth comes out. Young Lionel repents and is ultimately forgiven, and, after a moment of doubt, the old man forgives Reignald, who renounces his foxlike behavior. The Lionels and Reignald are present at the banquet in Wincott's house in the last scene; except for an account of the activities in the Lionel house given in old Wincott's house, there is no other relationship between the two plots.[2]

In his suggestive essay on *Hamlet,* Mr. Francis Fergusson proposes a method of analysis for the plays of Shakespeare:

> The situation, the moral and metaphysical "scene" of the drama, is presented only as one character after another sees and reflects it; and the action of the drama as a whole is presented only as each character in turn actualizes it in his story and according to his lights. This is as much as to say that the various stories with their diverse casts of characters are analogous, and that the drama as a whole is therefore "one by analogy" only. It does not have the literal and rational unity of the single logically and causally connected chain of events or story. And if we are to grasp a novel of Henry James or a play by Shakespeare, we must be prepared to follow these shifting perspectives, as we move from character to character and from story to story, trying, as we go, to divine the supreme analogue, the underlying theme, to which they all point in their various ways.[3]

Such a "supreme analogue" underlies both actions of *The English Traveller*: it is the familiar theme of appearance and reality, which Heywood had employed already in *The Royal King and the Loyal Sub-*

---

[2] Freda L. Townsend, "The Artistry of Thomas Heywood's Double Plots," *PQ,* XXV (1946), 114, notes that *"The English Traveller* is the only one of Heywood's double-plot plays which fails in the opening act to provide a natural transition from one action to the other, to make it appear, at the beginning, that the second action is in some sense an outgrowth of the first."

[3] *The Idea of a Theater* (Princeton, 1949), p. 104.

ject and *A Woman Killed with Kindness.*[4] In the main plot, as in *A Woman Killed,* that theme is developed with respect to fidelity in love; in the subplot it is generalized.

The hero of the play is clearly young Geraldine, and his discovery of the truth, a discovery which the audience makes at the same time as he does, constitutes a moral education for him. From the outset he is explicitly concerned with the relation of seeming to being:

> I should be loath
> Professe in outward show to be one Man.
> And prooue my selfe another.

> (p. 12)

The character through whom his education is effected, and who is therefore a focal character in the plot, is Wincott's wife; and it is above all through her, and young Geraldine's perception of her, that the theme of the play is developed.

From the moment when she is first described, Wincott's wife's relationship with her husband is seen as somewhat problematical. Of all the characters in the play, she alone has no name of her own: she is identified solely by her role as the old man's wife. The very first line describing her is delivered by Roger the Clown, servant of Wincott, who suggests that this is a typical marriage of "cold Ianuary and lusty May," subject to all the ills of such marriages (p. 8). This is a comedy; two young intimates of Wincott's house are reminded by a clown of a standard farce situation represented by the marriage: the audience at this point must have a stock response which hints how the rest of the action is going to work.[5] But immediately we are told that this is an unusual marriage, and the terms in which Dalavill describes the virtues of Mistress Wincott, and the sympathy between the two, make us realize that the play is going to develop in a fashion different from what we expect. Dalavill as much as says that the expectations of farce are not to be satisfied by this noble situation, and the audience is made to feel that the play will deal with human relations in a different manner from that of the customary literary treatment. That Dalavill, ultimately the real villain in

---

4 Extended analysis of the two plays would be out of place here, but one need only note such lines as, " 'Tis geenrall thorow the world, each state esteemes / A man not what he is, but what he seemes," *The Royal King and Loyall Subject,* ed. Kate Watkins Tibbals, University of Pennsylvania Series in Philology and Literature, XII (Philadelphia, 1906), III.259–260, or remember Heywood's ironic emphasis through much of *A Woman Killed* on Frankford's happy state of deception.

5 For a brief description of the characters of *The English Traveller* in terms of the conventions of Roman comedy, see Marvin T. Herrick, *Tragicomedy: Its Origins and Development in Italy, France, and England,* Illinois Studies in Language and Literature, XXXIX (Urbana, 1955), p. 285. For pertinent descriptions of the conventions of various Elizabethan dramatic genres, see W. W. Main, "Dramaturgical Norms in the Elizabethan Repertory," *SP,* LIV (1957), 128–148.

this marriage, now makes the exonerating statement, cannot yet be significant to the audience. Note, however, that Dalavill supplants a conventional and unfair account of the marriage by a deeper kind of understanding; and note that Heywood will later disclose that the man who makes us see what seems, through most of the play, to be the truth, is the man who will violate that "truth."

Dalavill's good report of the marriage is finally substantiated in a private scene (II.i) between young Geraldine and Wincott's wife. If the audience has any lingering suspicions that there will be an affair between the two young people (Dalavill is excluded from such an affair because of his courtship of Prudentilla, and his apparent lack of interest), this scene makes it perfectly clear that values animate the action of the couple which exist in a different world from the worlds of Roman comedy and the fabliau. Young Geraldine and Wincott's wife, conscious of a deep and long-lived mutual attraction, both show an impressive self-restraint and concern for honor as they pledge never to deceive Wincott; their vow to marry each other a suitable period of time after the expected death of old Wincott—an event which they anticipate with muted sadness —is thoroughly virtuous, and involves renunciation by young Geraldine of interest in any other woman. Through this much of the second act, then, the audience has been shown that a situation potentially capable of leading to predictable farce is charged with decent and intense emotions, and with principles not commonly expected in the stage event.

As the plot moves forward, Heywood produces a kind of reversal strangely characteristic of *The English Traveller*. We have just seen a good relationship purged of all its suggestions of evil; now the suggestions are vigorously renewed. Dalavill, whose motives at this point are not clear to the audience, suggests to old Geraldine that there is an illicit affair between young Geraldine and Wincott's wife. "The audience is as much surprised as old Geraldine."[6] Dalavill's behavior seems gratuitous, like that of Iago, since we have seen him so far only in the role of sympathetic friend to young Geraldine, and Heywood suggests this apparent gratuitousness by making Dalavill actually echo the language of Iago: "yet introath, / I thinke they both are honest"; "for as I liue, / I thinke, they both are honest" (pp. 43–44). The effect of Dalavill's evil report is to keep young Geraldine away from the house of Wincott, since he is as desirous as his father to preserve the good name of that house; the audience is not convinced by the charges, because they have seen the true relationship between the young people. Once again, as at the beginning of the play, a virtuous relationship is seen as evil; but whereas the audience was previously ready to believe in the evil because their expectations of comic convention had been aroused, they do not

6 R. G. Martin, "The Technical Development of Thomas Heywood," unpublished dissertation (Harvard, 1910), p. 651.

believe in this report, and recognize its basis in appearance rather than in fact.

The play seems to be making a point at this stage about the involvement of evil appearance in a good reality. Young Geraldine, because of the sanctity of his vow to Wincott's wife not to consider any other wife but her, is unable to clear up his father's suspicions by obeying old Geraldine's request that he marry; the result is that the old man continues to suspect the behavior of his son, who is actually acting out of almost excessive scrupulosity, rather than out of the evil principles his refusal suggests. Old Geraldine watches an innocent scene in which Wincott begs that young Geraldine accompany the Wincotts home from the Geraldines, and feels constrained to note "How men are borne / To woe their owne disasters?" (p. 45)—a comment we shall see returning in the subplot in an equally ironic context. When young Geraldine has convinced his father of his virtue, he agrees, in order to prove his innocence, to stay away from Wincott's house: to avoid evil appearances, he must abandon a situation in which there has been nothing but good. Again, when the young man reluctantly accepts Wincott's request for an interview, in order that he may cast no shadow on the reputation of the house he takes care to arrive at midnight, and to arrange that the garden gate be open so that he may slip in unperceived. No one else in the house must know of his visit. The meeting thus covertly arranged bears all the marks of an assignation with Wincott's wife—but the meeting is really with the husband!

The denouement of the plot concerning Wincott's wife involves her unmasking: the good appearance she has so firmly established in the eyes of young Geraldine and the audience must be destroyed. Before the scenes in which Heywood accomplishes the disillusionment (IV.iii, IV.iv) there is only one hint that Mistress Wincott has been dishonest. Bess, her chambermaid, suggests to young Geraldine that Dalavill's constant presence in the house is due to an affair with the old man's wife. Characteristically, both of young Geraldine's steadfastness and of the obscurity of the truth presented throughout the play, Geraldine angrily denies the slander, so strongly as perhaps to leave the audience even more convinced of Mistress Wincott's innocence. Bess's answer to young Geraldine's defense of his friend reverberates with overtones of much more than this one problem in the play: "Come, come, he is, what he is; and that the end will prooue" (p. 56).[7]

The whole problem of appearance as it is embodied in his friends becomes most excruciating and most explicit for young Geraldine in the final scene. At Wincott's banquet he has no intention of telling what he knows, but, left alone for a minute with Mistress Wincott, he discovers that she intends to use all her charms and her virtuous appearance to

---

7 Heywood had already given a similar remark, charged with the same irony, to the title character of *The Wise Woman of Hogsdon* (1604): "I am as I am, and there's an end" (*Dramatic Works*, V, 296).

lure him into an explanation of his absence and a return to her company. He tries vainly to put her off, but her hypocrisy and her importunate demands for signs of affection goad him into a fury which he cannot restrain, and he tells her what he has seen. His sensitivity to the problem of deceptive appearance in behavior has already been established. Now, like Shakespeare's Troilus able at last to see both the appearance and the reality simultaneously, young Geraldine finds the discrepancy between them more than he can bear:

> Shee almost makes me question what I know,
> An Hereticke vnto my owne belief:
> Oh thou mankinds seducer.

(p. 89)

For the audience, too, the series of changes in the relationship between what Mistress Wincott seems to be and what she is has come full circle. Heywood has suggested at the outset that she is a woman who will act according to certain comic conventions; he has surprised the audience by betraying the expectations he has set up, and presenting her as a woman whose virtue is superior to that of the traditional, fabliau character in her situation; then, having convinced the audience of her purity, he has demonstrated that this apparently saintly woman has been deceiving not only her husband, but also her best friend and confidant, her betrothed. The audience, who know the truth about her, must find ironic satisfaction in watching her, practically at the moment of her death, still attempting to mask that truth. Like young Geraldine, they look at once on semblance and actuality.

The subplot presents, worked out in an entirely different manner but again involving the ironic manipulation of dramatic convention, a set of variations on the same theme.[8] The situation is one of complex and

---

[8] Previous critics of *The English Traveller* have found no such relation between the two plots. T. S. Eliot, "Thomas Heywood," *Selected Essays* (New York, 1950), p. 155, who thinks that "in *The English Traveller*...Heywood found his best plot," tosses off the subplot as a "clumsy failure." Madeleine Doran, *Endeavors of Art* (Madison, 1954), pp. 296–97, cites the play as an example of how "the introduction of a secondary plot interlaced through the main one...may dilute the effect of the principal story." F. S. Boas, *An Introduction to Stuart Drama* (Oxford, 1946), p. 181, asserts that the "subplot...is very loosely related to the main action." R. G. Martin (pp. 666–667) charges that "the connection between the two plots is of the most artificial description, even slighter than that which links the two stories in *Woman Killed*." Miss Townsend (pp. 110–111) couples *The English Traveller* with *The Captives* (I agree with her judgment on the latter play): "In neither play can there be discerned a theme which gives unity." Most recently, and with more perception of intention than his predecessors, Michel Grivelet, *Thomas Heywood et le Drame Domestique Élizabéthain* (Paris, 1957), p. 376, finds in the double plot of *The English Traveller* "une de ces dissonances qui, si elles nous choquent aujourd'hui, étaient peut-être dans le goût du temps de Heywood et qui ne sont pas, en tous cas, l'effet du hasard mais certainement calculées."

yet obvious deception. Put in charge of his father's house and money because he appears trustworthy, young Lionel has abandoned all scruple and turned the once respectable home into the lowest kind of house. But his understanding of the situation is no more accurate than his father's. For young Lionel, glorying in his first moments of freedom, thinks he is lord of the house, and his servant Reignald encourages him in that belief:

> YOUNG LIONEL: Who in my fathers absence should command, Saue
> I only his sonne?
> REIGNALD: It is but iustice.
> YOUNG LIONEL: For am not I now Lord?
> REIGNALD: *Dominus fac totum.*
> And am not I your Steward?

> (pp. 16–17)

But the fact is that Reignald is master in the house: he arranges the entertainment, controls the money, and treats the house as his own. He even tells another servant that he is "the mighty Lord and Senescall / Of this great house and castle" (p. 14).

If the theme develops in the main plot chiefly through the role played by Mistress Wincott, it does so in the subplot through the actions of Reignald. To a certain point the epitome of the standard comic servant running away with his master's house, Reignald makes his way by brilliant manipulation of the actual situations in which he is involved, and of their appearances. When old Lionel returns unexpectedly, the servant is able not only to allay the old man's suspicions, but even to make young Lionel appear virtuous and thrifty—in the very presence of a usurer who is trying to collect young Lionel's debts! Reignald keeps old Lionel out of his own house, disguising the evil in the riotous building by a cock-and-bull story of far more serious evil, involving murder and ghosts. Often in both plots of *The English Traveller* one feels as if one were playing with a set of Chinese boxes within boxes. For example, the story Reignald tells old Lionel is, itself, about a man being trapped by evil in the guise of good. It should be noted too that Reignald's "Braine and Art" (p. 41) succeed in tricking the neighbor Ricott, who mistakenly thinks he is fully acquainted with Reignald's motives and plans, into assisting him.

But it is a different kind of trick which makes Reignald the remarkable character he is. Reignald should remind the audience of Jonson's Face: conducting the revels in the absence of the master of the house, inviting in low and miscellaneous friends, throwing the house into ill repute among the neighbors, locking the door against the master and warning him away from touching the doorknob upon his return, being left to hold the fort alone for his accomplices, and keeping the master off for a night by a fictitious story of what has occurred within. The audience is probably familiar with Face; they remember the independent connivances of Brainworm, who works for old and young Knowell and at the expense of both; and they will think of Mosca, who fleeces his own master more thoroughly than he does anyone else. Hence they must expect that Reignald will feel no sense of obligation to anyone. And Reignald announces to the audience that he is just this kind of untrustworthy servant:

> What fooles are these,
> To trust their ruin'd fortunes to his hands,
> That hath betrai'd his own; And make themselues
> Prisoner to one deserues to lie for all,
> As being cause of all.

> (pp. 36–37)

The lines anticipate old Geraldine's "How men are borne / To woe their owne disasters?" and are equally ironic for the audience. Old Geraldine's speech has not given a true picture of the situation, for Wincott is not courting his own disaster by trusting in young Geraldine. Likewise, Reignald is clearly established as a conniving, unprincipled servant-Vice, accountable only to his own wit; yet, like other characters in the play, he disappoints the audience's expectations and turns out not to be what he has seemed. For immediately after the speech just cited he announces to the audience that "something prompts me" to take any risk necessary to protect young Lionel against his father. He will "Art...with Knauery join" to serve his young master, out of a "seruants love." The effect is one of great surprise, to see the "mighty Lord and Senescall" of the house voluntarily assuming this role of loyal retainer.

The essence of Reignald's game is "smooth Dissembling meet with Impudence" (p. 37). He cozens all; we have already examined the way in which he plays on appearances with young and old Lionel (and, it might be added, with their neighbor Ricott). It is this faculty, of being able—until old Lionel beats him at his own game—to see both the appearance and the reality at once, which gives Reignald his power over the other characters; it is also what relates him to the main plot. For, in less comic fashion, young Geraldine comes precisely to Reignald's point of view at the end of the play: he too can see the truth behind the mask as he beholds the mask. Young Geraldine recognizes the disguise as evil; and Reignald too, caught in a trap of his own making and spared only by his master's grace, comes to acknowledge the evil of pretending that things are not what they seem. Hence he renounces playing on others' capacity to be gulled:

> I was the Fox,
> But I from hencefoorth, will no more the Cox-
> Combe, put vpon your pate.

> (p. 85)

Thus both plots involve the unmasking of a dissembler, and, in different degrees because the degree of sinning is different, the penance of the dissembler. It is interesting to note that when old Lionel exposes Reignald, though he is fully aware of Reignald's tricks now, he first pretends not to know them, just as young Geraldine is to do in the other plot with Mistress Wincott. And just as Mistress Wincott is accused of the wrong crime in the first part of the play, Reignald is held most accountable for the murder of young Lionel, and almost loses his life for this crime which has never taken place.

Through another element of the subplot Heywood again deceives the audience. Young Lionel has a mistress by the name of Blanda, a courtesan who frequents the house in the company of her bawd, Scapha. Hardly has the relationship between young Lionel and Blanda been established as that between young rioter and courtesan when a new aspect appears: young Lionel treats Blanda and his affair with her seriously, almost morally. He acts as if really in love with her, speaks of "an affection fixt, and Permanent" (p. 21) and of his soul being at peace with her. So much does Blanda seem to be in love with him that Scapha must caution her against being excessively loyal and monogamous. All of this is still comic, and done without much emphasis, but young Lionel and Blanda consistently treat each other with a fidelity not to be expected on the conventional stage between two such young people. The most revealing lines come at the end of this scene. Young Lionel and another rioter have arranged the evening's entertainment, to include wenches. Overhearing the last arrangement, Blanda asks young Lionel what he is up to; he makes a feeble excuse and then says, in a curtain aside, "In youth there is a Fate, that sways us still, / To know what's Good, and yet pursue what's Ill" (p. 23). "What's Good" is Blanda the courtesan, "what's Ill" the wenches with whom he is planning to be entertained. Just as happened, then, when the audience discovered that the conventionally comic account of the Wincotts' marriage as that of January and May did not conform to non-comic realities, the conventional situation of young blood and courtesan becomes transformed before their eyes into something else. And once again the audience is later informed that it has been deceived: at the end of the play young Lionel willingly dismisses the courtesan as a "wanton," admitting that he did not love her (p. 83). Ultimately it is the conventional not the individual nature of the relationship which shapes its course. May does deceive January; young men drop their mistresses as "Shaddowes, Toyes and Dreames" (*loc. cit.*). The same play which has told us that people should not be treated as comic stereotypes ends by making its characters conform to just those stereotypes.

Heywood plays on the "supreme analogue" of *The English Traveller* through yet another deception. In no other play—not even in *The Wise Woman of Hogsdon,* another comedy of chicanery—does Heywod withhold essential information from the audience. But here we never learn whether or not Dalavill has been deceiving Wincott and young Geraldine from the beginning. At the outset he seems socially isolated from the other characters, and before long he seems even morally isolated. During a conversation in which the Wincotts and Geraldines express their obligation and friendship to each other, Dalavill objects, aside, to the economic metaphor in which they couch their sentiments. He acts as if he has a higher morality, a deeper sensibility, than theirs. And yet it is just after this moment (p. 42) that he denounces young Geraldine's apparent affair with Mistress Wincott. This bewildering of the audience is accomplished with the utmost virtuosity. A means of averting suspicion from Dalavill throughout the first two thirds of the play is the suggestion that there is going to be a second subplot, involving a courtship between Prudentilla and Dalavill. Nothing ever comes of it; in fact, Prudentilla has nothing at all to say in the latter part of the play. But in several scenes, especially II.i, where the couple flirt and whisper, audience expectations are certainly aroused—and deceived. Whether Dalavill is reprobate in all respects we do not know; whether he is the complete hypocrite, or sometimes honest and sometimes not, we are never told. R. G. Martin complains that Dalavill's

> villainy, instead of being motivated before it takes place, is presented first under the guise of benevolence, and with no indication of its true nature, and is explained only after it has been discovered by young Geraldine. Heywood does not appear to have thought him out carefully beforehand.... He is so smooth a dissembler that *there is reason to fear that he deceives the audience as well as old Geraldine*.... In this respect he is, I think, the sole exception to Heywood's general rule of never leaving the spectators in doubt as to the character or intentions of his people.[9]

Likewise, Mistress Wincott remains a problem. Martin feels that Heywood's failure to tell the audience whether, at the time she plights her troth to young Geraldine, she is already Dalavill's mistress, is the result of dramaturgic clumsiness.[10] But these authorial silences are so consistent with the theme of the play, and, like other aspects of the comedy, involve the audience itself so deeply in the problem of the determination of the truth, that it is hard to believe they are accidental. Their effect on the reader is strangely disturbing: we are left with a sense of some appearances too well preserved, some realities too mysterious, for probing.

Of *The English Traveller* one might say, as Fergusson has said of *Hamlet,* that the "action is illumined from so many angles that we have an embarrassment of riches; the problem is not to demonstrate that the play moves in ironic parallels but rather to show that they add up to

---

9 Pp. 662–664; italics mine.
10 P. 664.

something—are intended to convey (with however rich a profusion)—
an underlying unity of theme."[11] In a play constructed according to a
principle of "analogy," we should not be surprised to find the "supreme
analogue" reflected by many facets—even by the title. Who is the English
traveller?[12] At first blush one is tempted to assume that it is old Lionel,
who has been abroad on the seas, and whose return is so central to the
subplot. But, as with *The Changeling,* one is immediately struck by the
oddity of naming a play after a relatively minor character of the subplot;[13]
one could not conceive of *The Alchemist* being called *Lovewit.* Moreover, in the passage in which old Lionel's travels are most lengthily
described, the title of traveller is applied metaphorically to his son, who
has remained at home:

[11] P. 105. The "supreme analogue" of appearance and reality is reflected in a
number of subsidiary ways through both plots. The clown constantly plays on it;
two examples will serve. Having come from the house where young Lionel is
revelling, he announces at Wincott's house that he has been present at a massacre,
and describes in great detail the progress of the entire banquet in such terms as to
make his audience think, though he is being nothing but accurate and hardly even
metaphorical, that he is speaking of a brawl (pp. 24–27). A. H. Gilbert, "Thomas
Heywood's Debt to Plautus," *JEGP,* XII (1913), 597, notes that this description
is one of Heywood's few major additions to the source he otherwise follows so
scrupulously in his subplot. Later, when old Lionel is puzzling over Reignald's
strange account of murder and ghosts in his house, the clown describes to him,
very truthfully, what has been going on in the house, but in such a manner as to
reinforce old Lionel's notion that there are ghosts walking in it, and that crimes
have occurred (p. 75). The theme appears in a similarly playful manner in a conversation in which the bawd Scapha tries to teach Blanda that appearance, represented by clothes, matters less than what a woman is really like; she is unable to
understand, however, what the reality of character is, and so says that "that which
the garment couers," as opposed to the "outward habit," is manners, "sweet
carriage, / And Court behauiour" (p. 19). The closing lines of the play also touch
on this ubiquitous theme. Old Wincott has decided to feast rather than mourn for
his wife, whose death he accepts as her due. After the feast, because a man who
has lost his wife should mourn, and because he has no reason to make the cause of
her death public knowledge, he will put on mourning:

> Wee'le like some Gallants
> That Bury thrifty Fathers, think't no sinne,
> To weare Blacke without, but other Thoughts within.

(p. 95)

[12] C. F. Tucker Brooke, *A Literary History of England,* ed. A. C. Baugh (New
York, 1948), p. 547, comments that *The English Traveller* is strangely titled. In
his multiple-plot plays, Middleton more frequently than not uses the title to represent all the plots, and Dekker often alludes in his titles to all the plots of the play;
The English Traveller is the one case in which Heywood does so, although he does
play on the meaning of the title in *The Wise Woman of Hogsdon.*

[13] See the conclusive demonstration by Karl L. Holzknecht, "The Dramatic Structure of *The Changeling,*" *Renaissance Papers,* University of South Carolina
(1954), pp. 77–87, that the title of Middleton's play refers ironically to several
characters in both plots.

Wife, it grieues me much both for the young and old man, the one,
Graces his head with care, endures the parching heat and biting cold,
The terrours of the Lands, and feares at Sea in trauell, onely to gain
Some competent estate to leaue his sonne;
Whiles all that Merchandize, through Gulfes, Crosse-Tides,
Pirats and Stormes, he brings so farr, Th'other
Heere Shipwrackes in the Harbour.

(p. 27)

One recalls, in this connection, the marvelous description which young
Geraldine offers (pp. 28–29) of the party at the house being run by
young Lionel, in which all present suddenly imagine, under the influence
of spirits playful and alcoholic, that the house is a ship laboring through
a storm at sea, and its occupants the crew.[14] Continued throughout the
scene, the conceit suggests that young Lionel, as well as his father, can
be regarded as the "traveller."

But the confusion is deeper even than this. For when young Geraldine,
in the main plot, discovers the infidelity of Mistress Wincott, he decides
impulsively to leave England and "Trauell till / Age snow vpon this
Head. . . . / To seeke out place, where no two such can liue" (p. 70).
As a result of this decision the farewell dinner, the denouement of the
play, takes place. Recalling that as the play opens young Geraldine
speaks at length of the trip all over the world that he has just concluded,
we must think that *he* is the English traveller. Ultimately, however, he
decides not to travel, remains in England, and becomes Wincott's heir.
At this point a new candidate appears. The clown, sent to seek out the
perfidious Dalavill, returns with the news that "Hee went presently
to the Stable, put the Sadle vpon his Horse, put his Foote into the
Stirrupe, clapt his Spurres into his sides, and away hee's Gallopt,
as if hee were to ride for a Race for a Wager," to which Wincott replies,
"All our ill lucks goe with him, farewell hee" (p. 94). The only man
travelling at the end is Dalavill. Who the traveller is remains an unresolved question. Once again, through the unconventional treatment of
a convention, Heywood's play reflects the theme of life as a mystery, the
solution to which lies hidden behind any one of a number of appearances.

Recurring frequently in the play, often of course associated with the
motif of travelling, is the poetic image of the sea, which runs through
both plots. Its ironic appearance in the subplot, to describe the house
of a man who is himself away at sea, has already been noted. After young
Geraldine's tale of the pretended sea-storm in the Lionels' house, we see
young Lionel carrying on the fancy with his riotous friends. Numerous
jokes are based on the conceit; among them, young Lionel refers to

---

[14] Gilbert observes that the entire matter of the sea is an original addition of
Heywood's to the source.

his father's being at sea, and applies that condition metaphorically to himself:

> These are the Marine gods, to whom my father
> In his long voyage prayes too; Cannot they
> That brought vs to our Hauen, bury him
> In their Abisse? For if he safe ariue,
> I with these Sailors, Syrens, and what not,
> Am sure heere to be shipwracket.
>
> (p. 33)

Reignald, entering shortly after, announces the unexpected return of the owner in a continuation of the metaphor:

> We are all Lost, Split, Shipwrackt, and vndone,
> This place is a meere quick-sands. . . .
> We and all ours, are in one turbulent Sea
> Of Fear, Dispaire, Disaster and mischace swallowed;
> Your father, Sir. . . . Landed, and at hand.
>
> (p. 34)

When old Lionel finally arrives at his house, the image reappears in a beautiful stroke of irony. The old man unsuspectingly meets his servant Reignald at the door of his house, a house which has been laboriously identified through the last two scenes as a kind of sea. Bidding Reignald discharge the sailors, he issues further instructions:

> These special things,
> And of most value, weele not trust aboord;
> Meethinkes they are not safe till they see home,
> And there repose, where we will rest our selues,
> And bid farewell to Trauell; for I voew,
> After this houre no more to trust the Seas,
> Nor throw mee to such danger.
>
> (p. 37)

Old Lionel has weathered the storms of the world's seas only to return to seas far more evil. Heywood seems to be presenting the world as a sea in which what appears to be a safe harbor may not necessarily be so—again appearance and reality—and we are not surprised to find the motif of the harbor recurring later in the subplot. Reignald, driven by all his victims to the roof of the house of which he has recently been master, shouts down in explanation of his climbing: "It hath bin my Harbour long, and now it must bee my Sanctuary" (p. 81).

The same images appear in the main plot, where their meaning is made somewhat more clear. In fact, the first long speech of the play couches in the metaphor of the sea a discussion of whether one proceeds more successfully in life by a knowledge of "Theoricke" or by experience (p. 7). What course is one to steer in the sea of life, and how may one go about it best? Dalavill raises the question. And Dalavill voices the image for its last appearance in the play. After Mistress Wincott has scornfully cast him aside, and he realizes that his fortunes in Wincott's house are finished, he exclaims, as he runs off the stage, "The storme's comming, I must prouide for harbour" (p. 93). Like the comic villain of the other plot, he has found his harbor finally untrustworthy.

Dalavill and Reignald have been shipwrecked on the metaphoric seas upon which each sails. Through this image Heywood expresses most explicitly the moral of his play. It is obvious that Reignald and Dalavill have not had the right idea of what constitutes good sailing: both have relied on "Braine" and "Theoricke," as each recognizes about himself (pp. 41, 7). Requesting his son to demonstrate his dedication to the good life by giving up the company of the Wincotts, Old Geraldine admonishes him:

> You are growne perfect man, and now you float
> Like to a well built Vessell; 'Tweene two Currents,
> Vertue and Vice; Take this, you steere to harbour
> Take that, to eminent shipwracke.
>
> (p. 46)

Life and love, then, are presented in the play as a sea of uncertainty and possible shipwreck, in which the only secure harbor can be reached by virtue; the only characters in the play whose fortunes are worse at the end than they were at the beginning are those who violate the moral law, who deceive. Like the theme of appearance and reality, this idea runs through both plots, as we have seen; and in at least two cases— that of the motif of the apparently safe harbor, and that of the moment at which old Lionel, standing in front of the "sea" of his house, vows never more to trust the seas—the theme of appearance and reality seems to be intimately related to the image of the sea. The moral violations in the action, leading to "shipwreck," are all crimes of deception, of misusing the false appearances of things. Thus the two motifs are elements of the same underlying idea, that life is uncertain when things are not what they seem. The idea has been presented not only through the action and language of the play, but also through a consistent manipulation of dramatic convention. In his treatment of the title, the rioter-courtesan relationship, the witty servant, the marriage of January and May, and the deceptive suggestion of a second subplot, Heywood has created meaningful effects by upsetting dramatic formulas. This unifying and thematically significant device, of cheating the audience by suggesting that certain conventions will be observed and then not observing them, forces the audience, like the characters of the play, to see the disparity between things as they seem and things as they are, primarily links the several plots, and reveals the theme of the whole play; and this device contributes much toward making *The English Traveller* one of the great plays of its age.

THOMAS HEYWOOD

Adams, Henry Hitch. *English Domestic, or Homiletic Tragedy: 1575–1642.* New York, 1943, pp. 144–159.

Berry, Lloyd E. "A Note on Heywood's *A Woman Killed with Kindness,*" *MLR,* LVIII (1963), 64–65.

Brown, Arthur. "Thomas Heywood's Dramatic Art," in *Essays on Shakespeare and the Elizabethan Drama in Honor of Hardin Craig,* ed. Richard Hosley. Columbia, Missouri, 1962, pp. 327–339.

Cook, David. *"A Woman Killed with Kindness:* An Unshakespearian Tragedy," *ES,* XLV (1964), 353–372.

Coursen, Herbert R., Jr. "The Subplot of *A Woman Killed with Kindness,*" *ELN,* II (1965), 180–185.

Craig, Hardin. *The Enchanted Glass: The Elizabethan Mind in Literature.* New York, 1936, pp. 128–136.

Eliot, T. S. *Selected Essays.* New Edition. New York, 1950, pp. 149–158.

Grivelet, Michel. *Thomas Heywood et le Drame Domestique Élizabéthain.* Paris, 1957, pp. 195–232.

_____ "The Simplicity of Thomas Heywood," in *Shakespeare Survey 14.* Cambridge, Eng., 1961, pp. 56–65.

Hooper, A. G. "Heywood's *A Woman Killed with Kindness,*" *ESA,* IV (1961), 54–57.

McDermott, John J. "Henryson's *Testament of Cresseid* and Heywood's *A Woman Killed With Kindness.*" *RenQ,* XX (1967), 16–21.

McNeir, Waldo F. "Heywood's Sources for the Main Plot of *A Woman Killed with Kindness,*" in *Studies in the English Renaissance Drama in Memory of Karl Holzknecht,* ed. Josephine W. Bennett, Oscar Cargill, and Vernon Hall, Jr. New York, 1958, pp. 189–211.

Prior, Moody E. *The Language of Tragedy.* New York, 1947, pp. 93–99.

Ribner, Irving. *Jacobean Tragedy: The Quest for Moral Order.* New York and London, pp. 51–58.

Smith, Hallett D. *"A Woman Killed with Kindness,*" *PMLA,* LIII (1939), 138–147.

Spacks, Patricia Meyer. "Honor and Perception in *A Woman Killed with Kindness,*" *MLQ,* XX (1959), 321–332.

Thorp, Willard. *The Triumph of Realism in Elizabethan Drama: 1558–1612.* Princeton, 1928, pp. 110–113.

Townsend, Freda L. "The Artistry of Heywood's Double Plots," *PQ,* XXV (1946), 97–119.

Van Fossen, R. W., ed. *A Woman Killed with Kindness.* The Revels Plays. London and Cambridge, Mass., 1961, pp. xxvii–lviii.

Ben Jonson

JONSON'S REVISION OF
EVERY MAN IN HIS HUMOR *

J. A. Bryant, Jr.

JONSON's adaptation of the structures of Roman comedy is too large a subject for detailed consideration in a single essay, but the general outline of the story is clear enough. As might be expected, his earliest extant comedies, *The Case Is Altered* (1597) and *Every Man in His Humor* (1598), show unmistakably the influence of Terentian structural conventions. By contrast, *Every Man out of His Humor* (1599) and the two comical satires that followed, *Cynthia's Revels* and *The Poetaster*, represent a conscious attempt to break away from the restrictions of those conventions and find a form more suited to the "elegancie and disposition" of the times.[1] Between the last of these, however, and his writing of *Volpone* early in 1606 Jonson apparently decided that the old Terentian pattern might have its uses after all and thereafter, even in the remarkably complex *Bartholomew Fair*, always worked with some recognizable version of it. The really interesting part of the story—which unfortunately cannot be dealt with here—is the way in which Jonson made the structure of these mature plays serve as part of the action, participate in it, and contribute to the meaning of the whole. He had done something like this, too, in *The Case Is Altered*, perhaps without

* From *Studies in Philology*, Vol. 59, 1962, pp. 641–650. Reprinted by permission of the editor and The University of North Carolina Press.

1 See the Induction to *Every Man out of His Humour*, 247–270. Quotations from Jonson's plays in this essay are all taken from *Ben Jonson*, ed. C. H. Herford and Percy Simpson, Vol. III (Oxford, 1927).

fully realizing what he was about; but he had done nothing at all like it in the original version of *Every Man in His Humor,* the structure of which, for all its Terentian sturdiness, was mere scaffolding, something to hold the scenes together and keep them in balance. Apparently neither of these early plays pleased the poet Jonson who put together the Folio of 1616. He ignored *The Case Is Altered* entirely and reshaped *Every Man in His Humor* so successfully that it has kept a place of high honor in his work ever since. The primary purpose of this essay is to show what happened to the structure of *Every Man in* in that revision, but it begins with a brief discussion of *The Case Is Altered,* which nowadays usually gets only passing notice as a misguided attempt to complicate further a couple of already complex Plautine intrigues.

It is customary to say that Plautus's plays are characterized by relatively simple intrigues and intrinsically amusing scenes of broad comedy; those of the more sophisticated Terence, by a more complex intrigue, usually consisting of two interdependent strands. Jonson apparently tried to work something of both varieties of Roman comedy into his *Case Is Altered.* To the matter of the *Captivi,* which deals with the efforts of a father to recover his son, he added that of the *Aulularia,* which deals with the efforts of a miser to protect a pot of gold from his daughter's two suitors. Then, having discarded very little and having added a great deal of his own, he proceeded to make the two Plautine plots work together in a neat Terentian fashion. The result is something that informed readers have been reluctant to pronounce either very Plautine or very Terentian, though it has in it both the traditional complexity of Terentian comedy and an abundance of those immediately appealing scenes of broad comedy that helped to give Plautus's plays their special character. "Romantic" is the term most frequently applied to *The Case Is Altered;*[2] and one must admit that the term is justified, since the focus of interest in the play is clearly on the emotionally appealing business of Camillo-Gasper and the love affair of Paulo and Rachel. Miss Freda L. Townsend, who sees this well enough, feels that Jonson could not possibly have intended it so and complains that he has here allowed the romantic parts of the play to attract attention that ought properly to have been distributed evenly among all the parts of the plot.[3]

It is just possible that Miss Townsend has marked as a blemish something that she might more properly have praised as a beauty. The Phaedria of Plautus's *Aulularia* is a girl of damaged character as well as one of lowly station; her greatest potential virtue is her father's gold.

---

[2] Some critics prefer "semi-romantic" or "quasi-romantic"; see, for example, F. S. Boas, *Stuart Drama* (Oxford, 1946), p. 50, and C. H. Herford, *Ben Jonson,* I (Oxford, 1925), p. 311. John J. Enek, however, has registered a somewhat different view of the play; see his *Jonson and the Comic Truth* (Madison, Wisconsin, 1957), p. 24.

[3] *Apologie for* Bartholmew Fayre. *The Art of Jonson's Comedies* (New York, 1947), p. 41.

Jonson's Rachel has only superficial disadvantages; and it is clear, or should be, that his multiplication of her suitors from two to five serves the primary purpose of establishing her as the virtuous and aristocratic young lady she eventually proves in fact to be and thus a worthy object of Paulo's affections. Among her suitors only the stupid Onion, whose main business in the intrigue is to steal the gold, fails to contribute positively to the definition of Rachel's character. Christophero sees her domestic qualities, the Count sees her great natural dignity, and Angelo, in addition to being attracted by her undeniable physical qualifications provides a test of her constancy. Placing these suitors on an equal footing with Paulo would have rendered Jonson's expansion of his original pointless, a complication for complication's sake. As it is, this particular complication of Jonson's Plautine-Terentian potpourri helps to focus attention on the one thing that gives *The Case Is Altered* its integrity as a play: the action which brings the two lovers together at the end.

The true friendship of Chamont and Gaspar-Camillo, greatly expanded by Jonson from some suggestions in the *Captivi* and introduced at the beginning of Act IV, participates significantly in the same action. Mechanically speaking, of course, it effects Paulo's return home and makes complete denouement possible; but it does considerably more than that. For one thing, the friendship between Chamont and Gasper contrasts sharply with the specious friendship between Angelo and Paulo, showing clearly what honor and constancy are and representing dramatically the kind of attachment of which Paulo would be capable, given a proper opportunity. For another, it enables Gaspar, who is also the long-lost Camillo and therefore Paulo's own flesh and blood, to serve as a substitute focus for the audience's attention until Paulo himself is ready to reappear. When Paulo does return to the stage, he proves quite capable of speaking and acting honorably in his own person; but before that, as the responses of both Phoenixella and the Count amply testify, his brother has successfully projected an anticipatory image of honorable behavior for him and thus made it possible for Paulo (of whom we have really seen very little) to assume convincingly a position of dignity with Rachel in the last act. In short, the new intrigue that Jonson has fashioned from two unrelated sources works to establish a credible image of constancy in human relations and with a fair degree of effectiveness focuses that image on the reunited lovers.

When Paulo finally gets home, he discovers that much has changed during his absence: the identity of the old man whom he had previously thought of as his prospective father-in-law, the character of his father, the integrity of his friend, and even the name and station of his beloved. No one at home, it seems, has entirely escaped the alterations and counter-alterations of "case," which mark the various steps in the denouement of Jonson's ingenious intrigue. Yet the main point of the play is that all these alterations of case do not affect Paulo's integrity or the love he feels for Rachel and she for him. "I see that honours flames

cannot be hid," he says, "No more than lightening in the blackest cloud."[4]
The world turns round, and time brings in its changes; but these lovers
stand firm. This is the serious base of the play, defined—perhaps somewhat overdefined—by the intrigue which Jonson has erected upon it.
The fact remains, however, that Jonson has required his intrigue to do
something more here than hold the attention of his audience. It stands
for the aspect of mutability in human affairs, it defines characters that
a run-of-the-mill writer of intrigue comedy might have been content to
postulate, and it justifies on ethical grounds a denouement that would
almost certainly have got by any Elizabethan audience on the force of
convention alone.

Thus at the point at which specimens of Jonson's dramatic work begin
to be available to us we can see that he was already capable of making
the intrigue of a play serve its function as a significant part of a larger
action. As I suggested earlier, he continued to do this throughout most
of the rest of his career. The one important exception is the version of
Every Man in His Humor which he gave to the stage in 1598 and allowed
to be published three years later.

On the surface, *Every Man in His Humor* would seem to be just the
sort of thing a Roman playwright might have turned out had he been
writing at the close of the Elizabethan period. Almost no detail in it
does not admit of some comparison with Roman comedy.[5] There is the
familiar "suspect world" of pretenders, parasites, and four-flushers. There
is also the young man whose descent into that world has caused the
concern of a father who has almost forgotten what it means to be
youthful. There is the witty servant, loyal to the young man but eager
for sport for sport's sake. And, finally, there is the young girl, enmeshed
in the "suspect world" but altogether worthy of the young man, whose
only fault is that he is young, rebellious, and adventurous. The action of
the intrigue is the young man's acquisition of the young girl, effected
through the help of the loyal servant, who gulls the young man's father.
At the end a disinterested person (Clement) brings about the reconciliation of the principal parties, much as Lysimachus makes possible the
denouement of Plautus's *Mercator*.

The structure of the play also shows the influence of Roman comedy.[6]
Act I gives the *protasis*, the exposition of the principal characters, the
situation, and the accidents which set everything off. Acts II and IV
are devoted almost exclusively to the business of getting impediments out
of the way. In Act II the wily servant, here called Musco, works alone;
in Act IV he works in conjunction with the friend, Prospero. But the

---

4 V. xii. 103–104.

5 See Henry Holland Carter, ed., *Every Man in His Humor,* Yale Studies in
English, LII (New Haven, 1921), pp. lxxxv–xcvi.

6 The pattern is that familiar Terentian one which T. W. Baldwin has dealt with
at length in his *Shakespeare's Five-Act Structure* (Urbana, Illinois, 1947).

result of their maneuvering in both of these acts is the pairing of the lovers and the gulling of the cautious protectors who would keep them apart. As in most Roman comedy, Act III is *epitasis,* the stirring of all the difficulties. Here at the center of the play we have the two wild scenes at Thorello's, or Kitely's, punctuated by a view of the elder Lorenzo's discomforture at Justice Clement's and concluded by another forward thrust in the action when Prospero promises to secure Hesperida for the young Lorenzo. Act V shows the result of all the plotting and with the aid of Justice Clement brings an end to all the suspicions, vindication to the virtuous young people, and judgment to the fools.

Admirable as this construction is, it does not keep *Every Man in His Humor* from failing to measure up to the superficially cruder *The Case Is Altered.* In the earlier play Jonson had made his intrigue meaningful. It stood for the way of the world, which tests the virtuous and the foolish alike and enables us to tell one from the other. In the first version of *Every Man in His Humor* he required his intrigue to be little more than a correctly constructed showcase designed to hold attention and exhibit the contents. The result is that such meaning as Jonson has put into this play actually works against the intrigue rather than with it and ends up as so much moralizing, just as meaningful out of the showcase as in it.

One area of meaning in the play has to do with the young hero's "addiction" to poetry. In a speech in the first scene, retained practically intact in the Folio of 1616, Lorenzo senior calls this the "one vain course of study" that his son affects; yet in neither version of the play do we get any indication until the last scene that the son is very seriously concerned with poetry, good or bad. We do learn in the poetry reading scene (III.iv in 1601 and IV.i in 1616) that the young man can distinguish readily between literary affectation and genuine inspiration, but most of the activity of the play is concerned with other matters. In the first version of the play, however, Jonson gave to young Lorenzo an impressive setpiece, thirty-one lines long, in defence of true poets and poetry.[7] This had the unfortunate effect of suggesting that most of the action had somehow been beside the point, and Jonson deleted it in his revision for the Folio.

Another area of meaning has to do with the much discussed business of humor. Jonson's explanation in *Every Man out* of the way he intended to apply the theory of humors, "by *Metaphore,*" is well known:

> when some one peculiar quality
> Doth so possesse a man, that it doth draw
> All his affects, his spirits, and his powers,
> In their confluctions, all to runne one way,
> This may be truly said to be a Humour.

(Induction, 105–109)

---

[7] V. iii. 313–343.

Such affectations as wearing a pied feather or the three-piled ruff, he went on to say, simply mark a man as a ridiculous ape fit for scourging. Henry Snuggs pointed out some time ago that this passage helps us to distinguish among the various "humor" characters of *Every Man in*,[8] and it undoubtedly does, provided we take the Folio version as our text. Yet the nice set of distinctions set forth in the Induction to *Every Man out* reads almost like an attempt at justification after the fact when applied to the earlier *Every Man in*. There Lorenzo senior and Thorello are still only vaguely humor characters in the primary sense, and they tend to line up with the other fools in a broad rationale for the presentation of folly, which the sensible characters are expected to recognize and avoid. It was to this area of the play that Jonson seems to have addressed himself most assiduously when he settled down to the task of revising it.

Henry Holland Carter has listed and classified most of the changes in his edition of the two versions of the play.[9] A great many of these have to do with bringing the play up to date—that is, with transforming the Italianate surface of the play to one recognizably English in names of characters, names of places, and diction. But the importance of this kind of change is slight in comparison with the importance of Jonson's decision to abandon the defense of poetry in *Every Man in*, already mentioned, and his decision to integrate the humor business with the action and the structure of the play. This second decision, which had more to do than anything else with the present status of *Every Man in* among Jonson's better comedies, is evident in two major kinds of change.

The first of these is Jonson's addition to the Folio of passages that turn the elder Lorenzo, or Knowell, from the stereotype of a distressed father into a convincing portrait of a man racked with anxiety and strengthen the portrait of the conventionally apprehensive Thorello, or Kitely. In the Quarto Jonson has Lorenzo senior declare:

> My labouring spirit being late opprest
> With my sonnes follie, can embrace no rest,
> Till it hath plotted by aduise and skill,
> How to reduce him from affected will
> To reasons manage.

> (II. ii. 1–5)

Then he has the old gentleman go on for thirty-one lines more, giving an academic speech on the need to govern passions by the reason. There is nothing in these lines to indicate directly that Lorenzo senior "can embrace no rest." The speech is as calm and deliberate as Reason itself; and it ends, furthermore, with the assertion that even in young Lorenzo, who has much abused the faculty, reason may still prove strong. The

---

8 Henry L. Snuggs, "The Comic Humours: A New Interpretation," *PMLA,* LXII (1947), pp. 114–122.

9 Carter, pp. xxxi–lvii.

speech given to Knowell at the corresponding point in the Folio is quite different. It begins:

> I cannot loose the thought, yet, of this letter,
> Sent to my sonne: nor leaue t'admire the change
> Of manners, and the breeding of our youth,
> Within the kingdome, since my selfe was one.

(II. v. 1–4)

The sixty-two lines that follow clearly present the elder Knowell's humor. Everything has gone wrong, he fears. Youth no longer respects age, and age no longer presents a good example for youth; the world has become a pitfall for the unwary. He congratulates himself that he has never allowed his son to become contaminated by it:

> Well, I thanke heauen, I neuer yet was he,
> That trauail'd with my sonne, before sixteene,
> To shew him, the *Venetian cortezans.*
> Nor read the grammar of cheating, I had made
> To my sharpe boy, at twelue. . . .
>   Neither haue I
> Drest snailes, or mushromes curiously before him,
> Perfum'd my sauces, and taught him to make 'hem. . . .
> My sonne, I hope, hath met within my threshold,
> None of these houshold precedents; which are strong,
> And swift, to rape youth, to their precipice.

(II. v. 44–48, 51–53, 58–60)

After reading this, we understand why Edward Knowell has momentarily kicked over the traces and why his father is half crazed with anxiety at the thought of losing the one thing he has for so long singlemindedly sought to control. In the Quarto young Lorenzo was a young man lured from his home by a special devotion to Mistress Poesy; in the Folio, as Edward Knowell, he has become the image of a more typical young man driven from home at the point of his maturity by the need to escape his father's excessive watchfulness. Kitely's humor was pretty well developed in both versions of the play, though Jonson enhanced it with a few deft touches in the Folio version.[10] Yet in neither play is Kitely's humor the prime mover; Kitely is a genuine humor character but one principally on exhibition, more moved than moving. In the Folio it is Knowell's humor that sets the whole action in motion, and that action in turn brings about the rectification of all the genuine humor and the exposure of all the folly.

The second great alteration that Jonson made in *Every Man in* had to do with the structure. The Quarto, as we have already seen, was constructed like a Latin comedy. But Jonson's decision to convert the folly of the elder Lorenzo into the spiritually shattering humor of Old

---

[10] See especially Quarto III. i and Folio III. iii.

Knowell was like deciding to pour gasoline into a machine that had originally been designed to run on kerosene. It meant that the old pattern, with its presentation in the first act, its "crank up" (Musco's machinations) in the second, simply would not do. What was needed was a new design, one that would allow for a slow but steady beginning and a rapid acceleration after that to carry the whole action forward to the end in one uninterrupted thrust. The new design of *Every Man in* gives us something like that. Act I presents the elder Knowell's potentially explosive concern for his son and the accident of the letter which sets it off. Act II incorporates the Musco-Brainworm business, to which Jonson had originally given the prominence of isolation in a single act, but subordinates it to Kitely's explosive concern for his wife and sister, set in motion finally by Cob's chance remark. Thus the first two acts of the Folio *Every Man in His Humor* operate very much like a two-stage firing and lead directly into the rapid forward movement of Act III which flows into Act IV without a break. In his original version Jonson arranged that Musco's machinations in Act II should lead directly to the gathering at Kitely's and that the machinations of both Musco and young Prospero in Act IV should lead directly to the second gathering in Cob's house, which he placed along with the denouement at Clement's in a rather long Act V. In the final version the two gatherings are treated simply as two stages of one great movement—distributed over two acts, it is true, but welded together by a single scene at Kitely's, which serves as both the end of Act III and the beginning of Act IV. The revised Act V thus contains only the scene at Justice Clement's with its clarifications, rebukes, and general reconciliation.

I have used the analogy of a machine to illustrate the mechanics of Jonson's revised structure for *Every Man in,* but there is a much better analogy and one which Jonson himself was probably aware of. The action of this play now parallels the predictable course of a disease, moving from symptoms to aggravation to crisis to cure. That is to say, the structure of the play, like the main characters in it, participates in the analogy which the title suggests. We can say that Acts I and II present the accumulation of symptoms, Act III the aggravation, Act IV the crisis, and Act V the cure, sought by those who are potentially capable of normality and thrust upon those who are incorrigible fools. The machinations of Brainworm, Knowell, and the others, the erratic behavior of the fools, and the instances of pure chance are all secondary factors in the forward movement of the whole. What really makes the revised *Every Man in His Humor* move is the humor characters, and these move in the way they do because they are what they are; and the meaning of their movement is symbolized in the external structure of the dramatic poem which presents them. For this reason, *Every Man in His Humor,* in the form in which we commonly read it now, is Jonson's first and only fully realized humor play and a minor masterpiece of its kind.

We may say, then, that Jonson's adaptation of the Roman-comedy intrigue developed in the following way. With *The Case Is Altered* he brought the device in its conventional form under control, augmented its function, and made it define character and provide part of the meaning of the action. Thus he early established for himself the possibility of using the intrigue of Roman comedy in a new and significant way. With *Every Man in His Humor,* however, having let himself be distracted by a fascination with the humor theory (which he still saw simply as a device for characterization) and by a growing preoccupation with defining the role of poetry in society, he sought to add more meanings than a conventional intrigue, could conveniently carry. The conventional intrigue, therefore, for all its perfection, was ready to be discarded; and indeed it virtually was discarded in the three plays that followed. It was not until 1604 that Jonson again sought in a play solely of his own devising to make significant use of something resembling the conventional five-act intrigue that had itself provided meaning for his early *The Case Is Altered.* The artistic and popular success of Jonson's work during the decade that followed is a matter of simple record. Thus it was that before he could permit a second publication of the phenomenally popular *Every Man in His Humor* and let it stand with *Volpone, Epicœne,* and *The Alchemist,* he cut away the superfluous moralizing about poetry and reshaped his play to make it a humor play all over, speaking with a single voice and saying only what it was capable of saying as a whole play and nothing more.

See other studies in Jonson bibliography (below, pp. 253–254).

THE DOUBLE PLOT IN *VOLPONE* *

Jonas A. Barish

FOR more than two centuries literary critics have been satisfied to dismiss the subplot of *Volpone* as irrelevant and discordant, because of its lack

* Reprinted from *Modern Philology,* Vol. 51, pp. 83–92 by permission of The University of Chicago Press. Copyright 1953 by The University of Chicago.

of overt connection with the main plot. Jonson's most sympathetic admirers have been unable to account for the presence of Sir Politic Would-be, Lady Would-be, and Peregrine any more satisfactorily than by styling them a "makeweight" or a kind of comic relief to offset the "sustained gloom" of the chief action.[1] Without questioning the orthodox opinion that the links of intrigue between the two plots are frail, one may nevertheless protest against a view of drama which criticizes a play exclusively in terms of physical action. What appears peripheral on the level of intrigue may conceal other kinds of relevance. And it is on the thematic level that the presence of the Would-be's can be justified and their peculiar antics related to the major motifs of the play.

John D. Rea, in his edition of *Volpone,* seems to have been the first to notice that Sir Politic Would-be, like the characters of the main plot, has his niche in the common beast fable:[2] he is Sir Pol, the chattering poll parrot, and his wife is a deadlier specimen of the same species. Rea's accurate insistence on the loquaciousness of the parrot, however, must be supplemented by recalling that parrots not only habitually chatter, they mimic. This banal but important little item of bird lore offers a thread whereby we may find our way through the complex thematic structure of the play. For Sir Politic and Lady Would-be function to a large extent precisely as mimics. They imitate their environment, and without knowing it they travesty the actions of the main characters. In so doing, they perform the function of burlesque traditional to comic subplots in English drama, and they make possible the added density and complexity of vision to which the device of the burlesque subplot lends itself.

His effort to Italianize himself takes the form, with Sir Politic, of an obsession with plots, secrets of state, and Machiavellian intrigue. His wife, on the other hand, apes the local styles in dress and cosmetics, reads the Italian poets, and tries to rival the lascivious Venetians in their own game of seduction.

Further, and more specifically, however, Sir Politic and Lady Would-be caricature the actors of the main plot. Sir Pol figures as a comic

---

1 The quoted phrases are from George Saintsbury, *A History of Elizabethan Literature* (New York, 1912), p. 181. For substantially the same view see John Addington Symonds, *Ben Jonson* ("English Worthies" series [New York, 1886]), p. 86; Maurice Castelain, *Ben Jonson* (Paris, 1907), p. 301; G. Gregory Smith, *Ben Jonson* ("English Men of Letters" series [London,, 1919]), p. 111; C. H. Herford and Percy Simpson, (eds.), *Ben Jonson* (Oxford, 1925–50), II, 64; and Arthur Sale (ed.), *Volpone* (London, 1951), pp. vii, 176. Recent studies of Jonson by Townsend, Sackton, and others intimate some uneasiness about the canonical view of the subplot in *Volpone* but do not seriously challenge it.

2 (New Haven, 1919), p. xxxiii. The further possibility advanced by Rea (pp. xxx–xliii) and sharply challenged by the Simpsons (IX, 680–82), that Sir Politic was intended as a caricature of Sir Henry Wotton, need not be dealt with here. The identification is by no means certain, and if it were, it would not materially affect the present analysis of Sir Politic, whose role transcends mere personal satire.

distortion of Volpone. As his name implies, he is the would-be politician, the speculator *manqué*, the unsuccessful enterpriser. Volpone, by contrast, is the real politician, the successful enterpriser, whose every stratagem succeeds almost beyond expectation. Sir Pol, like Volpone, is infatuated with his own ingenuity, and like Volpone he nurses his get-rich-quick schemes; but none of these ever progresses beyond the talking stage. While Volpone continues to load his coffers with the treasures that pour in from his dupes, Sir Pol continues to haggle over vegetables in the market and to annotate the purchase of toothpicks.

Lady Would-be, for her part, joins the dizzy game of legacy-hunting. Her antics caricature the more sinister gestures of Corvino, Voltore, and Corbaccio. She is jealous, like Corvino, as meaninglessly and perversely erudite as Voltore, and like Corbaccio, she makes compromising proposals to Mosca which leave her at the mercy of his blackmail. But, like her husband, Lady Would-be is incapable of doing anything to the purpose, and when she plays into Mosca's hands in the fourth act, she becomes the most egregious of the dupes because she is the blindest.

We do not learn of the existence of the Would-be's until the close of the first act,[3] and then only in a scrap of dialogue between Mosca and Volpone. Mosca's panegyric on Celia, following his sarcasms about Lady Would-be, serves to initiate a contrast which prevails throughout the play, between the households of Corvino and Sir Politic. If Corvino's besetting vice is jealousy, that of Sir Pol is uxoriousness, and the contrast enlarges itself into a difference between the brutal, obsessive passions of Italy and the milder eccentricities, the acquired follies or humors, of England. The contrast continues to unfold in the opening scene of Act II, where Sir Politic talks to his new acquaintance, Peregrine. Peregrine, it should be mentioned, probably belongs to the beast fable himself, as the pilgrim falcon. A case for this possibility would have to be based on the habits of hawks, commonly trained to hunt other birds. One then might find propriety in the fact of the falcon's hunting the parrot in the play. In Jonson's Epigram LXXXV (Herford and Simpson, VIII, 55), the hawk is described as a bird sacred to Apollo, since it pursues the truth, strikes at ignorance, and makes the fool its quarry. All these activities are performed by Peregrine via-à-vis Sir Politic.

In the initial scene between them, three chief ideas are developed, all of cardinal importance to the play and all interrelated. The first is the notion of monstrosity. Monstrosity has already made its spectacular appearance in the person of Androgyno and in the passage on Volpone's misbegotten offspring. We are, thereby, already familiar with the moral

---

[3] For the sake of brevity, this discussion will confine itself as closely as possible to the scenes actually involving the Would-be's. Jonson's sources, which are legion for this play, have been assembled both by Rea and by Herford and Simpson in their editions but will not be considered here. All citations to *Volpone* will be from Herford and Simpson, Vol. V.

abnormality of Venice and its inhabitants. The present passage, with its reports of strange marvels sighted in England—a lion whelping in the Tower, a whale discovered in the Thames, porpoises above the bridge— introduces us to an order of monsters more comic than those to be met with in Venice, but to monsters nonetheless, in the proper sense of the word. Sir Pol's prodigies are distant echoes of the moral earthquake rocking Venice, a looking glass for England whereby that country is warned to heed the lesson of the Italian state lest its own follies turn to vices and destroy it.

The enactment of the interlude in the first act, by placing the soul of the fool in the body of the hermaphrodite, has already established an identification between folly and monstrosity.[4] Appropriately enough, then, having discussed monsters, Peregrine and Sir Pol turn to speak of the ·death of a famous fool, thus reinforcing the link between the two ideas. Sir Pol's excessive reaction to the event prompts Peregrine to inquire maliciously into a possible parentage between the two, and his companion innocently to deny it. The joke here, that Sir Pol is kin to the dead fool through their mutual folly if not through family, merges into a larger reflection on the ubiquity of folly, picking up that suggestion by ricochet, as it were, from the interlude in Act I. When Peregrine asks, "I hope / You thought him not immortall?" (Act II, scene i, lines 55–56), the question implies its own Jonsonian answer: Master Stone, the fool, is not immortal, but his folly lives on incarnate in hundreds of fools like Sir Politic, much as the soul of Pythagoras, in the interlude, invested the body of one fool after another for thousands of years, only to reach its final and most fitting avatar in the person of Androgyno.

The colloquy concerning the Mamuluchi introduces the third chief motif of the scene, that of mimicry. This passage, where baboons are described in various quasi-human postures,[5] acquires added irony from the fact that it is recited by the parrot, the imitative animal par excellence, and also from the fact that the activities of the baboons, like those of Master Stone, the fool, consist chiefly of spying and intriguing and therefore differ so little from the way Sir Pol himself attempts to imitate the Italians.

The arrival of Volpone disguised as a mountebank produces the expected confrontation between the archknave and the complete gull,

---

[4] For an analysis of the first interlude and its importance to the play as a whole see Harry Levin, "Jonson's Metempsychosis," *PQ,* XXII (1943), 231–39.

[5] Rea quotes from Edward Topsel's chapter "Of the Cynocephale, or Baboun" in *The Historie of Four-footed Beastes* (1607): "It is the error of vulgar people to think that *Baboons* are men, differing only in the face or visage. . . . They will imitate all humane actions, loving wonderfully to wear garments. . .they are as lustful and venerous as Goats, attempting to defile all sorts of women" (Rea, p. 178).

the latter hopelessly hypnotized by the eloquence of the former. Volpone commences by disdaining certain imputations that have been cast on him by professional rivals. By way of counterattack, he accuses them of not knowing their trade, of being mere *"ground* Ciarlitani," or spurious mountebanks. If there is any doubt about the application of the passage to Sir Politic, it is settled by that individual's cry of admiration: "Note but his bearing, and contempt of these" (II, 2, 58). Sir Politic thus plays charlatan to Volpone's mountebank as, within the larger frame of the play, he plays parrot to Volpone's fox. But Volpone has brought along his own misshapen child, the dwarf Nano, as an accredited imitator. Nano, who fills the role of Zan Fritada, the zany, is the domesticated mimic, the conscious mimic, as Androgyno is the conscious fool, while Sir Pol remains the unconscious mimic and the unconscious fool.

Volpone, pursuing his attack on imitators, assails them for trying to copy his elixir: *"Indeed, very many haue assay'd, like apes in imitation of that, which is really and essentially in mee, to make of this oyle"* (II, 2, 149–50). What is "really and essentially" in Volpone we know already to be monstrosity, so that to imitate Volpone (as Sir Politic does) is to imitate the unnatural, and therefore, in a sense, to place one's self at two removes from nature. But Volpone believes himself, not without justification, to be inimitable. The wretched practitioners who try to duplicate his ointment end in disaster. *"Poore wretches!"* he concludes, *"I rather pittie their folly, and indiscretion, then their losse of time, and money; for those may be recouered by industrie: but to bee a foole borne, is a disease incurable"* (II, 2, 157–59). At this moment all that would be needed to drive home the application of Volpone's *sententia* would be a pause on his part, followed by a significant look from Peregrine to Sir Pol.[6] But the situation conceals a further irony. Volpone's aphorism applies to himself. Before long, he, the archknave, will have proved the greatest fool, and this despite the versatility which enables him to transcend for the moment his own preferences, in order to cater to the prejudices of the public. Paradoxically, in this scene, speaking out of character, Volpone utters truths which reverse the premises of his former behavior. In Act I, gold, the great goddess, served him as sovereign remedy and omnipotent healer. For the saltimbanco Scoto of Mantua, peddling his fraudulent elixir, newer and relatively truer axioms celebrate the treasure of health: *"O, health! health! the blessing of the rich! the riches of the poore!"* (II, 2, 84–85). But with the application of this facile maxim, error descends again. The new truth proves to be only

---

6 A proper staging of the scene would involve, I think, placing Sir Pol fairly close to Volpone, so that the two stare each other in the face, the one collecting with ardor every flower of rhetoric that falls from the other. At this moment, Volpone himself might stop to gaze into the infatuated countenance before him; by now Sir Pol's credulity is as apparent to him as it is to Peregrine.

a distorted half-truth. In place of gold, Volpone offers only his humbug ointment as the *"most soueraigne, and approued remedie"* (II, 2, 103–4). The real point, and he has made it himself, escapes him: to be a fool born is a disease incurable, and it is this disease to which he himself is destined to succumb.

The *"little remembrance"* which Volpone now presents to Celia proves to be a cosmetic powder with virtues more miraculous than those of the *oglio* itself. It is the powder *"That made* VENVS *a goddesse (giuen her by* APOLLO) *that kept her perpetually yong, clear'd her wrincles, firm'd her gummes, fill'd her skin, colour'd her haire; from her, deriu'd to* HELEN, *and at the sack of* Troy *(vnfortunately) lost: till now, in this our age, it was as happily recouer'd, by a studious Antiquarie...who sent a moyetie of it, to the court of* France...*wherewith the ladies there, now, colour theire haire"* (II, 2, 235–43). Thus the history of the powder parallels the metempsychoses of Pythagoras. Like Pythagoras' soul, the powder began its career as a gift from Apollo, and in its transmigrations through the goddess of love, the whore of Sparta, and the court ladies of France, it serves to underline the ancient lineage of vanity as a special case of the folly rehearsed in the interlude.

Mosca's opening soliloquy in Act III shows that this excellent counter-feiter is himself, like his master, obsessed by the notion of imitators. His contempt for ordinary parasites suggests that there is a hierarchy of coun-terfeits, ranging from those who are deeply and essentially false (like himself) to those who practice falsity out of mere affectation, who are, so to speak, falsely false and therefore, again, at two removes from nature. The shift of scene back to Volpone's house produces still another variation on the theme of mimicry. In order to beguile their master from his boredom, the trio of grotesques stage an impromptu interlude, dominated by Nano, who claims that the dwarf can please a rich man better than the eunuch or the hermaphrodite. The dwarf, explains Nano, is little, and pretty:

> *Else, why doe men say to a creature of my shape,*
> *So soone as they see him, it's a pritty little ape?*
> *And, why a pritty ape? but for pleasing imitation*
> *Of greater mens action, in a ridiculous fashion*

[III, 3, 11–14]

The first interlude, it may be recalled again, established an identification between folly and the unnatural. The present fragment confirms a further identity between mimicry and deformity, already hinted at in the mountebank scene where Nano appeared as the zany, or mimic, to Vol-pone's Scoto. At this point one may represent some of the relationships in the play diagrammatically as follows:

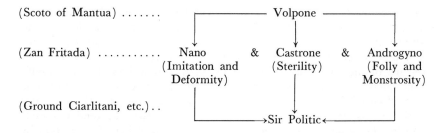

Since Volpone has (presumptively at least) sired both Nano and Androg-yno, and since Sir Pol combines the chief attributes of both, one may, with the aid of the diagram, infer what is already emerging plainly in context, that mimicry itself is something monstrous and abnormal. It is unnatural for baboons and apes and parrots to counterfeit human behavior. It is equally unnatural for men to imitate beasts. It argues a perversion of their essential humanity. It is not for nothing, then, that the chief characters of the play fit into one zoological classification or another. As men, they duplicate the habits of beasts; as beasts, they brutishly travesty humanity. They belong to the genus *monster*—half man, half brute—that order of fabulous creatures whose common denominator is their unnaturalness, their lack of adherence to whatever category of being nature has assigned them.

The arrival of Lady Would-be, fuming and fussing over her toilet, and snapping at her servingwomen, provides still a further object lesson in falsity. Here, as so often in Jonson, face physic symbolizes the painted surface hiding the rotten inside; the cosmetic care of the face signifies the neglect of the soul. It signifies equally an attachment to appearances, an incapacity to look beyond the superficies of life or truth. The powder which Volpone offered to Celia and which Celia did not need, since her beauty was of the platonic sort that revealed the purity of her soul, might with more justice have been given to Lady Would-be, and it is Lady Would-be who deserves the epithet of "lady *vanitie*" (II, 5, 21) with which Corvino, in his jealous tantrum, has stigmatized Celia.

The scene between Lady Would-be and Volpone serves partly as a burlesque of the parallel scenes in Act I between Volpone and the other *captatores*. All the essential ingredients of those scenes reappear, but scrambled and topsy-turvy. Once again Volpone feigns sickness, but this time it is in self-defense against the terrible oratory of Lady Would-be. Once again remedies are prescribed, but these are neither Corbaccio's deadly opiate nor his *aurum palpabile* offered as pump-priming, but the fantastic assortment of old wives' restoratives dredged up from Lady Would-be's infernal memory. She rains down the hailstones of her learning on the helpless Volpone, until the archrogue, anticipating the judgment to be rendered on him in Act V, cries out in despair: "Before I fayned diseases, now I haue one" (III, 4, 62). The whole episode is a rich application of the principle of comic justice. If in the final denouement Volpone suffers the penalty of vice, here he reaps the more ludicrous reward of his own folly. Trapped by Lady Would-be's rhetoric, itself a consequence of his own scheming, he is finally driven to pronounce himself cured. But the talking machine grinds on, and only Mosca's happy notion of exciting her jealousy, as he has previously aroused Corvino's, and for the same purpose, succeeds in getting rid of her. As her contribution to Volpone's coffers, she leaves behind a wrought cap of her own making; this forms a suitably ridiculous contrast to the treasures earlier offered by Corvino, Corbaccio, and Voltore.

The same scene serves as introduction and comic distortion of the scene immediately to follow between Volpone and Celia. Celia's unearthly purity is made to seem even more unearthly by its contrast to Lady Would-be's lecherousness, this latter apparent in the lady's addiction to cosmetics, in her slips of the tongue, and in her barely disguised sexual overtures. Lady Would-be's attempted seduction of Volpone having been thwarted, the stage is set for Volpone's attempted seduction of Celia. Volpone commences his wooing with a characteristic boast: "I, before / I would haue left my practice, for thy loue," he swears, "In varying figures, I would haue contended / With the blue PROTEVS, or the horned *Floud*" (III, 7, 150–53). Justifiably proud of his powers of disguise, Volpone emphasizes them further by citing a past occasion on which he masqueraded in the ambiguous role of Antinous, Nero's favorite. Embarking on an enumeration of the exotic splendors in store for Celia, he reserves as his final inducement the promise that she will participate, with him, in transmutations without end: "Whil'st we, in changed shapes, act OVIDS tales" (the *Metamorphoses,* of course),

> Thou, like EVROPA now, and I like IOVE,
> Then I like MARS, and thou like ERYCINE,
> So, of the rest, till we haue quite run through
> And weary'd all the fables of the gods.
> Then will I haue thee in more moderne formes,
> Attired like some sprightly dame of *France,*
> Braue *Tuscan* lady, or proud Spanish beauty.

> [III, 7, 221–28]

We have already witnessed, in the first interlude, the metempsychoses of folly and, in the powder offered to Celia in Act II, the transmigrations of vanity. Now, as a climax to his eloquence, Volpone rehearses the metamorphoses of lust. Jonson thus endows his central themes with vertical depth in time as well as horizontal extension in space. Folly, vanity, lust, have been, are, will be. At any given moment their practitioners are legion, and often interchangeable.

It is at this point that Celia's refusal crystallizes into a repudiation of folly, vanity, and lust combined and that her behavior contrasts most sharply with that of Lady Would-be. The recollection of Lady Would-be lacquering her face and making indecent advances to Volpone brings into sharper focus Celia's sudden horror at her own beauty, and her plea that her face be flayed or smeared with poison, in order to undo the lust she has aroused. If, for Lady Would-be, the cosmetic art is a necessary preliminary to sexual conquest, its opposite, the disfigurement of the face, becomes for Celia the badge of chastity. Where Lady Would-be strives to adopt Italian vices for her own, Celia's gestures as well as her name demonstrate her alienation from the moral and spiritual province of Venice.

Act IV carries us back into the open street, where Sir Pol, ignorant of the plot developing at Volpone's house, continues babbling of plots in terms which ordinarily have one meaning for him and another for the audience. After a patronizing recital of "instructions" to Peregrine on methods of deportment in Venice, he confides suddenly that his money-making projects need only the assistance of one trusty henchman in order to be put into instant execution. Evidently he is hinting that Peregrine undertake that assignment and thus play Mosca to his Volpone. But Peregrine contents himself with inquiring into the particulars of the plots. The most elaborate of these proves to be a way to protect Venice from the plague by using onions as an index to the state of infection on ships entering the harbor. This mad scheme, with its echo of Volpone's claim to have distributed his *oglio* under official patent to all the commonwealths of Christendom, serves chiefly to remind us again of the moral plague prevailing in Venice and of the incomprehension of that fact on the part of those characters who prattle most about disease and cure.

The ensuing scene parodies the episode in Act II where Corvino discovers his wife in conversation with the mountebank. Just as Corvino interrupts Volpone while the latter is advertising his medicine, so Lady Would-be bursts in on Sir Politic as the knight is dilating on his schemes and projects. As Corvino babbles jealously of lechers and satyrs, so Lady Would-be jabbers of land sirens, lewd harlots, and fricatrices. Corvino beats away the mountebank. Lady Would-be rails at Peregrine. Both harp on "honor," and both discard that term as soon as it becomes an inconvenience, Corvino when it becomes an obstacle to his plan of inheritance, Lady Would-be when she discovers that Peregrine is no harlot in disguise, but a young gentleman. As for Sir Politic, though he too plays his part in the little impromptu from the *commedia dell' arte,* he remains, unlike Volpone, quite oblivious to the fact. Actually, Sir Pol reenacts not the role of "Signior FLAMINIO," the lover in disguise—that part, however reluctantly assumed, belongs to Peregrine—but the female role, the "FRANCISCINA," guarded by a jealous "PANTALONE *di besogniosi*" (II, 3, 3–8). The confusion of sexes symbolized in Androgyno, in the indiscriminate journeyings of the soul of Pythagoras, in Volpone's masquerade as Antinous, in Lady Would-be's error, as well as in the reversed masculine-feminine roles of Sir Pol and Lady Would-be, con-tributes its own kind of abnormality to the deformity of the moral atmosphere chiefly figured by the metamorphoses of beasts into men. And if one regards Sir Politic's unxoriousness as a kind of metaphoric emasculation, one may then equate him with Castrone, as he has already been equated with Nano and Androgyno, to make the pattern of mimicry complete.[7]

The fourth-act trial starts with justice and concludes with a perversion of it. The monsters begotten by Volpone, the prodigies and portents that exercised such a hypnotic effect on Sir Pol, now make a lavish and climactic reappearance in the language of the scene. First they designate their proper objects. But as Voltore begins to exercise his baleful rhetoric, the parlance of unnaturalness, appropriate to the guilty, begins to turn against the innocent. Corbaccio disavows his son for "the meere portent of nature"; he is "an vtter stranger" to his loins, a "Monster of men, swine, goate, wolfe, parricide" (IV, 5, 108–12). Finally Lady Would-be arrives, the eternal parrot, to give testimony which virtually clinches the case against Celia:

> Out, thou *chameleon* harlot; now, thine eies
> Vie teares with the *hyaena*.
>
> [IV, 6, 2–3]

The beast characters in the play display an unerring faculty for describ-ing the innocent as beasts. Corvino has already called Celia a crocodile, referring to that animal's notorious ability to imitate human tears, and Lady Would-be, though she has her unnatural natural history somewhat confused, invokes another creature famous for its powers of mimicry, the hyena, as well as the even more versatile chameleon.

The juxtaposition of the hyena and the chameleon reminds one that there is a point at which the ideas of metamorphosis and mimicry coalesce. The chameleon, shifting its colors to blend itself with its environment, indulges in a highly developed form of protective mimicry. Volpone carries the principle a step further. He goes through his restless series of transformations not as a shield but in order to prey on his own kind, to satisfy something in his unnatural nature which demands inces-

---

[7] Actually, Florio's *Worlde of Wordes* (1598) denfies *Castrone* not only as "a gelded man," but as "a noddie, a meacocke, a cuckold, a ninnie, a gull" (quoted in Rea, p. 144). Any of these will serve as accurate epithets for Sir Pol, with the possible exception of "cuckold," and if that designation does not fit it is not owing to any lack of effort on Lady Would-be's part.

sant changing of shape and form. But knavery and credulity, mimicry and metamorphosis, alike reflect aspects of one basic folly: the folly of becoming, or trying to become, what one is not, the cardinal sin of losing one's nature. Only Bonario and Celia, of all the creatures in the play, never ape others, never change their shapes, never act contrary to their essential natures. And in the unnatural state of Venice it is chiefly they, the unchanging ones, who are attacked as hyenas and chameleons.

Volpone, in short, may be read as a comic restatement of a theme familiar in Shakespeare's plays of the same period, the theme of disorder. Order figures here not as social balance or political hierarchy, but as a principle of differentiation in nature whereby each species, each sex, maintains its separate identity. With the loss of clear-cut divisions between man and beast, between beast and beast, between male and female, all creatures become monsters. The basic structure of nature is violated. The astronomical portents discussed earlier by Sir Pol and Peregrine in connection with animal prodigies reflect the upheaval of the cosmos itself following the degeneracy of man.

But by this time, justice has become as monstrous as its participants, and the *avocatori* close the session piously intoning their horror at the unnaturalness of Celia and Bonario. Volpone's last and greatest hoax is destined to set the balance of nature right again. It starts, however, with one more act of unnaturalness. Volpone, a monster, who therefore occupies no fixed place in the order of created beings, feigns death and thus symbolically demonstrates his lack of status. One by one the inheritors file in for the legacy, only to find that they have been duped by Mosca.

The first to receive her dismissal is Lady Would-be. Having made overtures to both Mosca and Volpone, she is in a position to be summarily blackmailed. "Goe home," advises Mosca, "and vse the poore sir POL, your knight, well; / For feare I tell some riddles: go, be melancholique" (V, 3, 44–45). Thus the learned lady who knew so many bizarre ways of curing Volpone's melancholy now has the opportunity to treat herself for the same ailment, and so do her colleagues. The value of this scene consists partly in its inflicting comic justice on the legacy-hunters before the *avocatori* render their sterner legal judgments, just as Volpone has already, in Lady Would-be, met a comic foretaste of the retribution which overtakes him at the *Scrutineo.* But since the parrot, for all its shrillness, remains less venal than the crow or vulture, the untrussing of Lady Would-be goes no further. In the realm of the severer truths, vice and folly may appear as different aspects of a similar spiritual malaise. In the realm of poetic justice, however, a distinction continues to be practiced. Vice, which is criminal and attacks others, must suffer public correction, whereas folly, a disease essentially self-destructive, may be dealt with in private and without the assistance of constituted authority. For Lady Would-be it is sufficient that, awakened to some sense of her own folly, she vows to quit Venice and take to sea "for physick."

And so with her preposterous knight, Sir Politic, whom we now encounter for the last time, the victim of a private plot which performs the same service of mortification for him that the final trial scene does for Volpone. The *mercatori* enlisted by Peregrine perform the office of the *avocatori* who pronounce sentence on Volpone, and the divulging of the pathetic notebook, with its scraps from playbooks, becomes the burlesque substitute for the exposure of Volpone's will, in bringing on the disaster. Peregrine, echoing Voltore's suggestion that Volpone be tested on the strappado, warns Sir Pol that his persecutors will put him to the rack. Whereupon the knight remembers an "engine" he has designed against just such emergencies, a tortoise shell. And to the disgust of three hundred years of literary critics he climbs into the ungainly object, playing possum after the fashion of his model, Volpone, who has feigned death in the foregoing scene. The arrival of the merchants brings on the catastrophe:

> MERCATORI 1: What
> Are you, sir?
> PEREGRINE: I am a merchant, that came heere
> To looke vpon this tortoyse.
> MERCATORI 3: How?
> MERCATORI 1: St. MARKE!
> What beast is this?
> PEREGRINE: It is a fish.
> MERCATORI 2: Come out, here.
> PEREGRINE: Nay, you may strike him, sir, and tread vpon him:
> Hee'll beare a cart.

[V, 4, 62–67]

Eventually, by stamping and poking, they goad Sir Politic out of his exoskeleton. The scene thus rephrases in a vein of broadest tomfoolery the essential question of the play: "What kind of creatures are these?" Throughout the action one has seen beasts aping men and men imitating beasts on the moral and psychological levels. Here the theme of mimicry reaches its literal climax in an episode of farce, where the most imitative of the characters puts on the physical integument of an animal and the hired pranksters stand about debating its probable zoological classification. The final unshelling of the tortoise, a parallel to the uncasing of the fox in the last scene, arouses further comment from the merchants:

> MERCATORI 1: 'Twere a rare motion, to be seene, in *Fleet-street!*
> MERCATORI 2: I, i'the terme.
> MERCATORI 1: Or *Smithfield,* in the faire.

[V, 4, 77–78]

Sir Politic, thus, so inquisitive about prodigies, has finally become one himself, a specimen fit to be housed among the freaks of Smithfield or amid the half-natural, half-artificial curiosities of Fleet Street. With the knowledge that he is destined to become a victim of the kind of curiosity he himself has exhibited, his disillusionment is complete and his chastisement effected. He and Lady Would-be, the only survivors, in this play, of Jonson's earlier humor characters, are now "out of their humor," purged of their imitative folly by the strong medicine of ridicule.

Public punishment, however, awaits the actors of the main plot. Jonson is not sporting here with human follies like those of the Would-be's, but dealing grimly with inhuman crimes. The names of fabulous monsters, basilisks and chimeras, continue to echo in our ears as the catastrophe approaches, fastening themselves at last onto their proper objects, the conspirators in the game of *captatio*. Voltore's spurious fit spells out in concrete theatrical terms his unnatural status and the lesson pointed by the *avocatori:* "These possesse wealth, as sicke men possesse feuers, / Which, trulyer, may be said to possesse them" (V, 12, 101–2). The delivery of Volpone's substance to the *Incurabili* places a final and proper valuation on the medicinal powers of gold. The imprisonment of Volpone is specifically designed to give him the opportunity to acquire in reality the diseases he has mimicked and the leisure to ponder the accuracy of his own text: to be a fool born is a disease incurable. Voltore and Corbaccio are henceforth to be secluded from their fellow-men like the unnatural specimens they are, while Corvino's animality is to be the object of a public display more devastating than Sir Politic's brief masquerade as a tortoise.

Thus on successive levels of low comedy and high justice, the monsters of folly and the monsters of vice suffer purgation, exposed as the sort of misshapen marvels they themselves have chattered about so freely. The relative harmlessness of Sir Pol's downfall serves to differentiate his folly from the viciousness of the Venetians, but the many parallels between his catastrophe and theirs warn us that his kind of folly is sufficiently virulent after all, is closely related to graver sins, and, if it persists in imitating them, must ultimately fall under the same condemnation.

If these observations are accurate, it should be clear in what sense the subplot of the Would-be's is relevant to the total structure of *Volpone.* Starting from a contrast between Italian vice and English folly, Jonson personifies the latter in two brainless English travelers, makes their folly consist chiefly in mimicry of Italian vice, and Italian vice itself, in its purest form, consist of the more comprehensive form of mimicry we have termed "metamorphosis," thus bringing the two aspects of evil together into the same moral universe and under a common moral judgment; with the use of the beast fable he binds the two together dramatically, and by the distribution of poetic justice he preserves the distinction between them. Each of the episodes involving the Would-be's, including the much despised incident of the tortoise, thus serves a definite dramatic purpose, and one may conclude, then, that the subplot adds a fresh dimension and a profounder insight without which *Volpone,* though it might be a neater play, would also be a poorer and a thinner one.

VOLPONE

Arnold, Judd. "The Double Plot in *Volpone:* A Note on Jonsonian Dramatic Structure," *SCN,* XXIII, No. 4 (1965), item 4.

Davison, P. H. *"Volpone* and the Old Comedy," *MLQ,* XXIV (1963), 151–157.

Dessen, Alan C. *"Volpone* and the Late Morality Tradition," *MLQ,* XXV (1964), 383–399.

Donaldson, Ian. "Jonson's Tortoise," *RES,* XIX (1968), 162–166.

Goldberg, S. L. "Folly into Crime: The Catastrophe of *Volpone,"* *MLQ,* XX (1959), 233–242.

Hawkins, Harriett. "Folly, Incurable Disease, and *Volpone,"* *SEL,* VIII (1968), 335–348.

Kernan, Alvin B., ed. *Ben Jonson:* Volpone. The Yale Ben Jonson. New Haven, 1962, pp. 1–26.

Levin, Harry. *"Jonson's Metempsychosis,"* *PQ,* XXII (1943), 231–239.

Mills, Lloyd L. "Barish's 'The Double Plot' Supplemented: The Tortoise Symbolism," *Serif,* IV (1967), 25–28.

Miller, Joyce. *"Volpone:* A Study of Dramatic Ambiguity," in *Studies in English Language and Literature,* ed. Alice Shalvi and A. A. Mendilow. Scripta Hierosolymitana, pubs. of the Hebrew University, 17. Jerusalem, 1966, pp. 35–95.

Nash, Ralph. "The Comic Intent of *Volpone,"* *SP,* XLIV (1947), 26–40.

Weld, John S. "Christian Comedy: *Volpone,"* *SP,* LI (1954), 172–193.

See other studies in Jonson bibliography (below, pp. 253–254).

———◆———

THE ALCHEMIST : COMIC INTRIGUE *

Paul Goodman

DOUBLENESS OF COMIC CHARACTERS

In the last chapter we started from "seriousness" as an essential relation between the character and his action; let us now explore the relation

* Reprinted from *The Structure of Literature* by permission of The University of Chicago Press. Copyright 1954 by The University of Chicago.

between a base character and his action. This is "comic" when the intrigue can be reversed or even be deflated (come to nothing), and still the character is not destroyed; yet the intrigue is the intrigue *of* the character in the sense that in part it follows from him and follows from a part of him. This is what I mean by an "accidental" connection. It will be seen at once that a character of comedy has two aspects: that which is destroyed and that which survives in, let us say, "normalcy." Most of the possibilities of this comic relation occur in *The Alchemist.*

1. The character may be composed simply of a comic trait necessary for the intrigue and of the normal trait of being a man, as when a man persists in a single illusion and then awakes from it. When a play is made mainly of such characters, we have a comedy of situation, and we sympathize with the persons in their return to normalcy. In broader kinds of farce such a character is a straight man, brought into the comedy by his accidental connection with the broader comedians and afterward of no further interest.

2. On the contrary, the disposition to comic intrigues, whether as a butt or as an initiator, may be strongly developed, so that, even after the deflation, the mask survives as a name of ridicule. We think of the mask and not the normal man. These are the humors, and the Jonsonian comedy is mainly comedy of humors, as here the simpleton Abel, Sir Epicure Mammon, the stormy Kastril, the materialistic Puritan.

3. Or not only the comic but also the normal may be strongly developed, as when the deflation of the intrigue purges the normal man of an error or humor. So Surly comes to recognize in himself that "same foolish vice of honesty." Honesty and the need to expose rogues, these are of course humors among the Jonsonian Lovewits and Truewits. For Jonson the flawless normal man is urbane; he knows his way around. But we can see how this same combination of the comic and normal may easily verge on the tragic, as in *Le Misanthrope,* where the disposition to a comic intrigue is really a tragic flaw for a man who is not urbanely normal but serious.

4. On the contrary again, what seems to be a merely comical disposition, such as gluttony, knavery, deviltry, may be so apt for any eventuality that it survives every deflation and proves in the end to be a lively way of normal life. Let us call these traits Wits, like Face, Falstaff (at the end of the first part of *Henry IV*), Figaro, Scapin, or Schweik. In relation to these witty knaves, the other characters are dupes and butts.

5. Or it may be the normal or even heroic part of the character that is most developed and that, in detachment, permits or enjoys or profits by the comedy, like Lovewit or Prince Hal or even Theseus in *A Midsummer Night's Dream.* This is the Urbane.

6. A completely deflatable trait is a Buffoon. Mostly this would occur in passing.

BUFFOONERY AND THE UNDERLYING DRIVES

Comic traits are base because they generate superficial or accidental relations that in the end do not make any difference. But they are not completely absurd, because they generate determinate probable intrigues. A character completely absurd could enter at any time, and from him anything could be expected; he would be the object merely of indifference or contempt.

Yet, since the comic intrigue is combined of the accidental relations of accidental relations, when the combination reaches the utmost limits of accidentality, all the comic characters and their actions tend to become ad libitum, at sea. There is a pervasive buffoonery. Consider Kastril, for example: at the climax he might do or say anything.

What is it, at such a moment, that makes the comedy most delicious and not merely contemptible, since it is apparently so devoid of sense? Obviously it is the emergence of the more elementary but *by no means formless* underlying drives, wanton destructiveness and animal lubricity. Compared with the intricacy of the plot, this underlying part is a dim background, everywhere suggested in the incidents, gestures, language, innuendo, but never given a plot. But, when the plot itself turns to chaos, this part abides and makes sense. A comedy where all "human values" are absolutely deflated proves to be a fertility ritual of the highest human value.

So we shall see that the normalcy that survives the explosion of the comedy, as a resolution, is not the normalcy of everyday but is a lively normalcy, man in a wanton mood. The comic and normal parts of the comic characters are integrally related for this lively function.

COMIC INTRIGUE

Expansion

The combination of incidents probable from the wits, dupes, and humors is, as a whole, the comic intrigue. And it is immediately evident that such an intrigue, unlike the serious plot, is more than the acting-out of the characters, for some comic events befall the characters not as they choose or as is in their disposition but simply because, with quite other ends in view, they have entered the situation. Since the situation is accidentally related to some, it can be accidentally related to others, and, by a compounding of accidents, characters who originally have nothing to do with one another are thrown together. Thus, Surly comes disguised as the amorous Don; Dol, the appropriate bawd, is occupied elsewhere; the Don must have some woman, and Dame Pliant, who has come on other business, happens to be only other woman; so Surly is thrown with Dame Pliant. Here indeed we have a case not merely of comic probability but of comic necessity (for it depends on the exhaustion of the possibilities), yet it is absurd. In extreme cases mere juxtaposition is a sufficient generator of comic incidents, as in the famous tradition of multi-occupied closets.

Such an intrigue is naturally divergent and expansive, freely introducing new complications, whereas the tragic plot converges to remove just the complexity that it has. Thus one might diagram the action of *The Alchemist* as a kind of expanding balloon. In general, as the strands of action are more numerous, the unity among them all becomes more accidental to each—the characters become more distracted, the pace more dizzy, the probability more heady and tenuous. (This explains why melodrama, the climactic coming-together of many serious plots—the attack of the Indians, the attempt on the heroine, the coming of the soldiers from the post—is likely to become uproariously funny.)

Probability and Reversal

The strands of a comic action may cross by normal probability, as when a character plans to do something and does it. Or by a comic probability: the characters are thrown into new, unmeant, and still more accidental situations that they have to cope with. Then the comedy is heightened if these new situations surprisingly provoke new traits of characters that have a comic compatibility with the previous traits and intentions. Thus, disappointed at the explosion of the stone, Sir Epicure is provoked to the remorseful outcry, "O my voluptuous mind! I am justly punished" (IV, 5).

This is a comic reversal. But we must make an important distinction. The new situation may be one of continuing comedy or of the return to normalcy (deflation to absolutely naught). Unlike the reversals of tragedy, comic reversals are not brought on by discoveries; rather, they compound the errors. Tragic reversals are apprehensive and fearful, but these heighten daring and bewilderment, or the daring to be bewildered.

In this context we may make a further distinction of the characters in plays like *The Alchemist.* The humors and dupes are subject to continual comic reversals; but the Alchemist himself is the agent of reversals. He knows what is going on; therefore, he is not reversed; he is, however, exposed in the general deflation to normalcy. But Face and Lovewit, the witty and the urbane, are not subject to the deflation either.

Obviously it is the hallmark of Jonsonian comedy to fill out this whole line: humors, knaves, wits, and the urbane. Jonson gives us a hierarchy of malicious intelligence. In *The Alchemist* the hierarchy is kept neat, and the effect is pleasant throughout; Lovewit, the urbane, is not involved in the comedy as an agent, and so he may pleasantly profit from the spoils set free by laughter, namely, sex and an heiress. But perhaps *Volpone* is more profoundly Jonsonian: the Fox is both onlooker and agent; he lusts in the malicious intelligence itself, not in the profits: "Oh more than if I had enjoyed the wench: the pleasure of all womankind's not like it." This is cruel.

(Correspondingly, in Jonson's comedies the underlying suggestiveness is rarely very warm. There is plenty of lubricity but little pornographic excitement. A typical verse: "For she must milk his epididymus." We have the remarkable case of great comedy that is not funny; we are not invited to let go to belly laughter.)

License and Deflation

Ordinarily we expect normal thoughts and feelings to be effective causes, for mistakes and misunderstandings to right themselves, etc. Thus, special comic conditions are prerequisite for comic probability, the compounding of accidents and errors. In a sense every humor provides such conditions. Mammon wills to believe anything that will make him rich, Dame Pliant wants any husband, and the gull wants to be gulled. (And, philosophically considered, no special conditions are required for comic complication; the ordinary illusions of people are obviously self-compounding. To a disinterested view, life is at least as comic and serious as it is "normal.")

Often, however, the poet provides a special comic license to compound errors, in a special place and for a limited time. One is licensed to be mad on St. John's Day or to play tricks on April Fools'. Wine and the party spirit give a license for dirty jokes. In *The Alchemist* the master of the house is away, and this gives a license; the comic complication depends on the erroneous belief that he will be gone for a fortnight. Then we may simply define for plays like *The Alchemist:* Normalcy is the part of the play after the revoking of the comic license (return of Lovewit at the end of Act IV). The reversal to normalcy is the deflation. (Revoking the license is, of course, analogous to discovery and the deflation to the tragic reversal.)

Many comedies are not deflated to normalcy. *The Clouds,* for example, ends with the establishment of the Cloud-Cuckoo Utopia; what need for a deflation? *The Acharnians* is not deflated for the opposite reason; the proposition of the end is witty and true. Comedies that can end undeflated have a peculiar heady glory (and socially are more aphrodisiac).

On the other hand, sentimental comedies, those in which we sympathize with the romantic couple (socially, a vicarious outlet), require the removal of the comic conditions, the revoking of license, in order that the lovers may be no longer anxious. In such cases there is often a comic miracle to clear up the difficulties. This may be a windfall, like the inheritance that falls to Léandre in *Le Médecin magré lui* and nullifies the old man's objection to the marriage (for his humor is stubborn; he could not be made urbane). A windfall is the removal of comic conditions that are not deflatable; and there are likely to be such stubborn conditions in sentimental comedies because the sympathetic (noncomic) lovers are not likely to be involved for only comic reasons—

they would avoid merely comic complication and go off by themselves. The structure, the gratuitous probability, of such windfalls is analogous to the *deus ex machina:* the comic complication has come to a threatening impasse, but the lovers are deserving of better than deflation, etc.

The formal comic license issued and revoked by Jonson is characteristic of his art: he is the controlling comic master who will neither allow a sympathetic plot strand nor, on the other hand, let the comic malice release a libido that carries everything before it.

THE BEGINNING

We may now speak of the beginning, the middle, and the ending.

The beginning is the comic license and the agents who generate the intrigue, not subject to comic reversals but subject to revoking of the license. In *The Alchemist,* Act I, scene 1, could be regarded as a sufficient beginning: the trio who generate the intrigue, the dupes they practice on, the likelihood of a later disruption within the trio because of their quarrels and rivalry (making probable the deflation), and the possible return of the master of the house (revoking the license). The rest follows from this.

But comedy is expansive, and it may be said also that each new humor introduces new comic conditions. Thus in a comedy of this type the effect depends not on a distinction between the beginning and the middle but rather on the continual expansion of the possibilities of accident. This is different from tragedies like *Oedipus,* where each new entrance (e.g., the Messenger from Corinth) eliminates an alternative in the converging plot strands.

THE MIDDLE

In the middle the intrigue is enlarged (1) by the introduction of new humors (start of Acts II and III) and (2) by the combination of the previous combinations. The new humors are introduced with a certain probability from what has preceded, as Tribulation enters because he has lead roofing to sell to Sir Epicure for projection; yet each humor has peculiarities that serve as starting places for new trails.

But what principle, then, determines the magnitude of a play so enlarged? For the principle of tragedy, "just what is necessary to produce the reversal," has no place here. Why should not the balloon expand indefinitely, introducing ever new humors and their complications? This question may be answered by two related considerations drawn from the limits of the comic intrigue in itself and from the relation of the intrigue to normalcy.

First, the compounding of accidents cannot be indefinitely comic; after a while it reaches the random or trivial. This occurs when the potentiality of the humors to operate in new reversals has been exhausted. If new humors are introduced with which the previous humors can no longer react, we would no longer have one play. Thus, the plight of Surly when the bellicose Kastril turns on him as the cheat is near the limit; it is only because Kastril has been developed as such a buffoon that this climax of buffoonery is sensible. And that Ananias should now turn on the Spanish fiend with his ruff of pride and his idolatrous breeches is simply wondrous. The next moment would be absurd, but Jonson, of course, allows no next moment. (We might think of a sequence of expansion somewhat as follows: the comic, the buffoon, the absurd, the trivial.)

Second, the probable return of normalcy sets a limit to the comic expansion. But this is integrally probable from what is happening to the intrigue; for we must remember that all the characters have a normal component, and, as the intrigue becomes too tenuous and absurd, the characters must return to normalcy, for otherwise they would be destroyed completely: they would be madmen and not characters of comedy. Thus, we must expect Surly to call the police; but the police and the crowd have not been handled at all, so they need not now be dupes. Another aspect of this is that the comic expansion begins to touch themes that by convention are only normal; thus Jonson cannot allow the chastity of Dame Pliant to be actually comic but only to threaten to be so; so in the comic crisis at the end of Act IV we are near the deflation. Again, from previous to the expansion, there is the probability of the return of normalcy: Lovewit must return, for the possibility was mentioned in the beginning; the license is for a limited time and place. To give another example, at the beginning of *A Midsummer Night's Dream* we are told that "Four nights will quickly dream away the time [of waiting]"; but these nights pass in due course, and then the dreamlike probability is over. And, as with the limited time, so with the place: when the madness becomes so violent that it overflows among the neighbors, there is a deflation. Thus in *Les Précieuses ridicules* the spectacular motion, noise, and crowding of the dance (scene 12) is a sufficient inflation and makes probable the entry of the irate suitors with their sticks.

THE ENDING: COMIC FEELINGS

The deflation of the comic intrigue is the beginning of the ending. The humors are destroyed. The incidents of the ending comprise the salvaging of what survives in normalcy.

Let us choose this turning point in the plot to discuss the kinds of laughter. (The kinds of comic laughter fit in the spectrum between the giggling of embarrassment on one extreme and the gurgling of animal satisfaction on the other.)

The deflation of the humors is malicious laughter, energized by released destructiveness and made safe by contempt or indifference. The succession of the normal persons to the humors is the belly laughter of the released underlying drives. And the resolution is a kind of happy smiling and chuckling.

We have argued above that the audience identifies not with this or that particular character but with the world of the work as a whole, a space and time and drama. In discussing the feelings of comedy, it is essential to bear this in mind. With tragedy, everything centers in the end in the protagonist, so that what is felt for him is not far from what is felt during the work. But with comedy, no such thing.

Malicious laughter is roused in a titillating or embarrassed way by the forethought of the reversals; it is roused restrainedly by every reversal; and it is is aroused unrestrainedly at the deflation or reduction of the comedy to absolutely nought. This is the moment of greatest absurdity: "All goes up in fume." Obviously this laughter is not identification with what is deflated; usually it is explained as a laughter of superiority (identification with the author?), that we are *not* that; it is base, we are superior. But I think the case is simpler; it is that we *are,* we are left, even in the dangerous activity of mocking, destroying, childishly laying about us. No superiority or contempt need be inferred; when it is strongly present, the comedy passes over into satire and invective. The energy of ordinarily suppressed destructiveness bursts out laughing. It is as though the base intrigue that we have been following has become a burden, and we are glad to annihilate it.

But then why have we involved ourselves in it from the beginning? It is because of the suggestion of the more elementary animal drives that accompanies the intrigue of base aims and vices. We do not identify with the characters, knaves, and humors, but we identify with their world, which is after all compact of simple childish wants. At the deflation the comic characters are destroyed; they carry off with them the shame and the base imputation. But the point is that what is left is not nothing, but normal persons, we ourselves—nobody has been hurt. Then comes the loud laughter of the released instincts that have all along been suggested; we have allowed ourselves successfully to be seduced. Toward this end the comic reversals and the absorption in the increasingly absurd are capital, for they surprise and distract us, and we find ourselves out further than we intended to go, or even than we knew. We are astonished to be laughing from our bellies. There is no sense to it; it is never "so funny as all that"; but that's just the point.

JONSON'S COMIC FEELINGS

Jonson is extremely malicious (and satiric), but he is weak in deep laughter. There is not enough suggestiveness. He presents gluttony but little gusto, and lechery but almost no pornography; only the scatological part is strongly felt, and this expresses itself not so much in excretion as in hostility. (Compare the good nature of a really dirty comedy like *Ubu.*)

On the other hand, Jonson, especially in *The Alchemist,* is glorious in the smiling and chuckling of the resolution, the satisfaction of the cat that has lapped up the cream. We are left with a normalcy that is lively indeed. For other poets liveliness means mainly a wedding, and Jonson nods in this direction by assigning the pretty rich girl to Lovewit: it is the prize of urbanity; there is no romatic nonsense. But what he is mainly concerned with is that poetic justice be given to intelligence and skill, and he works this out in the nicest detail.

Face gets off free. In the beginning, Face and Subtile seemed almost formally identical; but, as the intrigue progresses, we find Face infinitely various, while Subtile is handled more and more as an expert in one line; therefore, Subtile is deflatable, but Face is not. (So in Gogol's "Gamblers" the master-cardsharp is taken by the all-round crooks.) Face is a wit; he can operate in normalcy, where normalcy belongs to a Lovewit, not a Surly who has the vice of honesty. Subtile is not punished, for he was so skilful. The surprising adequacy to normal conditions of what seemed to be a deflatable trait (knavery) is glorious. Glory is the survival, and reward, of a comic trait in the resolution. Glory is the discovery that a deflatable talent is a wit.

I have said that the officers and the crowd are not handled as dupes. Yet surely there is a sense in which they, and *a fortiori* the normal Sir Epicure and Surly, are made ridiculous by Lovewit and Face. But this is the comic world of everyday, not of accident. Herein one may get "Happiness...though with some small strain of his own candour" (V, 5, l. 483). We may take this as the comic thought of the resolution; it is a philosophical truth. (Note that the poet has to apologize for it, for it is not quite the morality of the audience.)

CHARACTERS AS ASPECTS OF THE PLOT

In a rough way the characters are introduced as foils: the intrigue is expanded by the interplay of contraries. Dapper and Drugger are dupes, the simpleton and the fool; they make no long speeches. Sir Epicure and Tribulation, the contrary vices, are heroic humors; they make long speeches; and, in the mutual dealing between lust and puritanism, each is secretly subject to the vice of the other. The foil between the friends, Sir Epicure and Surly, expresses an important structural moment, the humorous-normal; it is a probability within the intrigue for the ultimate deflation. Surly and Lovewit, again, are foils in that both aspire for the normal prize, the rich marriage; here the lively-normal or urbane has succession over the humorous-normal. Lastly, Face and the Alchemist are foils. Subtile is the comic genius who gives his name to this particular intrigue, but Face is a wit who can survive for any Jonsonian sequel. Thus Face and Lovewit, the witty and the urbane, are universal characters, not involved in a particular intrigue; and this is expressed by having these two appear together before the curtain (V, 5, ll. 484 *ad fin.*). They can address the audience directly, since they are no longer "in" the play.

The humors are "unsympathetic"; that is, they are completely deflatable without reconstitution. Thus the comedy of humors tends to be a little cruel; and where the humor is involved with a person's happiness and station, as in *Volpone* or in *Le Misanthrope, L'Avare,* and *Tartuffe,* we pass easily from comedy to tragic satire, from the heroic humor to the tragic flow. The comic talents, the knaves or shrewd fools, on the other hand, are in a certain sense "like the audience"; they have a cleverness that anyone might wish for himself. Thus their deflation calls for such reconstitution as is possible in normalcy. (We might say this formally as follows: The fact that these talents survive so many comic reversals creates a presumption of permanence also in the deflation, which is the last reversal; whereas the fact that the humors are always being reversed implies that they will be reversed out of existence.)

SPECTACLE

Spectacular disguises and hiding places imply a comic intrigue, accidental connections. In serious plays the disguises are for the most part natural, deep-going traits, as that Orestes does not recognize Iphigenia because of the lapse of time. And hiding places are not serious, because it is not the local place of the actor but his character and thought that must save or destroy him. A disguise on the scene, for instance Surly as the Don, presents us with two traits at once; it is the foretaste of a comic reversal. And, in general, the ability to assume different disguises is a comic talent; it sets intrigues in motion. To be named "Face" is to be a universal wit and to survive. In the setting of *The Alchemist* there are many rooms, from each one of which threatens to emerge a fatal secret, and, of course, Dapper is waiting in the privy.

Further, the spectacle of many persons engaged in heterogeneous occupations is comic; it promises accidental connections. So the Don is pleasure-bound, the Alchemist busy with his retorts, Dol as the Queen of Faerie is waving her wand, Face has his medals, and the carriers are bringing on the leaden roofs of the churches of the elect. Out of this potpourri the disguised actors frequently make asides and out-of-character grimaces, which may be in some other character or "real" and out of the play, normalcy. But the "reality" of the actor is itself comic in the ideality of the theater.

By means of spectacle there are quick reversals and deflations, unmaskings. To be hit with a soft pie is a quick reversal of superficial dignity. When the intrigue is thickly starred with such spectacular reversals, not much prepared, we have the effect of slapstick.

On the other hand, a very effective expression of normalcy is the presence of the normal crowd as opposed to the comic company, for the anonymous crowd is not a humor. Bergson remarks on this well when he says that monstrosities develop in private and are destroyed by publicity. The crowd is active and vociferous but homogeneous and anonymous; it is lively and normal. The crowded comic company is active, vociferous, and heterogeneous. And, following the convention of Roman comedy, we see in *The Alchemist* the contrast of Inside the House, where there is comic license, and Outside, normalcy pounding at the door.

The Time, nearly continuous with the drama, is exhilaratingly crowded. The relation between continuous time and the comedy of juxtaposition is obvious, for where there are many actions, and all of them must be carried on at once, accidental relations are inevitable. Jonson makes good use also of the neoclassical acts, the entrances and curtains: the end of Act I, scene 1, is the end of the formal beginning; Act II, scene 1, and Act III, scene 1, introduce the major heroic humors; and Act V, scene 1, is the entrance of the normal crowd, lively and noisy enough to avoid a letdown after the climax.

DICTION

The dramatic irony of comedy is jokes. In serious plays ironic speech makes even the spare lines of the plot more fatally simple; but jokes fly off in every direction, and each one is a reversal of thought and a deflation of intention. Slapstick is the multitudinous and unprepared deflation of comic appearance, jokes of comic thought. So the feeling of the whole becomes heady and unpredictable. (But, if once the jokes become predictable, the whole falls like a wet cake.)

In an important class of cases it is pointless to distinguish comic thought from comic diction, namely, where laughter is roused by the deflation of sense to sound, as in puns. Speech is sound significant by convention; the comedian breaks the convention. Puns are usually trivial (e.g., Drugger's "angels" are also coins), but Jonson is a master of the sophisms that turn on form of sentences rather than the composition of meanings, what sounds like sense (e.g., Face on Dapper's birth caul: "How! swear by your fac, and in a thing so known unto the Doctor? how shall he then believe you i' the other matter?"). The matter-of-fact tone, the wild absurdity, the careful logic; it is a kind of fun that is as rich as can be, and yet we are not invited to let go but to keep pent up and finally mellowing within us the philosophic wine of how ridiculous the world is. Then a whole character may be deflated to a sound, as we are assured that Dapper is no "chiaus."

The scientific arguments of a Subtile or a Sganarelle are, of course, the same comedy of sophisms. But Molière on the physicians is not savorous but sharp (it is mere folly); he turns the comedy outward in presistent satire; whereas the learned Jonson savors and dreams of learned men, and it is mere folly.

The reduction of character and plot to sound is very marked in those plays (not *The Alchemist*) that employ elaborate comic rhythms; for example, in *The Acharnians* the cretics of the Chorus are so warlike and striking that the soldiers become singers and chorus boys. Gilbert and Sullivan are English masters in this kind and also in the patter songs of individuals.

In general, when the rhythm is kept subordinate to the thought and action, regular rhythm dignifies and ennobles. A simple smooth rhythm that does not call attention to itself makes the speech serious; iambic rhythm elevates colloquial speech. The tack that Jonson takes, however, is to handle the iambics roughly, to bring the music *down* to colloquial speech, and this is a comic diction. Compare an excited moment in *Oedipus* with one in *The Alchemist:* in the tragedy the verse is climactically cut to hemistichs, but in the comedy to six speeches to a pentameter (e.g., I, 1, l. 107). Naturally the audience cannot hear such a meter, but that too is one of Jonson's learned jokes. Also, the crowded heterogeneous scene fits with broken rhythms.

We must not overlook the long speeches in *The Alchemist,* those that most directly give the heroic humors. They are of the lineage of Horace and Martial and just as good. Thus, the marvelous characteristic rhapsodies of Sir Epicure: "Come on, sir. Now you set your foot on shore..." (II, 1, ll. 1 ff.); "I will have all my beds blown up, not stuft..." (II, 2, ll. 145 ff.); "We'll therefore go with all, my girl, and live / In a free state..." (IV, 1, ll. 156 ff.); or Tribulation's "The children of perdition are oft-times / Made instruments..." (III, 1, ll. 15 ff.). These, with their compactness of idea and firm march of sound, are truly heroic. They are laughable, not part by part but as wholes; this is epic comedy. At the other extreme the dupes do not express themselves at all, as if speech were too grand for them, but the adaptable Face speaks up for them: "'Slight, I bring you no cheating Clim-o'-the Cloughs..." (I, 2, ll. 244 ff.), or "This is my friend Abel, an honest fellow..." (I, 3, ll. 396 ff.).

Insults and obscenity belong to comedy, both for their malice and to create the suggestive atmosphere of the deep laughter. In the first seven lines of *The Alchemist* we have farting, shitting, and pissing; and we proceed thence to uncomplimentary personal remarks. (I have previously suggested that the cruel use of the excretory is the characteristic libido of Jonson.)

The so-called speech of low characters and any other emphasis on individual tricks of speech (e.g., the dialect of Lucas in *Le Médecin malgré lui*) may or may not be comic, depending on the structure. If the thought, and especially the sentiment, is strongly developed, as in Wordsworth, then the speech appears as a halting attempt to be serious with inadequate means, and the effect is pathetic; but if, by the emphasis, the character is reduced to the mere eccentric use of words, the effect is comic. The particular Jonsonian mixture of base speech and Marlovian high rhetoric is quite his own. He does not mean it to be bombastic and satiric, and it is not; it is not comic but simply strange, the soaring dreams of a gross animal body (indeed, the daring comparison that comes to mind is *L'Après-midi d'un faune!*). And this gross beauty, again, he involves with a matter-of-fact naturalism and an acutely intelligent appraisal of the types of the town.

Finally, there is a good deal of actual "topical reference": to the actual statute of sorcery, to a real highwayman, a current "Persian" incident, etc. Such random actual reference tends to trivialize tragedy, reducing it to the level of news, "his tragedy has become a *fait divers*"— unless, of course, there is one great unified reference to an important current event, in which case the tragedy becomes a kind of tract for the times. In comedies like *The Alchemist,* however, the references to actuality provide a ballast, a comic normalcy of reality continuous with the normalcy of the humors. Such comedy verges into social satire. (Quite different is the effort to use the topical reference as a joke, like a radio comedian; the laughter is then often embarrassed, for the audience is unwilling to deflate the actual world to nought.)

THE ALCHEMIST

Blissett, William. "The Venter Tripartite in *The Alchemist,*" *SEL,* VIII (1968), 323–334.

Brown, Douglas, ed. *The Alchemist.* The New Mermaids. London, 1966, pp. xii–xxiv.

Dessen, Alan C. *"The Alchemist:* Jonson's 'Estates' Play," *RenD,* VII (1964), 35–54.

Hill, Edgar Duncan. "Jonson's *Alchemist* and the Literature of Alchemy," *PMLA,* LXI (1945), 699–710.

Hoy, Cyrus. "The Pretended Piety of Jonson's Alchemist," in *Renaissance Papers 1955,* ed. Allan H. Gilbert. Columbia, S.C., and Durham, N.C., 1955, pp. 15–19.

Knoll, Robert E. "How to Read *The Alchemist,*" *CE,* XXI (1960), 456–460.

Mares, F. H., ed. *The Alchemist.* The Revels Plays. Cambridge, Mass., 1967, pp. xxxi–lxxix.

Parr, Johnstone. *Tamburlaine's Malady and Other Essays.* Tuscaloosa, Alabama, 1953, pp. 107–111.

Steane, J. B., ed. *The Alchemist.* London, 1967.

Thayer, C. G. "Theme and Structure in *The Alchemist,*" *ELH,* XXVI (1959), 23–35.

See other studies in Jonson bibliography (below, pp. 253–254).

BEN JONSON

Every Man In His Humour = EMI   *Alchemist* = A
Every Man Out Of His Humour = EMO   *Bartholomew Fair* = BF
Volpone = V   *Epicene* = E

Bacon, Wallace A. "The Magnetic Field: The Structure of Jonson's Comedies," *HLQ*, XIX (February 1956), 121–153.

Barish, Jonas, A., ed. *Ben Jonson: A Collection of Critical Essays.* Englewood Cliffs, N.J., 1963.

_____. *Ben Jonson and the Language of Prose Comedy.* Cambridge, Mass., 1960, pp. 98–104 and 130–141 (EMI), 104–113 (EMO), 147–186 (E), 187–239 (BF).

Baum, Helen Watts. *The Satiric and Didactic in Ben Jonson's Comedies.* Chapel Hill, N.C., 1947, pp. 71–76 (A), 126–131 (BF), 165–182 (V).

Boas, Frederick S. *An Introduction to Stuart Drama.* Oxford, 1946, pp. 49–55 (EMI), 106–110 (V), 110–113 (E), 113–117 (A), 117–120 (BF).

Campbell, Oscar J. *Comicall Satyre and Shakespeare's Troilus and Cressida.* San Marino, Calif., 1938, pp. 54–81 (EMO).

Cunningham, John E. *Elizabethan and Early Stuart Drama.* London, 1965, pp. 61–65 (EMI), 65–67 (V), 67–68 (A).

Eliot, T. E. *Selected Essays.* New Edition. New York, 1950, pp. 127–139 (E).

Enck, John J. *Jonson and the Comic Truth.* Madison, Wis., 1957, pp. 43–59 (EMO), 110–131 (V), 132–150 (E), 151–171 (A), 188–208 (BF).

Gardner, Thomas. " 'A Parodie! A Parodie!' " in *Lebende Antike: Symposion für Rudolf Sühnel,* ed. Horst Meller and Hans-Joachim Zimmerman. Berlin, 1967, pp. 197–206.

Gibbons, Brian. *Jacobean City Comedy: A Study of Satiric Plays by Jonson, Marston and Middleton,* Cambridge, Mass., 1968, pp. 69–73 (EMI), 73–75 (EMO), 124–129 (V), 169–178 (A), 178–189 (BF).

Gottwald, Maria. "Ben Jonson's Theory of Comedy," *GW*, X (1966), 31–53.

Hays, H. R. "Satire and Identification: An Introduction to Ben Jonson," *Kenyon Review,* XIX (1957), 267–283.

Heffner, Ray L., Jr. "Unifying Symbols in the Comedy of Ben Jonson," in *English Stage Comedy,* ed. W. K. Wimsatt. English Institute Essays (1954). New York, 1955, pp. 74–97 (BF, E).

Herford, C. H., and Percy Simpson, eds. *Ben Jonson.* 11 vols. Oxford, 1925–1952, I, 335–357 (EMI); II, 49–65 (V), 67–84 (E), 99–109 (A), 131–145 (BF).

Hussey, Maurice, ed. *Jonson and the Cavaliers.* London and New York, 1964.

Kernan, Alvin. *The Cankered Muse: Satire of the English Renaissance.* New Haven, 1959, pp. 150–91.

Knights, L. C. "Ben Jonson, Dramatist," in *The Age of Shakespeare,* ed. Boris Ford. Baltimore, 1955, pp. 302–317.

_____. *Drama and Society in the Age of Jonson.* London, 1937, pp. 200–206 (V), 206–210 (A).

Knoll, Robert E. *Ben Jonson's Plays: An Introduction.* Lincoln, Nebraska, 1964, pp. 31–40 (EMI), 45–52 (EMO), 79–104 (V), 106–117 (E), 117–135 (A), 145–162 (BF).

Partridge, Edward B. "Ben Jonson: The Makings of the Dramatist (1599–1602)," in *Elizabethan Theatre,* ed. John Russell Brown and Bernard Harris. Stratford-upon-Avon Studies 9. London, 1966, pp. 221–244.

_____. *The Broken Compass: A Study of the Major Comedies of Ben Jonson.* New York, 1958, pp. 70–113 (V), 114–160 (A), 161–177 (E).

Ransom, John Crowe. *The New Criticism.* Norfolk, Conn., 1941, pp. 158–175.

Seymour-Smith, Martin, ed. *Every Man in His Humour.* The New Mermaids, London, 1967, pp. xv–xxi.

Snuggs, Henry L. "The Comic Humours: A New Interpretation," *PMLA,* LXII (1947), 114–119 (EMI, EMO).

Thayer, C. G. *Ben Jonson: Studies in the Plays.* Norman, Oklahoma, 1963, pp. 17–25 (EMI), 25–32 (EMO), 50–66 (V), 66–84 (E), 84–111 (A), 128–156 (BF).

Townsend, Freda L. *Apologie for Bartholomew Fayre: The Art of Jonson's Comedies.* London and New York, 1947, pp. 58–62 (V), 62–66 (E), 66–70 (A), 71–76 (BF).

John Marston

THE MALCONTENT :
VIRTUOUS MACHIAVELLIANISM *

Philip J. Finkelpearl

MARSTON modestly admits in the preface to *The Fawne* that *"above better desert"* he has been *"fortunate in these stage-pleasings."*[1] There is reason to believe that his work was usually well-received in the circles I have been describing, but with *The Malcontent* in 1604 he momentarily achieved a wider popularity.[2] Three quartos of this play were required

* Reprinted by permission of the publishers, from Philip J. Finkelpearl, *John Marston of the Middle Temple: An Elizabethan Dramatist in His Social Setting.* Cambridge, Mass.: Harvard University Press; copyright 1968 by The President and Fellows of Harvard College.

[1] *The Plays of John Marston*, ed. H. Harvey Wood (Edinburgh, 1934–1939), II, 143. All page citations in the text refer to Volume I of this edition.

[2] Nothing has been discovered to dislodge E. K. Chambers' conclusion (*The Elizabethan Stage* [Oxford, 1923], III, 432) that *The Malcontent* "is Marston's first play for the Queen's Revels after the formation of the syndicate early in 1604." G. K. Hunter in "English Folly and Italian Vice," *Jacobean Theatre*, Stratford-upon-Avon Studies 1 (London, 1960), p. 100, mentions that *The Malcontent* reflects "much borrowing from Guarini's *Pastor Fido.*" Following Hunter's suggestion, Bernard Harris in his edition of *The Malcontent*, New Mermaid Series (London, 1967), has demonstrated that Marston drew heavily, often nearly verbatim, on an anonymous English translation entitled *Il Pastor Fido or the Faithfull*

in less than six months, and the King's Men judged it to have a broad enough appeal for production at the Globe.[3] The reasons are not hard to discover. It has an exciting plot with a multitude of surprising twists, and in the Hamlet-like title figure Marston created a fascinating role worthy of the actor who played it, Richard Burbage.

But even with Burbage and the other immortals, a production of *The Malcontent* in the vast open spaces of the Globe must have been unsatisfactory. The cramped, claustrophobic setting of a private theater is absolutely essential to Marston's purposes. Using techniques reminiscent of German Expressionist drama of the 1920s, the play opens in a barrage of olfactory, aural, and oral effects to evoke the atmosphere:

> The vilest out of tune Musicke being heard.
>
> [Enter BILIOSO and PRAEPASSO.]
>
> BILIOSO: Why how now? are ye mad? or drunke? or both? or what?
> PRAEPASSO: Are ye building *Babilon* there?
> BILIOSO: Heer's a noyse in Court, you thinke you are in a Taverne, do you not?
> PRAEPASSO: You thinke you are in a brothell house doe you not? This roome is ill sented. [*Enter one with a perfume.*] So; perfume; perfume; some upon me, I pray thee: The Duke is upon instant entrance; so, make place there. [p. 145] Heere round about is hell [p. 204] in a world...turnde upside downe [p. 177].

In this heightened version of the world of *What You Will,* men are constantly "bewitched" (p. 157) and "beseld" (p. 165) by their senses. They are helpless before those who would inflame them:

> in an *Italian* lascivious Pallace, a Lady gardianlesse,
> Left to the push of all allurement,
> The strongest incitements to immodestie,
> To have her bound, incensed with wanton sweetes,
> Her veines fild hie with heating delicates,
> Soft rest, sweete Musick, amorous Masquerers, lascivious banquets,
> sinne it selfe gilt ore, strong phantasie tricking up strange delights,
> presenting it dressed pleasingly to sence, sence leading it unto the

---

Shepheard (London, 1602). Perhaps it was awareness of this fact that led Edward Phillips, *Theatrum Poetarum* (London, 1675), p. 113, to ascribe to Marston "the *Faithfull Sheapherd* a Pastoral"—although this attribution is almost certainly incorrect. Discovery of this source effectively refutes those who would revive E. E. Stoll's theory that *The Malcontent* dates from 1600 and precedes *Hamlet;* it must postdate the translation of 1602. And in view of Marston's heavy reliance on a notoriously poor translation, this discovery also casts doubt on Marston's mastery of Italian.

[3] After a thorough study of the quartos, M. L. Wine, ed., *The Malcontent,* Regents Renaissance Drama Series (Lincoln, Neb., 1964), p. xv, concluded that since the augmented version "has indications of authorial revision," it was not really pirated.

soule, confirmed with potent example, impudent custome inticed by
that great bawd opportunitie, thus being prepar'd, clap to her easie
eare, youth in good clothes, well shapt, rich, faire-spoken, promising-
noble, ardent bloud-full, wittie, flattering: *Ulisses* absent, O *Ithaca,*
can chastest *Penelope,* hold out.[4]

(p. 179)

Through such speeches and through symbolic actions Marston takes
great pains throughout the play to create an atmosphere of overpowering,
nearly irresistible corruption. Life in the palace is imaged by a symbolic
dance (Act IV, Scene 2) which is far removed from Davies' heavenly
ritual of love and harmony. Instead, it is a "brawle"—the pun alludes to
a complex French dance—resembling in its meaningless intricacy and
confusion a "maze" where "honor" is lost (p. 188).

Atmosphere and action are inextricably intertwined in this play; each
infects the other. In the second act, for example, the Duke plans to catch
his wife in the arms of her latest lover, having been informed of the
tryst by her former lover. What could have occupied one scene is broken
into three with each of these punctuated by scenes in other parts of the
palace. First we see the new lover slip into the duchess' chamber while the
old lover (the worst villain in the play) exults in his imminent vengeance
(II, 1). Then we hear court ladies exchange dirty jokes about cuckolding
and aphrodisiacs with the Malcontent, Malevole (II, 2), after which the
scene shifts to the last-minute preparations of the group of courtiers who
are to break in upon the lovers (II, 3). Once more there is a shift to
the ladies who make amoral comments about the necessity of caring for
their beauty as they sip a newly concocted "posset," a beautifier and
"restorative" (II, 4). At the end of the scene we hear music emanating
from the duchess' chamber to remind us of what is going on there, and
only then do we see the violent scene in which the duchess is publicly
disgraced and her lover wounded (II, 5). The cause-effect relationship
between these apparently disparate activities is clear. Women who have
such matters on their minds will fall into such situations. When the
speech about the dangers in an "*Italian* lascivious Pallace" (quoted
above) is delivered a few scenes later, its truth has already been demonstrated.

The usphot of the action I have just summarized is that the villainous
Mendoza regains his position as the Duchess' lover and as the Duke's
favorite and successor. Moreover, his cunning plot, concocted at a moment
when he seemed to have been outfoxed, leads to further success. Angered

---

[4] It has been customary to set this entire passage as poetry although all three
quartos show a portion of it as prose. I prefer to leave it as printed because
Marston appears to have taken some pains with the text and because it is characteristic of Malevole's speeches to hover ambiguously between poetry and prose.
Moreover some of the lines in this passage resist being chopped into pentameters.

by her public humiliation, the Duchess resolves to revenge herself on her husband. In an instant she invents a plot which reveals her own high competence in the intricacies of *Realpolitik:*

> Ile make thee Duke, we are of *Medices,*
> *Florence* our friend, in court my faction
> Not meanly strength-full; the Duke then dead,
> We well prepar'd for change: the multitude
> Irresolutely reeling: we in force:
> Our partie seconded: the kingdom mazde:
> No doubt of swift successe all shall be grac'd.

(p. 171)

The activities just described are normal in the palace, the *"unquiet studies"* of these discontented creatures, in the words of Marston's preface, *"labor innovation, contempt of holy policie, reverent comely superioritie, and establisht unity"* (p. 139). Politically, they engage in usurpations, domestically, in cuckolding. In the Duke's palace the two activities are connected. To gratify these linked appetites, one must be able to plot. The Duchess Aurelia's effortless mastery of this art comes to her naturally because she is a Medici, but there are other great technicians of plotting. The form of the play can be described as a structure of progressively cunning plots; through them, the usurping Duke Pietro is usurped, and the successful usurper, Mendoza, is in turn usurped by the rightful duke, Altofronto, who has been masking as the Malcontent, Malevole. In this atmosphere, plotting is as natural as breathing.

In addition to linking atmosphere and action better than in his previous plays, Marston has also inhabited the palace with a more fully realized set of characters. The villainous Mendoza is a satiric portrait, but Marston endows him with the ability to express his physical pleasure at being a prince's favorite in remarkably vivid images:

> to have a generall timerous respect, observe a man, a statefull scilence in his presence: solitarinesse in his absence, a confused hum and busie murmure of obsequious suters trayning him; the cloth held up, and waye proclaimed before him; Petitionary vassailes licking the pavement with their slavish knees, whilst some odde pallace *Lampreel's* that ingender with Snakes, and are full of eyes on both sides with a kinde of insinuated humblenesse fixe all their delightes upon his browe.

(p. 154)

In addition to reaching "the Olympus of favor" (p. 154), he is ravished by his role as the Duchess' lover. When his ideal situation is threatened, he defends himself with great cunning because he remembers precisely what it feels like to be a menial:

> Shall I whose very humme, strooke all heads bare,
> Whose face made scilence: creaking of whose shooe

Forc'd the most private passages flie ope,
Scrape like a servile dog at some latch'd doore?
Learne now to make a leg? and cry beseech ye,
Pray yee, is such a Lord within? be aw'd
At some odde ushers scoft formality?
First seare my braines: *Unde cadis non quo refert.*

(p. 163)

The Senecan tag is not a revenge play cliché. It is an association which naturally springs to the mind of a Machiavellian. Mendoza is frequently a comic figure, but he is fully imagined and credible.

The Duchess Aurelia is a much slighter portrait, but Marston successfully captures the image of a haughty, passionate aristocrat. She reacts with defiance and extravagant indifference to the public exposure of her immoral conduct and with equally extravagant contrition after she is betrayed by her lover. She dances defiantly when her husband's death is announced, but after her conversion she wears a "mourning habit" and interrupts courtly revels by reciting pious poetry (p. 211).[5]

The weak usurper, Duke Pietro, is also conceived with some psychological subtlety. He is a puppet set up by an outside power and manipulated by Mendoza. Inept at politics, he is, fittingly, also a cuckold. It is this predicament which troubles him most, for his repentant wife's words at the end of the play confirm what we have already seen: "As the soule lov'd the body, so lov'd he" (p. 195). When Pietro is finally compelled to take vengeance, Marston does not use the situation as a pretext for stale jokes about cuckoldry. He makes him into a pitiable and sympathetic figure:

I strike but yet like him that gainst stone walles
Directs his shafts, reboundes in his owne face,
My Ladies shame is mine, O God tis mine.
Therefore I doe conjure all secrecie,
Let it be as very little as may be; pray yee, as may be?
Make frightlesse entrance, salute her with soft eyes,
Staine nought with blood—onely *Ferneze* dies,
But not before her browes: O Gentlemen
God knowes I love her, nothing els, but this,
I am not well.

(pp. 166–167)

5 As Arthur H. Bullen discovered, this poem is by Thomas Bastard, the schoolmate of Hoskins, Davies, and Wotton. Thus the insertion of this passage is an inner circle allusion, which through Marston's designation of the author as an "honest Priest" (p. 211), constitutes a compliment to a friend of several important Middle Templars. Marston's joke on p. 150 about the disappearance of simony in the next age may also have been derived from Bastard's epigram "Ad Thymum," *Chrestoleros* (London, 1598), p. 113.

The request to "salute her with soft eyes" is a delicate touch; it prepares us for Pietro's eventual moral regeneration. He has been living in a fool's paradise, and he eloquently attests to the pain of learning the truth:

> I am not unlike to some sickman,
> That long desired hurtfull drinke; at last
> Swilles in and drinkes his last, ending at once
> Both life and thirst: O would I nere had knowne
> My owne dishonour: good God, that men should
> Desire to search out that, which being found kils all
> Their joye of life: to taste the tree of Knowledge,
> And then be driven out of Paradice.

(p. 174)

Pietro is a convincing combination of sensitivity and weakness. He provides a subtle contrast to the two other figures who take their turns as Duke. He lacks the passionate intensity of the one and the moral stature of the other.

These are the main ingredients of the world which the hero must set right. Dispossessed of his kingdom and sentenced to exile, the rightful Duke of Genoa, Altofronto, remains at court in the disguise of a "malcontent." This term, which seems to have entered the language in the 1580's, denotes a clearly defined type. A man of some parts developed by education and foreign travel, the malcontent was poor, usually unemployed, and obsessed by a sense of unrewarded merit; often he was melancholic. Thus he was a prime source of danger to the kingdom since he was readily available for schemes against the established order. In these he could be relied on to employ special skills acquired in Italy for plotting and murder. As many scholars have pointed out, malcontents were only in part a literary construction. Economic and political conditions fostered his appearance late in Elizabeth's reign, and in fact such men did sow some discord, as Henry Cuffe's role in the Earl of Essex's uprising illustrates. By the time of this play, the malcontent had become a stock figure on the stage. Nevertheless there must have been special interest attached to a play with this title, written by an author with a reputation for "malcontentedness."[6] The evidence of the preface, the "Prologus," and the Induction indicates that some members of the audience interpreted the play *"with subtilitie (as deepe as hell)"* (p. 139). Marston claimed that it was *"over-cunning"* (p. 139) to ferret out contemporary allusions, but as we shall see, a few clear examples have survived.

Even if Marston did not conceive the play as having a specific con-

---

[6] See the epigram to Marston by John Davies of Hereford, *The Scourge of Folly* (London, 1610), p. 105, which begins: "Thy *Male-content,* or, *Malecontentedness* / Hath made thee change thy Muse as some do gesse."

temporary application, this play, with its suggestively political title, is primarily about the conduct of politics in a world "turnde upside downe" (p. 177). From the first moments it is apparent that the Malcontent is an agent of discord. It is he who produces the "vilest out of tune Musicke" offstage, and his first speech, blurted from the same place, is the verbal equivalent of this discord:

> Yaugh, godaman, what do'st thou there: Dukes *Ganimed Junoes* jealous of thy long stockings: shadowe of a woman, what wouldst Weesell? thou lambe a Court: what doost thou bleat for? a you smooth chind Catamite!
>
> .(p. 145)

This clash of obscene discords seems to mirror a "soule. . .at variance (within her selfe)" (p. 146), as the Duke says in his character sketch of the Malcontent. Although "his speach is halter-worthy at al howers," the Duke has licensed him to speak freely in order to help him to "understand those weakenesses which others flattery palliates" (p. 146). Thus the title figure with the name that means "ill will" appears to be a domesticated malcontent, a Lord of Misrule authorized to castigate the Duke and his courtiers. He goes at it with wild abandon, changing his direction at every moment:

> PIETRO: But what's the common newes abroade *Malevole,* thou dogst rumor still.
> MALEVOLE: Common newes? why common wordes are, God save yee, Fare yee well: common actions, Flattery and Cosenage: common things, Women and Cuckolds: and how do's my little *Ferrard:* a yee lecherous Animal, my little Ferret, he goes sucking up & downe the Pallace into every Hens nest like a Weesell: & to what doost thou addict thy time to now, more then to those Antique painted drabs that are still affected of yong Courtiers, Flattery, Pride, & Venery.
>
> (p. 147)

This passage has elements of traditional Tudor satire: the abstractions of the Ship of Fools, the use of the beast fable, and moral commonplaces. But the rapid shifts and the colloquial style charge Malevole's satiric prose with a vitality Marston rarely achieved in his verse satires. In these passages, he adopts the manner of a vaudeville entertainer, stringing together a seemingly random series of jests suitable for preservation in a "table-booke," as the character Sly mentions in the Induction (p. 141). But the role of entertainer which Altofronto adopts is part of a more complicated disguise. In an original twist, Marston's figure is a true malcontent posing as a malcontent. As a dispossessed duke, Altofronto has a perfect right to the character of a malcontent. When he describes his malcontented state without his verbal disguise, there is none of Malevole's broad, gross-jawed style:

> in night all creatures sleepe,
> Onely the Malecontent that gainst his fate,
> Repines and quarrels, alas hees goodman tell-clocke;
> His sallow jaw-bones sincke with wasting mone,
> Whilst others beds are downe, his pillowes stone.

(p. 178)

To regain his kingdom he adopts as his disguise an "affected straine" which allows him to indulge in *"Free speach"*:

> I may speake foolishly, I knavishly,
> Alwaies carelesly, yet no one thinkes it fashion
> To poize my breath, "for he that laughs and strikes,
> Is lightly felt, or seldome strucke againe.

(pp. 150–151)

The special quality to Malevole's manner springs from the fact that he is acting: Marston makes us hear the effort it requires for him to sustain his wild and whirling words:

> Sir *Tristram Trimtram* come aloft, Jacke-a-napes with a whim wham, heres a Knight of the lande of *Catito* shall play at trap with any Page in Europe; Doe the sword daunce, with any Morris-dauncer in Christendome; ride at the Ring till the finne of his eyes looke as blew as the welkin, and runne the wilde-goose chase even with *Pompey* the huge.

(p. 148)

Through Pietro's comment, "You runne..." (p. 148), Marston suggests his attitude toward Malevole's style. It is not the idiosyncratic manner of an amusing character like Tucca, nor the acerb commentary of a "pure" malcontent like Bosola, nor a stage version of madness. It is designed to convey a sense of the pressure on someone who is acting a part which is not natural to him and which he occasionally finds odious: "O God, how loathsome this toying is to mee, that a Duke should be forc'd to foole it: well, *Stultorum plena sunt omnia,* better play the foole Lord, then be the foole Lord" (p. 204). He resembles the court fool Passarello, a professional comedian who finds his job a "drudgery" (p. 160) in a world of "loose vanities" (p. 162). "Stultorum plena sunt omnia" is a true saying because if you are not a fool naturally, the world will force you to become one.

The strain and wildness of Malevole's language are justified by his personal plight and by his need for a disguise. The language has the further value of providing an ideal medium in which to express a special view of the world. Malevole is a kind of visionary who sees the waking world as a perpetual nightmare. His "dreams" are the reality which others cannot see:

PIETRO: Dreame, what dreamst?

MALEVOLE: Why me thinkes I see that Signior pawn his footcloth: that *Metreza* her Plate: this madam takes phisick: that that tother *Mounsieur* may minister to her: here is a Pander Jeweld: there is a fellow in shift of Satten this day, that could not shift a shirt tother night: here a *Paris* supports that *Hellen:* theres a Ladie *Guinever* bears up that sir *Lancelot.* Dreames, dreames, visions, fantasies, *Chimeras,* imaginations, trickes, conceits.

(pp. 147–148)

Throughout the play, Malevole's goal is to make people see the world as his "dreams" have revealed it to him, to make them see how "strange" (to use his recurrent phrase) and vile and unnatural it is. He wants to convert them to his "faith" that, as Pietro comes to realize, "All is damnation, wickedness extreame, there is no faith in man" (p. 193). Sometimes he shows them the invisible truth by inventing an appropriate visual metaphor: "Muckhill overspread with fresh snow" (p. 147), "pigeon house...smooth, round, and white without, and full of holes and stinke within" (p. 153). Sometimes he makes people "see" by the detailed evocation of a vivid, concrete picture, as when he describes Aurelia's adultery to Pietro. To excerpt one example from a long speech, he says that even when she does yield *"Hymeneall* sweetes,"

> the thaw of her delight
> Flowes from lewde heate of apprehension,
> Onely from strange imaginations rankenes,
> That formes the adulterers presence in her soule,
> And makes her thinke she clips the foule knaves loines.

(p. 149)

Pietro reels before Malevole's "Hydeous imagination" (p. 150), but Malevole, in a speech that constitutes one of the most famous expressions of "Jacobean melancholy," forces him to see more and greater horrors:

> th' art but in danger to loose a Dukedome, thinke this: this earth is the only grave and *Golgotha* wherein all things that live must rotte: tis but the draught wherein the heavenly bodies discharge their corruption, the very muckhill on which the sublunarie orbes cast their excrement: man is the slime of this dongue-pit, and Princes are the governours of these men: for, for our soules, they are as free as Emperoures, all of one peece, there goes but a paire of sheeres betwixt an Emperoure and the sonne of a bagpiper: only the dying, dressing, pressing, glossing, makes the difference: now, what art thou like to lose?
>
> *A jaylers office to keepe men in bonds,*
> *Whilst toyle and treason, all lifes good confounds.*

(p. 197)

This is the generality to which every detail in the play has been contributing; it is a moving elaboration of Antonio's realization in *Antonio's Revenge* that men are "vermine bred of putrifacted slime" (p. 118). Nor do any subsequent events in the play, not even the "happy" ending, modify its force. Nevertheless, for Malevole, the "Golgotha" speech is also a piece of rhetoric designed to induce Pietro to give up his claim to the dukedom. He responds correctly: "I heere renounce for ever Regency: O *Altofront,* I wrong thee to supplant thy right" (p. 197). Step by step, the malcontent has educated the usurper to recognize the worthlessness of his office in order that he, Altofronto, may regain it. The only difference between an emperor and a bagpiper is "a paire of sheeres," but Altofronto prefers his own clothes.

Thus the "Golgotha" speech is true, but it is also cunning. It illustrates an art which Altofronto has acquired and mastered. He had lost his dukedom, he explains, because

> I wanted those old instruments of state,
> Dissemblance and suspect: I could not time it *Celso,*
> My throane stood like a point in midd'st of a circle,
> To all of equall neerenesse, bore with none:
> Raind all alike, so slept in fearlesse vertue,
> Suspectles; too suspectles: till the crowde:
> (Still liquerous of untried noveltics)
> Impatient with severer government:
> Made strong with *Florence:* banisht *Altofront.*

> (p. 151)

Since then he has learned to "time it" by waiting for his chance and by prodding his enemies toward their ruin. The experience has taught him that "we are all Philosophicall Monarkes or naturall fooles" (p. 152). Either you stand stiffly aloof from the world, a Stoic sage, speaking sententiously like Altofronto and his impregnable, virtuous wife while your kingdom is stolen away, or you immerse yourself in the world with all its degradation and horror and become nature's fool. To paraphrase, "the Emperor Aurelius may be a model for a Philosophicall Monarke, but don't live in an *Italian* lascivious pallace without Machiavelli."

Thus it is that Malevole can improve on one of Mendoza's plots so impressively that he inspires the unabashed compliment: "ô unpeerable invention, rare, Thou God of pollicie! it hunnies me" (p. 183). Malevole has indeed become the "unpeerable" god of policy in a contest with masters. He can exchange aphrodisiac recipes with court ladies and Machiavellian aphorisms with Mendoza, he can convert Pietro and Aurelia, insult Bilioso with obscene jokes, and most importantly, he can fool Mendoza "most powerfully" (p. 180) with his disguise. But after bragging about this last accomplishment, he betrays an interesting confusion (whether in Marston or Altofronto it is impossible to say). He says caustically that Mendoza

> faine would claspe with me: he is the true slave,
> That will put on the most affected grace,
> For some vilde second cause.

(p. 181)

Obviously Altofronto is doing the same thing. He is putting on an affected "gracelessness" for a "second cause" which he has shown to be "vilde": the regaining of his "jaylers office" as duke.

Whether or not Marston intended Altofronto's remark to be an unwitting partial self-condemnation, other passages suggest that Altofronto's left hand has different values from his right.[7] After Pietro has relinquished the dukedom, Altofronto comments on his act in a speech which begins with pious platitudes and ends with a Machiavellian sententia:

> Who doubts of providence,
> That sees this change, a heartie faith to all:
> *He needes must rise, who can no lower fall,*
> *For still impetuous* Vicissitude
> *Towzeth the world, then let no maze intrude*
> Upon your spirits: wonder not I rise,
> *For who can sincke, that close can temporize?*
> The time growes ripe for action, Ile detect
> My privat'st plot, lest ignorance feare suspect:
> Let's cloase to counsell, leave the rest to fate,
> *Mature discretion is the life of state.*

(p. 198)

Altofronto's position shifts with each sentence. He first claims that Pietro's conversion should buttress faith in a presiding moral order, but then uses his own rise to demonstrate Fortune's continuing influence on events in this world; he was so low, that vicissitude had no direction in which to push him but upwards! Earlier in the play, speaking in the guise of an amoral malcontent, he had said to Mendoza, "only busie fortune towses, and the provident chaunces blends them together; Ile give you a symilie: did you ere see a Well with 2. buckets, whilst one comes up full to be emptied, another goes downe emptie to be filled; such is the state of all humanitie" (p. 181). One man rises at the expense of another: Pietro up, Altofronto down; Mendoza up, Pietro down;

---

7 Even the name "Altofronto" has equivocal implications. According to the most famous book of physiognomy of the period, Joannis Baptista Porta's *De humana physiognomonia* (Ursel, 1601), p. 127, an "alta frons" signifies firmness and bravery: "Qui frontem altam habent, pertinaces vel audaces sunt." On the other hand, Malevole says to the cuckold Bilioso, "you have a passing high forehead" (p. 152). As a duke who has been usurped, having a name associated with cuckoldom would not be out of place for Altofronto.

Altofronto up, Mendoza down. "This *Genoas* last yeares Duke" (p. 151) gets another turn. But more important than the power of Fortune is his own recent acquisition of "mature discretion." He has learned how to "time it."

The morality which Altofronto is forced to adopt sounds like Mendoza's, but the parallel which Marston develops more fully is that between Malevole and the most immoral figure in the play, the bawd Maquerelle. After Mendoza has gained power in Act V, Malevole asks her what she thinks of "this transformation of state now" (p. 201). Her reply is the sexual equivalent of his political metaphor of the two buckets:

> wee women always note, the falling of the one, is the rising of the other: . . . as for example, I have two court dogges, the most fawning curres. . . . now I, like lady Fortune, sometimes love this dog, sometimes raise that dog.
>
> (pp. 201–202)

She plays Lady Fortune in sexual matters, having brought an uncountable number of "maidenheads. . . to the blocke" (p. 203), just as Malevole manipulates political fortunes. She is the "God of pollicie" in her realm, with her cunning advances in the technology of adultery (p. 161), her possets and restoratives, her tricks for seduction. She is a Machiavelli of the bed chamber who constantly counsels "discretion" (e.g., p. 186) and mastery of the art of "timing it" (e.g., p. 202). As early as the first act, Malevole hints at some kind of relationship between himself and Maquerelle (p. 148), and in the last act he excuses an action by saying that he did it "as baudes go to Church, for fashion sake" (p. 197). A successful politician, Marston shows, must be something of a bawd.

This parallel makes it clear that the "malcontent" is a more complicated figure than he is often thought to be. He is not merely an upholder of virtue whose disguise allows him to satirize everyone at will in an extension of the author's manner. Despite his high moral standards, he has learned the black arts required to manipulate men, as his final plot demonstrates. In an original variant on the formulaic concluding masque of the revenge play, all but one of the masquers whom Malevole employs are apparent murder victims of Mendoza. The villain's response, consistent with the theme Marston has been developing, emphasizes that Altofronto has succeeded in turning dreams into reality:

> Are we surprizde? What strange delusions mocke
> Our sences, do I dreame? or have I dreamt
> This two daies space? where am I?
>
> (p. 213)

The reign of the devil has been overthrown, the good are redeemed, the bad are punished. But it is important to notice that Marston does not make extravagant claims for the effect of the experience on the lascivious palace creatures. The courtier Ferneze had been the first of Mendoza's victims after having succeeded him as the Duchess' lover. Rescued by Malevole, he was treated to a moral sermon on the evil effects of lust. During the masque of the revengers he dances with the dissolute Bianca, and his first act on returning to the court is to try to seduce her. With Maquerelle instantly involving herself in the transaction as she had in his earlier effort at seduction, Ferneze's regeneration is not a conspicuous success.

Nevertheless we are back in the virtuous and rational reign of Duke Altofronto, as we see from his just but merciful meting out of punishment. Turning to the archvillain, Mendoza, he refuses to kill him, explaining that a true monarch, someone with a *"glorious soule,"* disdains to hurt a peasant "prostrat at my feete" (p. 214). Aside from a few hasty lines to tuck in loose ends, the private theater text concludes on this note of self-satisfied grandeur. However, when Marston lengthened the play for public theater performance, he added thirteen lines to Altofronto's speech. These lines are important because they discuss directly the central political problem of the play, how to be both "good" and a "king." Altofronto begins by moralizing about the action of the play:

> O, I have seen strange accidents of state!—
> The flatterer like the Ivy clip the Oke,
> And wast it to the hart: lust so confirm'd
> That the black act of sinne it selfe not shamd
> To be termde Courtship.

(p. 214)

Mendoza had made his way by a combination of flattery and lust as had the courtier Bilioso. But since such activity was not unknown in courts closer than Genoa, Altofronto aims the rest of his oracular speech at the great and sinful rulers of the world:

> O they that are as great as be their sinnes,
> Let them remember that th' inconstant people,
> Love many Princes meerely for their faces,
> And outward shewes: and they do covet more
> To have a sight of these men then of their vertues,
> Yet thus much let the great ones still conceale,
> When they observe not Heavens imposd conditions,
> They are no Kings, but forfeit their commissions.

(p. 214)

The people are not loyal to a prince because he is virtuous. As Altofronto has learned to his cost, they are "Impatient with severer government" (p. 151) and want "outward shewes," impressive appearances. But a king cannot commit immoral acts with impunity. He must be a moral ruler or Heaven will see to his fall. The problem is how to square the requirements of Heaven with those of politics. Altofronto's answer is centered on the word "conceale," the crucial importance of which is often obscured by an emendation (to "conceive") for which there is no textual justification. Altofronto has learned that however virtuous you are, you must conceal it. You can be a philosophical monarch only if you act like a natural fool. You must temporize and pretend to play the game even if it means becoming something of a bawd.

In addition to its general political relevance, this passage was apparently understood to have a contemporary political meaning. In the corrected version of the third quarto, the words "Princes" and "Kings" were changed to "men," the censor suppressing what must have been interpreted as a blow at King James. The claim that kings forfeit their commissions when they fail to observe heaven's conditions would have sounded like a clear rejection of James's cherished doctrine of Divine Right. Marston's attitude must have been nurtured in the nursery of liberty where he was residing; certainly it would have been approved by many in his audience. With this play Marston began to skirmish in very dangerous territory, as a brief passage from the first quarto demonstrates:

> BEAN [CHA]: And is not sinnior S. *Andrew Iaques* a gallant fellow now.
> MAQUERELLE: By my maiden-head la, honour and hee agrees as well together, as a satten sute and wollen stockings.[8]

That this was a hit at James, and a brutal one at that, is confirmed by the elimination of *"Iaques"* in the second quarto, which thus changed the passage to a general indictment of the Scots. At the same time that *"Iaques"* was eliminated, Marston inserted verses (after the "Epilogus" in the second quarto and designated as the "Prologue" in the third quarto) which attack *"too nice-brained cunning"* for wresting *"each hurtlesse thought to private sence"* (p. 216). These two revisions of the first quarto suggest that *The Malcontent* has a place in the series of politically indiscreet plays for which the Children of the Queen's Revels became notorious.

This is not to suggest that *The Malcontent* was in any important way an attack on the monarch, but its political theme does constitute advice in the "Mirror for Magistrates" tradition to which so many Inns of Court writers had contributed. This political theme did not require the overt statement of the added lines; it is visible in the shorter, private theater version. Early in the first act Malevole mentions the importance of temporizing, and in the world which Marston depicts, only cunning and concealed virtue can survive. Malevole's disguise guards him from real danger, but this does not diminish the insidious nature of the atmosphere he is combating. His role is exemplary. As a satirist and teacher, he shows what the world is; as a god of policy, he shows how to cope with it. It is a joke on the world that an outsider has mastered its tricks, but he

---

8 First quarto, *The Malcontent* (London, 1604), sig. H2v.

can do nothing to eliminate the atmosphere or to regenerate the vermin who pollute it and are in turn polluted by it.

I have been discussing the political and moral implications of *The Malcontent*, but it was through a theatrical innovation that Marston made these moral complexities appear convincing and relevant. He transformed the convention of the disguised revenger by endowing its separate halves with essentially distinct personalities; Malevole-Altofronto has many of the characteristics of a "double" figure. I do not know how much is gained by describing these two halves as the "superego" and the "id"; nonetheless some signs of that eternal struggle are perceptible, indeed are exploited as part of the total pattern of the play. Thus Malevole-Altofronto impinges on our consciousness at a deeper level than most of Marston's intellectually conceived characters. A further contribution to the richness of the theatrical experience—particularly apparent with the addition of John Webster's Induction in the third quarto, where Burbage appears onstage before the play begins—results from the employment of Malevole as an actor playing the role of an actor. There is no Pirandello-like metaphysics in this device. Role-playing is shown to be a physical necessity for moral man in an immoral society. The pestilential atmosphere communicated through the charged rhetoric and the "Expressionist" stage techniques constitutes Marston's most successful representation of a morally debilitated world. He had shown a comic version of this in *What You Will*, but there the characters tend simply to be mouthpieces of simple ideas. In the *Antonio* plays the satiric background is very imperfectly linked to the concerns of the main characters. *The Malcontent* achieves a meaningful union of these components. It possesses the immediacy and credibility of a nightmare.

Because of the play's symbolic and dreamlike atmosphere, its relationship to Marston's audience is not as immediate as usual. For example, his protagonist, for the first time, is not a young man. But its ultimate relevance to this audience is of the same order that most of his plays had because its substructure is that of the initiation ritual. It is a demonstration of what it must cost the morally innocent to participate in a degraded society. In this play, Marston's terms are political, but with some exceptions he confines his treatment to general matters of conduct and ethics. In contrast, when he next wrote a play with a disguised duke in an Italian palace, *The Fawne* (1606), his aims were far more immediate and specific. As he learned more about "S. *Andrew Iaques*," his speech became, like Malevole's, "halter-worthy at al howers."

JOHN MARSTON

Allen, Morse Shepard. *The Satire of John Marston*. Columbus, Ohio, 1920, pp. 140–148.

Axelrad, Albert José. *Un Malcontent Élizabéthain: John Marston (1576–1634)*. Paris, 1955, pp. 275–284.

Boas, Frederick S. *An Introduction to Stuart Drama*. Oxford, 1946, pp. 132–147.

Campbell, Oscar J. *Comicall Satyre and Shakespeare's Troilus and Cressida*. San Marino, Calif., 1938, pp. 135–184.

Caputi, Anthony. *John Marston, Satirist*. Ithaca, N.Y., 1961

Cross, Gustav. "Marston, Montaigne, and Morality: *The Dutch Courtezan* Reconsidered," *ELH*, XXVII (1960), 30–43.

_____. "The Retrograde Genius of John Marston," *REL*, II (October 1961), 19–27.

Eliot, T. S. "John Marston," in *Elizabethan Essays*. London, 1934, pp. 177–195.

Gibbons, Brian. *Jacobean City Comedy: A Study of Satiric Plays by Jonson, Marston and Middleton*. Cambridge, Mass., 1968, pp. 98–104.

Hunter, G. K. "English Folly and Italian Vice: The Moral Landscape of John Marston," in *Jacobean Theatre*, ed. John Russell Brown. Stratford-upon-Avon Studies 1. London and New York, 1960, pp. 85–111.

Ingram, Reginald W. "Marston, Old or New Elizabethan," *HAB*, XVII (1966), 19–26.

Kernan, Alvin. *The Cankered Muse: Satire of the English Renaissance*. New Haven, 1959, pp. 211–219.

Keyishian, Harry. "Dekker's *Whore* and Marston's *Courtesan*," *ELN*, IV (1967), 261–266.

Korninger, Siegfried. "John Marston und die Bedeutung des *Malcontent*," in *Festschrift...Theodor Spira*, ed. Helmut Viebrock and Willi Erzgräber. Heidelberg, 1961, pp. 152–163.

McDonald, Charles Osborne. *The Rhetoric of Tragedy: Form in Stuart Drama*. Amherst, Mass., 1966, pp. 161–178.

Ornstein, Robert. *The Moral Vision of Jacobean Tragedy*. Madison, Wis., 1960 (reprinted 1965), pp. 159–163.

Pellegrini, Guiliano. *Il Teatro di John Marston*. Pisa, 1952, pp. 121–157.

Peter, John. *Complaint and Satire in Early English Literature*. Oxford, 1956, pp. 219–254.

Schoenbaum, Samuel. "The Precarious Balance of John Marston," *PMLA*, LXVII (1952), 1069–1078.

Spencer, Theodore. "Reason and Passion in Marston's *The Dutch Courtezan*," *Criterion*, XIII (1934), 586–594.

Stoll, Elmer Edgar. "Shakespeare, Marston, and the Malcontent Type," *MP* (1906), 281–303.

Tomlinson, T. B. *A Study of Elizabethan and Jacobean Tragedy*. Cambridge, Eng., and Melbourne, 1964, pp. 215–223.

Wine, M. L., ed. *The Dutch Courtesan*. Regents Renaissance Drama Series. Lincoln, Nebraska, 1965, pp. xii–xxiv.

Zall, Paul M. "John Marston, Moralist," *ELH*, XX (1953), 186–193.

John Webster

" COURTLY REWARD AND PUNISHMENT " :
AN INTERPRETATION OF *THE WHITE DEVIL* *

Travis Bogard

THE opening scene in *The White Devil* states the theme of the play:
the evils of courtly reward and punishment.

> LODOVICO: Banish'd!
> ANTONELLI: It griev'd me much to hear the sentence.
> LODOVICO: Ha, Ha, ô *Democritus* thy Gods
>   That govern the whole world! Courtly reward
>   And punishment.

(I. i. 1)

The rest of the scene is concerned with the development of this statement
and the establishment of the theme. Lodovico has been banished, and his
friends Gasparo and Antonelli attempt to calm him by pointing out that
there was some justice in the sentence. They join in one of Webster's
accusatory duets and try to show Lodovico the error of his prodigal way
of life in Rome. But Lodovico counters their assertions by asking what
justice there is in his punishment when greater criminals go untouched,

* From *The Tragic Satire of John Webster*. Berkeley and Los Angeles, 1955, pp.
119–128. Reprinted by permission of the University of California Press. The reading here presented is excerpted from a larger section of Professor Bogard's book.

and such men as the Duke of Brachiano, who "by close panderism seeks to prostitute / The honour of *Vittoria Corombona*," are permitted to remain in Rome. Is this the reward of service? It would have been better to have been condemned to death. He concludes,

> This is the world's alms; pray make use of it—
> Great men sell sheep thus, to be cut in pieces,
> When first they have shorn them bare and sold their fleeces.

> (I. i 60)

During Lodovico's lament and his friends' remonstrances, the larger theme, which is styled "courtly reward and punishment," is divided into three parts for later development: first, the rotten prodigality of court life; second, the evils of a social system in which sycophants flatter a lord for an uncertain living; third, the treachery of a prince's capricious "justice." These are the chief aspects of the theme which appear in action and comment throughout the play, and Webster never loses sight of them. Indeed, at the very end, Vittoria and Flamineo, dying, speak words that bear home these ideas.

> VITTORIA: O happy they that never saw the Court,
>   "Nor ever knew great Man but by report.   *Vittoria dies.*
> FLAMINEO: ...Let all that belong to Great men remember th' old
>   wives' tradition, to be like the Lions i'th' Tower on Can-
>   dlemas day, to mourn if the Sun shine, for fear of the
>   pitiful remainder of winter to come.

> (V, vi, 261, 268)

Thus, at the last moment in the life of his tragic heroine, Webster restates the theme that he set forth in the opening of the play.

Between the preliminary statement and the final summation, Webster develops the aspects of courtly reward and punishment as they were defined at the outset.

The corruption and extravagance of court life are constantly in evidence. Cornelia interrupts the lavishly staged assignation of her daughter and Brachiano and makes explicit their lascivious wickedness. When she and Flamineo are left alone, their dialogue widens the thematic implications of the exemplary scene just played. Flamineo turns on his mother in a rage that she should therefore interfere with his hopes for preferment. How, he asks, can one be virtuous, when one is at the mercy of a corrupt world? Why must he resort to pandering his sister except that his father's prodigality consumed his estate and left him penniless? What has he learned in his university days and in his experience at court?

> Conspiring with a beard
> Made me a Graduate—then to this Duke's service—
> I visited the Court, whence I return'd

> More courteous, more lecherous by far,
> But not a suit the richer.
>
> (I, ii, 316)

Such statements early in the play serve to fix in the minds of the audience the corruption of the court. The succeeding episodes of brawling, treachery, lust, and murder all become exemplifications of this first subdivision of the main theme.

Coupled with illustrations of the prodigal corruptions of the courts are numerous statements regarding the scramble for courtly reward. Flamineo describes his youth in terms of such activity. It is a degrading experience, dangerous and dishonorable.

> Remember this you slave, when knaves come to preferment
> they rise as gallowses are raised i'th' low countries,
> one upon another's shoulders.
>
> (II, i, 316)

Throughout the play, Flamineo is interested only in obtaining preferment, even if he must prostitute his sister. He is a professional at the game of courtly reward. There is no suggestion of affection for Brachiano, or even of loyalty. Everything he does for the Duke is motivated by cynical self-interest. He recognizes his activity as being essentially predatory, but, more important to him, insecure and unprofitable. Nevertheless, he has no alternate way of life, and if he had, it is doubtful that he would choose it. The struggle for courtly reward is too thoroughly ingrained in him as a way of life to allow him to change.

In his quarrel with Marcello preceding the arraignment scene, Flamineo states fully his thought on the subject. When Marcello accuses his brother of procuring their sister for Brachiano, Flamineo replies that it has been to the interests both of himself and of Vittoria to serve Brachiano, and adds,

>   thou art a soldier,
> Followest the great Duke, feedest his victories,
> As witches do their serviceable spirits,
> Even with thy prodigal blood—what hast got
> But like the wealth of Captains, a poor handful?—
> Which in thy palm thou bear'st, as men hold water—
> Seeking to grip it fast, the frail reward
> Steals through thy fingers. . . .
> Thou hast scarce maintenance
> To keep thee in fresh shamois. . . .
> And thus when we have even poured our selves,
> Into great fights, for their ambition
> Or idle spleen, how shall we find reward? . . .
> Alas the poorest of their forc'd dislikes

At a limb proffers, but at heart it strikes:
This is lamented doctrine.

(III, i, 38, 57)

What Flamineo means is that any service rendered to a prince is folly. All a courtier can hope is that if he bends pliantly to the whims of his lord, he may be thrown scraps. There is no distinction, in Flamineo's mind, between Marcello's honest soldiering and his own dishonest route to preferment. The results for both will be poverty and perhaps such punishment as Lodovico has earlier received for similar services.

It is important that Flamineo have no illusions about courtly reward. He predicts his own failure, yet still hopes to avoid it. In the end, when hope is gone, he becomes a powerful example of the folly of pursuing preferment. All that he prophesies comes ironically true. Courtly reward has played him false. The man who knows the game is cast down from his prince to his death. When even the professional cannot succeed, what remains to be said for such a way of life, other than that it is dangerous folly?

The third aspect of the central theme, the cruelty, treachery, and injustice of a prince's vengeance, is exemplified by the behavior of Brachiano and of Francisco and Monticelso. Brachiano poisons his wife. Francisco and Monticelso indicate their willingness to ruin Vittoria and her lover even at the cost of Camillo's life. These princes will stop at nothing. Their ruthlessness is made clear in Act IV, scene i, where much of the dialogue is given to thematic statement. Here Francisco is shown putting off Monticelso's incitement to revenge by a pious dissertation on the evils of starting a war against Brachiano. Monticelso, however, counsels treachery, not open warfare.

Bear your wrongs conceal'd
And, patient as the Tortoise, let this Camel
Stalk o'er your back unbruis'd: sleep with the Lion,
And let this brood of secure foolish mice
Play with your nostrils, till the time be ripe
For th' bloody audit, and the fatal gripe:
Aim like a cunning fowler, close one eye,
That you the better may your game espy.

(IV, i, 16)

This is an explicit statement of the manner in which princes work their punishments. Although Francisco appears to disclaim such methods, when Monticelso leaves the stage momentarily the Duke informs the audience that he is plotting just such treachery. He feels, however, that Monticelso is not to be trusted and states that he prefers to work alone. Princely treachery is thus translated from precept into dog-eat-dog action.

During the fifth act the theme is fully developed, and its three divisions are woven inextricably into the action. The marriage of Brachiano and

Vittoria seems to Flamineo an assurance that at last he will gain preferment.

> In all the weary minutes of my life,
> Day ne'er broke up till now. This marriage
> Confirms me happy.
>
> (V, i, 1)

Life for the first time is promising, and Flamineo's prospects belie his prophecies, but, in the ironic scene that follows, Brachiano enters and with splendid munificence assigns the Moor, Mulinassar, a "competent pension" in return for his proffered services. It is a clear example of the courtly reward which Flamineo has sought, but neither he nor Brachiano knows that Mulinassar is Francisco, disguised in pursuit of his treacherous revenge. Francisco is a realization, in dramatic terms, of the concept of princely vengeance. As an instrument of courtly punishment, Francisco is presented with a courtly reward. The two concepts merge, and from the resultant irony arises the foreshadowing of disaster to the good fortune which Flamineo thought to have.

Francisco joints his henchmen Lodovico and Gasparo to discuss the possible ways of murdering Brachiano. Lodovico takes an inhuman relish in plotting the crime so that it will stand out as a work of art in an age of diabolical killings. But Francisco puts an end to such virtuosity by demanding the quickest and surest way. This development of the cruelty of courtly punishment is interrupted by Flamineo, who warns Francisco of the fickleness of princes and the capriciousness of their promises. He tells Francisco to get the promised reward in his hands before he counts on it. Even with fair prospects before him, Flamineo has no trust in the liberality of princes.

The evil life of the courts is exhibited in the sequence. Marcello becomes enraged at Zanche's boast that she will marry Flamineo. When Flamineo elects to defend her, the brothers quarrel, and Marcello sends his sword to Flamineo as a challenge. Flamineo returns the sword by stabbing it in Marcello's back, and Marcello dies, attributing his death to Vittoria's attempt "to rise by all dishonest means." Yet to come is an exemplification of this truth and of other warnings inherent in the theme.

Flamineo sees his prospects ruined. Brachiano punishes him cruelly for Marcello's death by forcing him to sue for renewed pardon each day of his life. This capricious punishment is meted out because Flamineo once dared to "brave" him in the House of Convertites. Flamineo now realizes that all hope for courtly reward is gone. Neither he nor Brachiano realizes, however, that even as the one sentences the other, courtly punishment and courtly vengeance are again being exemplified, for, at the rear of the stage, Lodovico is sprinkling Brachiano's helmet with poison. When the great Duke is next seen, he is shrieking for an armorer to tear off the burning mask. In his fury he condemns the armorer to torture; without hope of recovery, he can only wait for death.

At this point, Webster introduces a new element in the theme which links with the conception of the fickleness of court sycophants: the horror and loneliness that surround the deaths of princes. Brachiano's torment is set off against Flamineo's unfeeling commentary on the "solitariness ...about dying Princes." But Webster relied on more forceful means than choral comment to dramatize his theme. A few moments later, Brachiano is brought in on his deathbed. Alone with him, Lodovico and Gasparo torment him with his sins and strangle him. His dying cry, "*Vittoria! Vittoria!*"—in itself an ironic comment on his defeat—calls his court about him. Vittoria, when she realizes he is dead, rushes from the unbearable room. The others murmur, "Rest to his soul," and at this point Flamineo resumes his commentary. Francisco observes with a note of wonder that Vittoria takes Brachiano's death so heavily. Flamineo shrugs:

> O yes, yes;
> Had women navigable rivers in their eyes
> They would dispend them all;...I'll tell thee,
> These are but Moonish shades of griefs or fears,
> There's nothing sooner dry than women's tears.
> Why here's an end of all my harvest, he has given me nothing.
> Court promises! Let wisemen count them curst,
> For while you live he that scores best pays worst.

(V, iii, 183, 192)

He continues in the same vein, repeating much that he has previously said about the solitary deaths of princes, and exemplifying his statement by his conduct. As he leaves the stage, Zanche, Vittoria's Moorish maid, enters. The maid has become enamored of Francisco in his Moor's disguise, and, by way of courtship, exchanges lewd "dreams" with her prospective lover:

> ZANCHE: Methought sir, you came stealing to my bed.
> FRANCISCO: Wilt thou believe me sweeting?—by this light
>   I was a-dreamt on thee too: for methought
>   I saw thee naked....
>   And lest thou shouldst take cold, I covered thee
>   With this Irish mantle.
> ZANCHE: Verily I did dream,
>   You were somewhat bold with me; but to come to't—
> LODOVICO: How? How? I hope you will not go to it here....
> FRANCISCO: When I threw the mantle o'er thee, thou didst laugh
>   Exceedingly methought....And cried'st out,
>   The hair did tickle thee....
> LODOVICO: Mark her I prithee, she simpers like the suds
>   A Collier hath been wash'd in.

(V, iii, 232, 249)

Lodovico has told Brachiano that he will be forgotten before his funeral sermon, and Zanche and Francisco provide the living proof. For, as they speak, Brachiano's body lies on the bed in full view of the audience! Webster says much about the solitary deaths of princes, but nowhere does he dramatize it so effectively as by juxtaposing Brachiano's death with the scene between these "lovers." The great Duke dies, not in glory, not even in peace, but in torment. Any residual illusion of greatness about his death is dispersed by the callous scene between his murderer and the Duchess' servant.

Brachiano's death leaves Flamineo still some hope for preferment. The Duke has settled his estate upon Vittoria until his son Giovanni comes of age. Flamineo's first move is to court the boy. Giovanni, however, will have nothing to do with him and forbids him the court. In a last effort, Flamineo goes to test Vittoria's bounty and to "sum up all these horrors." Vittoria gives him nothing for his services but Cain's portion—"A most courtly Patent to beg by." He tests her once more by the mock death and only proves her ingratitude further. All he can do now is to kill her. But he is interrupted by Lodovico and Gasparo, who inflict the last of Francisco's courtly punishments. The brother and sister die, and their murderer is led away to torture, exulting in their deaths. As he goes, the audience is permitted to shudder once more at the terrible fanaticism of courtly punishment. Lodovico says,

> I do glory yet,
> That I can call this act mine own: For my part ,
> The rack, the gallows, and the torturing wheel
> Shall be but sound sleeps to me, here's my rest—
> "I limn'd this night-piece and it was my best."

> (V, vi, 295)

The spectacle of courtly reward and punishment has run its course; the horrors are summed up; the courtly way of life is seen without illusion. And, though Lodovico's words are the final statement of any single aspect of the theme, all themes find their summation in the couplet Vittoria speaks as she dies:

> "O happy they that never saw the Court,
> Nor ever knew great Man but by report."

> (V, vi, 261)

See other studies in Webster bibliography (below, pp. 289–291).

THE DUCHESS OF MALFI:
STYLES OF CEREMONY *

James L. Calderwood

IN his review article, 'Motives in *Malfi*' (*Essays in Criticism*, October 1959) McD. Emslie presents an interesting departure from what has been, until recently, a prevailing fashion in Webster criticism—the careful examination not so much of the plays themselves but of their literary failings. For critics with this sort of aim, Webster has been a fairly easy mark. Admissions are not difficult to make: Webster's plots are replete with the most un-Aristotelian contingencies and blind alleys; his verse, happily suited to the aphorism, is only rarely able to sustain itself well beyond a couple of lines; his action is uncomfortably near to being melodramatic; his characterisation is often either vague or else too neatly Theophrastian; and finally—a fault for which some of his critics have been unable to forgive him—his plays were not written by Shakespeare. Underlying much of the specific criticism of Webster is a general distaste for his philosophy, or, more accurately, for his lack of a philosophy, for his failure to supply in his plays a governing moral perspective. For example, W. A. Edwards finds ['John Webster', *Determinations,* ed. F. R. Leavis (London, 1934), p. 176] that 'in Webster's tragedies there is no such internal scale [as that provided in *Hamlet*] to measure depravity'. Ian Jack holds a similar view ['The Case of John Webster', *Scrutiny,* XVI (March, 1949), p. 38]: 'If one reads through [both plays] noting down the *sententia* and moralising asides, one finds oneself in possession of a definite attempt at a "philosophy", a moral to the tale'. However, Jack finds that the tale itself is altogether too discrete from the attempted moral. He concludes (p. 43) that the plays exemplify Webster's 'artistic insincerity' and that Webster himself is a 'decadent in the sense that he is incapable of realising the whole of life in the form in which it revealed itself to the Elizabethans'.

The argument of Edwards and Jack, however it may apply to *The White Devil*, seems wholly untenable with respect to *The Duchess of Malfi*. Certainly no one, I think, denies that the later play has an abundance of depravity and is embarrassingly rich in unintegrated

* From *Essays in Criticism,* Vol. 12, 1962, pp. 133–147. Copyright © 1962 by F. W. Bateson. Reprinted by permission of the publisher.

moral comment, or that there are excrescenees of plot and inconsistencies of character. But these faults can be granted without our having to concede either that the play is a dramatic failure or that Webster is morally despicable. On the contrary, the view offered here is that the play is, among other things, a powerful and subtle articulation of a thoroughly Elizabethan theme—the relationship between individual impulse and societal norms, specifically the religious and political doctrine of Degree. And I shall suggest that Webster, far from failing to present an 'internal scale to measure depravity', is entirely willing to test evil against good. His principal dramatic means to this end is his employment of ceremony and ritual for the evaluation of private action. My intention here is to examine several crucial scenes in order to suggest how Webster's use of ceremony helps clarify some of the rather vexing problems of action, motivation, and character.

In a play which focuses so largely upon revenge and violence, motivation is unusually important. In the corruption scene of Act I Ferdinand, referring to the Duchess, says to Bosola: 'she's a yong widowe, / I would not have her marry againe.'

> BOSOLA: No, Sir?
> FERDINAND: Doe not you ask the reason: but be satisfied, I say I would not.

Bosola, whether satisfied or not, does not ask the reason; but critics have not been so easily put off. What Ferdinand later calls his 'mayne cause' —his hope to have gained 'An infinite masse of Treasure by her death' (IV, ii, 304) had she died without remarrying—has been unanimously disallowed by critics for having no dramatic confirmation elsewhere. On the other hand, most critics have acknowledged as at least plausible the case made by F. L. Lucas and supported by Clifford Leech that Ferdinand acts from incestuous jealousy. But Leech himself is not very happy with his proposal, for after all, he finds, 'Ferdinand leaves us perplexed, not quite certain of the dramatist's purpose' [*John Webster* (London, 1951), p. 105]. However, the perplexity which he complains of is discredited— or at least so I am convinced—by his own findings. A certain haziness of motivation need not result from a corresponding haziness of authorial purpose but may be deliberately built into a character: it is Ferdinand who is unsure of himself, not Webster. From Ferdinand's 'Doe not you ask the reason'—certainly an answer that makes us want to ask the reason—we can assume either that he does not understand the grounds of his behaviour or that he prefers not to state them. But a flat refusal to discuss the matter is surely a poor means of concealing information, especially from a man who has been singled out precisely because he is an adept at ferreting facts. Ferdinand's brusqueness here suggests a lack of self-awareness, not so much an irritation at being questioned as a failure ever to have asked himself the same question.

It is in the following exchanges between the Duchess and her brothers that we should expect to find an indication of the motives underlying the demonic punishments of Act 4. There is clearly, even before the offence, a pressure behind Ferdinand's speech that is absent from his brother's. The Cardinal is willing to consider the prospect of a remarriage provided it involves 'the addition, Honor'; Ferdinand categorically forbids it: 'Marry? they are most luxurious, / Will wed twice'. It is Ferdinand who harps upon the sensual temptations of remarriage—'luxurious' (i.e., lecherous), 'those joyes, / Those lustful pleasures', his Lamprey metaphor; and he associates sensuality with corruption and disease—'Their livers are more spotted / Then *Lebans* sheepe'—an association which he dwells upon again, most significantly, later in the play. Taking a cue from the Cardinal, however, Ferdinand does insert one important non-sensual objection to the Duchess' possible remarriage: he likens private marriage to 'the irregular Crab, / Which though't goes backward, thinkes that it goes right, / Because it goes its owne way'. This is essentially an argument from Degree: the reliance upon private choice, especially when that choice descends upon an inferior, constitutes an infringement of the rigidly established social hierarchy and is, ultimately, an attack upon cosmological order.

There is by no means sufficient evidence here to persuade us one way or another about the brothers' opposition to a possible remarriage. However, the Duchess provides us a critical perspective to the scene when she suggests that the brotherly duet has been a piece of staged ceremony: 'I thinke this speech betweene you both was studied, / It came so roundly off'. The sequence of mutually supported and elaborated arguments has seemed impressive; but the stylisation to which the Duchess calls attention enables us to observe a schism between the form and the content of their objections. For in actuality the brothers have offered only the appearance of an argument, not any logical grounds for opposition, but merely opposition. What they have said is simply that they do not want the Duchess to remarry, but their motives have been left unclarified. Ferdinand's emotional antagonism—we cannot at this point give it a more precise title—has been both partly obfuscated and superficially ennobled by the ritual formality of a 'studied' presentation. Since the brothers are wholly unaware that Antonio or anyone else is a potential, much less a favoured, suitor, their argument from Degree is entirely irrelevant, at best hypothetical. But as we shall see, it is not irrelevant structurally: the hypothetical attack upon order becomes actual after the brothers' exit, when the Duchess reverses the courtly tradition in her wooing of Antonio. By comparing these two brief scenes, as well as others later on, we shall find that Webster, at times so cavalier in his disregard of dramatic consistency, can at other times unify apparently discrete elements of action by remarkably subtle nexuses of imagery and structure.

The Duchess conducts her courtship of Antonio as a staged ceremony which is in effect a casting off of the essential values represented in ceremony. As a depersonalised, formalised expression of belief and emotion, ceremony is necessarily in the service of supra-individual interests, and its participants make at least a gesture of indorsing those interests by voluntarily restricting the free play of private emotion to the symbolic pattern prescribed by the ceremonial role. Although ceremony and ritual are by no means prohibitive of individual expression—but merely impose a form upon the content of private experience—they are confirmations of order, of an order that exists to some extent regardless of the individual, even if the individual is a Duchess. Indeed, as Antonio's first speech in the play implies, it is precisely because the individual here is a Duchess—the political and moral exemplar who, if corrupt, causes 'Death, and diseases through the whole land,—that her conduct has serious and even tragic implications. For what the Duchess is engaging in here is not properly ceremony but ceremony-in-reverse, a form of deceremonialisation by which she divests herself of the responsibilities of her social role.

The Duchess' defection from Degree is not simply the product of impetuosity; after her brothers' exit her determination to assert herself is couched in convincing terms: 'if all my royall kindred / Lay in my way unto this marriage: / I'll'd make them my low foote-steps'. Nor, as her last remark to Cariola indicates, is she unaware of the broader implications of her action:

> wish me good speed
> For I am going into a wildernesse,
> Where I shall find nor path, nor friendly clewe
> To be my guide.

This journey beyond the restrictions, but also the safeguards, of Degree into a 'wildernesse' where her only guides are the dictates of private impulse cannot help reminding us of Ferdinand's warning about "the irregular Crab, / Which though't goes backward, thinkes that it goes right, / Because it goes its owne way'. But the Duchess' 'owne way' is not a random one. The "wildernesse" into which she goes may be thoroughly disordered, but her means of getting there are quite systematic.

She first establishes Degree with almost ritual formality. As Antonio enters, at her bidding, her greeting is an expression of superiority: 'I sent for you, Sit downe'. This is of course ironic, and charminingly so in the light of her intentions; but it is also the initial step towards a moral infraction the gravity of which charm fails to dissipate. It is also significant, particularly in a scene which makes a symbolic point of bodily positions, that at the beginning the audience is presented with a view of Antonio seated and the Duchess standing above him, prepared to dictate her 'will'. She quickly forces an opportunity to use the word *husband,* and then with considerable psychological subtlety suggests her concern about 'What's laid up for to-morrow', which, coming hard after the word 'expence,' seems to regard Antonio in his inferior role as treasurer—and so he interprets it; but then she corrects him by explaining that she meant 'What's layd up yonder for me', that is, in heaven, which gently insinuates Antonio into an equality with her as fellow mortal. Further promptings by the Duchess, the most important of which are of a ceremonial nature—the transfer of the ring (463), the symbolic elevation of rank (481-2)—lead Antonio to realise 'whereto [her] favours tend', but though he is tempted by ambition, he remains uncomfortably aware of his 'unworthinesse', of his prescribed station in the hierarchy of Degree. To the Duchess, for whom Degree is by this time irrelevant, his hesitance is puzzling: 'Sir, he confident, / What is't distracts you?' Despite his later reminder about her brothers, it is not fear of violence that is troubling Antonio: it is made sufficiently clear that he is an excellent soldier, a man of proved courage and ability. It is also made sufficiently clear that he is an honourable man, one who would be honest, as he says, 'were there nor heaven, nor hell'. Indeed, his distraction here could only be felt by an honourable man, for it stems from a conflict between private desire and societal values. Part of the irony of the courtship scene is that the Duchess abandons Degree in wooing the one man who thoroughly endorses Degree: his opening lines in Act I display his admiration for the French king who sought 'to reduce both State, and People / To a fix'd Order'. It is in the light of Antonio's reluctance to overturn Degree that Webster, by a kind of literary counterpoint, enables us to judge the nature of the Duchess' conduct. For the ceremonial revelation of her feelings to Antonio is necessitated by the inhibitions of Degree. The 'great', she says,

> Are forc'd to expresse our violent passions
> In ridles, and in dreames, and leave the path
> Of simple vertue, which was never made
> To seeme the thing it is not.

It is surely a perversion of terminology when the 'path of simple vertue' —which echoes her earlier image of the pathless 'wildernesse'—has become representative of uninhibited passion. Having discarded her own loyalties to 'fix'd Order', she has nevertheless been utilising until now the symbolic forms of order—ceremony and ritual—as psychological weapons designed to overcome Antonio's more entrenched loyalties and to release the passions which those loyalties have so far successfully constrained. Her final resort is to dispense altogether with ceremony and Degree; if he will not rise to her station, she will descend to his: 'I do here put off all vaine ceremony, / And only doe appeare to you a yong widow / That claimes you for her husband'. It is a telling expedient, and with it Antonio's last resistance breaks. It is characteristic of him that he is unable either to deceive effectively—witness the way he falls apart in II, iii, when forced into deceptions—or to cope with deception. But it must be admitted that the Duchess' techniques—first establishing, then suddenly relaxing the formalities of Degree—have been unusually subtle, and, coupled with his own desires, difficult to resist.

Near the conclusion of this movement away from Degree and towards the release of 'violent passions', we have another brief ritual gesture as the Duchess puts her arms around Antonio and then orders him to kneel. It is a fitting end, for the gesture is merely a gesture; far from endorsing ceremony and the values it represents, the Duchess engages in a profane parody, employing the ritual solemnities of Degree to confirm and sanction the autonomy of private impulse, the symbols of order to proclaim the ascendancy of disorder. Of her brothers she says:

> Do not thinke of them,
> All discord, without this circumference
> Is onely to be pittied, and not feared:
> Yet, should they know it, time will easily
> Scatter the tempest.

The imagery here, and in the following passages which use musical metaphors (551–4), is strongly reminiscent of Ulysses' famous speech on Degree in *Troilus and Cressida*: 'Take but degree away, untune that string, / And, hark, what discord follows' (I, iii, 109–10 ff.).[1] Degree taken away, discord does indeed follow; but for the moment the lovers seek within the circumference of their own arms to create a private universe, to elevate 'violent passion' to the status of a self-sufficient moral law. The attempt may have its romantic appeal, but the Duchess' speech displays a disrespect for external realities which is, as the remainder of the play demonstrates, dangerously naïve. It is left to Cariola to conclude the scene on a note of ominousness: 'Whether the spirit of greatnes, or of woman / Raigne most in her, I know not, but it shewes / A fearefull madnes. I owe her much of pitty'.

If we are correct in assuming that Webster is using ceremony as a dramatic device to explore subtleties of character and action, we should expect it to be used again in other critical scenes. The tragic ironies of the Duchess' speech about 'discord' indicate that Webster was anticipating the dramatic future. The audience is prepared for the next appearance of Ferdinand and the Cardinal, is awaiting with a certain amount of suspense the brothers' reactions to the marriage. In II. iv, where those

---

1 In some respects Webster's entire play is a comment on Shakespeare's passage, even to the point of Ferdinand's becoming, like 'appetite', a 'universal wolf' eating himself up in madness. Incidentally, there is another parallel with Shakespeare that has gone unmentioned: in IV, ii, Bosola, denied reward for his services to Ferdinand, says, 'I stand like one / The long hath ta'ne a sweet, and golden dreame. / I am angry with my selfe, now that I wake' (349–50), which appears to be an echo of Posthumous' speech in *Cymbeline* (V, iv, 127–9), 'And so I am awake. Poor wretches, that depend / On greatness' favour, dream as I have done, / Wake, and find nothing.'.

reactions are presented, Webster is clearly conscious of the logical and structural claims imposed upon him by Act I. The 'tempest' which the Duchess felt time would scatter has now arisen in the form of Ferdinand's intemperate anger; the association is made exact as the Cardinal says, 'Why doe you make your selfe / So wild a Tempest?' Ferdinand wishes the metaphor were literal fact: 'Would I could be one...' Ferdinand also embodies the 'discord' of which the Duchess was so disdainful: he produces 'this intemperate noyce', and is admonished by the Cardinal, 'Come, put your selfe / In tune'. His anger, we may think, is perhaps a vastly amplified echo of Antonio's 'distraction'—that is, that just as Antonio hesitated to overturn Degree, so Ferdinand rages because it has been overturned. But this would hardly explain the Cardinal's relative calmness, his utter inability to comprehend his brother's reactions: 'You flie beyond your reason'; 'Are you starke mad?' Only if we accept the unmistakable suggestions of incestuous jealousy in this scene does Ferdinand's behaviour become more understandable for us than for the Cardinal.

The psychological development here is roughly the reverse of that in Act I. Instead of casting off ceremony to reveal underlying passions, Ferdinand moves from passion to the cloaking of passion in ceremonial robes, from disorder to order. His opening line, 'I have this night dig'd up a man-drake', is meaningfully ambiguous, carrying not only the primary notion of madness but a secondary, sexual implication as well. What is merely implication at this point becomes manifest when Ferdinand's sense of injury shifts to the source of injury:

> Me thinkes I see her laughing,
> Excellent *Hyenna*—talke to me somewhat, quickly,
> Or my imagination will carry me
> To see her, in the shamefull act of sinne.

To this point, and somewhat beyond it, Ferdinand seems wholly lacking in self-awareness; his jealously receives direct expression in anger, but he is conscious only of anger, and mistakenly assumes that the Cardinal is reacting similarly. But when he tortures himself with images of the Duchess 'in the shamefull act' (56–9) he has clearly gone beyond anything that the Cardinal is feeling. The intensity of his experience is attested by his failure even to hear the Cardinal's 'You flie beyond your reason'. Lost to the immediate situation, he directly addresses his sister from his imaginative station as voyeur (62–4). Dumbfounded by this display, the Cardinal remonstrates with a metaphor that is more accurate than he realises:

> this intemperate noyce,
> Fitly resembles deafe-mens shrill discourse,
> Who talke aloud, thinking all other men
> To have their imperfection.

Although Ferdinand is unconscious of the nature of his 'imperfection', he has supposed a similar violence of reaction on the part of his brother. It is only now that he senses a difference between them. Immediately he withdraws, knowing that he has somehow exposed himself. His next lines—'Have not you, / My palsy?'—mark an abrupt shift of tone: outwardly directed anger recoils, turns inward, gives way to self-suspicion. The question is wary, the diction ambiguous enough to suggest shaking anger and perhaps also his half-awareness of a deeper motivation springing from bodily disturbance. The Cardinal's reply is significant:

> Yes—I can be angry
> Without this rupture—there is not in nature
> A thing, that makes man so deform'd, so beastly,
> As doth intemperate anger...

The thought moves from the personal to the general, from the admission of private but controlled anger to an explanation of the necessity of control. Disordered passions, whether specifically sexual or not, represent a deviation from the nature of, from what is proper to, man; it is not Ferdinand's impulse to violence that the Cardinal objects to, it is the unrestrained disorder of that impulse. The parallel with the Duchess is obvious: both have become threats to society by departing from communal patterns of ordered behaviour, by representing the chaos of uninhibited private action. But the parallel ends there. Ferdinand has not deliberately violated Degree in order to release passion; indeed, his very lack of deliberation, the spontaneity of his giving way to emotion, has released to the surface a deformity of man's nature. Although both of them enter a 'wildernesse', the Duchess seeks to establish private order amid public disorder, to forge a circumference of harmony in the centre of discord. Secure of self, conscious of her own identity, she conceives of 'wildernesse' as being purely external. But Ferdinand blunders into a chaos within himself. Nearly losing complete control of himself, he discovers a self he would prefer to lose. Ultimately he does lose himself all ways, in madness; and ultimately the Duchess retains her self, even triumphantly reasserts her identity despite all Ferdinand can do to destroy her.

Webster's problem now is a delicate one. Unless the prolonged torture and demonic killing of the Duchess have some amount of communal sanction, he will have produced, not tragedy, but only melodrama. Having already suggested the potential tragic justification by presenting the Duchess' marriage as a violation of Degree, he now runs the risk of causing Ferdinand to exact disproportionate retribution as a private agent; the nexus between crime and punishment is in danger of breaking. Webster's solution is to cement that nexus by an inversion of the process which led to the crime.

Throughout II, iv, Ferdinand employs the imagery which will lead him from private to at least a semblance of public revenge. From the beginning his mind dwells upon purgation:

> We must not now use Balsamum, but fire,
> The smarting cupping-glasse, for that's the meane
> To purge infected blood, (such blood as hers:).

If the sin is of the blood, as Vittoria's was in *The White Devil*, the blood must pay for it. But this medical imagery, which suggests an impulse towards impersonal action—Ferdinand as agent of society, the physician-priest who will restore order by destroying disorder—is unconvincing in light of the private animus manifest in Ferdinand's outbursts. But there is, as we noted, a shift of tone following the Cardinal's remonstrance about 'deafe-mens shrill discourse', a shift of tone which mirrors Ferdinand's shift in self-consciousness. After the Cardinal's next speech, which concludes with an exhortation to order—'Come, put your selfe / In tune'—Ferdinand, already sobered by self-doubt, returns a premeditated answer:

> So—I will onely study to seeme
> The thing I am not...

To pause briefly here, we should note the verbal echo from Act I where the Duchess, lamenting the inhibitions imposed by greatness, spoke of 'simple vertue, which was never made / To seeme the thing it is not' (513–14), just before she 'put off all vaine ceremony'. Here, however, Ferdinand intends just the reverse—to submit passion to order, or at least to the appearance of order. He continues:

> ...I could kill her now,
> In you, or in my selfe, for I do thinke
> It is some sinne in us, Heaven doth revenge
> By her.

This is an entirely new turn of thought, to which the Cardinal can only react with amazement: 'Are you starke mad?' But this is a far cry from madness. If we have been correct in gauging his growth of self-awareness, Ferdinand's acknowledgement of 'some sinne in us' which requires expiation employs the plural 'us' merely as a cover: the sin is within him alone, and he knows it. More significant, however, is his identification of his with the Duchess' sin, the linking of his latent desire with her realized desire; for here is precisely the association needed to justify his revenge upon her and to expiate his own latent sin: he can now truly quench his 'wild-fire' with her 'whores blood'. What would have been merely a private act of violence now assumes the status of ritual purgation, with the Duchess as sacrificial scapegoat and Ferdinand, already her judge, as physician-priest-executioner who seeks the purgation of his own tainted blood in the purging of hers. Before the scene closes, Ferdinand reverts to the language of violence once more, but it is clear that he has found his solution. His final speech reveals an attitude far more terrifying than his earlier bluster, for it portends not merely an uninhibited, formless act of revenge but a patient, controlled, impersonal ceremony which will culminate with the Duchess' execution.

All of this is not of course to suggest that the highly ceremonialised murder of IV, ii, is justified merely because it is ceremonial, nor that Ferdinand is genuinely identified with moral order merely because he converts an essentially private vengeance into the appearance of public justice. Ferdinand's role is obviously synthetic, an attempt to dignify incestuous frustrations that urge him to retaliation. Yet by restraining his desire for immediate vengeance, and, more important, by transforming it and his sexual desires as well into elements of a formal process, he makes a gesture of sublimation which, even though synthetic, suggests a confirmation of order. It is a gesture entirely appropriate to the nature of the Duchess' marriage, for if the crime is against society, the punishment must in some sense proceed from society. It is owing to this ritualisation of vengeance that we apprehend the inevitability of disaster so important in tragedy, an inevitability which arises only from our consciousness of extra-personal forces working out the fate of the protagonist.[2]

In IV, i, the ritual begins. The Duchess has been imprisoned for an indeterminate period. Ferdinand consults Bosola about her behaviour, sems satisfied to learn of her nobility. But when Bosola remarks that her blood is not altogether subdued, indeed that her very imprisonment away from Antonio 'Makes her too passionately apprehend / Those pleasures she's kept from', Ferdinand responds with his own brand of passion:

> Curse upon her!
> I will no longer study in the booke
> Of anothers heart: informe her what I told you.

The nature of his feelings and the difficulty with which he keeps them subjected to the demands of ceremony are always most apparent when some sensual reference to the Duchess' 'whores blood' reignites his 'wildfire'. But he always manages to regain control, to depersonalise the issue. When Bosola remonstrates with him (142–6) and unfortunately mentions the Duchess' delicate skinne', Ferdinand's reply again reveals a momentary breakdown of his role: 'Damne her, that body of hers...' He resolves upon further torments: so long as the sacrificial victim lives, so long as the Duchess' blood remains unregenerate, the latent sin within himself continues unpurged. More drastic purgatives having been planned, he resumes his role: 'Intemperate agues, make Physitians cruell' (170).

In IV, ii, a new development occurs. The increasing imbalance of Ferdinand's mind is suggested by his changing to a form of homeopathic treatment in which the mad are to heal the mad. He is still attempting to purge himself by proxy, but his employment of madmen symbolises

---

2 For the relationship between private action and communal order, I am indebted to Professor Robert B. Heilman's excellent book on *Othello—Magic in the Web* (Lexington, Kentucky, 1956)—and especially to his chapter. 'Othello: Action and Language', pp. 137–168.

his own approaching madness. His identification of his own sin with that of the Duchess has led him to impute to her, not just sensuality, but all of his aberrations. The strain of holding in balance the conflicting demands of the synthetic role and private passion, the inevitable self-injury involved in destroying the object of desire, and the impossibility of genuinely purging himself by means of another—all are contributing to Ferdinand's mental disintegration. As the Duchess grows more con-firmed in her personal identity (139), he begins to lose all sense of identity in that 'wildernesse' within him.

The conclusion of the ritual is the Duchess' sacrificial death. Bosola engages in his own form of depersonalisation, assuming the role of bellman both to conceal and to dignify his participation in what he has come to regard as an extravagant cruelty. Ironically enough, the ceremony designed to purify Ferdinand has served to purify Bosola, for by experi-encing the Duchess' integrity of self it is he who has metamorphosed from an impersonal agent of Ferdinand's malice to a responsible indi-vidual capable of the independent action he performs in the last act of the play.

In the dialogue with Bosola over the Duchess' body, Ferdinand, rapidly nearing madness, achieves what appears to be a form of *anagnorisis*. He acknowledges both the fact and the injustice of the private act of vengeance: 'I bad thee, when I was distracted of my wits, / Goe kill my dearest friend, and thou has don't' (298–9). But the admission of injustice is in the abstract, and, qualified by the emphasis upon Bosola as efficient cause and by the claim of mental distraction, it is in effect merely a denial of personal responsibility. Appeals to justification on the grounds of ritual authority—Ferdinand as physician-priest serving society—are con-spicuously absent. For evaluation from that point of view, however, we have only to wait a few lines, until Ferdinand says:

> By what authority did'st thou execute
> This bloody sentence?
> BOSOLA: By yours—
> FERDINAND: Mine? was I her Judge?
> Did any ceremoniall forme of Law,
> Doombe her to not-Being?

The denial of 'any ceremoniall forme of Law', of any communally sanctioned process by which revenge was executed, is aimed at depriving Bosola of reward, but instead deprives Ferdinand himself of that super-ficial ennoblement of motive which he had sought through an alliance with the forms of order. It is one of Ferdinand's last rational utterances, and it is thoroughly appropriate that as he approaches the disaster of mind which is correlative with the Duchess' death, Webster chooses to illumine the nature of Ferdinand's revenge by the same dramatic tech-nique with which he illumined the nature of her offence: it is Webster's final use of ceremony as an 'internal scale to measure depravity'.

JOHN WEBSTER

Duchess of Malfi = DM   *White Devil* = WD

Allison, Alexander W. "Ethical Themes in *The Duchess of Malfi*," *SEL*, IV (1964), 263–273.

Baldini, Gabriele. *John Webster e il linguaggio della tragedia.* Rome, 1953, pp. 56–150 (WD), 151–173 (DM).

Benjamin, Edwin B. "Patterns of Morality in *The White Devil*," *ES*, XLVI (1965), 1–15.

Boas, Frederick S. *An Introduction to Stuart Drama.* Oxford, 1946, pp. 194–198 (WD); 198–203 (DM).

Bogard, Travis. *The Tragic Satire of John Webster.* Los Angeles and Berkeley, 1955, pp. 131–141 (DM).

Boklund, Gunnar. *The Duchess of Malfi: Sources, Themes, Characters.* Cambridge, Mass., 1962.

_____. *The Source of the White Devil.* Uppsala and Cambridge, Mass., 1957, pp. 133–185.

Bowers, Fredson T. *Elizabethan Revenge Tragedy, 1587–1642.* Princeton, 1940, pp. 179–183 (WD).

Bradbrook, Muriel C. *Themes and Conventions of Elizabethan Tragedy.* Cambridge, Eng., 1957, pp. 186–195 (WD), 195–209 (DM).

_____. "Two Notes Upon Webster," *MLR*, XLII (1947), 281–291.

Brennan, Elizabeth M., ed. *The Duchess of Malfi.* The New Mermaids. London, 1964, pp. xii–xxvi.

_____. "The Relationship between Brother and Sister in the Plays of John Webster," *MLR*, LVIII (1963), 488–494.

Brooke, Rupert. *John Webster and the Elizabethan Drama.* New York, 1916, pp. 98–104 (WD), 104–109 (DM), 123–162.

Brown, John Russell, ed. *The White Devil.* The Revels Plays. Cambridge, Mass., 1960, pp. xxviii–lviii.

_____, ed. *The Duchess of Malfi.* The Revels Plays. Cambridge, Mass., 1964, pp. xli–lv.

Cecil, David. *Poets and Story-Tellers.* London, 1949, pp. 25–43.

Cunningham, John E. *Elizabethan and Early Stuart Drama.* London, 1965, pp. 94–101.

Davies, Cecil W. "The Structure of *The Duchess of Malfi*: An Approach," *English*, XII (1958), 89–93.

Dent, R. W. "The White Devil, or Vittoria Corombona?" *RenD*, IX (1966), 179–203.

Driscoll, James P. "Integrity of Life in *The Duchess of Malfi*," *DramS*, VI (1967), 42–53.

Edwards, W. A. "John Webster," in *Determinations: Critical Essays*, ed. F. R. Leavis. London, 1934, pp. 155–178.

Ekeblad, Inga-Stina. "The 'Impure Art' of John Webster," *RES*, IX (1958), 235–267.

_____. "Webster's Constructional Rhythm," *ELH*, XXIV (1957), 165–176.

Ellis-Fermor, Una. *The Jacobean Drama*. 4th rev. ed. London, 1958, pp. 170–191.

Empson, William. " 'Mine Eyes Dazzle,' " *EIC*, XIV (1964), 80–86 (review of Clifford Leech, *Webster: The Duchess of Malfi*, London, 1963).

Emslie, McD. "Motives in *Malfi*," *EIC*, IX (1959), 391–405.

Fieler, Frank B. "The Eight Madmen in *The Duchess of Malfi*," *SEL*, VII (1967), 343–350.

Franklin, H. Bruce. "The Trial Scene of Webster's *The White Devil* Examined in Terms of Renaissance Rhetoric," *SEL*, I (1961), 35–51.

Gill, Roma. " 'Quaintly Done': A Reading of *The White Devil*," *E & S*, XIX (1966), 41–59.

Hurt, James R. "Inverted Rituals in Webster's *The White Devil*," *JEGP*, LXI (1962), 42–47.

Jack, Ian. "The Case of John Webster," *Scrutiny*, XVI (1949), 33–43.

Jenkins, Harold. "The Tragedy of Revenge in Shakespeare and Webster," in *Shakespeare Survey 14*. Cambridge, Eng., 1961, pp. 49–53 (WD), 53–55 (DM).

Kernan, Alvin. *The Cankered Muse: Satire of the English Renaissance*. New Haven, 1959, pp. 232–242 (DM).

Layman, B. J. "The Equilibrium of Opposites in *The White Devil*: A Reinterpretation," *PMLA*, LXXIV (1959), 336–347.

Leech, Clifford, *John Webster: A Critical Study*. London, 1951, pp. 29–57 (WD), 58–89 (DM).

Lucas, F. L., ed. *The White Devil*. Rev. ed. London, 1959, pp. 38–45.

_____, ed. *The Duchess of Malfi*. Rev. ed. London, 1959, pp. 28–35.

Luecke, Jane Marie, O. S. B. "*The Duchess of Malfi*: Comic and Satiric Confusion in a Tragedy," *SEL*, IV (1964), 275–290.

McDonald, Charles Osborne. *The Rhetoric of Tragedy: Form in Stuart Drama*. Amherst, Mass., 1966, pp. 269–313 (WD).

Moore, Don D. *John Webster and His Critics, 1617–1964*. Louisiana State University Studies, Humanities Series 17. Baton Rouge, 1966.

Mooschein, Henry, "A Note on *The White Devil*," *N & Q*, XIII (1966), 296.

Mulryne, J. R. "*The White Devil* and *The Duchess of Malfi*," in *Jacobean Theatre*, ed. John Russell Brown. Stratford-upon-Avon Studies 1. New York, 1960, pp. 85–111.

Ornstein, Robert. *The Moral Vision of Jacobean Tragedy*. Madison, Wisconsin, 1960 (reprinted 1965), pp. 129–130, 140–148 (DM), 129–140 (WD).

Price, Hereward T. "The Function of Imagery in Webster," *PMLA*, LXX (1955), 717–739.

Prior, Moody E. *The Language of Tragedy*. New York, 1947, pp. 119–135.

Rabkin, Norman. *Twentieth Century Interpretations of The Duchess of Malfi*. Englewood Cliffs, 1968.

Ribner, Irving. *Jacobean Tragedy: The Quest for Moral Order*. New York and London, 1962, pp. 100–108 (WD), 108–122 (DM).

_____. "Webster's Italian Tragedies," *TDR* V, No. 3 (1961), 106–118.

Ridley, M. R. *Second Thoughts: More Studies in Literature*. London, 1965, pp. 76–90, 108–110, 123–132 (WD); 90–106, 110–123, 123–132 (DM).

Riewald, J. G. "Shakespeare Burlesque in John Webster's *The Duchess of Malfi*," *ES*, XLV (1964), Supp., pp. 177–189.

Scott-Kilvert, Ian. *John Webster*. Writers and their Work, No. 175. London, 1964, pp. 16–23 (WD), 23–29 (DM).

Sensabaugh, George F. "Tragic Effect in Webster's *The White Devil*," *SEL*, V (1965), 345–361.

Smith, James. "The Tragedy of Blood," *Scrutiny*, VIII (1939), 265–280.

Stoll, E. E. *John Webster*. Boston, 1905, pp. 116–132.

Stroup, Thomas B. "Flamineo and the 'Comfortable Words,'" *RenP*, 1964 (pub. 1965), pp. 12–16.

Thayer, C. G. "The Ambiguity of Bosola," *SP*, LIV (1957), 162–171.

Tomlinson, T. B. *A Study of Elizabethan and Jacobean Tragedy*. Cambridge, Eng. and Melbourne, 1964, pp. 132–157 (DM), 229–237 (WD).

Vernon, P. F. "The Duchess of Malfi's Guilt," *N & Q*, X (1963), 335–338.

Wright, Louis B., and Virginia A. LaMar, eds. *The Tragedy of the Duchess of Malfi*. Folger General Reader's Edition. New York, 1959.

George Chapman

BUSSY D'AMBOIS
AND CHAPMAN'S CONCEPTION OF TRAGEDY *

Jean Jacquot

THE fact that a discerning critic like T. M. Parrott, the editor of Chapman's *Tragedies,* with an intimate knowledge of the play and its background, saw Bussy D'Ambois as an embodiment of Roman *virtus,* shows that, however reprehensible this hero's conduct may be at times, his courage and self-reliance are also worthy of admiration. The character is not easy to interpret in terms of Chapman's philosophy, and Ennis Rees[1] is right in thinking that it is of crucial importance for an understanding of the poet's tragic world.

Now Rees thinks that earlier critics misunderstood the tragedies "with remarkable consistency," and he is so consistent in his irritation with them that one expects him to conclude his book by declaring

> The work that I was born to do, is done.

The work is scholarly, and a valuable contribution to the study of the plays, but, in my opinion, its method calls for some objections. Firstly,

---

* From G. A. Bonnard, ed., *English Studies Today: Second Series,* Bern: A. Francke AG Verlag, 1961, pp. 129–141. Reprinted by permission of the publisher.

[1] *The Tragedies of George Chapman: Renaissance Ethics in Action,* Cambridge (Mass.), 1954.

the coherence of Chapman's ethical and religious thinking is now well established, but his philosophy is not something so static and intemporal as the sphere of Parmenides, nor does it exclude internal development, change of emphasis, or contradiction. In his works the Platonic, Stoic, and Christian elements of which he attempted the synthesis do not always appear in the same proportion or relation. His changes of personal and political allegiance, his varying response to contemporary history must also be taken into account. Therefore quoting extensively from his later works to elucidate an early play is not perhaps the safest procedure.

Secondly, earlier critics have pointed out that Chapman made use of irony to reveal the insincerity or folly of his characters, and that sometimes their outbursts of rhetoric should be taken with a grain of salt. Rees elaborates the suggestion, and scores a point by showing that the poet considered irony as one of Homer's devices in the delineation of character, and that, in the *Iliad,* a man who was not good might sometimes fall "upon sentence and good matter in his speeches."[2] But one may be tempted to see irony in the play when there is no hint of it in the text. There are cases when a character, say Bussy, employs mythology, or imagery, or maxims in a way which is in such contradiction to his behaviour that no erudite member of the audience could have missed the point. Now as Rees thinks that Bussy is by no means virtuous, but only seems so because the other characters are still worse, he tends to dismiss as pretence or illusion *all* the virtuous language in the play. If he is right, how did Chapman make himself understood? After all the play owed much of its lasting success to Bussy's impassioned speeches, which contain some of Chapman's finest poetry, and even the discerning playgoer may have been carried away by admiration, just as modern critics were, until Rees decided that these speeches were to be entirely interpreted as Chapman's ironic comments on an unworthy character.

Lastly, when he feels that 'irony' will not carry him any further, Rees resorts to 'convention' as a system of interpretation. For instance, in his attempt to deny the genuine elevation of thought of Bussy's last utterances, he asserts that while Monsieur's caricature at the end of Act III reveals the real features of the character, the encomium, by the same Monsieur, of Bussy who is about to face death, is just a concession to the tragic convention that the hero must die nobly. Unfortunately the claim runs against his main line of argument. Chapman, who insisted on originality and was capable of challenging received opinion, would certainly not have obscured the ethical and religious issues of the play at a crucial moment for the sake of convention. By omitting the significant fact that Bussy forgives his enemies and offers his life as a means of reconciling Montsurry and his wife, by dismissing the concluding statement on Bussy's fate—"Farewell, brave relics of a complete man, etc."—

[2] *Ibid.,* pp. 38–39.

as a "final effort in the direction of pathos" while it is an answer to the lament of the dying hero, by disconnecting these two speeches and inverting their order, Rees succeeds in eschewing a real discussion of the main problem of the play: does Bussy achieve spiritual salvation and, if so, can this be considered the outcome of earlier developments, or must we admit that the play lacks coherence?

I have always felt that, if I had cleared up a number of points in my earlier study of this play,[3] I had been unable to find a satisfactory answer to the problem I have just mentioned. This is why I welcomed the opportunity that was given me of again examining the play and its relation to the other tragedies when I was asked to prepare a critical edition and a translation of it.[4] What I submit here to your judgment is a mere outline of an interpretation that would require substantial quotations and references, and a detailed discussion of imagery and classical reminiscences.

Chapman declared, in the often-quoted dedication of *The Revenge of Bussy D'Ambois,* that the subject of tragedy "is not truth, but things like truth", and "the authentical truth of either person or action" should not be expected in such poems, which have an ethical purpose. But this should not lead us to believe that the historical background of each play could conveniently be dismissed in a footnote. To understand his meaning, we must know how he handles his material, and why he alters the facts. In *Bussy* we find him surprisingly well informed of the career of his hero, though the biographical sources were only published after the play.

To give a single instance: it had been hitherto impossible to find an historical basis for the fact that in the play Monsieur, not the King, betrays the secret of Bussy's amours. But a seventeenth-century historian, Antoine Varillas,[5] refers to two traditions, one of which lays the ultimate responsibility of the murder on Monsieur. Bussy's conduct and fate were much commented on in France, England and the Low Countries, and remained a theme for moral discussion many years after his murder. Chapman shared this interest in what the age considered such a significant case. Contemporary judgments on Bussy vary from the severity of L'Estoile, who praises his indomitable courage and noble ambition, but thinks that his vices and insufficient fear of God caused his untimely death, to the hyperbolic "tombeaux" which promise immortality and heavenly bliss to the hero who fought so gallantly against treacherous enemies. As for Pierre de Dampmartin, a new examination of his *Bonheur de la Cour*[6] has convinced me that this book is undoubtedly the

---

3 *George Chapman. Sa vie, sa poésie, son théâtre, sa pensée,* Paris, 1951, Ch. V.

4 Due to appear in June 1960, in Fernand Aubier's "Collection billingue", Paris.

5 *Histoire de Henry* III, 1694 ed., I, 573–575.

6 *Du Bon-heur de la Cour, et vraye félicité de l'homme,* Anvers, 1592.

source of the first scene of *Bussy*, and that it helped Chapman considerably in setting the tragic story in its ethical perspective. Now for Dampmartin the question of knowing whether one can make a career at court and remain virtuous is worth discussing; he does not deny the generosity of Bussy's aspirations but points out that he had no clear idea of the supreme good. If he preferred an active life, and affairs of state, he should not have become unduly attached to the power and riches that go with them.

When the hero states, in his first soliloquy, that poverty and virtue go together, he says so because he finds the grapes too sour, but the poet did not think that it should necessarily be so. The theme of *De Guiana,* and of the masque for the marriage of princess Elizabeth, is the reconciliation of riches with honour (in the sense of virtue). In Chapman's eyes Somerset did not cease to be virtuous because he acquired huge riches, but when James's minion met with adversity, the poet exhorted him to bear it stoically. It seems to follow that in the play Bussy is not to be blamed for attempting to become a courtier and remain virtuous, but for lacking clear principles of conduct.

His entry at court shows, in the best vein of the comedy of humours, that he has no sense of decorum. But the gentlemen who insult him only notice the outward man in his rich new coat, they fail to realise his valour. Now we may have little sympathy with a moral code that requires the shedding of blood for the satisfaction of offended honour, but we cannot have it both ways. If we admit that, in the later play, Clermont's duty of avenging his brother is one which "no sixteenth century gentleman could have neglected," and if we think that Montsurry is ignoble because he refuses the challenge[7], then Bussy is no more to blame for killing offenders who, like men of honour, have accepted the fight, than his brother Clermont is for killing Montsurry after forcing him to fight. And the pursuit of private vengeance is surely as detrimental to the laws of the realm in one case as in the other.

Bussy's plea for the right to do himself justice seems based on a letter of the historical Bussy which was quoted with praise by connoisseurs of this "spice" of honour, like Brantôme. But he claims too much, according to the ethics of the play, when he pretends to be a law unto himself because he has such imperfect control over his passions. Even so there is one passion which he thoroughly dominates, and that is fear, and there is one good which he enjoys but is not afraid of losing, and that is his own life. Chapman adopts the highest epic strain in his narration of the fight (based on an exploit of the real Bussy which the connoisseurs compared to the fight of the Horatii and the Curiatii) and gives Homeric stature to Bussy's opponents, the "perfumed musk-cats" of the previous

---

7 Rees, *op. cit.,* p. 109, quoting Una Ellis-Fermor.

scene. He obviously wants to impress upon us that the hero is no mere braggart, but has a fiery nature, and is "a spirit beyond the reach of fear". And by doing so he seeks to win our admiration, so that Bussy's claim should seem less extravagant, and the king's pardon more credible.

Bussy shows himself unscrupulous when he receives money from Monsieur, who wants his help to usurp the crown, and then passes to the service of the king. Yet the king is the better master of the two (or if you prefer, he is not the worse). His protection of Bussy may be based on calculation as well as sympathy. But this does not compare with Monsieur's perfidy. And while the latter is a self-revealing villain, Chapman attributes to Henry's part a number of lines of gnomic character without any obvious hint that they are spoken hypocritically. I am inclined to believe that he is weak but well-meaning, and rather ineffective in his efforts towards conciliation. But whatever his character, he is the legitimate sovereign and in this sense a better master than Monsieur. And this is worth noticing since Chapman deliberately alters historical data, the real Bussy having left the king for the service of Monsieur.

The French nobleman was involved in state affairs, but Bussy's diatribes against those who undermine the authority of Henry are the only indication, in the tragedy, of his attempts to play a political part. As his own conduct is not beyond reproach, he is not in the best position to anatomize corruption. And in his role as the king's eagle he only succeeds in renewing his quarrel with de Guise and troubling the peace of the court. The duke is the first to attack, but Bussy is only too glad of this opportunity to truss such a big fowl. Yet, in this scene, as later with Monsieur during the banquet, Bussy appears as the man of comparatively low birth who has nothing but his courage to rely on, and whose outspokenness attracts the hatred of powerful lords who will stop at no treachery in their pursuit of revenge.

We know that Chapman had no mean opinion of martial virtue. And he gave much thought to the problem of the adaptation to the circumstances of civil life of the warrior who is expected to develop, to use Platonic language, the irascible parts of his soul. Only the best, like Clermont, can achieve rational control over their aggressive passions without stifling them. But in the absence of this control, the warrior may damage his integrity by indulging in the concupiscible passions which occupy the lowest degree in this threefold hierarchy. This is what happens when the favourite of Mars becomes the minion of Venus, and Bussy the lover of Montsurry's wife. Tamyra's indignant reply to Monsieur's advances, her deft handling of her husband's credulity, her inward lust and outward show of virtue, the Friar's stratagem which enables Bussy to win her, all this is in Chapman's best comic vein with, of course, grave undertones that give us a sense of impending tragedy. Tamyra's reflections on the force of destiny are naturally self-deceptive, though her complaint that

> Our bodies are but thick clouds to our souls

echoes a feeling to be found frequently in Chapman's gnomic verse. There is no fatality here; had the storm raised in the blood been reformed by reason (II, ii, i. 141), it would not have culminated in the scene of raving jealousy where Montsurry becomes his own torturer as well as Tamyra's. Bussy will pay a bitter price for his belief that:

> Sin is a coward, madam, and insults
> But on our weakness in his truest valour.

(III, i, ll. 20–21)

Monsieur and Guise are not slow in discovering that a cunning stag can be caught "where he rutteth with his hind," and Bussy's intrigue gives them a means of ensnaring him.

Here we must say a word of the invocations of spirits to which the Friar and Bussy have recourse in their attempt to ward off the attack. D. P. Walker's recent book[8] confirms that many learned men of the Renaissance were deeply interested in forms of knowledge and activity grounded in the belief that *spiritus* is the link between the World and its Soul as well as between man's body and his soul. Chapman possessed, and valued, a compendium of neo-Platonic and Hermetic treatises on demons in Ficino's translation. His description of the blessed spirit of Homer in *The Tears of Peace* bears evidence of familiarity with such sources, which also throw much light on the magic scenes in *Bussy*. The same can be said of Agrippa's widely-diffused *Occulta philosophia*, which he seems to have known, since an example of the effects of imagination which occurs in the book, is alluded to in the play (II, ii, ll. 175–179).

According to this tradition, the Friar's practices are not evil in themselves, they might even become as beneficent as Prospero's. But he lacks the piety and purity of heart which are required of a true magician whose mind must become united to the highest powers in order to command the spirits below them. He only succeeds in impressing them by outward ceremony and binding them by formulae. Those which appear have more in common with the rather lower orders in the demonic hierarchy of say, Iamblichus, than with the devils of medieval tradition, though there are some hints that Behemoth is one of the fallen angels.

Because the Friar and the lovers he seeks to protect are involved in passions, the spirits he conjures up are of impure substance, their predictions are confused, they can help the body only in a limited and rather bungling way, but they cannot free the soul from the bonds of

---

8 *Spiritual and Demonic Magic from Ficino to Campanella,* London, 1958.

destiny. The moral implication is obvious: Bussy will derive no benefit from their assistance. His own invocation (V, iii, ll. 41–53), clad in splendid verse, with its dim intuition of the doctrine dear to Chapman that the sun is but an image of the true source of light which is concealed in darkness, is misguided.

As for the Friar's ghost it is not, as I once thought, a mere stage commodity. The Friar uses his priestly authority, and Christian doctrine, in an effort to moderate the husband's fury. He may be concerned primarily with protecting his own life as well as Tamyra's. But it is important to notice that, for the first time, principles of charity are formulated in the play, and from this point onwards, as a being of flesh and blood or as a ghost, he is bent, first on preventing the murder of Bussy, then on helping the hero to make the best of death, lastly on reconciling Tamyra and her husband. During the last scene, he acts and speaks as if he were the spokesman of religion and justice. It is easy to deny all value to his words because he is a "pandar priest," but then this concluding scene will cease to have either structure or meaning. We hear from his ghost what became of him after he died of shock when seeing Tamyra tortured. His soul is "unrested" (V, iv, l. 153); in other words he expiates his sins, and here already satisfaction is given to a principle of proportion and justice. But we learn from the Hermetic and neo-Platonic tradition, as it was reinterpreted during the Renaissance in an attempt to conciliate it with Christian belief, that corrupt souls remain attracted by matter and exposed to earthly suffering. Instead of ascending to the abode of the gods they go to the underworld where they suffer, but they may appear as shadows, assist their friends and frighten their enemies, and in so doing may become the instruments of divine justice.

This is exactly what happens in the play, and after accomplishing his work on the scene of tragedy, the Ghost clearly states, in lines which are omitted in the revised version, that now he will do penance, "strike his terrors inwards," and inflict "earthly affliction" upon himself alone. At an earlier point, when he appears to Tamyra, she complains that man's "power to live is given to no end, but t'have power to grieve" (V, iv, ll. 13–14). He answers briefly, in the 1641 quarto, that "it is the misery of our creation." But in the earlier text he gave a fuller answer:

> Tis the just curse of our abus'd creation,
> Which we must suffer here, and scape hereafter;
> He hath the great mind that submits to all
> He sees inevitable; he the small
> That carps at earth, and her foundation shakes,
> And rather than himself, will mend his maker.

In these deleted lines, the statement that suffering is the consequence of sin, and that by securing our salvation we may be delivered from evil, is followed by a stoical precept which constitutes the core of the philosophy of Epictetus and will become Clermont's rule of conduct in the second play. This adds force to our argument that however unworthy he may have been as a priest, the terrible effects of sin in this world and the next have induced repentance, and he may be considered an exponent of the ethical and religious meaning of the play. That he is used by a power greater than his own appears clearly from his own words—"a fate doth ravish me", "my power is limited"—and all his efforts to prevent the murder of his friend are frustrated. I see two reasons for this: Bussy pays the price of blood for the sin of adultery *and* he must find in death the means of achieving true greatness.

The motive of retribution receives ironic emphasis when Montsurry, disguised in the Friar's robe, leads the credulous Bussy to his mistress. But at this moment he is already prepared to face death with his usual courage. He may have undertaken Tamyra's conquest in a cynical mood, but according to the code of honour which binds a gentleman to risk his own life to avenge an offence, he must also defend the reputation of his mistress, and this he pledged himself to do as soon as he became her lover (III, i, l. 35 ff.). For the same reason he neglects the Spirit's warning that her hand will kill him. He believes, as he must, that she will not do it unless she is forced, and rather suffer many deaths than do it. And he decides that if he fails to come when she calls, because this might cost him his life, he will behave like a coward:

> I must fare well, however, though I die
> My death consenting with his [the Spirit's] augury.

(V, iii, ll. 70–82)

A moment later he says of the letter written in her blood, which he receives from the disguised husband:

> Or how it multiplies my blood with spirit
> And makes me apt t'encounter Death and Hell.

The whole episode, we have seen, is fraught with irony, and Tamyra has little in common with the poet's own mistress, Philosophy, the true elixir. But Chapman, as a true disciple of Ficino, loved to speak of the conversion from the life of the body to that of the soul in terms of this refining and invigorating process:

> Spirit to flesh, and soul to spirit giving.[9]

The allusion to it, at this point, is significant. And a careful study of the imagery of the play, which is in such harmony with its subject matter, would confirm this. The violent perturbation of the blood and its humours, the turbulence and lawlessness of passions and their cosmic equivalents, the elemental forces, are its recurring themes. According to Monsieur's virulent satire, Bussy's gall turns his blood to poison, and the grosser elements, earth and water, form "a toad-pool that stands in

---

9 *A Coronet for his Mistress Philosophy,* sonnet 2.

[his] complexion" (III, ii, ll. 450–457). But at an earlier point we get a different picture from the narration of Bussy's epic fight. Here the combatants, and Bussy in particular, are all fire and spirits, and the idea of a purification of the blood, not through sheer violence, but through courage and indifference to death, is elaborated in flaming imagery. And this I believe helps us to understand the purification of the hero in his final ordeal, when he gives Montsurry the sword into which his fight "has still'd inherent valour with charms of *spirit*."

Before this takes place, Chapman introduces a scene where Monsieur comments with de Guise on the fate of the man who is about to fall into their trap. Monsieur judges of the event according to his own materialistic philosophy: Nature works at random, and there is no proportion between the gifts she may lavish upon a man and the end for which she has created him. For instance Bussy, who is "young, learned, valiant, virtuous and full mann'd," is going to meet an undeserved death. Guise remarks that this is the view of worldly men. It is true enough, and we find the same problem discussed, from the opposite point of view, in *Caesar and Pompey*, by Cato who justifies his faith in immortality, by proving that "Nature works in all things to an end", and there is "a proportion betwixt the ends of those things and their primes" (IV, v, l. 97 ff.).

But why, at the very moment when Bussy's decision to face death precipitates the tragic issue, is Monsieur made to dwell on the hero's high gifts, while congratulating himself on his worldly wisdom? No doubt to remind us that if adultery is the immediate cause of his death, Bussy is uprooted because he is not a hollow tree through which the winds sing, but a solid one which offers resistance to them. And that if his grave imperfections have appeared in other scenes, his unusual merits must not be forgotten. And finally that man's destiny is not limited to this world, and there may be more proportion between Bussy's creation and his end than Monsieur can think of.

In the final scene, after putting the murderers to flight, Bussy challenges the husband to a single combat, thinking that he can still defend Tamyra's reputation with his sword. Then he is shot from behind, at the very moment when, as his mistress's request, he spares Montsurry whom he holds at his mercy. His valour and the gentleman's code of honour have helped him a long way towards making the best of an end which might have been ignominious, while his "politic" enemies have disgraced themselves. But now he must do more than face danger in the full vigour of his faculties, he must experience in his agony the divorce of body and soul and the vanity of this life.

He models his attitude on Roman stoicism and declares he bears as equal thought of life and death, which is now more difficult to achieve than in action. He seeks consolation in the survival of his fame, and this is expressed in magnificent lines. But the Ghost interferes with a brutal injunction: he must not indulge in self-pity, he must forgive his murderers. Now the forgiving of offences is the most difficult thing to accept, according to the code of honour by which he has lived. He forgives, no doubt, because this is the only way left of showing greatness. And he does something even more Christian in forgiving Montsurry (though hiring murderers to achieve vengeance is a greater crime than adultery) and in offering his life in reparation of the wrong Montsurry has suffered, and as a means for Tamyra to obtain her husband's pardon.

> Now let me pray you that my weighty blood
> Laid in one scale of your impartial spleen,
> May sway the forfeit of my worthy love
> Weigh'd in the other; and be reconcil'd
> With all forgiveness to your matchless wife.

(V, iv, lll. 119–123)

No one can deny that this request is inspired by a true sense of charity and justice, and that in so behaving Bussy has shown himself a complete man. Following his example, Tamyra asks to be forgiven for being the cause of his death. This revelation, and the sight of her tortured body, break his heart. And he dies expressing the fear that he will be unable to reach the firmament. Then comes as an answer the Friar's valediction:

> Farewell, brave relics of a complete man
> Look up and see thy spirit made a star;
> Join flames with Hercules——

(Ibid., l. 147 ff.)

The Ghost then addresses Montsurry as a "son of the earth," and bids him threateningly to perform "christian reconcilement" with his wife and heal the wounds "manlessly digg'd in her." Finally Montsurry forgives, but rejects reconciliation, and Tamyra decides to live in penitence.

When the Ghost exhorted the transfigured Bussy to "join flames with Hercules," the contemporary playgoer with a modicum of classical learning could not miss the allusion to the death and resurrection of the mythical hero on his funeral pile. He would have already recognised a paraphrase of the Senecan chorus lamenting the fate of Hercules in Bussy's address to his fame (V, iv, l. 98 ff.). And with the aptness of the Renaissance mind to apply myth, he would have discerned in *Hercules Oetaeus* the underlying pattern of the final scene of our play.[10] A detailed comparison would take too much time and I shall limit myself to a few points of resemblance.

The dying Bussy, like Hercules, is struck by an invisible enemy with which he cannot struggle face to face, he complains to Heaven of his

---

[10] Direct borrowings were noticed by F. S. Boas and T. M. Parrott, and there are valuable suggestions for a comparative study of the two plays in A. S. Ferguson, "The Plays of George Chapman," *MLR*, XIII (1918), 1–24.

unworthy end, and decides to compensate this by supporting pain and death unflinchingly. Tamyra, in her last speeches, over-indulges in self-pity and remorse, like Dejanira (and also Alcmene). And of course, the letter written in blood, like the tunic steeped in blood, is the cause of the hero's death. But Hercules destroys the poisonous fire in a sacrificial fire, and with it the earthly part of his nature which came from woman and mortality, and liberates the divine part. When Bussy comes to the bitterest moment of his ordeal, and Chapman's lines become a thick cluster of Senecan images, he sees himself, like Hercules, as a defeated Titan buried under Pindus and Ossa, and like him feels a devouring fire. Thus he expiates his carnal attachment, and is purified of the grosser elements of his nature.

Hercules and the commiserating chorus thought that he would go to the underworld, to the realm of the dead, and so did Bussy (tell them "that D'Ambois now is hasting / To the eternal dwellers" translates "dic ad aeternos properare manes Herculem"). Both heroes aspired to Heaven but thought they had failed to reach it, and died complaining of the "frail condition of strength, valour, virtue." And while the voice of the transfigured Hercules announces that he has ascended to the throne of his celestial Father, the Umbra reveals that Bussy's spirit is made a star. Both have achieved this through their courage. The last word on Bussy's virtue is to be found in Seneca's play: *virtus in astra tendit, in mortem timor.*

We must add that the moralizing of the Herculean myth by the Stoics was continued by the Christians, and, as Marcel Simon has shown,[11] the process of assimilating the hero to Christ reached its culminating point in the Renaissance, when he was represented on his pyre, with the legend *consummatum est*. For the proud like Bussy the imitation of Hercules is easier than the imitation of Christ. Seneca's protagonist is a warrior, capable of violent outbursts of passion, and in his agony he is not exempt from self-pity or self-glorification. But Bussy goes further than Hercules. The latter gives his bow to his friend, Bussy gives his sword to his enemy, and forgives, and throws his life into the scales to make up for the offence his sin has caused.

This interpretation of the play may be rejected, or perfected by others, but it is the only I can think of that accounts for its unity and makes sense of its final scenes. One thing is certain, we cannot think of *Bussy D'Ambois* in simple terms of punishment for vice according to Baldwin's definition of tragedy in the *Mirror for Magistrates*.[12] Chapman's tragic art is something more complex than the mechanical application of ethical

---

11 *Hercule et le Christianisme*, Paris, 1955.

12 "For here as in a looking-glass, you shall see (if any vice be in you) how the like has been punished in other heretofore; whereby admonished, I trust it will be a good occasion to move you to the sooner amendment"; ed. L. B. Campbell, Cambridge University Press, 1938, pp. 65–66. Quoted by Rees, *op. cit.*, p. 29.

formulae. Because in his non-dramatic poems he condemns in general terms men who lack "true learning," it does not follow that a highly individualized figure like Bussy is incapable of inner development, and of the instinctive discovery, through tragic experience, of the means of preserving his spiritual integrity.

This must be kept in mind in our judgments on Byron, though he is far more guilty than Bussy and is executed for relapsing in treason, after being given every opportunity of rehabilitation.

But though we are shown, throughout *The Conspiracy* and *The Tragedy of Byron,* his pride and treachery, and not his glorious past, it is clearly indicated, when he first appears on the stage, that his error results from noble, but utterly misguided aspiration, and we find, in his soliloquy, celestial imagery reminiscent of *Hercules Oetaeus,* though he will more and more resemble *Hercules furens.* His phases of revolt and dejection, his self-commiseration, his struggle with the fear of death, his efforts to face the destiny of his soul before the executioner delivers the final stroke, form an impressive tragic spectacle. And though he was utterly unprepared for the ordeal he finds at last the force to recognize his guilt, and its moral causes, to persuade his brothers that his death is just and they must remain loyal to the king, and to draw the lesson of his errors for all "statists." It will not do to say with Rees that this is just convention, and that towards the end Chapman gradually prepares "his audience for the 'change' which is to occur in Byron at the very last in order that he may die 'nobly.'" Nor to affirm that though he remains the same proud man until the end and never repents he becomes the poet's mouthpiece and is brought "to an articulation of the moral inherent in the structure of these ten acts."[13] Nor will it serve to deny flatly, as Marcello Pagnini does, that the hero feels "il fremito della sua anima immortale."[14] What else can he mean when he says:

> I feel her free:
> How she doth rouse and like a falcon stretch
> Her silver wings, as threatening Death with death
> At whom I joyfully will cast her off.

And again in the very last lines:

> Strike, strike, O strike; fly, fly commanding soul,
> And on thy wings for this thy body's breath
> Bear the eternal victory of Death!

While the moral lesson is made perfectly clear, we are reminded by a soldier in the crowd that for all his guilt Byron far outweighs "the King's chief minion," and though the sentence is just, the sight of this ruined life should fill us with sorrow. Earthly condition is indeed miser-

---

13 Rees, *op. cit.,* pp. 88–90.

14 *Forme e motivi nelle poesie e nelle tragedie di George Chapman,* Firenze, 1957, p. 206. I discuss this book in a review, in a forthcoming number of *Etudes anglaises.*

able if a man of Byron's mettle may become the slave of error and passions. Again, this does not extenuate responsibility but, though he has greatly injured his soul, it seems, when death approaches, when he is stripped of all worldly goods and the bonds of flesh are severed one after the other, that his soul recovers some of its pristine brilliance, and that the inner core has remained uncorrupted.

Chapman's dualism, and pessimism regarding this life, help us to understand Byron's "change." The same applies to heroes like Cato or Clermont who attempt to live virtuously without eluding any of their duties, but finally commit suicide.

I shall deal briefly with Clermont's relation to Bussy. Chapman tells us that he possesses, like his brother, great natural gifts and also true "learning," which the other lacked, that is to say a clear view of virtuous ends, and control over his passions. Clermont wins our sympathy by his efforts to act without injuring his moral integrity, and *The Revenge of Bussy D'Ambois* owes much of its interest to the dramatic conflict of ethics and politics and the beautiful formulation of the precepts of Epictetus. It is planned as a sequel to the earlier play and is also meant to form a contrast with it. If de Guise is idealised, and, though one of Bussy's murderers, becomes the friend of Clermont, who himself is made to justify the massacre of the Huguenots, this may be accounted for, partly at least, by Chapman's change of patron, and of political allegiance.[15] If Bussy's ghost appears to Clermont, and asks to be revenged upon Montsurry, it is no doubt because the obligation puts Clermont's principles to a severe test. This has an historical basis in the attitude of Bussy's family, though Clermont himself is a fictitious character. But it completely destroys the moral and religious meaning of the tragic close of the earlier play in which the dying Bussy *forgives* Montsurry. His Ghost is now made to require vengeance in the name of eternal justice, but what he did before he died satisfied both charity and justice. In spite of this Chapman confirms that Bussy has achieved spiritual salvation, according to the prediction of the Friar's ghost. In the *Revenge,* Tamyra repeats that Bussy's spirit was not earthly, and ascended to the sphere of fire (I, ii, ll. 16–18). And Clermont says of him that reason and justice are "perform'd / In spirits ten parts more than fleshy men" (V, i, ll. 112–113), which can only indicate that his moral state has considerably improved in the other world. The deeper significance of the appearance of Bussy's ghost is that men who pretend to possess "learning" and "holiness of life" have something to learn from the example of Bussy who died fearlessly, and this is why Bussy's ghost is made to express a doctrine as dear to Chapman as to the stoic Clermont, that man must strive to become God's image:

> To live to Him, is to do all things fitting
> His image, in which, like Himself, we live;

15 Cf. my *Chapman,* pp. 48–49 and 175 ff.

To be His image is to do those things
That make us deathless, which by death is only
Doing those deeds that fit eternity...

(V, i, ll. 87–91)

CHAPMAN AND BUSSY D'AMBOIS

Adams, Robert P. "Critical Myths and Chapman's Original *Bussy D'Ambois*," *RenD*, IX (1966), 141–161.

Barber, C. L. "The Ambivalence of *Bussy D'Ambois*," *REL*, II (1961), 38–44.

Battenhouse, Roy W. "Chapman and the Nature of Man," *ELH*, XII (1945), 87–107.

Bement, Peter. "The Imagery of Darkness and of Light in Chapman's *Bussy D'Ambois*," *SP*, LXIV (1967), 187–198.

Boas, Frederick S. *An Introduction to Stuart Drama*. Oxford, 1946, pp. 13–41.

Brooke, Nicholas, ed. *Bussy D'Ambois*. The Revels Plays. Cambridge, Mass., and London, 1964, pp. xxvi–lxxiv.

Craig, Hardin. "Ethics in the Jacobean Drama: The Case of Chapman," in *Essays in Dramatic Literature: The Parrott Presentation Volume*, ed. Hardin Craig. Princeton, 1935, pp. 25–46.

Decap, Roger. "Bussy d'Amboise héros tragique: Sur le *Bussy d'Amboise* de George Chapman," in *Hommage à Paul Dottin, Caliban*, III (1966), 97–114. (Special issue, Annales publiées trimestriellement par la Faculté des Lettres et Sciences Humaines de Toulouse, N.S. II, Fasc. 1, janvier.)

Ellis, Havelock. *From Marlowe to Shaw*, ed. John Gawsworth. London, 1950, pp. 41–94.

Ellis-Fermor, Una. *The Jacobean Drama*. 4th rev. ed. London, 1958, pp. 53–76.

Evans, Maurice, ed. *Bussy D'Ambois*. The New Mermaids. London and New York, 1965, pp. x–xxvii.

Ferguson, A. S. "The Plays of George Chapman," *MLR*, XIII (1918), 1–24.

Herring, Thelma. "Chapman and an Aspect of Modern Criticism," *RenD*, VIII (1965), 153–179.

Hibbard, G. R. "George Chapman: Tragedy and the Providential View of History." *ShS*, XX (1967), 27–31.

Higgins, Michael H. "The Development of the 'Senecal Man'; Chapman's *Bussy d'Ambois* and Some Precursors," *RES*, XXIII (1947), 24–42.

Jacquot, Jean. *George Chapman (1559–1634): sa vie, sa poésie, son théâtre, sa pensée*. Paris, 1951, pp. 131–143.

Lordi, Robert J., ed. *Bussy D'Ambois*. Regents Renaissance Drama Series. Lincoln, Nebraska, 1964.

Kennedy, Charles W. "Political Theory in the Plays of George Chapman," in *Essays in Dramatic Literature: The Parrott Presentation Volume*, ed. Hardin Craig. Princeton, 1935, pp. 73–86.

MacLure, Millar. *George Chapman: A Critical Study.* Toronto, 1966, pp. 113–125.

McCollom, William G. "The Tragic Hero and Chapman's *Bussy d'Ambois,*" *UTQ,* XVIII (1949), 227–233.

McDonald, Charles Osborne. *The Rhetoric of Tragedy: Form in Stuart Drama.* Amherst, Mass., 1966, pp. 179–224.

Muir, Edwin. " 'Royal Man': Notes on the Tragedies of George Chapman," in *Essays on Literature and Society.* London, 1949, pp. 20–30.

Ornstein, Robert. *The Moral Vision of Jacobean Tragedy.* Madison, Wis., 1960 (reprinted 1965), pp. 50–60.

Pagnini, Marcello. *Forme e motivi nelle poesie e nelle tragedie di George Chapman.* Florence, 1957, pp. 172–189, *et passim.*

Parrott, Thomas Marc, ed. *The Plays and Poems of George Chapman: The Tragedies.* London, 1910, pp. 541–546.

Perkinson, Richard H. "Nature and the Tragic Hero in Chapman's Bussy Plays," *MLQ,* III (1942), 263–285.

Prior, Moody E. *The Language of Tragedy.* New York, 1947, pp. 104–112.

Rees, Ennis, Jr. *The Tragedies of George Chapman: Renaissance Ethics in Action.* Cambridge, Mass., 1954, pp. 29–50.

Ribner, Irving. "Character and Theme in Chapman's *Bussy D'Ambois,*" *ELH,* XXVI (1959), 482–496.

——————. *Jacobean Tragedy: The Quest for Moral Order.* New York and London, 1962, pp. 23–35.

Schwartz, Elias. "Seneca, Homer, and Chapman's *Bussy D'Ambois,*" *JEGP,* LVI (1957), 163–176.

Smith, James. "Revaluations (VII): George Chapman," *Scrutiny,* III (1935), 339–350; IV (1935), 45–61.

Spens, Janet. "Chapman's Ethical Thought," *Essays and Studies,* XI (1925), 145–169.

Spivack, Charlotte. *George Chapman.* New York, 1967.

Tomlinson, T. B. *A Study of Elizabethan and Jacobean Tragedy.* Cambridge, Eng., and Melbourne, 1964, pp. 256–261.

Ure, Peter. "Chapman as Translator and Tragic Playwright," in *The Age of Shakespeare,* ed. Boris Ford. Baltimore, 1955, pp. 318–333.

——————. "Chapman's Tragedies," in *Jacobean Theatre,* ed. John Russell Brown. Stratford-upon-Avon Studies 1. New York, 1960, pp. 227–247.

Waddington, Raymond B. "Prometheus and Hercules: The Dialectic of Bussy *D'Ambois,*" *ELH,* XXXIV (1967), 21–48.

Waith, Eugene M. *The Herculean Hero in Marlowe, Chapman, Shakespeare,* and Dryden. New York and London, 1962, pp. 88–111, *et passim.*

Weiler, John William. *George Chapman—The Effect of Stoicism upon His Tragedies.* New York, 1949, pp. 21–51.

Cyril Tourneur

THE REVENGER'S TRAGEDY:
A STUDY IN IRONY *

Peter Lisca

In his edition of Cyril Tourneur (1930), Mr. Allardyce Nicoll remarked that Tourneur's use of "dramatic and tragic irony" had been "somewhat neglected." Thirty years later, Mr. Nicoll's observation still stands.[1] This neglect is curious not only because *The Revenger's Tragedy* is suffused with irony, but also because this irony bears heavily on what has been (except for the question of authorship)[2] the most discussed aspect of

* From *Philological Quarterly* (The University of Iowa), Vol. 38, 1959, pp. 242–251. Reprinted by permission of the editors.

[1] Ironically, the most complete discussion of irony in *The Revenger's Tragedy* is found in *Middleton's Tragedies* (New York, 1955), pp. 16–22. But Mr. Samuel Schoenbaum's discussion does not pay adequate attention to verbal irony. And his presentation of dramatic irony consists mostly of what Miss Bradbrook was so careful to avoid—four pages of plot summary.

[2] Recognition of the important role of irony in *The Revenger's Tragedy* might also cause those forces engaged in the Tourneur-Middleton controversy to realign themselves. As Mr. Samuel Schoenbaum pointed out in "The Revenger's Tragedy and Middleton's Moral Outlook," *N & Q*, CXCVI (1951), 8–10, four years before his *Middleton's Tragedies*, Middleton's use of irony implies a moral framework and thus strengthens the argument for his authorship of *The Revenger's Tragedy*, which, unlike Middleton's plays, is obviously moralistic. Similarly, Mr. R. A. Foakes admits ("On the Authorship of *The Revenger's Tragedy*," *MLR*, XLVII

that play, its morality.[3] It is my argument not only that the moral attitude expressed in *The Revenger's Tragedy* proceeds from a Christian point of view (the Puritan),[4] but that Tourneur objectifies this moral attitude by his use of an intense and ubiquitous irony on two levels: action and language.

Miss M. C. Bradbrook, writing of *The Revenger's Tragedy*, states that she has "counted a list of twenty-two ironic reversals" (actually a small fraction of the number), but begs that "to cite them would be tedious and unimpressive."[5] It is not my intention to rush in where Miss Bradbrook fears to tread, but rather to examine Tourneur's techniques of dramatic and verbal irony with a view toward establishing their role in the play. For the appreciation of dramatic irony it will suffice to examine the plethora of ironic incidents peripheral to just one of the play's major intrigues, that of Ambitioso and Supervacuo, sons of the Duchess by a previous marriage.

Their intrigue begins in Act I, scene ii, when they offer consolation to their blood brother, who has received a deferred judgment for raping Antonio's wife:

> AMBITIOSO: Brother, this makes for thee;
> Feare not, wee'll haue a trick to set thee free.
> JUNIOR: Brother, I will expect it from you both;
> And in that hope I rest.

> (I. ii.)[6]

In the light of subsequent developments, these statements of devotion

---

[1953], 129–138), as did E. H. C. Oliphant before him (*TLS,* Dec. 18, 1930), that the strongest argument against Middleton's authorship is the "moral fervour" of the play.

[3] On this question of the play's morality, critics have ranged from William Archer, who calls Tourneur "a sanguinary maniac" (*The Old Drama and the New* [Boston, 1923], p. 73), and T. S. Eliot, who speaks of the play's "loathing and disgust of humanity" (*Elizabethan Essays* [London, 1934] p. 129), to R. A. Foakes, E. H. C. Oliphant, Samuel Schoenbaum (*supra*) and John Peter (note 14 below), who are convinced of the play's moral intention. See also L. G. Salingar's "*The Revenger's Tragedy* and the Morality Tradition," *Scrutiny,* VI (1938), 402–422; also his "Tourneur and the Tragedy of Revenge," *The Age of Shakespeare,* ed. Boris Ford (Penguin Books, 1955), pp. 334–354.

[4] It is not the purpose of this paper to read into *The Revenger's Tragedy* Tourneur's private moral attitude. But the reader who does not object to inferring the artist's personal opinions from his work will perceive that because irony, unlike image clusters and symbols, cannot be unconscious, the following discussion throws light on Tourneur as well as the play. This insight would be supported by *The Transformed Metamorphoses* and *The Atlantic Tragedy.*

[5] *Themes and Conventions of Elizabethan Tragedy* (Cambridge, 1935), p. 165.

[6] Citations from Tourneur in my text are to *The Plays and Poems of Cyril Tourneur,* Vol. II, ed. John Churton Collins (London, 1878).

and trust are purest irony, for the two brothers' machinations become
so complicated that they secure the opposite effect. At the instigation of
Vindici (in disguise as Piato) and expecting to find his bastard brother
(Spurio) in the arms of the Duchess, Lussurioso charges into his stepmother's chamber yelling, "Villaine! Strumpet!" He finds instead his
father, the Duke, who promptly promises his wife Lussurioso's death.
Supervacuo and Ambitioso, jealous of Lussurioso's position as heir, plot
to ensure his fate while pretending to plead for him:

> AMBITIOSO: Now brother, let our hate and loue be wouen
> So subtilly together, that in speaking one word for his life,
> We may make three for his death.

(II. ii.)

Despite their craft ("forgiue him, good my Lord: hee's your owne sonne /
And I must needs say 'twas the villier done.") the Duke apprehends their
purpose well and ironically pretends to be moved to forgiveness. The
brothers then show their true hand and the crafty old Duke, intending to
draw them out, gives them a death seal for Lussurioso, whom he immediately and secretly frees. In their zeal the brothers ignore the slower
procedure of law and, circumventing the judge, present this seal directly
to the jailer. Further, they order the execution of their "brother" to be
private. Both these efforts, of course, ensure the death of their own blood
brother, whom they had pledged to set free.

The scene in prison is full of ironic interplay. The condemned younger
brother, trusting to his two brothers' efforts, misunderstands the keeper's
news and is joyful:

> KEEPER: Bad newes my Lord, I am discharg'd of you.
> JUNIOR: Slave call 'st thou that bad newes? I thanke you brothers.

(III. iv.)

He dies cursing his brothers, convinced they have betrayed him. Even he,
however, has an ironic sense of humor: "My fault was sweet sport, which
the world approues / I dye for that which euery woman loues" (III. iv).

The next scene is that of the Duke's murder by Vindici and Hippolito.
Immediately after this (ignorant of the fact) the two brothers come on
stage, and the first lines are (*Ambi.*), "Was not his execution rarely
plotted? / We are the Duke's sonnes now" (III. vi). Thinking that they
have effected Lussurioso's death, they quarrel for the honor of the plot's
conception. Having agreed that "the glory be shar'd equally," they begin
to plot the escape of their younger brother, whom they think to be still
in prison. At this moment an officer enters to present them with the
severed head (concealed) and they put on a display of mock sorrow
which is interrupted by the entrance of Lussurioso, whom they are pretending to mourn. When the actual events become clear to them, they

accuse each other of the mis-fired plot with the same vehemence with which each had previously claimed it for himself.

It is difficult to see where Tourneur has missed a single opportunity for ironic reversal, and it is the ubiquitousness of this irony which imparts, even to the plot, a sense of unity.[7] Other intrigues in the play, such as the murder of the Duke, the self-elimination of the brothers, and Vindici's tempting of his own sister are equally complex in their ironies, and these intrigues contribute to the total impression for which the drama strives and in terms of which it must be judged. Mr. F. T. Bowers is of the devil's party and does not know it when he says, "There are so many intrigues that the revenger loses control and is lost in the maze. The opposing forces are stronger than he, and he is frequently of no purpose in the plot," and "Tourneur has so constructed his play that the conflict chiefly occurs among the foes of the revenger without the revenger's instigation."[8] For *The Revenger's Tragedy* does not attempt to trace out the war of good with evil, nor the self-division of good, but rather the intestinal division of evil itself, a division which while seeming to lead to multiplication ironically ends in cross-cancellation. It is through this function that such minor intrigues as, for another example, the illicit relationship between the Duke's bastard son and the Duchess are central to the play's theme. Sin begets sin begets sin; but the sin of murder cancels all.

This saturation with irony on the level of action is paralleled and intensified by Tourneur's use of verbal irony. There is in *The Revenger's Tragedy,* of course, that species of comic irony whereby a character's lines simply convey to other characters a meaning the opposite of what he intended—for example the whole interchange between the imprisoned brother and his keeper. But Tourneur's consummate verbal irony can be perceived best by its more subtle manifestation in three forms: puns, personifications, and images of metamorphosis. The most important of these is the last, which for its full appreciation requires a review of the play's opening scene.

It has been remarked of this scene, and justly, that "There is hardly a more effective opening scene in Elizabethan drama. . . ."[9] There is the stage effect itself: the pomp and circumstance of a lively procession,

---

7 In her *Themes and Conventions of Elizabethan Tragedy,* M. C. Bradbrook makes an excellent observation on the dramatic structure of *The Revenger's Tragedy:* "The narrative is formalized as well as the characters. Hence some of the incidents which at first sight seem episodic strengthen the main structure of the play, which is an enlarged series of peripeteia" (p. 165).

8 *Elizabethan Revenge Tragedy* (Princeton, 1940), pp. 136, 137.

9 T. M. Parrot and R. H. Ball, *A Short View of Elizabethan Tragedy* (New York, 1943), p. 216.

dominated (probably from above) by the cloaked figure of Vindici and a grinning skull. There is also Vindici's opening speech:

> ...O, that marrow-lesse age
> Should stuffe the hollow bones with dambd desires
> And 'stead of heate kindle infernal fires
> Within the spend-thrift veynes of a drye Duke,
> A parcht and juicelesse luxur. O God! One
> That has scarce bloud inough to liue upon,—
> And hee to ryot it like a sonne and heyre?
> O the thought of that
> Turnes my abused heart-strings into fret.

This opening speech of some fifty lines presents the play's central irony in verse, as the physical scene of rich earthly values (the procession) is contrasted to the "bare bone" of the skull ("thou shell of death") in whose presence the procession moves. It is ironic that in the imminent shadow of death man should strive to damn himself; that with his sure knowledge of the steadfast and enduring bone he should pamper his "three-pilde flesh." Vindici closes this speech with an address to the skull:

> Aduance thee, O thou terror to fat folkes
> To haue their costly three-pilde flesh worne off
> As bare as this;—for banquets, ease, and laughter
> Can make great men, as greatnesse goes by clay;
> But wise men little are more great than they.

These lines, pantomimed in the physical scene, present the basic moral attitude against which Tourneur skillfully plays his images of metamorphosis to have them rebound as irony.

Vindici's lines everywhere demonstrate a zest for this game—transforming beauty into ugliness, goodness into evil, enduring values into ephemera. When, disguised as Piato, he is inducing his mother to ensure his sister's surrender to Lussurioso:

> Who'd sit at home in a neglected roome,
> Dealing her short-liu'd beauty to the pictures
> That are as uselesse as old men? When those,
> Poorer in face and fortunes than herselfe,
> Walke with a hundred Acres on their backs,
> Faire Meadowes cut into Greene fore parts—oh
> It was the greatest blessing euer happened to woman
> When Farmers' sonnes agreed, and met agen
> To wash their hands, and come up Gentlemen.
> The common wealth has flourisht, euer since
> Lands that were mete by the Rod,—that labor's spar'd,—
> Taylors ride downe and measure 'em by the year.

> Faire trees, those comely fore-tops of the Field
> Are cut to maintaine head-tires, much untold.
>
> (II. i.)

Again when Vindici is trying to convince Lussurioso that he is fit for the role of Pandar:

> I haue seene Patrimonies washt a' peices,
> Fruit-fields turnd into bastards,
> And in a world of Acres
> Not so much dust due to the heire t'was left to
> As would well grauell a petition.
>
> (I. iii.)

And when, still in disguise, he reproves his mother:

> The words I brought
> Might well haue made indifferent honest naught.
> A right good woman in these days is changde
> Into white money, with lesse labour farre.
>
> (II. ii.)

Vindici is so obsessed with this imagery of metamorphosis that it breaks out not only in set speeches, but also in his most casual remarks.[10] Even his dead betrothed, whose skull he carries, was once "able to ha' made a Usurer's sonne / Melt all his patrimony in a kiss. . . ." (I. i)

This kind of imagery is not limited to Vindici. The members of the court are themselves aware that the time is out of joint. The bastard Spurio turns "one incestuous kiss" into a key which "picks open hell" and claims that "if the truth were knowne" his father was "some stirring dish" after "some gluttoneous dinner." (I. ii) The Duke boasts that "Many a beauty" has he "turn'd to poyson," (II. ii) and Lussurioso that he has the power "To reare up Towers from cottages." (IV. i) The "younger son," standing trial for rape, says of his victim, "Her beauty was ordayned to be my scaffold. . . ." (I. ii) Supervacuo knows that "Fayths are bought and sold / Oths in these daies are but the skin of gold." (III. i) And Antonio remarks that the rape of his wife took place "When torch-light made an artificiall noone. . . ." (I. iv)

The irony of this imagery of metamorphosis and its centrality to the play's moral content, obvious from the opening speech, rises to its climax

---

10 In his "Tourneur and the Tragedy of Revenge," L. G. Salingar remarks that ". . . nowhere, outside of Shakespeare and Jonson, is the essence of the drama—the symbolization of evil—so firmly embedded in its imagery, in the sensory impact, the movement, the inner tension of its words" (p. 342). See also U. M. Ellis-Fermor, "The Imagery of *The Revenger's Tragedie* and *The Atheist's Tragedie*," *MLR*, XXX (1935) 289–301.

of expression just before Vindici and his brother Hippolito murder the Duke, when, using the skull as a reminder of enduring values, Vindici asks, "Does the Silke-worme expend her yellow labours / For thee?... Does euery proud and self-afflecting Dame / Camphire her face for this, and grieue her Maker / In sinfull baths of milke?...see / Ladies, with false formes / You deceiue men, but cannot deceiue wormes." (III. v)

Another variety of verbal irony, though a less important one, is Tourneur's use of personifications which share in the imagery of metamorphosis. "Chastity" captures no unicorns; unlike Britomart, she subdues no errant knights. Rather, she is a "foolish Country-girl." (II. i) "Virginity is "paradise lokt. up. . . .'And 'twas decreed that man should keep the key. . . ." (II. i) "Honestie" is "but heauen's beggar." (II. i) "Incest" is "but a Veniall Sinne." (I. ii) It is "Impudence" who is "Goddesse of the pallace, Mistris of Mistresses" and it is to her that "the costly-perfum'd people pray." (I. iii) As the virtuous Castiza remarks, "The world's so changed one shape into another, / It is a wise childe now that knowes her mother." (II. i)

A more important manifestation of verbal irony is Tourneur's use of puns. When Miss Bradbrook says that "Tourneur's puns are the most awkward and ineffectual of all the Elizabethans, especially his obscene ones,"[11] she is missing a good deal. For Tourneur's puns are not excesses of wit unrelated to the play, but, like his images of metamorphosis and his personifications, they are instruments of a mordant irony. Of course, there are a few puns which may be called "ineffectual" in the sense that they are not instrumental; but they are not "awkward."[12] When Vindici remarks on the "Bare-headed vassailes that had nere the fortune / to keep on their owne Hats, but let hornes weare 'em" (II. i), when he swears on his sword to "dis-heire" Lussurioso (I. iii), or when he asks at the end of the play, "May we not set as well as the Duke's sonne?" (V. iii) he is not being any more awkward than those two great punsters, Hamlet and Othello. Even those puns to which Miss Bradbrook most objects ("especially his obscene ones") are unobtrusive parts of the play's surface idiom. The pun on "male" in "That woman is all male whome none can Enter," (II. i) the pun on "performance" in "O what it is to haue a old-coole Duke / To bee as slack in tongue, as in performance," (I. ii) the puns on "nose" and "Boxe" in "It is the sweetest Boxe that ere my nose came nye," (II. i) and the possible pun on "secretary" in "You were his mid-night secretary" (I. i) : these are not the results of

<hr>

11 Bradbrook, p. 172.

12 In his study, "Eight Types of Puns," *PMLA*, LXXI (1956), Mr. James Brown defines the two basic forms of "bad" puns: ". . . the one makes use of a forced or false lexical ambiguity; the other sometimes brutally manipulates contexts so as to utilize ambiguities fetched from afar" (Note 4, p. 16).

brutally manipulated contexts, and they are too much a part of the play's web of incest and adultery to be "ineffectual."

Of prime concern to us at this point, however, are those puns whose peculiar effectiveness resides in some irony, an irony created by moral context. When Vindici, disguised as Piato, attempts to convince his mother she should play the pander to her own daughter, she replies, "Oh fie, fie! the riches of the world cannot hire a mother to such a most unnaturall taske." To which Vindici answers,

> No, but a thousand Angells can[.]
> Men haue no power, Angells must worke you to't.
> The world descends into such base-borne euills
> That forty Angells can make fourscore diuills.

(II. i.)

If this pun on "Angells" is compared to the following pun on "cuffe," occurring in the same scene and under almost identical circumstances, a significant difference in effect will be perceived. After being struck a blow by his sister for playing the pander to her, Vindici exclaims that this is "The finest drawne-work cuffe that ere was worn..." Unlike the double meaning of "Angells," the sartorial and pugilistic meanings of "cuffe" are related only on an auditory level; they do not penetrate each other and are not subsumed in some third meaning or effect arising from their juxtaposition in a particular context. The pun on "Angells" achieves irony because Vindici's juxtaposition of the two meanings is a measure of the extent he believes his world to be out of joint. Angels, ostensibly agents of salvation, have become agents of damnation.

It is in the presence of this moral context that irony is released when Lussurioso, giving Vindici money for pandering, says, "So thou'rt confirm'd in mee / And thus I enter thee," a parody of the sacrament which is enforced when Vindici, in an aside, refers to Lussurioso as an "Indian Diuill." (I. iii) This moral context, and hence irony, is also present when Vindici assures Lussurioso that some people "had rather be damn'd indeed than damn'd in colours." Vindici's reference to his "bony" lady with the "graue" look, just before the Duke kisses the skull and is poisoned, is another example of the *pun ironic,* as is his reference to Grace: "Saue *Grace* the bawde I seldome heare Grace nam'd." (I. iii)

That Vindici is fully conscious of the play's dramatic and verbal ironies is proved not only by his skillful utilization of them, but also by his occasional outbursts of self-applause: "O rare, delectable, happy, ravishing!" or "I'm in a throng of happy apprehensions!" Miss Bradbrook objects to these outbursts, maintaining that "This kind of consciousness belongs rather to the author than the character...."[13] If this were true, it would completely demolish the play. Vindici must be and is supremely

13 Bradbrook, p. 167.

aware of the play's ironies. This awareness is not only a part of his character, but the mainspring of his actions. In this connection it is significant that his magnificent opening speech sets up moral justice in abstract and impersonal terms—in the principle, not the particular. Remove this moral awareness, deprive Vindici of that double role as good and evil which he shares with other great revengers of Elizabethan and Jacobean drama, and his actions *do* become wanton atrocities, a string of horrors perpetrated by a lunatic.

If there should still persist a doubt as to the sincere moral framework posited by this irony, there remain Vindici's explicit references. Concerning secret lust:

> ...and in the morning
> When they are up and drest, and their maske on
> Who can perceiue this, saue that eternal eye
> That sees through flesh and all?

(I. iii.)

When his mother agrees to play pander to his sister:

> Why does not heauen turne black, or with a frowne
> Undoo the world? why does not the earth start up
> And strike the sinnes that tread uppon't. . . .

(II. i.)

When showing the skull to his brother:

> ...here's an eye
> Able to tempt a great man—to serue God.
>
> · · · · · · · · · · · ·
>
> ...and is not he absurd
> Whose fortunes are upon their faces set
> That feare no other God but winde and wet?

(III. ii.)

When Lussurioso lies about his commands to Piato:

> Has not heauen an eare? Is all lightning wasted?

(IV. ii.)

Again when Lussuriso hires Vindici to skill himself (Piato) :

> O thou almighty patience! 'tis my wonder
> That such a fellow, impudent and wicked
> Should not be clouen as he stood,
> Or with a secret winde burst open.
> Is there no thunder left? or is't kept up
> In stock for heauier vengeance?

(IV. ii.)

Because of these and numerous similar passages it is difficult to grasp what Miss Ellis-Fermor means when she writes, "...Tourneur excludes in his first play [*R. T.*] specific or implicit references to that universe of the spirit to which Chapman and Webster in their different ways give positive or negative testimony.... He...appears to accept a world order inherently evil."[14] Mr. C. V. Boyer does not overlook these passages, but he takes "the moral censures which [Tourneur] puts into Vindici's mouth" as the author's unsuccessful attempts "to elicit some sympathy for his hero by suggesting piety."[15]

Perhaps if all references to the "universe of the spirit" were as obvious as these we would be correct in calling them, as does Miss Ellis-Fermor, "perfunctory and unconvincing"[16] (though they seem sincere enough in or out of context). But the successful function of verbal irony in *The Revenger's Tragedy* is to keep firmly and continually before us the moral basis of the grim revenger's deeds—the contrast between his moral awareness and his deeds providing in itself another irony.

The final irony of the play is that of Vindici's fate. In his very first speech, he asks, "...who ere knew / Murder unpayed?" But by the beginning of Act V, when he himself is an unsuspected murderer, he boasts, "Thus much by wit a deep Reuenger can / When murder's knowne; to be the cleerest man / ...and with as bould an eye / Survey his body as the standers by." And when a court noble remarks that "No doubt but time / Will make the murderer bring forth him-selfe," Vindici replies, "He were an Asse then, y' faith!" Yet it is through his own full admission, motivated by pride, that he confesses his own and his brother's guilt: " 'Twas somewhat witty carried, tho' we say it. / 'Twas we two murder'd him." After they are sentenced to a "speedy execution" by Antonio, Vindici remarks,

> 'Tis time to die when we're our selues our foes
> When murders shut deeds closse, this curse does seale 'em,
> If none disclose 'em they themselves reueale 'em!
> This murder might haue slept in tonglesse brasse
> But for our selues, and the world dyed an asse.

Thus Vindici is aware of even the final irony; and that moral balance

[14] *The Jacobean Drama* (London, 1936), p. 153.

[15] *The Hero as Villain in Elizabethan Tragedy* (New York, 1914), p. 152. In another essay, *"The Revenger's Tragedy* Reconsidered," *Essays in Criticism* VI (1956), 131–142, Mr. John Peter, although convinced of the play's positive moral framework, comes to a similar conclusion, taking these passages to be examples of "intrusive moral comment" by the author.

[16] Ellis-Fermor, p. 173.

on whose behalf he had sinned so earnestly is restored only with his own death.

See other studies in *The Revenger's Tragedy* bibliography (below, pp. 327–329).

TRAGICAL SATIRE AND
THE REVENGER'S TRAGEDY *

Alvin Kernan

AFTER a particularly elevated passage describing the Roman matron's habit of poisoning a husband with whom she becomes bored, Juvenal's satirist pauses to remark that while satire may now appear to be wearing the tragic boot and declaiming a grand theme in Sophoclean tones, murder has become so commonplace in Rome that it is a fitting subject for a genre which ordinarily deals with fools rather than villains and with follies rather than crimes.[1] Though the lines are clearly ironic, they also provide a justification for the Juvenalian type of satire in which the satirist seems always on the verge of stepping over onto tragic ground. If the world is totally depraved and such great crimes as murder and incest are ordinary practice, then the follies with which satire usually sports are mere foibles unworthy of serious discussion. In this potentially tragic world the satirist will be required to show sterner virtues and employ more vicious methods of correction than are needed by the satirist who works in less dangerous surroundings.

The Elizabethans were well aware of the close relation of satire to tragedy. Some critics thought that satire had its origins in tragedy, and John Milton could remind his readers that "a Satyr as it was borne out of a *Tragedy*, so ought to resemble his parentage, to strike high, and

---

* From Alvin Kernan, *The Cankered Muse: Satire of the English Renaissance.* Copyright © 1959 by Yale University Press Inc. Reprinted by permission of Yale University Press.

[1] Satire VI, lines 634–40.

adventure dangerously at the most eminent vices among the greatest persons, and not to creepe into every blinde Taphouse that fears a Constable more then a Satyr."[2] John Marston, probably taking his cue from Juvenal, could warn his Muse after an attack on a Machiavel not to venture on tragic ground:

> Bold-faced Satire, strain not over-high,
> But laugh and chuck at meaner gullery.

(Pigmalion, II, 105–6)

The attraction of the tragic for the Elizabethan authors of formal satire is evident in their choice of sensational subject matter, their use of certain features of the high style, and their frequent references to "high flight" of their satires or to the fact that their Muse stalks "a loftier gate than Satyres use." This interest in the tragic aspects of satire found full expression in the satiric scene, the satirist, and the plots of some of the new satiric plays.

The same types of fools are usually present in these plays: the dissolute courtier, the rack-rent landlord, the cuckold, the fop, the epicure, and the empty-headed, gullible, immoral ladies of fashion who care only for new lovers, new clothes, and new gossip. But these characters are given a sinister turn, and mixed among them are more dangerous types: the flatterer, the Machiavel, the parasite, the traitor, and men whose lust and greed are cast in a heroic mold. The fools become the instruments of the villains, and the stakes of the struggle are now life, thrones, honor, power. The scene is no longer the London street or the houses of the well-to-do, but more perilous and mysterious places. The fools and villains now crowd in threatening masses on the plains of Troy, or press in on the remnants of virtue in the palace of Tiberius. The satirist finds himself isolated in the symbolic setting of the desert after he has banished himself from Athens, or he makes his way about the dark "Italian lascivious palace." Our surest method of finding our way into this world of tragic satire is, again, to follow the fortunes of the satirist.

.   .   .

No discussion of the Elizabethan satirist would be complete without reference to the manner in which he was fitted into the tragedy of blood-revenge. We have already noted that Juvenalian satire has a tendency toward the tragic and that, conversely, most tragic heroes have pronounced satiric qualities; but the Elizabethan blood-revenger is a special instance of the tragic hero and similar to the satirist in many

---

[2] "An Apology for Smectymnuus," ed. H. M. Ayres in *The Works of John Milton,* ed. F. A. Patterson *et al.* (New York, 1931), III, Part 1, p. 329.

ways.[3] Both figures, for example, find themselves in a world where virtue has been dispossessed by vice and in a once healthy society now become morally sick. Both are unable to hold their tongues but discover in themselves an agonized compulsion to reveal the truth by speaking out, and to unmask the world's pretenses to virtue by clever arrangement of events and scene. Both find it necessary, though for somewhat different reasons, to probe to the very source of infection in the state and cut it out of the body politic. The traditional metaphorical tools employed for this work by the satirist, the surgical probe and caustic medicine, blend readily with the actual tools of the revenger, the sword and the cup of poison.

Hamlet is, of course, the greatest instance of the combination of the two roles. He is not only the Prince of Denmark called on to revenge his father's foul murder and clear the throne of the usurper, but is also the surgeon satirist, the "scourge and minister," who finds the time "out of joint," and feels that he must "set it right." When he enters reading from that "satirical rogue"—Juvenal,[4] no doubt—who says that "old men have grey beards...and...a plentiful lack of wit"; when he holds up the picture of Old Hamlet and Claudius to Gertrude for comparison; when he catalogues the miseries of existence for the honest and sensitive man, "the law's delay, the insolence of office"; or when he mockingly comments in the graveyard on the dusty end of the great lawyer, the splendid courtier, and the cunning politician, Hamlet is very close to the satirist in subject, style, tone, and method. But the Hamlet whose will is "puzzled," who can wonder, "What should such fellows as I do crawling between earth and heaven?" has a complexity, a depth, and a speculative turn of mind which carry him far beyond the limited vision of the satirist, and, for that matter, of the blood-revenger. And the world in which he must move, for all its surface resemblance to the satiric scene, has a corresponding complexity and mystery about it which force him constantly to ponder and revise his earlier ideas. A discussion of *Hamlet* would for these reasons lead us away from satire and into the tragic world.

3 There is a certain appropriateness in the union of the Juvenalian satirist and the hero of the blood-revenge tragedy, for both figures were originally closely allied. Seneca's plays, the source of Elizabethan revenge tragedy, and Juvenal's satires were both literary products of the post-Augustan Roman Empire, and in both, despite the differences of genre, we find similar "heroes" dealing with amoral, corrupt societies. The Senecan tragic hero has as little ability to change his ideas through suffering as the rocklike satirist of Juvenal. The former maintains his virtue by enduring without change whatever miseries the world loads on him, while the latter maintains his virtue by never ceasing to speak out and tell the world the truth about itself.

4 Gilbert Highet, *Juvenal the Satirist* (New York, 1954), p. 213, suggests that Hamlet is here reading from Juvenal's Satire X.

But in Tourneur's *The Revenger's Tragedy* (1607), the satiric qualities of the scene, hero, and plot are not absorbed by the tragic, though they are ultimately modified by something like a tragic view of character and action. The story of the play is simple: some years before the action begins the Duke of a nameless Italian state has caused the deaths of Vendici's betrothed, Gloriana, and his father. Disguised as Piato, a malcontent, Vendici makes his way into the court, where he serves as royal pander, sows mischief, and arranges the death of the Duke. Then shifting to his own person he contrives the death of the Duke's heir, Lussurioso. At the end of the play Vendici, after proudly admitting his hand in these murders, is ordered executed, along with his brother Hippolito, by the new Duke, a just and honest man who has suffered much under the old regime.

The setting for this action is an Italian ducal palace populated with the usual villains and fools. The Duke is no more than a doddering, but still dangerous, old lecher continually searching for new objects for his lust. His legitimate son Lussurioso is equally lustful and clever, while his bastard Spurio plots against his brother and sleeps with his stepmother, the Duke's second wife. Her three sons by a previous marriage, Ambitioso, Supervacuo, and "Junior," are no more than vain, vicious young brutes. From this corrupted throne and family evil spreads out over the entire court and kingdom. Junior, surrounded by his cronies, rapes a young wife in the middle of a masquerade ball when her cries will be drowned by the music. The corruption of justice is revealed in his trial where he escapes death by the pleadings of the Duchess and the command of the Duke. The officers of state are mere toadies who hasten to do any bidding of those in power. Vendici's own family catches the general disease when he is sent by Lussurioso to buy his sister, Castiza, and persuade his mother to become a bawd. Castiza resists, but Gratiana, the mother, gives in to the lure of gold. Behind these specific events of the play, the language, primarily that of Vendici, brings into being the kingdom itself through which the infection spreads:

> Now tis full sea a bed over the world;
> Theres iugling of all sides; some that were Maides
> E'en at Sun set are now perhaps ith Toale-booke;
> This woman in immodest thin apparell
> Lets in her friend by water, here a Dame
> Cunning, nayles lether-hindges to a dore,
> To avoide proclamation.
> Now Cuckolds are a quoyning, apace, apace, apace, apace.
> And carefull sisters spinne that thread ith night,
> That does maintaine them and their bawdes ith daie![5]

---

[5] II.2.152–61. All citations of *The Revenger's Tragedy* are to *The Works of Cyril Tourneur,* ed. Allardyce Nicoll, London, Franfrolico Press, 1930.

This apocalyptic vision of the world outside the court being enfolded in the night of lust and self-interest is kept before us throughout the play by frequent references to the usual targets of Elizabethan satire, the yeomen's sons who "wash their hands, and come up Gentlemen" (II. i. 242), the tradesmen who take advantage of these fools and buy their land, the lady who bathes "in sinfull baths of milke,—when many an infant starves."[6] In short, this kingdom is the dense world of "three-pilde flesh," of hurried but aimless movement, casual carnality, and animal savagery usually created in satire, though here given a more sinister turn than is customary.

But if the details with which the scenes are fleshed out derive from Renaissance Italy—and Renaissance England—the supporting skeleton derives from another age. Still perceptible under the contemporary details are the old morality play structure and conception of character.[7] The ducal family—who, incidentally, are seven in number—retain their type names, Spurio, Ambitioso, Lussurioso. But the relationship of these characters to the morality play is suggested more by their woodenness, their lack of complexity, their single-mindedness, than by the use of devices such as type names. Each of them seems to be only a living vice, a personification of a single characteristic, and each of them moves in a mechanical, uncomplicated fashion toward satisfaction of his particular lust. It was Tourneur's genius to perceive, in an age when "realistic" dramatic characters had become the fashion and could be created by any fairly competent writer, that the only way of satisfactorily imaging a personality given over to vice is to portray it in the "flat" single-dimensional manner of the morality tradition. For characters of this kind have lost their complexity and the "reality" which comes from being fully alive. *The Revenger's Tragedy*, despite the exotic nature of some of the vice displayed in it and its blood-revenge plot, is conceptually very close to the world of the morality play in which the Seven Deadly Sins struggle with and very nearly succeed in overcoming such characters as Justice, Chastity, Honor, Love, Faithful Service, and Truth, who are represented

---

6 III.5.89. This speech of Vendici's extending from line 47 through line 119 provides an excellent example of the manner in which the Jacobean dramatist managed to extend the range of his satire. Rather than restricting his satiric voices to comments on the vices actually portrayed in the action, the playwright provided his satirists with speeches in which they describe a variety of fools and villains who seem to exist in a world just beyond the limits of the stage proper. In this speech, for example, Vendici attacks the swearer, the drunkard, the usurer, the proud courtesan, the noble who sells land to maintain her, the thief, the judge, the epicure; and he enlivens his attacks in the manner of verse satire by creating little scenes in which the sins are brought to life momentarily, e.g. a "selfe-affecting Dame" bathing in milk, and a riotous party in a brothel.

7 For a fuller discussion of this aspect of the play see L. G. Salingar, *"The Revenger's Tragedy* and the Morality Tradition," *Scrutiny, 6* (1938), 402–24.

in Tourneur's play, in a superficially realistic manner, by the courtiers, the judges, and the members of Vendici's family. As a result of this reduction of character to single vices and virtues, the satiric qualities of the scene are intensified, while the tragic quailties are diminished. For, as we have seen, characters in the satiric world are usually sketched in clear-cut blacks and whites. Neither satire nor Tourneur's play has any place for such bewilderingly complex and contradictory characters as Shakespeare's Gertrude, Claudius, Laertes, or even Polonius.

In keeping with the satiric tendencies of the scene, the hero of the play, Vendici, resembles the satirist more than he does the tragic hero. In his first appearance on stage he is placed in the same position in relation to the scene that the satirist in Juvenalian verse satire occupies. The stage is dark and over it passes a procession made up of the Duke, members of his family, and a train of court attendants carrying torches. As they pass silently, Vendici stands to one side unobserved and comments on them:

> Duke: royall letcher; goe, gray hayrde adultery,
> And thou his sonne, as impious steept as hee:
> And thou his bastard true-begott in evill:
> And thou his Dutchesse that will doe with Divill,
> Foure exlent Characters—O that marrow-lesse age,
> Would stuffe the hollow Bones with dambd desires,
> And stead of heate kindle infernall fires,
> Within the spend-thrift veynes of a drye Duke,
> A parcht and iulcelesse Luxur. O God! one
> That has scarce bloud inough to live upon.
> And hee to ryot it like a sonne and heyre?
> O the thought of that
> Turnes my abused heart-strings into fret.

(I.I.4–16)

The use of the word "Characters," i.e. set satirical portraits, suggests the close relationship of this scene and speech to the satiric tradition.

This initial scene establishes the perspective of the play. Seen from the outside, from the point of view of the audience, the *mise en scène* is that of formal satire with Vendici as satirist standing in the foreground and commenting on the activities and characters of the play proper, the world of the ducal court. This scenic effect is achieved in a number of ways during the course of *The Revenger's Tragedy*. Vendici may stand aside as he does in the first scene and simply address the audience directly while a dumb-show takes place on the stage proper; or he may appear alone on stage, or with his brother Hippolito, and deliver a long railing speech on human iniquity; or he may position himself in the foreground by employing irony, i.e. his speech may seem flattery to the self-blinded character to whom it is specifically addressed, while the audience understands that it is bitter sarcasm; or, finally, he may take advantage of the aside as he does in V.1.109 ff., where, as each obsequious courtier addresses some particular piece of outrageous flattery to the new Duke, Lussurioso, Vendici steps forward and delivers a withering comment to the audience.

But where the satirist in formal verse satire remains always outside the scene he describes, Vendici steps into it from time to time and becomes an actor in the world he loathes. Each time he does so, however, he puts on a disguise; first he assumes the person of the pander Piato, and then he uses his own name but a false character, that of a malcontent ready for any gainful employment. Whenever Vendici stands outside the scene he uses the standard tools of the satirist, words, to achieve his purpose of unmasking and punishing the villainy of the world; but when he steps into the play proper, intrigue and malicious meddling become his chief methods of operation. He tells Lussurioso that Spurio is in bed with the Duchess and sends him off to kill them; he tempts his mother with gold to become a bawd for her own daughter; he arranges an assignation for the old Duke, tricks him into kissing the poison-smeared lips of the skull of Gloriana, then treats him to the sight of Spurio embracing the Duchess; and at the end of the play he contrives a masque in which the dancers fall on Lussurioso and his party and kill them. Each of these activities, except the temptation of the mother, seems at first glance to be solely a function of Vendici's role as blood-revenger, for they are all retributions for what his family has suffered. But each of these events also achieves the satiric aim, it unmasks pretense and clears away illusion to reveal the truth.

This is plain enough in the scenes in which the Duchess is revealed as a whore, Lussurioso as a murderer, and Gratiana as a corruptible bawd, but in order to see how the murders of the old Duke and Lussurioso are achievements of the satiric end of unmasking villainy we must look briefly at what Vendici takes for reality. The majority of satirists are morally and socially oriented. That is, they trace the personal and social corruption they describe to the loss of certain ethical and social virtues, and they hope—in a hopeless way—to drive man back to these virtues by showing him how idiotic and depraved he has become. So they cut away the layers of pretense with which men cover themselves and reveal that underneath they are fools, animals, machines. But Vendici cuts a little deeper and discovers a further reality, the skull.[8] Perceiving that "lust is death" and that therefore the characters of the play who are

---

[8] Despite the traces of medieval otherworldliness present in this attitude, in a Renaissance context this somber vision of the world seems most immediately to be related to Calvinism. For a discussion of Tourneur's connections with this philosophy, see Michael Higgins, "The Influence of Calvinistic Thought in Tourneur's *Atheist's Tragedie*," *Review of English Studies*, 19 (1943), 255–62. The idea, already suggested in Ch. 3, that Juvenalian satire and the Calvinist view of the world and man are basically congenial is borne out to some degree by an interesting fact. John Calvin wrote only one poem, as far as we know, during his life, and that one poem contains an imitation of Juvenal. See Highet, *Juvenal the Satirist*, p. 212.

no more than ambulant sexual appetites are in reality dead, his satiric business of cutting away pretense can be realized only by cutting away the bodies of his enemies and reducing them to the reality of the skeleton. In this way the actions of the blood-revenger and the satirist are perfectly fused, and the pessimism and cruel methods of the Elizabethan satirist are given their ultimate expression.

The skull, that "terror to fat folkes," is Vendici's touchstone, the "steele glass" which he holds up to life to reflect its true image. Contemplating Gloriana's skull which he carries around as a memento mori, he asks it,

> Do's the Silke-worme expend her yellow labours
> For thee? for thee does she undoe herselfe?
> Are Lord-ships sold to maintaine Lady-ships
> For the poore benefit of a bewitching minute?
> Why dos yon fellow falsify hie-waies
> And put his life betweene the Judges lippes,
> To refine such a thing, keepes horse and men
> To beate their valours for her?
> Surely wee're all mad people. . . .

(III.5.75–83)

The skull here reduces all artificial beauty and all fancy dress to nonsense, and Vendici applies it with equal effectiveness to most of the usual forms of human vanity during the course of the play, proving again and again that you can "deceive men, but cannot deceive wormes." But his masterpiece, which combines both his functions as revenger and satirist, is the scene of revelation he arranges for the old Duke. Vendici's betrothed has some years earlier killed herself rather than submit to the Duke, and when the Duke commissions Vendici, now disguised as Piato, to find a young girl for him, Vendici dresses the skull in rich, hanging silks, veils it, and smears its lips with poison. Revenge is accomplished by leading the Duke to this "bony lady" and allowing him to kiss her in the belief that she is beautiful. This is more than revenge, for the scene that Vendici arranges here is the true image of lust. In his view of life, beauty is no more than a skull dressed in gorgeous coverings, the luxurious embrace is not life clasping life but death touching death, and the lecherous kiss is the seal on the death warrant.

The Duke does not die immediately of the poison, and Vendici arranges another scene of truth before finally dispatching him with the dagger. While his tongue is being eaten away by the poison, the Duke is forced to be a spectator at a meeting of his Duchess and his bastard, Spurio, in which they reveal their incestuous love for one another and their common hatred of the Duke. The first of Vendici's arranged scenes exposes in symbolic terms the true nature of the Duke's entire life and of lust in general, while the second scene restates the same truth in more realistic terms.

We have seen many times already that the satirist for all his attempts to present himself as merely honest in his evaluation of the world, no matter how grotesque his vision may be, inevitably reveals that he too is morally sick. This is as true of the satirist-revenger Vendici as it is of such obviously culpable creatures as Thersites or Macilente. In his reaction to the vicious, depraved world of the palace, his imagination has become infected, and, with the satirist's characteristic pessimism and lack of balance, he can see *only* rottenness, lust, and animality in the world. This narrowed and unhealthy view of life appears most clearly in the speeches in which he addresses the skull of Gloriana. When he reflects on her once living beauty, he can recall that,

> 'twas a face
> So farre beyond the artificiall shine
> Of any womans bought complexion
> That the uprightest man, (if such there be,
> That sinne but seaven times a day) broke custome
> And made up eight with looking after her.
> Oh she was able to ha made a Usurers sonne
> Melt all his patrimony in a kisse.

(I.1.23–30)

Even in thinking of the woman he loved he is unable to separate her beauty and virtue from the fleshly attraction it exerted in the sinful world. So obsessed does he become with the reality of the skull and the consequent meaninglessness of life and love that after a long discussion of how all living things come to the grave he can turn to Gloriana's skull and exclaim.

> And now me thinkes I cold e'en chide my selfe,
> For doating on her beauty.

(III.5.72–3)

The agonized conviction that all that lives is loathsome forces him to believe that any person not yet corrupted requires only the opportunity to become so. He tests this theory on his mother and sister when he is sent to them to persuade his sister, Castiza, to yield to Lussurioso. Castiza rejects the officer, but the mother after some urging gives in. The scene (II.i) is an excellent dramatization of the agonized and divided mind of the satirist. On one hand Vendici the son wants desperately to believe that his mother would not sell her own daughter, and this side of his nature is expressed in a series of asides such as, "I e'en quake to proceede, my spirit turnes edge" (line 122). On the other hand Vendici the satirist, scenting hidden corruption and unable to cease until he has uncovered it, can paint for Gratiana a tempting picture of the riches she will enjoy if she persuades her daughter, and can explain to her with oily plausibility,

You tooke great paines for her [Castiza]...,
Let her requite it now, tho it be but some;
You brought her forth, she may well bring you home.

(lines 113–15)

The sadistic delight with which the satirist in formal satire wields his whip and applies his burning medicines is translated in *The Revenger's Tragedy* to the blood lust of the revenger. Vendici not only sees his work of killing as necessary to reveal the truth about the world, but he comes to enjoy it and executes his victims with fiendish ingenuity and unnecessary cruelty. When he murders the old Duke he nails down his tongue with a dagger, threatens to tear up his eyelids "and make his eyes like Comets shine through bloud." He can exclaim with savage excitement —and bad critical judgment—"When the bad bleedes, then is the Tragedie good" (III.5.216). Vendici also resembles the satirist in his pride in his own ingenuity and his rhetorical skill. His brother Hippolito, who has a more practical turn of mind, can admire Vendici's long, railing speeches—"You flow well brother"—but again and again he is forced to break in on Vendici's excited explanations of elaborate schemes and sonorous speeches on human vanity to remind him of the workaday necessities of the situation.

Vendici also has the satirist's usual double nature, for he is at once the inspired prophet who sees that the depraved palace world is no more than a charnel house, and at the same time the very spirit of death itself. The play is thus a *danse macabre* in which one skeleton leads other skeletons to the grave. Vendici himself seems partially aware of his close relationship to the corruption he attacks so determinedly, for he remarks musingly,

My life's unnaturally to me, e'en compeld
As if I liv'd now when I should be dead.

(I.1.134–5)

By the end of *The Revenger's Tragedy* the traditional aims of both the blood revenger and the satirist have been achieved. The members of the viperish ducal family, the "nest of Dukes," who have destroyed Vendici's family and vitiated the kingdom have either been killed or banished—though there is some doubt about what happens to Supervacuo who simply disappears from the play after V.3.74. Antonio, the elderly noble whose wife was ravished by Spurio, is proclaimed the new duke; and Vendici's pun on Antonio's gray hair identifies his assumption of the throne with the return of the older and better society for which the satirist always strives:

Your hayre will make the silver age agen,
When there was fewer but more honest men.

(V.3.126–7)

At this point a satire could end—though it would be more optimistic than is usual—but Tourneur carries the action on to its logical conclusion. When the new Duke Antonio remarks on the strange manner in which the old Duke was murdered, Vendici, blinded by the satirist's usual delight with his own skill, cannot resist revealing that he and Hippolito were the murderers, and cannot help adding, with true craftsman's pride, "Twas some-what witty carried tho we say it." When Antonio expresses surprise, "You two?" Vendici preens himself a bit more, "None else ifaith my Lord nay twas well managde" V.3.142). Antonio's reaction is immediate: "Lay hands upon those villaines. . . . Beare 'em to speedy execution." His explanation for this action, that the brothers who found it so easy to murder one duke would find it equally easy to murder another, is a final judgment on the satirist-revenger. Except in certain rare moments of self-analysis Vendici, like other satirists, proudly exempts himself from his scene. He may move *in* a world of corruption, but he is not *of* it. Antonio, like the Elizabethan and Jacobean dramatists, sees, however, that the satirist-revenger is one with his world, one symptom of a generalized infection. Ironically, a thorough healing of the world then requires that the chief means for accomplishing that goal, the satirist-revenger, should himself be destroyed after his work is finished. Vendici in his last speech is half aware of this bitter necessity and can state the grim paradox which has been revealed:

> Tis time to die, when we are our selves our foes.

> (V.3.154)

These words, constituting as they do an attenuated tragic recognition, could never be spoken by the satirist, who always remains steadfast in his belief in his own righteousness. But Tourneur, like the other dramatists of his age, was unwilling to allow the tensions of the satiric character to remain unresolved or the narrow satiric view of the world to pass for reality unquestioned.

THE REVENGER'S TRAGEDY

Adams, Henry Hitch. "Cyril Tourneur on Revenge," *JEGP,* XLVIII (1949), 72–87.

Barker, R. H. *Thomas Middleton.* New York, 1958, pp. 64–75.

Boas, Frederick S. *An Introduction to Stuart Drama.* Oxford, 1946, pp. 214–218.

Bowers, Fredson T. *Elizabethan Revenge Tragedy: 1587–1642.* Princeton, 1940, pp. 132–138.

Bradbrook, Muriel C. *Themes and Conventions of Elizabethan Tragedy.* Cambridge, Eng., 1957, pp. 165–174, 185.

Ekeblad, Inga-Stina. "An Approach to Tourneur's Imagery," *MLR,* LIV (1959), 489–498.

_____. "On the Authorship of *The Revenger's Tragedy,*" *English Studies,* XLI (1960), 225–240.

Eliot, T. S. *Selected Essays.* New Edition. New York, 1950, pp. 159–169.

Ellis-Fermor, Una. "The Imagery of 'The Revenger's Tragedie' and 'The Atheist's Tragedie,'" *MLR,* XXX (1935), 289–301.

_____. *The Jacobean Drama.* 4th rev. ed. London, 1958, pp. 153–169.

Eluchère, Henri, ed. *La Tragédie du Vengeur.* Collection Bilingue des Classiques Étrangers. Paris, 1959.

Foakes, R. A. "On the Authorship of *The Revenger's Tragedy,*" *MLR,* XLVIII (1953), 129–138.

_____, ed. *The Revenger's Tragedy.* The Revels Plays. London, and Cambridge, Mass., 1966, pp. xix–lxix.

Gibbons, Brian, ed. *The Revenger's Tragedy.* The New Mermaids. London, 1967.

Jenkins, Harold. "Cyril Tourneur," *RES,* XVII (1941), 21–36.

Legouis, Pierre. "Réflexions sur la recherche des sources: à propos de la 'Tragedie du vengeur,'" *Etudes Anglaises,* XII (1959), 47–55.

Lockert, Lacy. "The Greatest of Elizabethan Melodramas," in *Essays in Dramatic Literature: The Parrott Presentation Volume,* ed. Hardin Craig. Princeton, 1935, pp. 103–126.

McDonald, Charles Osborne. *The Rhetoric of Tragedy: Form in Stuart Drama.* Amherst, Mass., 1966, pp. 225–266.

Murray, Peter B. *A Study of Cyril Tourneur.* Philadelphia and London, 1964, pp. 173–257.

Nicoll, Allardyce, ed. *The Works of Cyril Tourneur.* London, 1929–1930, pp. 38–46.

Oliphant, E. H. C. "Tourneur and Mr. T. S. Eliot," *SP,* XXXII (1935).

Ornstein, Robert. "The Ethical Design of *The Revenger's Tragedy,*" *ELH,* XXI (1954), 81–93.

_____. *The Moral Vision of Jacobean Tragedy.* Madison, Wis., 1960 (reprinted 1965), pp. 105–118.

Peter, John. *Complaint and Satire in Early English Literature.* Oxford, 1956, pp. 255–273. [Cf. *"The Revenger's Tragedy* Reconsidered," *EIC,* VI (1956), 131–143.]

Prior, Moody E. *The Language of Tragedy.* New York, 1947, pp. 135–144.

Ribner, Irving. *Jacobean Tragedy: The Quest for Moral Order.* New York and London, 1962, pp. 75–86.

Ross, Lawrence J., ed. *The Revenger's Tragedy.* Regents Renaissance Drama Series. Lincoln, Nebraska, 1966, pp. xxiii–xxx.

Salingar, L. G. " 'The Revenger's Tragedy' and the Morality Tradition," *Scrutiny*, VI (1938), 402–422.

_____. *"The Revenger's Tragedy:* Some Possible Sources," *MLR*, LX (1965), 3–12.

_____. "Tourneur and the Tragedy of Revenge," in *The Age of Shakespeare*, ed. Boris Ford. Baltimore, 1955, pp. 334–354.

Schoenbaum, Samuel. "Internal Evidence and the Attribution of Elizabethan Plays," *BNYPL*, LXV (1961), 102–124.

_____. *Middleton's Tragedies: A Critical Study.* New York, 1955, pp. 3–35.

_____. *"The Revenger's Tragedy:* Jacobean Dance of Death," *MLQ*, XV (1954), 201–207.

Tomlinson, T. B. "The Morality of Revenge: Tourneur's Critics," *EIC*, X (1960), 134–147.

_____. *A Study of Elizabethan and Jacobean Tragedy.* Cambridge, Eng., and Melbourne, 1964, pp. 97–131.

Francis Beaumont
and
John Fletcher

PHILASTER AND CYMBELINE *

Harold S. Wilson

AT the beginning of the present century Professor A. H. Thorndike advanced two notable contentions in his book *The Inflence of Beaumont and Fletcher on Shakespeare*.[1] The first was that Beaumont and Fletcher had introduced a new dramatic genre to the Jacobean stage during the first decade of the seventeenth century, the genre of the heroic romance, with such plays as *Philaster, The Maid's Tragedy,* and *A King and No King*. This contention has scarcely been challenged since he so ably presented it, and certainly not successfully challenged. His second contention, however—that Shakespeare followed the fashion set by Beaumont and Fletcher in writing *Cymbeline, The Winter's Tale,* and *The Tempest* —has proved more controversial, though this contention still carries

---

* From *English Institute Essays, 1951*. New York, 1952, pp. 146–167. Reprinted by permission of the Columbia University Press.

1 Worcester, Mass.: Press of Oliver B. Wood, 1901.

enough weight to have gained the notice of Granville-Barker[2] and to have been recently endorsed, with some qualifications, by critics of the distinction of Una Ellis-Fermor[3] and E. M. W. Tillyard.[4] I should like to re-examine Professor Thorndike's second contention in this paper, with particular reference to the analogy he draws between *Philaster* and *Cymbeline*.

First, however, we should notice, for the sake of dismissing them, certain gratuitous assumptions which color Professor Thorndike's argument and which have also commended themselves to various later writers. There is the assumption that Shakespeare's latest plays represent a diminution of Shakespeare's dramatic powers, an assumption based upon the feeling that *Cymbeline* and the plays which followed it are somehow inferior to *Antony and Cleopatra* and the other tragedies,[5] an assumption common to Professor Thorndike and Lytton Strachey,[6] but incapable of real demonstration, since the last plays are very different in form and purpose from the great tragedies. Then there is the view (to quote Professor Thorndike) "that Shakespere almost never invented dramatic types. In his earliest plays he was a versatile imitator of current forms, and in his later work he was constantly adapting dramatic types used by other men."[7] Shakespeare, it would seem, lacked the ability, so conspicuous in Beaumont and Fletcher, to mold his own dramatic form. Fortunately, he was clever at imitation and quick to follow the changing fashions set by others. If the Jacobean audiences demanded romances of the Beaumont and Fletcher cut, Shakespeare was their humble servant.

This part of Professor Thorndike's hypothesis is, of course, designed to bolster his main argument that *Cymbeline* is imitated from *Philaster* and Shakespeare's last group of plays from the Beaumont and Fletcher type of romance. These assumptions are unsupported by any real examination of the development of Shakespeare's dramatic form. It is simply asserted that Shakespeare was an "adapter and transformer"[8] of other men's work, and we are expected to take this extraordinary assertion as self-evident.

Finally, there is the circumstance, fortunate for Professor Thorndike's argument, that it has not proved possible to establish by external evidence whether *Philaster* preceded *Cymbeline* or *Cymbeline* preceded *Philaster*. Both plays belong to the period 1608–1610; that is all we may safely

---

2 *Prefaces to Shakespeare: second series,* London, 1935, p. 234.

3 *The Jacobean Drama,* London, 1936, p. 268.

4 *Shakespeare's Last Plays,* London, 1938, pp. 6–10.

5 *The Influence of Beaumont and Fletcher on Shakspere,* pp. 6, 142, 145.

6 *Books and Characters,* London, 1922, p. 60.

7 *The Influence of Beaumont and Fletcher on Shakspere,* p. 160.

8 *Ibid.*

assert about their dating. Professor Thorndike, of course, thinks it extremely likely that *Philaster* came first; but if some unlooked-for evidence should one day turn up to show that *Cymbeline* preceded *Philaster,* his hypothesis would be in a sad plight.

Yet although Professor Thorndike's case depends in some measure upon the question of dating and the apparatus of critical assumption that we are agreed, I hope, to dismiss as irrelevant or worse, his argument does not rest simply upon these insubstantial grounds. He bases his contention chiefly upon his demonstration that Beaumont and Fletcher did introduce a new type of dramatic romance to the Jacobean stage during the first decade of the seventeenth century, a type of play different from anything Shakespeare had written before *Cymbeline,* and upon a detailed analysis of the plot, characterization, style, and stage effects of *Philaster* and *Cymbeline* designed to show that the resemblances between these two plays cannot be accidental. To quote his summing up,

> there are enough specific similarities to make it very probable that one play was directly suggested by the other. When we remember that both plays were written at nearly the same time, for the same company, and by dramatists who must have been acquainted, the probability approaches certainty. . . . It is not only practically certain that *Philaster* was written for the King's Men while Shakspere was still writing for that company; it is also probable that it was written before *Cymbeline.* In that case we could not escape the conclusion that Shakspere was indebted to *Philaster.*[9]

Professor Thorndike assumes, with little further argument, that *The Winter's Tale* and *The Tempest* belong to the same type as *Cymbeline* and must therefore reflect a less specific, but still definite, influence of Beaumont and Fletcher.[10] With the latter suggestion we need not much concern ourselves, for the weight of Professor Thorndike's argument rests upon the analogy he traces between *Philaster* and *Cymbeline.* We shall accordingly treat that analogy as providing the only substantial ground of his conclusions.

Though it is a great commonplace, it may be remarked by way of preliminary that analogies are often misleading. In literary criticism, especially, they are dangerous tools. With something less than metaphysical ingenuity, one may draw analogies, more or less striking, between Sophocles' Queen Jocasta and the Wife of Bath or between *Paradise Lost* and *Tom Jones;* and what has actually been done with Shakespeare's *Tempest* in this line almost passes belief. By a tactful selection of criteria,

---

[9] *Ibid.,* pp. 156–157. The resemblance between the two plays had earlier been pointed out by B. Leonhardt (*Anglia,* VIII [1885], 424 ff.), who attributed the alleged "imitation" to Beaumont and Fletcher. See also C. M. Gayley, *Beaumont the Dramatist,* New York, 1914, pp. 390–391, and D. M. McKeithan, *The Debt to Shakespeare in the Beaumont and Fletcher Plays,* Austin, Texas, 1938.

[10] *The Influence of Beaumont and Fletcher on Shakspere,* pp. 161 ff.

it would not be too difficult to argue that both *Cymbeline* and *Philaster* are imitated from Robert Greene's *James IV* or from *King Lear*. The analogy with *Lear,* to take but one example from those here suggested,[11] might go like this: Cymbeline is Lear, with one ungrateful daughter instead of three. He is also the father of Arethusa. Iachimo is Edmund, turning his attentions upon Cordelia and Edgar, who are at once Imogen and Posthumus, Arethusa and Philaster. And surely Belarius is an unmistakable Kent, a little damaged by his long exile, whose *alter ego* is Bellario's father, the Lord Dion. So we might go on; but we have all played this game and need not further remind ourselves that analogy hunting comes easy to an irresponsible fancy.

Part of the trouble with Professor Thorndike's analogy between *Philaster* and *Cymbeline* is the highly selective nature of his criteria for comparison and a certain ambiguity about the criteria themselves. This is how Professor Thorndike compares the plots of the two plays:

> The historical narrative and the Italian expedition of Posthumus have no parallels in *Philaster,* and most of the Megra affair and the rising of the mob in *Philaster* have no parallels in *Cymbeline.* In the main, however, the plots are strikingly similar.
>
> Imogen, heiress to the throne, is destined by her royal father to marry his boorish step-son, Cloten; but she is wedded to a noble youth, Leonatus Posthumus. Arethusa, only daughter of the King of Calabria, is likewise destined by her father to marry the boorish Spanish prince, Pharamond, but she is in love with Philaster the rightful heir. Leonatus is favorably contrasted by the courtiers with Cloten, and so Philaster is contrasted with Pharamond. Both Leonatus and Philaster are driven from court by the royal fathers. As he is leaving Arethusa's apartments, Philaster has an encounter with Pharamond, and as Leonatus is leaving Imogen, he has an enocunter with Cloten. In the absence of Leonatus, Iachimo tries to seduce Imogen, and Pharamond makes similar proposals to Arethusa. Both are repulsed. Iachimo slanders Imogen to Leonatus, and Arethusa is falsely accused to Philaster by Dion. Imogen is brought to despair by Leonatus' letter charging her with unfaithfulness, and Arethusa is likewise in anguish when similarly upbraided to the face by Philaster. Each lover has a passionate soliloquy in which he denounces his mistress and all womankind. Imogen leaves the court in disguise to seek Leonatus and, after dismissing Pisanio, loses her way; and Arethusa parts from the hunting party to wander "O'er mountains, through brambles, pits, and floods." Both, because falsely slandered, wish to die. Each king is very much disturbed at his daughter's absence. Cymbeline accuses Pisanio of knowing where she is, and so Calabria accuses Dion. Arethusa is wounded by Philaster, and Imogen is struck down by Leonatus. Finally the disentanglements of the two plots are made in similar ways. In *Philaster,* Bellario explains that in spite of her page's clothes, she is a woman, and Megra confesses that she has falsely

---

11 The other suggested analogies, which are even less substantial, the ingenious reader may amuse himself with deciphering, or not, as he pleases.

slandered Arethusa. In *Cymbeline*, Imogen explains and Iachimo confesses. In *Philaster*, all are forgiven, even Megra and Pharamond; so in *Cymbeline* Iachimo is pardoned; and in each play the lovers are happily united under the king's favor.

These parallels indicate a close similarity between the two plots, yet after all the similarity does not lie so much in the stories as in the situations. The basis of the Imogen story is probably the ninth novel of the second day in the Decamerone. This story, the story of Iachimo's trick, forms no part of *Philaster*. To this Iachimo-Imogen story, however, Shakspere added a dozen or so situations which are almost exact counterparts of situations in *Philaster*.[12]

But a group of dramatic "situations" do not constitute a dramatic action. The situation of Philaster in the opening of his play roughly corresponds to the situation of Hamlet; the situation of Bellario approximates that of Shakespeare's Julia and Viola; and we might easily multiply similar parallels from *Much Ado* and other of the earlier Shakespearean comedies. But this does not mean that the plot of *Philaster* derives in any part from Shakespeare. The situations of the romantic plays of Shakespeare and of Beaumont and Fletcher are the materials of romance which they are every other playwright of their time used in common. To select certain stock romance situations from two plays like *Philaster* and *Cymbeline* and to conclude from this that one play must be imitated from the other is like comparing, let us say, the David of Verocchio and the Statue of Liberty and concluding that because they contain similar materials the one must be imitated from the other.

By means of this innocent confusion between "plot" and "situation," Professor Thorndike has, in fact, largely avoided comparing the conduct of the action in the two plays. Had he done so with any care, he must surely have concluded that they were very different.

Let us notice some of these differences. The plot of *Cymbeline* is a double plot in this sense: it is the story of what happened to Imogen and of what happened to her brothers. The two stories are not parallel and do not grow out of each other; each story has a separate exposition, a separate climax, and a distinct culmination. After we have followed Imogen's story for two whole acts, she wanders into her brothers' story by accident, and from then on the two stories are cleverly sandwiched together to produce a finely complicated climax.

The plot of *Philaster* is nothing like this. From beginning to end it is one story, the story of what happened to Philaster, and the fates of Arethusa and Bellario-Euphrasia are parallel and contrasted plot elements that depend upon Philaster's fate and support his story. The controlling idea of *Philaster*, again, has nothing to do with Shakespeare's *Cymbeline*, but rather finds its proper parallel in Fletcher's own *Faithful Shepherdess*.

---

[12] *The Influence of Beaumont and Fletcher on Shakspere*, pp. 152–154.

There we find disinterested love represented in Clorin; normal love in the pairs of Amoret and Perigot, Alexis and the reformed Chloe, Daphnis and the reformed Amarillis; lust in the Sullen Shepherd and the unregenerate Amarillis and Chloe. So in *Philaster,* Bellario-Euphrasia stands for disinterested love, Philaster and Arethusa for normal love, Megra and Pharamond for lust.

The main sources of *Cymbeline* are clear enough. Shakespeare retells, whether at first or second hand, the story of the ninth novel of the second day in Boccaccio's *Decameron* and adds certain materials from Holinshed for his framework and second plot. The sources of *Philaster* are by no means so clear (though no scholar likes to admit that the authors may have made up the story themselves); but it is at least clear that *Philaster* is not derived from Boccaccio or Holinshed. Shakespeare must have had a fine time with his sources if he had to watch the plot of *Philaster* constantly while he was juggling with Boccaccio and Holinshed. According to Professor Thorndike, Shakespeare would have had to turn from Boccaccio's story to elaborate traits and situations for Imogen suggested by the two characters of Arethusa and Bellario; and in modeling his Posthumus upon Philaster he must surely have felt embarrassed to recognize in Philaster traits of his own Hamlet.

But the really essential and decisive difference between the two plots lies in Shakespeare's technique of preparation as distinguished from the Beaumont and Fletcher technique of surprise. Coleridge long ago pointed it out: "Expectation in preference to surprize. . . . As the feeling with which we startle at a shooting star, compared with that of watching the sunrise at the pre-established moment, such and so low is surprize compared with expectation."[13]

In *Cymbeline* we are prepared to grasp the implications of each situation as it arises, as the actors themselves are not. The effect of such preparation is cumulative. We first see Posthumus's protestation of fidelity to Imogen:

> I will remain
> The loyal'st husband that did e'er plight troth.

We then learn of the Queen's poison plot, but neither the Queen, who gives the poison to Pisanio, Pisanio, who gives it to Imogen, nor Imogen, who ultimately takes it, knows what we learn from Cornelius, that it is actually but a sleeping potion. We witness the wager scene, learn all the circumstanaces of Iachimo's attempt, and see his successful ruse of concealment in Imogen's chamber whereby he betrays both Imogen and Posthumus. From then on (II, iii) we are prepared to observe the mounting irony of the succeeding action. Cloten comes in the morning with his musicians to serenade Imogen, and we have the comic moment

---

[13] "The Characteristics of Shakespeare," *Coleridge's Shakespearean Criticism,* ed. by T. M. Raysor, London, 1930, I, 225.

of his emphatic rejection. But the comedy is sharply interrupted by Imogen's discovery of the loss of her bracelet; and her premonitory

> I hope it be not gone to tell my lord
> That I kiss ought but he

reminds us poignantly that the consequences are likely to be far worse than even she knows. With all her high courage, she has no chance of avoiding the snare laid for her; we have seen it, but she has not.

The ensuing scenes gradually increase the sense of horror impending and closing in on its victim. We see Pisanio receive his instructions from Posthumus to kill Imogen on the way to Milford Haven; and though we are slightly reassured by Pisanio's

> I am ignorant in what I am commanded,

Imogen's rapturous outburst,

> O, for a horse with wings! Hear'st thou, Pisanio?
> He is at Milford Haven!

marks for us the beginning of her deepest pathos. The moment of her realization that she has been betrayed is supported for us by her impassioned denial and appeal to Pisanio, whose device of disguising her as a page brings about the reunion with her brothers at the cave of Belarius. Here, for a moment, the idyllic setting and the gentleness of her welcome bring a lull in Imogen's misfortunes; but the other shadow of the plot against her, set in motion by Pisanio's parting gift of the Queen's poison, soon closes in again. The sleeping Imogen is placed beside the headless body of Cloten, and she wakens, but dimly realizing her surroundings at first, as she finds the corpse half-concealed with flowers, and the flowers soaked in blood; then the dawning realization that there is no head, that the clothes, the very limbs seem to be her husband's, that Pisanio, as she thinks, has murdered him.

We know better; but it is not this knowledge that matters at the moment, it is Imogen's suffering. And all that separates it from the pathos of Lear's attempts to revive the dead Cordelia is that we are spared the recognition of the inevitability of it all. It comes close to tragedy, so close that in the reunion of Imogen and Posthumus at the end there can be no rejoicing, but only tenderness and tears. It is tragedy subdued to a gentler, a sentimental key, with a consequent loss of intensity. But it is by no means the Beaumont and Fletcher vein of sentimentality.

The opening situation of *Philaster* shows the hero in love with the Princess Arethusa, whose father intends to marry her to the cowardly Pharamond. Philaster presents his devoted page Bellario to Arethusa as a liaison in forwarding their love. Here is the first major difference in method. Bellario is represented to us as Bellario, a page. We do not learn her proper sex or identity or why she is devoted to Philaster until the very end; so complete is her disguise that her own father, Dion, does not recognize her; indeed, he never gives his daughter a thought, beyond casually mentioning near the beginning of the play (I, i, 333–35) that she has gone on a pilgrimage. We witness Imogen's disguise as a page and fully understand the circumstances of it. All the time she is disguised, our awareness of her identity allows us to understand not merely her actions but also her feelings, and this deepens the pathos of her predicament, especially in the denouement. There is no surprise and no trick about Imogen's disguise; the intention is to let us see all the springs of her actions and to feel the full significance for her of each following situation as it arises.

Bellario's situation actually offers considerable psychological possibilities, but they are deliberately ignored. Bellario loves Philaster and must act as his representative with the woman he loves, who (unlike Viola with the Duke and Olivia) also loves him. Furthermore, Bellario is falsely accused of illicit relations with Arethusa, and the man Bellario loves believes the calumny. Philaster unhesitatingly takes the word of Megra and the nobles against Arethusa, whom he loves, and the page, whose single-hearted devotion to himself he has already remarked. When he passionately accuses Bellario face to face, she sadly protests her innocence and her devotion to Philaster; but neither of them seeks an explanation of the misunderstanding, and Philaster's suspicions are but lulled, to rouse with new welcome when he finds Bellario bending over the fainting Arethusa in the hunting scene. He dismisses Bellario (though one might expect a man of such strong feelings to direct his first violence against her; as usual, she seeks no explanation or vindication, but sadly departs), and Philaster exhorts Arethusa to kill him. Since she declines, he wounds her. Philaster, himself wounded by the countryman who intervenes to protect Arethusa, then comes upon Bellario sleeping from exhaustion and wounds her as she lies asleep with this remarkable explanation:

> Hark! I am pursued. You gods,
> I'll take this offer'd means of my escape:
> They have no mark to know me but my blood,
> If she [i.e., Arethusa] be true; if false, let mischief light
> On all the world at once! Sword, print my wounds
> Upon this sleeping boy! I ha' none, I think,
> Are mortal, nor would I lay greater on thee.

The next instant Philaster repents what is surely the most astonishing lapse in any hero of Jacobean romance (though no comment is made upon it anywhere in the play) and urges Bellario to lay the blame for wounding Arethusa upon him, which she, of course, fails to do, taking it upon herself to protect him; then he crawls out of the bushes, where he has impulsively hidden, and assumes it himself, and both of them are arrested.

All of this is, of course, the most evident artifice, and we are not to pause and ask why Bellario and Arethusa and Philaster act at any particular moment as they do. The action is full of excitement, swift turns, and surprises; logical motivation and consistency of character are neglected, that each turn of the plot may be more unexpected than the last.

When the denouement comes, we see the King reconciled to the marriage of Arethusa and Philaster. There has perforce been some preparation for this through Philaster's quelling the popular uprising in his favor and the final discrediting of Pharamond. But the authors have one surprise left. The discredited Megra spitefully renews her accusation of Bellario. The king at once credits Megra and is bent only upon getting a confession from Bellario. He orders the page to be stripped and tortured. Philaster, who must be prevented from spoiling things, is tricked into an oath not to interfere. He offers to kill himself, but no one pays much attention to him. As Bellario is about to be stripped, she is obliged to break her oath (of which we hear now for the first time) and reveal herself as Euphrasia, the Lord Dion's daughter, dedicated to a hopeless love. She assures them that her love is selfless.

> Never, sir, will I
> Marry; it is a thing within my vow;
> But, if I may have leave to serve the princess,
> I shall have hope to live.

She, at least, has been consistent, and her role is the only element in the play which might tempt one to take it seriously. The beautiful lines she earlier speaks to Philaster:

> Alas, my lord, my life is not a thing
> Worthy your noble thoughts! 'tis not a life,
> 'Tis but a place of childhood thrown away

are of a piece with her modest renunciation at the end; but the picture of a tranquil *ménage-à-trois* with which the play closes is again too much for solemnity. "I, Philaster," says Arethusa majestically,

> Cannot be jealous, though you had a lady
> Drest like a page to serve you; nor will I
> Suspect her living here.—Come, live with me;
> Live free as I do. She that loves my lord,
> Cursed be the wife that hates her!

We might similarly consider the treatment of Arethusa. Her good name is traduced to her lover, as Imogen's is to Posthumus. But even to suggest the comparison is to see at once its absurdity. Arethusa makes a few rhetorical protestations when she is required to act:

> And I (the woful'st maid that ever lived,
> Forced with my hands to bring my lord to death)
> Do by the honour of a virgin swear
> To tell no hours beyond it!

But woeful she is not, unless in the figure she cuts beside the more attractive Bellario, who is obviously the feminine lead. For the most part, Arethusa preserves an inconspicuous calm throughout the tempestuous action to which she is submitted that at least saves her from being altogether ridiculous. Philaster is charming in his way, but he is closer to *opéra bouffe* or even musical comedy than to tragedy. Posthumus is not one of Shakespeare's strong characters. He is necessarily absent from the action during the middle part of the play, and he is built up for the climax by rather artificial means. But he has dignity and force in the difficult wager scene, and in the end he seems a fitting husband for Imogen, which is all that need be required of him. He lacks the volatility of Philaster, and certainly he is not half so much in love with easeful death. But he belongs in a serious play, and the other does not.

The other characters of *Philaster* are little more than conveniences of the plot. The King is a good cardboard tyrant, refreshing in his imperiousness because he always seems to know his own mind—which can hardly be said of Shakespeare's Cymbeline—even when he changes it abruptly as the plot requires. Since neither monarch has any clearly marked character, neither needs to reform in order to accept the culmination of events and preside benevolently at the end. Megra is a stock villainess, "a lascivious lady," like Chloe in *The Faithful Shepherdess*, except that she does not reform; and Pharamond is a stock villain, the cowardly lecher. Beaumont and Fletcher do not run the risk of puzzling their audience—to say nothing of later readers—with the subtler characterization of a Cloten, a bully too dull to know fear. Pharamond is lecherous, boastful, cowardly, and nothing more. The Calabrian lords are a faint and ineffectual chorus, with the prize for fatuity going to Dion, who leads the attempt to turn Philaster from his allegiance to the King by swearing that he has seen Arethusa's misbehavior with the page Bellario.

Thus, to belittle *Philaster* is not, of course, to do it justice. It is not meant to be a study of human pathos or human character, for all the high-pitched emotional tone of the piece, even to the relatively slight extent that *Cymbeline* is. *Philaster* is a lively series of incidents contrived with great ingenuity to provide constant excitement and surprise and to issue agreeably with the recognition and reward of virtue, the dismissal of the wicked in disgrace. And it is nothing more. *Cymbeline* is, by comparison, more old-fashioned in method, more complicated, and altogether more ambitious. At least as ingeniously plotted, it employs an utterly different method in the conduct of the action: preparation of the audience to perceive the dramatic ironies of situation, the pathos of character, the joys and sorrows of reunion; it aims at effecting the gratification of expectancy rather than the shock of surprise. *Cymbeline* admits all kinds of ancient romance conventions and stage devices in which Beaumont and Fletcher were little interested—stately pageants, riddles, masques, the god from the machine. The younger dramatists seem to have regarded such effects as unnecessary. Their new technique in the dramatic romance was actually a remarkable simplification of existing stage conventions. In *Philaster,* apart from the ingenious plotting there is scarcely any conspicuous stage device used save that of disguise—and that in the single example of Bellario. But they carried their economy much further, virtually eliminating character study and stripping the play down to the bare essentials of swift emotional dialogue and clever plot. One might say, if the figure would hold, that *Cymbeline* is a stately and somewhat overloaded Elizabethan matron, bejeweled and brocaded, with filmy laces, ruff, farthingale, and pelisse, old-fashioned and stiff in fashionable Jacobean society, but still imposing; *Philaster* is a court shepherdess under the Stuarts, sophisticated to extreme simplicity and as shallow as her simplicity would make her seem.

Cymbeline has fully as much artifice as *Philaster,* or more, as the foregoing figure would suggest, but it is directed to a more serious end. *Philaster* is written in the middling mood of pure recreation. Its stormy passions, its perils and reverses, are never meant to be taken seriously. It is like a ride on a roller coaster. It is breathless and exciting, and the whole technique is directed to keeping the roller coaster going through its dizzy swerves and plunges and recoveries, until the ride comes to a delicious end with everybody safe and sound and pleased with the fun— and it may be very good fun, if you happen to like it. Some people do not, and denounce it as a fraud or a menace; but this is not fair to the operators of the entertainment. They had no nefarious design upon the art of the drama, but only strove to amuse people and to make some money in the process.

We have now considered the plots and the characters of the two plays and found them to be in important ways unlike. I am enough of an Aristotelian to think that the action of a play is its essence, that the characters tend to take their natures from the nature of the action—if the playwrights knew their business, that is, as Shakespeare and Beaumont and Fletcher undoubtedly do. The characters of a play like *Cymbeline* are not extracted from suggestions in someone else's play and "stuck on" to the action as one mounts postage stamps in an album. Rather, the impression of character, however impressive or unimpressive it may be, emerges from the developing action, emerges as we watch the characters act. This impression of individual and recognizable characters is very much stronger and subtler in *Cymbeline* than in *Philaster;* and so it is not likely that any of the characters of *Cymbeline* is "imitated," in any meaningful sense, from the characters of *Philaster.*

It remains to speak of Professor Thorndike's two other criteria, the "style" (or, more precisely, the verse) of the two plays, and the "stage effects"; and this we may do rather briefly. If anyone believes that the verse of one play may be at all successfully imitated from the verse of another play which has an essentially different theme and structure, he does not, to my mind, have a very clear conception of what poetry is like. And as for the stage effects, if Shakespeare, who had been writing successful plays for at least fifteen years before Beaumont and Fletcher started, had to be prompted by these juniors in order to avail himself of the pageantry of the court masques in his last plays, then he must surely have suffered something like that mental crisis and indeed collapse, before or during his famous "last period," of which some critics would fain persuade us. Nothing short of a mental breakdown could explain this extraordinary loss of initiative and command over one of the familiar elements of stage technique that Shakespeare had made skillful use of in plays like *A Midsummer Night's Dream* and indeed most of the earlier comedies. The hypothesis of a mental collapse during Shakespeare's later years might attract us, were it not for the fact of the plays that he wrote during that time. Of course, there are those who say that the Earl of Oxford wrote them for him.

"The question of Beaumont and Fletcher's influence on Shakespeare," writes Dr. Tillyard, "has, in fact, been warehoused rather than disposed of for good."[14] This paper has attempted to take it out of the warehouse and air it a little. But it has also, I hope, a relevance to a more general issue—the issue of sources and analogues and what use we should make of them in literary criticism. The principle which this paper tends to support, it seems to me, is that the first and best analogue in considering any author's work is that author's other work. Our first critical obligation is to try to understand the author's whole work in all its interrelations. There are, to be sure, many aids to doing this outside the *corpus* of the author, and the study of his work in relation to its indubitable sources is one of the most important. But we must not confuse sources with partial analogues, nor should we venture to introduce the vague and dubious conception of "literary influence" to explain such partial analogues. For a great author like Shakespeare, we must never lose sight of the aim to comprehend his work as an organic and interrelated whole, growing as a tree grows from a young sapling until it towers above the forest. When we treat some casual or conjectural circumstance—that Beaumont and Fletcher may have written *Philaster* for Shakespeare's company; that this play or others like it enjoyed such popular success that Shakespeare was bound to imitate them—as of decisive critical importance, we not only imply a decided disparagement of Shakespeare's ability; we disregard the vital principle that Shakespeare's dramatic art was a continuous growth. If we would understand *Cymbeline,* or any other play of Shakespeare's, we must consider it primarily in relation to the whole body of his work,

---

[14] *Shakespeare's Last Plays,* p. 6.

in relation to this only indubitable evidence of his artistic growth. And the same holds for Beaumont and Fletcher. The best clue to *Philaster* is not in *Cymbeline* or any other play of Shakespeare, but in the other plays with which Beaumont and Fletcher, those enterprising and estimable collaborators, graced the Jacobean stage.

See other studies in Beaumont and Fletcher bibliography (below, pp. 361–362).

THE HIGH DESIGN OF
A KING AND NO KING *

Arthur Mizener

It is *A King and No King* which Dryden described as "the best of [Beaumont and Fletcher's] designs, the most approaching to antiquity, and the most conducing to move pity." Apparently it was the play's power to move him which determined this opinion, for he added: " 'Tis true, the faults of the plot are so evidently proved, that they can no longer be denied. The beauties of it must therefore lie. . . . in the lively touches of the passion."[1] These remarks come very close to implying that a play can be formally ordered, given design, in terms of "the lively touches of the passion" rather than assuming, as most neoclassic theory does, that these "lively touches" are minor elements which have by their nature to be subordinated to a design largely determined by the plot. And Dryden goes on to do some very queer things to the seventeenth-century concept of Nature in order to defend Beaumont and Fletcher

* Reprinted from *Modern Philology*, Vol. 38, 1940, pp. 133–154 by permission of The University of Chicago Press. Copyright 1953 by The University of Chicago.

1 "The Grounds of Criticism in Tragedy," *The Essays of John Dryden,* ed. W. P. Ker (Oxford, 1926), I, 212. What kind of faults of plot Dryden had in mind is indicated by his remarking a little earlier that "how defective Shakespeare and Fletcher have been in all their plots, Mr. Rymer has discovered in his criticisms" (p. 211).

on something like these grounds.[2] The reason for this stretching of the neoclassic theory is that Dryden feels *A King and No King* to be a better play than it can be shown to be by any analysis based on the strict interpretation of neoclassic theory which Rymer adopted. This is in effect to argue that the play is not a bad example of the best kind of tragedy but a good example of an "inferior sort of tragedies."[3]

Throughout the nineteenth century, however, the possibility of explaining the success of the Beaumont and Fletcher plays (for they are all alike in this respect) in this way was lost sight of. The nineteenth-century critics were intent on showing that all successful plays were functional in terms of character as they conceived it and presented the human situation in terms of their moral predilections.[4] They therefore

[2] "The beauties of [*A King and No King*] must therefore lie either in the lively touches of the passion; or we must conclude, as I think we may, that even in imperfect plots there are less degrees of Nature, by which some faint emotions of pity and terror are raised in us: . . . for nothing can move our nature, but by some natural reason, which works upon passions. And, since we acknowledge the effect, there must be something in the cause."

[3] Rymer suffered from none of Dryden's sensitivity and was content with the unqualified damnation of the play to which the strict application of neoclassic theory led: "The characters are all *improbable* and *unproper* in the highest degree, besides that both these, their actions and all the lines of the play run so wide from the *Plot,* that scarce ought could be imagin'd more contrary" (*The Tragedies of the Last Age* [1692], p. 59). But it is not to be supposed that Rymer, shrewd critic that he was, did not see what Beaumont and Fletcher were up to; it was just that he disliked what they were up to so much that he refused to grant it even a qualified validity: "Had some Author of the last age given us the character of *Phedra,* they (to thicken the *Plot*) would have brought her in burning of Churches, poisoning her Parents, prostituting her self to the Grooms, solliciting her Son face to face, with all the importunity and impudence they could imagin; and never have left dawbing so long as there might remain the least cranny for either *pity* or *probability.* They would never have left her, till she had swell'd to such a *Toad,* as nothing but an *audience of brass* could fit the sight of her" (*ibid.,* p. 92). This is an amusingly accurate description of the method of authors of the last age, however it ignores the frequently achieved intention behind the method and however ignorant it is of the flexibility of audiences in respect to moral and dramatc conventions.

[4] I have used the word "moral" in two commonly accepted but distinct senses in this essay. In the first sense the word refers to the established customs and manners of a particular age and society. In this sense of the word Beaumont and Fletcher seemed very moral to their own age and very immoral to the nineteenth century. This is the sense of the word in the above passage and in the quotation from Ward (n. 27); it is the sense which lies behind the quotation from Hazlitt below. In the second sense the word refers to some meaningful order of the universe in terms of which events and actions are felt to be good or bad. In this sense Beaumont and Fletcher are neither moral nor immoral by intention, though the underlying mood of their plays certainly implies a kind of sensationalism. It is in this sense of the word that I suppose the greatest plays to convince us of their truth. I do not believe there is any difficulty in distinguishing these two uses of the word, and it is almost impossible to avoid them, without awkward circumlocutions, in a paper of this kind.

undertook to show, and nothing is easier, that *A King and No King* was defective in plot, that is, that it was not formally ordered in terms of the narrative, and that, where it was not defective in plot, it was painfully lacking in regard for nineteenth-century decorum. This conclusion ought to have proved, as Rymer's conclusion ought to have, that Beaumont and Fletcher's play was a failure. Yet the best of the nineteenth-century critics continued to admit that the play in some sense succeeds. Hazlitt is a good example; he found, on the one hand, that "what may be called the love-scenes...have all the indecency and familiarity of a brothel," and, on the other, that the play was "superior in power and effect."[5]

The more or less explicit contradiction in these nineteenth-century judgments between the theoretical conclusion and the actual response to the play is the result of the assumption that narrative form is the only kind of form a play can have, that the narrative form must therefore of necessity be the bearer of the play's meaning and value, and that "the lively touches of the passion" must be subordinated to it. With the very greatest kind of plays this assumption is probably justified, for in the final analysis we are not satisfied to be moved by what we find on consideration not to be natural or morally true in the deepest sense. But there are not very many plays of this kind, and Beaumont and Fletcher's are not among them. Their plays are of a different kind, and critics who analyze them on an assumption not relevant to this kind are bound, if they are at all sensitive, to land in a contradiction between what they prove by analysis and what they feel about the plays.

It is the object of this essay to try to define the kind of play Beaumont and Fletcher wrote and to try to show how successfully they did so. The primary concern of their kind of play is to order its material, not in terms of narrative form, but in terms of what might be called emotional or psychological form. Beaumont and Fletcher's aim was to generate in the audience a patterned sequence of responses, a complex series of feelings and attitudes so stimulated and related as to give to each its maximum effectiveness and yet to keep all in harmonious balance. The ultimate ordering form in their plays is this emotional form, and the

---

5 "Lectures on the Dramatic Literature of the Age of Elizabeth," *Collected Works,* V, 252. This opinion, common to most of the early nineteenth-century critics, can be traced through the great historians of the drama to such diverse contemporary critics as Miss M. C. Bradbrook and P. E. More. The nineteenth-century critics will of course have little to do with Rymer, but the increasingly popular neoclassicism of Mr. Eliot, who in his ambiguous way finds Rymer "a critic of whom Dryden speaks highly, and of whom I should be tempted to speak more highly still" (*John Dryden,* p. 55), may yet revive not only the general but the specific argument of *The Tragedies of the Last Age.* More finds Rymer's remarks on *The Maid's Tragedy* "diabolically shrewd" (*With the Wits,* p. 6), and Miss Bradbrook's combination of moral and formal objections to Beaumont and Fletcher implies a similar attitude (see n. 28 below).

narrative, though necessarily the ostensible object, is actually with them only a means to the end of establishing this rich and careful arrangement of responses.[6]

There is nothing particularly novel about the idea that a complex of emotions generated by a loosely bound set of scenes—loosely bound, that is, as narrative—was the primary object of a Jacobean play. The consequences of approaching Beaumont and Fletcher this way have not, however, been very much considered. Yet Beaumont and Fletcher, perhaps more skilfully than most of their contemporaries, directed all the resources of their plays to the induction of such complexes of emotions; they learned, as so many Jacobean dramatists did not, how to manage character and event so that they became useful to this kind of play rather than irrelevant or at best intolerably confused. This is not to say that Webster, for example, constructed a less valuable pattern of responses. I mean only that Beaumont and Fletcher showed more skill in using narrative elements such as character and event to this end. While Webster, Ford, and Tourneur frequently sacrificed the narrative to the demands of emotional form, Beaumont and Fletcher not only showed less willingness to lose the advantage of the representational illusion of an ordered narrative but succeeded in finding out how to use it to further the effect of the emotional form.

It is probably at least in part because Beaumont and Fletcher constructed the narrative so carefully as a means of supporting and enriching the emotional form that critics have been able to suppose it was the end, the ultimate ordering form, and not merely a means, in their plays. There is not much chance that a critic will focus his attention exclusively on the narrative in Webster, for example.[7] But the skill with which Beaumont and Fletcher construct the narrative of their plays invites just this kind of misunderstanding.

There is plainly another reason, however, why critics have been unwilling to approach Beaumont and Fletcher as they approach Webster. Webster, though his range of feelings is narrow, appears sincere; it is felt that the mood his plays explore is serious. Critics are willing, therefore, not only to pass over the defective narrative in his plays but even to forgive him what are at least for us faults of the emotional form.[8]

6 "The power of [*A King and No King*] consists in the effective manner in which the feelings of the different persons are brought into play, balanced one against another, so as to form a sort of network of conflicting emotions. . . . The play is like a piece of music arranged in four parts, and performed all at once on different instruments" (*Quarterly Review*, LXXXIII [1848], 389). This anonymous essay is a striking exception to the general run of nineteenth-century criticism of Beaumont and Fletcher.

7 Unless he be William Archer; see *The Old Drama and the New*, pp. 52–62.

8 Webster's frequent failure to provide even the necessary minimum of motivation or to make a pretense at narrative logic probably needs no illustration. As for the emotional form, it is of course difficult to say how congruous the scenes which seem

But, though the range of feelings presented in a Beaumont and Fletcher play is by no means narrow, the lightness of the mood which seems to lie behind their emotional effects offends many critics.

I do not intend in this paper to argue with this judgment of the moral shortcomings which are supposed to inhere in the mood which Beaumont and Fletcher project with such skill in their plays.[9] It has already been discussed too much at the expense of ignoring the skill itself. Beaumont and Fletcher succeeded in writing plays embodying a mood into which their audience could enter wholeheartedly, and so found "(that which is the only grace and setting forth of a Tragedy) a full and understanding Auditory." And the dramatic presentation of that mood was accomplished through the use of a set of moral and dramatic conventions which were understood and accepted in Beaumont and Fletcher's day. Many of the charges, for example, which are made against their plays are the result of a failure to remember that "it was the letter and not the spirit of action that counted with Elizabethan [and to an even greater extent Jacobean] audiences."[10] The substitution of one woman for another, the repentance of villains, such tricks of plot as those by which an Arbaces or an Angelo is freed from the guilt of his evil impulses apparently had for these audiences no "moral valency" at all. It is perfectly understandable that such a baroque art as Beaumont and Fletcher's should offend critics of a serious cast of mind. But if there is to be any understanding of the exact nature of the mood

---

emotionally inharmonious to us appeared in Webster's own day, but such comic scenes as I. i. 83–150 and III. iii. 1–42 of *The Duchess of Malfi* seem to most modern readers failures, and Mr. Lucas has called attention to the disturbing effect of Webster's apparently awkward use of the conventional "cute" children and the "secret yet a certaine meane" for murder of the revenge play.

9 I do not mean to imply that in that ultimate critical judgment which is so largely a moral judgment these charges of immorality may not prove true; though I cannot believe that the attitude toward life implied by Beaumont and Fletcher's plays is not a reflection of the attitude which dominated the society for which they wrote and of which they were a part, rather than the result of any special immorality in them. Unlike Webster or Jonson, they were not seriously in revolt against the values of a large part of their world. Their plays are complex and delicate projections of one of the attitudes widespread in their day, just as Dekker's plays are a confused and crude projection of another. The moral quality implicit in both is not primarily a personal, but a group attitude; for "beide [Beaumont and Fletcher] nehmen von Anfang an unter den Literaten eine bevorzugte und exklusive Stellung ein, und beide betrachteten das Leben unter dem Gesichtswinkel der Aristocraten" (Philip Aronstein, "Die Moral des Beaumont-Fletcherschen Dramas," *Anglia,* XXXI [1908], 146).

10 M. C. Bradbrook, *Themes and Conventions of Elizabethan Tragedy,* p. 60. This fact undercuts even such considered judgments of narrative implication as G. O. Macaulay's observation that "an accidental discovery that the material conditions are not such as had been supposed is taken by Arbaces as an absolution from guilt, with which in fact it has little or nothing to do" (*Francis Beaumont,* p. 176).

embodied in their best plays, we shall simply have to grant them their right to the moral and dramatic conventions of their day by means of which that mood is given body and life. It will be time enough to condemn the mood of their plays, if we wish to, after they are understood.

A reader normally notices the narrative of a play first, and as you examine the narrative of *A King and No King* you are surprised—if you have read the textbooks—not only to discover how carefully planned the plot is, but to realize that there is a moral plainly implicit in that plot. To be sure, Beaumont and Fletcher are not particularly in earnest about it; they apparently care for it not so much because it is moral as because it can be used to arouse certain feelings in the audience. Nonetheless it is there, as it were, to justify the play at this level of interest.[11] Arbaces, for all his good qualities, is so domineering and proud that Gobrias feels he cannot reveal the truth until Arbaces' pride has been broken. He chooses as his means for breaking that pride, Panthea. If Arbaces comes to love Panthea enough, Gobrias is to be thought of as reasoning, his sense of omnipotence will be destroyed, and he will gladly give up his claim to royal birth. This scheme is a particularly clever one for Gobrias to have devised because it will also serve his desire to retain a high place for his son by making him Panthea's husband.[12] The psychology of character in this plot is simplified, as it so often is in Elizabethan plays, and one may question the probability of many of the incidents which

---

[11] There is a great deal of morality of this kind in Beaumont and Fletcher and a great deal of overt moralizing on the part of their characters, and it is all there because it is one of the most effective ways of stimulating certain interesting and exciting feelings in the audience. The great passages of moralizing in Shakespeare are deeply moving, but they are always moving in order that the moral significance of the action may come home to the hearts of men. Beaumont and Fletcher undoubtedly learned how to make morality moving from Shakespeare, but they were interested in learning how to achieve this effect, not because they had a significant action to bring home to their audience, but because they wished to be moving. It is their diabolical skill in using the profoundly moving ideas which their world inherited from an age of greater faith without taking responsibility for the moral implications of these ideas which offends critics like Mr. Eliot (see n. 15). One has only to contrast the scenes between Panthea and Arbaces with the scenes between Isabella and Angelo to see this difference in intention and its consequences. Beaumont and Fletcher's use of morality was apparently based on a clear understanding of the kind of interest their audience had in morality; cf. the following commendatory verses prefixed to the Second Folio:

> *Shakspear* was early up, and went so drest
> As for those *dawning* hours he knew was best;
> But when the Sun shone forth, *You Two* thought fit
> To wear just Robes, and leave off Trunk hose-Wit. . . .
> For *Yours* are not meer humours, gilded Strains:
> The fashion lost, Your massy Sence remains.

[12] See II. i. 40–62; Gobrias' unobtrusive insistence in the temptation scene, III. i; the skilful ambiguity of IV. i. 12–28; the pregnant "Now it is ripe," V. iv. 46; and finally Gobrias' explanation, V. iv. 246–50.

the dramatists force to play into Gobrias' hands, as Shakespeare forces chance to favor Iago and not to favor Romeo and Juliet. But these are conventional short cuts of all drama of the period; grant them, and this central plot is tightly knit.

Parallel to this main plot runs the minor story of Tigranes, Spaconia, and Lygones. It is attached to the main plot not only by the careful interrelation of the characters but by the balancing of the emotional relations between the four characters.[13] In general, this subplot is used as a contrast to the main plot. It is the Everlasting's canon against incest which hinders Arbaces and Panthea, and the helplessness of Arbaces' earthly power to destroy that canon is emphasized; what hinders Tigranes and Spaconia is mainly a lack of earthly power, the Everlasting being, presumably, a supporter of romantic love. Finally, there is the comic subplot built around Bessus. Bessus' plight is the comic version of Arbaces'. Like Arbaces, Bessus is boastful, and his troubles, like Arbaces', are the consequences of his boastfulness.[14]

It is impossible not to admire the ingenuity of this construction; yet most readers will probably feel that it is more ingenious than satisfying. The difficulty is most apparent in the case of Bessus; for all their skilful management of it, Beaumont and Fletcher do not seem really to care about the parallel between Bessus and Arbaces. The complex comparison of the attitudes of different kinds of people in the same basic dilemma in the typical Shakespeare play gives the reader a sense not only that the possible implications of the comparison are almost as multitudinous as those of life itself but that Shakespeare is serious about those implications. The form of the narrative, once one has granted the conventions of the Elizabethan theater, is a correlative of Shakespeare's own sense of the world: it is both verisimilar and meaningful. The reader feels none of this fundamental seriousness in Beaumont and Fletcher's parallel, and he does not because their narrative is not the correlative of a serious sense of the world, but only of a convenient and conventional one. Most of the Jacobean dramatists gave up trying to make their plays accord with both "reality and justice," with the moving and significant worlds

13 Tigranes is Arbaces' victim and prisoner; Spaconia is Panthea's waiting lady; Bessus is connected with the Tigranes-Spaconia plot by two carefully distributed scenes (I. ii. and V. i), on the one hand, and with the Arbaces-Panthea plot (especially by III. iii), on the other. The balance of emotional relations is prevented from becoming merely mechanical by Beaumont and Fletcher's failure to have Arbaces tempted by Spaconia and Panthea jealous of her.

14 Had it not been for Arbaces' pride, Gobrias' plot would not have been necessary. Bessus would never have met such difficulties had he not allowed the news of "Bessus' Desperate Redemption" to get abroad. " 'The harmony and degradation of colours,' from the upper to the under parts of this piece, are one of its merits. After listening to the sallies of Arbaces we can descend with ease to the brags of Bessus" (*Quarterly Review*, LXXXIII, 389).

of their imagination and the always more or less—but in their apprehensions unconquerably—discordant facts of the actual world. Most of them set about organizing the worlds of their plays in accord with their ideas of justice; but they succeeded only at the expense of keeping the narrative in accord with their sense of reality. Beaumont and Fletcher so organized the world of their plays, too, if one can describe the underlying mood which determined the pattern of the emotional form of their plays as a sense of justice. But they did not, in the process, allow the narrative form to lose all formal order. They gave the narrative of their plays a pattern; but it is not a morally significant pattern, and its great complexity is not determined by any complexity of meaning but exists because a complex narrative is itself exciting, as well as the means of providing the maximum number of exciting moments.

It is for this reason that the reader feels none of the seriousness, finds none of the moral significance, in the parallel between Arbaces and Bessus which he does in the structurally similar parallels in Shakespeare's plays. And this same lack of significance can be traced through the rest of the play's structure. There is no serious meaning to be found in the elaborate interrelation of the main plot and the subplot. And in the main plot the light of our attention is, if the narrative were actually the means for giving the play form and significance, in the wrong place: Gobrias' scheming, which provides the trial of Arbaces and Panthea, is so in the shadow that we are scarcely able to detect it, and the tragic moral implications of that trial are not only never fully developed, but sometimes scandalously neglected; Beaumont and Fletcher's only contingent interest in them is most apparent when the characters are moralizing most violently. We are forced into the realization that, despite the care and skill with which Beaumont and Fletcher have constructed the narrative of this play, they are interested not so much in having it carry a serious meaning as in using it to support and enrich an emotional form; this is the significant form of the play. In spite of their great care for the narrative, the focus of attention in *A King and No King,* as in all their plays, is the emotional form, just as it is in the plays of any typical Jacobean dramatist. No more than in the cases of Webster or Tourneur or Ford, therefore, is it a really relevant objection to Beaumont and Fletcher that the feelings displayed by a character or generated in the audience by a scene are found, on close examination, to be out of proportion to the narrative situation which ostensibly justifies their existence.

The successful creation of a formal structure of this kind depends, in the first place, on an ability to display with elegance, with a kind of detached eloquence, the attitudes presented. It depends, in the second place, on an ability to vary and repeat these attitudes in such a way as to give the pattern which they form richness and interest. The coolness, the artificiality, the "insincerity" of the emotional displays in Beaumont and Fletcher's plays is the deliberately calculated means by which they give the necessary weight to the particular attitude presented.[15] Consider, for example, Arbaces' great speech in the first scene of Act III of *A King and No King:*

> My sister!—Is she dead? If it be so,
> Speak boldly to me, for I am a man,
> And dare not quarrel with divinity;
> And do not think to cozen me with this.
> I see you all are mute, and stand amazed,
> Fearful to answer me: it is too true,
> A decreed instant cuts off every life,
> For which to mourn is to repine: she died
> A virgin though, more innocent than sleep,
> As clear as her own eyes; and blessedness
> Eternal waits upon her where she is:
> I know she could not make a wish to change
> Her state for new; and you shall see me bear
> My crosses like a man. We all must die;
> And she hath taught us how.

This speech would verge on the extravagant in almost any play. It is in a manner the simplicity and grandeur of which is reserved by the greatest dramatists for the moment when the hero becomes morally certain of the tragic fact of the play, in this case the death of Arbaces' sister. "Detached from its context," to quote Mr. Eliot again, "this looks like the verse of the greater poets."[16] But if you turn to the context of the speech, you find that it is not, as it would be in "the greater poets," any such climactic speech; it is not, that is to say, the poetic exploitation of a situation carefully built up in terms of plot and character; it has not, in this sense, any roots in the soil of the narrative form. And when you look at the speech more closely, you detect in it a kind of elegant and controlled exaggeration which is almost never found in Shakespeare's voice as if the dramatists and their audience wished to make the most they could of a particular feeling short of allowing it to become patently absurd in its exaggeration, because their interest was in that feeling and

---

15 T. S. Eliot (*Selected Essays, 1917–1932,* p. 135) calls this dependence "upon a clever appeal to emotions and associations which they have not themselves grasped." But Beaumont and Fletcher have grasped everything that is relevant to their purpose. It may be that this purpose excludes everything that is important about these emotions and associations in Mr. Eliot's estimation, and his estimation may be right. But to call Beaumont and Fletcher's use of them merely clever is to imply the lack of any steady purpose whatsoever behind it, and that implication is, I think, false.

16 *Ibid.*

not in the character and situation of which it is supposedly the result.[17]

What this speech shows, in other words, is that Beaumont and Fletcher had a highly developed sense of just how far they could push a given feeling without pitching the whole speech over the edge into the abyss of absurdity. Their insistence on retaining for the speech its appearance of being justified by situation and character is largely owing to their realization that by giving the speech an appearance of justification they could push the feeling a good deal further without producing this disaster. Thus, though neither the kind nor degree of response demanded by this speech is actually justified in terms of Arbaces' character and the situation, Beaumont and Fletcher show an immense and deceptive ingenuity in making it appear that it is. And they elaborate this deception with such ingenuity because by doing so they can lull themselves and the audience into accepting and enjoying a kind and degree of emotion which would otherwise seem merely absurd. Consider this ingenuity for a moment. Arbaces knows that his sister is not dead but kneeling before him, and he knows too that he is in love with her. Looked at from the point of view of the narrative, therefore, these are the words of a proud man driven to playing for time in a desperate situation, and there is much in the speech which, for an audience with its attention not fixed directly on the moral significance of character, will encourage this view of its purpose. It is clever dramatic irony on the authors' part, for example, to have the man who has just discovered himself desperately in love with his sister say that for him she is dead. It may seem to the audience simply further evidence of the authors' concern for the moral implications of character that Arbaces, who has always thought of himself

---

[17] One very intelligent reader of this essay has said that the contrast with Shakespeare here is unfortunate because Shakespeare does linger over certain emotional passages and because Beaumont and Fletcher, in fact, learned the trick of handling such effects from him. This objection suggests that I have not made my point clear. Certainly Shakespeare lingers over emotional passages, but almost never simply for the sake of the emotion. Gertrude's description of Ophelia's death is a convenient example, and it not only lingers over Ophelia's death but does so in a lyric and ostensibly incongruous fashion, as if Shakespeare were ignoring for the moment the question of what attitude in the audience is dramatically relevant here. Yet this feeling and the weight given it are justified, for this blossom of Shakespeare's imagination has its roots firmly imbedded in the desire and horror which the narrative is about. Ophelia is the play's figure of perfect innocence and purity, and her death is a triumph over the forces of mortality; they cannot touch her. It is a sea change into something rich and strange, a thing of flowers and music (Shakespeare's characteristic imagery for purity and spiritual harmony), in contrast to all other visions of death in the play which emphasize the degradation and disgust, the defeat of death. Beaumont and Fletcher certainly learned from Shakespeare a great deal about how to manage the responses of the audience, but what they learned they put to very different uses.

as a godlike hero, should, in this moment of discovering his own sinful-
ness, realize that "I am a man / And dare not quarrel with divinity."
And Arbaces' tender concern for his sister's virginity may easily be
thought to have no other function than to reveal his revulsion from his
incestuous impulse. Even his closing words may appear to be a necessarily
concealed prayer for strength to bear his own crosses.

All this is calculated to encourage an audience to believe that this
stimulating speech is no more than a legitimate exploitation of character
and situation, that the excitement really has been justified by them. Yet
on careful examination it is quite clear that character and situation are
not the center of Beaumont and Fletcher's interest here, that everything
in the speech is primarily directed to arousing in the audience a feeling
which is both in degree and in kind not so justified. The speech lacks
the tone of irony and bitterness which it must have if it is to be taken
as the words of a man in the midst of self-discovery. Its tone is one of
elegiac simplicity and dignity, of graceful pathos. It was plainly written
with a view to extracting all the pity possible from the thought of a
sister dead, in spite of the narrative irrelevance of that pity at this
point. All the details of the speech, including those discussed in the
previous paragraph, are so presented as to demand of the audience, not
such a response as the situation and character might be justified in
demanding, but a response which could be justified only if Panthea were
really dead, and only then if this were the culminating disaster of the
play for Arbaces.

This is the characteristic relationship in Beaumont and Fletcher
between the narrative and "the lively touches of the passion." A dramatic
situation is created which, usually with some ingenuity, is made to appear
to justify the speech; that speech is then written, not so much for the
purpose of exploiting the feelings which grow out of character and situation, the feelings which in terms of the narrative justify the speech—
though that purpose is never wholly neglected. It is written primarily
to exploit a feeling which contrasts with, parallels, or resolves the
patterned sequences of emotions which have, in precisely the same way,
been exploited in the speeches which form its context.

Arbaces' speech is climactic, then, not in the sense that it forms a
climax in the narrative development; any reader looking at it in its
context will see that its appearance of climaxing a tragic narrative is a
skilfully devised trick. It is climactic in the sense that it resolves a complex sequence of emotional tones, the tension of which has become almost
intolerable. The sequence is worth looking at closely, since it is, in little,
a Beaumont and Fletcher play: the method of its construction is the
method they use in dealing with the larger units of the play as a whole.

This sequence begins with an introductory passage in which Arbaces'
supposed mother, Arane, kneeling before him, is graciously forgiven for
having plotted his death. Panthea then kneels before Arbaces and speaks

as if the whole purpose of her life had been fulfilled by the mere privilege of looking at him; the attitude is adoration, an emotion ostensibly justified by the fact that Arbaces is supposedly Panthea's kingly brother; but it is plainly out of all proportion to this narrative justification. Arbaces' response to this speech is in startling contrast, not only with Panthea's words, but with his treatment of Arane a moment before, though Arane would have murdered him and Panthea is all adoration.

GOBRIAS: Why does not your majesty speak?
ARBACES: To Whom?
GOBRIAS: To the princess.

Panthea then strikes another note, trembling fear that Arbaces looks upon her as "some loathed thing." Once more Gobrias intervenes.

GOBRIAS: Sir, you should speak to her.
ARBACES: Ho!

And once more Panthea strikes in, now with the attitude of one conscious of her unworthiness, who pleads for a word of kindness for simple mercy's sake.

This time it is Tigranes who is shocked by Arbaces' apparent brutality and who urges him to speak. Tigranes, Arbaces' prisoner and the man he has chosen for his sister's husband, is secretly pledged to Spaconia. Throughout this scene the theme of his growing love for Panthea gradually emerges until, for a moment near the end, it dominates the scene. This speech is its first appearance; Arbaces answers it with a long aside which makes it clear to the audience that he has been confounded by the discovery that he is passionately in love with his own sister. This aside is followed by an aside from Tigranes in which he indicates *his* growing love for Panthea.[18]

Once more Panthea speaks; this time with half-jesting pathos she begs Arbaces to speak, if only to save her modesty. Now it is Mardonius, the bluff soldier, who urges Arbaces to speak; and, with another startling shift in emotional tone, Arbaces turns to Panthea with grave courtesy:[19]

---

[18] The narrative structure here is typical. There is great ingenuity in this manipulation of the situation in such a way as to produce parallel attitudes at the same moment which require the same concealment in these two very differently situated characters in parallel and interlocked but nevertheless different plots. But there is no serious significance in this paralleling of the attitudes of Arbaces and Tigranes. The very ingenuity of it is itself exciting, and it is the means of providing the clash which occurs a moment later between these two characters; and that is its purpose.

[19] "Startling," but not without its appearance of narrative justification. In terms of the narrative Arbaces is the desperate man playing for time. As usual, this motive is a trick—it does not really justify the speech—but it is sufficient to motivate the action if the audience's attention is focused where it should be, for in that case this motivation will be at the periphery of attention, not enough in focus for its inadequacy to become apparent.

You mean this lady: lift her from the earth;
Why do you kneel so long?—Alas,
Madam, your beauty uses to command,
And not to beg! What is your suit to me?
It shall be granted; yet the time is short,
And my affairs are great.—But where's my sister?
I bade she should be brought.

The tension of this moment is then held through a series of short speeches, each of which seems inevitably to be the last which can be spoken before Arbaces must publicly recognize Panthea:

MARDONIUS (*aside*):   What, is he mad?
ARBACES: Gobrias, where is she?
GOBRIAS: Sir?
ARBACES: Where is she, man?
GOBRIAS: Who, sir?
ARBACES: Who! hast thou forgot? my sister.
GOBRIAS: Your sister, sir!
ARBACES: Your sister, sir! Some one that hath a wit,
              Answer where is she.
GOBRIAS: Do you not see her there?
ARBACES: Where?
GOBRIAS: There?
ARBACES: There! Where?
MARDONIUS: 'Slight, there: are you blind?
ARBACES: Which do you mean? that little one?
GOBRIAS: No, sir.
ARBACES: No, sir! Why, do you mock me? I can see
              No other here but that petitioning lady.
GOBRIAS: That's she.
ARBACES: Away!
GOBRIAS: Sir, it is she.
ARBACES: 'Tis false.
GOBRIAS: Is it?[20]
ARBACES: As hell! by Heaven, as false as hell!

And then, after the anger and fear and bewilderment of this sequence, after the intolerable pitch of tension that has been reached and then held through this virtuoso passage, the sequence is resolved by Arbaces' astonishing elegy for his dead sister.[21]

[20] A good example of Beaumont and Fletcher's very great cleverness in using the narrative to support and intensify the emotional pattern. Gobrias knows that it is false; it is his scheme to have Arbaces fall violently in love with Panthea, and then to reveal that she is not his sister. It was for the sake of this kind of emotional effect that Beaumont and Fletcher were loath to give up a carefully constructed narrative and seldom allowed a speech which has not some appearance of narrative justification.

[21] The sequence of emotional attitudes is resolved, but not the dramatic situation (see below). This passage is also a good example of the way Beaumont and

Throughout this passage Beaumont and Fletcher are concerned primarily neither to develop the characters nor to bring out the moral implications of the action. Their primary concern is to arouse in the audience, at each step, the feeling which is a psychologically dramatic successor to the feeling aroused by the previous speech. And this purpose requires the introduction of a series of attitudes on the part of the characters which makes it appear, from the point of view of the narrative, that these characters are not only strained to the breaking point for a mere momentary effect which comes to nothing but made to speak at great length while only apparently advancing the plot.

The scene-by-scene and act-by-act construction of the play has the same purpose in view and the same consequences. The remainder of the first scene of Act III, for example, is made up of a series of passages of exactly the same kind as the one analyzed above; and each of these passages is adjusted to the preceding and succeeding passages with the same care for the emotional pattern in the audience's mind as is shown in the arrangement of the individual speeches within these passages. As soon as the elegiac mood of Arbaces' speech which closes the first passage has been exhausted, Gobrias once more reminds the king that Panthea is his sister. At this Arbaces takes another line:

> Here pronounce him traitor,
> The direct plotter of my death, that names
> Or thinks her for my sister. . . .

In terms of the narrative, Arbaces is here displaying the passionate side of his nature, established in Act I. In terms of the emotional form, this speech is a skilful modulation of the pathos of his previous elegiac speech; for, though this is the impassioned anger of a man unaccustomed to denial, it is asserted on a hopeless case, against nature itself; the more angry Arbaces becomes, the more pathetic he appears, "a sight most pitiful in the meanest wretch, / Past speaking of in a king."

After a speech from Panthea, Arbaces is given a third modulation of pathos:

> I will hear no more.
> Why should there be such music in a voice,
> And sin for me to hear it. . . ?

a speech which ends with his sinking exhausted on the throne.

At this pause Tigranes steps forward to address Panthea. The passage which follows is beautifully balanced against the preceding passage. Panthea, distracted by grief and uncertainty, is yet gentle and gracious; the simple pathos which has been hers from the start shows in this

---

Fletcher use the varying speed of their verse to reinforce the emotional pattern: the abrupt, hurried exchange of questions and answers sets off with maximum effectiveness the slow and solemn regularity of Arbaces' elegy.

passage with a new and touching dignity. Tigranes is eager to show his devotion to her but is restrained by the presence of Spaconia, whose asides are at once a choral commentary on the dialogue and, as the expression of another much-wronged woman's sorrows, a kind of complementary grief to Panthea's. The passage, so far as the feelings presented are concerned, is a variation on the previous one, with Tigranes replacing Arbaces. Gradually Arbaces recovers, and the audience's attention is brought back to his feeling—now jealous suspicion of Tigranes—by the series of ominously cryptic questions which he asks. Tigranes becomes more and more angry under this questioning, and Arbaces more and more certain that his jealousy is justified, until, in helpless rage, he orders Tigranes imprisoned.

As the clashing anger of this passage dies away, Gobrias once more reminds Arbaces of the presence of his sister, and, in immediate and striking contrast to his anger of the moment before, Arbaces turns to Panthea, kneels, and begs her forgiveness. Panthea kneels with him, and there follows a passage of suspiciously extravagant affection, tense with the audience's knowledge that certainly Arbaces and perhaps Panthea are playing with fire in this attempt to pretend that their mutual feelings are only natural.[22] Arbaces kisses Panthea "to make this knot the stronger" and then, with a brief aside—"I wade in sin, / And foolishly entice myself along"—turns abruptly away and orders Panthea imprisoned. Thus the scene shifts back to anger and violence, though to a kind subtly different from that of the exchange between Arbaces and Tigranes a moment before. As Panthea is carried off to prison, Arbaces returns to the despairing rage at his own powerlessness which appeared in his second speech in the scene, though now that feeling is more despair than rage:

> Why should you, that have made me stand in war
> Like Fate itself, cutting what threads I pleased,
> Decree such an unworthy end of me
> And all my glories?

At the end of this speech, once more faint with exhaustion, he is led out by Mardonius, and the emotional pattern of the scene is completed with a Hamlet-inspired dying fall:

> Wilt thou hereafter, when they talk of me,
> As thou shalt hear, nothing but infamy,
> Remember some of these things? . . .
> I prithee, do;
> For thou shalt never see me so again.

From the narrative point of view this scene is full of wild starts and

---

[22] The scene is, in its ironic way, a tribute to the skill with which Beaumont could adapt Shakespearean effects to his own purposes (cf. *King Lear,* IV. vii. 59 ff.).

changes on the part of the characters and of bewildering and apparently profitless backing and filling on the part of the story. But in term of the audience's psychology the form of the scene is firm and clear, for all its richness and variety.[23]

The form of the act can also be defined only in these terms. Miss Bradbrook has remarked that the coarsening of the poetic fiber can be clearly seen in Beaumont and Fletcher's blurring of the tragic and comic. In the sense that the contrasting of the tragic and comic, like the contrasting of other moods in the audience, has no serious functional purpose in terms of the narrative, this comment is true. But in terms of the emotional form, Beaumont and Fletcher's comic contrasts are clear-cut and carefully calculated. The first scene of Act III, for example, is followed by a comic seene in which Bessus faces the ridiculous consequences of his newly acquired and embarrassing reputation for courage, as Arbaces has just faced the tragic fact of his sudden and passionate love for Panthea. This contrast, as Miss Bradbrook suggests, proves nothing morally, and there appears to be little justification for the considerable space which is devoted to the rather pointless business of Bessus' cowardice; in terms of the narrative, in other words, the variation from tragic to comic here and throughout the play seems to be purposeless and random. The scene can, in fact, be justified only in terms of the psychology of the audience; its relationship to the previous scene is of the same kind as the relationship which exists between speech and speech within the scene. In terms of the narrative, such justification as it has is tricky but meaningless, but psychologically it shifts the audience's attention to a set of feelings, parallel but of a different kind, and it also prevents the law of diminishing returns from asserting itself, as it would if the dramatists attempted to follow scene 1 immediately with scene 3.

After this comic scene, however, it is possible to return to the tragic theme of Panthea and Arbaces. The basic form of scene 3 is simpler than that of scene 1; the audience watches Arbaces slowly working himself up to the point where he can request Mardonius' aid in fulfilling his shameful desire, and presumably it thrills to Mardonius' manful refusal and pities Arbaces as he wilts before Mardonius' righteousness. Scarcely has Arbaces repented his request when Bessus enters and Arbaces is once more tempted. Bessus accepts the commission eagerly, so eagerly that Arbaces is horrified and once more repents. The scene is Beaumont and Fletcher's version of the familiar good-angel, bad-angel scene and, in the way it plays down the larger implications of such a scene, it is an

---

[23] The plot of a Beaumont and Fletcher play is more obviously repetitive than the plot of a play in which narrative form is the ordering form, since Beaumont and Fletcher can afford to go to greater lengths in holding a particular situation in order to exploit its emotional possibilities.

instructive example of the skill with which Beaumont and Fletcher collected the cash while only pretending not to let the credit go.[24]

Probably Beaumont and Fletcher's very real talent for narrative construction shows most clearly in the act-by-act organization of the play. The complicated story which is necessary for their kind of play, if the emotional climaxes it requires are not to be obviously arbitrary and therefore difficult to accept, is handled with such ease and with so very little direct exposition, and the narrative interest is so carefully carried over when new material is introduced, that only detailed analysis is likely to reveal how elaborate the plot really is. Yet, for all this display of narrative skill, Beaumont and Fletcher build their play around emotional, rather than narrative, climaxes. The climax of Act I, for example, is clearly Arbaces' display of passionate anger; true, this passionate quality is the "tragic flaw" in Arbaces' character, but it is not the cause of his tragic dilemma; it exists not so much for the sake of the action as a whole as because, in conjunction with the plot, it provides some sort of narrative justification for Arbaces' extravagant and varied emotions, which are so important a part of the emotional form. The climax of Act II is perhaps Spaconia's display of pathos; in any event, there is no narrative climax in this act, no obligatory scene. The last three acts have similar climaxes, each a little tenser than its predecessor. In so far as they depend on suspense—on whether Arbaces will yield to desire— they depend on the narrative for their effect. But in the sense that the narrative is the local habitation of an important meaning, as in *Doctor Faustus,* which has some superficially comparable scenes, and the climaxes moments when the choice between good and evil must be made, they are not narrative climaxes at all. Once more Beaumont and Fletcher are in these scenes using the narrative effect of suspense to support and

---

[24] Miss Bradbrook is concerned (p. 242) over the fact that "when Arbaces asks Bessus to procure his sister for him. Bessus' assent is far more convincing than the King' indignation." In the sense of the firmness with which they are rooted in character and situation, the attitudes of both characters are in no serious sense convincing. In general, it is easier, I should suppose, to believe in the king's revulsion from, than in the pander's extraordinary enthusiasm for, this crime. But I think Miss Bradbrook means that Bessus is made to display an enthusiasm greater than Arbaces' revulsion. This is true, but it does not prove that Beaumont and Fletcher loved viciousness more than goodness. The scene shows, rather, that they were not seriously concerned about either, and from a strictly prudential point of view that may very well be a worse condition for their souls to have been in than if they had loved evil, for as Mr. Eliot has observed, "so far as we do evil or good, we are human; and it is better, in a paradoxical way, to do evil than to do nothing: at least, we exist" (*Essays,* p. 344). What is dramatically relevant here, however, is the fact that Bessus' enthusiasm not only must parallel—with variations —Arbaces' desire of a moment before, but must also contrast with Mardonius' previous and Arbaces' present horror. It obviously needs extreme emphasis.

enrich an emotional climax, rather than using emotional effects to support and enrich a narrative climax.[25]

The climax of the third act is the first meeting between Panthea and Arbaces, with its elaborate emotional composition, its use of events as one more way of inducing a patterned sequence of psychologically effective attitudes in the audience. The climax of the fourth act is the second meeting between the two lovers, a meeting perceptibly tenser for the audience than that of the third act because Arbaces' confession to Panthea and Panthea's "For I could wish as heartily as you, / I were no sister to you" bring the two so much closer to disaster. This sequence reaches its logical culmination in the fifth act, when Arbaces finally surrenders to his desire.[26] The expectation of action aroused by Arbaces'

> It is resolved: I bore it whilst I could;
> I can no more. Hell, open all thy gates,
> And I will through them: . . .

is held suspended through a passage between him and Mardonius in which he displays the tortured cynicism of his determination to do what he knows to be sin, and through a passage in which he accuses Gobrias of having fostered his love for Panthea. The audience's attention is then partly deflected from the expectation that Arbaces will act on his sinful desire by the first part of Gobrias' revelation and Arbaces' anger at Arane as he understands Gobrias to be telling him he is a bastard. Each of these notes is held as long as possible, both for its own sake and for the sake of maintaining the suspense. Finally, however, Gobrias is permitted to tell Arbaces enough to make him listen to the rest, and Arbaces

---

[25] "The blossoms of Beaumont and Fletcher's imagination draw no sustenance from the soil, but are cut and slightly withered flowers stuck into sand," as Mr. Eliot so wittily says (*Essays*, p. 135). And this is one way to put it, though probably an exaggerated way, for I think Dryden was right that "nothing can move our nature, but by some natural reason, which works upon passions. And, since we acknowledge the effect, there must be something in the cause." It may be that Beaumont and Fletcher's flowers are of an artificial variety and have been trained to grow in a garden whose formal arrangement is very different from the arrangement of more natural gardens, but such artificial gardens have life and form, however much we may deplore a preference for them.

[26] This is perhaps the place to mention a problem which is far too complex to be dealt with in this essay. All the climactic scenes of *A King and No King,* indeed all the scenes which are of any real importance to the emotional form of the play, are assigned to Beaumont in the usual distribution, concerning which there is, as Chambers says, "practical unanimity." This fact suggests that the form I am describing was the creation of Beaumont. I believe this implication is false, though I have not space to present the arguments here. The mere fact, however, that the experts are almost equally unanimous in giving the magnificent opening scene of Act IV of *The Maid's Tragedy* to Fletcher is enough to cast serious doubt on it (see E. H. C. Oliphant, *The Plays of Beaumont and Fletcher,* pp. 168–69, 182–83).

shifts abruptly from anger and despair to what G. C. Macaulay well called "a sudden violent patience":

> I'll lie, and listen here as reverently   [*Lies down*]
> As to an angel: if I breath too loud,
> Tell me; for I would be as still as night.

Gobrias' story is quickly told, Arbaces rises almost mad with joy, and on this note the play is quickly brought to an end.[27]

The ordering form of *A King and No King*—and it is the form of all the tragedies and tragicomedies that Beaumont and Fletcher wrote together—is a pattern of responses in the mind of the audience, a subtle and artful arrangement of "the lively touches of the passion." Like *A King and No King*, the typical Beaumont and Fletcher play is an excitingly elaborate affair of lath and plaster whose imposing pretense that it is a massive narrative structure is in part a device for making the audience accept the elaboration and in part a means of adding to the excitement by the charm of its own ingenuity. Its characters and narrative are given the maximum of decorative elaboration, and, though Beaumont and Fletcher are careful that the decoration shall always appear to be a part of some functional detail in the narrative, actually the significant and ordering form of the structure is not the narrative pattern, clever as that always is, but the pattern of decoration. Just as in another kind of play the meaning implicit in character and situation is intensified by a subordinate pattern of more narrowly poetic effects, so in Beaumont and Fletcher these carefully ordered poetic effects are made richer and more complex by the narrative pattern. If the ideal play of the critical imagination of the nineteenth century may be said to have been functional in terms of character and narrative, then Beaumont and Fletcher's plays are strictly baroque.

Most critics would, I believe, agree that plays which are functional in terms of Nature, in the widest sense of the word, constitute a superior kind; if they do, then Beaumont and Fletcher's baroque plays represent an inferior kind. But that kind is certainly superior to the kind represented by the ideal play of the nineteenth-century critics' imagination, which is functional in terms of character only in a very mundane and individualist sense, and in terms of a nature whose vitality has been dissipated by a scientific and utilitarian conception of it. There is something to be said for Rymer's attitude toward Beaumont and Fletcher; he knew what they were up to and damned them by comparison with

---

27 Ward's comment on Arbaces' fantastic attitude here is a striking tribute to its effectiveness, especially since he is convinced that the immorality of the play on the narrative level is an artistic flaw: "...while reprobating both from a moral and from an artistic point of view the nature of the solution, we feel that rarely has joy been more vividly depleted than in the last scene, where Arbaces finds himself delivered from the unutterable oppression of a criminal passion, and at the same time free to indulge a lawful love" (*A History of English Dramatic Literature*, II, 678).

a kind of play whose superiority is at least arguable. But the nineteenth century, misunderstanding them, damned their plays as bad examples of a kind which they do not represent and which is inferior to the kind they do.

There is not much to be gained from a discussion of Beaumont and Fletcher's plays which assumes that they represent a kind they do not, nor is the situation visibly improved if the critic goes on to offer a simple moralistic explanation of their failure to be something their authors never sought to make them. It seems to me obvious that there is something radically wrong with the usual approach to Beaumont and Fletcher when it can lead so acute a critic as Miss Bradbrook into the assumption of a simple relationship between the historical, the strictly literary, and the moral kinds of decadence.[28]

We would be nearer to understanding Beaumont and Fletcher and thus to being able to judge them justly if we had never strayed from the conception of their purpose, which lies behind Herrick's lines for the First Folio:

> Here's words with lines, and lines with Scenes consent,
> To raise an Act to full astonishment; . . .
> Love lyes a bleeding here, *Evadne* there
> Swells with brave rage, yet comely every where,
> Here's a *mad lover,* there that high designe
> Of *King and no King.* . . .

[28] "It is not surprising . . . to find [in Beaumont and Fletcher] a taste for the more extraordinary sexual themes (rape, impotence, incest) combined with a blurring of the aesthetic difference between tragedy and comedy and the moral distinction between right and wrong" (p. 243).

BEAUMONT AND FLETCHER

Adkins, M. G. M. "The Citizens in *Philaster:* Their Function and Significance," *SP,* XLIII (1946), 203–212.

Appleton, William W. *Beaumont and Fletcher: A Critical Study.* London, 1956, pp. 29–41.

Boas, Frederick S. *An Introduction to Stuart Drama.* Oxford, 1946, pp. 257–266.

Bradbrook, Muriel C. *Themes and Conventions of Elizabethan Tragedy.* Cambridge, Eng., 1935, pp. 240–250.

Cunningham, John E. *Elizabethan and Early Stuart Drama.* London, 1965, pp. 82–86.

Davison, Peter. "The Serious Concerns of *Philaster,*" *ELH,* XXX (1963), 1–15.

Danby, John Francis. *Poets on Fortune's Hill: Studies in Sidney, Shakespeare, Beaumont & Fletcher.* London, 1952, pp. 162–183.

Edwards, Philip. "The Danger not the Death: The Art of John Fletcher," in *Jacobean Theatre,* ed. John Russell Brown. Stratford-upon-Avon Studies 1. New York, 1960, pp. 159–177.

Ellis-Fermor, Una. *The Jacobean Drama.* 4th rev. ed. London, 1958, pp. 201–226.

Leech, Clifford. "The Dramatic Style of John Fletcher," in *English Studies Today: Second Series,* ed. G. A. Bonnard. Bern, 1961, pp. 143–157.

_____. *The John Fletcher Plays.* London, and Cambridge, Mass., 1962, 16–21, 78–100, *et passim.*

Ornstein, Robert. *The Moral Vision of Jacobean Tragedy.* Madison, Wis., 1960 (reprinted 1965), pp. 168–169, 178–179.

Schutt, J. H. *"Philaster* Considered as a Work of Literary Art," *English Studies,* VI (1924), 81–87.

Thorndike, Ashley H., ed. *The Maid's Tragedy and Philaster.* Boston, 1906, pp. xix–xx, xxv–xl.

Turner, Robert K., Jr., ed. *A King and No King.* Regents Renaissance Drama Series. Lincoln, Nebraska, 1964, pp. xv–xxvi.

_____. "The Morality of *A King and No King,*" in *RenP (for 1958–1960),* ed. George Walton Williams. Durham, N.C., 1961, 93–103.

Waith, Eugene M. *The Pattern of Tragicomedy in Beaumont and Fletcher.* New Haven, 1952, pp. 15–19, 27–42.

Wallis, Lawrence B. *Fletcher, Beaumont & Company: Entertainers to the Jacobean Gentry.* New York, 1947, pp. 163–180, 220–228, 234–245.

Thomas Middleton
and
William Rowley

THE CHANGELING
AND THE TRAGEDY OF DAMNATION *

Helen Gardner

In both *Dr. Faustus* and *Macbeth* what astounds our imagination is the spectacle of the hero's suffering, the exploration of the nature of separation, intermittent in *Dr. Faustus,* but sustained throughout the play in *Macbeth*. Macbeth never loses that horror at himself which made him gaze upon his "hangman's hands" as if they were not his. What he does is a perpetual offence to what he is, and he never ceases to feel it. The horror implicit in the exact Latin of Aquinas is here made vivid to the imagination: "ideo non oportet, quamvis naturaliter inclinentur ad bonum, quod motus virtutis in eis sit, vel esse possit."

* From Helen Gardner, "Milton's 'Satan' and the Theme of Damnation in Elizabethan Tragedy," *English Studies, 1948,* pp. 46–66. Reprinted by permission of the author.

At first sight *The Changeling* appears a very different play from either *Dr. Faustus* or *Macbeth*, though Beatrice-Joanna has sometimes been compared with Lady Macbeth because of the lack of imagination she shows when she incites to murder. The supernatural, which broods over *Macbeth* and is essential to the story of *Dr. Faustus*, becomes here only a perfunctory acknowledgment of the popular taste for ghosts of murdered men. Beatrice-Joanna makes her choice and instigates to crime, prompted only by her passion for Alsemero, with no "supernatural solicitings" to disturb her judgment. But though this is true literally, Middleton gains an effect that is beyond the natural by the wonderful invention of De Flores.[1]

The alterations that Middleton made in his source are very remarkable; all the play's most memorable situations are invented. The story as told by Reynolds is flat and pointless, as the following summary shows.[2]

> The opening situation is the same as in the play: Beatrice-Joanna, who meets Alsemero at Mass by chance, is being urged by her father to marry Alonzo Piracquo. She has never liked Piracquo and is at once attracted by Alsemero. The story develops slowly with Beatrice-Joanna removed to the country, and corresponding clandestinely with Alsemero, who at last comes secretly to see her, admitted by her waiting woman, Diaphanta. Beatrice-Joanna tells him "before *Piracquo* be in another World, there is no hope for *Alsemero* to inioy her for his wife in this"; whereupon Alsemero proposes to send him a challenge. But Beatrice-Joanna makes him promise not to meddle, and swears she can manage her father. The secret meeting is reported to her father, and she realizes that he is set upon her match with Piracquo, and so "after shee had ruminated, and runne ouer many bloody designes: the diuell, who neuer flies from those that follow him, proffers her an inuention as execrable as damnable. There is a Gallant young Gentleman, of the Garrison of the Castle, who follows her father, that to her knowledge doth deepely honour, and dearely affect her: yea, she knowes, that at her request he will not sticke to murther *Piracquo*: his name is *Signiour Antonio de Flores*."
>
> Beatrice-Joanna then sends for de Flores and "with many flattering smiles, and sugered speeches, acquaints him with her purpose and desire, making him many promises of kindenesse and courtesies." De Flores is so "intangled in the snares of her beautie, that hee freely promiseth to dispatch *Piracquo*; and so they first consult, and then agree vpon the manner how." The murder is committed just as in

---

1 Since the problem of authorship does not affect my argument, I use Middleton's name for brevity, instead of speaking of Middleton and Rowley.

2 John Reynolds, *God's Revenge against Murder,* 1621, Book I, History IV, pp. 105–46.

the play, except that de Flores cuts off no finger for proof. He then tells Beatrice-Joanna what he has done, "who doth heereat infinitly reioyce, and thankes him with many kisses."

Piracquo's disappearance is accepted as a mystery; Beatrice-Joanna hints to her lover that Piracquo is dead "but in such palliating tearmes, that thereby shee may delude and carry away his iudgement, from imagining, that shee had the least shadow, or finger heerein." Her father withdraws his objections and "heere our two Louers, to their exceeding great content, and infinite ioy, are vnited, and by the bond of marriage of two persons made one."

But after three happy months, Alsemero suddenly becomes jealous, and begins to restrain his wife's liberty. She complains to her father, but his remonstrances are useless, and Alsemero carries her off to the country. Her father sends de Flores to her with a letter, and de Flores "salutes and kisseth her, with many amorous embracings and dalliances." She bids him visit her often as her lover. Alsemero is told of the *liaison* by Diaphanta, and accuses Beatrice-Joanna of infidelity. She, "in seeking to conceale her whoredome, must discouer her murther," and tells Alsemero that she has to show courtesy to de Flores, because he got rid of Piracquo for her. Alsemero, who is unaffected by the revelation of the murder, charges her to admit de Flores no more; but she continues with the affair, and being caught is killed with her paramour by Alsemero. At the trial Alsemero is acquitted of murder, when Diaphanta swears to the fact of adultery. But the author regards him as guilty of concealing the murder of Piracquo, and arranges a fit punishment for him too. He is challenged by Piracquo's younger brother, Tomaso, and by using treachery in the duel kills him. For this he is seized, and after confessing the truth is executed.

The power of Middleton's play lies in something which is quite absent from the source: the absolute contrast at the beginning and the identity at the close of Beatrice-Joanna and De Flores. She is young, beautiful, a virgin, and of secure rank; he is no "Gallant young Gentleman", but a despised serving-man, an "ominous ill-fac'd fellow", one of those broken soldiers of fortune who are so common in Jacobean tragedy, and he bears the marks of a dissolute life on his face. Middleton is usually praised and rightly for the intense realism of his characterization, and particularly for the two studies of Beatrice-Joanna and De Flores; but there is more than realism here. What Mephistophilis is to Faustus, what the "supernatural solicitings" and the horror of the deed are to Macbeth, De Flores is to Beatrice-Joanna. He is repulsive and she has a strong instinctive loathing of him. She too sins against her nature, when she accepts the thing her nature most loathes as the instrument of her will. The deed comes to her mind through him, because she recognizes him as a suitable instrument. She is horrified when Alsemero suggests a challenge. She is afraid he may be killed, or that the law may step in and seize him. Her instinct tells her that he is an innocent man, and so she remembers another who is not:

> Blood-guiltiness becomes a fouler visage;—
> And now I think on one; I was to blame,
> I ha' marr'd so good a market with my scorn.[3]

It has been said that Beatrice-Joanna has no moral sense: that she is irresponsible, and only develops a sense of responsibility at the close of the play. This is true in a sense; but it might be truer to say that she develops a moral consciousness through her violation of what is fundamentally a moral instinct and a very deep one: the instinct which tells her that De Flores is her opposite.

Middleton's handling of the centre of his play is just as striking. In the centre of *Macbeth* we have the banquet, the concrete image of a hollow kingship; in the centre of *The Changeling* is the marriage that is no marriage. On her wedding night, Beatrice-Joanna has to send her waiting-woman to her husband's bed; we see her outside the door in a frenzy of jealousy and impatience. She too has given away her "eternal jewel" and got nothing in exchange. The three months of happiness in the source have disappeared, as did the ten years of prosperous kingship in Holinshed. Beatrice-Joanna might say of her married state as Macbeth does of his kingship: "To be thus is nothing." She employs De Flores to get Alsemero. She loses Alsemero and gets De Flores. She becomes "the deed's creature". In the end she recognizes her link with him and what she has become and sees herself as defiled and defiling. Like Faustus, who continues to affirm his bargain, like Macbeth who adds murder to murder, she too is involved in repetition of the original act; she has again to employ De Flores for her safety; he becomes to her "a wondrous necessary man" and she comments: "Here's man worth loving," as he makes his preparations for the dispatch of Diaphanta.

With the same sense of the implications of his theme, Middleton makes Alsemero absolutely innocent of any complicity. Beatrice-Joanna and De Flores tower over the play, as Macbeth and Lady Macbeth, and Faustus and Mephistophilis do. Alsemero's function is not to interest us in himself, but to be a standard by which we see what has happened to Beatrice-Joanna. He was to be her reward, and so, in an ironic sense, he is, when he turns upon her with horror and cries: "O, thou art all deform'd!" She makes a last despairing effort with a lie: "Remember, I am true unto your bed"; to which Alsemero replies:

---

[3] Quotations from *The Changeling* are from *The Works of Thomas Middleton* edited by A. H. Bullen, 1885–86, Vol. VI.

The bed itself's a charnel, the sheets shrouds
For murder'd carcasses.

At last she tells the truth, and the truth of the play emerges.

BEATRICE-JOANNA: Alsemero, I'm a stranger to your bed;
Your bed was cozen'd on the nuptial night,
For which your false bride died.

DE FLORES: Yes, and the while I coupled with your mate
At barley break; now we are left in hell.

VERMANDERO: We are all there, it circumscribes us here.[4]

[4] The echo from *Dr. Faustus* can hardly be accidental.

Hell hath no limits, nor is circumscrib'd
In one self place; but where we are is hell,
And where hell is, there must we ever be.

See other studies in bibliography for *The Changeling* (below, pp. 376–377).

———————

THE DRAMATIC STRUCTURE OF
THE CHANGELING *

Karl L. Holzknecht

OF *The Changeling* by Thomas Middleton and William Rowley, Professor F. S. Boas has recently written: "It is highly paradoxical that one of the most grimly powerful of Stuart tragedies should take its title from a character in a farcical underplot which has the loosest relation to the main action."[1] Years before A. C. Swinburne had said much the same thing: "The underplot from which it most unluckily and absurdly derives

* From *Renaissance Papers, A Selection of Papers Presented at The Renaissance Meeting in the Southeastern States,* ed. Allan H. Gilbert. Orangeburg, 1954, pp. 77–87. Reprinted by permission of the University of South Carolina Press, and Hennig Cohen, managing editor of the series.

[1] *Introduction to Stuart Drama,* Oxford, 1946, p. 241.

its title is very stupid, rather coarse and almost vulgar"; then he described the play as Middleton and Rowley's greatest and "a work which should suffice to make either name immortal."[2] Here are three points about this drama upon which most critics, early and late, seem to be agreed: *The Changeling* is a masterpiece marred by an irrelevant inferior subplot; the play is unfortunately named after a character in the secondary action; and as a whole it is poorly constructed.[3]

It is not the purpose of the present paper to defend the doubtful artistry of mad-house scenes intended to be comic, or even the ingenuity of a lover who becomes an inmate of a lunatic asylum to carry on his amorous intrigues. It is rather to demonstrate: (a) that *The Changeling* is not named after Antonio, the pretended madman who alone is called "the changeling" in the original *dramatis personae;* (b) that persistence in this belief leads to an incomplete and imperfect understanding of the technique of Middleton and Rowley; and (c) that by ringing variations on the theme of transformation, involving several seventeenth-century meanings of the word "changeling" and several "changelings," the authors have produced a play which is structurally sounder than is sometimes supposed.[4]

---

[2] Introduction, *Thomas Middleton,* The Mermaid Series, 1887, p. xxxv. The essay is reprinted in *The Age of Shakespeare,* London, 1908.

[3] The following opinions are typical. The underplot is "thin and clumsily connected with the main story" (P. G. Wiggin, *An Inquiry into the Authorship of the Middleton-Rowley Plays,* Radcliffe Monographs, IX, 1897, p. 43). "Rowley's underplot and some of Middleton's intermediate action do what they can to deform a play which, but for them, would be a noble and complete masterpiece" (Arthur Symons, "Middleton and Rowley," *Cambridge History of English Literature,* VI, p. 77, reprinted in *Studies in the Elizabethan Drama,* London, 1919). "It is a pity that the silly underplot should have given its name to a tragedy that ranks among the very finest in the language" (E. H. C. Oliphant, *Shakespeare and His Fellow Dramatists,* New York, 1929, II, 905). "It is a grievous commentary on public taste that the title alludes to the leading figure of the foolish underplot" (Hazelton Spencer, *Elizabethan Plays,* Boston, 1933, p. 1015). "The avowedly comic sub-plot could. . .be detached without damage and the resulting tragedy would stand as one of the most compact and pitiless in this drama" (Una Ellis-Fermor, *The Jacobean Drama,* London, 1936, p. 144). "*The Changeling* is an illustration of the dual plot construction common at the time. . . . A superbly conceived main-plot is disfigured by a trashy comic sub-plot. . . . The mad-house scenes. . .are worthless in themselves, revolting to modern taste, exhibiting Rowley's coarse and clumsy humor at its worst; they are united to the main-plot in the flimsiest fashion; the only connection between the two actions is that Antonio and Franciscus are for a time suspected of Piracquo's murder, and the final scene is almost ruined by the intrusions of these buffoons" (J. S. P. Tatlock and R. G. Martin, *Representative English Plays,* Second Editon, New York, 1938, p. 384).

[4] *The Changeling,* which dates from 1622; is based without change of characters upon History IV of Book I of John Reynolds' *The Triumphs of God's Revenge Against the Crying and Execrable Sin of Murther. Expressed in Thirty Several Tragical Histories* (1621, and reprinted frequently). But changes in the plot, made by Middleton and Rowley, alter both the psychology and the ethics of the play, as

Seeds for the misconception concerning the title-role of the play seem to have been sown in the very first edition of 1653. There in the original *dramatis personae* list Antonio

> This love's knight-errant, who hath made adventure
> For purchase of [Isabella's] love

is designated as "the changeling," but nowhere else in the text does the word occur.[5] From "the" instead of "a," later confusion has apparently sprung.[6] Yet the term "changeling" might be applied, not to one, but to several persons in the play, and in more than one sense. *The New English Dictionary* offers at least four meanings of the word, all in good use in the seventeenth century:

(1) One given to change; a fickle or inconstant person; a waverer, turncoat, renegade.
(2) A person or thing (surreptitiously) put in exchange for another.
(3) *Spec.* A child secretly substituted for another in infancy; *esp.* a child (usually stupid or ugly) supposed to have been left by fairies in exchange for one stolen.
(4) A half-witted person, idiot, imbecile.

(a) The heroine, Beatrice Joanna, in her fickleness and inconstancy is an example of (1). As T. S. Eliot has pointed out, hers is the tragedy

---

well as simplify it. The prefatory summary follows: "Beatrice-Joanna, to marry Alsemero, causeth De Flores to murder Alfonso Piracquo, who was a Suter to her. Alsemero marries her, and finding De Flores and her in adultery, kills them both. Thomaso Piracquo challengeth Alsemero for his Brother's death. Alsemero kills him treacherously in the field, and is beheaded for the same, and his body thrown into the sea. At his Execution he confesseth, that, his Wife and De Flores murthered Alfonso Piracquo. Their bodies are taken up out of their graves, then burnt, and their ashes thrown into the air." The Diaphanta story of the substitute bride is a folk tale told in the *Gesta Romanorum*. The sub-plot is an addition, but in the very next story in Reynolds the name of one of the principals is Alibius.

5 The role of Antonio appears to have been popular on the early stage; in the famous frontispiece to Kirkman's *The Wits, or Sport Upon Sport* (1622), a collection of abridged plays performed during the Commonwealth period, there is a figure called "Changeling." It may represent Antonio. But in the book itself there is no abridgement of this play. Perhaps there existed a droll which for some reason was omitted from the collection. See the edition of *The Wits* by John James Elson, New Haven, 1932, Appendix II.

6 How widespread is the belief that the play is carelessly titled can be appreciated by observing that both of the standard editions of Middleton make the assumption: *Works*, ed. Alexander Dyce (1840), IV, 206; and *Works*, ed. A. B. Bullen (1885), I, lxix, n. To the quotations included in the above note may be added the following popular works: *Chief Elizabethan Dramatists*, 1939 edition, p. 859; *English Drama, 1580–1642*, ed. C. F. T. Brooke and N. B. Paradise, 1933, p. 912; *Elizabethan and Stuart Plays* ed. C. R. Baskervill, Virgil B. Heltzel, and A. H. Nethercoat, 1934, p. 1280; and *A Survey-Outline of English Literature*, by William Bradley Otis and Morriss H. Needleman, 1938, p. 237.

of the "not naturally bad, but irresponsible and undeveloped nature caught in the consequences of its own action."[7] She follows her own whims, taking the easiest way, without once facing the cost, and the play is a study of her spiritual degeneration. As the drama opens the beautiful daughter of Vermandero, governor of the castle of Alicante, has discovered that her eyes and her heart could be mistaken. She has permitted herself to be betrothed by her father to Alonzo de Piracquo, a man she does not love. Then, only five days later, she finds "a giddy turning in her" (I. i. 164); outside a church she flirts with Alsemero, a complete stranger, and falls in love with him. She has changed her mind:

> Sure my eyes were mistaken;
> This was the man was meant me. That he should come
> So near his time and miss it.

(I. i. 88 ff.)

Her chagrin is all the greater when she learns that Alsemero is the son of a friend of her father's, and, hence, an eligible suitor—had he not come a week too late. Here is Beatrice Joanna's tragedy. Ironically, she thinks she now sees with "the eyes of judgment" (II. i. 13), "with intellectual eyesight" (II. i. 19). But in her new love for Alsemero and her desire to be rid of her old love Piracquo, she deludes her own judgment and easily wins the service of a murderer by flattering the one man she loathes. Ironically, too, it is the valorous Alsemero's suggestion that he send a challenge to Piracquo that prompts her crime (II. ii. 28 ff.). And when the deed is done, De Flores, the realist, understands her flightiness better than she does; greed for gold is unknown to him; his price is a share in Beatrice Joanna's changeling affections. Thus for her, "murder is followed by more sins"; she is "the deed's creature," transformed and known for what she is by the fiend she has made her tool and must make her third love:

> Why, 'tis impossible thou canst be so wicked,
> Or shelter such a cunning cruelty,
> To make his death the murderer of my honor!
> Thy language is so bold and vicious
> I cannot see which way I can forgive it
> With any modesty.

But she is met with an obdurate:

> Pish! you forget yourself;
> A woman dipp'd in blood, and talk of modesty!...
>   Do you urge me,
> Though thou writ'st maid, thou whore in thy affection [i. e., base desire]
> 'Twas chang'd from thy first love, and that's a kind

---

[7] "Thomas Middleton," in *For Lancelot Andrewes,* London, 1928, p. 104.

Of whoredom in thy heart; and he's chang'd now
To bring thy second on, thy Alsemero,
Whom, by all sweets that ever darkness tasted,
If I enjoy thee not, thou ne'er enjoy'st!

(III. iv. 128 ff.)

Such is the penalty which sin exacts of this proud beauty that as she sinks deeper she comes first to endure and then to love the hairy, pimply, dog-faced creature whose very sight had once been poison to her:

When w'are used
To a hard face, 'tis not so unpleasing;
It mends still in opinion, hourly mends;
I see it by experience.

(I. ii. 87–90)

I'm forced to love you now,
'Cause thou provid'st so carefully for my honour....
How rare is that man's speed!
How heartily he serves me! his face loathes one;
But look upon his care, who would not love him?
The East is not more beauteous than his service....
Here's a man worth loving!

(V. i. 48 ff.)[8]

Yet at the end, when hypocrisy can no longer save her, and she is confronted by the truth, Beatrice Joanna, the moral changeling, betrays De Flores as readily as she had hired him. With only the excuse that all she has done was for love of Alsemero, the unhappy girl confesses to adultery, murder, and deception, still professes her loathing for De Flores, and blames the stars, not her own self-will, for her ruin. Throughout Beatrice Joanna is completely without moral sense, and the play is a study of the deterioration of her character from beauty to deformity.

To some extent, but by contrast in a wholly favorable way, the hero Alsemero is also a "changeling" of the first type. A confirmed bachelor before the play opens, he has been unsusceptible to beauty until by chance he meets Beatrice Joanna, and he puzzles his friend Jasperino by his capricious delay about continuing his travels:

Lover I'm sure y'are none; the Stoic was
Found in you long ago; your mother nor

---

8 It is significant that the source of this play contains no suggestion of De Flores' deformity or the physical horror he at first inspires in Beatrice Joanna. Instead, his counterpart in the source is described as "a gallant young Gentleman" who for a long time had loved Beatrice Joanna. To attain her end, with "flattering smiles and sugared speeches," she feeds "his hopes with the air of her promises, and he is so caught and entangled in the snares of her beauty."

> Best friends, who have set snares of beauty, ay,
> And choice ones too, could never trap you that way.
>
> (I. i. 36 ff.)

But when Jasperino sees Alsemero accost Beatrice Joanna, he perceives how love may transform a man:

> The laws of the Medes are chang'd sure; salute a woman! He kisses too; wonderful! Where learnt he this? And does it perfectly too. In my .conscience, he ne'er rehears'd it before.
>
> (I. i. 57 ff.)

(b) Diaphanta, waiting woman to Beatrice Joanna, is an illustration of the second meaning of "changeling" cited above. She is the substitute bride Beatrice Joanna remorselessly persuades to take her place in the dark when she fears her own loss of virtue will be detected. "As good a soul as ever lady countenanced" (V. i. 101), Diaphanta at first is worthy of the honest, if cajoling, love of Jasperino. But she has weaknesses which prove her undoing. "'Tis a nice piece gold cannot purchase" (IV. i. 57), and the dowerless girl accepts without too much question a bribe to go to Alsemero's bed when lusty Beatrice Joanna pretends to be

> the most timorous virgin
> That ever shrunk at man's name
>
> (IV. iv. 118-9)

rather than risk discovery. Thus greed without scruple is responsible for Diaphanta's acceptance of the exchange and for her transformation from honor to dishonor. The changeling Diaphanta stays too long, and, torn by jealousy and fear, Beatrice Joanna must get rid of her second, if partly unwitting, accomplice. Apparently the necessity had not occurred to Beatrice Joanna until the realistic De Flores advised extreme measures and urged the need of a general fire alarm to justify Diaphanta's wandering so far from her chamber. Then, though she is utterly without conscience, Beatrice Joanna is almost as slow in understanding his drift as she had been before:

> BEATRICE: How? Fire, sir? That may endanger the whole house.
> DE FLORES: You talk of danger when your Fame's on fire.
>
> (V. i. 34 ff.)

(c) Finally, in the disguises they adopt for amorous purposes, not only Antonio, but also Franciscus, represents a fourth kind of "changeling," the pseudo imbecile and madman who contrast grimly with the real varieties in Dr. Alibius' sanatorium for half-wits and lunatics. They are comic pretenders which the Elizabethans would have recognized as variations of a familiar stage type.

But these transformations and changes are only a part of what unifies the play; main-plot and sub-plot, far from being flimsily held together, are actually parallels of action.[9] The more obvious has already been alluded to; the story of Alsemero and Beatrice Joanna is paralleled by that of Jasperino and Diaphanta. Both are flirtations which ripen into honorable love, only to be wrecked by thoughtlessness and irresponsible desire. A second parallel is perhaps less obvious; the "quadrangle" in which the spoiled, proud Beatrice Joanna is involved is matched on another social plane by that in which boredom rather than viciousness entangles Isabella, the wife of Dr. Alibius.[10]

Bound by the will of her father, who has betrothed her to Alonzo de Piracquo,

> A courtier and a gallant enrich'd
> With many fair and noble ornaments,

> (I. i. 222–3)

Beatrice Joanna nevertheless in Alsemero finds reason to rebel against the fetters laid by custom upon her freedom, and resorts to desperate means to break them.

In the underplot, for different reasons, Isabella, the beautiful wife of the jealous old specialist in mental diseases, resents the shackles that are laid on her. She is kept in a pinfold, watched at every turn, dependent for her social life upon imbeciles and madmen. Her spirit is at the breaking point. Moreover, Alibius has taken every precaution that the affections of his young wife shall have no opportunity to waver. He does not fear the brain-sick unfortunates in his house—they are but idiots, fools, and madmen. But he is uneasy about the daily visitants to these inmates, especially comely, well-dressed gallants with quick enticing eyes. These are shrewd temptations to clandestine love affairs, and Alibius sets his trusty Lollio to watch his lady and to take care that those who come to see idiots and madmen see no more than they came for.

It is this situation which offers the opportunity for mischief and black-mail to parallel the main plot. Lollio increases Isabella's temptation and provides her with two objects for the affection she owes her husband. He shows her their latest arrival, Franciscus, "the handsomest, discreet-est madman," who is a poet mad for love. And the pretended lunatic sings her a song. Then Lollio brings in Antonio, but is called away by other duties. The disguised idiot—the "changeling" of the original *dramatis personae*—reveals himself to Isabella as a gentleman whose love for her has wrought his transformation. He kisses her, but however great

---

[9] The thematic connection of the comic sub-plot with the main-plot of this play was first suggested by William Empson in *Some Versions of Pastoral*, London, 1935, pp. 48–52, and further developed by Miss M. C. Bradbrook in her *Themes and Conventions of Elizabethan Tragedy*, Cambridge, 1935, pp. 213–224.

[10] It is not without significance that Alibius is an amateur physician (IV. i. 20).

the provocation may be for Isabella to avenge herself upon her suspicious old husband, she does not succumb to it. She merely assures Antonio that she will not expose him; that is all the favor he may expect (III. iii. 168–71).

Their encounter has an unexpected sequel, however, which the resourceful Isabella is quite capable of handling. From his concealment Lollio has seen and heard everything, and when he returns from putting Antonio away, he grossly makes advances he had not dared before, and demands of his mistress the same price for silence which De Flores had exacted from Beatrice Joanna:

> Come sweet rogue; kiss me, my little Lacedaemonian; let me feel how thy pulses beat. Thou hast a thing about thee would do a man pleasure. I'll lay my hand on't.
>
> (III. iii. 256 ff.)

But Isabella's reply is the reverse of Beatrice Joanna's:

> Be silent, mute,
> Mute as a statue, or his injunction
> For me enjoying, shall be to cut thy throat;
> I'll do it, though for no other purpose; and
> Be sure he'll not refuse it.
>
> (*Ibid.*, 264 ff.)

Old Lollio can only murmur:

> My share, that's all;
> I'll have my fool's part with you.
>
> (*Ibid.*, 268 ff.)

That is all De Flores had demanded of Beatrice Joanna. Later Isabella joins the madmen's morris, which is to dance at Beatrice Joanna's wedding, and in her madwoman's disguise makes advances to Antonio. But obtusely the fool does not recognize her, and in disgust she remains faithful to her husband. When Lollio reiterates his claim, Isabella can reply with less indignation but with more assurance:

> The first place is thine, believe it, Lollio,
> If I do fall.
>
> (IV. iii. 47–8)

Thus there develops in the maligned subplot which is said to be so loosely connected with the rest of the play a comparatively innocent parallel to the central situation in the main plot: a young woman has every provocation and every opportunity for wavering but does not, and a servant tries to blackmail his lady for a share in her supposed frailty. In both plots what had been alluded to as "love's tame madness" (II. i.

THE DRAMATIC STRUCTURE OF *THE CHANGELING*   375

153) "shapes and transshapes, destroys and builds again" (IV. iii. 25–26).
The similarity of love and madness is often reiterated:

> O heaven! Is this the waning moon?
> Does love turn fool, run mad, and all at once?
> Sirrah, here's a madman akin to the fool too,
> A lunatic lover.

(IV. iii. 1–4)

Isabella's exclamation is provoked by her transformed lovers, but it
applies equally to other persons in the play.

The parallelism, however, does not end here. A few scenes later Lollio
keeps both Antonio and Franciscus encouraged by news of rivals, and
by assuring each that the lady prefers him to his rival, but must have
some proof of his love to her. The dialogue which follows has a familiar
ring:

> FRANCISCUS: There I meet my wishes.
> LOLLIO: That will not serve, you must meet her enemy and yours.
> FRANCISCUS: He's dead already. . . . Show me the man.
> LOLLIO: Ay, that's a right course now; see him before you kill
>   in any case; and yet it needs not go so far neither. 'Tis
>   but a fool that haunts the house and my mistress in the
>   shape of an idiot; bang but his fool's coat well-
>   favouredly, and 'tis well.

(IV. iii. 212 ff.)

At the close of the tragedy all of these unifying themes, these mad
transformations various kind of love have wrought, these parallel stories,
are brought together. Vermandero produces the two suspects of Piracquo's
murder:

> Beseech you, hear me; these two have been disguised
> E'er since the deed was done.

Alsemero brings out two others

> That were more close disguised than you two could be
> E'er since the deed was done.

Then the grief-stricken husband summarizes the effect which the changeling moon has had on Beatrice, De Flores, and himself:

> Here is beauty chang'd
> To ugly whoredom;[11] here servant-obedience
> To master sin, imperious murder;
> I, a suppos'd husband, chang'd embraces
> With wantonness,—but that was paid before.

---

[11] Cf. De Flores on Beatrice's change in III. iv. 144 ff. (quoted on p. 370, above);
also V. iii. 33 and 56.

He turns to Tomaso de Piracquo, who had sought to avenge his brother's murder upon Alsemero,[12] but discovered his error in time:

> Your change is come too, from an ignorant wrath
> To knowing friendship.—Are there any more on's?

Antonio, one of the suspects of the murder, speaks up:

> Yes, sir, I was chang'd too from a little ass as I was to a great fool as I am; and had like to ha' been chang'd to the gallows, but that you know that my innocence always excuses me.

Franciscus adds:

> I was chang'd from a little wit to be stark mad,
> Almost for the same purpose.

Then, turning to her husband, Isabella says:

> Your change is still behind [i.e., lagging, to come in the future]
> But deserve best your transformation:
> You are a jealous coxcomb, keep schools of folly,
> And teach your scholars how to break your own head.

To this veiled threat Alibius replies:

> I see all apparent, wife, and will change now
> Into a better husband, and never keep
> Scholars that shall be wiser than myself.

Here is a neat unifying conclusion to what, in the Elizabethan manner, is a well-made play.

---

[12] Tomaso's quarrel also has a "changeling" basis in that Alsemero had taken his brother's place in Beatrice Joanna's affections:

> I should have a brother in your place;
> How treachery and malice have disposed of him
> I'm bound to inquire of him which holds his right,
> Which never could come fairly. (IV. ii. 70–73).

THE CHANGELING

Barker, Richard H. *Thomas Middleton.* New York, 1958, pp. 121–131.

Bawcutt, N. W., ed. *The Changeling.* The Revels Plays. Cambridge, Mass., 1958, pp. xlv–lxviii.

Black, Matthew W., ed. *The Changeling.* Mathew Carey Library, Philadelphia and London, 1966.

Boas, Frederick S. *An Introduction to Stuart Drama.* Oxford, 1946, pp. 241–245.

Bradbrook, Muriel C. *Theme and Conventions of Elizabethan Tragedy.* Cambridge, Eng., 1936 (reprinted 1957), pp. 213–224, 234–239.

Eliot, T. S. *Selected Essays.* New Edition. New York, 1950, pp. 140–148.

Ellis-Fermor, Una. *Jacobean Drama,* 4th rev. ed., London, 1958, pp. 144–149.

Empson, William. *Some Versions of Pastoral.* London, 1935, pp. 48–52.

Engelberg, Edward. "Tragic Blindness in *The Changeling* and *Women Beware Women,*" *MLQ,* XXII (1962), 20–28.

Farr, Dorothy M. *"The Changeling,"* *MLR,* LXII (1967), 586–597.

Hibbard, G. R. "The Tragedies of Thomas Middleton and the Decadence of the Drama," *Renaissance and Modern Studies* (University of Nottingham), I (1957), 35–64.

Jump, John D. "Middleton's Tragedies," in *The Age of Shakespeare,* ed. Boris Ford. Baltimore, 1955, pp. 361–368.

Kehler, Dorothea. "Rings and Jewels in *The Changeling,*" *ELN,* V (1967), 15–17.

Ornstein, Robert. *The Moral Vision of Jacobean Tragedy.* Madison, Wis., 1960 (reprinted 1965), pp. 179–190.

Ribner, Irving. *Jacobean Tragedy: The Quest for Moral Order.* New York and London, 1962, pp. 126–137.

Ricks, Christopher. "The Moral and Poetic Structure of *The Changeling,*" *EIC,* X (1960), 290–306.

Schoenbaum, Samuel. *Middleton's Tragedies: A Critical Study.* New York, 1955, pp. 132–150.

Thomson, Patricia, ed. *The Changeling.* The New Mermaids. London, 1964, pp. xi–xxviii.

Tomlinson, T. B. *A Study of Elizabethan and Jacobean Tragedy.* Cambridge, Eng., and Melbourne, 1964, pp. 185–212.

Williams, George Walton, ed. *The Changeling.* Regents Renaissance Drama Series. Lincoln, Nebraska, 1966, pp. ix–xxiv.

Philip Massinger

SOCIAL MORALITY IN
A NEW WAY TO PAY OLD DEBTS *

L. C. Knights

THE first symptom of decadence that we notice in Massinger is his dependence on Shakespeare. Canon Cruickshank gives a close-packed page to "a few examples of the imitation of incidents," and over seven pages to "parallels in thought and diction."[1] The nature of this indebtedness is discussed by Mr. Eliot, who concludes that,

> Massinger's feeling for language had outstripped his feeling for things; that his eye and his vocabulary were not in co-operation.... Every vital development in language is a development of feeling as well. The verse of Shakespeare and the major Shakespearian dramatists is an innovation of this kind, a true mutation of species. The verse practised by Massinger is a different verse from that of his predecessors; but it is not a development based on, or resulting from, a new way of feeling. On the contrary it seems to lead us away from feeling altogether.[2]

Massinger not only imitates Shakespeare, he repeats his imitations and he repeats himself. There is not only dilution, there is a tendency toward

* From L. C. Knights, *Drama and Society in the Age of Jonson*. London, Chatto and Windus, 1937, pp. 270–280. Reprinted by permission of Chatto and Windus, Ltd.

[1] A. H. Cruickshank, *Philip Massinger*, pp. 77–81, 163–168.
[2] *Elizabethan Essays*, pp. 159–160.

stereotyped feelings and perceptions. And besides the influence of Shakespeare there is the influence of Jonson, most potent in *The City Madam*.

> In by-corners of
> This sacred room, silver in bags, heap'd up
> Like billets saw'd and ready for the fire,
> Unworthy to hold fellowship with bright gold
> That flow'd about the room, conceal'd itself.
> There needs no artificial light; the splendour
> Makes a perpetual day there, night and darkness
> By that still-burning lamp for ever banish'd!
> But when, guided by that, my eyes had made
> Discovery of the caskets, and they open'd,
> Each sparkling diamond from itself shot forth
> A pyramid of flames, and in the roof
> Fix'd it a glorious star, and made the place
> Heaven's abstract, or epitome!—rubies, sapphires,
> And ropes of orient pearl, these seen, I could not
> But look on with contempt. And yet I found
> What weak credulity could have no faith in,
> A treasure far exceeding these: here lay
> A manor bound fast in a skin of parchment,
> The wax continuing hard, the acres melting;
> Here a sure deed of gift for a market-town,
> If not redeem'd this day, which is not in
> The unthrift's power: there being scarce one shire
> In Wales or England, where my monies are not
> Lent out at usury, the certain hook
> To draw in more. I am sublimed! gross earth
> Supports me not; I walk on air.[3]

There is no need to quote Volpone's address to his gold;[4] it is clear where the central inspiration comes from. There is, besides, a minor borrowing from *Epicoene*,[5] and the speech ends with a reminiscence of *Sejanus*.[6] The play reveals other direct borrowings,[7] but what this speech

---

[3] *The City Madam*, III. iii (IV, 65). [Gifford's edition of the *Plays* is cited throughout by volume and page number directly following Act and Scene references.—Ed.]

[4] *Volpone*, I. i.

[5] *Epicoene*, II. i ("she feels not how the land drops away, nor the acres melt").

[6] "My roof receives me not; 'tis air I tread" (*Sejanus*, V. i).

[7] *E.g.*

> And when you appear
> Like Juno in full majesty, and my nieces
> Like Iris, Hebe, or what deities else...

Cf. *Volpone*, III. vi (to Celia) and, more particularly, *The Alchemist*, IV. i ("Thy wardrobe Richer than nature's," etc.). Cf. "A perpetuity of being"—*The City Madam*, V. iii (IV, 108)—and "a perpetuity of life and lust"—*The Alchemist*, IV. i. (repeated as "A perpetuity of pride and pleasure" in *The Bondman*, I. iii).

shows also is that Massinger is not a mere unconscious plagiarist. The passage has a life of its own, and it forms a genuinely original variation on the Jonsonian mode. Much more could be said about Massinger's verse. It is capable of sudden vividness—

> Think of the basket, wretches,
> And a coal-sack for a winding-sheet.[8]

and it is almost always a serviceable dramatic medium. It is, however, "the nearest approach to the language of real life at all compatible with a fixed metre,"[9] and its virtues—perspicuity and a freedom from "poeticisms"—too easily become vices.

> Now to you we'll discover
> The close design that brought us, with assurance,
> If you lend your aids to furnish us with that
> Which in the colony was not to be purchased,
> No merchant ever made such a return
> For his most precious venture, as you shall
> Receive from us.[10]

This is not verse at all, and passages of this kind reinforce Mr. Eliot's verdict that "if Massinger's age, 'without being exactly corrupt, lacks moral fibre,' Massinger's verse, without being exactly corrupt, suffers from cerebral anaemia"[11]—

> Old poets fancy, (your cramm'd wardrobes richer
> Than various natures,) and draw down the envy
> Of our western world upon you

(III, ii [IV, 63].)

though one has to add that it is far from being consistently anaemic.

Comment of this kind was necessary preliminary to a consideration of Massinger's handling of social themes in his...admirable comedy, *A New Way to Pay Old Debts....* Here, as the verse tells us to expect, we find that Massinger is derivative, but not, like Shirley, entirely dependent upon a literary common stock. His themes are drawn from the Jonsonian field, he breaks no fresh ground, and his manner of approach and presentation is obviously dependent upon Jonson's.... [His] play lives; it is not a mere *repetition* of work that had been done better. That is to say that there is fresh perception of a contemporary world, and the treatment shows that the tradition on which Jonson drew is active in Massinger, not a matter of inert convention.

---

[8] *The City Madam,* IV. iii. (IV, 86). The basket is the basket of food provided by charity for the poorest prisoners.

[9] Coleridge, *Lectures on Shakespeare* (Bohn Edition), p. 404.

[10] *The City Madam,* IV. i (IV, 95).

[11] *Elizabethan Essays,* p. 162.

In *A New Way to Pay Old Debts* (1621) Wellborn, ruined by his own prodigality and by the extortion of his uncle, Sir Giles Overreach, persuades Lady Allworth, whose late husband he had once helped in similar circumstances, to countenance a plot, and allows it to be understood that he is about to marry her. His credit immediately rises; to those who had turned on him in his degradation he is now "worthy Master Wellborn." Even Sir Giles insists on lending him a thousand pounds and protests his affection—while plotting to gain his lands when he shall have married the widow. Meanwhile Sir Giles has planned to marry his daughter, Margaret, to Lord Lovell, whose page, Tom Allworth, is in love with the girl. Lord Lovell helps the lovers, and Tom, instead of his lord, is secretly married to Margaret. By this time Overreach has been deprived of the lands extorted from Wellborn and the double disappointment drives him mad. Lord Lovell marries the widow, and Wellborn, determined to regain his reputation as well as his estate, goes abroad to fight in the wars.

The relationship between this play and Middleton's *A Trick to Catch the Old One* has been made too much of. Massinger borrows the central device of the plot—the hero's supposed engagement to a rich widow—but the scope and method are entirely different from Middleton's. In his comedies Middleton's inspiration derives from nothing more profound than the desire to make a play; Massinger does at least feel indignation at a contemporary enormity. It is commonly recognized that Sir Giles Overreach—"Cormorant Overreach" (I. i [III. 488])—is Sir Giles Mompesson. The play was produced shortly after his impeachment,[12] and the Christian name was probably sufficient indication for the first audience. As Gifford points out, Massinger refers to Mompesson's gold and silver thread monopoly in *The Bondman* (II. iii—1623).

> Here's another,
> Observe but what a cozening look he has!
> Hold up thy head, man; if, for drawing gallants
> Into mortgages for commodities, cheating heirs
> *With your new counterfeit gold thread,* and gumm'd velvets,
> He does not transcend all that went before him,
> *Call in his patent.*

Overreach, moreover, like Mompesson, has power over tavern keepers:

> For, from the tavern to the taphouse, all,
> On forfeiture of their licences, stand bound
> Ne'er to remember who their best guests were,
> If they grow poor,
>
> (I. i [III, 485])

---

[12] Schelling says that "the play was certainly on the stage by 1625," and quotes Fleay's opinion that the first performance took place in 1622 (*Elizabethan Drama,* II, p. 253). The Shakespeare Association's *Chart of Plays* (ed. W. P. Barrett), p. 38, places it in 1621, the year of the impeachment.

and Tapwell and Froth are represented as creatures of Sir Giles. Mompesson, it will be remembered, issued licences solely with an eye to his profit, ignoring his functions as a guardian of public order.[13]

But just as Dryden's Achitophel stands independently of the historic Shaftesbury, so Overreach is very much more than a portrait of a living person. *A New Way to Pay Old Debts* is a play—something made, not a mirror of persons and events. Overreach is created, though not quite consistently,[14] on Jonsonian lines.

MARRALL: I wonder,
          Still with your license, why, your worship having
          The power to put this thin-gut in commission,
          You are not in't yourself?
OVERREACH: Thou art a fool;
          In being out of office I am out of danger;
          Where, if I were a justice, besides the trouble,
          I might or out of wilfulness, or error,
          Run myself finely into a praemunire,
          And so become a prey to the informer.

[13] Gifford gives a quotation from Wilson's *Life and Reign of James I* (Fol. 155), which may be reproduced here:
"They [Mompesson and Michell] found out a new alchemistical way to make gold and silver lace with copper and other sophistical materials, to cozen and deceive the people. And so poisonous were the drugs that made up this deceitful composition, that they rotted the hands and arms, and brought lameness upon those that wrought it; some losing their eyes, and many their lives, by the venom of the vapours that came from it. . . . Sir Giles Mompesson had fortune enough in the country to make him happy, if that sphere could have contained him, but the vulgar and universal error of satiety with present enjoyments, made him too big for a rustical condition, and when he came at court he was too little for that, so that some novelty must be taken up to set him in *aequilibrio* to the place he was in, no matter what it was, let it be never so pestilent and mischievous to others, he cared not, so he found benefit by it. To him Michell is made compartner; a poor sneaking justice, that lived among the brothels near Clarton-well, whose clerk and he picked a livelihood out of those corners, giving warrants for what they did, besides anniversary stipends (the frequent revenue of some justices of those times) for conniving. This thing was a poisonous plant in its own nature, and the fitter to be an ingredient to such a composition—whereby he took liberty to be more ravenous upon poor people, to the grating of the bones, and sucking out the very marrow of their substance."
"From this apposite extract," says Gifford, "it will be sufficiently apparent not only from whence Massinger derived his principal character, but also where he found Marrall and Greedy. The 'speaking justice,' Michell, undoubtedly sat for the latter, and his clerk for the 'term-driving' Marrall; whose hopeful education will now enable the reader to account for his knowledge of the 'minerals, which he incorporated with the ink and wax' of Wellborn's bond" (III, 505–506).

[14] Mr. Eliot has pointed out the inconsistencies in the mode in which Overreach is presented. Massinger, that is, has not Jonson's complete sureness of purpose. A minor example is provided by the Justice, Greedy; he is admirably comic, but he has no part in the main design, as Jonson's minor figures have, and his exhibition of greed tends to become merely extraneous fooling.

> No, I'll have none of't; 'tis enough I keep
> Greedy at my devotion: so he serve
> My purposes, let him hang, or damn, I care not;
> Friendship is but a word.

(II. i [III, 503–504])

Those lines are spoken by a descendant of Barabas; other passages clearly relate Overreach to Volpone and Sir Epicure Mammon,[15] though as each example shows, Massinger is a creator inspired by his predecessors, not a mere imitator.

Throughout the play there is a sure grasp of the actual. Massinger, that is, observes the significant economic activities of the time, and sees their significance.[16]

> MARRALL: What course take you,
> With your good patience, to hedge in the manor
> Of your neighbour, master Frugal? as 'tis said
> He will nor sell, nor borrow, nor exchange;
> And his land lying in the midst of your many lordships
> Is a foul blemish.
>
> OVERREACH: I have thought on't, Marrall,
> And it shall take. I must have all men sellers,
> And I the only purchaser....
> I'll therefore buy some cottage near his manor,
> Which done, I'll make my men break ope his fences,
> Ride o'er his standing corn, and in the night
> Set fire on his barns, or break his cattle's legs:
> These trespasses draw on suits, and suits expenses,
> Which I can spare, but soon will beggar him.
> When I have harried him thus two or three year,
> Though he sue *in forma pauperis,* in spite
> Of all his thrift and care, he'll grow behind hand....
> Then, with the favour of my man of law,
> I will pretend some title: want will force him

---

15 *E.g.*   Spare for no cost; let my dressers crack with the weight
Of curious viands....
And let no plate be seen but what's pure gold,
Or·such whose workmanship exceeds the matter
That it is made of; let my choicest linen
Perfume the room, and, when we wash, the water,
With precious powders mix'd, so please my lord,
That he may with envy wish to bathe so ever.

(III. ii [III, 529–30])

—A good example of the poetic force that is generated by Massinger's carefully managed, cumulative constructions.

16 Cf. The Projector scenes in *The Emperor of the East,* and Timoleon's speeches to the senate in *The Bondman,* I. iii. Massinger also had keener *political* interests than most of his fellows. Cf. S. R. Gardiner, "The Political Element in Massinger," *The Contemporary Review,* August 1876.

> To put it to arbitrement; then, if he sell
> For half the value, he shall have ready money,
> And I possess his land.
>
> (II. i [III, 504–506])

Elsewhere Overreach describes himself as

> Extortioner, tyrant, cormorant, or intruder
> On my poor neighbour's right, or grand encloser
> Of what was common, to my private use,
>
> (IV. i [III, 553])

and his relationship with Greedy typifies the power of money over justice.[17] The reflection (if we call it that) is of course magnified—

> To have a usurer that starves himself. . . .
> To grow rich, and then purchase, is too common:
> But this Sir Giles feeds high, keeps many servants,
> Who must at his command do any outrage;
> Rich in his habit, vast in his expenses;
> Yet he to admiration still increases
> In wealth and lordships. . . .
> . . .No man dares reprove him.
> Such a spirit to dare, and power to do, were never
> Lodged so unluckily
>
> (II. ii [III, 517])

—but Overreach certainly represents the new aristocracy of wealth. It is not merely that he plans to marry his daughter to a lord, so that she may "write honourable, right honourable" and have the wives "of errant knights" to tie her shoes—in spite of the

> strange antipathy
> Between us and true gentry
>
> (II. i [III, 508])

—he is also conscious of his own social power:

> In birth! why art thou not my daughter,
> The blest child of my industry and wealth?
>
> .   .   .   .

[17]   . . .And yet
The chapfall'n justice did his part, returning,
For your advantage, the certificate,
Against his conscience, and his knowledge too,
With your good favour, to the utter ruin
Of the poor farmer.   (II. i [III, 503])
He frights men out of their estates,
And breaks through all law-nets, made to curb ill men,
As they were cobwebs.   (II. ii [III, 517])

> Be thou no enemy to thyself; my wealth
> Shall weigh his titles down, and make you equals.

> (III. ii [III, 532–534])

But more goes to the making of Overreach than typical traits. I do not think it is too much to say that he represents the traditional figure of Avarice—one of the Seven Deadly Sins. He is explicitly anti-Christian:

> I would be worldly wise; for the other wisdom
> That does prescribe us a well-govern'd life,
> And to do right to others, as ourselves,
> I value not an atom.

> (II. i [III, 504])

He instructs his daughter, Margaret,

> Learn any thing,
> And from any creature that may make thee great;
> From the devil himself,

> (III. ii [III, 535])

and her reply, "This is but devilish doctrine," both echoes Wellborn's retort to Marrall, "Thy religion! The devil's creed!" (II. i [III, 509]) and foreshadows the "atheistical assertions" that Overreach makes to Lord Lovell when he expects the latter to become his son-in-law:

> Then rest secure; not the hate of all mankind here,
> Nor fear of what can fall on me hereafter,
> Shall make me study aught but your advancement
> One story higher: an earl! if gold can do it.
> Dispute not my religion, nor my faith;
> Though I am born thus headlong by my will,
> You may make choice of what belief you please,
> To me they are equal.

> (IV. i [III, 553–554])

It would be foolish to make too much of isolated passages of this kind, but they help to bring out the theological-moral aspect of a scene such as that where Marrall—following the instructions of Overreach, "this blasphemous beat" (IV. i [III, 554])—attempts to drive Wellborn "to despair."[18] "Despair" had fairly definite religious connotations, and when Marrall fails to persuade Wellborn to hang himself—

---

18 The second half of II. i—

> Do anything to work him to despair,
> And 'tis thy masterpiece.

Miss Bradbrook has pointed out the references to religious "despair" in *The Duchess of Malfi.—Themes and Conventions of Elizabethan Tragedy*, pp. 195–212.

> Will you stay till you die in a ditch, or lice devour you?
> ...If you like not hanging, drown yourself; take some course
> For your reputation,

the religious theme is made explicit:

> 'Twill not do, dear tempter,
> With all the rhetoric the fiend hath taught you.
> I am as far as thou art from despair.

(II. i [III, 510])

A New Way to Pay Old Debts is a comedy, not a morality play, but that it is so much more than mere amusement is largely due to the way in which Massinger has drawn on and made his own the traditional attitude toward avarice and worldly ambition.

MASSINGER

Ball, Robert H. *The Amazing Career of Sir Giles Overreach.* Princeton, 1939.

Bennett, A. L. "The Moral Tone of Massinger's Dramas," *Papers on Language and Literature,* II (1966), 207–216.

Boas, Frederick S. *An Introduction to Stuart Drama.* Oxford, 1946, pp. 304–330.

Byrne, Muriel St. Clare, ed. *A New Way to Pay Old Debts.* London, 1949, pp. 5–16.

Chelli, Maurice. *Le Drame de Massinger.* Lyon, 1923, pp. 178–180, 279–282, *et passim.*

Craik, T. W., ed. *A New Way to Pay Old Debts.* The New Mermaids. London, 1964, pp. xii–xxii.

Cruickshank, A. H. *Philip Massinger.* New York, [1926].

Cunningham, John E. *Elizabethan and Early Stuart Drama.* London, 1965, pp. 102–107.

Dunn, Thomas A. *Philip Massinger: The Man and the Playwright.* Edinburgh, 1957, pp. 58–61, 122–125, 133–134.

Eliot, T. S. "Philip Massinger," in *Selected Essays, 1917–1932.* New York, 1932, pp. 181–195.

Enright, D. J. "Poetic Satire and Satire in Verse: A Consideration of Jonson and Massinger," *Scrutiny,* XVIII (1951–52), 211–223.

Gross, Allen. "Contemporary Politics in Massinger," *SEL,* VI (1966), 279–290.

_____ "Social Change and Philip Massinger," *SEL,* VII (1967), 329–342.

Quennell, Peter. *The Singular Preference: Portraits and Essays.* New York, 1953, pp. 37–43.

Spencer, Benjamin Townley. "Philip Massinger," in *Seventeenth Century Studies,* ed. Robert Shafter. Princeton, 1933, pp. 3–119.

John Ford

THE LAST JACOBEAN TRAGEDY *

Clifford Leech

PART of the fascination which...Jacobean tragedies hold for us lies in their shifting attitudes. We have the sense of being in a world like the one we have felt on our own pulses—where there is an uncertainty in the basis for judgment, where an ever-resurgent scepticism coexists with an inherited scheme of values. In that world the rebel can exercise a peculiar power over us, can never be quite denied our sympathy, yet can never firmly hold our approval.

But this kind of tragic writing had a comparatively short life in the seventeenth-century theatre.... Webster's tragedies are later than Shakespeare's, and Middleton's later still, but the tragic impulse does not remain long with either of them. By the end of James's reign the drama had ceased to make hardly endurable demands on the minds of its public.

It was in such a state of affairs that Ford set up as an independent dramatist. Earlier he had been associated with Dekker, in whose work Christian feeling is invariably strong, and Ford's own share in *The Witch of Edmonton, The Sun's Darling* and, we may believe, *The Spanish Gipsy* is by no means incompatible with his writing of *Christes Bloodie Sweat*. But we have noted in his non-dramatic writings a wide-

* From *John Ford and the Drama of His Time*. London, 1957, pp. 46, 48–64. Reprinted by permission of Chatto and Windus Ltd.

spreading interest in Elizabethan and Jacobean drama: Kyd and Marlowe, Shakespeare and Chapman, all left their casual imprint on his prose and verse. He had, moreover, in *Fames Memorial* and *Honor Trivmphant,* shown his preoccupation with the love of woman and beauty, a preoccupation which he perhaps over-strenuously disowned in *Christes Bloodie Sweat*:

> Loue is no god, as some of wicked times
> (Led with the dreaming dotage of their folly)
> Haue set him foorth in their lasciuious rimes,
> Bewitch'd with errors, and conceits vnholy:
>   It is a raging blood affections blind,
>   Which boiles both in the body and the mind.

In *Honor Trivmphant* he displayed a liking for paradox, and in *The Golden Meane* and *A Line of Life* his stoicism is presented with little reference to the Christian scheme. A man in whom these contrary impulses could flourish, and who had responded freely to the tragic writing of his youth, should not surprise us if he manages to re-create in one play, perhaps the first that he wrote independently,[1] the Jacobean tragic spirit. This indeed is his achievement in *'Tis Pity She's a Whore.*

Because it is a re-creation we shall find something of strain in it. Ford goes out of his way to shock his audience. Giovanni must not merely rebel, as Bussy d'Ambois does: he must proclaim himself atheist. His love must be not merely illicit, but incestuous. Not only must he kill Annabella, but he must make his last entry on the stage bearing her heart on the end of his dagger. The Jacobean writers had indeed cultivated the horrible and the shocking, needing to jolt an audience accustomed to tragedy, to prevent them from merely recognizing in disaster an old dramatic acquaintance. But there is something "operatic," something in the Fletcherian mode, in *'Tis Pity She's a Whore.* Though when he wrote it he was around forty years of age, Ford shows something of a mere desire to make our flesh creep. That needs to be said, but the criticism does not dispose of the play. The blemish is almost inevitable when a dramatist is working in circumstances of special difficulty, is aware that his audience is hardly to be made to share his view of things. This is indeed frequent in drama, from the *Electra* of Euripides to the plays of Mr. Sartre and the films of Mr. Luis Buñuel.

The main action of the play concerns the love of Giovanni and Annabella, a brother and sister. In the first scene Giovanni is confessing his love to the Friar Bonaventura, who is horrified and counsels prayer and fasting. Giovanni is already in a mood to challenge the Church's teaching, yet he agrees to try what the Friar recommends. Next we meet him

---

1 The dedication describes the play as "these first fruits of my leisure." G. E. Bentley, *The Jacobean and Caroline Stage,* III, 463–4, is unconvinced by this evidence, and certainly it is not to be relied on.

still consumed with passion, and he brings himself to tell Annabella of his condition. She reveals her own love for him, and for a time they live in secret joy, their relationship known only to the Friar and Annabella's gross servant Putana. Then Annabella is pregnant, and she agrees to marry her suitor Soranzo. He discovers her condition, and attempts to find out the identity of her lover. He treats her brutally, but the secret is safe with her, and she jeers at him and exults in her love—wanting to drive him to the point of killing her. Then, through a trick of Soranzo's servant Vasques, Putana is made to reveal that Giovanni is his sister's lover. Soranzo, planning revenge, invites all the city's nobles to a feast. Giovanni comes early, and Soranzo allows him to visit Annabella. The lovers realize their end must be near: Giovanni kills Annabella, and then comes among the assembly at the feast, proclaiming his love and the murder he has done, and displaying his sister's heart on his dagger. He kills Soranzo and is himself killed by a troupe of banditti whom Soranzo has hired for the achievement of his revenge. The father of the lovers dies of grief and horror, and the Cardinal, who is conveniently present, moralizes the play's ending.

There are two subordinate actions. Soranzo has formerly seduced Hippolita, the wife of Richardetto: she tries to win the help of Vasques, Soranzo's servant, in order to revenge herself on Soranzo; Vasques, however, is loyal to his master, and Hippolita dies by her own poison. Her husband Richardetto is believed to be dead, but he returns to the city in a physician's disguise, accompanied by his niece Philotis: he too plans Soranzo's death, but this leads only to the accidental killing of the comic Bergetto, a suitor of Annabella who has transferred his affections to Philotis. I have already commented on Ford's use of crude comedy to set off the high passion of his chief characters, but the subordinate actions in this play involving Hippolita and Richardetto have an additional function. They make us recognize the moral worthlessness of Soranzo. Otherwise our sympathy might have gone to him, the convenient husband, and away from Giovanni and Annabella. As it is, we care not one jot for his deception, and our sympathy remains with the brother-and-sister lovers. This firm separation of our symphty from Soranzo is finally ensured when, in V. iv, he permits Giovanni to visit Annabella once more, so that Giovanni may be killed fresh from the committing of sin. Those critics, incidentally, who take Hamlet literally in the prayer-scene should note the effect of this similar passage in Ford's play. Miss Sargeaunt is surely justified in her view that Maeterlinck, in his version of 'Tis Pity, was wrong to excise the Hippolita plot.[2] And, though the Bergetto affair is crude, we shall not enter fully into Ford's world unless we see his motive for introducing it, the contrast between the intensity and the reluctance of Giovanni's love and the casualness and easy pleasure of Bergetto's.

---

[2] M. Joan Sargeaunt, *John Ford*, Oxford, 1935, p. 108.

What, however, are we to make of the incest-story? In the opening
speech of the play the Friar forbids the wanton exploration of heaven's
decrees:

> Dispute no more in this; for know, young man,
> These are no school-points; nice philosophy
> May tolerate unlikely arguments,
> But Heaven admits no jest: wits that presum'd
> On wit too much, by striving how to prove
> There was no God with foolish grounds of art,
> Discover'd first the nearest way to hell,
> And fill'd the world with devilish atheism.
> Such questions, youth, are fond: far better 'tis
> To bless the sun than reason why it shines;
> Yet He thou talk'st of is above the sun.
> No more! I may not hear it.

(I. i.)

Later he admits that, were it not for revelation, there might be something in Giovanni's claims for liberty:

> O ignorance in knowledge! Long ago,
> How often have I warn'd thee this before!
> Indeed, if we were sure there were no Deity,
> Nor Heaven nor Hell, then to be led alone
> By Nature's light—as were philosophers
> Of elder times—might instance some defence.
> But 'tis not so: then, madman, thou wilt find
> That Nature is in Heaven's positions blind.

(II. v.)

This exclamation has been provoked by an argument of Giovanni's which
must remind us of Ford's theses in *Honor Trivmphant*.[3] Here he claims
that Annabella's physical beauty implies a beauty of soul and thus a
goodness in her love:

> Father, in this you are uncharitable;
> What I have done I'll prove both fit and good.
> It is a principle which you have taught,
> When I was yet your scholar, that the frame
> And composition of the mind doth follow
> The frame and composition of [the] body:
> So, where the body's furniture is *beauty,*
> The mind's must needs be *virtue*; which allow'd,
> Virtue itself is reason but refin'd,
> And love the quintessence of that: this proves,
> My sister's beauty being rarely fair
> Is rarely virtuous; chiefly in her love,

---

3 See Clifford Leech, *John Ford and the Drama of his Time,* London, 1957, p. 20.

And chiefly in that love, her love to me:
If hers to me, then so is mine to her;
Since in like causes are effects alike.

(II. v.)

When the lovers meet for the last time, Annabella is repentant for her sin and anxious to be reconciled to heaven, but Giovanni cannot believe in what "the schoolmen" teach:

> GIOVANNI: ...The schoolmen teach that all this globe of earth
> Shall be consum'd to ashes in a minute.
> ANNABELLA: So I have read too.
> GIOVANNI: But 'twere somewhat strange
> To see the waters burn: could I believe
> This might be true, I could believe as well
> There might be hell or heaven.
> ANNABELLA: That's most certain.
> GIOVANNI: A dream, a dream!

(V. v.)

Yet he attempts a compromise before the act of killing her. He hopes for her salvation and for some recognition that their incest may be distinguished from those unjustified by love:

> If ever after-times should hear
> Of our fast-knit affections, though perhaps
> The laws of conscience and of civil use
> May justly blame us, yet when they but know
> Our loves, that love will wipe away that rigour
> Which would in other incests be abhorr'd.

(V. v.)

Moreover, Ford repeatedly suggests here the idea of fate, which allows Giovanni no choice but to pursue his illicit love. Thus Giovanni views his situation before he has spoken to Annabella:

> Lost! I am lost! my fates have doom'd my death:
> The more I strive, I love; the more I love,
> The less I hope: I see my ruin certain.
> What judgment or endeavours could apply
> To my incurable and restless wounds,
> I throughly have examin'd, but in vain.
> O, that it were not in religion sin
> To make our love a god, and worship it!
> I have even wearied Heaven with prayers, dried up
> The spring of my continual tears, even starv'd
> My veins with daily fasts: what wit or art
> Could counsel, I have practis'd; but, alas,
> I find all these but dreams, and old men's tales,
> To fright unsteady youth; I'm still the same:
> Or I must speak, or burst. 'Tis not, I know,

My lust, but 'tis my fate that leads me on.

(I. iii.)

Before that he has protested that he will follow the Friar's counsel of prayer and fasting, but if it fails he will know that he cannot free himself from the fate that is on him:

All this I'll do, to free me from the rod
Of vengeance; else I'll swear my fate's my god.

(I. i.)

Yet, when the Friar tries to prevent Giovanni from attending Soranzo's feast, he defies prophecy as Bussy d'Ambois did in Chapman's play when he was warned not to go to his last assignation with his mistress:

FRIAR: Be rul'd, you shall not go.
GIOVANNI: Not go! stood Death
Threatening his armies of confounding plagues
With hosts of dangers hot as blazing stars,
I would be there: not go! yes, and resolve
To strike as deep in slaughter as they all;
For I will go.
    FRIAR: Go where thou wilt: I see
The wildness of thy fate draws to an end,
To a bad fearful end.

(V. iii.)

This, of course, is *hubris,* but Giovanni's arrogance is at times stronger still. We hear his triumphant words as he listens in the gallery while Soranzo woos Annabella, who is not yet conscious of her pregnancy:

SORANZO: Have you not will to love?
ANNABELLA: Not you.
SORANZO: Whom then?
ANNABELLA: That's as the fates infer.
GIOVANNI: [*aside*]. Of those I'm regent now.

(III. ii.)

And, seeing Annabella for the last time, he reproaches her for not recognizing the mastery of fate that he believes was almost his:

Thou art a faithless sister, else thou know'st,
Malice, or any treachery beside,
Would stoop to my bent brows: why, I hold fate
Clasp'd in my fist, and could command the course
Of time's eternal motion, hadst thou been
One thought more steady than an ebbing sea.

(V. v.)

So at his last entrance he exults in his anticipation of Soranzo's revenge, his ability, as he sees it, to dominate the course of events:

> SORANZO: But where's my brother Giovanni?
> *Enter GIOVANNI with a heart upon his dagger.*
> GIOVANNI: Here, here, Soranzo! trimm'd in reeking blood,
> That triumphs over death, proud in the spoil
> Of love and vengeance! Fate, or all the powers
> That guide the motions of immortal souls,
> Could not prevent me.
>
> (V. vi.)

From this it is a far cry to Giovanni's earlier belief that his guilt was not his responsibility because fate had decreed it. Like Tamburlaine, he has come to believe, despite the imminence of his destruction, that he holds "the Fates bound fast in iron chains." His arrogance is in sharp contrast to Annabella's passive acceptance of fate's decree as she knows her end near:

> Thou, precious Time, that swiftly rid'st in post
> Over the world, to finish-up the race
> Of my last fate, here stay thy restless course,
> And bear to ages that are yet unborn
> A wretched, woful woman's tragedy!...
> O, Giovanni, that hast had the spoil
> Of thine own virtues and my modest fame,
> Would thou hadst been less subject to those stars
> That luckless reign'd at my nativity!
>
> (V. i.)

The echo of *Faustus* here ("You stars that reigned at my nativity" [*Faustus,* V. ii] can hardly be accidental, and it brings with it the notion of a terrified submission. With this we can associate Richardetto's cry when he feels that the dénouement is near "there is One Above begins to work" (IV. ii).

There can be no doubt that in the planning of this play Ford had *Romeo and Juliet* in mind. The Friar, Giovanni's confidant, and Putana, the gross "tutoress" of Annabella, manifestly correspond to Friar Lawrence and the Nurse in Shakespeare's tragedy of love. The point is significant, for Shakespeare stressed that his lovers were "star-crossed," were not responsible for the catastrophe that awaited them. Ford, it is evident, sees the love of Giovanni and Annabella as an impulse that drives them to doom. Nevertheless, he sees Giovanni's growing arrogance as at once inevitable, splendid, and culpable.

To an early seventeenth-century tragic writer it is not surprising that a man's conduct should simultaneously present these different facets, and in Ford the opposition of pagan and Christian impulses is stronger than in most. Joined to his admiration for the adventurous Giovanni is the stern piety that had earlier shown itself in *Christes Bloodie Sweat*. Immediately before her marriage the Friar terrifies Annabella with a threat of hell, and it is in this passage that the play is closest to the poem. Here is the Friar:

> Ay, you are wretched, miserably wretched,
> Almost condemn'd alive. There is a place,—
> List, daughter!—in a black and hollow vault,
> Where day is never seen; there shines no sun,
> But flaming horror of consuming fires,
> A lightless sulphur, chok'd with smoky fogs
> Of an infected darkness: in this place
> Dwell many thousand thousand sundry sorts
> Of never-dying deaths: there damnèd souls
> Roar without pity; there are gluttons fed
> With toads and adders; there is burning oil
> Pour'd down the drunkard's throat; the usurer
> Is forc'd to sup whole draughts of molten gold;
> There is the murderer for ever stabb'd,
> Yet can he never die; there lies the wanton
> On racks of burning steel, whiles in his soul
> He feels the torment of his raging lust.
>   ANNABELLA: Mercy! O, mercy!
>   FRIAR: There stand these wretched things
> Who have dream'd out whole years in lawless sheets
> And secret incests, cursing one another.
> Then you will wish each kiss your brother gave
> Had been a dagger's point; then you shall hear
> How he will cry, "O, would my wicked sister
> Had first been damn'd, when she did yield to lust!"

                                                    (III. vi.)

Ford has achieved an eloquence of speech that was far beyond him a dozen years earlier, when the poem was written. But in devising the Friar's words he must have remembered the vision of hell that he had personally, not dramatically, represented. We cannot doubt that, when he wrote the play, the vision still had validity for him. Here is the poem's version:

> Here shall the *wantons* for a a downy bed,
> Be rackt on pallets of stil-burning steele:
> Here shall the *glutton,* that hath dayly fed,
> On choice of daintie diet, hourely feele
>   Worse meat then toads, & beyond time be drencht
>   In flames of fire, that neuer shall be quencht .
>
> Each moment shall the *killer,* be tormented
> With stabbes, that shall not so procure his death:
> The *drunkard* that would neuer be contented
> With drinking vp whole flagons at a breath,
>   Shalbe deni'd (as he with thirst is stung)
>   A drop of water for to coole his tongue.
>
> The *mony-hoording Miser* in his throat

> Shall swallow molten lead: the *spruce perfum'd*
> Shall smell most loathsome brimstone: he who wrote
> *Soule-killing rimes,* shall liuing be consum'd
>> By such a gnawing worme, that neuer dies,
>> And heare in stead of musicke hellish cries.[4]

At the end of *'Tis Pity* the situation is moralized by the Cardinal in sententious couplets, which stand in strong contrast to the last words of Giovanni, finding to the end his idea of heaven in Annabella's love:

> O, I bleed fast!
> Death, thou'rt a guest long look'd for; I embrace
> Thee and thy wounds: O, my last minute comes!
> Where'er I go, let me enjoy this grace,
> Freely to view my Annabella's face.

(V. vi.)

It was at this point, understandably, that Maeterlinck ended his version of the play, but to adapt Ford in this fashion is to conceal his complexity of view. He could at times see Giovanni as not merely arrogant but wholly unscrupulous in his course of evil. When wooing Annabella, he assures her:

> I have ask'd counsel of the holy church,
> Who tells me I may love you.

(I. iii.)

Yet nothing that the Friar has said to him could be legitimately twisted to mean this. At this moment his wooing becomes seduction.[5] Moreover, he administers to us a subtler shock when he claims that his pleasure in lying with Annabella has in no way been diminished since her marriage:

> Busy opinion is an idle fool,
> That, as a school-rod keeps a child in awe,
> Frights th' unexperienc'd temper of the mind:
> So did it me, who, ere my precious sister
> Was married, thought all taste of love would die
> In such a contract; but I find no change
> Of pleasure in this formal law of sports.
> She is still one to me, and every kiss
> As sweet and as delicious as the first
> I reap'd, when yet the privilege of youth
> Entitled her a virgin.

(V. iii.)

---

4 Two misprints are silently corrected here.

5 H. J. Oliver (*The Problem of John Ford,* London and New York, 1955, p. 89) has attempted to justify his words, suggesting that "the Friar's failure to prove a case against him is to Giovanni equivalent to condonation." But Giovanni had surely been taught to distinguish better than this.

The passage is primarily intended to display Giovanni's condition of *hubris*, as, near the point of catastrophe, he sets himself up more arrogantly against "Busy opinion" and rejoices in his mastery of pleasure; but also it suggests a coarsening of the character, his deterioration into an intriguer showing itself in his delight in the skill of his deception.[6]

Yet at the same time it is not merely Giovanni or destiny that is culpable. We have seen that the lovers hold our sympathy as no other character in the play holds it, how Ford takes pains to ensure that we shall waste no regard on Soranzo. And at one moment at least the Cardinal who moralizes the ending comes himself under a critical lash. Grimaldi has mistakenly killed the comic Bergetto and has then taken refuge with the Cardinal, who is his kinsman. When Bergetto's father Donado asks for justice, the Cardinal answers that he has received Grimaldi into the Pope's protection and will not give him up. Donado and his friend Florio protest against this ecclesiastical partiality:

> Donado: Is this a churchman's voice? dwells justice here?
> Florio: Justice is fled to Heaven, and comes no nearer.
> Soranzo!—was't for him? O, impudence!
> Had he the face to speak it, and not blush?
> Come, come, Donado, there's no help in this,
> When cardinals think murder's not amiss.
> Great men may do their wills, we must obey;
> But Heaven will judge them for't another day.

> (III. ix.)

So we may remember this when the Cardinal takes it upon himself to re-establish the rule of law at the end of the play, condemning Putana to be burned and declaring, of Annabella, "'Tis pity she's a whore."[7]

When in this way one analyzes Ford's attitude to his characters and their actions, one may feel only that confusion now hath made his masterpiece. But this, as we have seen, is the way of Jacobean tragedy. There is no simple faith in the man who rebels or in the law against which he rebels. There is a strong sense of sin, and of the arrogance that comes on a man as he hardens in sinning; there is a sense that he has had no choice; there is a sense that his fellows are not worthy of judging him. Above all, there is a strong sense of sympathy with the man who is apart from his fellows, making his challenge, facing his end. While we are close

---

[6] This passage was a source of bewilderment to Jacques du Tillet in his review of the performance of Maeterlinck's version (*Revue Bleue*, 4e Série, II [1894], 633–6).

[7] Mary E. Cocknower, "John Ford" (*Seventeenth Century Studies by Members of the Graduate School, University of Cincinnati*, Princeton, 1933, pp. 211–12), has suggested that the Cardinal's prompt confiscation of "all the gold and jewels, or whatever, ... to the pope's proper use" (V. vi) has a satiric tinge. If so—and it seems not unlikely—this would strengthen the audience's imperfection of sympathy with the Cardinal's judgment of Annabella.

to Giovanni, Ford keeps us remote from the cosmic scheme, at whose nature Giovanni or the Friar or the Cardinal may only guess. There is a pattern in things, which leads Giovanni from his first impulse of love for Annabella to his murder of her and his own virtual suicide, but we have only glimpses of what the pattern signifies.

In recent years we have become used to vastly differing interpretations of Shakespeare's major plays. There is a school of critics that sees Othello as winning salvation as he dies, holding Desdemona in a last embrace; there is another school that is sure of his damnation. There are those who see the world as well lost for Antony's and Cleopatra's love, and those who are impressed by the irony of Cleopatra's sensual imaginings of a heaven where Antony is waiting for her kiss or Iras's. It is not surprising, therefore, that *'Tis Pity She's a Whore* has similarly lent itself to a diversity of recent interpretation. Professor Sensabaugh sees Giovanni as Ford's sympathetic portrayal of the man who follows, and must follow, his love-impulse, being crushed by a society that will not recognize his need and the inevitability of its assertion.[8] Dr. Ewing, on the other hand, is willing to dispose of the whole matter by consulting Burton's *Anatomy of Melancholy* and by diagnosing in Giovanni a religious melancholy of the atheistic kind.[9] We could not have clearer indications of the danger of interpreting seventeenth-century tragedy either in the light of modern feeling or in the light of its contemporary psychology. According to Professor Sensabaugh,

> *'Tis Pity She's a Whore*...strikes the most decisive blow against the world's moral order. Here no subtle distinctions between whoredom and marriage arise; instead, the play makes an open problem of incest and thus queries the Christian idea of retributive justice.[10]

Yet we have seen that Ford, as we should indeed expect from his earlier writings, is sharply aware of sin and by no means an active unbeliever in the Christian cosmology. And Dr. Ewing's simple diagnosis leaves out of account the impulse to incest that goes along with, and indeed provokes, Giovanni's religious doubts, and the reciprocal love that Annabella feels for her brother. Mr. T. S. Eliot has declared Giovanni "almost a monster of egotism" and Annabella "virtually a moral defective."[11] To that one might reply that, if the company of monsters of egotism is uncongenial, one had better not read much of seventeenth-century tragedy, and that a sinner who comes to recognize her guilt and to pray for pardon is a moral defective of an unusual kind. Miss Sargeaunt has rightly taken Mr.

---

[8] G. F. Sensabaugh, *The Tragic Muse of John Ford* (Palo Alto, 1944), pp. 171–73, 186–88.

[9] S. Blaine Ewing, *Burtonian Melancholy in the Plays of John Ford,* Princeton Studies in English 19 (Princeton, 1940), pp. 71–76.

[10] Sensabaugh, p. 186.

[11] *Selected Essays,* New York, 1932, p. 198.

Eliot to task for this exhibition of imperfect sympathy, which is doubtless due to his understandable dislike of the overt expression of moral and cosmic uncertainties. But even she falls into the irrelevant judgment, concerning this brother and sister, that Annabella is "the better man of the two." She praises Annabella's clear-sighted recognition of her guilt in comparison with Giovanni's "attempts at a rational justification of their conduct."[12] But this is to give to Ford a sureness of belief that the play hardly warrants, and it runs counter to our deep involvement with Giovanni and the strong sympathy that both he and Annabella successfully demand.

Certainly we can make a distinction between them. For Giovanni we feel that "admiration," in both senses, that normally constitutes part of our response to the Jacobean hero. Professor Davril expresses the wish that he had stabbed himself immediately after dispatching his sister,[13] but this character is not one born to acquiesce: like Macbeth, like Bussy, he can take heart from a last confrontation of his enemies, and he perhaps outgoes precedent in the enjoyment of his last triumph. The conception of the hero and the violent course of action into which he enters constitute, in fact, the surest link between this play and the tragedies of Ford's predecessors, while Annabella belongs rather with the heroines of the plays that were to come. She has a close kinship with Bianca in *Love's Sacrifice,* who similarly falls into an illicit love-relationship and mocks at her husband in order to provoke her own death. And Annabella's final acquiescence in the march of events is characteristic of all Ford's heroines. She has not the strong individuality that characterizes her brother: she is nearer the dramatic symbol of error and suffering quietly borne. It is of her, not of Giovanni, that Maeterlink speaks when, in the preface to his version of the play, he declares that Ford achieves a vision of the undifferentiated human soul:

> Ford est descendu plus avant dans les ténèbres de la vie intérieure et générale. Il est allé jusqu'aux régions où toutes les âmes commencent à se ressembler entre elles parce qu' elles n'empruntent plus que peu de choses aux circonstances, et qu'à mesure que l'on descend ou que l'on monte (c'est tout un et il ne s'agit de dépasser le niveau de la vie aveugle et ordinaire) on s'approche de la grande source profonde, incolore, uniforme et commune de l'âme humaine.[14]

In conformity with this, and in contrast to her brother, Annabella has a discretion and gravity of speech, she can give a Racine-like eloquence to the simplest words:

---

12 Sargeaunt, p. 186.

13 Robert Davril, *Le Drame de John Ford,* Paris, 1954, p. 299.

14 *Annabella,* pp. xii–xiii. U. M. Ellis-Fermor, *The Jacobean Drama,* London, 1936, p. 228, has similarly found the secret of Ford's universality "in the knowledge of the ultimate oneness of the roots of human feeling and experience to which his concentration upon a few processes of the mind has led him."

Brother, dear brother, know what I have been,
And know that now there's but a dining-time
'Twixt us and our confusion.

(V. v.) [15]

She uses the term of family relationship, "brother," by which she has
thought of Giovanni for a longer time than their illicit love has endured;
the simple reference to "a dining-time" gives an immediacy, an association with a life we know, to her quiet and controlled speech; the word
"confusion" is restrained and generalized, yet ultimate. This is the accent
of Calantha in *The Broken Heart* when she recalled how "one news
straight came huddling on another Of death! and death! and death!" If
we take Ford's dramas as a whole, it is his women rather than his men
that remain in our minds. Giovanni, like the play he dominates, is something of a stranger in that world. But that does not diminish either his
stature or that of this last, belated Jacobean tragedy.

[15] As noted in *The Works of John Ford,* ed. William Gifford and Alexander Dyce,
3 vols., London, 1869, I, 198, there is a variant reading "dying time." This does,
of course, make good sense, but Annabella's reference, later in the same speech, to
the coming banquet as "an harbinger of death To you and me" strengthens the
case for reading "dining-time."

See other studies in Ford bibliography (below, pp. 404–405).

THE BROKEN HEART *

Robert Ornstein

IN contrast to the glowing life and passion of *'Tis Pity, The Broken
Heart* seems somewhat pale. The violence that erupts in the last act
does not so much quicken the dramatic action as add to the hidden
soul-destroying burden of silent griefs. An Elizabethan dramatist, one
imagines, would have cast *The Broken Heart* in the romantic mold of
Romeo and Juliet. He would have set upon the stage another tale of

* Reprinted with permission of the copyright owners, the Regents of the University of Wisconsin, from Robert Ornstein, *The Moral Vision of Jacobean
Tragedy,* 1965, the University of Wisconsin Press.

star-crossed lovers ruined by hostile circumstances. Ford is more interested, however, in emotional reaction than in romantic action. His play
begins after the most dramatic incidents of the fable have occurred. He
studies, as it were, the aftermath of romantic tragedy, the cumulative
shock of misery and frustration on the lives of Penthea, Orgilus, and those
who share their unhappy fates.

The tragedy of Penthea is to be betrayed by the three men who love
her: her brother, Ithocles, who for ambition forces her into a loathsome
marriage; her evil-minded "humorous" husband, Bassanes, who imprisons
her to possess her entirely; and her former lover, Orgilus, who tries to
seduce her from her marriage vows. To Ithocles and Bassanes, Penthea's
misery brings a redeeming awareness of the sins of ambition and jealousy.
Orgilus' spiritual fate is more uncertain. Although Penthea's death seals
his decision to murder Ithocles, his revenge is motivated as much by
self-pity and envy as by love; there is, in fact, a touch of Giovanni's
crazed vanity in his thought and actions. On the other hand, his misfortune demands our sympathy and he achieves in the acceptance of
death a dignity lacking in his struggle against the circumstances of his
life. His revenge is certainly immoral, but his claim to Penthea's love
is not explicitly refuted except by Penthea, whose feelings are ambivalent
if not contradictory.

By conventional standards Orgilus' love for another man's wife is
adulterous, even though Penthea's marriage was tyrannically enforced
and is a shameful travesty of the wedding vow. Before Ithocles interfered,
Penthea and Orgilus shared a chaste and "approved" affection. Indeed,
according to Elizabethan custom, they were "married" by plighting their
troth even though an official ceremony had not yet been performed.
When Orgilus confronts Penthea he does not place the rights of love
above the bond of marriage. He claims a wife, not a courtly mistress:
"I would possesse my wife, the equity / Of very reason bids me" (II. iii).
More than anyone else, Penthea is aware of the immorality of her
marriage; she feels violated, defiled, and even prostituted by her loveless
servitude. In effect she admits Orgilus' prior claim when she later says
to Ithocles:

> ...she that's wife to *Orgilus,* and lives
> In knowne Adultery with *Bassanes,*
> Is at the best a whore.

> (III. ii)

And yet when Orgilus presses his claim she denies it:

> How (*Orgilus*) by promise I was thine,
> The heavens doe witnesse; they can witnesse too

A rape done on my truth: how I doe love thee
Yet *Orgilus,* and yet, must best appeare
In tendering thy freedome; for I find
The constant preservation of thy merit,
By thy not daring to attempt my fame
With iniury of any loose conceit,
Which might give deeper wounds to discontents.

(II. iii)

When he continues to plead for her love, she turns on him angrily:

Uncivill Sir, forbeare,
Or I can turne affection into vengeance;
Your reputation (if you value any)
Lyes bleeding at my feet. Unworthy man,
If ever henceforth thou appeare in language,
Message, or letter to betray my frailty,
I'le call thy former protestations lust,
And curse my Starres for forfeit of my iudgement.
Goe thou, fit onely for disguise and walkes,
To hide thy shame: this once I spare thy life.

(II. iii)

We may admire Penthea's strength of will and still question her wisdom. We may wonder what value resides in an utterly meaningless dedication, or what purpose is served by fidelity to a marriage that exists in name only. By spurning Orgilus she condemns him as well as herself to a living death and ensures catastrophe. Perhaps in this instance Ford suggests that it would have been wiser to challenge circumstances than to submit passively. Perhaps it would have been more moral for Penthea to find happiness with Orgilus than to observe the "customary forme" of marriage.

How easy it is to falsify the central issue in *The Broken Heart* by reducing it to a simple conflict of values—the "promptings of the heart" versus "conventional morality."[1] Actually Ford's presentation of character leaves no doubt that Penthea is wiser as well as stronger than Orgilus, who advances the claim of love as an absolute that negates circumstances and time itself. Penthea does not deny that she was once promised to Orgilus, but she will not confuse the past with the present. Admitting the vileness of her marriage, she nevertheless accepts it as one of the irremediable accidents that distort the shape of men's lives. The opportunity for happiness which she and Orgilus once possessed no longer

---

[1] For a discussion of *The Broken Heart* as a "problem play," see S. P. Sherman, "Forde's Contribution to the Decadence of the Drama," Bang's *Materialien* (Louvain, 1908), **XXIII**, xi ff.

exists because they have themselves changed. Like Giovanni (indeed, like most of Ford's heroes), Orgilus is weaker than the woman he loves and crushed by a far lighter burden than she bears. The misery that makes her compassionate and generous makes him selfish and self-pitying. Although he attacks Ithocles' tyranny, he insists on the privilege of authorizing his own sister's marriage and enjoys the power even if he does not abuse it. Embittered, wretchedly frustrate, he enters into a labyrinth of deceptions and disguises that ends in murder and self-destruction.

Far more realistic than Orgilus, Penthea recognizes the true nature of the alternatives that face her. If she flees with Orgilus it must be outside society and law, without hope of the joyous fulfillment of marriage. If she refuses, Orgilus may yet find happiness and she will preserve intact the citadel of her mind. Her thoughts are pure even though her body is defiled; the shame of her "adultery" rests upon Ithocles. Thus while Orgilus' claim to Penthea is in the abstract just, he demonstrates his unworthiness of her by pressing it. She spurns him pityingly, aware of the gulf that has sprung between them, recognizing that he is "fit only for disguise" and a ruin of his former self. There is obviously more frustrate desire than selfless devotion in his plea. He speaks of Neoplatonic devotion but his imagery reveals the hunger of sensual appetite:

> All pleasures are but meere imagination,
> Feeding the hungry appetite with steame,
> And sight of banquet, whilst the body pines,
> Not relishing the reall tast of food. . . .

> (II. iii)

For Penthea, then, the choice is between an evil-minded husband who feverishly schemes to inter her alive and an embittered lover who feverishly schemes to steal her away. Both are ungenerous, both are wildly possessive. The gentle Penthea, who had almost attained the strength to endure her life with Bassanes, is crushed by the shock of Orgilus' betrayal.

Far from exalting the claim of individual desire over the bond of matrimony, *The Broken Heart,* like Ford's other tragedies, depicts the warping of love that cannot grow and mature. It is quite true that Giovanni and Orgilus express Ford's romantic idealism—his poetic worship of love—but they also betray that idealism by their jealousy and by their desire to possess rather than serve beauty. Indeed, the highest expression of love in Ford's drama is not the reckless ardor of Giovanni and Orgilus but the generous devotion of Annabella and Penthea.[2] And

---

2 Although I agree with Mr. Oliver (*The Problem of John Ford,* London, 1955, pp. 11–12) that we cannot take all the casuistry of *The Peers' Challenge* seriously

though Tecnicus is the official "philosopher" of *The Broken Heart,* it is Penthea who, expressing in the beauty of her own life the correspondence of poetic vision and moral knowledge, reaffirms the essential humanity of ethical ideals. If the portrayal of Penthea leaves any doubts about Ford's attitude towards marriage, those doubts are erased by the solemn beauty of Euphranea's betrothal and Calantha's wedding to Ithocles in death. . . .

. . . To a reader familiar only with the tragedies, confusion and sensationalism may seem more characteristic of Ford than the refinement and sensitivity which we find in *The Broken Heart.* Those who also study *The Lover's Melancholy, Perkin Warbeck,* and *The Lady's Trial,* however, will have a truer sense of Ford's quality. They will know a dramatist who did not always possess the tact required for the investigation of the darker ways of passion, but whose judgments were based on a clearly defined set of values. Indeed the very nature of Ford's subjects indicates that he wrote with a far greater ethical assurance than did his predecessors. In the absence of pervading skepticism, he was free to probe beneath the surface of conventional morality and to investigate the rare individual instance that proves the moral "rule." Because he was concerned with the individual rather than the typical, Ford does not offer universal truths. Instead each of his plays, perhaps even *Love's Sacrifice,* adds another fraction to a cumulative knowledge of the human heart.

Twentieth-century criticism has insisted upon Ford's "modernity," either by praising his psychological insights or by damning his "scientific" amoral view of the passions. I imagine, however, that we need no more modern a guide to Ford's view of character than the liberal ethic of *Biathanatos.* If Ford does not arrive at Donne's conclusion that "there is no externall act naturally evill," he shares Donne's knowledge that circumstances "condition" acts and give them their moral nature. Like Donne

---

nevertheless it does seem to express Ford's ideal of love. Perhaps the finest comment on Giovanni and Orgilus is the following passage from the *Challenge:* "For this, in the rules of affection, is text: whosoever truely love, and are truly of their ladies beloved, ought in their service to employ their endevours; more for the honour and deserving the continuance of their ladies good-will, than any way to respect the free-will of their owne heedlesse dispositions; else are they degenerate bastards, and apostates, revolting from the principals, and principall rules of sincere devotion. It is not ynough for any man, that hath by long suit, tedious imprecations, jeopardous hazard, toyle of bodie, griefe of mind, pitifull laments, obsequious fawnings, desperate passions, and passionate despaire, at length, for a meed or requitall to his unrest, gained the favourable acceptance of his most, and best desired ladie: . . . Perfect service, and serviceable loyaltie, is seene more cleerely in deserving love and maintaining it, than in attempting or laboring for it. How can any one be sayd truely to serve when he more respects the libertie of his owne affections, than the imposition of ladies' command?" (*Shakespeare Society Reprints* [London, 1843], pp. 10–11.)

he insists upon an ethical judgment that is individual, flexible, and humane, not rigid, dogmatic, and absolute. Like Donne he believes that moral values are shaped by the processes of life even as they in turn shape the nature of human relationships.

A modern dramatist might have viewed the tragic situation in *The Broken Heart* as an unresolvable dilemma that baffles judgment. Ford, however, challenges the reader to perceive those permanent values on which judgment rests. Although he lived in an age of warring factions, he wrote with a deeper sense of the communion between the individual and society than did Chapman or Webster. And unlike Middleton he had a clear view of the ideal in man's thought and conduct and a poignant awareness of the tragedy that befalls when the bonds of friendship, love, and devotion are warped or sundered.

JOHN FORD

Broken Heart = B   *'Tis Pity She's a Whore* = T

Adams, Henry Hitch. *English Domestic or, Homiletic Tragedy: 1575 to 1642.* New York, 1943, pp. 177–183.

Anderson, Donald K., Jr. "The Heart and the Banquet: Imagery in Ford's *'Tis Pity* and *The Broken Heart*," *SEL,* II (1962), 209–217.

Bawcutt, N. W. "Seneca and Ford's *'Tis Pity She's A Whore*." *N&Q,* XIV (1967), 215.

Blayney, Glenn H. "Convention, Plot, and Structure in *The Broken Heart*," *MP,* LVI (1958), 95–102.

Boas, Frederick S. *An Introduction to Stuart Drama.* Oxford, 1946, pp. 342–347 (B, T).

Burelbach, Frederick M., Jr. " 'The Truth' in John Ford's *The Broken Heart* Revisited," *N&Q,* XIV (1967), 211–212.

Bradbrook, Muriel C. *Themes and Conventions of Elizabethan Tragedy.* Cambridge, Eng., 1935, rptd. 1957, pp. 250–261.

Brissenden, Alan. "Impediments to Love: A Theme in John Ford," *RenD,* VII (1964), 95–102.

Carsaniga, Giovanni M. "The 'Truth' in John Ford's *The Broken Heart*," *CL,* X (1958), 344–348.

Cocknower, Mary Edith. "John Ford" in *Seventeenth Century Studies,* ed. Robert Shafer. Princeton, 1933, pp. 123–275.

Cunningham, John E. *Elizabethan and Early Stuart Drama.* London, 1965, pp. 109–113.

Davril, Robert. *Le Drame de John Ford.* Paris, 1954, pp. 163–168, 250–254, 264–268, 279–285, *et passim.*

Eliot, T. S. *Selected Essays.* (New Edition). New York, 1950, pp. 170–180.

Ellis-Fermor, Una. *The Jacobean Drama.* 4th rev. ed. London, 1958, pp. 227–246.

Ewing, S. Blaine. *Burtonian Melancholy in the Plays of John Ford.* Princeton, 1940, pp. 55–64 (B); 70–76 (T).

Hoy, Cyrus. " 'Ignorance in Knowledge': Marlowe's Faustus and Ford's Giovanni, " *MP,* LVII (1960), 145–154.

Homan, Sidney R., Jr. "Shakespeare and Dekker as Keys to Ford's *'Tis Pity She's a Whore,*" *SEL,* VII (1967), 269–276.

Kaufmann, R. J. "Ford's Tragic Perspective," *TSLL,* I (Winter 1960), 522–537, reprinted in *Elizabethan Drama,* ed. R. J. Kaufmann. (A Galaxy Book). New York, 1961, pp. 366–371 (T).

Leech, Clifford. *John Ford and the Drama of His Time.* London, 1957.

McDonald, Charles Osborne. *The Rhetoric of Tragedy: Form in Stuart Drama.* Amherst, Mass., 1966, pp. 314–333 (B).

Oliver, H. J. *The Problem of John Ford.* London, 1955, pp. 86–98.

Ornstein, Robert. *The Moral Vision of Jacobean Tragedy.* Madison, Wisconsin, 1960 (reprinted 1965), pp. 203–213 (T).

Quennell, Peter. *The Singular Preference: Portraits and Essays.* New York, 1953, pp. 30–36.

Ribner, Irving. *Jacobean Tragedy: The Quest for Moral Order.* New York and London, 1962, pp. 156–163 (B); 163–174 (T).

Sargeaunt, Margaret Joan. *John Ford.* Oxford, 1935, pp. 124–127.

Sensabaugh, George F., "John Ford Revisited," *SEL,* IV (1964), 195–216.

_____. *The Tragic Muse of John Ford.* Palo Alto, Calif., 1944, pp. 88–93.

Sherman, Stuart P., ed. *'Tis Pity Shees a Whore.* Boston, 1915, pp. xxiv–lv.

Tomlinson, T. B. *A Study of Elizabethan and Jacobean Tragedy.* Cambridge, Eng., and Melbourne, 1964, pp. 270–272 (B); 272–276 (T).

Ure, Peter. "Marriage and the Domestic Drama in Heywood and Ford," *ES,* XXXII (1951), 200–216.

Wilcox, John. "On Reading John Ford," *Shakespeare Assoc. Bulletin,* XXI (1946), 66–75.

Woolf, Virginia. "Notes on an Elizabethan Play," in *The Common Reader.* London, 1925, pp. 73–85.

James Shirley

ELIZABETHAN REVENGE TRAGEDY AND *THE CARDINAL* *

Fredson T. Bowers †

THE *Cardinal* (1641), Shirley's greatest tragedy, completes the trend by presenting in a brilliant fashion a clear-cut, coherent Kydian revenge tragedy, polished and simplified in his best manner. The play has been most often compared to *The Duchess of Malfi* because of consequences resulting when an interested person tries to enforce affection. This theme, however implicit in Webster's tragedy, was not put forward with the vigor found in *The Cardinal*,[1] and Ford's *Broken Heart* with its powerful lesson on freedom of choice seems more probable as the source for Shirley's special and conspicuous pleading.

The *Cardinal* is not an especially derivative play, however. Shirley

---

* From Fredson T. Bowers, *Elizabethan Revenge Tragedy, 1587–1642* (Princeton: Princeton University Press, 1940), pp. 228–234. Reprinted by permission of Princeton University Press.

† Mr. Bowers has been tracing Shirley's development as a dramatist reviving and typifying late Caroline interest in the conventions of the Elizabethan revenge play, "with its treatment of motives for revenge as a legitimate source of action and character, instead of a mere means of a pointing a practical moral."—ED.

[1]See especially the king's speech after the murder of Alvarez (III. ii) and Rosaura's dying forgiveness (V. iii).

went chiefly to *The Spanish Tragedy* for the larger construction of his plot, and though various other dramas contributed characters and incidents, these were chiefly used to bring the old Kydian tragedy up to date. An outline of *The Cardinal* fits almost point for point into the outline of Kyd's play. In both there is much preliminary action leading up to the murder which is to be revenged. In both this murder is committed by a jealous lover to rid himself of his rival who has won the heroine's heart. Both murderers are backed by intriguing villains who are anxious for the marriage to raise the fortunes of their houses. The murder calls forth the counter-revenge, which is ordered with extreme deceit and dissimulation including a feigned reconciliation. While Rosaura, like Hieronimo, goes mad from excessive grief, the portrayal of her madness is more closely allied to *Hamlet*, since she resolves to pretend insanity in order to deceive her enemies but from time to time lapses into actual distraction. Like *Hamlet* is the emphasis put upon her melancholy. A masque is used to commit a murder, a body is exhibited, ingenious deaths are contrived with great irony. An effect somewhat similar to Bel-Imperia's self-immolation after her revenge is secured in Hernando's suicide.

Various other details are taken from the dramas which developed the Kydian form. The lust of the villain for the victim of his schemes is prominent in such plays as *Antonio's Revenge* and *The Atheist's Tragedy*, although the closest resemblance comes in *Alphonsus, Emperor of Germany, The Bloody Brother,* and *Sicily and Naples,* from which last, perhaps, the particular form of the cardinal's revenge may have been borrowed. Hernando, the accomplice, has been compared to Bosola. It is true that in the disinterested quality of their revenges they bear a certain resemblance, but Bosola's previous position as accomplice to the villains is a wide variant, and a closer approach to type may be found in Hamond in *The Bloody Brother* who has been himself directly injured. Stephanos in *The Roman Actor* has the same disinterested motives, but other suggested parallels to Baltazar in *The Noble Spanish Soldier* and Ziriff in *Aglaura* are wide of the mark, as are comparisons of Hernando as revenger to Sciarrha and to Vindici.[2] Indeed, Hernando corresponds most closely in his position in the plot to Hermegild in the Albovine story.

These matters of influence aside, *The Cardinal* is an expert work of the theater. The situations are clear-cut, the action rapid, and the characters strongly drawn. Action, however, has taken the place of the Kydian emotion with its accompaniments of a hesitating, overwrought revenger, blood and thunder, and ghosts. Rosaura's madness does not come until late and is sparingly exhibited. One moment she is seen planning to pretend madness, and the next as insane in fact. Since this change from sanity to actual distraction is accomplished off-stage, the

---

[2] R. S. Forsythe, *The Relations of Shirley's Plays to the Elizabethan Drama* (Columbia University Press, 1914), p. 186.

audience is not permitted to see the slow disintegration of a mind as in *The Spanish Tragedy, Hamlet,* or *Antonio's Revenge.* Similarly, there is no hesitation, and much of the important planning of the intrigue is done off-stage. Pursuing an entirely different course from that of Kyd, Shirley has his characters do their thinking behind the scenes. All the audience sees is the thinking which has turned into action. Such a method makes invariably for a brisker play but a more shallow one; the polish has rubbed up the surface at the expense of the inner glow.

Yet the brilliance of Shirley's achievement, particularly when viewed in the light of the sterile treatment of revenge in the dilettante plays of his contemporaries, must not be minimized. If in bringing the old revenge tragedy up to date he has lost much of the emotion and the high tragedy of a soul on the rack, if his characters are slightly too facile in conceiving and acting revenge, he has at the same time sloughed off the bathos and hysteria, the rant and bombast, which at times had made the Kydian form a butt for laughter. His characters are ordinary persons in an ordinary world, who set about righting their wrongs as best they can. Some remnants of the older tradition persist, as in Rosaura's real madness under the weight of her burden and in the constant references to the religious and expiatory nature of the revenge for her dead lover Alvarez. Yet even if Rosaura's distraction does not fit too smoothly in the plot, the revengers' talk of sacrificing to the ghost of Alvarez is necessary to show the nobility of Hernando's character and the essential justice of the vengeance. Without it, Hernando would have been a malicious man exploiting Rosaura's grievance for his own small ends.

The plays of the fourth period, especially that group yet to be considered, show in general an extreme degeneration in the convention of revenge. Only perfunctory motivation and action are given to a serious Kydian blood-revenge; consequently, all the true Kydian ethical spirit, the moral approach to a vital problem of character, is entirely missing. Although his *Cardinal* is not entirely divorced from this fault, Shirley has created a true revenge tragedy in which the entire play centers upon blood-revenge for murder. Vengeance is not perfunctorily relegated to the background until it is time for the catastrophe, nor is it hidden in artificial obscurity of motive. He has achieved a nice balance of characters and situation; in pure construction and actability *The Cardinal* is one of the best of the Elizabethan revenge plays. Furthermore, there are evidences in his careful delineation of character that Shirley up to a certain point in the play intended a conception of life which would closely approach the ethical content of the best revenge tragedy.

The early, or Kydian, tragedy of revenge, had presented a hero-revenger who, forced by his overwhelming duty and outraged passion into too bloody courses, had lost all ethical adjustment to normal life and was eventually forced to pay the penalty in death. The necessarily treacherous and evil course of his revenge soon produced the feeling that he could not have been a good man even at the start, and we have such bad revengers in a good cause as Hoffman, Vindici, Maximus, and Francisco. The natural transition was thereupon made to the convention that revenge was the prerogative of villains alone, as exemplified in the villain plays *The Turk* and *Women Beware Women.* The realization grew, however, that good men did revenge, and that there still remained dramatic material in showing the results of their departure from heavenly and earthly laws on a practical plane of morality. A form of problem play, such as *The Fatal Dowry,* was produced. This form in the best plays yielded to the broader artistic conception of life as a balanced whole in which people are neither all good nor all bad. The justice of revenge was occasionally recognized but also its harms and cruelties in a social as well as a personal sense. *The White Devil, The Changeling, The Roman Actor, The Cruel Brother, The Broken Heart,* and *Love's Sacrifice* all in one way or another portray this feeling. Shirley himself in *The Maid's Revenge, Love's Cruelty,* and to some extent in the portrait of Sciarrha in *The Traitor* had written in this mood.

The Cardinal may roughly be placed in this genre although the conception is not so clear or consistent. The cardinal with his ambitious schemes is the real villain, and his murder is truly the catastrophe of the play. Columbo is not wholly an evil but more an overrough and cruel man who lacks entirely the finer sensibilities which would have released Rosaura from her painful contract. Shirley is forced to produce the conflict between Hernando and Columbo to provide sufficient motivation for Hernando's revenge, but even greater emphasis is laid on Hernando's generous espousal of Rosaura's wrongs so that he is in effect her champion. Hernando himself partakes a trifle too much of the overbloody nature of the misled revenger. His anger is rather too personal and pronounced, and he betrays himself when he fiercely desires the damnation of the cardinal's soul as well as the destruction of his body. Hernando, however, is definitely no hypocrite; and his expiatory death, while it does no more than forestall the certain justice of the king, places him in the ranks of those revengers who were willing to suffer death for a good cause. At any rate, the noble method of revenge by formal duel in which he engages Columbo should remove him from the category of a villain.

Rosaura, the duchess, is a more complex person. It is her misjudgment of Columbo's character which really produces the tragedy. Not strong enough to resist with frank integrity the combined pressure of king and cardinal, she has weakly allowed herself to give the impression of acquiescence to Columbo's courtship, and so has involuntarily deceived him in a serious matter which he cannot forgive. The feeble exercise of her wiles in the writing of the letter, the fatal misinterpretation which, owing to her past deceit, Columbo gives it, and finally the reckless and injudicious haste with which she accepts his playful release and rushes into marriage, form a pyramid of feminine error which, when dealing with a man of Columbo's nature, can lead only to tragic consequences. Moreover, feminine jealousy plays its part in her revenge. The last push is given to her resolution by Columbo's vengeful and ostentatious courting of one of her ladies-in-waiting. She plans to seeks a bloody revenge on Columbo and the cardinal, who she firmly believes instigated the murder of her Alvarez, and then to die.

So far her portrait has been that of a humanly faulty but not a vicious woman, and her resolution not to outlive her revenge has greatly purified her motives. Almost immediately, however, and with no perceptible motivation, she forgets her resolution and promises to marry Hernando if he is successful in her revenge. In consequence Rosaura allies herself to the hated class of Elizabethan husband-poisoners who had made the same promise to their accomplices, and, on the stage, to such villainesses as Rhodolinda in *Albovine* who had offered the same conditions to Paradine. This incident causes the most grievously blurred morality in Shirley's play, and is the one loose thread in his plot. Rosaura never refers to it again except in a distorted form in her ravings, which Hernando misapplies. Furthermore, the plan is never put into execution. Hernando kills himself immediately after he has stabbed the cardinal, in spite of his expressed eagerness of a few moments before to live to enjoy Rosaura. The insertion of the incident is puzzling, because immediately afterwards Shirley reverts to his former conception of Rosaura and never pursues farther the red herring of her villainy.

In her vengeance Rosaura is single-minded to a fault. She persistently believes that the cardinal instigated the murder of her husband and, in fact, accuses him to his face. Yet Shirley has given no indication of such a fact, and the cardinal's comments during the masque which precedes the murder show distinctly that he has no connection with it. He answers Rosaura with an eloquent denial and a spirited defense of his championing the cause of his nephew Columbo which should convince any audience that he was innocent of any connection with the murder. Rosaura pretends to believe him, but her acceptance is pure dissimulation, for on his departure she disclaims her feigned reconciliation and starts her plans for his murder. The cardinal has admittedly been guilty of corrupting his sovereign, of forcing Rosaura's match with Columbo, and of securing the reinstatement of Columbo after the murder of Alvarez. His brilliant and sound defense to Rosaura, however, places him in the minds of the audience as an erring ambitious man but not a murderer, and so not deserving of a revenge for that murder. Some sympathy must inevitably have been taken away from Rosaura on her refusal to believe him and on her immediate plans to secure his death for an act of which he was innocent.

So far the interpretation has been only what is latent in Shirley's text, and has avoided as much as possible that facile error of reading into Elizabethan plays the nuances and conceptions which may be present only in the critic's own mind. Such a warning is necessary when we find that the ordering of the catastrophe destroys the whole of the more subtle distinctions in character which seem to have been built up in the evolution of the plot. According to what has gone before we should expect to find a clearly expressed or implied moral, not only on the faultiness of the characters but also on the inevitability of the result; or at least we should expect a suggestion that Rosaura, while grievously wronged, had in her turn mistaken justice and committed wrong.

On the contrary, the characters who have been gray throughout the drama suddenly part into black and white. The cardinal, from whom all Machiavellism had been missing, appears with an absurd villainous scheme of rape and poison to revenge Columbo. When Hernando's stab foils his plans, the person whose eloquent and sincere defense has shown him to be merely a man and so deserving of some need of sympathy, suddenly turns black villain and, with atheistical deceit, tricks Rosaura to her death. Rosaura, certainly a femininely faulty woman, by the metamorphosis of the cardinal is transformed into a guiltless heroine, whose cruel fate is universally mourned with not the slightest hint of censure. The change is too sudden and too sweeping to be caused by anything other than a weakening of conception, the result of Shirley's occasional theatricality. The collapse in characterization of the cardinal, the key figure in the drama, into a mere stage villain is peculiarly similar to the metamorphosis of Barabas, caused by whatever means, from a creation of humanly villainous grandeur to a bogey man to frighten children. With the collapse of the cardinal all ethical spirit in the characterization vanishes. The play fails to fulfil its brilliant promise. Fletcherian theatricality has destroyed the real potentialities of the last great tragedy of revenge.

SHIRLEY

Boas, Frederick S. *An Introduction to Stuart Drama.* Oxford, 1946, pp. 352–378.

Bradbrook, Muriel. *Themes and Conventions of Elizabethan Tragedy.* Cambridge, Eng., 1935 (reprinted 1952), pp. 261–267.

Forker, Charles R., ed. *The Cardinal.* Bloomington, Indiana, 1964. pp. lxi–lxxi.

Forsythe, Robert Stanley. *The Relations of Shirley's Plays to the Elizabethan Drama.* New York, 1914.

Harbage, Alfred. *Cavalier Drama.* New York, 1936, pp. 74–80.

Lynch, Kathleen M. *The Social Mode of Restoration Comedy.* University of Michigan Publications (Language and Literature), III. New York, 1926, pp. 34–42.

Morton, Richard. "Deception and Social Dislocation: An Aspect of James Shirley's Drama," *RenD,* IX (1966), 227–245.

McGrath, Juliet J. "James Shirley's Uses of Language," *SEL,* VI (1966), 323–339.

Schelling, Felix E. "James Shirley and the Last of the Old Drama," in *English Drama.* London, 1914, pp. 204–233.